Johann Brazda (Ed.)

The Development of the Mutuality Principle in the Insurance Business

Volume I

The Development of the Mutuality Principle in the Insurance Business

An International Comparison

Volume I

edited by

Johann Brazda

LIT

Supported by funds of the Oesterreichische Nationalbank (Austrian Central Bank, Anniversary Fund, project number: 15773).

Bibliographic information published by the Deutsche Nationalbibliothek
The Deutsche Nationalbibliothek lists this publication in the Deutsche Nationalbibliografie; detailed bibliographic data are available in the Internet at http://dnb.dnb.de.

ISBN 978-3-643-90973-2 (pb)
ISBN 978-3-643-95973-7 (PDF)

A catalogue record for this book is available from the British Library.

Flössergasse 10
CH-8001 Zürich
Tel. +41 (0) 76-632 84 35
E-Mail: zuerich@lit-verlag.ch http://www.lit-verlag.ch

Distribution:

In the UK: Global Book Marketing, e-mail: mo@centralbooks.com
In North America: Independent Publishers Group, e-mail: orders@ipgbook.com
In Germany: LIT Verlag Fresnostr. 2, D-48159 Münster
Tel. +49 (0) 2 51-620 32 22, Fax +49 (0) 2 51-922 60 99, e-mail: vertrieb@lit-verlag.de

e-books are available at www.litwebshop.de

Contents

Volume I

Volume II

Acknowledgements

The editor of this book wants to express his gratitude to those who participated in its making. First I wish to thank the contributors, whose studies offer new insights into the emergence of the insurance business. Further I thank notably to Robert Schediwy who helped with correcting some of the translations. The original translation work was done by Gabiela Csulich, who struggled bravely against the slings and arrows of a foreign rather technical terminology. Additionally, I am also thankful for the generous support of the Forschungsverein für Genossenschaftswesen that made this publication possible. My son Daniel has provided invaluable help with the index.

Johann Brazda
Vienna, November 2019

Notes on Contributors

Brazda, Johann studied economics and philosophy at the University of Vienna. Since 1997 he has been professor teaching at the University of Vienna and the Humboldt University Berlin. He is involved in many international research projects concerning the changing structures of co-operatives and has numerous publications. One of his major works is "Consumer Co-operatives in a Changing World", vols. 1 and 2, Geneva: ICA 1989 (together with Robert Schediwy).

Csulich, Gabriela, PhD is scientific assistant at the Department of Co-operative studies at the Faculty of Business, Economics and Statistics of the University of Vienna.

Jagschitz, Florian is scientific assistant at the Department of Co-operative studies, University of Vienna. His focus lies on the history of Austrian co-operatives. He is also involved in scientific work for the Research Society for Development and History of Consumer Co-operatives (FGK).

Kurimoto, Akira is Professor of co-operative program at Institute for Solidarity-based Society, Hosei University, Tokyo. He served as Chair of the ICA (International Co-operative Alliance) Research Committee (2001-2005). He is Chair of the ICA Asia-Pacific Research Committee and the member of Steering Committee of the World Co-operative Monitor. His major research interests include co-operative laws, co-operative history, corporate governance, food supply chain, health and social care co-operatives and the social economy.

Lorenz, Richard is professional coach and consultant at bit Schulungscenter GmbH. In addition, he is also involved in scientific work at the Deparment of Co-operative studies, University of Vienna. His major research interests and scientific work include co-operatives, co-operative history, tourism economy and insurance economy.

Laurinkari, Juhani is Professor at the University of Kuopio (social policy) since 1.7.1994. The name of the University of Kuopio changed to the University of Eastern Finland 1.1.2010. He is a member and representative of Finland in AGI (Scientific Association of Academic Departments of Social Economy and Cooperation in German-speaking area of Europe) since 1982. He is a full Member of the European Academy of Sciences and Arts and since 2015 the Head of the Finnish delegation. His focus comprises cooperation and social economic.

Lovescher, Balázs, MSc., works for a global management consulting, technology and outsourcing service provider in the field of Finance and Risk Services.

Okada, Futoshi is Professor at College of Commerce, Nihon University, Tokyo. He is a board member of the Japanese Society of Insurance Science from 2014. He serves as an auditor of Japan CO-OP Insurance Consumers' Co-operative Federation (2009-). He has conducted researches on co-operative insurance since 2000. One of his recent work is "Reconsideration on Mutual: A Preparatory Work for its Conceptualization and its Application to the General Insurance Theory" (Japanese), The Journal of Insurance Science, No. 636 in 2017.

Onzo, Miho is Professor of insurance at School of Commerce, Takachiho University, Tokyo. She worked as Director of Asia Research Interaction Center (2008-2013) and served as Dean of School of Commerce (2013-2017). Her primary scholarly interest includes deregulation, internationalization, and social responsibility of the Japanese insurance industry. She has also researched on how co-operatives improve their members' participation.

Preiner, Stefan MSc., BSc. (WU) studied Economic and Social Science at the Vienna University of Business and Economics as well as International Business Administration at the University of Vienna. Worked as a member of the project research staff of the "Fachbereich für Genossenschaftswesen" at the Faculty of Business, Economics and Statistics of the University of Vienna from July 2018 until March 2019.

Schediwy, Robert studied law and economics at the University of Vienna and at Saint Louis University, Missouri (LLD and MA). He has taught at the University of Vienna, at Webster University Vienna and as associate professor at Kuopio University (Finland). Schediwy is the author and editor of numerous publications, mostly on co-operatives and related matters.

Wolfgang Werner, Prof. Dipl.-Ing. Dr., was the president of the Verband ländlicher Genossenschaften in Lower Austria and was head of the Dr. Rudolf-Rasser institute.

Zeman, Stefanie MSc., BSc. (WU), is an economist at the Austrian Workers' Compensation Board.

Table 37: Premium income and market share of Health Insurers in 1959		
	premium income	market share in percent
Austria Versicherungsverein auf Gegenseitigkeit	139,288	32.24
Wiener Städtische Wechselseitige Versicherungeanstalt	105,365	24.39
Merkur	86,294	19.97
Vers.-Anst. d. österr. Bundesländer A.G.	60,659	14.04
Collegialität	40,667	9.41

Source: Veröffentlichungen des Bundesministeriums für Finanzen.

areas, such as agriculture, industry, or transportation. Sector-specific characteristics of insurances resulted only from a legally obligation to sign an insurance contract. This obligation is restricted to a few insurance sectors and opposed to the otherwise general voluntary nature of an insurance contract. Due to the differences, it does not surprise that the premium income in the various insurance sectors developed differently. The premiums increased the fastest regarding legal costs insurance, insurance against damage by natural forces, tap water insurance and household contents insurance. On the other hand, the premiums of fire, machinery, car accident, and hail insurances increased only slightly annually (see table 39).

The insurance penetration increased continuously from 2.03 percent in 1958 due to the economic upswing to 3.03 percent in 1969. It increased until 1960 constantly at the yearly rate of 0.10 percent, but was slowed down during the recession years 1961 (0.02), 1964 (0.03), and 1969 (0.05 percent).The insurance volume developed proportionally to the total gross premiums in connection with the Austrian population of each year. In 1958, the "average" Austrian citizen paid gross premiums to the amount of 399 Austrian Schilling per year to insurance companies and increased in average 11.8 percent per annum. During the years of the economic upswing the insurance volume increased to 1,362 Austrian Schilling in 1969, i.e. the sum had increased more than threefold (see figure 9).[273]

At the end of 1969, 39 domestic und 18 branches of foreign insurance companies existed in Austria. The latter were all joint stock com-

[273] Cf. *Rohrbach, W.* (1997), Der österreichische Versicherungsmarkt, in: Versicherungsgeschichte Österreichs, vol. V, Assekuranzmosaik des ausgehenden 20. Jahrhunderts, Vienna, p. 6.

Table 38: Share of the private insurance companies and the monetary and credit system for the creation of the gross domestic product

Year	Private insurers				monetary and credit system			
	Added value nominal in billion Austrian Schilling	Share of the GDP in percent	Real added value in billion Austrian Schilling	Share of the GDP in percent	Added value nominal in billion Austrian Schilling	Share of the GDP in percent	Real added value in billion Austrian Schilling	Share of the GDP in percent
1964	215	0.9	215	0.9	528	2.3	528	2.3
1970	367	1.0	361	1.2	1170	3.1	940	3.1

Source: *Szopo, P.* (1980), Die Entwicklung der österreichischen Privatversicherungswirtschaft seit 1959, in: Wifo-Monatsbericht 7.

Table 39: Gross premium income of the domestic direct business

Year	Life insurance		Health insurance		property and casualty insurance		Total
	in billion Austrian Schilling	In of the total gross premiums	in billion Austrian Schilling	In percent of the total gross premiums	in billion Austrian Schilling	In percent of the total gross premiums	in billion Austrian Schilling
1959	447	14,0	432	13.6	2,305	72.4	3,184
1961	597	14.4	562	13.5	2,994	72.1	4,153
1963	788	15.2	726	14.0	3,668	70.8	5,182
1965	1.071	16.1	908	13.7	4,674	70.2	6,652
1967	1.423	16.7	1,127	13.2	5,965	70.1	8,516
1969	1.798	17.3	1,487	14.4	7,078	68.3	10,363

Source: *Szopo, P.* (1980), Die Entwicklung der österreichischen Privatversicherungswirtschaft seit 1959, in: Wifo-Monatsbericht 7.

Table 40: Premium elasticities in the domestic direct business

Years	Life insurance	Health insurance	Non-life and accident insurance	Total
1959/1962	1.54	1.46	1.32	1.37
1962/1967	1.90	1.45	1.53	1.58
1967/1971	1.34	1.46	1.17	1.24

Source: *Szopo, P.* (1980), Die Entwicklung der österreichischen Privatversicherungswirtschaft seit 1959, in: Wifo-Monatsbericht 7.

Figure 9: Insurance penetration of the Austrian market between 1958 and 1969 in percent

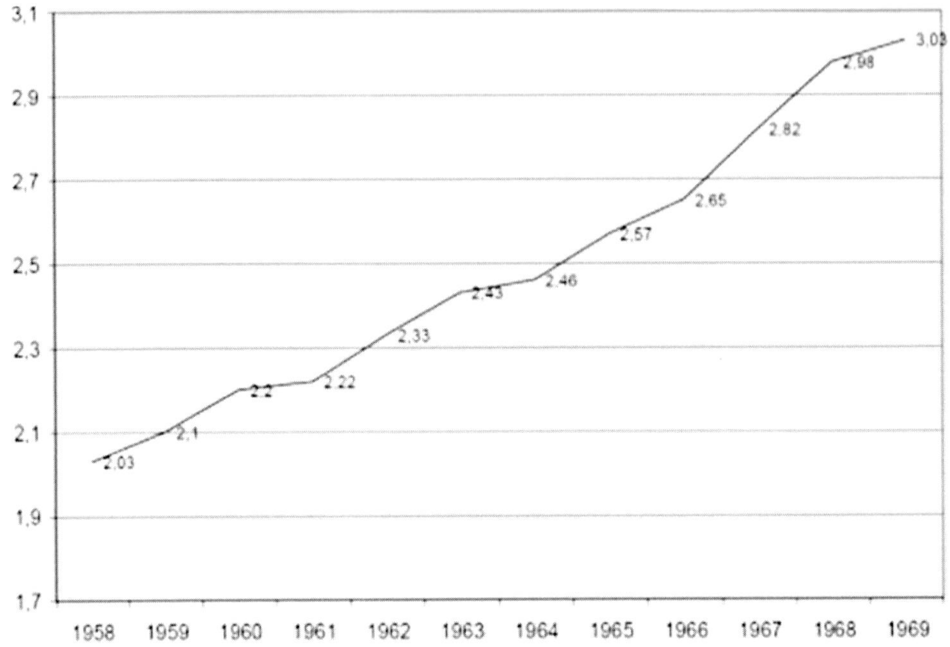

Source: VVO Annual report 2007 (Eigenverlag 2008), quoted in: *Kohlweg*, p. 137.

panies. The domestic companies comprised 20 joint stock companies, 13 mutual insurance societies, and 6 regional insurance institutions (Landesanstalten). Six new joint stock companies, three were foreign insurance companies were founded between 1955 and 1969.[274]

The insurance companies undertook property and casualty insurance, life insurance, and health insurance. 39 insurance companies were pure property and casualty insurers (from them 17 were foreign insurance stock companies)[275] and six pure life insurers (one was a foreign insurance stock company). From the remaining 12 composite insurers, eight were life, property, and casualty insurers, while three

[274] Foreign: "Nordstern Lebenversicherungs-AG", "Allianz Versicherungs-A.G." (1965), "Colonia Versicherung Aktiengesellschaft"; domestic: "DAS Der Automobil Schutz" (1955), "Garant Versicherungs-Aktiengesellschaft" (1958), "Raiffeisen-Lebensversicherungs A.G." (1969).

[275] There were also 108 small "Brandschaden- und Viehversicherungsvereine auf Gegenseitigkeit".

Figure 10: Total premium income, insurance payments and market share of mutual and stock insurance companies on the Austrian insurance market, 1959-1969

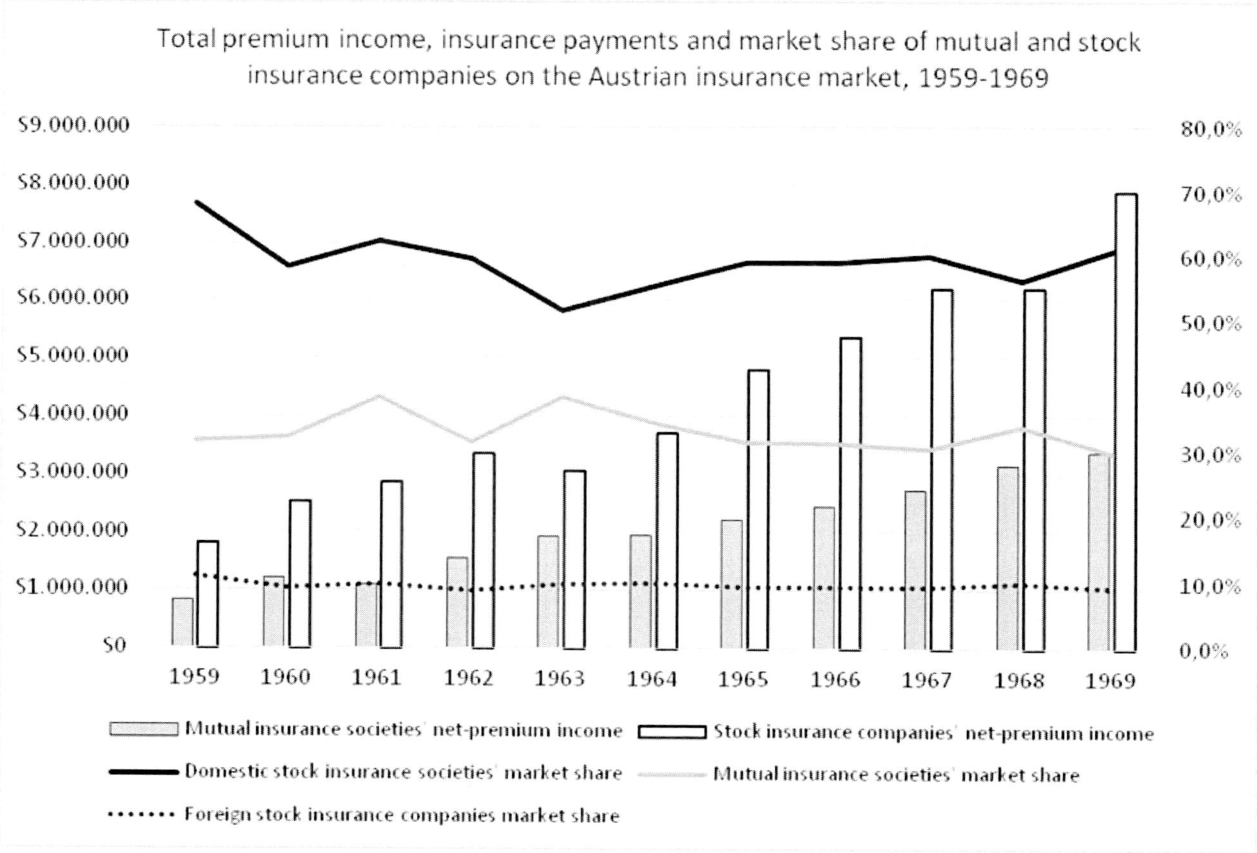

Source: Veröffentlichungen des Bundesministeriums für Finanzen.

were life and health insurers and one health, property, and casualty insurer, two insurance companies, the "Merkur Wechselseitige Krankenversicherungs-Anstalt" and the "Wiener Städtische Wechselseitige Versicherungsanstalt" offered all three insurance segments. In 1969, the largest insurance segment was property and casualty insurances with a market share of 68.8 percent regarding premiums, followed by life insurance with 17.3 percent, and health insurers with 14.4 percent.

In general, the period 1959-1969 was characterized by a high growth rate of premium income of the entire insurance industry (increase of the gross premiums of more than threefold), a development from which in particular joint stock companies with their ongoing market leadership benefitted the most. During the transition to a free insurance market (the end of the reconstruction of the insurance industry after 1945) from 1959 to 1963, the market share of mutuals increased (1959: 31.7 percent to 1963: 38.5 percent). However, the domestic joint stock companies' share increased again to 60.9 percent in 1969. On the other hand, foreign companies stagnated during this period with a share of 10 percent. It seems that the Austrian insurance market was not very attractive for foreign companies (see figure 10).

As mentioned before, the property and casualty insurance market lost its importance on the overall market between 1959 (72.4 percent) and 1969 (68.3 percent). Nevertheless, the market proportion regarding the legal forms remained constant due to its strong heterogeneity: in 1959, the ratios of mutuals (26.4 percent), domestic joint stock companies (65.3 percent), and foreign stock companies (8.4 percent) are similar to the ratios in 1969: mutuals (24.2 percent), domestic joint stock companies (65.7 percent), and foreign stock companies (7.9 percent) (see figure 11).

The property and casualty insurance market had the lowest concentration. The three largest companies had a total market share of 38.69 percent. The largest company was the "Erste Allgemeine Unfall und Schadenversicherung AG" with a market share of 13.79 percent, followed by "Wiener Städtische Wechselseitige Versicherung" on the second place, and the "Versicherungsanstalt der österreichischen Bundesländer" on the third (see table 41).

A retrospective view of the history of the Austrian insurance industry, in particular regarding the fire insurance segment, shows the endurance of mutuals, which total market share, was only between 8.24 and 5.48 during the period 1959 and 1969.

At first, mutuals dominated on the new life insurance and health insurance market, a trend that did not lasted very long (see figure 12).

Figure 11: Premium income, insurance payments and market share of mutual and stock property and casualty insurance companies on the Austrian insurance market, 1959-1969

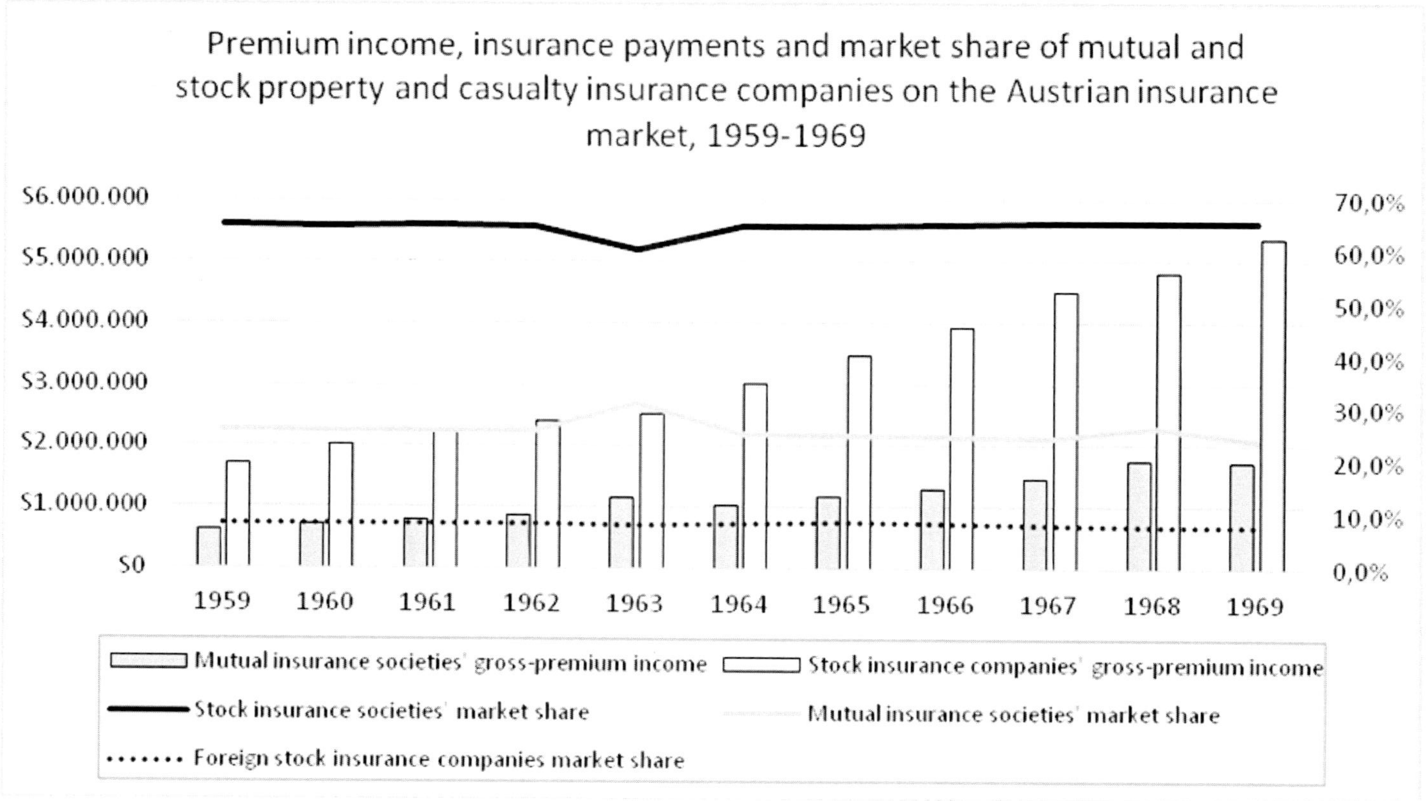

Source: Veröffentlichungen des Bundesministeriums für Finanzen

Figure 12: Premium income, insurance payments and market share of mutual and stock life insurance companies on the Austrian insurance market, 1960-1969

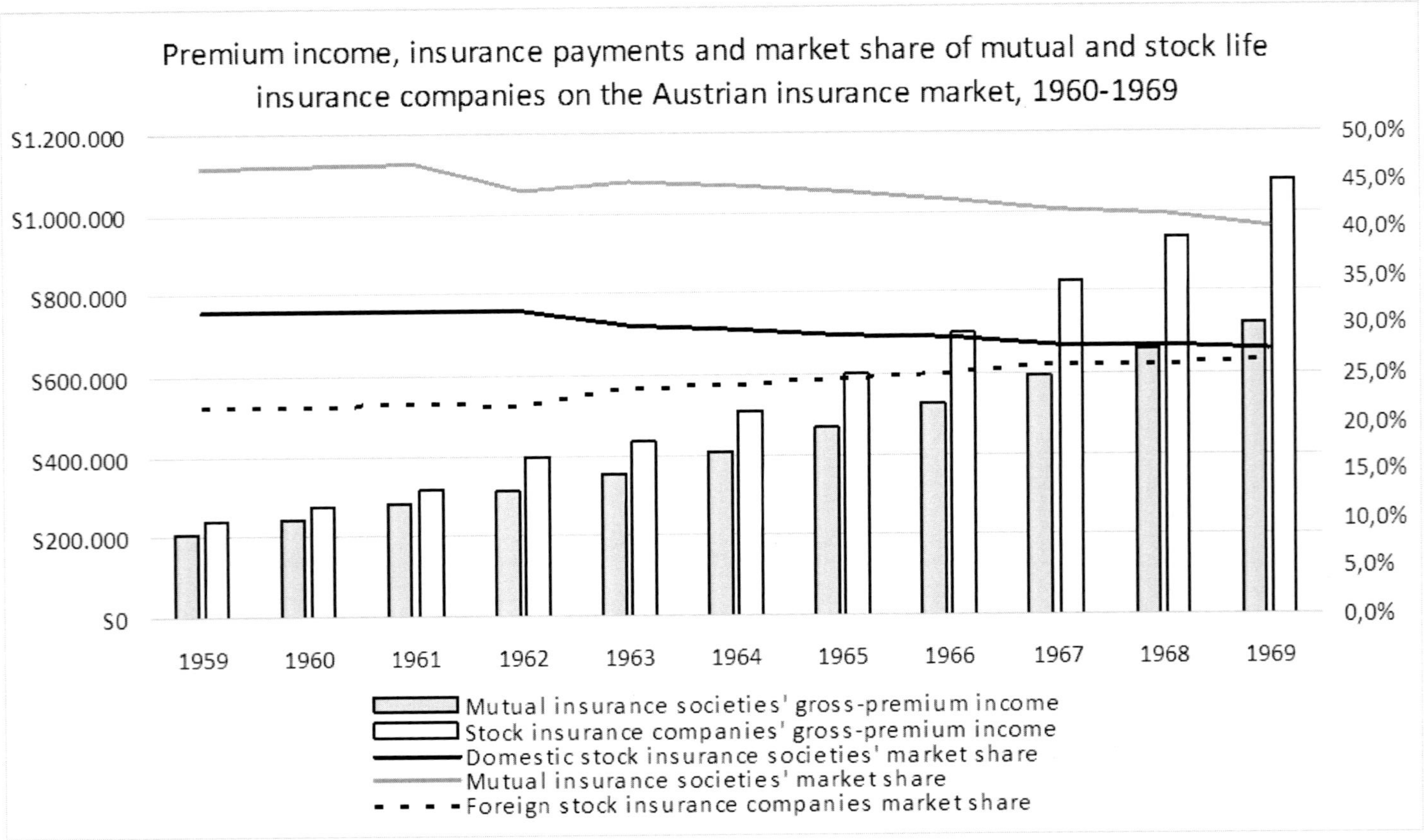

Source: Veröffentlichungen des Bundesministeriums für Finanzen

Table 41: Top 5 Property and Casualty Insurers on the Austrian insurance market in 1969			
name	direct gross premium income (in 1,000 Schilling)	market sharen in percent	gross insurance payments
Erste Allgemeine Unfall- und Schadens-Versicherungs-Gesellschaft	1.009.798	13.79	884.199
Wiener Städtische Wechselseitige Versicherungsanstalt	932.900	13.64	355.468
Versicherungsanstalt der österreichischen Bundesländer AG	820.916	11.26	376.389
Wiener Allianz Versicherungs-AG	806.373	10.11	261.124
Internationale Unfall- und Schadensversicherungs-AG (Interunfall)	554.293	7.84	247.155

Source: Veröffentlichungen des Bundesministeriums für Finanzen.

The Insurance Rebuilding Act influenced the benefits from health insurances until 1960: After the war, benefits and benefits limitations still existed, which lifting triggered an enormous increase in performance. As a result, the life insurance segment became the most expansive segment. Within ten years, the premium income increased from 447 Mio. (1959) to 11.798 Mio. (1969), which was a steep increase. At the same time, the demand profile of the policyholder changed evidently. While after the war primary industrial life insurances that were paid in the event of damage, such as funeral costs, ordinary life insurances, i.e. saving of capital for a future point in time, became common during the 1960s. With that, the life insurance market changed fundamentally. In 1964, group insurances developed, when for example a company had a master agreement with an insurance company. In that case, the insurance conditions were more reasonable, because the group was comprised under one contract.[276]

Regarding the legal forms, both mutuals and joint stock companies a decrease of their market shares. While mutuals started from a high market share in 1959 (46.4 percent) to a lower in 1969 (40.1 percent), the domestic stock companies' already low market share in 1959 (31.7 percent) decreased further (1969 27.7 percent). The winners of this development were foreign stock companies with an increasing market share from 22.0 percent in 1959 to 26.2 percent in 1969. Also the "Wiener Städtische Wechselseitige Versicherungsanstalt" was able to maintain its success course due to an expanding group formation.

[276] Cf. *Kohlweg, J.* (2009). Lebensversicherungen als Teil der Pensionsvorsorge in Österreich seit 1945, unpublished Masterthesis, Vienna, p. 49f.

The life insurance market was not so highly concentrated. The three largest companies had a total market share of 54.70 percent. The largest company, the "Assicurazioni Generali", with held 19.43 percent, while the "Wiener Städtische Wechselseitige Versicherungsanstalt" and the "Versicherungsanstalt der österreichischen Bundesländer AG" were the second and third largest life insurers (see table 42).

Table 42: Top 5 Life Insurers on the Austrian insurance market in 1969

name	direct gross premium income (in 1,000 Schilling)	market share in percent	gross insurance payments
Assicurazioni Generali, Direktion für Österreich	349,385	19.43	109,322
Wiener Städtische Wechselseitige Versicherungsanstalt	323,253	17.98	163,811
Versicherungsanstalt der österreichischen Bundesländer AG	299,595	16.66	140,119
Wiener Verein Lebens- und Bestattungsversicherung a. G	144,170	8.02	48,229
Österreichische Volksfürsorge Lebensversicherungs-AG	85,680	4.95	58,339

Source: Veröffentlichungen des Bundesministeriums für Finanzen.

The health insurance segment was a new type of insurance in Austria that had to prove itself during the years 1959 to 1969. After 1945, it had the advantages that for this insurance type neither the regulations of the law regarding the Schilling nor the restrictions of the Insurance Transaction Act applied to. As mentioned above, the direct domestic business dominated and the premium incomes increased continuously, while at the same time the group of people compulsorily insured with the National Insurance clearly expanded. The health insurers were able to compensate this process of ousting by expanding their supplementary insurance business – expansion of their range of products – and improving their service (e.g. introduction of blanket rate).[277] *Lehner* states that the awareness of people for health prevention due to the National Insurance was also an advantage for the

[277] Cf. *Dickinger, G.* (1999), Vom Krankenversicherer zum Gesundheitssicherer, Linz, p. 51.

Table 43: Top 5 Health Insurers on the Austrian insurance market in 1969			
name	direct gross premium income (in 1,000 Schilling)	market share in percent	gross insurance payments
Austria Versicherungsverein auf Gegenseitigkeit	409,439	27.54	223,985
Wiener Städtische Wechselseitige Versicherungeanstalt	391,148	26.31	281,261
Merkur	275,814	18.55	195,086
Vers.-Anst. d. österr. Bundesländer A.G.	212,795	14.31	156,037
Collegialität	103,460	6.96	62,498

Source: Veröffentlichungen des Bundesministeriums für Finanzen

private health insurance.[278] However, an important fact for the growth rate for health insurances was the cost increase triggered by hospitals and doctors' fees. As a result, the insurance contributions for the general class became insufficient and the resulting deficit had to be balanced out by the services of private insurers.[279]

In 1959, mutuals had still an outstanding market position with a market share of 87.2 percent, although with a continuously decreasing trend to 79.7 percent until 1969. Domestic joint stock companies, on the other hand, were able to catch up from year to year and increased their market share from 12.8 percent to 20.3 percent during this period (see figure 13). The "Austria Versicherungsverein auf Gegenseitigkeit" proved itself during this time by its group formation effort, which eventually brought it on the path of success. No foreign insurance companies undertook health insurances.

The health insurance market comprised only six companies during the period 1959 to 1969 and was so highly concentrated. The first three companies had a total market share of 72.40 percent. The largest insurer was the "Austria Versicherungsverein auf Gegenseitigkeit" with a market share of 27.54 percent, followed by the "Wiener Städtische Wechselseitige Versicherung" (26.31 percent), and the "Merkur Wechselseitige Versicherungsanstalt" (18.55 percent) on the third place. With the exception of two, all other companies offering health insurances were mutuals (see table 43).

[278] Cf. *Lehner, U.* (1988), Staat und Versicherung in Österreich, in: Versicherungsgeschichte Österreichs, vol. III, Das Zeitalter des modernen Versicherungswesens, Vienna, p. 858.

[279] Cf. *Dickinger, G.* (1999), Vom Krankenversicherer zum Gesundheitssicherer, Linz, p. 55.

Figure 13: Premium income, insurance payments and market share of mutual and stock health insurance companies on the Austrian insurance market, 1959-1969

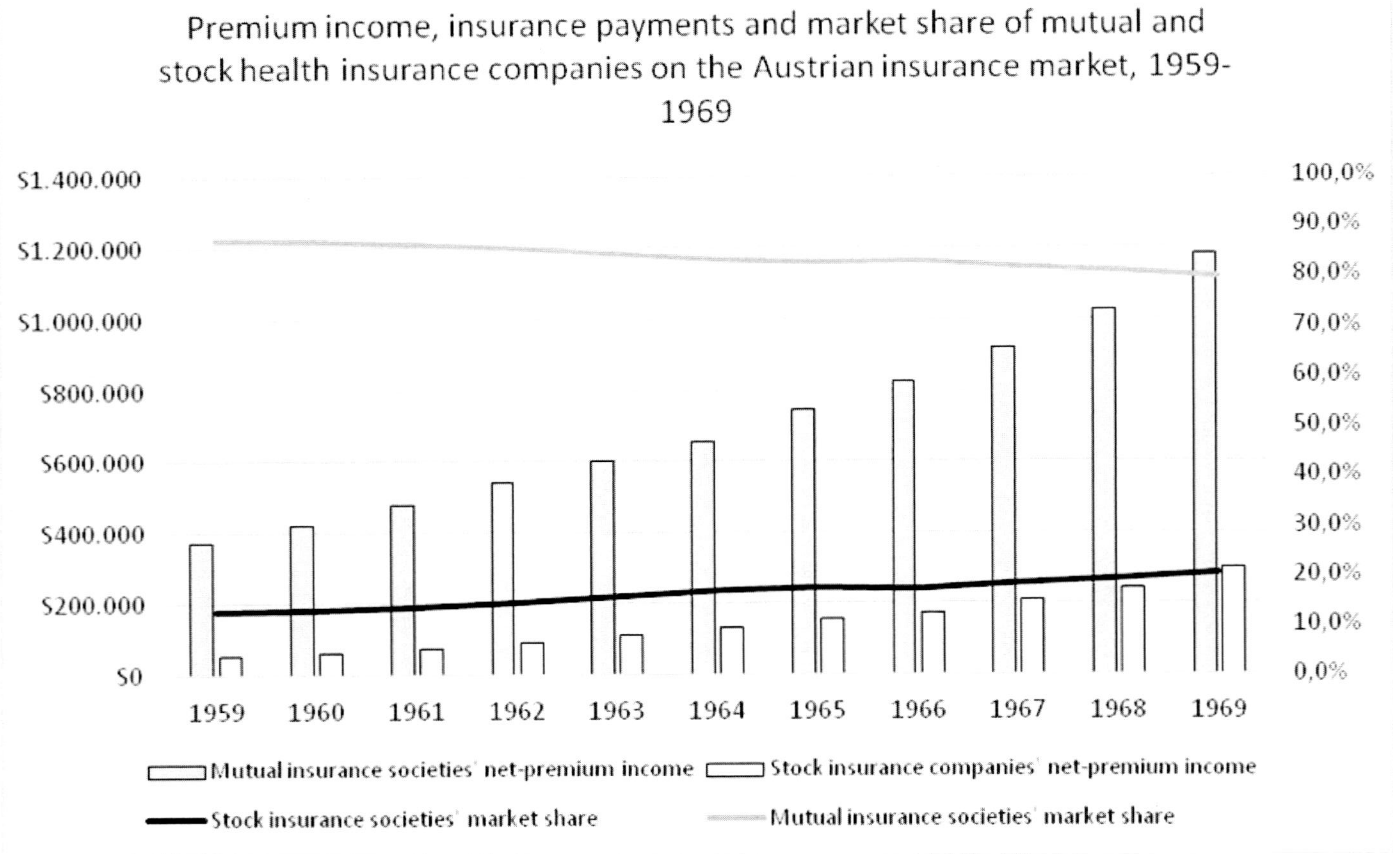

Source: Veröffentlichungen des Bundesministeriums für Finanzen.

Bibliography

Baran, P. (2015), Das Österreichische Versicherungsaufsichtsrecht, Vienna

Baumgartner, I. (2003), 175 Jahre Grazer Wechselseitige, Festschrift anlässlich des 175-jährigen Jubiläums der Grazer Wechselseitigen Versicherung, Graz

Borscheid, P. (2012), Europe: Overview, in: *Borscheid, P. / Haueter, N.* (eds.): World Insurance, Oxford

Braun, H. (1963), Geschichte der Lebensversicherung und der Lebensversicherungstechnik, Berlin

Bridgewater, A. (1995), The Modern Mutual Insurance Company in Britain, in: *Preiner, W.* (ed.) Grundlagen des Versicherungsvereins auf Gegenseitigkeit, Köln/Göttingen

Dickinger, G. (1999), Vom Krankenversicherer zum Gesundheitssicherer, Linz

Die österreichischen Assecuranz-Gesellschaften im Jahre 1892, in: Mittheilungen und Miscellen, Statistische Monatsschrift XX. Jahrgang

Egl, H. (1988), Maktstrukturen der österreichischen Versicherungswirtschaft zwischen 1925 und 1938, in: Versicherungsgeschichte Österreichs, vol. III, Das Zeitalter des modernen Versicherungswesens,Vienna

Egl, H. / Ludwig, B. (1988), Die Geschichte der Feuerversicherung von 1873 bis 1918, in: Die Ära des klassischen Versicherungswesens, Versicherungsgeschichte Österreichs, vol. II, Vienna

Ehrenberger, H. (1987), Die Geschäftsresultate der österr.-ungar. Lebensversicherungs-Gesellschaften und der ausländischen Lebens-Versicherungs-Gesellschaften in Oesterreich im Jahre 1886, in: Mittheilungen und Miscellen, Statistische Monatsschrift XIII

Ehrenzweig, A. (1929), Die Rechtsordnung der Vertragssicherung. Vienna. p. 501f.; *Rohrbach, W.*, Versicherungsgeschichte Österreichs, vol. I, Von den Anfängen bis zum Börsenkrach des Jahres 1873, Vienna 1988

Fachini E. (1888), Entstehung, Grundsätze und Entwicklung des Versicherungswesens in Österreich-Ungarn, Vienna

Fenyves, A. / Korinek, S. (1999), Das österreichische Versicherungsaufsichtsrecht im Überblick, in: Zeitschrift für Verwaltung, 24. Jahrgang 2

Gedenkschrift zum fünfzigjährigen Bestände des Ersten allgemeinen Beamten-Vereines der österreichisch-ungarischen Monarchie, Vienna 1915

Gollowitsch, J. (1950), Die geschichtliche Entwicklung des österreichischen Versicherungswesens bis zur Zulassung ausländischer Gesellschaften, Graz

Good, D. (1986), Der wirtschaftliche Aufstieg des Habsburgerreiches, Vienna

Hannak, K. (1969), Die Rechtsform der Landes-Versicherungsanstalten, in: Die Versicherungs-Rundschau. Heft 2

Herzfeld, E. (1896), Bemerkungen zum neuen österreichischen Assekuranzregulativ, in: Zeitschrift für die gesamte Versicherungs-Wissenschaft 2

Hollmayer, A. (2000), Makrodaten der Österreichischen Assekuranz 1875-2000, in: Versicherungsgeschichte Österreichs, vol. VI, An der Schwelle zum 3. Jahrtausend – Retrospektiven und Perspektiven, Vienna

Homburg, A. Legitimität des öffentlichen Versicherungswesens in der Bundesrepublik Deutschland. Vienna 2004 *Homburg, A.* Legitimität des öffentlichen Versicherungswesens in der Bundesrepublik Deutschland. Vienna 2004

Ilwof, F. (1879), Geschichte der wechselseitigen Brandschaden-Versicherungs-Anstalt in Graz von 1829 bis 1879. Graz

Israel, B. (1886) Die Geschäfts-Resultate der österr.-ungar. und der ausländischen Lebensversicherungs-Gesellschaften in Oesterreich-Ungarn im Jahre 1885, in: Mittheilungen und Miscellen, Statistische Monatsschrift XII Jahrgang

Israel, B. (1888), Die Geschäftsresultate der österr.-ungar. Lebensversicherungs-Gesellschaften und der ausländischen Lebens-Versicherungs-Gesellschaften in Oesterreich im Jahre 1887, in: Mittheilungen und Miscellen, Statistische Monatsschrift XIV Jahrgang

Israel, B. (1889), Die Feuerversicherungs-Gesellschaften in Oesterreich während der Jahre 1878-87, in: Mittheilungen und Miscellen, Statistische Monatsschrift XV. Jahrgang

Israel, B. (1889), Die Geschäftsresultate der österr.-ungar. Lebensversicherungs-Gesellschaften und der ausländischen Lebens-Versicherungs-Gesellschaften in Oesterreich im Jahre 1888, in: Mittheilungen und Miscellen, Statistische Monatsschrift XV Jahrgang

Jobst, C. / Kernbauer, H. (2016), Die Bank. Das Geld. Der Staat Nationalbank und Währungspolitik in Österreich 1816-2016, Frankfurt a.M.

Kalss, S. / Burger, C. / Eckert, G. (2003), Die Entwicklung des österreichischen Aktienrechts, Vienna

Koch, P. (2012), Geschichte der Versicherungswirtschaft in Deutschland, Karlsruhe

Kohlweg, J. (2009). Lebensversicherungen als Teil der Pensionsvorsorge in Österreich seit 1945, unpublished Masterthesis, Vienna

Kraus, H. (1971), Versicherungsaufsichtsrecht – Eine Studie zum deutschen und zum österreichischen Recht, in: Forschungen aus Staat und Recht, vol. 16, Vienna

Kraus, H. (1971), Versicherungsaufsichtsrecht – Eine Studie zum deutschen und zum österreichischen Recht, in: Forschungen aus Staat und Recht, vol. 16, Vienna

Krejci, H. / Weilinger, A. (ed.) (1988), Österreichisches Versicherungsrecht. Gesetze, Verordnungen und ausgewählte Materialien. Vienna

Krickl, R. (1893), Die österreichischen Assecuranz-Gesellschaften im Jahre 1891, in: Mittheilungen und Miscellen Statistische Monatsschrift XIX Jahrgang

Krickl, R. (1895), Die österreichischen Assecuranz-Gesellschaften im Jahre 1893, in: Mittheilungen und Miscellen, Statistische Monatsschrift XXI Jahrgang

Krickl, R. (1896), Die österreichischen Assecuranz-Gesellschaften im Jahre 1894, in: Mittheilungen und Miscellen, Statistische Monatsschrift XXII Jahrgang

Krickl, R. (1897), Die österreichischen Assecuranz-Gesellschaften im Jahre 1895, in: Mittheilungen und Miscellen, Statistische Monatsschrift XXIII Jahrgang

Krickl, R. (1898), Die österreichischen Assecuranz-Gesellschaften im Jahre 1896, in: Mittheilungen und Miscellen, Statistische Monatsschrift XXIV Jahrgang

Lehner, U. (1988), Das Versicherungswesen in der Zweiten Republik, in: Versicherungsgeschichte Österreichs, vol. III, Das Zeitalter des modernen Versicherungswesens, Vienna

Introduction

Gabriela Csulich

1. Defining "insurance"

On Sunday morning on the 2nd of September 1666, the people of London were woken by the sounds of bells announcing a catastrophic disaster that should alter the city of London and the insurance business forever. It started in Pudding Lane in the shop of the king's baker, *Thomas Farrinor*. The sparks from his oven fell onto some dry flour sacks, they caught fire, and flames spread through the house, down Pudding Lane and into the nearby streets. Soon the city of London was filled with smoke and the sky was red with huge flames from the fire. By Monday, 300 houses had burned down and 100,000 people were homeless. On Monday September 8th 1666, the London Gazette published the following article about the catastrophic event. "On the second instant at one of the clock in the Morning there hapned to break out, a sad in deplorable fire, in Pudding Lane, neer New Fish-street, which falling out at that hour of the night, and in a quarter of the town so close built with wooden pitched houses spread itself so far before day, and with such distraction to the inhabitants and Neighbours, that care was not taken for the timely preventing the further diffusion of it, by pulling down houses, as ought to have been; so that this lamentable Fire in a short time became too big to be mastred by any Engines or working neer it."[1]

The outbreak of a fire of such magnitude had to have consequences for the city of London[2] as well as for the development of the insurance business in general. It was unique that in London various organizational forms for fire insurers developed.

This diversity of organizational forms for fire insurance companies resulted directly from the formation of a modern state. This development was also closely connected with the evolving capitalism as well as with England's political and territorial independence from the Eu-

[1] The London Gazette, September 1666; Monday September 3, to Monday September 10, 1666, p. 1, https://greatfireoflondon.net/london-gazette-1666/ (29.11.2019).

[2] Stimulated the most concerted attempt to apply science and the law to the problem.

ropean mainland since the 1630s. The English Civil War (1642 to 1649) generated the change from a feudal social order to a middle class society. In the beginning, the social and political process of modernisation was coordinated by a strong central political power, but ended much earlier compared to the European mainland in 1688 with the Glorious Revolution, the introduction of the Bill of Rights and a new sight for private property. Moreover, these events marked a watershed by changing Britain into a constitutional monarchy and into an enlightened and parliamentary state.[3] With regard to the economic and financial changes during this period, London became the world's largest fire insurance market as well as a melting pot for all at this time existing organizational forms, a public corporation initiated by the city council in 1680, a capital-orientated joint stock company (1681), self-help organizations such as a friendly society (1684) and a mutual fire insurance company (1696). The latter existed successfully more than 100 years. In Germany and Austria, on the other hand, the reasons for choosing the organizational form of fire insurances differed, a fact that will be explained later in this study.

However, the question how to insure and prevent such catastrophic events is difficult to answer, because it is important to consider the zeitgeist of this period, too. Many European countries had faced before great fires that destroyed buildings and livelihoods, drove people into poverty and hardship. People had accepted their faith perceiving it as a punishment or providence by God and turning with prayers to a forgivable divine being. This incident in London, however, shattered the belief middle many Britons below the middling classes and generated the idea to face natural disasters and to make them to something "insurable" and not to another moral lesson. But what exactly is insurance and how can it be put into practice?

Legally, an insurance is a contract, characterized by an insurance policy, in which an individual or entity gets financial protection or compensation against losses from an insurance company. Such insurance companies have usually been formed as capital-orientated joint stock companies or mutual companies, sometimes also as public institutions. From a historical point of view, mutuals and joint stock companies developed differently. The mutual form of help, based on a support system concerning situations in which an individual has to join others to "secure together what one cannot secure alone" without the requirement of capital formation, is the earliest organizational form. A

[3] Cf. *Kees van der Pijl* (1996), Vordenker der Weltpolitik Einführung in die internationale Politik aus ideengeschichtlicher Perspektive, Opladen 1996, p. 55. According to *Paerson* also the Protestantism was an important factor to try such methods of self help in the face of calamities (Cf. *Pearson, R.* (2004), Insuring the Industrial Revolution. Fire insurance in Great Britain, 1700-1850, London, p. 3).

similar form of organization offering insurances and compensation is a friendly society, an association that combines mutual aid and fraternalism. Its philosophy is based on the Christian value of neighbourliness emphasizing cooperation and mutual aid. Friendly societies had their origin in the United Kingdom respectively Ireland and were precursors of modern insurers focusing on helping their members in the event of illness or death, and later even of fire.

On the other hand, insurance companies are closely connected with the development of monetary economies. During the middle ages Venice started to develop into the centre of commerce, drawing merchants from all parts of Europe to the city in the Mediterranean area by offering economic freedom. In Venice, it was possible to buy and sell goods from the Orient and the Occident. There Europe evolved into a place where neither religion nor culture was important as long as profit was involved. This led to the development of capitalism, in particular for merchants and traders, who joined and formed associations to establish merchant fleets. However, pirates and storms endangered such journeys, and, therefore, the merchants' investments. The transport over hundreds of kilometers on land was also a dangerous enterprise for goods and the life of the merchants. To handle this major problem, Italian merchants modernized the way of payments by developing a bill of exchange.[4]

Therefore, two different approaches resulted for the development respectively increase of risks:

- the transportation itself
- the temporal difference between performance and counter-performance respectively the time span the trade flows needed in this period

At the same time, new organizational forms such as guilds were introduced to covering risk. With an exchange bill, the seller was now able to change his assets into cash on every market. This form of cashless payment revolutionized the trade business and led to the foundation of banks and eventually to granting loans for interests. Money developed from a form of payment to a good of its own, i.e. to capital, and merchants became capitalists who founded the first financial institutions in Europe. With such economic power armed, merchants used their position to influence political decisions by demanding privileges, e.g. trade monopolies, taxes and tariffs, instead of interests.

---

[4] It all started in northern Italy, where the first real insurance transactions, mainly covering goods-in-transit against the perils of transportation, became a customary incident of trade, in the province of Lombardy from where the daring and adventurous merchants spread their practice of insurance to every conceivable trading town of the European continent.

At the beginning of the 13th century, approximately 1,000 conurbations were established near market places, cathedral cities, and castles. In the 14th century, 3,000 cities existed in the middle of Europe. During this time, urban development started too, when more and people came to towns for work and more accommodations were needed. With newly built timber houses and warehouses, insurances were necessary to protect these buildings. The phenomenon of urbanization happened everywhere, a development that made insurances, as capital-orientated companies or mutuals, international due to the further development of the capitalism and the insurance industry to something expanding across political, ethnic, religious, and cultural borders.

Several trends can be identified when looking at the various historical, political, and geographical events that shaped the insurance business in general.

- Firstly, the perception of fires and catastrophic events by the population changed over time. While originally people regarded them as punishment or providence of god, the industrial revolution transformed them into insurable risks. Moreover, scientific innovations and technological progress led to debates about rationality and the concept of nature.[5]
- Secondly, catastrophic events such as major fires in metropolises led to impulses of developing the insurance business and of taking measures to prevent and contain fires on a larger scale. Examples for such changes can be found in Great Britain with the "Great Fire in London" (1666) or in Germany with huge fires in Hamburg in 1606, 1626, and 1676. A similar effect had the large fires in Copenhagen (1728), in Chicago (1871) and Boston (1916), but also in Japan (1955 in Niigate City) that changed the people's perception about the existing efficiency of fire alarms and fire-fighting systems.
- Thirdly, although these events effected the development of insurances, the realization and foundation of insurance companies differed in the various countries regarding organizational form, time line, economic impact, and acceptance by the people and the governments immensely. While in Great Britain people joined together to distribute risks, choosing freely the organizational form of the insurance company, such as mutuals, joint stock companies, or friendly societies, in Germany the fire insurance was perceived as a public responsible of the cities and counties, starting with Hamburg in 1677. Therefore, this form of public insurance companies was initiated from above. Moreover, the membership was obligatory in these public institutions and had a large financial fund, a fact that will be explained later in this paper.
- In the Austrian-Hungarian monarchy, the first foundations of insurance companies were delayed due to difficult state formations during the

5 Cf. *Pearson, R.* (2004), Insuring the Industrial Revolution. Fire insurance in Great Britain, 1700-1850, London, p. 1.

reign of Empress *Maria Theresia* (Trieste since 1754). With establishing so-called "Landesanstalten" (regional insurance institutions) during the 1820s, no clear decision between capital-orientated companies, public institutions, and mutuals was made.[6]

- Finally, a geographical trend regarding marine insurances respectively transport insurances can be observed. The latter was not only the first line of insurance business, originating back to the ancient world, it also included a geographical element that can be traced back to the Mediterranean trade of the late Middle Ages. During this time, capitalism developed and traders became important figures. At that time, a merchant or banker acted as an individual underwriter for a merchant seeking insurance, while a broker connected them as an intermediary. The insurance as a product of this transaction was usually short term ranging from weeks to more than a year for maritime trades. From the Mediterranean area, the maritime insurance business expanded to the Northern European countries, to the Netherlands and from there via merchants to London, Germany, and Trieste that was part of the Austrian Hungarian monarchy during the 18th century. In this line of insurance, joint stock companies dominated the market, while mutuals became strong in the fire insurance business. In the 19th century, the maritime insurance segment generated also the development of the so-called P & I clubs, mutual companies that are specialised in transport insurances, in Norway and in the northern parts of Britain. These clubs started from small mutual companies, usually regional limited, and became successful global companies until today.

2. From god's punishment to insurable risk

As mentioned above, the basic concept of risk management is to spreading risks over a group of people to avoid unbearable suffering for e.g. families or small groups of people. This concept can be found, for example, during the 9th century, when people from various clans joined by oath helped each other in the event of fire, hail, or transport hazards. When simultaneously to the industrial revolution this way of supporting each other developed into organizational forms, two types of companies became the most common ones in many countries world-

[6] These insurance companies, so-called "Landesanstalten", based their premiums calculation on the procedure of adjustable contributions. Although this was common practice in many countries before fix premiums were introduced, this method became problematic when people started to use insurances for their own financial advantage by burning down their own houses and claiming the insurance money. Their actions made nonsense of the original idea of mutual help and support.

wide[7], mutuals and capital-orientated joint stock companies. These two types differ in such way that the policyholders of mutuals are the owners of the company and usually members of the company, while an insurance joint stock company, on the other hand, is owned by its shareholders. However, the product both organizational forms sell is not tangible; it is rather based on trust and expectation. The policyholders trust the insurer that for paying a certain amount of money, they will receive financial coverage for future losses in the event of e.g. fire, hail, or death. In case of a whole-term life insurance, the policyholder's claim is even made by someone else. On the other hand, the insurer had to make it clear that the company remains solvent in the future and guarantees that the risk is insurable.[8] Originally, the to-be insured risks comprised mainly fire hazards and transport issues, over time and due to the industrial revolution support for illnesses, deaths, and impoverishment became crucial. Insurances became so a way to improve the circumstances of the working class and, therefore, concerned to handle the social question.[9]

Over time, associations developed into organized societies and eventually into insurers with the aim to distribute risks among their members, which is the core element of mutual insurance societies. Mutual help is therefore the most elementary and simplest form of insurance. In such organized form, the process of spreading risks are practiced via regular contributions and developed gradually from voluntary contributions in form of mutual help to societies and institutions based on membership, either voluntary or compulsory, and monetary contributions. In countries like the Netherlands or the United Kingdom, societies and organizations based on the mutuality principle emerged during the 17th and 18th century, while one of the earliest mutual fire societies can be found in Germany, when in 1591, the building owners in Hamburg established the first mutual fire contract on voluntary basis. This development, however, was challenged when, as mentioned above, major fires showed the inadequacy of the existing fire preventing system. Consequently, the City Council founded in 1676 a public fire insurance fund ("Hamburger Feuerkasse"), replacing the current fire contracts and transferring their assets into the fund. The new established and very successful public fire institution based on compulsory membership of all property owners in Hamburg. Although the rise of the insurance business in Britain was also generated by a catastrophic event,

---

[7] The exceptions were, as mentioned above, Germany, Austria, and Scandinavia.

[8] Cf. *Pearson, R.* (2010), Introduction: Towards an international history of insurance, in: *Pearson, R.* (eds.) (2010). The development of international insurance, London, p. 1.

[9] Cf. *Brazda, J., Csulich, G., Zeman, St.* (2018), Das Gegenseitigkeitsprinzip im Versicherungswesen aus historisch-analytischer Sicht, in: *Brazda, J.; Blisse, H.* (eds.). Beiträge zur kritischen Genossenschaftsforschung, Vienna, p. 47.

the Great Fire of London (1666), the people initiated the modern fire insurance business. This catastrophe made it evident that the existing fire protection measures and compensation methods were insufficient. This included the many local cooperatives or collective schemes, such as "briefs". These official letters authorizing collections, sometimes compulsory, supported the victims of fires, but were unable to handle the problems of such epic proportion. Although the humanitarian aspect was the focus of these collections organized via parishes, they became open to fraudulent behaviour.[10]

At the same time, the movement of Enlightenment had a major impact on the concept of insurance. While originally people perceived fires and natural disasters such as earthquakes as a punishment by god, the notion of Enlightenment changed the European view of nature in general and with that, the idea of managing catastrophes respectively risks. In this situation private insurance companies, i.e. mutuals, capital-orientated joint stock companies as well as friendly societies (in the United Kingdom), evolved, becoming protectors of private property by insuring buildings. The ideology of preserving private property is an important issue in Great Britain and even acknowledged in the constitutional settlement of 1688. Property, in particular of the aristocracy and upper middle class, was a symbol of wealth and influence and supported as well as differentiated the social classes from each other. Consequently, securing property became a crucial factor.[11]

A similar trend regarding fire insurances can be found in the Nordic states such as Norway or Denmark. For example, a major fire generated in Copenhagen in 1728 the development of the fire insurance industry. In Norway, insurance companies were modelled after Danish enterprises and in 1753 the first Norwegian fire insurance "Christianiæ Byes Brand Assurance Casse" started its business as a voluntary, independent, and private organization, insuring buildings. The questions of how to prevent fire hazards and compensate damage became an issue not only in European countries, the growing cities in the United States were also confronted with such problems. Among the first established insurance companies, two mutuals were founded, in 1731 in Charleston (1731) and in 1752 in Philadelphia, providing insurances for selected houses within their towns. These first insurers modelled themselves af-

[10] Cf. *Ismay, P.* (2018), Trust among strangers. Friendly Societies in Modern Britain, Cambridge, p. 36f.; *Ismay, P.* (2010), Trust among strangers: Securing British Modernity `by way of friendly society,' 1780s-1870s; unpublished Dissertation University of California, Berkeley, p. 17.

[11] Cf. *Pearson, R.* (2004), Insuring the Industrial Revolution. Fire insurance in Great Britain, 1700-1850, London, p. 2f.

ter British marine and fire insurers, who were already well established by the eighteenth century[12]

3. Insurance industry and the industrialization

With new technological and scientific developments, the industry and the trade expanded their business overseas, leading to a thriving economy. New factories were built and the process of population growth, urban expansion and the rise in property values started to accelerate. People who migrated to cities needed accommodations and the growing industry needed more warehouses to store their goods for national and international trade. The cities became larger and overpopulated and with that fire hazards by combustible goods and buildings with stoves or manufacturing purposes became more frequent than ever. Insurance companies were challenged by this development. Firstly, they had to assess these new forms of risks and, secondly, they had to offer new insurance lines to cover the rising demand of fire and later of life assurances. The evaluation of possible future risks, however, needed to be based on risk scenarios that were built on probability allowing quantifying such hazards.[13]

These scientific innovations became known during the 18th century, but their actual use by the existing insurance companies took several decades or even longer. In the United Kingdom, for example, fire insurance companies competed against each other at the beginning of the 19th century to match the accelerated pace of the already fast industrial and commercial development that had started in the 18th century. The urban population grew steadily and England became an urban nation by developing large cities such as London. The insurance business reacted to this new development with fierce competition between insur-

---

[12] Cf. *Pearson, R.; Yoneyama, T.* (2015), Corporate forms and organizational choice in international insurance. An overview of the history and theory, in: *Pearson, R.; Yoneyama, T.* (eds.). Corporate forms and organizational choice in international insurance, Oxford, pp. 2-4.

[13] Cf. *Carter, R. L.; Falush, P.* (2009), The British Insurance Industry since 1900. The Era of Transformation, Houndmills, p. 118; https://apps.derstandard.at/privacywall/story/2000109264301/makrooekonomische-entwicklungen-unter-unsicherheit (3.10.2019); *Schredelseker, K.* (2005), Zur Entwicklung des finanz- und risikowirtschaftlichen Denkens, in: *Spremann, K.* (ed.). Versicherungen im Umbruch Werte schaffen, Risiken managen, Kunden gewinnen, Berlin, p. 513f.

ance companies. This situation became even more hostile due to two foundation waves of companies, the first during the 1820s and 1830s and the second after 1834. During this time, the dominance of the joint stock companies became evident, mutuals lost gradually business to the stock companies due to financial problems, followed by a wave of demutualization. By the early 1820s, the fifteen largest fire insurers in the United Kingdom were capital-orientated companies.[14]

In the Austrian-Hungarian monarchy, on the other hand, the insurance industry started, with the exception of transport insurance, not before the 1820 and was hindered by the unevenly industrial development in the different regions of the monarchy. At first, the insurance business was concentrated in Cisleithanien where the manufacturing production was located, i.e. in Bohemian-Moravian, the Austrian-Silesian areas, the Vienna Basin as well as East-Styria and parts of Carinthia. At the same time, the insurance industry functioned as a supporter of the industrialization by creating new insurance sectors. *Ritter von Högelmüller* generated the idea of protecting losses by fires by establishing fire insurance companies. His original concept was modelled after the German public fire insurances, but due to the Emperor's resolution (1819) insurance companies had to be private enterprises in the Austrian-Hungarian monarchy. As a result, his companies were "Landesanstalten" i.e. mutuals under governmental protection and with premiums based on adjustable instead of fixed premiums. Over time, however, large fires and fraudulent behaviour of members economically challenged these companies.[15]

In the United States, the beginning of the industrialization and the increase of world trade generated an early and vigorous growth of the insurance industry. Additionally, this development was supported by immigrants who brought the concept of insurance to the United States. However, the enormous changes of the economic life and the effects of the industrial revolution required a new way of managing risks, such as workplace accidents, by monetary compensation.[16] Consequently, the US life insurance market became important, although the first pure life insurance company, the "Pennsylvania Company for Insurance on Lives and Granting Annuities", had already been established in 1812.

---

[14] Cf. *Pearson, R.; Yoneyama, T.* (2015), Corporate forms and organizational choice in international insurance. An overview of the history and theory, in: *Pearson, R.; Yoneyama, T.* (eds.). Corporate forms and organizational choice in international insurance, Oxford, p. 5f.

[15] Cf. *Brazda, J.* Mutual insurance society in Austria Developments of a principle. (study in this publication).

[16] Cf. *Pearson, R.*, Organizational Forms in Insurance. A comparison of the USA and Germany during Industrialization, in: *Pearson, R., Yoneyama, T.* (ed.) (2015), Corporate Forms and Organizational Choice in International Insurance, Oxford, p. 115.

During the 1830s, the development of more accurate mortality tables were used by two joint-stock companies, the "New York Life Insurance and Trust" and the "Baltimore Life Insurance", to successfully expand their business offering better premium rate structures and an extending agency network. By 1840, the "New York Life Insurance and Trust" accounted for more than half of the life insurances sold in the USA.[17] Due to a banking crisis in 1837[18], mutual companies became important players on the insurance market for the next two decades by offering low prices and life insurance policies without a time limit.[19] In Japan, the first mutual insurance "Dai-ichi Life Insurance" (1902) was established as a starting point for the rise of mutuals. It is important to note that in Japan insurance co-operatives are a crucial factor for the insurance industry.[20]

In Europe, the modern form of the life insurance sector did not emerge before the 18th century and became closely connected with the social question. Early forms of life insurances can already be found in Germany and Austria, establishing societies such as "Knappschaften" that offered miners benefits in the event of illness, accident, or death. By 1850, such societies had even become compulsory in the German mining industry and continued until the 20th century. From the 17th century onwards, mutual societies were established to provide for widows and children in the form of a permanent annuity in the event of the death of their spouses. These societies can be found across Europe and were restricted to particular groups such as physicians, lawyers, or military officers. In England (1692) and Austria (1727), the states provided pensions and disability allowances for essential state employees.[21] This type of insurance offered by the state can be regarded as an early form of social insurance for the group of governmental staff.

---

17 Cf. *Loftin, G., Xie, X.* (2007), The United States Insurance Market: Characteristics and Trends, in: *Cummins, J.D., Venard, B.* (ed.): Handbook of international insurances. Between Global Dynamics and Local Contingencies, New York, p. 26; Cf. *Brazda, J.* chapter about the US insurance market.

18 The economic crisis of 1837 was one of the biggest in the US history. The reason was a speculative bubble that burst on May 10, 1837 in New York, when every bank stopped the convertibility of the paper currency into gold or silver; Cf. *Lepler, J.* (2013), The Many Panics of 1837: People, Politics, and the Creation of a Transatlantic Financial Crisis, New York.

19 Cf. Swiss Re, Are Mutual Insurers an Endangered Species, in: Sigma, no. 4/1999, p. 11.

20 Cf. *Okada, F., Onzo, M., Kurimoto, A.* Mutual insurance and co-operative Kyosai in Japan (chapter about Japan in this book).

21 *Pearson, R.; Yoneyama, T.* (2015), Corporate forms and organizational choice in international insurance. An overview of the history and theory, in: *Pearson, R.; Yoneyama, T.* (eds.) (2015). Corporate forms and organizational choice in international insurance, Oxford, p. 8.

An early form of private capital-orientated life insurances took the form of the tontine, a contribution scheme in which annual payments were distributed among the surviving members. In the early 18th century, life insurances in the forms of private tontines, reversionary annuities, and mutual contribution schemes were launched in London. In 1762, the mutual "Society for Equitable Insurances on Lives and Survivorships" was established introducing age-specific premiums. Although joint stock companies dominated the new life insurance market at first, by the late 19th century British mutual life insurers were considerably more efficient than capital-orientated companies regarding costs and management. These companies were able to distribute higher surpluses on with-profits policies, had better returns on their investments, and survived longer.[22]

During the industrial revolution, the concept of mutual societies spread across Europe, serving as a precursor of the modern welfare state by covering the main social risks. In Germany, mutuals were closely connected with the compulsory social security system and were incorporated in the existing scheme. In other countries, mutuals developed complementary insurance schemes and offered other types of insurances. Mostly, many European countries endorsed eventually public social insurance systems and health services, guaranteeing different forms of benefits, pensions, or allowances.[23] In Norway and Finland, for example, mutuals became an important part of social economy.[24] Mutual societies continued to function alongside the government's social security system and maintained an important role in most of the European countries.

---

22 *Pearson, R.; Yoneyama, T.* (2015), Corporate forms and organizational choice in international insurance. An overview of the history and theory, in: *Pearson, R.; Yoneyama, T.* (eds.) (2015). Corporate forms and organizational choice in international insurance, Oxford, p. 8f.

23 Cf. *Grijpstra, D., Broek, S., Buiskool, B., Plooij, M.* (2011), The Role of Mutual Societies in the 21st century. Brussels: European Parliament, p. 15; *Archambault, E.* (2009), Mutual Organizations, mutual societies. In: *Anheier, H; Toepler, S.* (eds), International Encyclopedia of Civil Society, Berlin, p. 2f.

24 Cf. Cf. *Laurinkari, J.* Mutual Associations in the Finnish Insurance System; *Lovescher, B.* Mutual Insurance and limited companies in the Norwegian insurance industry (both studies in this publication).

4. Regulations of the insurance business

The insurance industry was based from the beginning on two contrary business forms, on the one hand, on a risk community with the mutuality principle in its core, and, on the other hand, on the capital-orientated company. At the same time, the conversion of the insurance business from a bureaucratic small business to a large enterprise based on commercial-mathematical principles offered more opportunities for misuse by swindle and lack of understanding compared to other economic sectors. The policyholder in particular was endangered not being able to evaluate continuously the business practice of the insurer let alone to control it. This was also true for the public, because the insurance industry influenced soon the national economy as well as the entire society. This concerned the potential destruction of values, the business activities, the saving attitude of the population, the guarantee of a continued existence, the improvement of the social situation of the individual as well as of entire families, and the capital formation by the insurance business. In this situation, the primary responsible of the governmental insurance supervision was to intervene in a preventative, advisory, managing and leading way.[25] The forms of insurance supervision comprise compulsory disclosure and/or normative system (e.g. in the United Kingdom) as well as systems of substantive state supervision (e.g. in the United States). The latter method was also evident in Germany and Austria, states in which the legal procedures for mutuals were from the beginning part of state supervision regulations.

United Kingdom

From the middle of the 19th century onwards, improvements regarding legal regulations of insurance companies were made. In the United Kingdom regulations for life insurances were established in the years 1870, 1872, and 1909, followed by norms for the non-life sector in 1909. All these regulations were based on the principles of freedom and publicity, i.e. compulsory disclosure and in particular normative procedures. In addition to legal regulations, British companies also started to initiate cooperation as a reaction to mergers and competitions. Due to an intensifying of cooperation between companies periodic price-setting meetings among companies became necessary and, as a result, regular after 1840. From 1853 onwards, the co-operating offices were known as the "Tariff Offices" and the series of meetings since 1842 resulted in

[25] Cf. *Ogris, W.* (1988), Zur Entwicklung des Versicherungsaufsichtsrechts und des Versicherungsvertragsrechts in Österreich von der Mitte des 19. Jahrhunderts bis zum Ende der Monarchie, in: Die Ära des klassischen Versicherungswesens, Versicherungsgeschichte Österreichs, vol. II, Vienna, p. 21.

the creation of a formal tariff organization, the "Fire Offices Committee" (FOC), in 1868. Their tariff agreements altered permanently the fire business since the mid-19th century and the FOC dominated the insurance business until the 1970s when the tariff control declined.[26] Nowadays, the British lawmaker seemed to favour the co-existing of capital-orientated and mutual companies, supporting mutuals by allowing external financial sponsors. However, the involved companies opposed this legal proposal vehemently.

Germany

In Germany, on the other hand, a structure of normative state supervision was favoured. The system of giving out licences for insurance companies had started around the 1850s. It was limited, however, due to the fragmentation of Germany into numerous states. Finally, in 1901, an insurance supervision act was enacted that can be regarded as a nation-wide, homogeneous, and very progressive supervision law. It is based on control as well as on a licence procedure, principles that influenced the development in Austria considerably and which are nowadays still valid.

Finland and Norway

Scandinavia countries such as Finland and Norway have a tendency towards the progressive German insurance supervision law.

Austria

In Austria, mutual insurance companies were regulated according to the act regulating clubs and associations (1852). As a result, they were part of the governmental procedures based on licences and control while their business activities were under governmental supervision.

However, at the end of the 19th century, the Austrian lawmaker thought about to dissolve mutual companies due to scandalous business practice of some insurance enterprises including corruption and manipulations during the general meeting by abusing voting rights or using front men. Moreover, the bankruptcy of the mutual life insurance society "Austria" generated the enactment of a new insurance regulation in 1896, mostly as a reaction to the public outrage caused by this insolvency. The main watershed for the Austrian insurance industry was when the German Insurance Supervision Act (ISA, VAG) from 1901 was enacted 1939 in Austria and all other previous laws were repealed due to the National Socialist regime. The newly introduced German Insurance Supervision Act kept valid in Austria as transitional law even after the end of WW II. It was replaced by the Austrian Insur-

[26] Cf. *Cockerell, H.A.L.; Green, E.* (1976), The British insurance business 1547-1970, London, p. 23; *Pearson, R.* (2004), Insuring the Industrial Revolution, London, p. 215f.

ance Supervision Act (ISA, VAG) in 1978 and eventually by the ISA of 2016. It is important to note that during the phase of capitalization, the Austrian lawmaker offered mutuals the opportunity to convert into joint stock companies but, in contrast to the United States and Finland, not vice versa.

United States

In the United States, the regulatory authority for insurance companies follows a non-intervention policy regarding the organizational forms of insurance companies. The legal regulations are developed on a state-by-state basis encouraging the creation of state-based local insurance markets instead of a national one. Insurance supervisors, on the other hand, had coordinated their tasks nationally. In 1855, an insurance department was established in Massachusetts, followed by one in New York (1859). The latter was a model for the regulatory authority, supervision regulations, and the control of insurance companies in other federal states. The aim was to establish a broad governmental supervision based on the principle of an extensive governmental influence on the business activities of private insurance companies, starting with giving out licenses, followed by continuous supervision of the management, and including if necessary a direct intervention into the company's operational management. However, any changes concerning the insurance business were always closely connected with the regulatory authority. Moreover, in contrast to Austria, both re- and demutualization are lawful, a possibility that may explain the process of continuous conversions of insurance companies.

Spain

The regulation that established the arrangement of private insurance firms in Spain was the "registration and inspection of insurance firm act" of 1908 that created also a supervisory authority. Before this law came into force, insurance companies entered and exited the Spanish market very frequently. Forty percent of the insurance enterprises that were on the Spanish market during the 19th century withdrew from the market within the first five years of their business activities. The main reason for their failure was that they were established under weak technical and financial conditions. This fact revealed the need for legislation that established homogeneous norms for entering the market and operating on it.

At the beginning of the 20th century, the insurers in Spain were specialized in one line of business. The increase in competition during the first decades of the century promoted the diversification of the most important insurance firms in addition to setting up cartels among them to control the market. This diversification process was reinforced by the insurance law of 1954 that allowed insurance companies to extend

their activity to other lines of business without costs. However, this law did not have the necessary tools to perform effective arrangement and supervision, and it was not able to evaluate the market situation.

During the 1960s, regulations of the Spanish insurance industry was characterized by an interventionist policy. The control authority established not only the tariff system but also unified models of contracts. At the end of the 1970s, a new era began, when in 1978 a royal decree improved the Spanish insurance industry by establishing solvency restrictions for companies operating in Spain. These limits were more comparable to the solvency restrictions for firms operating in other European countries. In 1982, negotiations on Spain's membership in the EEC were advanced. This process culminated in a private arrangement law in 1984 that comprised all private insurance companies under the control of the Spanish supervisory authority. The solvency standards classified the private insurance firms into stocks, mutuals, branches of foreign enterprises, social benefit institutions, and cooperatives. Moreover, it encouraged mergers and acquisitions in the insurance industry to establish insurers that would be financially stronger, more efficient (demutualizations) and more competitive, both nationally and internationally.In 1995, a new law on the arrangement and supervision of the insurance industry incorporated the rules that apply to all the countries belonging to the European Economic Area. With the 1995 law, social benefit institutions were adapted to the regulation of private insurance firms.

In 1995, a new law on the arrangement and supervision of the insurance industry incorporated the rules that apply to all countries belonging to the European Economic Area. With the Act of 1995, social benefit institutions were adapted to the regulation of private insurance firms. The articles enacted in this law along with modified articles have been combined in a revised text on the private insurance supervision and arrangement law (TRLOSSP). This manuscript was approved by royal decree in 2004, and it forms the basic legislation on supervision and arrangement of insurers.

Since 2016, the supervision of insurance companies in Spain is mainly governed by rules originating from the European Union and deriving from the Solvency II Directive. The laws and regulations comprise the Act 20/2015, for ordination, supervision and solvency of insurance, and reinsurance undertakings (LOSSEAR) as well as the Royal Decree 1060/2015, approving the regulations for ordination, management and solvency of insurance and reinsurance undertakings (ROSSEAR).

Japan

When looking at the development of the Japanese insurance market after WW II, the reorganization and the intense regulation of the market is evident. Since the 1950s, the governmental supervision took

the form of protectionism by the state and promoted the business of the existing insurance companies. While mutuals benefitted from this development on the life insurance market, joint stock companies were supported in the non-life insurance segment during the second half of the 20th century. The newly introduced regulations did not lead to competition and rivalry between companies regarding different prices and products. At the same time, the regulations prevented that other insurance companies entered the insurance market. The intense supervision of the Japanese insurance market had the aim to create circumstances in which even the most inefficient insurance companies were profitable. For example, premium rates were fixed on a level that made all insurance business lucrative, preventing so insolvency and bankruptcy. Although the governmental supervision differed regarding the life and non-life segment, the aim was the same. As a result, the companies were able to maintain or even increase their market shares until the 1980s. Mutuals, for example, had a market share of more than 90 percent based on annual premium income and insurance sum and were able to maintain this high level on the life insurance market until the 1980s. Joint stock companies, on the other hand, dominated the non-life sector similarly. Nevertheless, the supervision led to a process of assimilation of the operative characteristics by the few insurance joint stock companies in the life insurance sector. The latter distributed high annual dividends to their policyholders but only a small amount of their profits to their shareholders. Moreover, the insurance products of both mutuals and joint stock companies were almost identical due to the intense governmental supervision. The constant growth of the Japanese insurance industry ended at the beginning of the 1990s when the economic bubble burst, followed by years of economic depression, reforms and deregulation leading to a liberalization of the Japanese insurance market.

The question that arises now in this context is: Did the insurance supervisory authority influence organizational forms, mutuals and stock companies, in the countries investigated in this publication? When looking at the historical development, three forms are evident:

- The insurance supervisory authority was neutral regarding the different organizational forms of insurance companies.
- The regulatory authority recognized the co-existence of mutuals and stock companies.
- The controlling authority regards mutuals not as an adequate organizational form for the insurance business and favours a change of legal forms into capital-orientated companies.

While in the United States, the lawmaker decided for a non-intervention policy regarding organizational forms, in Norway and Finland,

mutuals are legally supported, and in Germany and Japan, both legal forms are equal. On the other hand, in Austria and Spain the lawmakers and therefore the supervision authorities favour the adaptation of mutuals towards capital-orientated companies.

5. From increasing capital to demutualization

As mentioned above, decisions about future risks are based on event risk scenarios that are built on probability allowing quantifying them.[27] This fact allowed the insurance business to evolve as a resource for the protection against financial losses caused by unpredictable events during the 19th century. With the support of insurances, losses of or damage to property, business interruption, or legal liability to compensate third parties for their damage could have been managed. With the turn of the century, however, the principle of bearing of risks mutually became increasingly obsolete for mutual insurance companies and many companies progressively moved funds into equities to secure the benefits of capital growth and later to evade inflation. This investment practice was mainly determined by considerations based on economic, stock market, and political interests.[28] With that development, the motivation of insurance companies has changed gradually and lastingly, instead of focusing on risks their prime goal became eventually the increase of capital.

A possible way to raise capital for mutuals is demutualization, which is legally the "process of converting a mutual insurance company which is owned by its policyholders into a publicly traded stock company owned by shareholders, pursuant to a plan of conversion approved by policyholders and state regulators".[29] During the demutualization process of an insurance company, the value of the policies will be

[27] Cf. *Carter, R. L.; Falush, P.* (2009), The British Insurance Industry since 1900. The Era of Transformation, Basingstoke, p. 118; https://apps.derstandard.at/privacywall/story/2000109264301/makrooekonomische-entwicklungen-unter-unsicherheit (3.10.2019); *Schredelseker, K.* (2005), Zur Entwicklung des finanz- und risikowirtschaftlichen Denkens, in: *Spremann, K.* (ed.). Versicherungen im Umbruch Werte schaffen, Risiken managen, Kunden gewinnen, Berlin, p. 513f.

[28] Cf. *Carter, R. L.; Falush, P.* (2009), The British Insurance Industry since 1900, Basingstoke, p. 117; XV.

[29] *Chugh, L., Meador, J. W.* (2006), Demutualization in the Life Insurance Industry: A Study of Effectiveness. In: Review of Business, 27(1), p. 3.

turned into traded stocks and policyholders become stock investors. The United States acted as a pioneer regarding demutualization (full, sponsored). During the 1980s, major changes in the macro environment, i.e. the opening of the capital market, as well as the political and legal structure happened that clearly presented the various weaknesses of mutuals. Demutualization waves as well as hundreds of mergers and acquisitions followed, in particular in the health insurance sector, converting mutuals rapidly into stock companies. Although, the first demutualization waves started during the 1980s, the most important ones happened in the late 20th and early 21st century. Due to the Gramm-Leach-Bliley Act in 1999, the financial markets in the USA had developed and grown. Insurers came then under pressure to strengthen their insurance business as well as to expand into new financial services markets. Consequently, the access to equity capital was regarded as an increasingly important and eventually essential factor to survive. Under these circumstances, the insurance industry in general and the life insurance sector in particular shifted from the mutual organizational form to the joint stock company form.[30]

The phenomenon of demutualization started to spread from the United States to other countries, in particular to Europe where the first conversions can be observed since the late 1980s. This trend continued until the outbreak of the financial crisis in 2008. Before that event the largest life insurer in the United States, "Prudential Life", successfully demutualized in December 2001 as well major companies in Japan (e.g. "Dai-Chi Life Insurance"), and in the United Kingdom there was a demutualization wave in the late 1980s among mutual life insurance companies.[31] Compared to that, in Germany, no mutual insurance company has so far chosen the possibility of a full demutualization.

The Spanish insurance industry experienced a dramatic restructuring process during the 1980s and 1990s. At this time the government began tightening solvency standards and encouraging mergers and acquisitions in the insurance industry to create insurers that would be financially stronger, more efficient, and more competitive both nationally and internationally. Demutualization played in this restructuring an important role. In the 1980s, many mutuals were transformed into stocks as a way to get significant infusions of new capital. Substantial increases in capital were required to operate in the different lines of insurance by the insurance law of 1984 but also mutuals were transformed into social benefit institutions. The wave of demutualization had ended at the beginning of the 2000s years.

[30] Cf. *Zanjani, G.* (2007), Regulation, Capital, and the Evolution of Organizational Form in U.S. Life Insurance, in: American Economic Review 97, p. 973.

[31] Cf. Swiss Re, Are Mutual Insurers an Endangered Species, in: Sigma, no. 4/1999.

Nevertheless, even after the crisis, major demutualization processes occurred, e.g. in Norway when the mutual company "Gjensidige Forsikring BA" converted into a public limited company (2010) or when in Finland in 2014 "RÖF", the mutual parent company of the "Alandia insurance group", converted into a limited liability insurance company and subsequently merged with its subsidiary.[32] Although the huge number of demutualized companies suggests that the capital-orientated form has become more attractive for many mutual insurers, the financial crisis in 2008 stopped not only the demutualization trend but even reversed the process. At this time, remutualization was an interesting choice for companies in Europe.[33] For example in Finland, remutualization happened when in 2014 "Tapiola" and "Local Insurance" merged. This merger involved two types of mutual societies and more than 20 separate legal entities. The new company group, the "LocalTapiola Group", which is owned by its customers, was established in 2014 by emerging the "Local Insurance Mutual Company" and the "Tapiola General Mutual Insurance".

In addition to demutualization waves, the clear distinction between mutuals and joint stock companies, which has already became fuzzy, vanished and three holding forms have evolved. These new organizational forms comprise a wide range of elements of existing legal forms.

- In Germany developed since the 1970s insurance groups and enterprises (holdings) with insurers as parent companies due to the supervisory principles regarding the separation of insurance lines.
- In Austria and the United States, holding companies developed during the 1990s, which at the first look seem to be similar. However, these constructions were based in the United States on capital-orientated principles. It is important to note that Austria can be regarded as a precursor regarding the establishment of the mutual holding organizational form. Although both models were initiated by companies and not by the regulatory authorities, they differed. The main difference between both mutual holding constructions is that the Austrian model was originally founded as a temporary solution in the event of a full demutualization. However, this concept worked so well that it was further developed into an ownerless private foundation by a change of legal regulations. In contrast, in the United States a mutual holding construction was regarded as a sustainable solution, which in almost all federal states has already been put to practice.

[32] Cf. https://www.vikingline.com/investors/stock-exchange-releases/published-2014/de-mutualisation-and-merger-within-the-alandia-insurance-group1/ (20.12.2019)

[33] *Battilani P., Schröter H.G.* (2011), Demutualization and its problems, in: *Battliani, P; H.G. Schröter, H. G.* (eds.) (2011), The Co operative Business Movement 1950 to the Present, Cambridge, p. 155.

On the other hand new mutuals still emerge, for example in Austria, the "Muki" in 2004 and the "RVV" in 2016.

6. Insurance history as an international project

The selection of the studies for this book has already showed that mutual insurance history is a research field that has to be analyzed internationally. While the precursors of insurance can be traced back to the ancient world, later developments were influenced by regional political and economic factors that generated the insurance business in the various countries at different periods. However, major events such as large fires and catastrophes occurred in many cities making people aware of the fire hazards and the necessity to prevent and compensate such damage. Finally, the insurance industry became a global phenomenon generated by the industrial revolution, scientific innovations as well as overseas trade. With the new globalization of the insurance business in the late 20th century, insurers had to face major changes regarding the structure of the business. Markets became liberated and capitalised due to the rising globalization waves, while multinational companies started to expand their business into all regions of the world[34], a phenomena that the authors of the studies kept well in mind. Therefore, the main intention of this publication is to present the development of mutuals from an international point of view, including the historical roots and characteristics of each country by referring to most important academic research in the field.

The country studies in this publication are grouped according to their historical development in various categories, starting with the United Kingdom and Germany as examples for precursors of the insurance industry, followed by Finland and Norway, countries in which mutuals are closely connected with social economy. The four studies about Austria and the one about the insurance market in the United States present a historical overview as well as the evolving of new organizational forms of insurance companies (mutual holding companies). Japan and Spain are used as examples for economies in which the insurance industry developed late. Finally, the book closes with a study about the insurance business from an international point of view.

[34] *Pearson, R.* (2010), Introduction: Towards an international history of insurance, in: *Pearson, R.* (eds.) (2010). The development of international insurance, p. 19f.

This publication has been many years in the making with the goal to contribute new insights into the development of mutual insurance societies from a historical as well as economic perspective. It is hoped that this book will be regarded as an important contribution to the development of the mutual insurance industry.

Bibliography

Alemany, R., Guillén, M. (2013). The History of the Insurance Market in Spain. Assurances et gestion des risques, 81 (1-2).

Archambault, E. (2009). Mutual Organizations, mutual societies. In: *Anheier, H; Toepler, S.* (eds), International Encyclopedia of Civil Society, Berlin.

Battilani, P., Schröter, H.G. (2011). Demutualization and its problems, in: *Battliani, P; H.G. Schröter, H. G.* (eds.) (2011), The Cooperative Business Movement 1950 to the Present. Cambridge.

Brazda, J., Csulich, G., Zeman, St. (2018). Das Gegenseitigkeitsprinzip im Versicherungswesen aus historisch-analytischer Sicht, in: *Brazda, J.; Blisse, H.* (eds.). Beiträge zur kritischen Genossenschaftsforschung, Vienna.

Carter, R. L.; Falush, P. (2009). The British Insurance Industry since 1900. The Era of Transformation, Houndmills.

Casares, G.T., Caruana, L., García Ruiz, J. L., Manzano Martos, A., Pons, J. (2014), Historia del seguro en Espana. Fundación Mapfre, Madrid.

Chugh, L., Meador, J. W. (2006). Demutualization in the Life Insurance Industry: A Study of Effectiveness, in: Review of Business, 27(1).

Cockerell, H.A.L.; Green, E. (1976). The British insurance business 1547-1970, London..

Grijpstra, D., Broek, S., Buiskool, B., Plooij, M. (2011). The Role of Mutual Societies in the 21st century. Brussels: European Parliament.

Ismay, P. (2010). Trust among strangers: Securing British Modernity `by way of friendly society,' 1780s-1870s; unpublished Dissertation University of California, Berkeley.

Ismay, P. (2018). Trust among strangers. Friendly Societies in Modern Britain, Cambridge.

Koch, P. (2012). Geschichte der Versicherungswirtschaft in Deutschland, Karlsruhe.

Lepler, J. (2013). The Many Panics of 1837: People, Politics, and the Creation of a Transatlantic Financial Crisis, New York.

Loftin, G., Xie, X. (2007),.The United States Insurance Market: Characteristics and Trends, in: *Cummins, J.D., Venard, B.* (ed.): Handbook of international insurances. Between Global Dynamics and Local Contingencies, New York.

Ogris, W. (1988). Zur Entwicklung des Versicherungsaufsichtsrechts und des Versicherungsvertragsrechts in Österreich von der Mitte des 19. Jahrhunderts bis zum Ende der Monarchie, in: Die Ära des klassischen Versicherungswesens, Versicherungsgeschichte Österreichs, vol. II, Vienna.

Pearson, R. (2004). Insuring the Industrial Revolution. Fire insurance in Great Britain, 1700-1850, London.

Pearson, R. (2010). Introduction: Towards an international history of insurance, in: *Pearson, R.* (eds.) (2010). The development of international insurance, London.

Pearson, R. Yoneyama, T. (2015). Corporate forms and organizational choice in international insurance. An overview of the history and theory, in: *Pearson, R.; Yoneyama, T.* (eds.) (2015). Corporate forms and organizational choice in international insurance, Oxford.

Schredelseker, K. (2005). Zur Entwicklung des finanz- und risikowirtschaftlichen Denkens, in: *Spremann, K.* (ed.). Versicherungen im Umbruch Werte schaffen, Risiken managen, Kunden gewinnen, Berlin.

Swiss Re Corporate History (ed.), A History of US Insurance, Zurich 2013.

Swiss Re, Are Mutual Insurers an Endangered Species, in: Sigma, no. 4/1999.

Zanjani, G. (2007). Regulation, Capital, and the Evolution of Organizational Form in U.S. Life Insurance, in: American Economic Review 97 (2007).

https://apps.derstandard.at/privacywall/story/2000109264301/makrooekonomische-entwicklungen-unter-unsicherheit (3.10.2019).

https://greatfireoflondon.net/london-gazette-1666/ (29.11.2019), The London Gazette, September 1666; Monday September 3, to Monday September 10, 1666.

https://www.vikingline.com/investors/stock-exchange-releases/published-2014/de-mutualisation-and-merger-within-the-alandia-insurance-group1/ (20.12.2019)

Country	Until 16th century	16th to 18th century	18th and 19th century	1900-1980	1980s-1990s	1990s onwards
	Early precursors of insurance companies; transport and fire insurances dominated; "health insurance" limited to specific groups and/or offered by church.	*Influence of Enlightenment led to development of "insurable risks" in different organisational forms; catastrophes were no longer perceived as "God's punishment".*	*Insurance industry generated Industrial Revolution; mutuals became important insurers in specific sectors; various organizational forms developed.*	*Focus of insurance industry changed from risk management to raising capital; after WWI and WWII restructuring of the insurance industry was crucial; new insurance sectors developed; European Common Market.*	*Changes in macro economy structures led to demutualisation waves – became global phenomena; market is dominated by joint stock companies.*	*Development of new organisational forms; opening of the markets and deregulation; few occurrences of remu-tualization; remaining mutuals in specific insurance sectors.*
Great Britain	secular and religious friendly societies since the sixteenth century social risks were distributed with charity briefs under the authority of the king.	a marine insurance sector was established triggered by Britain's dominance as a naval power; "Lloyd's coffee house" in London became a centre of information about insurance; after Great Fire (1666) various organizational forms of fire insurances developed: firstly an individual underwriter (1667) (transformed in a joint stock company in 1681), secondly, a public corporation (1680), thirdly, a friendly society (1684) and finally, a mutual (1696); mutuals adopted joint stocks business structures to survive on changing and more complex market.	Britain became the centre of trade and commerce of the world and London developed into the centre of the insur-ance industry; rise of the joint stock companies and phase of mergers and acquisitions; only the mutual "P&I clubs" (transport insurance) remained important; development of classification and tariff systems to form standards (fire insurance); rise of the life insur-ance sector due to the middle class; industrial life assurance for the working class (offered by friendly societies).	amalgamation of fire insurance companies and emerge of new lines of insurances (e.g. accident, plate glass, railway insurances) led to composite insurers; friendly societies became main underwriter for industrial life insurance (1950s to 1990s); mutual life insurers successful until mid-1960, later outperformed by stock companies.	mutuals hold notable position within general insurance industry; more and more mutual life insurance com-panies demutualised to gain access to external capital.	after the demutualization wave and an all-time low in 2007, mutuals' market share in-creased steadily but remains low compared to stocks; friendly societies offer additional insurance products for services that are not provided by the government.

Country	Until 16th century	16th to 18th century	18th and 19th century	1900-1980	1980s-1990s	1990s onwards
Germany	"Knappschaften" and guilds for special professional groups since 1150; charity briefs by public and clerical authorities; marine insurances based on the Dutch model since 1588.	guilds based on mutual support for widows and orphans since 1636; public mutual fire institutions ("Feuersozietäten") in several big cities since 1677.	several new societies based on mutuality were established at the end of the 18th century, e.g. by *Arnoldi* ("Gothaer") – nationwide business of mutuals.	increasing risk awareness; during 1920s merger phase; between 1933 and 1945: insurance industry was under the influence of the National Socialist Party; after WWII economic upswing started and reforms followed.	1989 the German reunification of the insurance companies.	since 1994 privatization of the public insurances; increasing competition, take-overs, and mergers of com-panies to horizontal and subordinated groups; formation of mutual insurance society groups by integrating via joint stock companies.
Finland	roots of fire damage claims in Swedish speaking part of Finland (Middle Ages)	common accountability for fire damage among the rural population (17th century)	changes at the end of 19th century (Industrial Revolution): statuary mutual insurance;	at the beginning of the 20th century fire insurance was the main insurance type of mutual insurances; mutual insurance companies for different social classes developed (interwar period); after WW II: welfare state developed using insurance business; insurance regarded as collective help; conflicts between profit seeking and key elements of social economy arose.	after the financial deregulation in the 1980s, the stock company form gained popularity	restructuring arrangements in the insurance sector both externally and internally; since 2014 demutualization ("Alandia insurance group") and remutualization ("LocalTapiola Group"); concentration of the insurance market.

Country	Until 16th century	16th to 18th century	18th and 19th century	1900-1980	1980s-1990s	1990s onwards
Norway		foreign insurance companies dominated till the end of the 18th century	balance between risks and advantages in form of trans-portation insurances regarding merchant shipping and fishery as well as mutual help in local villages in case of fire; modelled after the Danish companies; end of 19th century marine insurance decreased eco-nomically, dissolution of companies.	beginning of 20th century: Norwegian P&I Clubs (Protection and Indemnity) Skuld and Gard founded (based on mutuality); only few mutual transport insurers due to the financial crisis of the 1920s and the fierce competition between Norwegian and foreign insurers; the mutual insurance companies were not prepared for inter-national competition, because of their small size and large number on the market; fire insurance companies decreased between 1960 and 1970 due to nume-rous mergers	the discovery of North Sea oil resulted in strong economic years for mutual insurance companies	since 2010 demutualization waves

Country	Until 16th century	16th to 18th century	18th and 19th century	1900-1980	1980s-1990s	1990s onwards
Austria	"Knappschaften" and guilds for special professional groups	private small local mutual societies (Bauernassekuranzen) – fire insurance; stock companies: transport insurance (Trieste)	"mutual" fire insurance companies (regional public institutions: Landesanstalten); life insurance companies; development of industrial insurance societies and national mutual insurance societies; stock market crash (1873), mutuals became composite insurers.	end of Austrian-Hungarian monarchy (1918), fragmentation of insurance industry; hyperinflation; many mergers/group formation ("Wiener Städtische"); bankruptcy of the "Phoenix" life insurance company (1936); "Anschluss" in 1938; after WW II: second wave of group formations.	demutualisation of industrial insurance societies	group formations; since 1991 creation of the Austrian mutual holding company model: mutual insurers transferred their operative insurance business to a joint stock company and continue the mutual association in form of an asset management society or since 2005 in the form of an private foundations; foundation of 2 new mutuals (Muki: 2004, RVV: 2016);
USA		during 18th century first American regional insurers in both forms: stock companies and mutualism (modelled after British marine and fire insurers); *Benjamin Franklin* founding father of mutualism.	vigorous growth of the insurance industry during the industrialization; immigrants influenced insurance industry; fierce competition due to capital requirements; different state insurance regulations influenced development of organizational forms.	development of additional insurance branches (windstorm, casualty, automobile, theft insurance) dominated by mutuals.	change in macro environment (opening of the capital market), political and legal structure led to demutualization (full, sponsored) especially in the life and health insurance sector; mutuals had weaknesses; in 1990s hundreds of mergers and acquisitions.	foundation of MIHC (Mutual insurance holding company).

Country	Until 16th century	16th to 18th century	18th and 19th century	1900-1980	1980s-1990s	1990s onwards
Spain	11th and 12th century: Christian brotherhoods ("cofradias") to help each other.	clerical system of cofradias and hermandades de socorros mutuos developed (social provisions)	secular authorities took this system out of the hands of clerics; wave of hermandades de socorros at the end of 18th century; foundation of Hermandades con-trolled by the crown via state institutions (montepios) offered insurances for certain groups of professions and trades; constant restrictive legislative changes; 2nd half of 19th century: expansion of the insurance sector and its diversifi-cation; founding of insurance companies of French capital ("La Unión and El Fénix Español").	turn of the century: insurance sector grew rapidly; during *Franco* regime in the field of social security mutualism was favoured focussing on the welfare of certain key industries represented by "friendly" unions.	after the end of the *Franco* dictatorship a process of liberalization started in the insurance sector which brought the mutualistic sector nearer to the commercial insurance sector; the largest mutualistic institutions took the character of regular enterprises and turned into multinational or transnational players; many smaller mutualities had to be liquidated.	Since 1990 demutualization wave; between 2000 and 2012 acquisitions and mergers.

Country	Until 16th century	16th to 18th century	18th and 19th century	1900-1980	1980s-1990s	1990s onwards
Japan			The first insurance companies (marine, transport, and fire insurers) since the 2nd half of the 19th century; end of 19th century first life joint stock companies.	1902: 1st mutual insurance "Dai-ichi Life Insurance"; rise of mutuals; before WWII: industrial co-operatives tried to enter insurance sector; after WWII: mutualisation wave in the life insurance sector as part of the economic democratization process; mutuals dominate life insurance market; development of insurance cooperatives as the third form of enterprise (since the 1940s).	time period characterised by governmental control on the insurance market; end of foundation wave and prohibition of foreign insurance companies; mutuals dominate life insurance sector; joint stock companies dominate non-life sector; Japan became second largest insurance market in the world.	From the mid-1990s onwards transformation process due to the Japanese financial crisis (early 1990s); gradual deregulation of the insurance market; development of holding companies and opening of the market for foreign insurers; period of crisis in the life insurance sector; since 2000: indirect demutualization and merger wave; co-existence of three organizational forms on the insurance market; dominance of joint stock companies in the life insurance sector; co-existence and adaption of the different organisational forms.

Part I.
The Pioneers of the Insurance Business

The Development of the Insurance System in Great Britain

Gabriela Csulich, Stefan Preiner

1. Early developments in the insurance business

When looking at the history of the insurance business it is crucial to investigate the development of insurances in Britain. With Britain's rise to become an economic super power during the 18th and 19th century, the insurance industry started to become an essential part of this economic development. The foundations can be found in political and financial changes at the end of the 17th century. From a political point of view, the end of the reign of *Charles II* and of the House of *Stuarts* in 1688 marked a watershed in Britain's history. With the following "Glorious Revolution" and the Bill of Rights, the rights of Parliament towards the monarch were strengthened. Britain was gradually transformed into an enlightened and parliamentary state. With regard to the economic and financial changes during this period, London became the world's largest fire insurance market. This dominated position held especially the marine insurance business. At the same time, central banks and a stock market were established. By the middle of the 19th century, Britain became the centre of trade and commerce of the world and with that, London developed to become the centre of the insurance industry.[1]

Various insurance sectors such as marine, fire, and life, however, developed differently. While the marine insurance business was undertaken by individuals and established its importance during the 17th century, generated by Britain's dominance as a naval power, the importance of fire insurances developed slowly and was connected to a changing world view. When people started to perceive fires as an insurable risk and not as "punishment by god", the modern fire insurance business was born. In this initial phase, fire insurance was relatively

---

1 Cf. *Pearson, R.* (2012), United Kingdom: Pioneering insurance internationally. In: *Borscheid, P.*; *Haueter, N. V.* (eds.). World insurance. The evolution of a global risk network. Oxford, p. 67.

unregulated, privately funded, and many associations were mutuals.[2] Life assurance[3], on the other hand, began to take off at the end of the 17th century due to the introduction of mortality tables by *Edmund Halley* and became a national business by the mid-19th century due to affordable industrial life insurances provided in particular by Friendly Societies[4] and legal developments such as the Poor House Legislation.[5]

1.1 Marine insurance

The marine insurance during the 16th century differed immensely from its later form. In this period, merchants, who functioned as underwriters, dominated the marine insurance sector by carrying their business with usually insufficient capital resources. Often this was done with highly speculative methods. Moreover, the crucial information for the ship owners and insurers about the ships, weather, ports, pirates etc., usually provided by *Lloyd's*, was at best incomplete. However, the information was crucial to estimate risks and therefore the premiums.[6] With establishing the Royal Exchange in 1570, where merchants were able to discuss their business, and the Chamber of Assurances in 1576, where all policies had to be registered to prevent malpractices such as double or over-insurance, the marine insurance sector developed further. With the new created Royal Exchange, it was now possible to move away from the location in Lombard Street, where, originally, merchants met twice a day to deal with bargains, insurance, and exchange. This kind of institution was modelled after the practice of merchants in Antwerp.[7] Finally, in 1601 the "Act touching Policies Assurances used among merchants" (43 Eliz., C.12) was enacted and established a court that was exclusively concerned with insurance cases. Although the merchants never favoured this institution and the Assurance Chamber had ceased activity by the end of the 17th century[8], the Act itself

2 Cf. *MacLeod J.* (2018), England and Scotland, in: *Hellwege, P.* (ed.). A comparative history of insurance law in Europe. A research agenda, Berlin, p. 166.

3 The distinction between insurance and assurance is based on an uncertain respectively certain event. An insurance provides against a loss in case something happened (e.g. fire damage), while an assurance is connected with a certain event, i.e. in case of a life assurance, the death of the policyholder. Cf. *Clayton, G.* (1971), British insurance. London, p. 74.

4 Cf. *MacLeod J.* (2018), England and Scotland, p. 168.

5 Cf. *Pearson, R.* (1990), Thrift or dissipation? The business of life assurance in the early nineteenth century. Economic History Review, 2nd ser., XLIII, 2 (1990), pp. 236-254.

6 Cf. *Clayton, G.* (1971), British insurance, p. 31.

7 Cf. *Raynes, H. E.* (1948), A history of British insurance. London, p. 42.

8 Cf. *MacLeod J.* (2018), England and Scotland, p. 159.

can be regarded as the first legislative attempt to regulate the marine insurance sector.[9] Moreover, as *Raynes* points out, the Chamber of Assurances "was instrumental in moulding marine insurance" and can be regarded as "the forerunner of the later organized market for individual underwriting", i.e. *Lloyd's* coffeehouse. Due to its work a formal marine policy developed.[10]

The 16th century was the period in which English became the dominant language for insurance policies and a period in which insurance practice and custom was established in England.[11] However, in the 17th century, marine insurance underwriting had still not developed into a specialised business and people had to search for insurers in various places such as private offices, the Royal Exchange, and in many coffeehouses.[12] Marine insurance was still carried out by private insurers, usually merchants, who shared their risks among each other. During this time, *Lloyd's* coffee house became the centre of information. For the first time, information about shipping movements and political developments was collected and from 1692 on published in a weekly newspaper, a forerunner of *Lloyd's List* (1734).[13] Although *Lloyd's* was the centre of information, it was not the centre of insurance underwriting. This situation changed when during the "South Sea Bubble"[14] in 1720, merchants started petitioning for a more secure marine insurance in form of charted corporations. They were opposed by other merchants and private underwriters who claimed that a monopoly would endanger free trade. Their fear was that private underwriters would be forced out

---

9 Cf. *Raynes, H. E.* (1948), A history of British insurance, p. 63; *Clayton, G.* (1971), British insurance. p. 32.

10 Cf. *Raynes, H. E.* (1948), A history of British insurance, p. 63.

11 Cf. *MacLeod, J.* (2018), England Scotland, p. 160f.

12 Cf. *Clayton, G.* (1971), British insurance, p. 52f.

13 Cf. *Pearson, R.; Doe, H.* (2015), Organizational choice in UK marine insurance, in: *Pearson, R.; Yoneyama, T.* (2015), Corporate forms and organizational choice in international insurance, Oxford, p. 48.

14 The South Sea Bubble was a speculation mania that ruined many British investors in 1720. The bubble centred on the fortunes of the South Sea Company, founded in 1711, to trade in particular slaves, with Spanish America, on the assumption that the War of the Spanish Succession would end with a treaty permitting such trade. The company's stock, with a guaranteed interest of 6 percent, sold well, but the peace treaty of Utrecht made with Spain in 1713 imposed an annual tax on imported slaves and allowed the company to send only one ship each year for general trade. Investors, who were unable to buy South Sea stocks, were persuaded by overly optimistic company promoters or downright swindlers into unwise investments. By September, the market had collapsed. Many investors were ruined, and the House of Commons ordered an inquiry, which showed that at least three ministers had accepted bribes and speculated. Many of the company's directors were disgraced. Cf. https://www.britannica.com/event/South-Sea-Bubble, retrieval: 30.04.2019.

of the market.[15] As *Clayton* points out, with the establishment of two-chartered joint stock companies, the "Royal Exchange Assurance Corporation" and the "London Assurance Corporation", as the sole marine insurers, the rise of *Lloyd's* as an underwriter started.[16] Although these two companies had the monopoly on corporate marine insurance until 1824, they were forced to apply for additional charters to write fire and life insurances, because their shares lost value when the "South Sea Bubble" finally burst. As *Pearson* and *Doe* point out, the market share of both companies was never higher than 10 percent in the marine insurance sector but was still more profitable than the fire and life insurance segments.[17] Moreover, other companies were not influenced by the expansion of both companies, because the insurance business maintained its diversity. In addition to the two-chartered companies, joint stock companies and mutuals were established underwriting fire and life as well as individual underwriters in the marine segment.[18] At the end of the 18th century, mutual societies developed specialised in shipping insurance due to their part-ownerships of ressels or their needs to supply their insurance. These friendly societies were not in conflict with the chartered companies, because each member was underwriting a share in the risks for which he was responsible. This fractional share holding form had the advantage that their membership was restricted to a small number of owners known to each other and the members and the ship could be selected carefully. This form of association was later regulated by maritime law and stated that each ship was considered as a separate enterprise and consisted of a number of transferable shares. In 1823, a maximum of 64 shares and 32 owners was fixed (Registry Act, 4 Geo. IV, 1823, c. 41). These P&I (Marine Protection and Indemnity) Clubs comprised the local ship owners focussing in particular on costal and short-sea trades that could be made several voyages within a year. Although a few associations were established in London, most of them had their origin in the North of England based on the coal transport trade.[19] Towards the end of the 18th century, the Selected Committee on Marine Insurance estimated that approximately 20 associations of ship-owners existed offering marine insurances of their members' ships.[20] As *Pearson* and *Doe* point out, the main goals of these societies

---

[15] Cf. *Kingston, C.* (2007), Marine insurance in Britain and America, 1720-1844: A comparative institutional analysis. Journal of Economic History, No. 67(2), p. 383f.

[16] Cf. *Clayton, G.* (1971), British insurance, p. 54f.

[17] Cf. *Pearson, R.; Doe, H.* (2015), Organizational choice in UK marine insurance, p. 49f.

[18] Cf. *MacLeod, J.* (2018), England Scotland, p. 167.

[19] Cf. *Raynes, H. E.* (1948), A history of British insurance, p. 186f; *Pearson, R.; Doe, H.* (2015), Organizational choice in UK marine insurance, p. 53f.

[20] Cf. *Cockerell, H.A.L.; Green, E.* (1976), The British insurance business 1547-1970. An introduction and guide to historical records in the United Kingdom, London, p. 6.

were risk selection and "monitoring of moral hazard for the benefit of the membership as a whole". They were able to provide lower insurance premiums and more specialised insurances, e.g. collisions at sea, that were not covered by *Lloyd's*. These mutuals were small specialised insurers limited to local areas and based on local knowledge and small pools of risks. Although these associations were never in competition with *Lloyd's* or the chartered corporations, they were able to underwrite a large number of risks. For example, in 1810 the "London Union Society" had 100 ships insured, the "Brixham Shipping Association" insured over 120,000 Pounds of risks, and the "West Country clubs" were able to underwrite 474 ships by 1854. It is interesting that these associations had never an important position in the marine insurance business, probably because of their extremely cautious policy: they declined all inferior risks and had higher premiums.[21] However, many of these clubs failed and had to close their business during the 19th century. One the one hand, some owners of "bad ships" established mutual insurance clubs and went on underwriting them until the ships went down, and on the other hand, owners of ships in good conditionsfunded bad risks that led to heavy losses.[22]

1.2 Fire insurance

When looking at the development of the fire insurance industry in Britain. The Great Fire of London in 1666 is usually perceived as the starting point. However, large fires that burned down more than forty or fifty houses were common in Europe after 1633. Most of them resulted from an increase of population, the disregard of fire regulations, and from London becoming the centre of trade. The latter is crucial because with new forms of trades, more warehouses with more flammable products were needed and with the expansion of British overseas trade, shipbuilding boomed. Most of the ressels were built by using flammable substances and fire-prone materials. Moreover, this specialised industry was located near the Thames, where also imported substances such as saltpetre for manufacturing gunpowder, brimstone for fireworks, oil, rum, or brandy were stored in warehouses. All these products could been found in large quantities and contributed to the inferno of 1666[23]

[21] Cf. *Cockerell, H.A.L.*; *Green, E.* (1976), The British insurance business 1547-1970, p. 6; *Pearson, R.; Doe, H.* (2015), Organizational choice in UK marine insurance, p. 56; *Bridgewater, A.* (1995), The modern mutual insurance company in Britain. In: *Peiner, W.* Grundlagen des Versicherungsvereins auf Gegenseitigkeit, Köln, p. 34.

[22] Cf. *Cockerell, H.A.L.*; *Green, E.* (1976), The British insurance business 1547-1970, p. 6.

[23] Cf. *Garrioch, D.* (2016), 1666 and London's fire history: a re-evaluation. The Historical Journal 59(2), p. 320; 331f.

that generated a psychological impact, which led to a re-evaluation of fire insurances in general. One of the first results to improve the situation for the fire victims was the Rebuilding Act of 1667 stating that instead of the 13,000 destroyed houses only 9,000 were to be rebuilt with brick or stone imposing specific norms regarding the thickness of walls and the position of doors. Although these regulations were rudimentary and inadequate, they were, nevertheless, the "first systematic attempt to reduce the risk of fire" and therefore essential for the development of fire insurance.[24] Rebuilding parts of London was also seen as the opportunity for making money by establishing fire insurance offices. The first was set up in 1667 by *Nicholas Barbon* in form of an individual underwriter, as it was already common for marine insurances, insuring buildings and houses. It was "settled on a found of ground rents, to answer in case of loss".[25] Small mutual fire insurances, however, were not established after the Great Fire. *Walford* points out that this belief is a misunderstanding due to the foundation of some contribution offices during this time. These offices only granted policies for particular sums, charged a premium and collected a proportion of loss in the event of fire.[26] Moreover, *Walford* and *Griswold* state that after the Great Fire an Association for friendly insurance against fire had been established in various Scottish towns. Unfortunately, no records have survived regarding these foundations. It is possible that they referred to the in 1720 founded Friendly Society in Edinburgh. Moreover, *Stewart* believes that Friendly Societies for Mutual Insurance had been established in various Scottish towns. These societies were either the above-mentioned contribution offices or *Steward* confused it with the later founded Society in Edinburgh.[27]

By the end of the 17th century, the existence of four companies with different business goals can be verified. Firstly, a joint stock company (1681) established by *Nicholas Barbon*, secondly, a corporation founded by the City of London (1680), thirdly, the "Mutual Friendly Society for Securing Houses from losses by Fire" (1684), and finally, the "Mutual Amicable Contributors for Insuring from Loss by Fire" ("Hand-in-Hand") in 1696. Until 1680, *Nicholas Barbon* worked as an independent fire underwriter, but was then forced to establish a company in form of a partnership due to massive financial losses. In September 1681, he founded the first fire joint stock company (or proprietary) for fire insurance in London, the so-called "Insurance Office for House". It was based on the monetary risk of its founders "without

24 Cf. *Clayton, G.* (1971), British insurance, p. 36.

25 *Relton, F. B.* (1893), An account of the fire insurance companies. Associations, institutions, projects, and schemes, pp. 20-22.

26 Cf. Statistical Journal, September 1877 qtd. in: *Relton, F. B.* (1893), An account of the fire insurance companies, p. 18f.

27 Cf. *Relton, F. B.* (1893), An account of the fire insurance companies, p. 23f.

special legal or corporate power". As a "mere partnership with a joint stock capital" *Barbon's* company did not legally interfere with the Act of Monopolies[28] (1610) that prohibited the foundation of insurance companies.[29] His "Fire Office", respectively the "Phoenix Office" since 1705, was a partnership based on a fund vested in trustees to secure that the undertakers fulfilled their insurance contracts for which they were personally responsible.[30]

Both *Barbon's* joint stock company as well as the corporation founded by the City of London (1681) based on *Newbold's* mutual insurance scheme[31] from 1674, revised 1678/79.[32] The clatter ompany was described as an "abortive experiment in municipal insurance". In contrast to Germany and its long tradition of public insurance companies starting with the "Hamburger Feuerkasse" in 1676[33], the London public fire office lasted only for a short time. Maybe the problem was that without the legislative protection and the monopoly position like in Germany the competition was a constant struggle. In November 1682, the company ceased writing fire insurances and refunded the premiums it had collected. The reason is probably that influential people did not believe that insurances should be organized by the government respectively they believed more in a free and independent insurance market regulated by supply and demand.

The third established company was the "Mutual Friendly Society for Securing Housed from losses by Fire" (known as the "Friendly Society") in 1684. As a mutual society, it was based on the contributions of their members in the event of loss (30s for each 100 Pounds). The contracts were limited to seven years, the members had no share in the profits and paid an annual premium. Moreover, they were obliged to deposit a proportion of the amount insured as security, but the fund was regarded as a "guarantee of the undertaker's good faith". Each member had to deposit a proportion of the amount insured that was returned after the contract expired. Additionally, they paid an annual premium,

[28] This was a proclamation by King James I. against Grants and Monopolies (confirmed by Act 21 James I, cap 3, 1623) and prohibited the foundation of Speculative Associations or the raise of transferable stocks with the exception of "Charters to Corporations, Municipal or Trading". Cf. *Relton, F. B.* (1893), An account of the fire insurance companies, p. 10f.

[29] Cf. *Relton, F. B.* (1893), An account of the fire insurance companies, p. 27f.

[30] Cf. *Raynes, H. E.* (1948), A history of British insurance, p. 80.

[31] Cf. *Relton, F. B.* (1893), An account of the fire insurance companies, p. 24f.

[32] Cf. *Clayton, G.* (1971), British insurance, p. 37f.

[33] The compulsory "Feuerkasse" in Hamburg, in which all property owners had to insure, was founded in 1676 and was very successful for a long time. Cf. *Pearson, R.* (2002), Mutuality tested, p. 23.

for example 1s 4d per 100 Pounds for brick buildings.[34] This means that the people paid up front an amount of money indicating their commitment to contribute for rebuilding any members' house. Moreover, they had to sign a contract binding them to do so. The creators, *Henry Spelman* and *William Hale*, capitalized on the concept of a friendly society so far that they did not rely on that neighbours would fulfil their social obligations to help each other.[35]

The rivalry between the "Fire Office" and the "Friendly Society" that heated up during this time was solved by giving the "Fire Office" a monopoly for one year and then fire insurance should be alternated quarterly between these two companies. A solution that never actually was realized, because the market demanded a rapidly expansion of fire insurances. However, it is interesting that *Barbon* offered in addition to premium type insurances mutual contributions since 1693, a business concept that was also copied by other companies. The reason may be that the "Friendly Society" was successful. By 1706, the "Friendly Society" had insured 18,000 houses, i.e. it had also around 18,000 members.[36]

Within the next couple of years, new companies emerged offering security and attractive terms for their customers. Among them was the fourth company established at the end of the 17th century, the mutual "Amicable Contributors for Insuring from Loss by Fire" (1696), renamed "Hand-in-Hand" in 1706, which existed until 1905. The company proposed profits to their members derived from the investment of their original deposits. Moreover, the policyholders paid an annual premium and were liable to any loss up to ten shillings per 100 Pounds of their insured money. The "Hand-in-Hand" became fast a successful company and by 1704, it had already issued 7,313 policies.[37]

The original proposal of the "Hand-in-Hand" when it was established included a comparison between the company and the "Friendly Society". It stated that the 7 years insurance of the "Hand-in-Hand" will cost only 25s and even will be repaid by the interest of the money, while the "Friendly Society" was much more expensive. The following proposal compares both companies:

[34] Cf. *Clayton, G.* (1971), British insurance, p. 39; *Cockerell, H.A.L.*; *Green, E.* (1976), The British insurance business 1547-1970, p. 18; *Bridgewater, A.* (1995), The modern mutual insurance company in Britain, p. 29.

[35] Cf. *Ismay, P.* (2018), Trust among strangers. Friendly Societies in Modern Britain, p. 40.

[36] Cf. *Clayton, G.* (1971), British insurance, p. 39; *Ismay, P.* (2018), Trust among strangers. Friendly Societies in Modern Britain, p. 41.

[37] Cf. *Raynes, H. E.* (1948), A history of British insurance, p. 89; *Ismay, P.* (2018), Trust among strangers, p. 40.

Table 1: Comparison of the "Amicable Contributors" ("Hand-in-Hand") and the "Friendly Society"

Amicable Contributors (Hand-in-Hand)				Friendly Society			
Paid down for insuring 100l. 7 years	£ 0	s. 12	d. 0	Paid down for insuring 100l. 7 years	£ 1	s. 1	d. 0
				Of which annual payments for 7 years are	0	9	4
Contribution to losses by fires (paid by yearly dividend/profits)	0	00	0	Contribution to losses by fire for 7 years not less than	0	7	0
There will be returned	0 0	12 10	0 0	Interest for 9s paid her more than at the "Amicable Contributors" for 7 years to, at 6 per cent	0	3	8
Remains expended in all	£ 020			Remains expended in all	£ 100		

Source: *Relton, F. B.* (1893). An account of the fire insurance companies. Associations, institutions, projects, and schemes, p. 72.

The "Friendly Society" did not only compete with *Barbon's* office that had introduced insurances by mutual contribution but also with the "Hand-in-Hand". As a result, the "Friendly Society" issued a note that stated "This Office insures for the same money as the Amicable Contributors or Hand-in-Hand Office, who have settled no real fund for payment of such losses as may happen". Moreover, the company published a proposal as a reply to the statement of the "Hand-in-Hand", in which the advantages of the "Friendly Society" were emphasized.[38] For example, it is stated that:

- The "Friendly Society" had always returned the deposit punctually, while the "Hand-in-Hand" did not return money unless the member demands it.
- The "Friendly Society" has two good funds: its fund is secured eight times of the "greatest loss it ever sustained" by land and settled by various trustees.
- The "Friendly Society" also emphasized that no other office had settled any land security for insuring mutual contribution and that those companies only pretend that the deposit is a security, while the deposit

[38] Cf. *Relton, F. B.* (1893), An account of the fire insurance companies. Associations, institutions, projects, and schemes, pp. 63-65.

can be easily embezzled "shewn by several precedent examples of a late land bank".

- The members of the "Friendly Society" are not liable to penalties, while members of the "Hand-in-Hand" forfeit double the rate with all their deposit and benefit of insuring when forgetting to pay their contribution for a few days.
- The members of the "Hand-in-Hand" have to contribute to charges regarding office rent, taxes, expenses of watermen, cashiers etc.

At the turn of the century, six companies dominated the insurance market: three mutual societies, the "Hand-in-Hand" (1696), the "Union Fire Office" (1714), and the "Westminster Fire Office" (1717), two chartered corporations, the "Royal Exchange Assurance" and the "London Assurance Corporation", as well as a private stock company, the "Sun Fire Office" (1710). The "Sun Fire Office"[39] was founded by *Charles Povey* and was organized as a partnership with 24 partners and incorporated in 1726 as the "Sun Insurance Office".[40]

Three features characterized these early fire insurers: firstly, many of them were initially successful, secondly, they limited their business to London, and thirdly, 3 out of six companies were mutuals. At the beginning of the 18th century, the mutual form had the advantage that insurers had not to calculate the insurance costs in advance but was able to bind their members for seven years, which stabilized their future business. The three mutuals used the "deposit and call system", which means that all policyholders were members and entitled to participate in profits. With regard to the "Hand-in-Hand", each policy was for one house and for a term of seven years. Originally, members paid 2s 6d for the deposit, a deposit of 5s per 100 Pounds insured for a brick-built house, and an annual premium of 1s, usually to cover the administrative costs. Moreover, each member was liable to contribute regarding the costs of claims of the company up to 10 percent per policy. In return, the members received an annual dividend. All three mutuals held a general meeting, the "Hand-in-Hand" held it initially twice a year. A board of 20 directors were elected, each for one year, but only 10 of them might be re-elected for a second term. There was no specific quorum for the general meeting and the directors had the power to elect six trustees, in whose names all assets were held, and who carried out the business without referring to the members. The directors alone had the power to appoint or remove the trustees. Amendments

---

39 In 1706, the first incorporated insurance company, the Company of London Insurers, was founded, and established the partnership known as the Sun Fire Office in 1710. Cf. *Outreville, J. F.* (1998), Theory and practice of insurance, Dordrecht, p. 19; *Raven, J.* (2014), Publishing business in eighteenth-century England, p. 104.

40 Cf. *Outreville, J. F.* (1998), Theory and practice of insurance, p. 19.

were made to rectify these flaws, e.g. in 1722, a quorum of 48 was introduced for the general meeting and the number of board members were increased to 24. In all three mutuals the full board met weekly or fortnightly, although the "Hand-in-Hand" and the "Union Fire Office" had a sub-board of five directors that met twice a week and had the power to make bylaws. The latter were later submitted to the full board and had to be ratified by a majority. The "Union Fire Office" and "Westminster Fire Office" modelled their constitutions on the "Hand-in-Hand" to reduce set-up costs and to limit competition.[41]

During the 1720s, rates were adjusted and the staff was monitored regarding bookkeeping methods. This became necessary when the "Union Fire Office" was confronted with the problem that members whose policy was expiring were liable for the losses of the company since its foundation. Instead of a return of their deposit, they faced a substantial retrospective call. The reason was that the directors of the "Union Fire Office" had neglected to fix rates for the members' contribution towards losses. After electing new directors and an inspection, the relation between the members and board improved.[42]

The business scope of all three mutual companies, however, was rather limited. While the "Hand-in-Hand" insured buildings and from 1805 on goods, the "Union Fire Office" insured goods and merchandise against fire in London and Westminster, and the "Westminster Fire Office" provided fire insurances for buildings and houses for the citizens of Westminster.[43] Only the stock company "Sun Fire Office" had a wider fire insurance market, attempted to insure property outside London by 1710, and underwrote goods and buildings in the same policy. The company also acquired several local companies in the later half of the 18th century when many new fire offices failed and were merged with other companies.[44] Moreover, the three mutual offices were closely connected to each other. For example, the "Union Fire Office" was the sister office of the "Hand-in-Hand", underwriting goods in the buildings insured by the "Hand-in-Hand", and the "Westminster Fire Office" was established by members of the "Hand-in-Hand".[45] Nevertheless, the three mutuals together earned more than 50 percent of the total income of all fire underwriting in the capital for the first two-thirds of the century, a time in which London accounted for more than 70 percent of all fire-insured

[41] Cf. *Pearson, R.* (2002), Mutuality tested: The rise and fall of mutual fire insurance offices in eighteenth-century London. Business History, vol. 44, no. 4, October 2002, p. 5f.

[42] Cf. *Pearson, R.* (2002), Mutuality tested, p. 8f.

[43] Cf. *Pearson, R.* (2004), Insuring the Industrial Revolution. Fire insurance in Great Britain, 1700-1850, Aldershot, p. 62; *Bridgewater, A.* (1995), The modern mutual insurance company in Britain, p. 29.

[44] Cf., *A.* (1995), The modern mutual insurance company in Britain, p. 29.

[45] Cf. *Pearson, R.* (2004), Insuring the Industrial Revolution, p. 62f.

property in Britain (cf. table 2).[46] Only these six companies survived beyond 1720 and ruled the insurance market for the next 60 years.

Table 2: London fire insurance market shares 1725-1795[47]

Year	Hand-in-Hand	Union Fire Office	Westminster Fire Office	Total market share of the 3 mutuals	Sun Fire Office	Royal Exchange Assurance (REA)	London Assurance Corporation	Phoenix	Total London premiums in Pounds
1725	37	5	3	45	36	11	9	-	33,482
1730	34	6	3	43	32	15	11	-	42,896
1735	38	8	4	50	29	11	11	-	44,414
1740	39	9	4	52	28	9	11	-	47,050
1745	39	9	5	53	28	8	10	-	47,486
1750	39	11	6	56	27	9	9	-	55,354
1755	36	12	6	54	27	10	9	-	64,860
1760	34	12	7	53	28	11	8	-	74,009
1765	29	14	7	50	34	10	7	-	94,029
1770	26	12	6	44	40	11	6	-	110,805
1775	21	11	7	39	43	12	6	-	122,191
1780	20	10	7	37	46	13	5	-	125,434
1785	14	6	7	27	44	12	5	12	116,732
1790	11	4	6	21	38	12	4	25	139,093
1795	8	2	4	14	37	14	4	30	165,715

Table 2 shows that the market share (estimated by premium income and the average of five years) of the three mutuals rose from 45 percent in 1725 to its peak with 56 percent in 1750 and then decreased, first slowly, then dramatically to 14 percent in 1795. This development can be explained by the difficulties these three mutuals had to face by 1800 and which nearly destroyed them. During the second half of the 18th century, the London mutuals had to sell stocks to pay the increasing insurance claims. This development was aggravated when, at the same time, the price of the funds decreased and the need of the companies to sell increased. As a result, the companies had to sell at a loss and their range of gilts narrowed. The "Hand-in-Hand" had eight categories of stocks in 1768; in 1781 the company had only one. While the "Hand-in-Hand" and the "Westminster Fire Office" survived by structural reforms, the "Union Fire Office", however, demutualized

[46] Cf. *Cockerell, H.A.L.*; *Green, E.* (1976), The British insurance business 1547-1970, p. 19; *Pearson, R.* (2002), Mutuality tested, p. 1f.

[47] Adapted from *Pearson, R.* (2004), Insuring the Industrial Revolution. p. 66f.

in 1805.[48] The latter finally made three major reforms by introducing annual and short-term insurances, marketing was extended outside London and built almost exclusively on annual insurances, and finally issuing 300,000 Pounds in 1,500 shares with 10 percent paid up. The capital supported the company doing business and by 1813, insurances increased to 6.1m Pounds.[49]

Table 2 demonstrates that the growth of the insurance business during the 18th century is in particular based on business in London. While the total premiums in 1725 were 33,482 Pounds, they increased almost fivefold to 165,715 Pounds in 1795 (cf. table 2). When looking at the market share in general, the "Hand-in-Hand" had always the largest market share of the three mutuals, respectively the "Sun Fire Office", with a peak of 46 percent in 1780, the largest of the joint stock companies. However, the "Sun Fire Office's" market share stabilized itself after the 1730s and the "Royal Exchange Assurance's" (REA) decreased during the second quarter of the 18th century before the company was able to recover during the 1750s. The "London Assurance Corporation" developed similarly but declined continuously until the end of the 18th century. With the foundation of the "Phoenix Fire Office" in 1782 under the name "New Fire Office" and renamed in 1785 (in 1901 renamed "Phoenix Assurance Company Ltd.") by the London sugar refiners, the market share of all other insurers became smaller. This development even became more evident with the collaboration of the "Sun Fire Office", the "Phoenix Fire Office" and the "Royal Exchange Assurance" (REA) that pressed the market share of the remaining even further.[50] The company expanded its trading connection and established the world's first foreign sales network for fire insurance. By 1815, 42 agents worked for the company in Europe, North America, the West Indies, at Buenos Aires, and the Cape and its overseas insurance accounted for half of its premium income by the 1820s.[51]

When looking at the business development of the "Friendly Society" and the "Hand-in-Hand" during the 18th century, the latter was able to increase its market share and premium rates by 1760 and became one of the main insurers in London. However, later the market changed and their geographical limitation to London with an increase of fires became a huge disadvantage for the business. Mutuals' subscription arrangements were limited to the London membership and therefore prohibited them to expand business to the fire insurance market outside of the capital. As a result, those companies missed the opportunities

48 Cf. *Pearson, R.* (2002), Mutuality tested, p. 21; *Pearson, R.* (2004), Insuring the Industrial Revolution. p. 331.

49 Cf. *Pearson, R.* (2002), Mutuality tested, p. 21.

50 Cf. *Pearson, R.* (2002), Mutuality tested, p. 68f.

51 Cf. *Pearson, R.; Doe, H.* (2015), Organizational choice in UK marine insurance, p. 70.

of gaining a much higher growth rate by expanding their business to provincial cities where the first industrialization efforts led to a higher need of fire insurances.[52]

By 1790, 7 fire companies existed in London and 14 outside the capital. Within the next 25 years, 30 offices were founded in Scotland, Ireland, and in the English countries and 10 more in London and by 1810, 51 fire insurances existed in the United Kingdom. Most of the new companies founded in the provinces were joint stock companies. However, at least nine mutuals were established between 1784 and 1809. These mutuals were the following[53]:

- "Suffolk & General Fire Office" (founded as a partnership in 1802 and became a mutual company as the "Suffolk Amicable" in 1809),
- "Devizes" (1784)
- "Norwich Mutual" (1785)
- "Norwich Union Fire Insurance Society" (1797)
- "Essex Equitable" (1802)
- "Finchingfield" (1804)
- "Wooler" (Northumberland, 1805)
- "Norwich Equitable" (1807), and
- "Anchor" (Norwich, 1808)

Although these mutuals were small companies, they flourished due to a highly selective membership and a tendency to minimize risks. Although the "Norwich Union Fire Insurance Society" tried to spread risks nationally, it was forced to merge with the "Norwich General Assurance Company" (founded in 1790 as a partnership). It eventually demutualized in 1821 due to the financial crisis during the 1720s.[54] The founder of the "Norwich Union Fire Insurance Society", *Thomas Bignold*, also established the "Norwich Union Life Insurance Society" in 1808 that was able to continue as a mutual company.[55]

1.3 Life Assurance

Life assurance is based on a life assurance policy that requires that the insuring company pays a sum of money after a specific period of time or at the death of the insured. The policy can be temporary, i.e.

---

[52] Cf. *Clayton, G.* (1971), British insurance, p. 40; *Cockerell, H.A.L.*; *Green, E.* (1976), The British insurance business 1547-1970, p. 19.

[53] Cf. *Pearson, R.* (2004), Insuring the Industrial Revolution. p. 162.

[54] Cf. *Pearson, R.* (2002), Mutuality tested, p. 24.

[55] Cf. *Bridgewater, A.* (1995), The modern mutual insurance company in Britain, p. 30; *Pearson, R.* (2004), Insuring the Industrial Revolution. p. 163.

a payment in the event of the insured dying during a fixed term, a whole life assurance, i.e. a payment after the death of the insured, or an endowment assurance, i.e. a payment after a fixed period of time or earlier if the insured dies during this time. For this type of insurance, the insurer needs information about the policyholder to assess the risk and therefore the premium which is based on the age, health, occupation, or the movement of the policyholder and compares then this information with the long time "mortality experience" of the life assurance company.[56]

In Britain, life assurance existed since the late 16th century and was limited to term assurance on business partners and merchants. In this period, life assurance was closely connected with the development of maritime trade, because when merchants underwrote maritime risks they also often insured the life of the captain, and probably important members of the crew, for the duration of the journey.[57] In general, life assurance policies were limited to a couple of months, only few were longer than a year. These short-term policies hindered the development of the life assurance business. Nevertheless, between 1696 and 1721 over 60 life assurance offices with approximately 12,000 policyholders existed.[58] Most life assurances were based on co-operative redistributive schemes the so-called "assurances in way of friendly society". Two forms existed, the contributorship and the mortuary tontine. The contributorship was based on a fixed sum paid by the members when someone died. Therefore, this insurance form had variable fees and fixed death benefits. The mortuary tontine, on the other hand, had fixed annual dues and a common fund that was divided equally among its members, i.e. fixed fees but variable death benefits.[59] However, at the end of the 17th century, the possibility of establishing funds developed making the payment of annuities with benefit of survivorship[60] possible. Several unsuccessful attempts of establishing such system were made, including one in 1699 by the "Society for Assurance of Widows and Orphans" founded by *Mr. Standfield*. This society lasted only 14 years, but was established as a mutual benefaction with 2,000 subscribers whose members paid to the widow of a subscriber 5s each (a total of approximately 500 Pounds). With this foundation, the type

[56] Cf. *Cockerell, H.A.L.*; *Green, E.* (1976), The British insurance business 1547-1970, p. 34.

[57] Cf. *Cockerell, H.A.L.*; *Green, E.* (1976), The British insurance business 1547-1970, p. 34; *Clayton, G.* (1971), British insurance, p. 63.

[58] Cf. *Clark, G.* (1997), Life insurance in the society and culture of London, 1700-75. Urban History, vol. 24, pt. 1 (May 1997), p. 18.

[59] Cf. *Clark, G.* (1997), Life insurance, p. 21.

[60] Survivorship benefit means that when subscribes to the fund die the survivors received proportionally increased annuities. Cf. *Clayton, G.* (1971), British insurance, p. 64; 75.

of life assurance acquired a mutual and co-operative character with a non-specialist clientele as policyholders.[61] From the type of such a mutual benefaction, it was just a short way to mutual assurance societies with premiums that were shared among the descendants of those who died. The amount of money depended on the number of death per annum. This scheme was used by the "Amicable Society for Perpetual Assurance Office" that was founded on July 25, 1706 by *William Talbot* (Bishop of Oxford) and *Sir Thomas Allen* (2nd Baronet and investor) under a charter of *Queen Anne*.[62] The company existed until 1866 when the "Norwich Union Life Insurance Society" acquired it. The company's philosophy was that their policies should be used for philanthropic work, for example to "the augmentation of poor (clerical) livings; to the propagation of Christianity in foreign parts; to charity schools; the relief of poor debtors, and to any such excellent design".[63] The philanthropic idea appealed in particular to the main clientele of life assurances, the middle class comprised by professionals and commercial people. This social class had modest capital and was wealthy enough to support social and charitable work, but not so rich that they were immune to the horrors of the workhouse and debtors' prison. Moreover, almost three-quarters of its members lived in London, the rest in the counties southeast of the capital and closely connected to the city. Poverty was also regarded as a way to moral corruption and therefore life assurance societies were closely connected with strong moral reforming impulses of the middle class at the beginning of the 18th century. The various motives to become members of such societies were, on the one hand, to guarantee that they would remain their social class and to avoid declining into the ranks of the poor, and, on the other hand, to be part of a co-operative charitable initiative and helping less fortunate people.[64] During the 18th century, a trend is evident that such life assurance societies comprised donors as well as beneficiaries of charity and poor relief.

The philanthropic philosophy of the "Amicable Society for Perpetual Assurance Office" claimed to be the first mutual life assurance society established in the world, while *Outreville* named the above-mentioned "Society for Assurance of Widows and Orphans" as the first mutual life assurance. Nevertheless, the "Amicable Society for Perpetual Assurance Office" had the monopoly in life assurance until the "London Insurance Corporation" and the "Royal Exchange Assurance Corporation" were founded in 1721.[65] It is important to note that in this period company

61 Cf. *Clark, G.* (1997), Life insurance, p. 20.

62 https://heritage.aviva.com/our-history/companies/a/amicable-society/ (07.03.2019)

63 *Clark, G.* (1997), Life insurance, p. 22.

64 Cf. *Clark, G.* (1997), Life insurance, p. 22f.

65 Cf. *Outreville, J. F.* (1998), Theory and practice of insurance, 22.

offering life assurances adopted the organisation of joint stock companies, a fashionable trend among business firms and charity societies. Therefore, policyholders held, like shareholders, also a portion of the society.[66] In the beginning, the membership of the "Amicable Society for Perpetual Assurance Office" was limited to 2,000[67], raised to 4,000 by 1790[68], to 16,000 in 1823[69] and to 32,000 in 1836[70] due to its success. The members, who had to be between 12 and 45 years old, paid a fixed annual sum (six Pounds 4 Shillings)[71] and were entitled to have a maximum of three shares. The "London Insurance Corporation's" and the "Royal Exchange Assurance Corporation's" scheme was also based on an age limit of 45 years for their policyholders and on same annual premiums for all members independently of their age and health. In 1807, the "Amicable Society for Perpetual Assurance Office" obtained a new charter to broaden its aims and adopt the improved methods used by other assurance offices. Under the new charter, premiums varied depending on the age and circumstances of each member.[72]

This type of life assurance scheme, however, had no firm scientific foundation. To assess the premiums and risks for policyholders over 45 years by doing research into rates and developing mortality statistics, a complex interest and probability theory is necessary, which did not exist in the first quarter of the 18th century.[73] Although the first life table was written by *Edmund Haley* in 1693, it took until the 1750s when *James Dobson*, a mathematician and actuary, was refused a life assurance policy due to his age that this type of life assurance scheme was questioned. *Dobson* developed a scheme for basing life premiums on the age and expectation of lives assured and tried to receive a Royal Charter in 1761. Although it was refused and he died in 1757, his disciple *Edward Rowe Mores* adopted his scheme and established the "Society for Equitable Assurances on Lives and Survivorships" in 1762. The company became "The Old Equitable Life Insurance Company" and wrote whole life insurance policies at a level premium, i.e. the premiums varied according to the age of the policyholder.[74] This mutual society offered life assurances on a whole basis, on a term basis (a fixed

[66] Cf. *Clark, G.* (1997), Life insurance, p. 24.

[67] Cf. The charters, acts of Parliament, and by-laws of the corporation of the Amicable Society for a Perpetual Assurance Office, London 1854.

[68] Cf. Ibid. Article V, p. 55.

[69] Cf. Ibid. p. 89.

[70] Cf. Ibid. p. 96.

[71] Cf. Ibid. Article 12, p. 10.

[72] The charters, acts of Parliament, and by-laws of the corporation of the Amicable Society for a Perpetual Assurance Office, Article 2, p. 57.

[73] Cf. *Clayton, G.* (1971), British insurance, p. 65.

[74] Cf. *Outreville, J. F.* (1998), Theory and practice of insurance, p. 23; *Cockerell, H.A.L.*; *Green, E.* (1976), The British insurance business 1547-1970, p. 35.

number of years), or on a single year basis. The company developed strong scientific roots regarding premiums that were now based on the age of the policyholder, limitation of the number of insured, periodical valuations and distributions of profits as well as equitable surrender values. In 1781, it changed its premium policy and adopted the Northampton table, revisionary payments, and reduced its premiums in 1781 and 1786. With these guidelines, the "Society for Equitable Assurances on Lives and Survivorships" became the dominant life assurance company at the end of the 18th century. Its competitor the "Royal Exchange Company" offered life assurances with annual contracts since 1721 and expanded its small business in 1783 by offering whole life terms with level premiums with similar conditions as the "Society for Equitable Assurances on Lives and Survivorships". The "London Assurance Corporation" offered life assurances on a yearly basis but its business was for the most part of the 18th century rather small. In 1792, the first proprietary life office the "Westminster Society for Insurance of Lives and Survivorships" was founded under a deed of settlement. It was later merged with the "Guardian Assurance Company" in 1863. The "Pelican Life Insurance", a branch of the "Phoenix", was established as a proprietary company in 1797 and with similar guidelines as the "Westminster Society for Insurance of Lives and Survivorships". At the end of the 18th century, six life assurance offices can be found: two mutual companies, the "Amicable Society for Perpetual Assurance Office" and the "Society for Equitable Assurances on Lives and Survivorships", and four joint stock companies, the "Royal Exchange Company", the "London Assurance Corporation", the "Westminster Society for insurance upon lives and survivorships", and the "Pelican Life Insurance".[75]

The question of what is an insurable and non-insurable cargo is closely connected with the debate about slavery and how to place a financial value on a life. This became an important issue when in November 1781 the British slave ship *Zong* threw more than 130 African slaves over board to drown when the ship ran low on drinking water. The reasons were on the one side to ensure the survival of the passengers and the crew but also to receive insurance money for the loss of the slaves. If the slaves had died of water deprivation, the owners had not got any money. After the ship reached the next harbour, the owners claimed their insurance money. Usually slave shippers insured against two risks, firstly, a total loss of the ship and cargo and secondly, against loss of life due to insurrection. The case came to court and the owners claimed that the deliberately killing of slaves was legal. However, the presiding judge Lord Chief Justice *Mansfield* ruled against this case, due to new evidence being introduced suggesting the captain and crew had made mistakes. However, the judge stated that without

[75] Cf. *Clayton, G.* (1971), British insurance, p. 74.

their mistakes the owners' claim would have been valid and the killing legal. Nevertheless, the loss of slaves was still regarded as a general average loss. In contrast, the continental law by 1770 stated that if goods were damaged or lost by the fault of the insured party then the insurers did not had to pay. With regard to the *Zong*, the human cargo was regarded as a partial loss but the loss was made due to mistakes by the captain and the crew. As a result of these events, the abolishing movement in the late 18th and early 19th centuries was stimulated and the debate became a public issue. In 1788, the Parliament passed the Slave Trade Act 1788 that regulated the slave trade and limited the number of slaves per ship. In 1791, Parliament passed another law that prohibited insurance companies from reimbursing ship owners when slaves were thrown overboard. Finally, the British Slave Trade Act, which abolished British participation in the African slave trade, though not slavery itself, was passed in 1807 and in 1833 the Slavery Abolition Act 1833 abolished slavery throughout the British Empire.[76]

2. Financial crises, mergers, and industrial changes during the 19th century

2.1 Marine insurances after 1824

After the Bill to repeal the monopoly of the charted companies was enacted in 1824, the market structure changed favouring free trade and led to a domination of single companies in the marine insurance sector. This development, however, started a debate if joint stock companies, private underwriters, or mutual companies were the best choice to undertake marine insurance. While joint stock companies provided only less security than *Lloyd's* did, because the latter offered unlimited liability, others argued that mutuality was the better option for this insurance sector. They claimed that mutual companies had lower costs, offered cheaper insurances, less restricted claim settlements, and a close relationship between insurers and the merchants. Supporters of the joint stock companies' idea claim that stocks had more capital than

[76] Cf. *Lobban, M.* (2007), Slavery, insurance and the law. The Journal of Legal History 28(3), pp. 319-328; *Rupprecht, A.* (2007), A very uncommon case: Representations of the Zong and the British campaign to abolish the slave trade. The Journal of Legal History 28(3), pp. 329-346.

mutuals and were able to estimate the costs of insurance in advance, and payments were made without any delays.[77] Another idea was a kind of hybrid form of organization combining features of a joint stock and a mutual company. As a result, a plan developed to establish the "Indemnity Mutual Marine Assurance Company" in 1824 as a mutual company with members and a capital stock. However, this idea did not work out, because the managers were not able to find shareholders. At the same time they had to deal with losses at seas, debts and shareholders with financial problems. In 1827, the chairman of the company considered the mutual system as the main problem and eventually the company was opened to the public and functioned as a regular joint stock company. By 1832, the company insured more ships and cargoes than the "London Assurance Corporation".[78]

In the 1827, the "Alliance Marine Insurance Company" was founded. The latter and the "Indemnity Marine Assurance" were the exceptions to the numerous weak foundations that followed and only existed for a short time. One of those that lasted for more than two decades was the "London Maritime Assurance Company", founded in 1839 and liquidated in 1860. When the Joint Stock Companies Act was established in 1844, a period of speculation and the foundation of mostly unsuccessful companies followed. During the 1860s, the situation changed when the American marine insurance business was transferred to Britain due to the American Civil War. New companies such as the "London and Provincial", "Thames and Mercy", and the "Universal Marine Insurance" quickly had 40 percent of the London insurance market. Moreover, they held 63 percent of foreign companies in overseas, particularly in the USA, in 1900. However, German, Swiss, and Austrian companies still dominated the European inland transport insurance sector.[79] Although mutual shipowners survived the time after 1824 and despite the foundation of new mutual and joint stock companies, they often insured older vessels while new ones were underwritten at *Lloyd's*. The existing mutual "P&I clubs" insured only hulls and cargoes, while new founded clubs covered more liabilities. The reasons were that new legislations and judicial rulings were enacted, such as the Passenger Acts of 1842 and 1847, the Steam Navigation Act of 1846, and the Fatal Accidents Act of 1846 that increased the liabilities of shipowners. Also various merchant shipping acts from 1894 and the Workmen's Compensation Act of 1906 made shipowners responsible for their seamen and stevedores regarding illness and costs. This became a new and promising

[77] Cf. *Pearson, R.; Doe, H.* (2015), Organizational choice in UK marine insurance, p. 66f.

[78] Cf. *Raynes, H. E.* (1948), A history of British insurance, p. 317f.; *Pearson, R.; Doe, H.* (2015), Organizational choice in UK marine insurance, p. 58.

[79] Cf. *Pearson, R.; Doe, H.* (2015), Organizational choice in UK marine insurance, p. 59.

insurance sector due to a debate about safety at sea and the following legislation, e.g. regarding third-party risks. The latter had a long-term influence on the UK insurance market.[80]

Mutual P&I clubs also had the opportunity of offering protection and indemnity insurance to their members on a non-profit basis. The first was the "Shipowner's Mutual Protection Society" established in 1855 that still exists as a mutual P&I club, the "Britannia Steam Ship Insurance Association Limited" (Britannia), operating worldwide.[81] The principle was that members joined the club for a year, gave details about the to-be insured risks, paid the "advanced call"[82], a contribution calculated at the beginning of each insurance year, and were liable for additionally payments in the event of future losses. The P&I clubs became larger over time, however, after World War II the market had changed. While Britain had no longer the largest merchant fleet, other nations had expanded or rebuilt their fleets. As a result, British P&I clubs turned international and established the "International Group of P&I clubs". Today, shipowners still favour the mutuality principle as a very good option for marine insurance.[83]

As mentioned above, after the repeal of the monopoly held by the two chartered companies many new companies were founded, however, most of them did last only for a short time. At the turn of the century, the marine insurance market changed drastically. In 1899, 16 British marine companies existed underwriting purely marine insurances. Although they had large capital fundings and stood in direct competition to *Lloyd's*, all but one were taken-over by composite companies between 1905 and 1927. Three other companies, the "Commercial Union", and the two chartered companies, the "Royal Exchange Assurance Corporation" and the "London Assurance Corporation", transacted other types of insurances as well and maintained independent.[84] The following table shows that only one company, the "Sea Insurance" remained independent and was not merged, while all others were absorbed within the next twenty years.

---

[80] Cf. *Pearson, R.; Doe, H.* (2015), Organizational choice in UK marine insurance, p. 58; 61f.

[81] Cf. https://tindallriley.co.uk/company-profile/, 29.09.2019.

[82] The amount was calculated on an estimation made by the club's managers of the total income required for the next insurance year and the proportion of the income that each member has to pay for the vessel. Cf. *Pearson, R.; Doe, H.* (2015), Organizational choice in UK marine insurance, p. 62.

[83] Cf. *Pearson, R.; Doe, H.* (2015), Organizational choice in UK marine insurance, p. 64f.

[84] Cf. *Raynes, H. E.* (1948), A history of British insurance, p. 375; *Pearson, R.* (2012) United Kingdom: Pioneering insurance internationally, p. 75.

Table 3: The amalgamations of marine insurance companies without the three composite insurers at the beginning of the 20th century

Transferred to or shares purchased by	Companies	Year
Alliance Assurance	Alliance Marine & General (1824)	1905
Royal	British & Foreign (1863)	1909
Provincial	Hull Underwriters (1893)	1927
Northern Maritime	Indemnity Marine (1824)	1916
Yorkshire	London & Provincial (1860)	1913
	Ulster Marine (1887)	1918
London & Lancashire	Marine Limited (1836)	1917
	Standard Marine (1871)	1907
Scottish Union & National	Maritime (1864)	1914
Employers' Liability	Merchants Marine (1871)	1919
Union Marine & General (already controlled by Phoenix)	Northern Maritime (1863)	1917
North British	Ocean Marine (1859)	1907
Guardian	Reliance Marine (1885)	1916
Sea Insurance *Still independent*		
Liverpool & London & Globe	Thames & Mersey (1860)	1911
Phoenix	Union Marine (1863)	1911

Source: based on *Raynes, H. E.* (1948). A history of British insurance, p. 375.

Table 3 shows that the marine insurance market was dominated by joint stock companies and in particular by composite insurers. The table also demonstrates that one of the few mutual insurance companies, the "Indemnity Marine" (1824), ceased to exist when it merged with the "Northern Maritime Company". Overall, it can be said that during this period the insurance market became dominated by composite insurers. They increased their market power by absorbing sole fire, life, marine, and accident insurers. One of the largest composite insurers became the "Commercial Union", which took over 21 companies between 1900 and 1939.[85]

2.2 Fire insurance

The fire insurance sector during the 19th century was dominated by several events. Firstly, the sector saw an increase of joint stock companies controlling the market and the downfall of mutual insurances due

[85] Cf. *Pearson, R.,* (2012) United Kingdom: Pioneering insurance internationally, p. 75.

to more and more complex market structures. Secondly, two waves of foundations, the first during the 1820s to the 1830s and the second between 1834 and 1850, led to fierce competition between the companies. Thirdly, the various strategies of the companies to handle the competition including a huge merger and acquisition phase that influenced the British insurance market sustainable. Fourthly, the development of a tariff system and the foundation of the Fire Offices Committee (FOC). Additionally, the beginning of new non-life insurance segments, such as accident or plate glass insurances. Finally, the composite insurers emerged and changed the market structure drastically.

2.2.1 The rise of the joint stock companies

By the end of the 18th century, the three mutual companies, "Hand-in-Hand", "Westminster Fire Office", and "Union Fire Office", faced financial difficulties due to heavy losses caused by large fires during the 1760s, the early 1780s and the early 1790s. This development was the result of London's rapid population growth, waves of speculative buildings, and a long period of neglecting regulations. Additionally, the American and French wars led to higher costs for insurance companies. The losses of the three mutual companies increased by the end of the 18th century.[86] Table 4 shows the loss ratios of the three mutual fire offices from 1726 to 1800.

Table 4 Loss ratio of three mutual fire offices (average in percent)

Years	Union Fire Office	Hand-in-Hand	Westminster Fire Office
1726-1730	24.0	-	-
1731-1735	14.4	14.1	-
1736-1740	6.2	12.6	-
1741-1745	11.6	7.6	-
1746-1750	13.3	-	-
1751-1755	6.3	8.0	-
1756-1760	18.1	15.0	-
1761-1765	18.3	21.5	14.8
1766-1770	28.6	31.8	14.7
1771-1775	27.0	19.4	7.1
1776-1780	17.5	20.1	11.1
1781-1785	57.5	22.4	12.3
1786-1790	21.8	23.3	10.8
1791-1795*	52.9	30.7	15.2
1796-1800**	22.4	9.2	-

* Westminster's average is for 1790-1794
** Union's average is for 1795-1799
Source: *Pearson, R.* (2002). Mutuality tested, p. 11.

86 Cf. *Pearson, R.* (2002), Mutuality tested, p. 11.

Table 4 demonstrates that the "Westminster Fire Office" was the most successful company of the three mutuals during the second half of the 18th century. Its loss ratio was half of the "Hand-in-Hand's" and more than a third lower than the "Union Fire Office's" during the 1790s. According to *Pearson*, the "Westminster Fire Office" was even able to increase its market share until the 1780s. A time when the success of the "Hand-in-Hand" as well as the "Union Fire Office" had already began to decline. However, from 1770 to 1790 the "Westminster Fire Office's" profits decreased from 12 percent to 6 percent. Like other mutuals, it sold stocks and used members' deposits when the losses by fire were too heavy. The problems of the "Hand-in-Hand" started during the 1770s due to more competitors and an increase of fire damage. This led to a decline of members, from 39,000 in 1770 to 15,000 by the end of the 18th century.[87] The London market became much more complex, in particular the increase of hazardous insurances and the need to operate on different markets within London, made it necessary to extend the range of products and the area of business. While new technical knowledge regarding fire insurance became crucial, the management and staff of mutuals remained on the same level. The still used deposit and call system raised the costs of the members' insurance and great disadvantages arose when the market became instable. New companies were founded and competed with mutuals. These new offices were able to stabilize their business due to fresh capital from their business outside of London.[88]

Although joint stock companies also faced problems during this period, they were able to expand their business outside London by using the need for fire insurance in the industrial regions. Additionally, new fire offices in the provinces were established during the first decade of the 19th century. However, many rapidly industrializing regions were not able to sustain local offices like the "West Riding" or the "West of Scotland". For example, by 1810 all 15 fire offices competing in Liverpool were based outside the region. Between 1784 and 1815, only four fire offices existed in the Midlands and the north of England, 7 in East Anglia, 4 in the west of England, and 5 in Essex, Kent, Sussex, and Hampshire. Most of these fire offices were joint stock companies, although 9[89] were mutuals. London mutuals, on the other hand, could not use the strategy to expand their business outside the capital so easily

87 Cf. Ibid., p. 12f.

88 Cf. Ibid., p. 23.

89 Suffolk & General Fire Office (founded as a partnership in 1802 and became a mutual company as the Suffolk Amicable in 1809), Devizes (1784), Norwich Mutual (1785), Norwich Union Fire Insurance Society (1797), Essex Equitable (1802), Finchingfield (1804), Wooler (Northumberland, 1805), Norwich Equitable (1807), and Anchor (Norwich, 1808), Cf. *Pearson, R.* (2004), Insuring the Industrial Revolution, p. 178.

to improve their financial situation, because due to their organizational form their business was limited to London. The "Hand-in-Hand", located in London, was able to survive, probably due to low administrative costs, the improvement in loss ratios, and the extension of the office's business to the provinces in 1789. Additionally, it expanded its product range and offered insurances of goods and merchandise, including farm stocks, and introduced non-participating policies for annual insurances. The latter was also used for the new introduced life insurance sector in 1836. It offered the policyholders now lower premiums compared to those holdings offering with-profits policies for whole lives. It seems that the "Hand-in-Hand" survived its difficulties by adopting strategies of a joint stock company. The still used seven-year contracts became less and less attractive to customers. Therefore, it introduced annual and short-term policies, however, this was only possible by keeping annual policyholders outside a membership and out of the call and deposit system.[90] As a result, it became a mutual company with some non-member policyholders at the turn of the century, acting "more like a stock company without undergoing full demutualization".[91]

Table 5 shows that joint stock companies with the "Sun Fire Office" at the top dominated the insurance business. However, most of the London offices were not able to increase their premium income during the 1800s and early 1810s, partly because of a falling price trend regarding premium rates and because of falling rates on industrial and commercial risks. Moreover, the loss ratios were exceptional high at the end of the 18th century for the "Sun Fire Office" (82.9 percent) and the "Phoenix Fire Office" (91.9 percent). In general, the ratio of losses was much higher for the London offices than for offices in the provinces. While the existing offices had their worst results during the 1790s and early 1800s, new established offices such as the "Globe", the "Imperial", and the "Atlas" had to face such problems between 1812 and 1814. Only the "Norwich Union", a mutual company, and the "County Fire Office" (founded in 1807), a joint stock company, were the exceptions to this trend. Their premiums increased steadily and exceptionally, while their loss ratios remained rather low.[92]

---

[90] Cf. *Pearson, R.* (2002), Mutuality tested, p. 23f.

[91] Ibid., p. 15f.

[92] Cf. *Pearson, R.* (2004), Insuring the Industrial Revolution, p. 167; 170.

Table 5 Profitability of fire insurance companies in London and the provinces between 1791 and 1815

Company	1791-1795		1796-1800*		1801-1805**		1806-1810***		1811-1815****	
	Premiums	Losses	Premiums	Losses	Premiums	Losses	Premiums	Losses	Premiums	Losses
	London									
Sun	115,090	82.9	126,215	63.3	121,845	69.2	107,611	61.5	113,985	64.1
Phoenix#	71,210	91.9	98,742	51.3	120,099	59.9	88,555	55.5	85,273	52.5
REA	45,769	71.5	63,997	54.8	79,820	63.8	72,949	66.1	71,274	64.6
London Assurance	6,539	46.2	7,963	41.2	8,470	53.7	8,455	52.4	8,801	43.3
Globe					32,683	45.1	36,527	62.2	37,257	74.2
Imperial					35,035	39.3	59,131	70.1	58,749	76.3
County Fire Office							11,648	17.7	22,103	26.8
Atlas Assurance Company									19,903	81.9
	Provinces									
Wiltshire	996	31.5	2,432	39.2	3,661	60.8	4,161	33.9	4,4485	43.1
Bath Sun	823	40.3	807	4.4	960	24.9	1,265	9.7	1,405	47.5
Old Bath (Bath Fire Office)			1,388	155.9	1,551	13.3	1,554	18.9	1,577	16.1
Norwich Union			403	1.4	3,276	13.3	13,693	20.4	35,861	36.2
Kent Fire Office					3,759	21.7	7,368	45.4	7,975	20.1
Newcastle Upon Tyne Fire Office							4,811	53.4	4,220	47.4
Sheffield Fire Office							958	11.0	1,116	0.0
Glasgow Fire Insurance Company							3,429	66.7	-	-
Essex&Suffolk									3,939	25.9

The premiums are average annual premiums (UK business only), and the loss ratios are the percentage of premiums (annual averages).

* Old Bath 1798-1800, Norwich Union 1797-1800

** Globe 1804-05, Imperial 1803-05, Kent premiums 1802-05 and loss ratios 1802-07

*** County Fire Office 1807-10, Newcastle upon Tyne Fire Office 1808-10, Sheffield Fire Office 1809-10, Glasgow Fire Insurance Company 1804-12, Kent loss ratios 1808-10

**** Atlas Assurance Company 1812-14, Kent 1811-13 and 1815, Essex-Suffolk 1813-15

\# According to Pearson, the premiums differ slightly compared to another source (Cf. *Pearson, R.* (2004). Insuring the Industrial Revolution, p. 169)

Source: *Pearson, R.* (2004). Insuring the Industrial Revolution, p. 168f.

2.2.2 The two foundation waves

At the beginning of the 19th century, the competition among the fire insurance companies increased, but none of them were able to match the pace of the industrial and commercial development, which accelerated after the end of the war against France. The population grew steadily and England became an urban nation, where 54 percent of its citizens lived in towns, i.e. more than 2,000 inhabitants. For example, in 1811 London had 1 million residents while in 1851 it had grown to a town with 2.4 million citizens. Even in the provinces, the towns

grew fast and cities such as Liverpool, Glasgow, and Manchester had over 300,000 inhabitants, while Dublin, Birmingham and Edinburgh had a population of more than 200,000.[93] The growth of the population and the increase of the income of the middle class led to a competition between insurance offices, in particular between the long existing companies and the large number of recently founded. The fierce competition that became even hostile was gererated by two foundation waves. The first wave had its peak during the 1820s and 1830s and led to 26 new offices between 1821 and 1826 in England, 6 in Scotland, and 7 in Ireland. While some of them were rather small and existed only for a short time, other such as the "Guardian" and the "Alliance" grew to large companies with domestic and international business. During this time, the insurance industry was confronted with open price warfare and numerous take-overs. Some of the companies faced this development by forming alliances, such as the "Sun Fire Office", the "Phoenix Fire Office", and the "Royal Exchange Assurance". They worked together in form of a cartel that resulted in the largest market shares on the insurance market. However, with a wave of new foundations, e.g. the "British Fire" (1799), "Imperial" (1803), the "Globe" (1803), and with the growth of the existing fire offices the market share of these three companies reduced from 40.5 percent (1816-1820) to 31.3 percent (1826-1830). Also the market share of the mutual company "Hand-in-Hand" declined. Additionally, between 1824 and 1831, 17 companies ceased fire underwriting.[94]

The second wave of foundations was after 1834 during which 18 new offices were founded. During this time, the insurance market became more and more concentrated due to mergers, bankruptcies, and withdrawals. The three largest companies, the "Sun Fire Office", "Phoenix Fire Office", and the "Royal Exchange Assurance" were able to increase their total market share to 38.1 percent during the years 1836 and 1840. As a result, the cooperation between companies intensified and periodic price-setting meetings after 1840 became regular, which eventually led to a permanent tariff agreement between fire offices and the foundation of the Fire Offices Committee (FOC) in 1868.[95] Table 6 presents the development of the market shares and insured sums of the largest insurance companies between 1816 and 1850.

[93] Cf. *Pearson, R.* (2004), Insuring the Industrial Revolution, p. 180.

[94] Cf. *Cockerell, H.A.L.*; *Green, E.* (1976), The British insurance business 1547-1970, p. 21; *Pearson, R.* (2004), Insuring the Industrial Revolution, p. 182f.; *Pearson, R.* (2002), Growth, crisis and change in the insurance industry: a retrospect. Accounting, Business and Financial History, 12(3), November 2002, p. 494.

[95] Cf. *Pearson, R.* (2002), Growth, crisis and change in the insurance industry, p. 494.

Table 6: Market share and sums insured of the most prominent insurance offices between 1816 and 1850

Company	Market shares				Sums insured (in million Pounds)						
	1816-20	1826-30	1836-40	1846-50	1822	1825	1830	1835	1840	1845	1850
Sun	19.7	15.9	16.9	15.7	76.1	72.5	80.4	89.9	114.8	132.0	128.9
Phoenix	12.2	8.8	13.8	10.5	43.9	41.0	45.9	51.7	93.6	89.9	85.1
REA	8.6	6.6	7.4	6.5	34.3	31.1	34.6	41.8	51.4	54.2	54.7
Norwich	7.6	8.6	7.3	7.1	42.1	42.7	41.6	49.3	54.9	57.0	58.6
Imperial	6.2	3.9	3.2	3.8	22.1	20.6	18.1	18.5	21.1	32.3	30.9
County	5.1	6.1	5.0	5.0	26.0	28.0	29.4	33.4	36.8	40.3	41.9
Globe	5.0	3.5	3.5	2.8	18.4	16.8	17.6	19.5	22.6	23.6	22.9
British	2.8	2.2	2.0	-	9.0	9.9	10.5	11.9	12.98	-	-
Atlas	2.2	2.8	2.7	2.8	10.1	12.2	13.8	15.3	18.0	21.9	24.3
Protector	-	6.0	1.5	-	-	9.9	37.4	37.8	-	-	-
Guardian	-	4.1	3.7	2.6	9.6	18.2	20.7	22.3	22.8	21.4	21.8
Alliance		2.6	2.8	3.1	-	10.0	13.5	15.5	18.0	19.3	32.1
West of England	?	3.2	3.5	3.7	10.3	13.5	16.8	19.2	23.4	28.6	32.0
Manchester	-	2.2	2.2	1.5	-	9.9	11.2	12.6	14.3	12.3	13.2
Scottish Union	-	2.3	2.2	1.8	-	?	?	13.7	14.6	12.7	15.5

Source: *Pearson, R.* (2004). Insuring the Industrial Revolution, p. 182f

The table demonstrates that the British insurance market was dominated by joint stock companies. The only sizeable mutual company, “Norwich Union”, with a market share of 7.6 percent, was merged with “Norwich General Assurance Company” and eventually converted to a joint stock company in 1821. However, its market share did not increase after its merger, only the insured sums slightly increased. In contrast, the “Phoenix Fire Office’s” insured sum almost doubled while its market share decreased by 1850. When comparing the largest insurance companies in London between 1831 and 1850 (table 6), two mutual companies, the “Westminster Fire Office” and the “Hand-in-Hand”, can be found. The “Westminster Fire Office” was able to increase its rank from the 6th to the 5th between 1831 and 1840 and to maintain it in 1850. Moreover, the company increased its market share from 5.5 percent in 1831 to 6.7 percent and its insured capital from 10.1 to 14.9 million Pounds in 1850. The “Hand-in-Hand”, on the other hand, slightly declined regarding market share, from 4.2 in 1831 to 3.6 in 1840. Its insured capital also decreased from 7.7 to 7.3 million Pounds. As a result, it had lost its place of the top 10 insurance company by 1850 and the joint stock company “London Assurance Corporation” took its place. Table 7 demonstrates that in all three periods, the market share of the top 5 companies was above 50 percent, respectively above 60 percent in 1840. However, the “Sun Fire Office” and the “Protector”, later the “Phoenix Fire Office”, were the two dominant companies on the London market.

Table 7: The 10 largest insurance companies in London between 1831 and 1850

	1831			1840			1850		
Rank	Company	Million Pounds	Market share	Company	Million Pounds	Market share	Company	Million Pounds	Market share
1.	Sun	42.8	23.5	Sun	48.4	24.1	Sun	51.0	23.1
2.	Protector	22.4	12.3	Phoenix	33.3	16.5	Phoenix	27.1	12.2
3.	Phoenix	16.6	9.1	REA	18.1	9.0	REA	19.9	9.0
4.	Imperial	13.1	7.2	Imperial	13.0	6.5	Imperial	15.9	7.2
5.	REA	12.1	6.6	Westminster	12.5	6.2	Westminster	14.9	6.7
6.	Westminster	10.1	5.5	Globe	10.9	5.4	Union	10.2	4.6
7.	Globe	9.7	5.3	Alliance	10.5	5.2	Guardian	10.0	4.5
8.	Guardian	9.3	5.1	Guardian	9.5	4.7	Globe	9.8	4.4
9.	Alliance	9.2	5.0	Union	9.1	4.5	Alliance	9.7	4.4
10.	Hand-in-Hand	7.7	4.2	Hand-in-Hand	7.3	3.6	London Assurance Company	9.6	4.4
Total million Pounds		**182.3**		Total million Pounds	**201.3**		Total million Pounds	**221.3**	
Market share top 5 companies			**58.7**	Market share top 5 companies		**62.3**	Market share top 5 companies		**58.2**
Number of offices		**15**		Number of offices	**21**		Number of offices	**26**	

Source: *Pearson, R.* (2004). Insuring the Industrial Revolution, p. 187.

In general, the number of offices in London increased but the average sum insured fell. On the other hand, the market outside London was able to expand faster than the number of offices. Like the London market, the ranking among the insurance companies maintained stable. Table 8 presents the 10 largest insurance companies in the provinces and shows that the "Sun Fire Office" and the "Phoenix Fire Office" became the leading offices between 1831 and 1850 with 69.9 million Pounds insured respectively 53.2. Their market shares, however, were up to a maximum of 15 percent, which is lower compared to their market share in London. Nevertheless, it is evident that both companies were the leading players of the insurance market in London as well as in the provinces. In contrast to London, no mutual companies could be found among the ten largest offices.[96]

[96] Cf. *Pearson, R.* (2004), Insuring the Industrial Revolution, p. 186; 191.

Table 8: The 10 largest provincial insurance companies between 1831 and 1850

	1831			1840			1850		
Rank	Company	Million Pounds	Market share	Company	Million Pounds	Market share	Company	Million Pounds	Market share
1.	Norwich Union	45.6	14.3	Sun	59.6	15.0	Sun	69.8	14.5
2.	Sun	39.9	12.5	Phoenix	55.6	14.0	Phoenix	53.2	11.1
3.	Phoenix	29.7	9.3	Norwich Union	45.1	11.4	Norwich Union	48.9	10.2
4.	County	26.7	8.3	REA	28.6	7.2	West of England	30.9	6.4
5.	REA	24.3	7.6	County	24.7	6.2	REA	30.3	6.3
6.	Protector	17.4	5.5	West of England	22.5	5.7	County	28.3	5.9
7.	West of England	17.1	5.4	MFLAC	13.9	3.5	Alliance	20.0	4.2
8.	Guardian	11.9	3.7	Guardian	12.7	3.2	Atlas	15.5	3.2
9.	MFLAC	11.6	3.6	Atlas	10.7	2.7	Imperial	14.3	3.0
10.	Atlas	8.3	2.6	Globe	10.7	2.7	MFLAC	12.8	2.7
Total million Pounds		**319.3**		Total million Pounds	**396.6**		Total million Pounds	**480.6**	
Market share top 5 companies			**52.0**	Market share top 5 companies		**53.8**	Market share top 5 companies		**48.5**
Number of offices		**39**		Number of offices	**43**		Number of offices	**46**	

Source: *Pearson, R.* (2004). Insuring the Industrial Revolution, p. 188.

2.2.3 The merger and acquisition phase

During the second wave of foundation and the increasing competition of insurance companies, several London and Scottish companies employed a merger and acquisition strategy, a tactic that affected the British insurance industry sustainable. Between 1782 and 1850, 50 fire insurance companies were either merged or acquired; however, 40 of them took place after the first foundation wave in 1825. Between 1825 and 1831, 14 companies with 9 percent of the UK market were merged. From 1835 to 1850, 26 offices holding a combined market share of approximately 15 percent at that time were purchased. It is interesting that most of these acquisitions were made by the largest companies. For example, the “Phoenix Fire Office” purchased 8 offices with insurance sums of 51 million Pounds, the “Protector” 6 offices with 35 million Pounds insurance sum, and the “Sun Fire Office” acquired 14 offices with a total of 32 million Pounds insurance sum. Additionally, 7 other companies bought fire offices, while at least 6 takeovers were unsuccessful. These acquisitions were the reason for the termination of underwriting insurances of more than three-quarters of the companies during the second quarter of the 19th century.[97] The largest merger during the second wave of mergers took place in 1836 when the “Phoenix Fire Office” took over the “Protector”, the fourth largest fire

97 Cf. *Pearson, R.* (2004), Insuring the Industrial Revolution, p. 202.

office in the country. With this, the "Phoenix Fire Office" was able to increase its market share from 10 to 14 percent. The dominance of the joint stock companies in the fire insurance business is even more obvious when looking at the British insurance market in general. Between 1835 and 1848 the "Sun Fire Office", the "Phoenix Fire Office", the "Alliance Assurance", and the "Imperial" purchased together 21 companies that comprised 15 percent of the market.[98] Table 9 demonstrates the numerous mergers by the largest insurance companies by the mid-19th century.

Table 9: The mergers of the insurance companies between 1825 and 1849

Purchasing Company	Year of merger	Company absorbed/Foundation date
Protector	1825	British Commercial (1820)
	1827	Hope (1807)
	1827	Beacon (1821)
	1828	Eagle (1807)
	1828	Albion (1805)
	1831	Berkshire, Gloucestershire (1824)
Guardian	1826	Sussex County (1824)
	1829	Commercial (Dublin) (1799)
Phoenix	1827	Royal Irish (1823)
	1828	East Kent (1824)
	1830	Palladium (1824)
	1830	Hertford, Cambridge (1824)
	1837	Protector (1825)
	1839	Metellus (1823)
	1841	Reading (1823)
	1844	English & Scottish Law (1840)
Sun	1827	Old Bath (1767)
	1829	Finchingfield (1804)
	1835	Salamander (1790)
	1836	North & South Shields (1826)
	1837	Bristol Crown (1718)
	1838	Bath Sun (1776)
	1839	Coventry & Warwickshire (1836)
	1839	Hibernian (1824)
	1841	Glasgow (1803)
	1843	Leicestershire (1834)
	1843	British (1799)
	1847	Friendly Society of Edinburgh (1720)
	1847	Winchester & South of England (1841)
	1848	Preston & North Lancashire (1845)

98 Cf. *Pearson, R.* (2004), Insuring the Industrial Revolution, p.202.

Leeds & Yorkshire	1838	Newcastle & North of England (1835)
Imperial	1840	Bristol (1769)
	1842	York & London (1834)
	1844	Bristol Union (1818)
Scottish National	1844	County & City (Perth) (1824)
Alliance	1847	Insurance Co. of Scotland (1821)
	1850	Suffolk Amicable (1802)
Northern	1844	Western (1844)
	1845	Bon Accord (1845)
Scottish Union	1849	Hercules (1809)

Source: Adapted from *Pearson, R.* (2004). Insuring the Industrial Revolution, p. 200f.

Table 9 shows that with the exception of one company, the "Friendly Society of Edinburgh" established in 1720, all acquired offices were joint stock companies, many of which had only existed for a very short time.

2.2.4 The tariff system

Apart from mergers and acquisitions, the companies started to respond to the new foundation wave by talking about the premium rates. The "Phoenix Fire Office", the "Sun Fire Office", and the "Royal Exchange Assurance" formed a cartel that led to regular price-setting meetings, and, as a result, to a reduction of the rates on ordinary residential property in 1825 as well as to an increase of the mercantile rates in 1826. However, not all companies fulfilled their agreements; for example, the "Sun Fire Office" reduced rates on London dock warehouses and expanded its rate reduction even to non-residential property in London. By the end of the 1820s, the competition became fiercer and the London offices felt even more threatened by the numerous foundations. Eventually, the price reduction failed its purpose, because it damaged the business relations between the companies and increased uncontrolled premium changes. The latter led to a raise of premium rates for particular risk types without a common agreement between the offices. Other companies tried to economise their business by abandoning non-profitable insurance sectors such as woollen or cotton mills that endangered the incomes of insurance agencies in industrial towns.[99] It is important to note that since the end of the 18th century, fire insurance was classified into three risk categories, common, hazardous, and doubly hazardous risks and some companies such as the "Sun Fire Office" had additionally special ratings for mills, stock,

[99] Cf. *Pearson, R.* (2004), Insuring the Industrial Revolution, p. 197f.

and buildings with stoves or oven used for manufacturing processes. These sectors became now non-profitable.[100]

Like the offices in London, the Scottish offices started to have similar meetings regarding a common tariff of premiums under the patronage of the "Association of Managers of Fire Insurance Offices" in 1829. The Edinburgh companies agreed on minimum rates for cotton, mills, flax mills, and distilleries with the main offices in London by the end of 1829, followed by an agreement among the Scottish offices, e.g. Manchester, Leeds, in 1830 on wooden mills. In England in contrast to Scotland, no organization managing the tariffs existed, therefore, agreements between the London and the provincial offices were at best temporarily successful.[101] Nevertheless, a cotton mill tariff was established in 1842. Its three classification classes and the requirement of certain standards signified an advanced stage of fire insurances. It comprised a careful surveying of fire risks and evaluated the sources and spreading of fires. The establishment of the cotton mill tariff had a model function. However, not all companies adhered to the tariff agreements, some of them offered a rate below the strict interpretation of the tariff, while others had never agreed to them. For example, the "Cotton Spinners' Mutual Fire Insurance Association" in Manchester charged the same contribution from their members as the tariff companies but reduced those when fire-extinguishing appliances were installed.[102]

From 1853 onwards, the co-operating offices were known as the "Tariff Offices" and the series of meetings since 1842 resulted in the creation of a formal tariff organization, the "Fire Offices Committee", in 1868. Originally, the committee comprised 19 London companies, 17 country companies as well as 9 Scottish, 3 Irish, and 2 foreign companies. Their tariff agreements altered permanently the fire business since the mid-19th century and the FOC dominated the insurance business until the 1970s when the tariff control declined.[103]

2.2.5 Amalgamation of offices at the end of the 19th century

At the end of the 19th century, 30 fire offices, with head offices in England and Scotland, that had a yearly premium income of more than 100,000 Pounds existed. Half of these offices merged or became associated with other offices during the first quarter of the 20th century. The

[100] Cf. *Raynes, H. E.* (1948), A history of British insurance, p. 332.

[101] Cf. *Cockerell, H.A.L.; Green, E.* (1976), The British insurance business 1547-1970, p. 22.

[102] Cf. *Raynes, H. E.* (1948), A history of British insurance, p. 340f.

[103] Cf. *Cockerell, H.A.L.; Green, E.* (1976), The British insurance business 1547-1970, p. 23; *Pearson, R.* (2004), Insuring the Industrial Revolution, p. 215f.

following table presents the 15 fire offices that were merged or allied with 7 other offices.

Table 10: Amalgamation of fire offices between 1900 and 1925

Absorbed by or allied with	Office	Fire insurance premium income in 1898 (in Pounds)	Year
Alliance	Imperial	612,545	1902
	County Fire	283,545	1906
	Westminster Fire	105,663	1906
	Law Fire	151,816	1907
London & Lancs.	Equitable Fire & Accident	214,459	1901
	Law Union & Crown	137,909	1919
Commercial Union	Palatine	663,465	1900
	Hand-in-Hand	109,150	1905
	Scottish Alliance (at first to Union in 1903)	155,463	1907
	Union	456,808	1907
Royal	Lancashire	705,788	1901
	Liverpool & London & Globe	1,500,793	1919
Atlas (fire business)	Manchester	831,218	1904
Norwich Union Life	Norwich Union Fire	941,011	1925
Yorkshire	Lion	190,333	1902

Source: Based on *Raynes, H. E.* (1948). A history of British insurance, p. 377.

One of the merged offices was the mutual company "Hand-in-Hand" that had been founded in 1696 and was finally absorbed by the "Commercial Union" ceasing to exist in 1905. Its developments was marked by some growth mixed with a lot of stagnation during the 19th century. Its life assurance business (1836) was successful, but its fire insurance segment declined. The latter is evident when looking at its premiums in 1898. The table shows that the "Hand-in-Hand" had with 109,150 Pounds the second lowest premium income in 1898, only the "Westminster Fire Office's" income was with 105,663 Pounds even lower. However, it is important to keep in mind that the fire offices in table 10 had a yearly premium income of more than 100,000 Pounds, a fact that made them rather larger in comparison to many other existing companies. The economic success of the "Westminster Fire Office" was also mixed during the 19th century. It had heavy losses but also some

increases during the last quarter of the 19th century, mostly due to administrative reforms and the foundation of provincial offices.[104] On the other hand, the highest premium income had the "Liverpool & London & Globe" with 1,500,793 Pounds, more than 10 times higher than the "Hand-in-Hand". Finally, after these mergers only the following 15 fire offices remained. These were the "Alliance", "Atlas", "Caledonian", "Commercial Union", "Guardian", "London & Lancashire", "London Assurance", "North British, Northern", "Phoenix Fire Office", "Royal", "Royal Exchange", "Scottish Union and National", "Sun Fire Office", "Yorkshire", all of which being stock companies, and the "Norwich Fire", classifying as a mutual as by then being a wholly owned subsidiary of the mutual life insurer. With these mergers, the structure of the British insurance market changed and a small group of extremely powerful composite companies emerged from the previous existing local, marine (local and national), fire, life, and accident companies that were the norm until the end of the 19th century.[105]

2.2.6 Accident insurances

With the change of the markets and the industrial developments, the new insurance segment "accident insurance" evolved in 1844 due to the enactment of the Joint Stock Companies Act. As mentioned above, accident insurance became an important part of the marine insurance business by making sure the safety of the crew and the passengers. The term "accident insurance" comprises all types of commercial insurances other than marine, fire, or life insurance business. The main types of this new insurance covered the accidental loss of or damage to property, accidental injury, or sickness as well as liability due to accidents. However, the various types were overlapping and the term was rather vague. Additionally, insurances such as fidelity guarantee, steam boiler, and plate-glass insurances were not included in this new branch initially.[106]

The development of accident insurance in its original meaning as a "protection against personal accidents" was a product of the rise of the railways. Originally, personal insurances were the sole field of friendly societies, now, however, many companies that wrote personal accidents were formed under the Companies Act. Between 1845 and 1850, 13 companies were registered against railway accidents, but only two were finally founded and carried on business, namely the "Railway Passengers Assurance Company" (1849) and the "Railway Assurance

[104] Cf. *Pearson, R.* (2002), Mutuality tested, p. 22.

[105] Cf. *Raynes, H. E.* (1948), A history of British insurance, p. 377; *Clayton, G.* (1971), British insurance, p. 135f.

[106] Cf. *Raynes, H. E.* (1948), A history of British insurance, p. 283.

Company" (1850). Two years later, the business of the latter was transferred to the "Accidental Death Company" (1850), which covered all types of accidental deaths. In 1867, it was merged with the "Accident Insurance Company" and reorganized. Finally, in 1906 the company was merged with the "Commercial Union" at a time when composite insurers started their accident insurance segment by acquiring such companies. Personal accident insurance was based either on a fix sum in the event of accidental death or the loss of a limp or an eye, or on a weekly rate covering a compensation for partial disablement. The latter was extended to all kinds of sicknesses by the established "Sickness and Accidental Assurance Association" (later the "Century Insurance Company") in 1885. The company's policyholders were middle class people from the professional class who wanted to be insured against temporary as well as permanent sickness. In case of the first event, allowances were paid for the first six months, while in the other case payments were made for the entire duration of the illness.[107] One of the few companies that was founded as a friendly society (in 1884) and later converted into a mutual company (1920) was the "Medical Sickness Annuity and Assurance Society", established by medical practitioners, offering sickness insurance, pensions, and life insurances for their members.[108] In 1850, 6 different types of accident insurances existed in Britain and Europe and by World War I approximately 50 types were available in Britain and the USA. Most of these new accident insurance types, such as contract employers' liability, public liability, steam boiler, elevator, or sprinkler insurances were offered at first by *Lloyd's* and by non-tariff offices. The existing fire insurers did not follow this new trend at first and fell behind. They established their own small accident departments and later took over existing offices to create giant composite insurance companies.[109]

Mutual companies, however, became rather strong in the new segment of plate-glass insurance, which also belonged to accident insurances. In 1852, after the taxes for glass decreased, the "Plate Glass Insurance Company of London" was established and kept its independence until 1910 when it was merged with the "Commercial Union". Initially it insured solely plate glass but extended its business scope to all types of glass, a business strategy that made this company very successful. Its competitor became the "National Provincial Plate Glass Insurance Company" (1854) and after several name changes, it was incorporated into the "Royal Exchange group" in 1909. Mutual glass insurers started to form in provincial towns, because plate glass in-

[107] Cf. *Cockerell, H.A.L.*; *Green, E.* (1976), The British insurance business 1547-1970, p. 48f; *Clayton, G.* (1971), British insurance, p. 116.

[108] Cf. *Bridgewater, A.* (1995), The modern mutual insurance company in Britain, p. 32.

[109] Cf. *Pearson, R.* (2002), Growth, crisis and change in the insurance industry, p. 492f.

surance was usually closely connected with shop fronts and therefore this type of insurance needed in particular local promotions and local control. The first was the "Huddersfield Mutual Plate Glass Insurance Company" of 1854. Others followed and most of them were small companies of a semi-mutual type: "Halifax" (1871), "Bath and West of England" (1872), "Bradford" (1874), "Torquay" (1885), "Ipswich Mutual" (1886), "Nottingham" (1886) and "Isle of Wight" (1889).

In 1890, 40 companies existed that transacted plate-glass business, including composite insurers. The following 23 companies conducted purely plate-glass insurance:

Table 11: Larger Plate Glass insurance companies mentioned in the insurance register (1890)

Company	Foundation Year
Plate Glass Insurance Company of London	1852
National Provincial Plate Glass Insurance Company	1854
Norwich and London (also accident insurance)	1856
London and General	1861
Guardian	1863
Liverpool	1866
Scottish Plate Glass	1870
The Bath and West and England	1871
Caledonian	1871
London and County	1873
Bradford Plate Glass Mutual	1874
Lancashire Plate Glass	1876
Ulster Plate Glass	1878
British and Irish	1880
Commercial	1880
Standard (of Scotland)	1880
West of Scotland	1880
Hull and Eastern Counties Mutual	1881
Mutual	1884
Blackburn Plate Glass	1886
Northern	1888
Provident	1886
York and District	1888

Source: The insurance register. Containing, with other information, a record of the yearly progress and the present financial position of British insurance Associations (1890), p. 70; 9ff.

Among these companies, four were mutual companies and among them the "Bradford Plate Glass Mutual" (1874) and the later founded "Derby Mutual" (1890) were larger companies.[110] The plate-glass business was a successful insurance segment and so 55 new companies were established between 1900 and 1909.[111]

2.3 Life assurances

The life assurance business started to grow during the 19th century. From the 1820s onwards, the life assurance sector became highly competitive. The premiums, however, were still calculated by mortality tables from the 18th century and were rather inaccurate. Additionally, many new companies were highly speculative, often without sufficient capital basis, or even fraudulent. In 1853, the "Selected Committee" inquired such complications and discovered various problems.[112]

While in 1800, only 9 life assurance companies, 2 mutuals and 7 joint stock companies existed, 463 companies, excluding friendly societies and annuity societies, operated during the 19th century. Life assurances were dominated by middle class policyholders, a social class that started to think about their family's security and economic stability. The development of life assurance companies is, therefore, regarded as a typical Victorian middle-class institution, although by 1850 the largest companies had also policyholders from other social classes.[113]

The three large life insurers, the mutual "Norwich Union Life Insurance Society", the "Manchester Fire& Life Assurance Company" (M.F.L.A.C.), and the "Law Life Assurance Society" (L.L.A.S.) had policyholders from various social classes, including people from the gentry, farmers, craftsmen, or servants.

---

110 The insurance register. Containing, with other information, a record of the yearly progress and the present financial position of British insurance Associations. (1899), p. 12ff.

111 Cf. *Cockerell, H.A.L.*; *Green, E.* (1976), The British insurance business 1547-1970, p. 50; *Raynes, H. E.* (1948), A history of British insurance, p. 292f.

112 Cf. *Pearson, R.* (1990), Thrift or dissipation?, p. 237; *O'Brien, C; Fenn, P.* (2012), Mutual life insurers, p. 325.

113 Cf. *Pearson, R.* (1990), Thrift or dissipation?, p. 237.

Table 12: Occupational structure of life policyholders (in percent)

Policyholders	Norwich Union Life Insurance Society (1808-17)	Manchester Fire& Life Assurance Company (M.F.L.A.C.) (1846)	Law Life Assurance Society (L.L.A.S.) (1824-42)
Gentlemen, Esq., nobility	14.24	16.25	29.90
Merchants, manufactures	20.18	28.75	7.27
Brewers, maltsters, millers	1.24	1.10	0.80
Professions	24.62	21.90	30.42
Farmers	5.43	6.06	3.19
Agents, factors	2.07	2.71	0.60
Govt. officials (includes military)	4.27	1.65	6.75
Victuallers, retailers, bookkeepers	5.97	5.17	2.22
Craftsmen	4.81	1.98	2.45
Labourers, servants	0.31	0.50	0.11
Minors	1.38	0.81	0.13
Others*			
Total sum assured	£2,578,078	£605,618	£870,731
Total policies	4,019	950**	845

* Includes wives, spinsters comprising 7.65 percent of M.F.L.A.C., and 12.19 percent of L.L.A.S. sums assured

** Excludes 59 joint-lives and survivor-ships to make a comparison with Norwich Union Life Insurance Society possible.

Source: *Pearson, R.* (1990). Thrift or dissipation?, p. 248.

Table 12 demonstrates that most policyholders of the mutual "Norwich Union Life Insurance Society" were from the social class of professions (20.18 percent) followed by merchants and manufacturers (20.18 percent). The latter was the largest group of policyholders for the "M.F.L.A.C." (28.75 percent), while the professions (21.90 percent) were on the second place. On the other hand, the "L.L.A.S." had with 29.90 percent the highest share in the social group of gentlemen (nobility), while both other companies had 14.24 respectively 16.25 percent policyholders in this social class. This does not surprise, because the "Norwich Union Life Insurance Society" and the "M.F.L.A.C." were provincial insurers, while "L.L.A.S." was a London company.

The life assurance market was highly divided, not only socially but also economically. While in London most policyholders were wealthy, the provincial policyholders had less financial capacities. The provinces were also divided geographically that comprised regions with different assurance requirements. Nevertheless, in 1846, two-thirds of all companies offering life assurances in Britain had their head office in London, because it was the most lucrative market.[114]

[114] Cf. *Pearson, R.* (1990), Thrift or dissipation?, p. 246.

Table 13: Development of mutual life assurance companies and joint stock companies during the 19th century

Year		Mutuals	Joint stock companies
1800-1804	New	0	1
	Discontinued	0	0
	at the end of period	2	8
1805-1809	New	2	8
	Discontinued	0	0
	at the end of period	4	16
18010-1814	New	0	3
	Discontinued	0	0
	at the end of period	4	19
1815-1819	New	1	2
	Discontinued	0	0
	at the end of period	5	21
1820-1824	New	0	24
	Discontinued	0	1
	at the end of period	5	44
1825-1829	New	1	7
	Discontinued	0	7
	at the end of period	6	44
1830-1834	New	3	7
	Discontinued	0	0
	at the end of period	10*	50*
1835-1839	New	7	24
	Discontinued	0	3
	at the end of period	17	71
1840-1844	New	7	24
	Discontinued	1	11
	at the end of period	24*	83*
1845-1849	New	11	44
	Discontinued	1	16
	at the end of period	35*	110*
1850-1854	New	6	74
	Discontinued	3	33

	at the end of period	38	151
1855-1859	New	2	28
	Discontinued	11	70
	at the end of period	29	109
1860-1864	New	6	29
	Discontinued	3	36
	at the end of period	32	102
1865-1869	New	2	25
	Discontinued	8	39
	at the end of period	26	88
1870-1874	New	1	8
	Discontinued	1	7
	at the end of period	26	89
1875-1879	New	0	3
	Discontinued	0	10
	at the end of period	26	82
1880-1884	New	1	2
	Discontinued	2	8
	at the end of period	25	76
1885-1889	New	1	3
	Discontinued	1	8
	at the end of period	25	71
1890-1894	New	0	3
	Discontinued	1	11
	at the end of period	24	63
1895-1899	New	0	8
	Discontinued	1	2
	at the end of period	23	69
Total at the end of the period		92	

* Denotes a firm converting from joint stock company to mutual status.
Source: *O'Brien, C; Fenn, P.* (2012). Mutual life insurers, p. 327.

Table 13 and figure 1 show the development of the life assurance industry distinguished between mutual and joint stock companies during the 19th century.

Figure 1: Development of mutual life assurance companies and joint stock companies during the 19th century

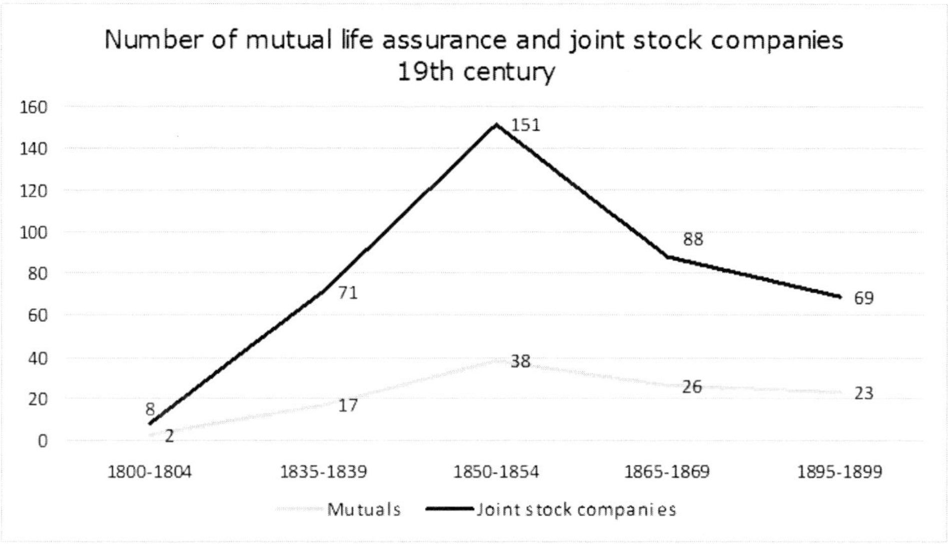

Source: *O'Brien, C; Fenn, P.* (2012). Mutual life insurers, p. 327.

Table 13 and figure 1 demonstrate that both mutual and joint stock companies increased regarding their numbers. Both organizational forms rose from a low number, 2 mutuals and 8 joint stock companies, to 17 respectively 71 by 1839 and had a peak after the introduction of the Joint Stock Companies Act in 1844 (151 joint stock companies and 38 mutuals). In the following period, 170 out of 219 between 1843 and 1870 established companies disappeared and the fraudulent activities of many companies led to the first major parliamentary regulation in the United Kingdom regarding the insurance industry, the Act of 1870. In 1870, the Life Assurance Companies Act was enacted and stated for the first time a minimum capital requirement for life insurers. From this time on, life insurance companies had to deposit 20,000 Pounds before they were allowed to be registered. Moreover, they were required to prepare actuarial reports and deposit them with the Board of Trade.

As a result, the numbers of both organizational forms decreased, i.e. less new companies were established, because new companies had to meet the capital requirements[115]

It is interesting that although many life assurance companies did not existed for a long time during the 19th century, most mutual companies lasted with a medium time of 26 years. As mentioned above, the failure of many companies was based on their fraudulent business, e.g. the "Independent and West Middlesex stock company" failed in 1838 due to non-existing capital. Others ceased to exist due to mergers, for example the two mutual companies "Albert" and "European company" acquired 33 respectively 38 companies, but failed both in 1869 respectively 1872.[116] The nevertheless longer survival of mutuals had several reasons. Firstly, their cost efficiency was lower or compared to stock companies better. For example, they were able to reduce costs by having directors who worked without fees. Secondly, in terms of total net premiums, mutuals were larger and usually older than stock companies. According to *O'Brien and Fenn*, the effect of the company's age on costs was highly significant and negative, however, the negative effects weakened with age.[117] Additionally, three joint stock companies converted to mutuals during the 19th century, the "Scottish Amicable" (1826) in 1832, the "Economic Assurance" in 1839, and the "National Life" in 1847. The reasons were divers and included mostly financial reasons, however, the "National Life" stated that the public opinion changed in favour of the Mutual Assurance Principle, which led finally to their decision to convert into a mutual company.[118]

In addition to the regular life assurance a new type emerged during the 1850s, the industrial life assurance. This insurance type was in particular to satisfy the needs of the working class who had small weekly incomes and wanted to have the necessary savings for funerals rather than to provide for family members after death. In 1848, the "Prudential Mutual Insurance Investment and Loan Association" was founded and became the dominant insurer for this type of insurances.[119] Between 1830 and 1850, it became common to take out loans on existing life assurance policies and the newly founded "Prudential Mutual Insurance Investment and Loan Association" advertised this type of loans to clergymen for repairs of their parsonages, to young men to pay their lawyer's entrance fees, or to tradesmen to raise capital. British life assurance companies also started to invest in property, for example in 1864, the "British Empire Mutual Life" bought land in Camberwell

---

[115] Cf. *O'Brien, C; Fenn, P.* (2012), Mutual life insurers, p. 326.; *Pearson, R.* (2012) United Kingdom: Pioneering insurance internationally, p. 81.

[116] Cf. *O'Brien, C; Fenn, P.* (2012), Mutual life insurers, p. 338ff.

[117] Cf. Ibid., p. 342.

[118] Cf. Ibid., p. 330.

[119] Cf. *Pearson, R.* (2012) United Kingdom: Pioneering insurance internationally, p. 82.

and built a partnership with the "Perpetual Investment and Building Society housing estates". Additionally, companies invested in overseas, e.g. in railways or in stocks and shares, and expanded so their business scope immensely.[120]

Friendly societies are insofar important for the formation of mutual life assurance companies, because they encouraged mutuals to take an interest in this type of insurance sector. Friendly societies received a legal basis and protection in 1793. Their aim was to provide support for their members or their dependents in sickness or in the event of death. They were based on contributions and offered benefits both governed by rules: However, many of these societies were incapable to be successful due to the lack of financial and actuarial knowledge, for example by distributing future funds immediately into benefits. Therefore, many contributions were insufficient to provide the promised benefits for their members. Under the Friendly Society Act (1834), it was possible to establish mutual life assurance companies, some of them such as the "Clergy Mutual, the Friend's Provident", the "National Provident" and the "Provident Clerks" (or "Provident Life") have existed more than a century.[121] According to *Walford*, in 1844 80 life assurance companies existed, however, this number includes also friendly societies. In 1846, he stated that of 52 insurance companies, 24 operated life insurances.[122] However, in 1850 no registered friendly society was able to insure more than 100 Pounds on a life or 30 Pounds on an annuity, a level at which most of the insurance companies started their business. According to *Pearson*, 30,000 friendly societies and 500 saving banks a well as 200 insurance companies can be found in mid-19th century. All these different institutions had different social parameters similar to the different social classes during this period.[123] Therefore, it is crucial to look briefly at the development of friendly societies in Britain.

3. Friendly Societies

Mutual benefit societies grew fast at the end of the 18th century and by 1801, approximately 7,200 friendly societies existed in England

[120] Cf. *Cockerell, H.A.L.*; *Green, E.* (1976), The British insurance business 1547-1970, p. 70f.

[121] Cf. *Raynes, H. E.* (1948), A history of British insurance, p. 260f.

[122] Cf. *Walford, C.* (1886), History of Life Assurance in the United Kingdom (conclusion), JIA 26 (1886-1887), p. 439f.

[123] Cf. *Pearson, R.* (1990), Thrift or dissipation?, p. 253.

and Wales with a combined membership of 648,000. Only two years later, the total number of friendly societies had increased to 9,672 with 704,350 members. Many of the societies were established between 1780 and 1815, and by 1815, they counted around 925,429 members in Britain and Wales. During the 1830s, the industry grew rapidly and with it the working class. The Poor Law Amendment Act of 1834 generated the fear of most working people ending up in workhouses. As a result, many people looked for help by joining friendly societies. However, by 1850 many of these societies ceased to exist due to the unemployment of their members or by emerging of other organisations such as saving banks, Mechanics' Institutes and Methodism. This trend changed when during the 1850s many friendly societies grew fast until World War I.[124]

The institution of friendly societies of the 19th century was the largest social movement and provided social security for millions of people from the working class. This type of organisation offered social welfare in the event of unemployment due to illness, accident but also money for funerals etc..[125] Friendly societies were usually founded and controlled by a group of trustees or honorary members from the middle or upper class, while members were usually from the working class, comprising in particular artisans. They offered sickness and death benefits, arranged medical aid for their members, and some of them even offered pensions. However, unemployment payments were rather rare. The financial benefits varied between the numerous societies but usually the sickness benefit was a significant proportion of the wage of a worker, while death or funeral benefits ranged between 10 and 12 Pounds for a member and 6 to 10 Pounds to a member's wife. Additionally, friendly societies established educational institutes offering lectures and libraries.[126]

The philosophy of which friendly societies was based on can be found in the Christian value of neighbourliness emphasising cooperation and mutual aid. Additionally, these societies became part of local credit networks based on the word of the borrower and the trust of the lender in small communities, usually parishes. However, the social pressure to fulfil one's obligation was high. Over time, the communities altered due to economic and social changes and people migrated to larger villages and into towns but also new people came to these small communities. The latter changed the perception of neighbourliness and friendly soci-

---

[124] Cf. *Neave, D.* (1996), Friendly Societies in Great Britain, in: *Linden, M. van der* (ed.) (1996), Social security mutualism. The comparative history of mutual benefit societies, p. 46ff.

[125] Cf. *Ismay, P.* (2018), Trust among strangers. Friendly Societies in Modern Britain, p. 2.

[126] Cf. *Neave, D.* (1996), Friendly Societies in Great Britain, pp. 53-56.

eties as a new form of trust between people developed.[127] Friendly societies were a combination of mutual aid and fraternalism and existed in towns as well as in provinces. With the emergence of insurance companies friendly societies were able to exist because they offered different types of social security by defining individual interests in the broadest way. Moreover, they encouraged people to believe that their interests are best protected within a small community and at the same time they contribute to the stability of this community.[128] It is important to note that the emergence of friendly societies was not connected with the demise of the charity brief[129], which was a preform of insurance, in particular for fire insurances, after the Great Fire of London (1666). As mentioned before, the Friendly Society (1684) established by *William Hale* and *Henry Spelman* capitalised on the concept of friendly societies. Nevertheless, fire insurances based on premiums were important to manage the collective risks after the Great Fire in London but did not have the impact of friendly societies when reinforcing the moral order and distributing all types of collective risks.[130] In 1793, the "Act for the Encouragement and Relief of Friendly Societies" was passed. It defined a Friendly Society as "a society of good fellowship for the purpose of raising from time to time, by voluntary contributions, a stock or fund for the mutual relief and maintenance of all and every member thereof, in old age, sickness, and infirmity, or for the relief of the widows and children of deceased members".[131] The Act stated that members of friendly societies were free from the laws of settlement that assigned poor people to a particular parish. The reason was that members of a friendly society had already proven to be able of hard work and they

---

[127] Cf. *Ismay, P.* (2018), Trust among strangers. Friendly Societies in Modern Britain, pp. 25-30.

[128] Cf. *Kowaleski, Wallace, E.* (2000), The needs of strangers: Friendly Societies and insurance societies in late eighteenth-century England. Eighteenth century life 24, pp. 53-72.

[129] A charity brief was a license granted by the crown to receive charity for losses that were too high for small communities to cover. A brief approved by the King's Seal was printed and distributed to every parish in Britain where it was read during the holy mess. Later the congregation would donate money that would then be remitted back to the royal patent office. Finally, the funds were distributed to the people or group in need. The charity brief was, therefore, a way of redistributing social risks, but, unfortunately, it was also open to fraudulent behavior. Cf. *Ismay, P.* (2018), Trust among strangers. Friendly Societies in Modern Britain, p. 36f.; *Ismay, P.* (2010), Trust among strangers: Securing British Modernity `by way of friendly society,' 1780s-1870s; unpublished Dissertation University of California, Berkeley, p. 17.

[130] Cf. *Ismay, P.* (2018), Trust among strangers. Friendly Societies in Modern Britain, p. 40f.

[131] *Beveridge, W.* (1948), Voluntary action; a report on methods of social advance, p. 21

had saved enough money to join a friendly society.[132] The general view was that friendly societies and its members were the "most reformist and Victorian value orientated" organisation respectively group of people. This means friendly societies were regarded as respectable and their members as hard-working, economically cautious and by embracing temperance. These habits were necessary as "practical safeguards against threats of poverty and economic insecurity". However, many friendly societies faced economically difficult times between 1820 and 1830, and numerous of them ceased to exist. With the Friendly Society Act of 1829, the government tried to centralize the system of the friendly society's rules, which led to fear and distrust of many members.[133] In 1834, the Poor Law Amendment Act of 1834 was enacted and the fear of living in workhouses increased dramatically, as a result, many and different friendly society branches were founded and the number of memberships accelerated again.

By the end of the 19th century, almost half of the adult male population were members of a friendly society. In 1877, 2,750,000 members could be found in a registered friendly society, a number that increased to 5,600,000 by 1904.

Table 14: Growth of registered friendly societies under the Act of 1875

Year	Number of Members	Funds in Pounds
1877	2,750,000	12,700,000
1887	3,600,000	20,000,000
1897	4,800,000	30,500,000
1904	5,600,000	41,000,000

Source: *Gosden,P.* (1961). The Friendly Societies in England 1815-1875, p. 91.

The growth and success of friendly societies in Britain started to fail at the end of the 19th century, when industrial insurance companies offered life assurances to the working class and became fast very competitive to friendly societies. In 1909, the state pension was introduced and in 1911, the National Insurance Act was enacted. The new legislation introduced a health insurance system for industrial workers based

[132] Cf. *Ismay, P.* (2018), Trust among strangers. Friendly Societies in Modern Britain, p. 65f.

[133] Cf. *Gosden, P.* (1973), Self-Help: Voluntary associations in the 19th century, p. 12.

on contributions from employers, the government, and the workers. The scheme, which came into effect in July 1912, was intended to create a national system of insurance for working people against illness and unemployment. All wage-earners aged between 16 and 70 were obliged to contribute 4d per week, while employers paid 3d and the state 2d. In return, workers were entitled to a level of free medical care and advice, and 7 shillings per week for a maximum of 15 weeks per year in the event of unemployment. Initially, the scheme was administered by approved societies, i.e. voluntary friendly societies authorized and underwritten by the government, and regulated by four Insurance Commissions.[134] However, the main requirement for friendly societies to take part in this scheme was to abolish all restrictions and barriers for memberships, and to be open to the whole population.[135] That meant that from now on members were "isolated" from the principle of mutuality. Moreover, it changed the internal structures of friendly societies to be able to administer the benefits. The benefits were now distributed through centralized friendly societies (trade unions) and collecting societies (insurance companies with employed agents to collect dues at their customers' houses).[136] Additionally, many new companies offering industrial insurances for the working class were able to cover better and more effective the needs of people regarding social security.

The Act itself can be regarded as one of the foundations of the modern welfare state and was part of the wider social welfare reforms of the Liberal Government between 1906 and 1915 under the Liberal Chancellor of the Exchequer *David Lloyd George*. In 1925, the Act was replaced by a newer system, when the Ministry of Health was charged with the administration of contributory pensions under the Old Age, Widows' and Orphans' Contributory Pensions Act. The system was eventually nationalized in 1945, with the creation of the Ministry for National Insurance. Many societies lost now their role as an approved society for the administration of state benefits, a function that was taken over by local executive councils in 1948. Finally, the National Insurance Act 1946 and National Assistance Act 1948 established the modern welfare state.[137]

The above mentioned development is also evident in the falling number of members in friendly societies from the late 19th century onwards.

---

[134] Cf. https://www.politics.co.uk/reference/national-insurance, 12.04.2019.

[135] Cf. *Cordery, S.* (2003), British Friendly Societies, 1750-1914, Palgrave Macmillan, p. 171.

[136] Cf. *Ismay, P.* (2018), Trust among strangers. Friendly Societies in Modern Britain, p. 207f.

[137] Cf. https://www.politics.co.uk/reference/national-insurance, 12.04.2019; *Neave, D.* (1996), Friendly Societies in Great Britain, p. 51.

Table 15: Great Britain: Development of registered Friendly Societies between 1877 and 1988

Year	Members	Funds in Pounds
1877	2,750,000	12,700,000
1887	3,600,000	20,000,000
1899	5,466,000	32,654,000
1905	6,164,000	41,795,000
1910	6,623,000	49,802,000
1920	7,216,226	67,486,406
1926	7,246,104	91,247,917
1930	7,679,093	108,591,642
1935	8,201,060	135,312,371
1945	8,720,000	192,829,000
1956	6,980,000	-
1961	5,917,000	257,910,000

Source: *Gosden,P.* (1961). The Friendly Societies in England 1815-1875, p. 91.

Although, as *Ismay* states, friendly societies saw a decline in memberships, they still exist and shifted their focus to social work by serving local communities and in particular elderly people. Moreover, some friendly societies provide financial services by offering members to buy into a collection of mutual schemes to reduce the costs of medical services that are not covered by the state.[138] However, it is important to keep in mind that a few friendly societies are still part of Great Britain's insurance market and they represent the largest proportion of mutual insurers on today's market.

[138] Cf. *Ismay, P.* (2018), Trust among strangers. Friendly Societies in Modern Britain, p. 211f.

4. The British Life insurance industry under the regulation of the Life Assurance Companies Act

In 1869, the “Albert Life Assurance Co.” got into serious financial trouble. These events motivated the British government to take steps towards a regulation of the nation’s life insurance market. After an era characterized by speculative ventures, mergers and acquisitions, the first British insurance legislation, namely the Life Assurance Companies Act of 1870 was introduced.[139] [140]

The Life Assurance Companies Act’s had the main objectives to place life insurance companies upon the same legal footing as the joint stock companies with respect to their legal constitution, powers of disposing of their business and others and on the other hand to provide policyholders with protection. The latter was achieved by mandatory publication of companies’ accounts as well as regular actuarial investigation of companies’ financial conditions.[141] [142] Stemming therefrom, main provisions included in the Life Assurance Companies Act can be divided into five main categories. These were provisions regarding legally required deposits, provisions regarding the separation of companies’ life insurance funds from other business segments, provisions regarding accounts, returns and other information for members required to be made public, provision regulating amalgamation and provisions regarding the winding up of companies.[143]

Under the provision regarding legally required deposit it was stated that a newly founded life insurance office was required to provide a sum of £20.000 as a security with the Accountant-General of the Court of Chancery in order to obtain a certificate of registration. This deposit was not returned until the life insurance company had been able to accumulate life assurance funds amounting to £40.000 out of its regular premium income. The requirement for deposits was however only applied to newly founded companies after the introduction of the act,

[139] Cf. *Raynes, H.* (1948), pp. 353, 355.
[140] Cf. *Pearson, R.* (2013), p. 12.
[141] Cf. *Booth, P.* (2007), p. 121.
[142] Cf. *Walford, C.* (1887), p. 456.
[143] Cf. *Raynes, H.* (1948), p. 355.

thus exempting already existent life insurers to provide such a security.[144] [145] [146]

Furthermore, the act introduced provisions requiring the separation of funds stemming from a company's life insurance business to any kind of other insurance business conducted. This implied that companies were required to keep a separate account for their life and annuity business as well as maintain a separate fund labelled "life assurance fund". In other words, insurance companies had to administer their life insurance business in such a way as if the company would operate no other kinds of business.[147]

In addition to deposit and separate life assurance funds requirements, the Life Assurance Companies Act also introduced provisions regarding the publication of company information with the objective to provide policyholders and shareholders alike with the possibility to truly estimate the financial position of companies. As stated in the act, life insurance companies were required to make annual returns of their receipts and expenditure as well as of their assets and liabilities. Moreover, companies became subject to regular actuarial investigations of their financial condition. Companies established after the introduction became required to undergo investigation into their financial condition by an actuary every five years, whereas companies already established prior to the act were only required to be investigated every ten years. Both annual accounts and periodical valuations were required to be submitted to the Board of Trade as well as provided to every policyholder and shareholder if being demanded by them.[148] [149]

Due to the foregoing period of imprudent amalgamation and merger activities within the country's life insurance industry as well as the resulting insurance insolvencies, the Life Assurance Companies Act also introduced provisions regarding the merger and winding up of life insurance companies. As laid out in the act companies deeming to perform an amalgamation became required to publically announce their plan as well as obtain approval from the Court of Chancery. Information regarding the planned process of the amalgamation had to be provided by companies to the court. In addition the act also demanded from companies to provide policyholders with material information relating to the proposed merger by each of the involved companies, whereas a veto against such plans could be imposed by policyholders,

[144] After the amendment of the Act in 1872 the 20,000 £ deposit was deemed to be part of a company's assurance funds.
[145] Cf. *Walford, C.* (1887), p. 456.
[146] Cf. *Raynes, H.* (1948), p. 355.
[147] Cf. *Raynes, H.* (1948), pp. 355-356.
[148] Cf. *Booth, P.* (2007), pp. 122-123;
[149] Cf. *Raynes, H.* (1948), pp. 356-357;

prohibiting the court to approve an amalgamation.[150] [151] With respect to an insolvency of a life insurance company, the Life Assurance Companies Act provided the court with the ability to order the winding up of a company if an application had been made by one or more policyholders or shareholders and if it was being proven that the company was in fact insolvent.[152] Moreover, "the court was not to give a hearing to petitions for winding-up until security for reasonable costs should be given and until a prima facie case should have been established."[153] Additionally, the court had the authority to prevent the winding-up of a company by instead ordering contracts to be operated further under a reduced insured sum and the company continuing to operate as a closed fund in the case of being potentially merged with a financially healthy company.[154]

While the Life Assurance Companies Act of 1870 had the objectives of providing higher protection to company policyholders and shareholders by addressing problems resulting from information asymmetry and the possible problem of time inconsistency "[...] leading to a lack of credibility of commitments made by long-term insurers"[155] critique that issues were partially insufficiently handled by the act can be voiced. First the fact that only newly founded life insurance companies were required to deposit a security, while existing companies were exempted from this provision, can be criticized. With the requirement for a security deposit being introduced for addressing the problem of life insurance nature of long-term commitment, it would have been plausible to apply respective provision to all life insurance companies. In addition, information publication requirements did not equip the Board of Trade with the right to penalize or fine life insurance companies. As a result, if the Board of Trade was being dissatisfied with returns and accounts submitted by a certain life insurance company, its officials could not do anything else besides entering into correspondence with respective company and to voice their concern publically.[156] The act therefore strongly followed the major principle of "freedom with publicity" with publications of accounts and valuations allowing external parties to evaluate a company's financial soundness and to take appropriate actions based upon their evaluation.

Despite several weaknesses, the Life Assurance Companies Act of 1870 was able to set an end to the prior era of speculative ventures and aggressive amalgamations and high number insolvencies. As shown by

[150] Cf. *Walford, C.* (1887), pp. 456-457.
[151] Cf. *Booth, P.* (2007), p. 123.
[152] Cf. *Raynes, H.* (1948), p. 358;
[153] *Raynes, H.* (1948), p. 358.
[154] Cf. *Booth, P.* (2007), pp. 123-124.
[155] *Booth, P.* (2007), p. 132.
[156] Cf. *Booth, P.* (2007), pp. 132-135.

Deuchar (1891, cf. *Booth* (2007), p. 127) the number of insolvencies occurring in the UK life insurance industry significantly reduced in the years after the introduction of the act. While a total of 177 companies were being dissolved between the years 1852 to 1869, only an amount of 72 companies were discontinued during the following sixteen years, whereas these discontinuations did mostly not occur due to solvency problems and did not include any failures of major life insurers.[157] At the same time also the numbers of mergers and acquisitions strongly declined in the aftermath of the introduction of the act in 1870. As stated by *Pearson* (2013, p. 12), the introduction of rigorous regulations in combination with the economic cool down of respective period of time led to the situation that only about twenty mergers took place during the 1870s and 1880s. A similar effect is reported by *White* (1887, p. 23), showing in his statistics that some forty life insurance companies ceased to exist between the years 1870 and 1888, including both, wound up companies and amalgamated ones. Nevertheless, also the number of companies being newly established was severely reduced in the aftermath of the introduction of the act, which can be related to the newly introduced 20,000 security required to be deposited by newly founded life insurance firms.[158] While there had been 92 newly established life insurance companies between the years 1852 to 1870, many of which failed within a rather short period of time, only eight new life insurance companies came into existence between the years 1871 to 1888, demonstrating the stagnation of the amount of new market entrants.[159] As a result, it appears that the new regulatory framework, created through the introduction of the Life Assurance Companies Act of 1870, had a stabilizing influence upon the UK life insurance market dynamics, reducing the amounts of insolvencies, while at the same time decreasing the possibilities for the establishment of new companies. Looking upon the development of market concentration in the life insurance industry for the period of time between 1870 and 1898, further evidence for this general assumption can be found. As can be seen in figure 2 market share controlled by the top five as well as top ten life insurance companies over the period of 1874 to 1899 increased continuously during respective period of time, while the total number of operating life insurance offices decreased slowly but steadily throughout the same era.

Here it can be mentioned, that with the “Scottish Widows Fund” one mutual life insurers was regularly present within the group of the top five UK life insurance companies within the period 1876 to 1904.[160] Moreover, when looking upon the group of the top ten life insurance

---

[157] Cf. *Booth, P.* (2007), p. 127, 133.

[158] Cf. *Deuchar* (1891), cf. *Booth, P.* (2007), p. 127.

[159] Cf. *White, W.* (1887), pp. 19, 25-28.

[160] Cf. *White, W.* (1890).

companies, it can be said that with companies such as the "National Provident" and the "Scottish Provident" additional mutual companies ranked among the largest UK life insurers in terms of premium income at some point during respective period of time.[161] In general, it can be said that mutual life insurance offices competed successfully with proprietary offices during the post-Life Assurance Company Act period until the beginning of the 20th century. Figure 2 shows the development of market share of mutual life insurance companies including ordinary as well as industrial life insurance operation. With a market share of 30.57 percent in 1874, 29.16 percent in 1880, and 28.37 percent in 1888, it can be clearly stated that mutual life offices represented and maintained an important role within the UK life insurance industry during the mid and late 19th century. Furthermore, with market share rates remaining very stable within the period of 1871 to 1890, the proposed stability resulting from the introduction of the Life Assurance Companies Act of 1870 can be inferred. With the mid and late 19th century being a period of steady growth of the Kingdom's life insurance industry, it seems that mutual life offices were on average growing almost at the same place as proprietary offices. Only during the last decade of the 19th century, with a drop of market share held by mutual life offices from 28.37 percent in 1888 to 21.9 percent in 1898, it appears that proprietary and composite offices slowly but steadily began to outperform mutual life offices in terms of growth of annual premium income recorded.

Here it can be seen that while the total number of life insurance companies on the UK market decreased during the three decades following the introduction of the Life Assurance Companies Act in 1870, the number of mutual life offices remained rather stable. As demonstrated in the figure, the number of mutual life offices reduced only by a total of one within the period of 1874 to 1898. At the same time, the number of proprietary offices decreased much stronger, with amalgamations occurring less often than before the introduction of the act, but still being performed regularly among the latter. On the other hand, while the mid and late 19th century saw the initiation of some new life insurance offices, none of these offices was of the mutual form. This is highly contrary to the pre-Life Assurance Companies Act period. Then a series of mutual life insurance offices were initiated between the years 1840 and 1869.[162] As a possible major reason explaining this new development the introduction of the newly required security deposit, amounting to a sum of 20,000, can be named. Here it seems that the nature of the mutual legal form of being unable to raise required capital from investors in exchange for an interest in the new company heavily restricted the

161 Cf. *White, W.* (1878), pp. 34-61, (1887), pp. 77-95, (1890), pp. 80-102.

162 Cf. *White, W.* (1887), pp. 25-28, p. 19.

Figure 2: Development of premium income and market share mutual life insurance companies

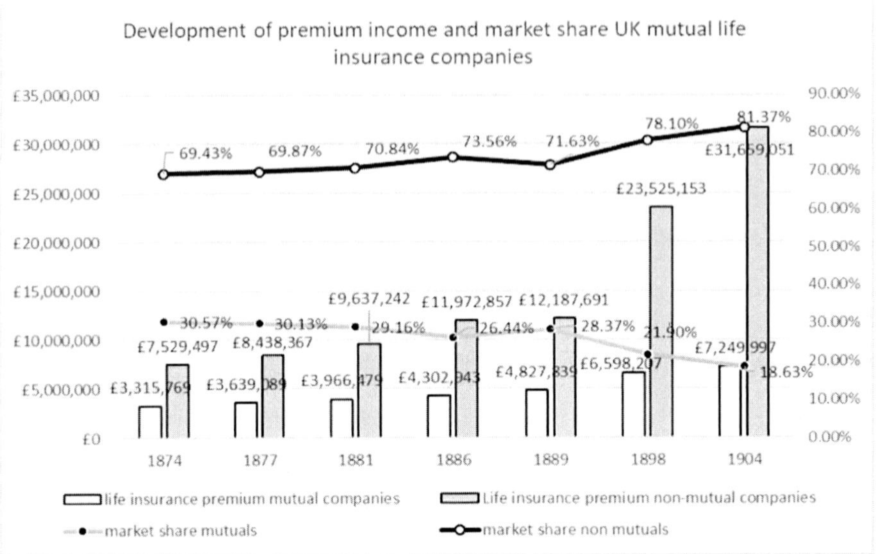

Source: *White, W.,* The Insurance Register (18xx), figures and data calculated by authors.

Figure 3: Development of the total number of mutual life insurance offices actively operating for the period 1874 to 1904.

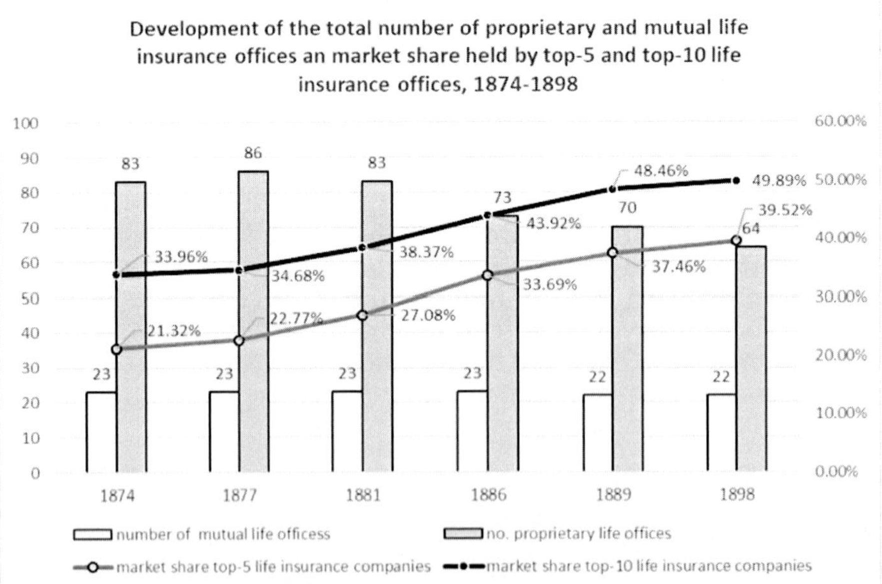

Source: *White, W.,* The Insurance Register (18xx), figures and data calculated by authors.

possibilities of new mutual life insurance offices being established once the British Life Assurance Companies Act was introduced in 1870.[163]

5. Great Britain's insurance industry development after World War II

Following the end of World War II the United Kingdom, though victorious, faced challenging economic circumstances. The nation's economy was geared towards the production of goods essential for the war effort and the British economy had experienced large losses of international trade due to the war. The nation itself owed large sums of debt to the United States resulting from the Lend & Lease Scheme and the wartime rationing of many raw materials still had to remain in place during the immediate post-war years. As a result, economic policies implemented during the immediate post war era largely focused around goals such as guaranteeing steady economic growth, reducing unemployment to a minimum, achieving a reasonable stability of internal purchasing power, and evening out the nation's highly negative balance of international payments. Economic policies did not fully succeed in meeting their goals, the United Kingdom nevertheless started to experience a period of high economic growth and low unemployment never experienced before. Also the overall private income of the general public lead to a continuous increase of peoples' standard of living.[164] [165]

With the increase of private income increasing the sum of property held increased as well. Subsequently, the demand for property and casualty insurance increased strongly too. At the same time, with more disposable income available to the general public, demand for life insurance products strongly increased as well. Life insurance became an investment vehicle.[166] Here, ordinary life insurance business contributed the most to the soaring life insurance market of the post-war United Kingdom, with growth rates of industrial life insurance business being steady but comparatively low throughout the 1950s, 60s and 70s, and ultimately starting to decrease during the early 1990s.[167] The following sub chapters will first provide an overview of the development of the UK's property and casualty insurance market, whereas the develop-

[163] Cf. *Booth, P.* (2007), p. 141.
[164] Cf. *Clayton, G.* (1971), pp. 201-208.
[165] Cf. *Carter & Falush* (2009), p. 42.
[166] Cf. *Clayton, G.* (1971), p. 211.
[167] Cf. *Carter & Falush* (2009), p. 64.

ment of the nation's life insurance industry will be examined afterwards. The role, mutual insurers played in the two separate insurance sectors, will also be examined respectively, as is the main intention of this chapter.

5.1 Development of the United Kingdom's property and casualty insurance industry during the second half of the 20th century

As mentioned above, the United Kingdom's property and casualty insurance industry experienced tremendous growth during the 1950s, 60s, 70s and with classes such as motor insurance and fire insurance among the major driving forces. Table 16 and 17 shows the development of insurance premium income generated by major lines of general insurance between the years 1949 to 1985, which demonstrate the tremendous increase of business operated by the UK general insurance sector during the second half of the 20th century.

Table 16: Worldwide premiums of major general insurance classes of UK insurance companies

	Fire	Accident	Marine, aviation and transportation	Total
1949	£147 Mio.	£171 Mio.	£53 Mio.	£371 Mio.
1960	£300 Mio.	£560 Mio.	£85 Mio.	£945 Mio.
1967	£465 Mio.	£1,020 Mio.	£140 Mio.	£1,625 Mio.
Increase 1949-1960	104.1%	227.5%	60.4%	154.7%
Increase 1960-1967	55.0%	82.1%	64.7%	72.0%
Increase 1949-1967	216.3%	496.5%	164.2%	338.0%

Source: *Carter & Falush* (2009), p. 42.

Table 17: UK general insurance premium development of British insurance companies

	Fire & Accident	Motor	Marine & Aviation	Total
1969	£383 Mio.	£213 Mio.	£97 Mio.	£693 Mio.
1975	£1,010 Mio.	£628 Mio.	£221 Mio.	£1,859 Mio.
1980	£2,411 Mio.	£1,564 Mio.	£320 Mio.	£4,295 Mio.
1985	£4,651 Mio.	£2,200 Mio.	£938 Mio.	£7,798 Mio.
Increase 1969-1975	163.7%	194.8%	127.8%	168.3%
Increase 1975-1980	138.7%	149.0%	44.8%	131.0%
Increase 1980-1985	92.9%	40.7%	193.1%	81.6%
Increase 1969-1985	1114.4%	932.9%	867.0%	1025.3%

Source: *Carter & Falush* (2009), p. 43.

It can be concluded from the tables that accident insurance classes, including motor insurance, were the fastest growing class of business during the 1950s and 1960s. This view is nevertheless somewhat tainted, as data presented above represents premium income originating from domestic and international business together. Only demonstrating domestic premium income development of UK general insurance operators for years 1969 to 1985, fire and accident insurance lines of business recorded the highest growth, by increasing a staggering 1,114.4 percent in terms of premium income. Similar can be said about motor insurance within the same time frame, generating annual premium incomes ten times higher in 1985 than in 1969.

While the United Kingdom's general insurance market grew as a whole throughout the first forty years of the second half of the 20th century, the insurance industry underwent several significant developments partially related to its growth in size. On the one hand the industry saw the founding of several new general insurance operators throughout the 1950s and 1960s, many of which entered the soaring market of motor insurance and/or fire insurance.[168] As an example, a total of 29 insurance companies alone entered the fire insurance market between the years 1945 and 1972.[169] Nevertheless, with many new

[168] Cf. *Pearson, R.* (2013), p. 18.
[169] Cf. *Carter & Falush* (2009), p. 83.

companies entering the nation's general insurance market, competition among companies increased heavily, leading among other to the development that motor insurers found themselves in a situation of experiencing substantial underwriting losses from 1970s onwards following the abandonment of the motor tariff by the Accident Offices' Association after being pressured to do so by ten leading tariff companies.[170] [171] [172]

Partly because of increased competition caused by the entrance of many new insurance companies, the UK's insurance industry experienced its first major wave of mergers and acquisitions during the years 1956 to 1968, leading to the subsequent disappearance of some of the UK's oldest insurance companies.[173] One main reason behind respective mergers was to increase competitiveness through the exploitation of scale and scope economies, allowing reducing companies' overall expense ratios. Moreover, with the majority of merging or acquiring companies being composite as well as fire and accident offices, the objective of geographical diversification and expansion of insurance services and lines of business offered can be named as the second major motivation for mentioned wave of amalgamations.[174] The following table lists major amalgamations having occurred between the years 1956 to 1968. Besides the majority of mergers and acquisitions occurring among proprietary composite insurance offices, the table also shows the participation of mutual insurance operators in respective amalgamation activities during the 1950s and 1960s. Notable examples of mutual participation are the acquisition of the "British Life Office" by the "Reliance Mutual Insurance Society Ltd.", the acquisition of the "Scottish Union" and the "Parcels" and "General" by the "Norwich Union" in 1959 and 1961 respectively and the amalgamation between the "National" and "Colonial" and the "National Employers Mutual" in 1960.[175]Another major cause by the increased competition among general insurance operators, especially in the segment of motor insurance business, as well as the previously mentioned abandonment of the motor tariff by the Accident Offices' Association on the 31st of December 1968, was the subsequent failure of a series of automobile insurers, many of which were only established recently in the wake of the roaring motor insurance market of the 1960s. Starting with the failure of the "Fire Auto & Marine Insurance Company" in 1966 a total of 23 companies operating in the automobile insurance sector became liquidated until 1971. Moreover, the abandonment of the motor tariff and the following increasing price competition also contributed to the

[170] Cf. *Pearson, R.* (2013), p. 18.
[171] Cf. *Carter & Falush* (2009), p. 45, 151.
[172] Cf. *Pearson, R.* (2002), p. 495.
[173] Cf. *Pearson, R.* (2013), p. 17.
[174] Cf. *Clayton, G.* (1971), pp. 219-220.
[175] Cf. *Clayton, G.* (1971), p. 219.

occurrence of a series of takeovers of automobile insurance operating companies during the same time period.[176] In 1971, the failure of one of the largest newly established motor insurers, namely the "Vehicle & General Insurance Company Ltd.", caused damages to yet another million insurance policyholders, forcing the government to take action. As a result, despite having recently tightened governmental regulation over British insurance companies with the introduction of the Part II of the Companies Act in 1967, the government introduced the Insurance Companies Amendment Act, 1973, with provisions of both legislations being consolidated only one year later under the Insurance Companies Act of 1974.[177]

Almost parallel to the dynamic developments on the nation's motor insurance sector, the UK's general insurance industry experienced the discontinuation and abolishment of the almost hundred-year-long existing fire tariff undertaken by the "Fire Offices Committee" (FOC) and later introduced various accident tariff practices undertaken by the "Accident Offices Association" (AOA). While the above-mentioned abolishment of the motor tariff, being set by the AOA, already occurred in 1968, tariff practices for insurance lines such as employers' liability insurance, engineering insurance and most importantly household fire insurance were all abandoned between years 1969 to 1971.[178] [179] Looking upon the segment of fire insurance in particular it can be said that the sector was highly concentrated with the top 5 fire insurance companies controlling 57 percent of the market in terms of annual premium collected. Of these five companies four were members of the FOC and thus tariff companies. Moreover, despite non-tariff companies being in control of slightly above 40 percent of the market, their competitive power was limited by the FOC's so-called "65/35 percent rule", which prohibited tariff companies to participate in large coinsured risk unless a minimum of 65 percent of such risk was placed with tariff companies. Due to the described situation and competitive practices 1968 the UK government referred the supply of fire insurance to the Monopolies Commission in 1968. In response the FOC voluntarily abandoned the household fire tariff on the 1st of January 1971. In 1972 the Commission issued its report, heavily criticizing the competitive practices of the FOC and further arguing that tariffs still in place strongly operate against the public interest. Despite that it was not until 1985 that commercial fire tariffs were kept in force.[180] Since then tariffs had been completely abandoned from the UK general insurance industry.

[176] Cf. *Pearson, R.* (2013), p. 18.
[177] Cf. *Carter & Falush* (2009), p. 193.
[178] Cf. *Pearson, R.* (2002), p. 495.
[179] Cf. *Carter & Falush* (2009), pp. 92-93, 153.
[180] Cf. Ibid.

Following the abandonment of the household fire tariff, motor tariff and tariffs for other lines of insurance competition intensified on the market throughout the following years. At the same time the number of foreign companies operating insurance in the UK increased steadily throughout the 1970s and 1980s. Furthermore, despite continuously high rates of growth in all major lines of general insurance business throughout the 1970s and 1980s, underwriting results of the major lines of fire insurance business and motor insurance business were undermined by a combination of mentioned intensification of business, inflation and a period of rising insurance claims, leading to the occurrence of underwriting losses in both major lines of business.[181] In the midst of these developments, the UK government passed yet another new Insurance Companies Act in 1982, consolidating all insurance legislation and introducing new regulations. Here it has to be mentioned that one of the major purposes of the act's introduction was also to bring UK legislation in line with requirements of the EEC Insurance Establishment Directives, a necessary step due to the United Kingdom's accession to the European Communities in 1973.[182]

After having provided an overview of the developments within major segments of the UK general insurance market during the 1950, 60s, 70s and 80s, the question remains how mutual insurers performed during respective period of time. Figure 4 and 5 show the development of premium income and market share of mutual insurers required to provide statement with the Board of Trade as stipulated under the Insurance Companies Act of 1958 and later the Companies Act 1967 and Insurance Companies Act of 1973.[183]

What can be seen first when looking upon the figures is the prior mentioned continuously high growth rate the general insurance market experienced throughout the time under investigation. Moreover, if looking only upon figure 5 it appears that while the market share of mutual insurance companies in the general insurance market somewhat fluctuated during the 1960s, it grew almost at a similar pace as was business of proprietary insurers, with mutuals only appearing to have grown slower between the years 1965 to 1967 and market share almost always staying between a 4-5 percent range in terms of total annual premium income. Nevertheless, it has to be mentioned here, that market share illustrated in figure 4 understates the actual market share of mutual insurers operating general insurance business during respective period of time. The reason for this circumstance is that

[181] Cf. Ibid., p. 152, 154.

[182] Cf. Ibid., p. 194.

[183] This includes a series of insurance association and societies of which not all are incorporated under the Companies Act, as well as many insurers labelled as "non-Act insurers" prior to the introduction of Part II of the Companies Act in 1967 from the year 1964 onwards.

Figure 4: Premium and market share development of mutual insurance companies on the general insurance market

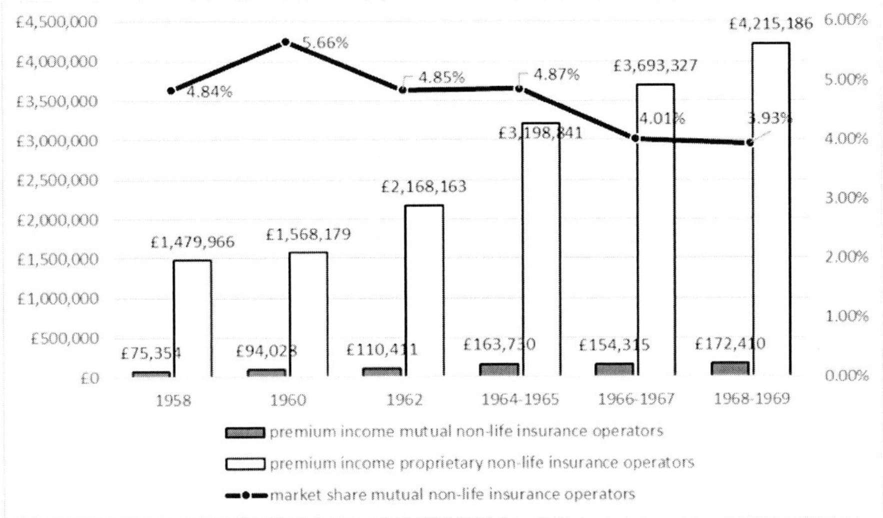

Source: *Board of Trade* (1969, 1971), figures and data calculated by authors.

Figure 5: Market share development general insurance business and market share mutual insurance operators under the Insurance Companies Act 1974/1982

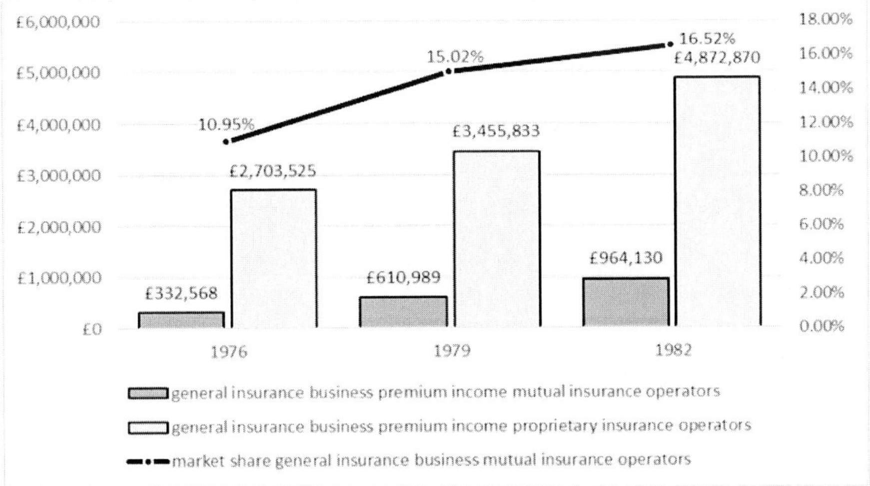

Source: Business Statistics Office – HMSO (1978, 1981, 1984), figures and data calculated by authors.

business statistics issued by the Board of Trade for the late 1950s and 1960s do not distinguish between domestic and overseas business in depicturing annual premium income. With overseas business representing a substantial part of business for several proprietary offices and the premium income stipulated in the statistics for foreign offices also including all their overseas business not operated in the United Kingdom, total premium income generated by insurance companies operating in the UK is overstated, leading to an underestimation of market share held by mutuals on the domestic general insurance market. Therefore, if ignoring business operation of overseas companies the market share for mutuals strongly increases and ranges between 8-10 percent for the period under consideration.

This estimation is further much more in line with calculated market share for business years depicted in figure 4. As can be seen in the figure market share held by mutual insurers on the general insurance market can be estimated to have accounted for slightly below 11 percent for the year 1976. Most interestingly, this market share increased throughout the following 6 years, as demonstrated in the graph, indicating that mutuals appear to have outgrown proprietary companies during respective period of time. As a result, market share held by mutuals in the general insurance market can be estimated to have been about 16.5 percent, being more than 5 percent higher in comparison to the mid-1970s.

Nevertheless, despite mutual insurers holding a notable position during respective period of time within the general insurance industry, it can be said that the market was highly dominated by proprietary offices, holding approximately 90 percent of market share during most parts of respective period of time. This argument of proprietary companies being more strongly present on the UK general insurance market is further strengthened by the fact that newly founded companies entering the general insurance market were almost exclusively of the proprietary type, with exceptions only to be found in some niche segments. As an example, mutual insurance organizations established during the 1980s in the segment of indemnity insurance can be mentioned, such as the "Bar Mutual", established in 1988 to provide compulsory indemnity insurance for barristers, the "Housing Association Mutual Insurance Association", starting to provide indemnity insurance to housing associations from 1987 onwards, PAMIA, initiated in 1989 to provide indemnity insurance for patent and trademark agents, and the "Solicitors Indemnity Mutual Insurance Association", providing indemnity insurance for solicitors since 1986.[184]

[184] Cf. *Carter & Falush* (2009), p. 95.

5.2 Development of the United Kingdom's life insurance market during the 2nd half of the 20th century and early new millennium

Similar to the property and casualty insurance industry, the United Kingdom's life insurance industry experienced a period of mostly continuous growth throughout between the 1950s and early 1990s. Despite that, the UK life insurance industry experienced several substantial changes throughout respective period of time, being caused by developments such as the decent of industrial life insurance as a major life insurance segment, the increase of competition through the entrance of new domestic and overseas competition, the increase of competition caused by the introduction of new underwriting and marketing techniques such as bancassurance and direct distribution channels, regulatory changes such as the abandonment of taxation benefits for life insurance policyholders in the form of the life assurance premium relief and last but not least the demise of mutual life insurance offices in the course of the demutualization wave of the 1990s. The following will provide a short overview of these developments and their effect onto the composition of the UK life insurance industry during respective period of time.

As already described earlier, industrial life insurance successfully developed as the second major life insurance segment parallel to ordinary life insurance in the UK insurance market and almost caught up to the latter segment in terms of annual premiums generated and total sum assured throughout the late 19th century and early decades of the 20th century. Thus, looking upon total premium income generated, it is not very unsurprising that with a total amount of £112.37 million of premium payments in 1947 industrial insurance accounted for a total of 41.4 percent of the entire UK life insurance business, whereas the remaining £158.9 million of premium payments generated includes both, income from ordinary as well as annuity business. As a result, industrial life insurance business was indeed the second major segment besides ordinary insurance on the UK life insurance market at the mid of the 20th century.[185]

A further specificity of the industrial life insurance segment was, that friendly societies operated a major share of total business generated, amounting to 18.9 percent in terms of total annual premium collected in 1947. Moreover, with a total of 115 societies in 1954 more friendly societies than life insurance companies were engaged in the

[185] Cf. *Johnston & Murphy* (1957), pp. 180-182, figures calculated by author.

underwriting of industrial life insurance business, with only around 14 of the latter operating respective insurance business.[186]

Despite the apparent success and popularity of industrial life insurance on the UK insurance market, industrial life insurance practices were regularly under heavy fire of public criticism throughout the late 19th century and first half of the 20th century. As already mentioned before in this chapter, this criticism mostly focused around three major points, being the high expense ratios in comparison to ordinary life insurance, industrial life insurance' high lapse ratios and finally its rather low returns generated for policyholders.[187] With these points of criticism regarding industrial life insurance business also being included in the 1942 *Beveridge* Report on "Social Insurance and Allied Services", public discussion regarding the potential nationalization or alternative mutualization of the industry were sparked once more in 1949 from within the ranks of the then ruling Labour Party. Nevertheless, for various reasons that shall not be discussed here in detail the idea of nationalization was soon to be dismissed in the following years.[188]

Here it shall be mentioned quickly with regards to the *Beveridge* Report, that it was this report on the basis of which the National Health Insurance (NHI) scheme, initiated in 1912, was abandoned in 1946 with the passing of the National Insurance Act of 1946. As mentioned previously, the NHI of 1912 was based upon the incorporation of existing friendly and industrial insurance societies as well as some trade unions as so-called registered societies, which performed the tasks of administering benefits, paid medical expenses through local insurance committees and managed the collection of social insurance premiums, all on a non-profit basis. Whereas this system highly contributed to the social security of the United Kingdom's workforce throughout its existence, it was far from perfect, with benefits varying locally and certain parts of the population, especially women, excluded from its benefits. Criticizing among others these weaknesses the *Beveridge* Report's therefore suggested the initiation of an extension and unification of social insurance under a unified state-run system, which was being performed by the Labour Government in 1946, despite heavy opposition from the National Confederation of Friendly Societies. As a result, friendly societies and industrial insurance societies were no longer involved in the national security service from 1946 onwards.[189]

The situation of industrial life insurance business representing a substantial part of the entire UK life insurance market changed sub-

[186] Cf. *Morrah* (1955), pp. 232-233.
[187] Cf. Ibid., pp. 88-89, 110-111.
[188] Cf. Ibid., pp. 193-196.
[189] Cf. *Whiteside, N.* (1999), p. 29, 32, 38-39.

stantially throughout the course of the second half of the 20th century. Even though industrial life insurance business grew steadily throughout the 1950s, 60s, 70s and 80s growth rates were substantially lower in comparison to ordinary life insurance business. Whereas the former experienced annual growth of business of approximately 7 percent during the period of 1965 to 1990, ordinary life insurance business experienced an average annual growth rate of almost 13.5 percent during the same period of time. Resulting from this development, industrial life insurance business generated annual premium income of only £1371 million in 1990, while ordinary life insurance business alone generated more than £12858 million in the same year, showing the comparatively slower rate of growth of industrial life business.[190]

Reasons named by literature for this development are different, ranging from industrial life insurance business' characteristics of chronically higher expense ratios and comparatively lower returns to the introduction of new types of ordinary life insurance products, boosting the sales of the latter. However, the plain and simple major reason for industrial life insurance' loss in significance on the UK life insurance market is that, with disposable income of the general populace increasing strongly throughout the second half of the 20th century, ordinary life insurance products with high saving capabilities appear of simply having been more attractive to customers, than industrial life insurance with its comparatively small return possibilities.[191]

From around the beginning of the 1990s onwards, total premium income resulting from industrial life insurance policies began to drop steadily, with the number of new industrial life policies annually sold already starting to drop since the mid-1980s. Consequently, insurance companies one by one ceased to underwrite industrial life insurance policies, with no new policies being sold by UK life insurance companies from the early 2000s onwards. At the same time, also the number of friendly societies underwriting industrial life insurance business decreased steadily. Whereas the number of collecting societies already reduced steadily throughout the second half of the 20th century, mainly due to mergers or acquisitions among societies themselves, the total number dropped further throughout the last decade of the 20th century from 30 in 1990 to a mere 14 by the end of 1999.[192] Moreover, while no new business of industrial life insurance was underwritten since the early 2000s, life insurance companies still recorded premium incomes of 247 million pounds stemming from industrial life policies still in force. Nevertheless, comparing this figure with the amount of premium generated by ordinary life insurance policies for the same year, totalling

[190] Cf. *Carter & Falush* (2009), p. 63.

[191] Cf. Ibid.

[192] Cf. Ibid.

at 41.5 billion pounds, the insignificancies of remaining industrial life insurance business at the beginning of the new millennium becomes visible.[193] From the perspective of friendly societies the downfall of industrial life insurance throughout the late 20th century can be interpreted as the loss of a previously important field of business.

As demonstrated above, ordinary life insurance business surged throughout the second half of the 20th century. While annual premium income of ordinary life insurance was 203.9 million pounds in 1950 it had increased to a total of 38.77 billion pounds 50 years later.[194] [195] Nevertheless, the segment of ordinary life insurance changed tremendously during respective period of time.

Starting from the 1960s onwards, new competition in the form of new domestic companies as well as newly introduced life insurance products as well as newly developed marketing channels began to change the industry. From the early 1960s onwards until the early 1970s, so-called unit-linked life insurance became popular on the UK life insurance market. At the same time new companies such as "Abbey Life", entered the UK market through selling unit-linked policies using direct sales forces. Moreover, life insurance offices began to diversify into new fields of business from the early 1970s onwards, also leading to the acquisition of property companies. In total, life insurance had moved from a product of protection to tax efficient savings product, with tax relieves on premiums granted to policyholders being a major selling point of life insurance and thus stimulant to the growth of life insurance business.[196] It was not until the introduction of the Finance Act of 1985 that tax relief granted for life insurance premiums were abandoned in an attempt "[…] to put all forms of savings on a level footing […]"[197].

Following the liberalization of the UK financial industry during the 1980s, causing the removal of old demarcation lines between the various segments of different financial services, financial institutions such as banks and building societies began to enter the insurance market quite aggressively.[198] Nevertheless, several British banks already performed first efforts to enter the life insurance industry as early as the 1960s. As an example Barclays Bank can be mentioned, which established its own life insurance company named "Barclays Life" in 1965.[199] From the late 1960s onwards also more and more foreign insurance companies attempted to enter the UK insurance market, leading to the acquisition of several established domestic insurance companies. This

193 Cf. Ibid.
194 Cf. *Johnston & Murphy* (1957), p. 181.
195 Cf. *Carter and Falush* (2009), p. 63.
196 Cf. Ibid, pp. 66-67.
197 *Carter and Falush* (2009), p. 67.
198 Cf. *Pearson, R.* (2013), p. 19.
199 *Carter and Falush* (2009), p. 70.

trend of performing market entrance through acquisition accelerated throughout the 1980s and also continued throughout the 1990s, such that by the end of 1999 no less than 18 British companies had been acquired by overseas insurers. In total the entrance of established companies, on the one hand from overseas markets and on the other hand from other areas of the domestic financial industry, changed the competitive landscape of the UK life insurance industry during respective period of time.[200] [201]

Considering these developments, the question arises how mutual life insurance offices performed and were able to cope with respective changes within the life insurance industry during respective period of time. In order to answer this question figure 6 and 7 state the development of total domestic (UK) premium income of mutual life insurance companies in comparison to proprietary life insurance offices between the years 1958 to 1982. Moreover, the figures demonstrate the development of market share held by mutual insurance companies on the UK life insurance market.

As can be seen from the figures, market share held by mutual life insurance companies remained rather stable throughout the late 1950s and first half of the 1960s. Only looking upon premium income of ordinary life insurance business as well as income generated from companies' annuity business, market share of mutual companies fluctuated between 42 percent to 49 percent during respective period of time. Including premium income generated by industrial life insurance business but not considering business operated by friendly societies, market share held somewhat decreases by about 8 percent for the years 1964 to 1966, demonstrating that mutual life insurance companies were less present in the industrial life insurance segment than were proprietary companies. Nevertheless, it can be concluded that during the period of 1958 to 1966 mutual life insurance companies grew at an almost same pace with proprietary offices, with both not outperforming the other.

However, from the mid-1960s onwards the observable situation changed, as proprietary companies appear to have outperformed mutual companies on the life insurance market from the year 1967 onwards. This can be seen by looking on the growth of annual premium collected by the two different types of life insurers. Despite the fact that both groups of insurance operators recorded steady growth rates from 1967 onwards, proprietary offices seemed to have outperformed mutual life insurance companies until the end of the 1970s, leading to the situation that mutual life insurance market share decreased notably, only being a mere 22.88 percent in terms of annual domestic premium income for the business year 1979. Looking upon this development, it

---

[200] Cf. *Pearson, R.* (2013), p. 19.
[201] Cf. *Carter and Falush* (2009), p. 162.

Figure 6: The development life insurance business insurance companies & market share mutual life insurance companies (annuities, ordinary & industrial business)

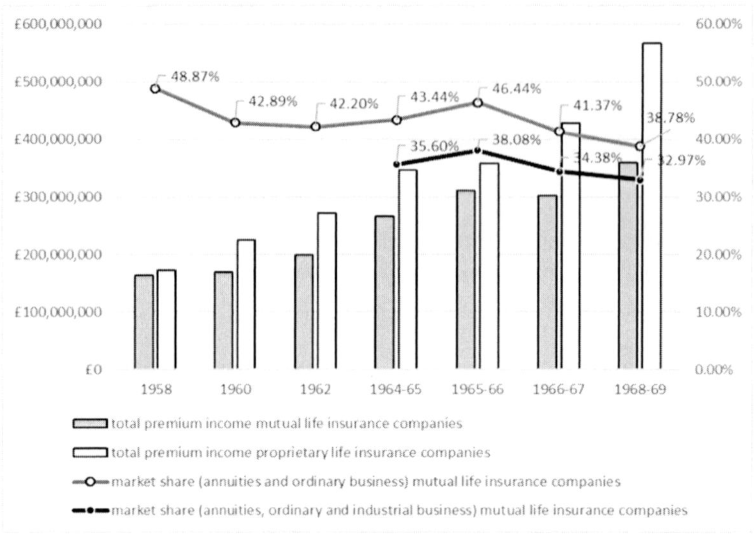

Source: Board of Trade (1959, 1961, 1963, 1969, 1971, 1972), figures and data calculated by author.

Figure 7: Market share development long-term insurance business and market share mutual insurance operators under the Insurance Companies Act 1974/1982.

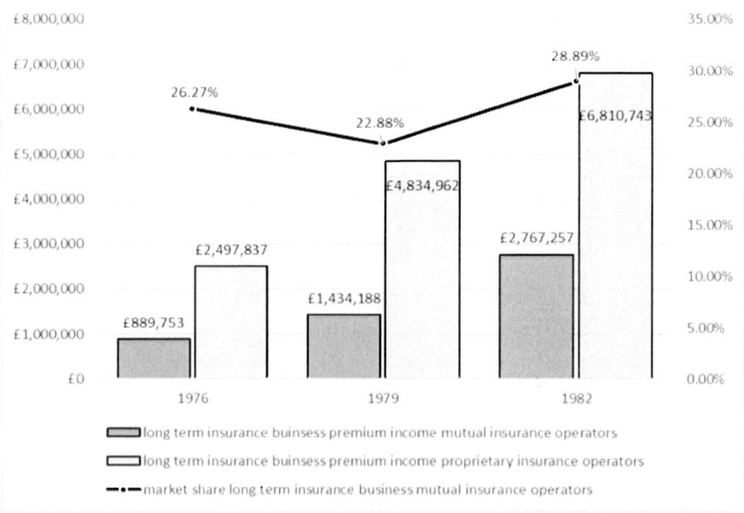

Source: Business Statistics Office – HMSO (1978, 1981, 1984), figures and data calculated by author.

could be inferred that mutual life insurance companies were able to less successfully cope with mentioned above market changes of the 1960s and 1970s in comparison to the proprietary rivals. On the other hand it has to be mentioned, that new competition more or the less exclusively arose in the form of new proprietary life insurers. Nevertheless, as shown in figure 6, mutual life insurance companies also seem to have outperformed proprietary insurers during the period of 1980 to 1982, accomplishing an overall higher premium growth, allowing them to reconquer market share to an amount of almost 29 percent of the domestic market. As a result, no decisive indication that one of the two types of life insurance companies was more capable to adapt to ongoing industry changes of respective period of time can be made from simple looking upon market share developments.

What can be concluded though is the fact that mutual companies were still in control of a substantial share of the UK life insurance market in the 1980s. This conclusion receives further support when looking upon table 18, showing the development sector share held by mutual and proprietary life insurance companies in terms of acquired new yearly premiums and new single premiums for the years 1988 to 1997.

Table 18: Sector share held by mutual and proprietary life insurance companies

	mutual companies		**proprietary compamnies**	
year	new yearly premiums	new single premiums	new yearly premiums	new single premiums
1988	40.3%	38.3%	59.7%	61.7%
1989	35.9%	39.9%	64.1%	60.1%
1990	35.8%	44.3%	64.2%	55.7%
1991	38.5%	44.5%	61.5%	55.5%
1992	38.4%	36.7%	61.6%	63.3%
1993	35.8%	34.5%	64.2%	65.5%
1994	33.0%	31.6%	67.0%	68.4%
1995	32.0%	29.3%	68.0%	70.7%
1996	32.3%	24.9%	67.7%	75.1%
1997	27.1%	22.8%	72.9%	77.2%

As demonstrated by the figures in the table, the market share held by mutual life insurance companies was substantial during the late 1980s, indicating the continuously strong presents of mutual companies on the UK life insurance market throughout the 1980s. However, if looking upon the development of the percentage of total premium income received from new policies underwritten, one can see a trend that from the early 1990s onwards mutual insurance companies' share of total new business underwritten reduced steadily, dropping from 40.3 percent and 38.3 percent in 1988 to a mere 27.1 percent and 22.8 percent respectively. As the major reason for this development, the wave of demutualization among mutual life insurance companies throughout starting in the late 1980s and lasting throughout the early 2000s can be named.[202]

Following the market entrance of new domestically established life insurance companies as well as of many foreign international insurance groups into the United Kingdom's life insurance market, competition increased steadily throughout the 1970s and 1980s. At the same time, the risk for mutual life insurers of being involved in the business of profit-participating life insurance during respective period of time due to increasing uncertainties on the financial markets. While the same was true for all life insurance companies, the risk experienced by mutual insurers heavily engaged in with-profit business was more severe, as mutual insurance companies, due to their nature of being mutual, are limited in gaining access to external capital in comparison to proprietary companies. As a result, the urge for many mutual insurance to demutualize and thus gain much better access to external capital market by being able to issue shares seemed to have increased during respective period of time, being somewhat pressured by large volumes of guaranteed policyholder dividend payments accounting for their inforce policies. An example of this situation is given by the "Standard Life", which after four years of stock market losses and remaining too long in a bear market, had to pursue the course of demutualization in order to cope with potential financial problems.[203] In short it can be therefore said that access to external capital markets seemed to have been the main motivation for mutual societies to undergo mutualization.

However, as mentioned by *Carter and Falush* (2007, p. 73), the consequences following the demutualization were not expected by former mutual insurance companies, as they found themselves particularly vulnerable to takeover, mainly by banks, building societies and foreign insurance company groups, which during the 1980s began to heavily push into the UK insurance market. While in 1991 a total of 27 mu-

[202] Cf. ABI (1999), p. 31.
[203] Cf. APPG (2006), p. 11.

tual life offices and two mutual composite offices existed in the UK life insurance industry, holding a market share of 46.9 percent in the segment of ordinary life insurance premiums, this number had almost reduced to zero until the early years of the new millennium. The table 19 provides an overview of the most notable demutualizations and following takeovers during respective period of time.

Table 19: Major demutualizations and acquisitions of former mutual life insurance companies between 1989 and 2006

Mutual Life insurance company	Acquiring Company
FS Assurance	Britannia Building Society* (1989)
London Life	Australian Mutual Provident* (1989)
Scottish Mutual	Abbey National plc (1991)
Scottish Equitable	AEGON (1994)
Clerical Medical & General	Halifax (1996)
Scottish Amicable	Prudential (1997)
Scottish Widows	Lloyds TSB (2000)
National Farmers Mutual (2000)	-
Royal London Mutual (2000)	-
Norwich Union Life (2000)	-
Scottish Life	Royal London Mutual* (2001)
Wesleyan (2006)	-
Standard Life (2006)	-

Source: *Carter and Falush* (2009), p. 74.

As a consequence of described wave of demutualization, market share held by mutual life insurance companies decreased significantly. Figure 7 demonstrates the development of mutual companies' share of new life business between the years 1996 to 2006, while table 20 shows the development of market share held in terms of premium income of ordinary life insurance business for the years 1987 to 1997. Both, the table and the figure show the demise of mutual life insurance com-

panies due to the wave of demutualization. While market share held still accounted for 46 percent in the ordinary life insurance segment in 1987, this figure had already dropped by 13 percent until 1997. Moreover, as shown in figure 8 mutual life insurance companies' market share of new business of single and regular premium products dropped below the ten percent mark in 2004 and 2006 respectively.

Table 20: Market share development of mutual life insurance companies and number of mutual insurers on the life insurance market.

	Market share in percent			Number of mutual life insurers		
	1987	1992	1997	1987	1992	1997
UK	46	48	33	58	57	47

Source: Sigma 4/1999, 1999; p. 21;[204]

Right during the pinnacle of the demutualization wave in the United Kingdom, the nation's life insurance industry experienced the failure of its second largest life insurance company in 2000, namely the "Equitable Life Assurance Society" ("Equitable Life"). Without going into too much detail, it can be said that this failure of one of Britain's oldest mutual life insurance office occurred due to large sums of with-profit policies containing guaranteed annuity options among its in-force business, falling market annuity rates and the inability of the company to legally lower bonus payments it guaranteed contractually to policyholders in the face of deteriorating market interest rates.[205] Explained plainly "Guaranteed Annuity Rate" (GAR) allowed policyholders a minimum pension payout and guaranteed bonuses on a maturity day. When these guarantees were written the most by "Equitable Life" during the 1960s, 70s and 80s inflation as well as market interest rates were high in the UK, therefore being of low concern to the mutual life insurer. As the inflation and interest rates became significantly throughout the

[204] Number of mutual life insurers includes several friendly societies.

[205] A detailed outline how these factors influenced each other and led to the deterioration of Equitable Life' financial position can be found in *O'Brian* (2006), page 189-195.

Figure 8: Mutual life insurance companies' market share development new insurance business underwritten

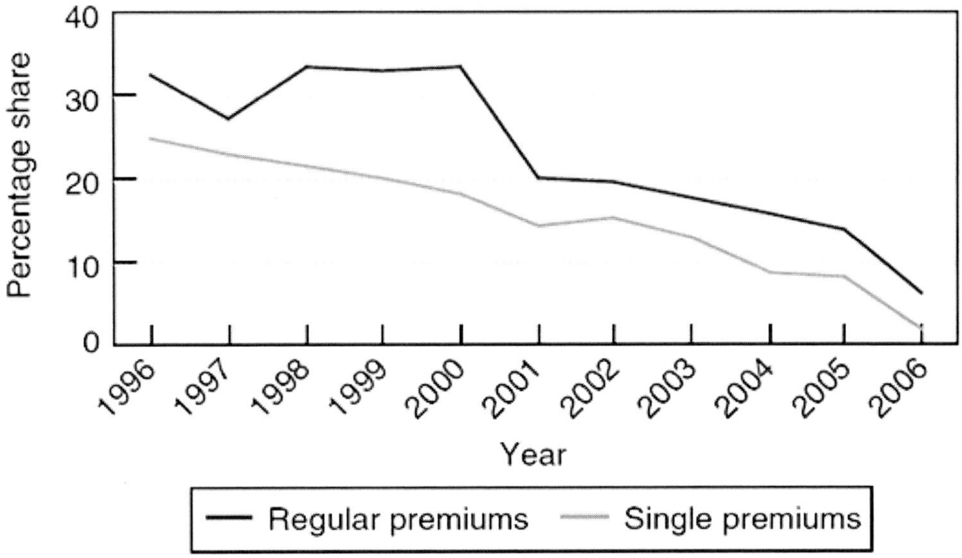

Source: *Carter & Falush* (2009), p. 74.

late 1990s and in 2000, it became almost impossible for the "Equitable Life" to pay out the guaranteed rates and their huge liabilities.[206]

Thus, with the beginning of the new millennium the company found itself in a critical financial position, forcing the company to offer itself to be taken over externally for the purpose of receiving a bail-out. When no potential buyer was found until December of the same year, the "Equitable Life" was forced to cease underwriting new business, with a new board being elected the following year and legal actions being taken against former directors and auditors.[207]

With one of the largest life insurance companies having severe financial troubles, the "United Kingdom's life insurance industry" was shaken, leading to the issue of a number of reports such as from the Treasury Select Committee (2001), the *Corley* Committee of the actuarial profession (2001), the *Baird* report (2001), the Parliamentary Ombudsman (2003) and the *Penrose* Report (2004), commissioned by the U.K. government itself.

[206] Cf. *Humphry, D.* (2017), pp. 114-115.
[207] Cf. *O'Brian, C.* (2006), pp. 192-193.

The *Penrose* report, substantial in detail, named reasons for the Equitable Life's failure as well as provided suggestions for potential solution for reducing the risk of the occurrence of similar failure in the future. On the one hand *Penrose* stated in his report that the flow of information within the company was poorly organized, that the collective skills of the board was not adequate for the tasks required, and there were no effective arrangements for ensuring that there were detailed examinations of actuarial reports that actuarial reports were regularly poorly examined. Moreover, the board was underestimating the critical situation the company sled into during the late 1990s due to not being well informed about the company's internal operations, being a result of above mentioned circumstances. As a whole, *Penrose* concluded that the internal structure of the company was very badly organized. Moreover, members were not included into the governance of the society, admittedly also due to their own ignorance with respect to their member rights and obligations, thus not performing any role of external supervision either. Finally yet importantly, adequate risk management systems were not being operated within the company.[208] [209]

Receiving *Penrose's* report in 2004, the UK parliament began discussing future actions for the improvement of regulations regarding the insurance industry. In 2004, the Parliament discussed the report about "Equitable Life", written by *Penrose* (2004), which stated his own opinions and possible solutions for the insurance sector, based on the experience of "Equitable Life". In the Parliament, it also was discussed about the future actions that the government should take in order to improve the conditions and regulations of the insurance sector.

Resulting from these considerations, new regulations of firms having liabilities stemming from with-profit policy over 500 million pounds were being formulated and introduced by the Financial Service Authority. These new regulations basically foresaw an extension of then applying Solvency I directives for with-profit insurance business. On the one hand the FSA introduced the concept of "Realistic Reporting for With-Profits business", requiring insurers to value guarantees and options as part of valuing with-profit liabilities. On the other hand the FSA introduced the Individual Capital Adequacy Standard (ICAS) regime, which took effect in 2005, whose purpose it was to guarantee that insurance companies would be financially equipped well enough in the case of heavy stress being experienced on its assets held, and there that companies would hold enough capital to cope with all possible risks and liabilities. Eleven years after the introduction of ICAS and changes made by FSA, Solvency II regime came into effect in the EU, which

[208] Cf. *Penrose* (2004), pp. 739-740.
[209] Cf. *O'Brian, C.* (2006), p. 199.

bore similarities to the already prior regulatory regime introduced as a consequence of the failure of the equitable Life Insurance Company.[210]

6. The recent development and current situation of mutual type insurers in the United Kingdom

The following subchapter provides an overview of the development of performance of UK mutual insurers in their domestic market. Doing so, this chapter looks upon the development of premium payments collected annually by mutual insurers as well as the thereof calculated market share held. As stated in the previous chapter, the overall market share held by mutual insurers in the UK dropped significantly throughout the 1990s and first five years of the 2000s due to a wave of demutualizations performed by mutual insurers especially in the life insurance sector.[211] This resulted into the situation that in 2006 market share held by mutuals in the overall UK market had dropped below 4.5 percent at the end of 2007, whereas in the life insurance market it had even dropped to a devastating 2.5 percent.[212] [213] [214]

Nevertheless, looking upon the development of the recent eleven years it can be said that the 2007 situation marked the historic low-point of mutuals' market share held in the United Kingdom's insurance sector, as since 2008 a mostly positive trend in terms of mutual market share could be identified. Table 21 and figure 9 show the development of market share held from 2007 to 2016. As can be seen in the table as well as from figure 9, mutual-type insurance operators in the UK were able to almost annually increase their market share held, expanding it to 8.7 percent until the end of 2016. This increase of overall market share resulted from both, an increase of market share in the life insurance as well as non-life insurance segment.[215]

---

[210] Cf. *Humphry, D.* (2017), pp. 115-119.

[211] For reasons of this development please refer to the previous chapter.

[212] Cf. ICMIF (2009), p. 2;

[213] Cf. ICMIF (2017), p. 4;

[214] Market share held by mutuals in the non-life insurance segment was 11.1 percent for the year 2007. This nevertheless shows the comparatively much larger size of the UK life insurance market in terms of total annual premium collected.

[215] Companies included into the group of mutual insurers for the calculation of their market share were not only those, which are directly of the mutual form, but also

Table 21: Development of premium income recorded and market share held by mutual/cooperative insurers in the United Kingdom, 2007-2016

year	premium income (in million GBP)	market share	life insurance segment market share	non-life insurance market share
2007	£11,764	4.4%	2.5%	11.1%
2008	£12,376	5.8%	3.7%	11.2%
2009	£13,840	6.9%	4.5%	12.6%
2010	£15,535	8.0%	5.4%	13.2%
2011	£15,946	8.0%	5.0%	14.2%
2012	£16,250	7.8%	4.9%	13.9%
2013	£15,823	7.6%	4.6%	13.7%
2014	£16,416	8.0%	5.3%	13.6%
2015	£17,897	8.3%	5.8%	13.3%
2016	£19.634	8.7%	6.6%	12.8%

Source: ICMIF (2017), pp. 3-4.

Especially in the life insurance market, UK mutual insurers were able to regain some foothold, by recording a 164 percent increase of market share held. Nevertheless, with a share of only 6.6 percent mutual insurers remain to be far from their original strength in respective segment before the period of severe demutualization. In the non-life insurance market, mutual insurers were able to increase their market share held from 11.1 percent in 2007 to 14.2 percent in 2011. However, despite solid growth rates of premium income since 2014, market share held by mutuals in the non-life insurance sector has been decreasing slowly ever since, resulting that by the end of 2016 mutual insurers control had reduced to a mere 12.8 percent of the market. Still, it can be said, that UK mutual insurers were able to gain market share in both market segments during the period of 2007 to 2016.

subsidiaries majority owned by mutual companies and societies as well as non-profit insurers, as defined by the ICMIF. For a more detailed definition please refer to the following source: ICMIF (2017), p. 3.

Figure 9: Development of premium income recorded and market share held by mutual/cooperative insurers in the United Kingdom, 2007-2016

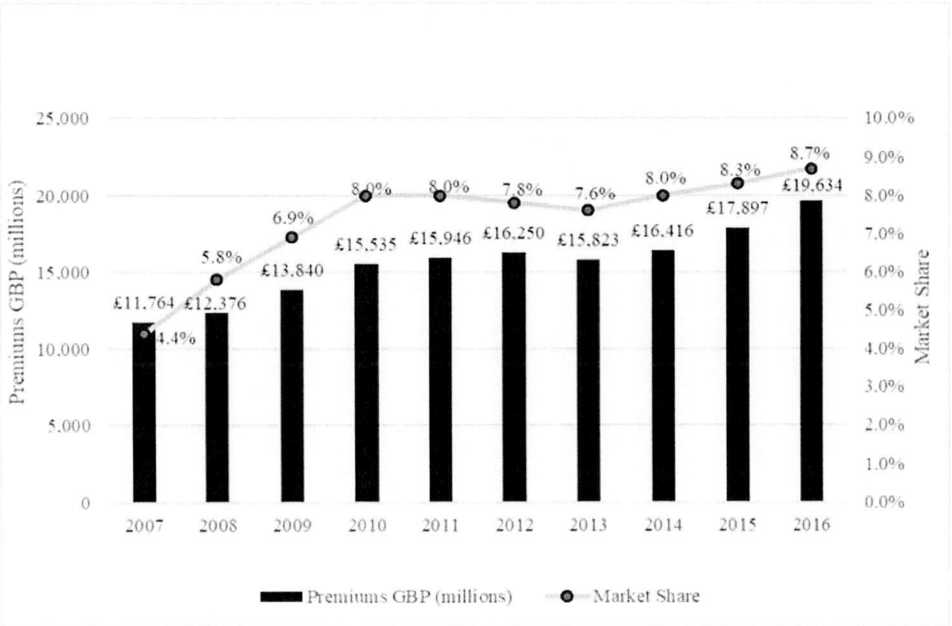

Source: ICMIF (2017), pp. 3-4.

Looking directly on the total numerical amount of premium payments collected annually it can be said that with a total of 19.63 billion UK pounds mutual insurers in the UK were able to increase their premium income by almost 67 percent between the years 2007 and 2016. This large increase of income especially resulted from extraordinary growth rates of business during the years of the economic crisis of 2009 and 2010 as well as during the current years of 2014 to 2016. Here it can be inferred from figures 10 and 11 that while the increase of premium income during the years 2009 and 2010 were mostly carried by solid growth rates of business in the non-life insurance sector, the more recent increase of growth of mutuals' premium payments resulted from a surge of premium income resulting from the life insurance business, with life insurance premium rates almost hitting the 10 billion pounds mark.

Figure 10: Development of insurance premium income recorded and market share held by mutual/cooperative insurers in the UK life insurance market, 2007-2016

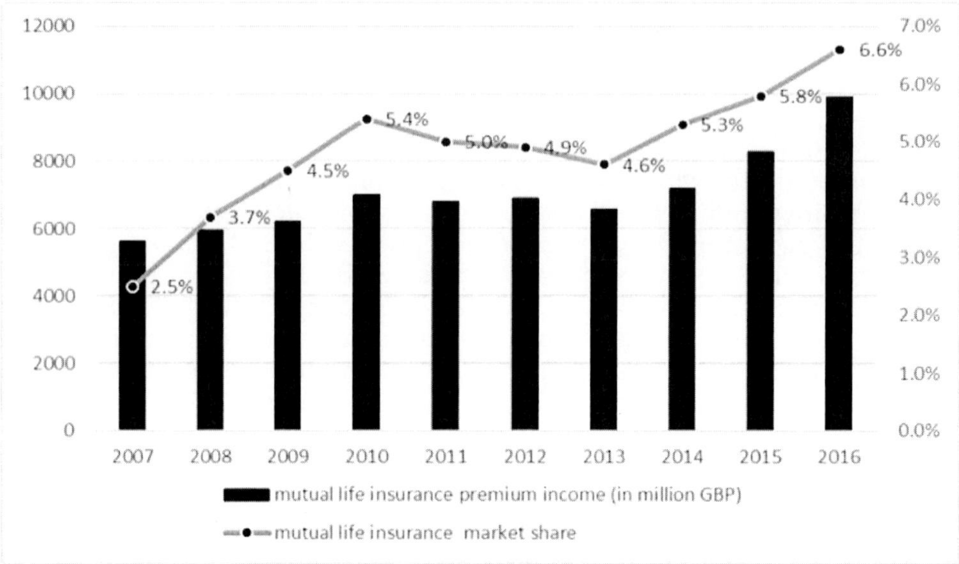

Source: ICMIF (2017), p. 4.

Figure 11: Development of insurance premium income recorded and market share held by mutual/cooperative insurers in the UK non-life insurance market, 2007-2016

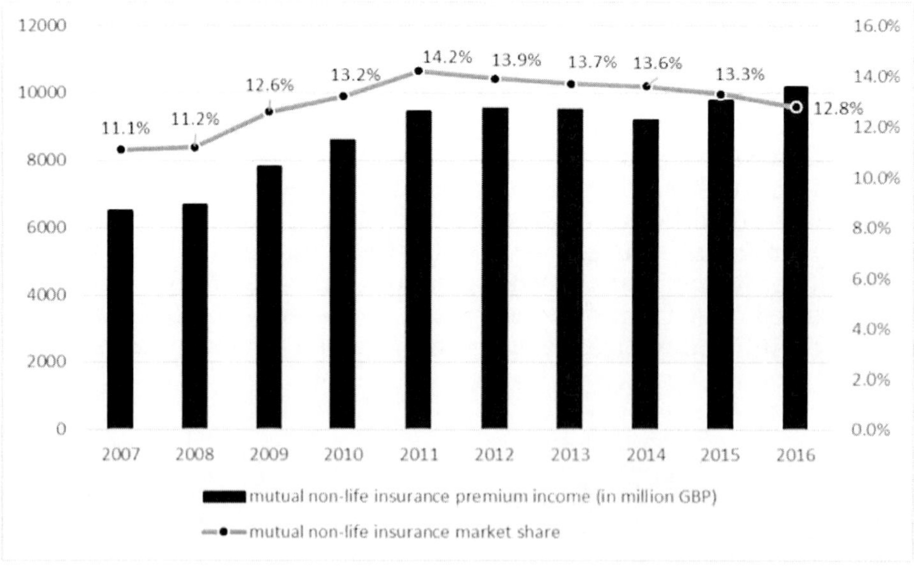

Source: ICMIF (2017), p. 4.

Whereas the overall development of annually collected premium payments was an overall positive one for mutual insurers in the UK between years 2007 and 2016, it does not fully explain the circumstance that mutuals were able to almost double their market share within this period of time. In fact a reason for the overall strong increase of market share during respective ten year period is the circumstance that the UK life insurance market experienced a significant decline in size, causing an overall deterioration of the UK insurance market, while mutual life insurers were not only able to maintain their annual premium income but to even expand it. While life insurance business generated approximately 211.7 billion pounds in 2007, this figure has dropped to only 144.4 billion pounds in 2016, representing a decline of almost 31.8 percent.[216] [217] Despite the country's non-life insurance market increasing in size during the same period of time, with annual premium income increasing from 57.8 billion pounds in 2007 to 70.2 billion pounds in 2016, gains in the non-life insurance segment were unable to compensate the severe losses experienced by the country's life insurance industry.[218] [219] Despite the strong decline of overall business in the life insurance sector and the therefrom resulting deterioration of the UK insurance market as whole, mutual insurers were on the contrary able to expand their life and non-life insurance business, explaining their strong increase in overall market share held during the period of 2007 to 2016. Nevertheless, considering the size of business operated by mutual insurers prior to the wave of demutualization of the 1990s and early 2000s, it can be said that mutual market share controlled nowadays remains to be comparatively small.

Despite the above presented overall growth of market share, it can be stated that the number of mutual insurers decreased from originally 208 mutual type insurers in 2007 to only 176 in 2015. Of these 176 mutual insurers, 101 were solely operating on the life insurance market, while 68 were solely operating in the non-life insurance market. The remaining five were composite insurers. Moreover, 141 out of mentioned 176 active mutual insurers were mutual or cooperative insurers in the legal form, while others comprised mostly out of subsidiaries majority-owned by financial mutuals or cooperatives and some were insurers of other legal forms that constitute as mutual-type organizations.[220] A more detailed depiction of the economic representation of these different types of mutual insurance operators is given by figure 12 for the en-

[216] Cf. Swiss Re (2009), p. 38.
[217] Cf. Swiss Re (2018), p. 41.
[218] Cf. Swiss Re (2009), p. 40.
[219] Cf. Swiss Re (2018), p. 43.
[220] Cf. AMICE/ICMIF (2018), p. 199.

tire mutual insurance market share over the years 2007 to 2015 and by figure 13 for the segments life and non-life insurance for the year 2015.

Figure 12: Development of total market share held by various types of mutual/cooperative insurers, 2007-2015

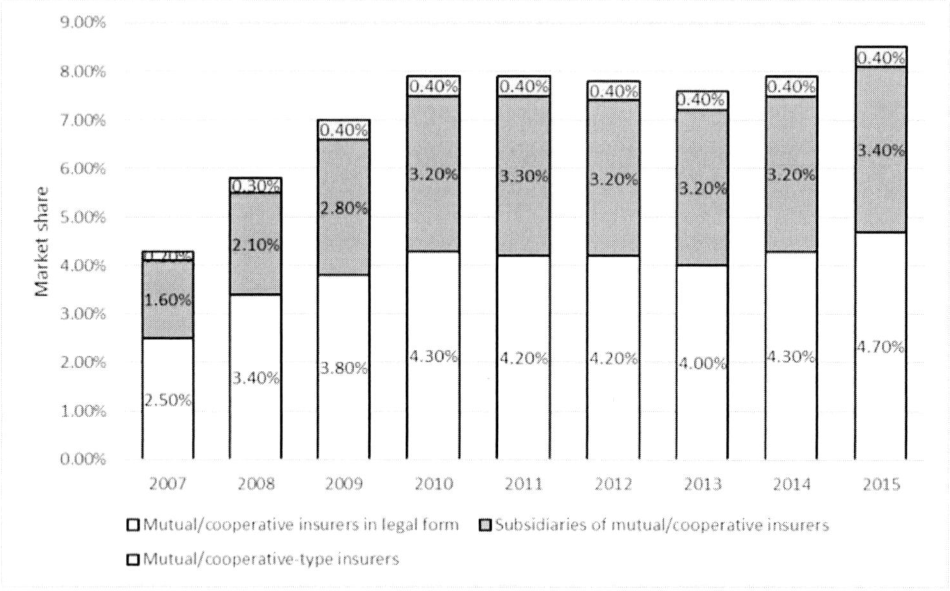

Source: AMICE/ICMIF (2018), p. 202.

As a last note it shall be mentioned, that during the recent period of extension of business and increase of market share held also the number of members and policyholders served by mutual insurers in the UK grew continuously. While it only was about 27.1 million in 2011, the number of members and policyholders recorded by mutual insurance operators in the UK had increased to about 30.7 million by the end of 2016.[221]

[221] ICMIF (2017), page 7.

Figure 13: Development of total market share held by various types of mutual/ cooperative insurers in the UK life and non-life insurance market of 2015

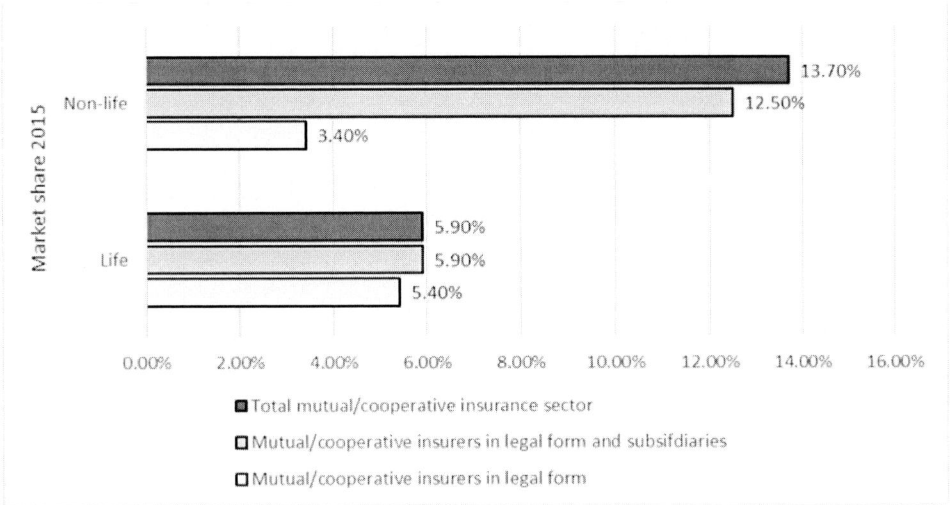

Source: AMICE/ICMIF (2018), p. 202.

7. Legal Framework and Regulations of Mutual-Type Insurances in UK

Whereas the majority of Western European countries established one or more separate specific legal forms for mutual insurers, the contrary can be said about the United Kingdom, as was already demonstrated in the above chapters. Thus an individual "mutual legal form" does not exist under the UK's legislation. Rather mutual insurers can be incorporated under various legal forms governed by various legal acts, representing the situation that the "being mutual" is broadly defined status that can be adopted by different legal forms. The following shall provide an overview of various legal forms, important regulatory authorities and important legislation, both national and trans-European, for insurance operators in the UK.

7.1 Different types and legal forms of mutual insurers under UK legislation

A demarcation of various legal forms optionally able to be chosen by mutual insurers in the United Kingdom is provided by the Financial Conduct Authority (FCA)[222] in the regulatory organization's handbook. Here it is stated that an insurance company can be classified as a mutual if

"(a) it is a body corporate that has no share capital (except a wholly owned subsidiary with no share capital but limited by guarantee), or
(b) it is a registered friendly society or incorporated friendly society, or
(c) a society registered or deemed to be registered under the Industrial and Provident Societies Act 1965 or under the Industrial and Provident Societies (Northern Ireland) Act 1969" (FCA Handbook, 2018, Glossary, ch.10).

Based on this classification mutual insurers in the UK must be established under one of the following five types of legal forms in the UK:[223] [224]

a) registered societies established under the Friendly Societies Acts 1992
b) the legal form of an unlimited company under the Companies Act of 2006.
c) a registered society under the Co-operative and Community Benefit Societies Act 2014[225] or a credit union

---

222 Here, it has to be mentioned that the main regulatory bodies of financial activities in the UK are the Financial Conduct Authority (FCA) and the Prudential Regulation Authority (PRA).
223 acc. to ICMIF (2018), p. 199.
224 acc. to *Shaw, et al.*, 2012, p. 327.
225 As of the 1st of August 2014 with the introduction of the new Co-operative and Community Benefit Societies Act, industrial and provident society originally established under the Industrial and Provident Societies Acts 1965 are labelled "registered societies". Moreover, the legal from is no longer available to be chosen by new undertakings, as with the introduction of the Co-operative and Community Benefit Societies Act 2014, the industrial and provident society legal form was replaced by two new legal forms, namely the co-operative society and the community benefit society (FCA, 2016b).

d) the legal form of a private company, which is either limited by shares or by guarantee and which falls under the regulations of the Companies Act of 2006.
e) a building society and
f) an EEA mutual society

Friendly societies are mutually-owned societies that are established either under the Friendly Societies Act of 1974 or the Friendly Societies Act of 1992. Before the two mentioned acts it was the Friendly Society Act 1947 regulating respective type of mutual insurers. Under this act friendly societies were able to operate in a multitude of different fields of activities differentiating these societies under different types of organizations such as "friendly societies, benevolent societies, cattle insurance societies, working men's clubs and specially authorized societies". Moreover, their activities were not exclusively restricted to financial support services such as providing sickness and unemployment benefits to its members and insuring livestock, as friendly societies were further allowed to perform activities such as running a social or sports clubs or managing allotments.[226]

Whereas the Act of 1947 has been abolished in the UK with the introduction of the Friendly Societies Act of 1974, the differentiation of fields of activity and thus type of organization is nowadays of importance, as regulatory requirements differ for various types of societies established under the act, based upon their field of activity. Broadly, two groups of activities are distinguished, being the group of unregulated activities and the group of regulated activities. Belonging to the former, activities "such as running a working man's club or providing discretionary benefits"[227] can be named. On the other hand, activities such as "carrying out contracts of insurance or paying non-discretionary benefits"[228] are classified as regulated activities. Based on activities performed, friendly societies are thus nowadays separated into regulated and unregulated friendly societies.[229]

One of the major differences between these two kinds of friendly societies is that societies performing regulated activates, including insurance services, have to be authorized by the Prudential Regulation Authority and are further subject to regulations and controls of the Financial Conduct Authority. Societies solely performing unregulated activates are exempted thereof. Furthermore requirements regarding annual reporting to authorities differ between the two types of societies, whereas a further distinction exists between directive and non-

226 Cf. FCA (2016a).
227 FCA (2016a).
228 FCA (2016a).
229 Cf. FCA (2016a).

directive societies.[230] In the case of a regulated society, which at the same time is also a directive one, an annually performed statement on annual returns and accounts has to be send to the FCA as well as PRA.[231] If a regulated society is distinguished as a non-directive one, the society further has to submit various valuation returns for its performed life and non-life insurance business.[232] In the case of an unregulated society statements regarding annual returns and final accounts only have to be submitted to the Financial Conduct Authority. Despite that, all societies under the Friendly Society Act 1992 have to be registered by the FCA.[233]

With the introduction of the 2014 Co-operative and Community Benefit Societies Act 2014, the former Industrial and Provident Societies Acts 1965 became replaced, with societies established under the act of 1965 now being subject to regulations of the former. As established in the new legislation, the legal form of a provident or industrial society cannot any longer be chosen as a legal form by a newly established society. In their place followed two new legal forms, namely the co-operative society and the community society. Despite that, already existing industrial and provident societies remain established under their original legal form, but are since August 1st 2014 deemed "pre-commencement societies.[234] Together all three legal forms represent so-called "registered societies", due to being obliged to register with the FCA and must further be authorized by the PRA if they want to provide regulated activities such as carrying out contracts of insurance.[235]

The rules related to the authorization and regulations are largely the same as for friendly societies. Moreover, societies have to pay for registration and further have to submit reports regarding their annual return and accounts on an annual basis.[236]

Besides above-mentioned legal forms, also a building society is established under the Building Society Act of 1986 is allowed to engage into insurance operations. Whereas building societies represent mutually-owned societies that traditionally focus on services such as banking and lending, with a heavy focus upon the mortgage business, they are also allowed under UK legislation to perform several other financial services including insurance. Identical to above mentioned legal forms

[230] A non-directive friendly society is a friendly society below the thresholds for inclusion in Solvency II and is thus not subject to EU life and non-life directives. Non-directive friendly societies are usually small scale societies that are subject to restrictions regarding the range of their insurance business.

[231] Cf. FCA (2016a), (2018).

[232] Cf. FCA (2018a).

[233] Cf. FCA (2016a).

[234] Cf. FCA (2016b).

[235] Cf. FCA (2016c), (2019).

[236] Cf. FCA (2016c).

building societies are authorized by the Prudential Regulation Authority (PRA) and regulated by Financial Conduct Authority (FCA).[237]

As demonstrated so far it can be seen that, contrary to most other European countries, mutual insurers in the UK may have a variety of legal forms, which are mutuals in their nature. In addition to those mutual legal forms, mutual insurers in the UK can further be established under legal forms primarily used for for-profit business activities under the general "Companies Act" of 2006. These available legal forms under the Companies Act of 2006 and suitable for mutual insurance activities are the "unlimited company with no share capital[238], the "private company limited by shares or guarantee" and until 2006 the "private company limited by private statute".[239] [240]

In addition to these legal forms, there are also member-owned protection organizations in the UK that from a legal perspective are not carrying out insurance business, but nevertheless provide insurance like services. Such organizations are referred to as "discretionary mutuals".[241] Only operating as quasi-insurers "discretionary mutuals" are not subject to the rules of the FCA. Nevertheless, of such organizations, being primarily of the legal form of a friendly society might be still obliged to register with the FCA and fall under its regulation, supposing they are providing any other kind of other "regulated activities" besides their discretionary benefit schemes. In such a case, societies also fall under the regulation of the PRA.[242]

Finally yet importantly, besides all above mentioned domestic legal forms available to mutual insurers in the UK, mutual companies and societies, which are operating their business in the UK, might also have their head office located in one of the European Economic Area (EEA) states. These insurers are labelled EEA firms under UK legislation, whereas the process of establishing their branches or agents in the UK is called "passporting". If a firm wants to extend its business that way into the United Kingdom, it has to make its home state supervising agency notify UK regulators about the company's intention of passporting to the UK market. Moreover, subsequent information has to be sending to the PRA allowing it to assess the suitability of the EEA insurance company to operate in the UK market.[243] Legal forms falling

[237] Cf. FCA (2016d).

[238] A prominent example of such a mutual would be the "Equitable Life".

[239] Examples of this particular type of mutual would be the "Cornish Mutual".

[240] Cf. *Shaw et al.* (2012), p. 330.

[241] Despite operating insurance like business, representatives of discretionary mutuals were successful to argue before court not tob e insurers. (*Shaw et al.* (2012), pp. 208-209).

[242] Cf. FCA (2019a).

[243] Cf. Bank of England (2019): "Passporting".

originating from a country of the EEA other than the UK and falling under the definition mutual society are the following:

a) "a body which is a European Cooperative Society for the purposes of Council Regulation;
b) a body which is established as a cooperative under the law of an EEA state as mentioned in that Regulation;
c) a body which is a cooperative or mutual undertaking of such description as the Treasury specify by order and which is established or operates in accordance with the laws of an EEA state or any of the Channel Islands or the Isle of Man"[244]

As demonstrated in the above, mutual insurers in the United Kingdom are existing under a multitude of different legal forms, demonstrating a clear difference in comparison to the majority of other European countries. Despite this situation, it has to be mentioned once more that the most common legal form of mutual insurers in the UK market is the one of the friendly society.

With a multitude of different legal forms available to operate mutual insurance in the United Kingdom a clear distinction between different terms for mutual insurers become important. The following provides a short overview of various terms and which types of legal forms they include:

a) The term mutual insurance company refers to all mutual insurers that are not a mutual society and thus are not incorporated as a friendly society, a registered society under the Co-operative and Community Benefit Societies Act of 2014 or as an EEA mutual society
b) On the other hand, the term mutual insurance society refers to all insurers that are established as a mutual society, therefore including the legal forms of a friendly society or a registered society under the Co-operative and Community Benefit Societies Act of 2014 or an EEA mutual society
c) The term mutual insurers describes all types of legal forms suitable for the performance of mutual insurance operations in the UK,
d) The term mutual as used in the Building Societies (Funding) and Mutual Societies (Transfers) Act 2007 refers to all mutual societies (friendly societies and registered societies) as well as some building societies and credit institutions,

[244] *Shaw et al.* (2012), p. 329.

e) Under the term financial mutuals fall all mutuals according to the above mentioned Act of 2007 as well as all mutual insurance companies that do not fall under respective Act,
f) Last but not least, the general term mutual refers to the all-financial as well as non-financial mutuals.[245]

7.2 Laws, regulations and authorities applicable and regulating mutual-type Insurance

Due to the multitude of different legal forms suitable for operating mutual insurance services mutual insurers in the UK market are further regulated by various legislative acts, partly mentioned the above stated. The following provides a list of the major legislative acts applying to the various types of mutual insurers in the UK:

a) Companies Act 2006
b) Friendly Societies Act 1992
c) Co-operative and Community Benefit Societies Act 2014
d) Building Societies (Funding) and Mutual Societies (Transfers) Act 2007
e) Building Societies Act 1986

Irrespective of the legal form, all mutuals operating regulated societies, which in general include insurance and re-insurance services, have to obtain authorization under the Financial Service and Markets Act 2000 in order to participate on the insurance market. Regulatory oversight of insurers operating in the UK is performed by the Financial Conduct Authority (FCA) and the Prudential Regulation Authority (PRA) as stated in the same act.[246]

7.3. The Financial Conduct Authority (FCA) and the Prudential Regulation Authority (PRA)

Today, the UK financial market is regulated by two regulatory agencies, namely the already prior mentioned Financial Conduct Authority (FCA) and Prudential Regulatory Authority (PRA).[247] Whereas the Financial Services and Markets Act 2000 originally established a single regulatory agency, namely the Financial Service Agency (FSA), regulatory changes in the form of the Solvency II directive and the introduction of new capital requirements, a change towards a dual-regulated

[245] Cf. *Shaw et al.* (2012), p. 330-331.
[246] Cf. Financial Services and Markets Act 2000, part IV, Permission to Carry on Regulated Activities.
[247] Cf. Financial Services and Markets Act 2000, part I-A, The Regulators.

scheme was decided to be performed, having the goal of improving the regulatory control over the financial sector. As a result the FSA was replaced by the FCA and the PRA in 2013.[248] [249] [250]

With the beginning of 2018 the Financial Conduct Authority (FCA) was responsible for the regulation of business activities of more than 58,000 financial service firms and financial marketers in the UK and acted as the prudential regulator for more than 18,000 of these companies.[251] On the other hand the Prudential Regulatory Authority (PRA) was the prudential regulator for approximately 1500 financial institutions including building societies, banks, insurers and credit unions. In both cases the major task of the prudential regulator is to "[...] promote the safety and soundness of the firms [...]"[252] being regulated. The regulatory mandates of the FCA and the PRA, despite being similar in nature, are thus different. Broadly speaking the FCA's responsibilities under the Financial Services and Markets Act 2000 as a regulator includes:

a) "regulating standards of conduct in retail and wholesale markets;
b) Supervising trading infrastructures that support those markets
c) The prudential supervision of firms that are not PRA-regulated; and
d) The functions of the UK Listing Authority"[253]

The major objective of the FCA is "[...] to ensure that the markets for financial services function well. Three operational objectives support this: securing an appropriate degree of protection for consumers (including wholesale consumers); protecting and enhancing the integrity of the UK financial system; and promoting effective competition in the interests of consumers in the markets for financial services."[254]

The responsibilities of the PRA, being incorporated within the Bank of England, consist mostly to conduct the authorisation of financial institutes wishing to operate in the UK as well as to act as the prudential supervisor of financial institutions falling under the categories individual deposit taker (includes banks, building societies and credit unions), insurer (including friendly societies in addition to regular

[248] Cf. *Shaw et al.* (2012), p. 329.

[249] Cf. Association of British Insurers (2018).

[250] Technically the FSA was renamed into the FCA, while part of the regulatory tasks formerly performed by the FSA were transferred to the PRA. (Cf. Financial Services and Markets Act 2000, Part I-A)

[251] Cf. FCA (2018b).

[252] Cf. Ibid.

[253] Bank of England (2018), p. 1.

[254] Ibid.

companies) and designated investment firm. With its activities the PRA's major objective is [...]to promote the safety and soundness of dual-regulated firms, and it is required to advance this objective primarily by seeking to minimise any adverse effects of firm failure on the UK financial system and to ensure that firms carry on their business in a way that avoids adverse effects on the system."[255] In addition the PRA has the goal to contribute to guarantee an appropriate degree of insurance policyholders' protection, through its prudential supervision of insurers active in the UK.[256]

Together the FCA and PRA represent the UK's 'Twin Peaks' micro regulatory system. Nevertheless, despite both agencies operating and fulfilling their regulatory tasks separately from each other, coordination and cooperation is important to be performed between the two regulators.

7.3 Authorization of Insurance Activities in the UK

With insurance services falling under the category of regulated activities, insurance operates in the UK have to apply for authorization to both, the FCA and the PRA. Entities allowed to file an application for authorization are:

a) "an individual;
b) a body corporate;
c) a partnership; or
d) an unincorporated association" (2018, part IV)."[257]

After authorization, insurance companies in the UK are only allowed to provide services for which they are particularly authorized. Legal forms that are required to obtain authorization include companies limited by shares or by guarantee, unlimited companies, societies which are established under the Co-operative and Community Benefit Societies Act 2014 and Friendly Societies established under the Friendly Societies Act of 1992.[258] Moreover, also Lloyd's underwriters must ob-

[255] Ibid., p. 2.
[256] Cf. Ibid., p. 2.
[257] Cf. Financial Services and Markets Act 2000, part IV, Permission to Carry on Regulated Activities.
[258] An EEA firm may not apply for permission under this section to carry on a regulated activity which it is, or would be, entitled to carry on in exercise of an EEA right, whether through a United Kingdom branch or by providing services in the United Kingdom. (Financial Services and Markets Act 2000, part IV, Permission to Carry on Regulated Activities.)

tain authorization in order to operate insurance services. In order to obtain authorization the PRA, companies must fulfil several threshold conditions as well as other PRA and FCA requirements. Moreover, an application is only successful if both regulatory bodies agree upon the authorization of the company.

While UK legislation splits insurance business in the UK into two segments, namely long-term and general insurance business, an insurer in the UK is allowed to operate one or both lines of business, given that the operation of particular line of business is permitted by the Act under which particular insurer has been established. In the case of operating both, long-term and general insurance business, the insurer has to obtain authorization for both lines of businesses separately, since life and non-life insurance service are threaded and regulated under UK legislation separately. Otherwise, it appears that there is no difference in regulations among different ownership (joint-stock and mutual) and legal forms. Furthermore, a composite insurer must separately manage its business of both to lines of business, meaning that profits and accounts of long-term and general insurance activities must be recorded completely separately, as if they would be performed by separate firms. Based on the premise, "[...] interests of policyholders of contracts of long-term insurance are not prejudiced by activities relating to the firm's general insurance business and the interests of policyholders of contracts of general insurance are not prejudiced by activities relating to the firm's long-term insurance business."[259] Moreover dividends to policyholders of long-term insurance contracts must only stem from activities relating to the insurer's long-term insurance business.[260]

7.4 Trans-European legislation on the insurance sector

Besides domestic legislation, insurance providers operating in the UK are further subject to directives issued by the European Union. In general it can be said that there are three major directives, which regulate insurance companies and markets within the EU.[261] Of those three the Solvency II directive, published for the first time in autumn 2009, but not coming into effect until the 1st of January 2016, can be labelled as the recently most important one. As mentioned in the above, it was this directive leading to the replacement of the FSA with the FCA and PRA in 2013 in the UK. The following shall shortly describe the Solvency II directive and its implications for UK regulation practice.

[259] PRA Rulebook: Solvency II Firms: Composites Instrument 2015, Section 2, 2.2.
[260] Cf. PRA Rulebook: Solvency II Firms: Composites Instrument 2015, Section 2, 2.2.
[261] Cf. *Grijpstra et al.* (2012), p. 38.

As stated in the FCA handbook, Solvency II is defined as "the Directive of the European Parliament and of the Council of 25 November 2009 on the taking-up and pursuit of the business of Insurance and Reinsurance".[262] The official overall goal of the Solvency II directive is to guarantee protection of insurance policyholders in the forthcoming establishment of a truly unified European insurance market. Doing so provisions of the Solvency II directive have the objective of fully harmonizing regulatory rules executed by regulatory agencies of the various EU member states.[263] [264] In other words, Solvency II directive wants to "[…] consolidate and expand the previously existing EU directives in the area of insurance and align that policy more clearly with the goal of creating a regulatory framework for primary insurance and reinsurance that achieves the greatest possible uniformity throughout Europe. Consequently, the Solvency II Framework Directive demands the creation of uniform conditions in the conduct of the insurance business throughout the internal market."[265]

The introduction of the Solvency II directive caused regulatory authorities of EU countries to adapt existing regulatory practices and provisions accordingly. In the UK, subsequent changes caused by the Solvency II directive were controlled and supervised by the Prudential Regulatory Authority. With respect to the applicability of Solvency II based provisions on mutual insurers in the UK it has to be stated that the PRA distinguishes between two types of insurers, namely directive (or Solvency II) firms and non-directive firms. While insurers of the former type are subject to Solvency II based provisions, latter are, due to the small scale of their operation, exempted from respective regulations. As stated in the PRA Handbook insurers with annual gross premium payments lower than 5 million € and gross technical provisions lower than 25 million € in general do not fall under Solvency II provisions. Nevertheless, further requirements to be account as a non-directive insurer are presented in detail in the PRA Handbook under the chapter Non-Solvency II Firms, Insurance General Application. For example, insurers operating re-insurance business which generates more than 500000 € of annual premium income or results in technical provisions of above 2.5 million €, are Solvency II firms, regardless of their size of business operations. Moreover, insurers operating in segments such as liability, credit and suretyship insurance are also always subject to Solvency II based provisions.[266]

---

[262] FCA (2019b).

[263] Cf. *Dreher, M.* (2015), p. 4.

[264] Cf. *Gründl et al.* (2016), p. 3.

[265] *Dreher, M.* (2015), p. 4.

[266] Cf. PRA Rulebook (2016), Non-SII Firms, UK Solvency II Firm, 2.3.

With respect to mutual insurers it can be said that, irrespective of their legal form, above presented classification of Solvency II and non-directive firms also applies to them. As a result mutual insurance companies under the Companies Act 2006, as well as the insurance operating societies under the Friendly Society Act 1992 and the Co-operative and Community Benefit Societies Act 2014 (if having to be registered with the PRA due to operating regulated activities such as insurance) can be either classified as directive mutual insurers or non-directive mutual insurers.[267] [268] Here it has to be mentioned, that further clarifications for friendly societies for falling under the "non-directive" classification do exist, extending the scope of non-directive societies.[269] Nevertheless in the case a friendly society is engaged in long-term or general insurance business , its annual gross premium is still not allowed to surpass 5 million € in order to be exempted from Solvency II based provisions.[270] Mutual insurance companies and societies being regarded as directive insurers are subject to the same provisions and thus regulated the same way as other non-mutual insurance operators in the UK.[271]

The following gives a short overview of the major concept of the Solvency II directive principle, which consists out of three pillars:

Pillar 1 defines solvency capital requirements of insurance operators. Here it is stated by the PRA that insurance operators classified as directive firms are required to have an adequate amount of funds based upon its solvency capital requirement (SCR) calculated in accordance to SCR rules. Generally speaking, this solvency capital requirement (SCR) shall include all the quantifiable risks that companies are exposed in their current business, "[…] including at least the non-life underwriting risk, life underwriting risk, health underwriting risk, market risk, credit risk, and operational risk"[272], quantifiable risks resulting from new expected business in the next 12 months and the risk of unexpected losses from existing business. The companies are required to report the calculation of their SCR to the PRA every year.[273]

The second pillar of the Solvency II directive defines required provisions regarding the corporate governance requirements for insurers. Here the PRA handbook states that solvency II firms must have stated

[267] Cf. FCA (2016c).

[268] Cf. PRA Rulebook (2016), Non-SII Firms, UK Solvency II Firm, 2.1-2.6.

[269] For further information refer to: http://www.prarulebook.co.uk/rulebook/Glossary/FullDefinition/53219/25-08-2015.

[270] Cf. PRA (2015).

[271] Cf. PRA Rulebook (2016), Non-SII Firms, UK Solvency II Firm.

[272] PRA Rulebook, Requirement to Hold Eligible Own Funds Covering the SCR, 3.3 (1).

[273] Cf. PRA Rulebook (2016), SII Firms, Solvency Capital Requirement – General Provisions.

their policies regarding risk management, internal control, internal audit and, when relevant, outsourcing, guarantee their enforcement, review them annually and adopt changes if deemed to be necessary due to newly evolving circumstances. Further specifications to each of these areas can be found in the PRA handbook under section SII Firms – Conditions Governing Business. Moreover, directive firms are required to annually produce and submit reports regarding a firm's assessment of its applied risk management and asset-liability management policies and procedures. The main purpose of the second pillar is thus to make European insurance markets more stable through enforcing regularity and continuity in the business of insurance operators.[274]

Pillar 3 contains provisions regarding the reporting and disclosure of reports and required to be submitted to the PRA and/or have to be published. According to the PRA Handbook UK insurance operators must establish and submit two kinds of reports, namely a regular supervisory report (RSR) and the Solvency and Financial Condition report (SFCR). Here, deadlines for submitting these reports had been set to continuously become shorter during the last three years, with reports for insurers' financial years ending throughout 2019 having to be submitted within a 14 weeks thereafter. Of the mentioned two reports the latter contains detailed information about a firm's business and performance, system of governance and adequacy of risk profile, a description of the risk exposure, risk concentration, risk mitigation and risk sensitivity, a description of assets, technical provisions and other liabilities held and recorded and a description of the capital management of the firm.[275] The RSR on the other hand must contain qualitative or quantitative elements, historic, current or prospective elements as well as data from internal or external sources, portraying "the nature, scale and complexity of the business of the firm, and in particular the risks inherent in that business"[276] The objective of provisions stemming from the third pillar is of course to enable the responsible regulatory agency, in this case the PRA, to evaluate the appropriateness of insurers' operations, risk and financial assessments as well as financial conditions and whether or not these are in compliance with provisions based upon the Solvency II directive.[277] [278]

[274] Cf. PRA Rulebook (2016), SII Firms, Conditions Governing Business, 2.1-3.11.
[275] Cf. PRA Rulebook (2016), SII Firms, Reporting, 3.1-3.8.
[276] PRA Rulebook (2016), SII Firms, Reporting, 2.4.
[277] Cf. PRA Rulebook (2016), SII Firms, Reporting, 2.1-3.8.
[278] Cf. PRA Rulebook (2016), SII Firms, Transitional Measures, 3.1-3.2.

7.5 Deferred Shares Act 2015

An often-argued major disadvantage of mutual insurers in comparison to their stock company counterparts is the formers' inability to raise additional funds on capital markets. While insurers of the latter group are able to raise capital through the issuance of new shares on equity markets, mutual insurers are unable to perform any similar measures of capitalization, due to policyholders being owners of the mutual insurance operator. As this situation also applies to UK mutual insurers, a new form of quasi-equity capitalization measures was proposed for mutual insurers with the draft of the Mutuals' Deferred Shares Act in 2015. Under the Deferred Shares Act from 2015 mutual-type insures, including those established under the UK Companies Act, the Friendly Societies Act from 1992 as well as others, would have become equipped with a new method of raising additional funds through the issuance of so-called "deferred shares".[279]

Similar to shares issued by stock companies, deferred shares would have allowed investors to participate in profits of mutuals in the form of dividends and would equip them with voting rights. However, the major difference between ordinary shares issued by stock companies and deferred shares of mutual type insurers is that in the case of the latter voting rights are restricted. As stated in the Mutuals' Deferred Shares Act, holders of deferred shares, regardless of the actual number of shares held, are equipped with only one ordinary vote, having the same weight as any vote of any policyholder allowed to participate in the general annual meeting of their mutual insurer.[280] Furthermore as stated by the HM Treasury it was foreseen in the event of introducing the act that mutuals would have been able to choose between two types of deferred shares, namely "ordinary" and "preference" deferred shares. The main distinction between these two types of shares was suggested to be in the level of subordination of the shareholder members' interests.[281] "The interests of 'ordinary' shareholders rank equal to the interests of nonshareholder members of the mutual, while those of 'preference' shareholders rank just above; both rank below policyholders and non-subordinated creditors."[282]

With the Mutuals' Deferred Shares Act having been proposed in 2015, it appears that the act can be seen as an action taken by the UK parliament to support mutual type insurers in meeting tightened capital requirements coming into effect under the introduction of the Solvency II directive in 2016. Nevertheless, after the end of consulta-

---

[279] Cf. Mutuals' Deferred Shares Act 2015, 1 (3), 3 (1).

[280] Cf. Mutuals' Deferred Shares Act 2015, 2 (1).

[281] Cf. HM Treasury (2016), p. 7.

[282] HM Treasury (2016), p. 7.

tion with respect to the proposed Act, "the government decided in October 2018 not to lay the new regulation, due to various reasons."[283] The position may be reconsidered if material factors change in the future.[284]

While the UK government's decision not to introduce the Act forestall a new source of funds for mutual insurers in the UK, it has to be mentioned, that according to estimations of the HM Treasury the practice of issuing deferred shares would have been a costly undertaking for most mutuals under the drafted regulations, with estimation for necessary investments per mutual insurer being around £100,000. Due to such costs, the HM Treasury predicted that in the event of an introduction of the act only large-scale mutual insurers would be able to use this new source of funding.[285]

8. Conclusion

During the 18th and 19th century, Britain's rise to an economic super power was closely connected with the development of the insurance business. At the same time, central banks and a stock market were established. By the middle of the 19th century, Britain turned into the centre of trade and commerce and London became the centre of the insurance industry. This development was also due to Britain's dominant position in the marine insurance business that was based on the monopoly of two chartered joint stock companies. After the Bill regarding the monopoly was repealed in 1824, many new single companies entered the marine insurance sector, while the rise of Lloyd's to an important insurer continued. At the turn of the century, the marine insurance market changed drastically by the rise of composite insurance companies which led to a phase of mergers between 1905 and 1927.

The development of fire insurance companies, on the other hand, was triggered by the Great Fire of London in 1666. Apart from an unsuccessful attempt to establish a public fire insurance institution in London, joint stock companies and mutuals controlled the fire insurance market, while friendly societies were limited to smaller towns. At the turn of the 17th century, three fire mutual insurance companies were founded in London and worked successfully until the 1760s. Later however, they faced financial difficulties due to heavy losses caused by

---

[283] A detailed outline of these reasons can be found in the literature source "HM Treasury (2018)" in the bibliography.

[284] HM Treasury (2018), p. 7.

[285] Cf. HM Treasury (2016), p. 13.

large fires. Their total market share dwindled from 45 percent in 1725 to 14 in 1795. During this period, the London market became much more complex, a development that favoured joint stock companies. Their numbers increased and soon they controlled the market, leading mutual insurances to their downfall. The existing fire mutuals either demutualized or changed their business strategies according to the work of joint stock companies. Two waves of foundations, the first during the 1820s to the 1830s and the second between 1834 and 1850, led to fierce competition between the companies. During this time, the insurance market became more and more concentrated due to mergers, bankruptcies, and withdrawals. As a result, companies developed various strategies to handle the competition including a huge merger and acquisition phase that influenced the British insurance market sustainable. Until the 1850s, the market share of the former successful mutuals dwindled under 7 percent. Additionally, the introduction of a tariff system, the foundation of the "Fire Offices Committee" (FOC) in 1868, and the beginning of new non-life insurance segments, such as accident or plate glass insurances altered permanently the insurance industry. In these new insurance segments, mutual companies became rather strong. Finally, the composite insurers emerged and changed the market structure drastically. At the end of the 19th century, a wave of amalgamation started and lasted until the 1920s.

Although life assurance existed in Britain since the late 16th century, it was limited to term assurance on business partners and merchants. These short-term policies hindered the development of the life assurance business. Nevertheless, between 1696 and 1721 over 60 life assurance office with approximately 12,000 policyholders existed. During the 18th century, many companies offering life assurances by adopting the organisation form of joint stock companies, a fashionable trend among business firms and charity societies. At the end of the 18th century, six life assurance offices existed, two mutuals and four joint stock companies. The life assurance business started to grow during the 19th century and from the 1820s onwards, it became highly competitive. While this insurance sector was dominated by middle class policyholders, friendly societies offered industrial insurances focusing on the working class. Therefore, the market was highly divided, socially as well as economically. While in London most policyholders were wealthy, the provincial policyholders had less financial capacities. Between 1800 and 1899, the number of mutual life assurance companies increased from 2 to 23, with a peak of 38 companies in 1850. At the same time, joint stock companies were able to rise their numbers from 8 to 69 and had a peak with 151 companies in 1850. Many of the companies established between 1843 and 1870 disappeared due to fraudulent activities and led eventually to the first major parliamen-

tary regulation in the United Kingdom insurance industry, the Life Assurance Companies Act (1870). With the introduction of this Act, a stabilization of the former turbulent life insurance business started and lasted the following three decades. During the same period, the market share held by proprietary offices increased steadily, despite the number of proprietary life insurance offices decreasing from 1877 onwards. This decrease of numbers of proprietary insurers was mainly due to various mergers and acquisitions, which occurred nevertheless much less frequently than during the period of the 1850s and 1860s. At the same time, the entrance of new insurance companies, especially mutual insurance companies, was reduced to a minimum due to new regulations put in place, such as required minimum capitalisation levels for new life insurance operators. Furthermore, a tremendously positive development of the UK's insurance industry occurred during the second half of the 20th century. The country's property and casualty as well as life insurance industry were able to expand tremendously their scope of business, resulting from steady economic growth as well as increasing wealth of the general population. At the same time, mutuals were able to maintain their relevance within the industry, despite fluctuating shares of market held and the entrance of many new proprietary insurance operators, especially in the segment of property and casualty insurance. It was not until the 1990s that, especially in the case of the life insurance industry, the strong presence of mutual insurance operators dwindled, which was caused by a wave of demutualization followed a wave a series of takeovers of many former mutual life insurance companies. This led to a severe decrease of market share held by mutual insurance companies, being especially drastic in the case of mutual life insurers, whose market share dropped to an all-time low of almost 4 percent during the mid-2000s. Lastly, looking upon the recent development of mutual insurance in the United Kingdom since 2007, a steady increase of market share can be recognized in both, the life and non-life insurance segment. Despite that, with the majority of traditional mutual insurance companies being gone from the market and the majority of mutual insurers being of the legal form of friendly societies, mutual insurers are anywhere both close to their past importance and visible presence in the United Kingdom's insurance market.

Bibliography

ABI (1999), Association of British Insurers, UK insurance and long-term savings.

AMICE/ICMIF (2018), Facts and figures: Mutual and cooperative insurance in Europe Vol 2, *AMICE aisbl & International Cooperative and Mutual Insurance Federation (ICMIF)*, Cheshire.

APPG (2006), Windfalls or Shortfalls? – The true cost of Demutualisation, The All-Party Parliamentary Group for Building Societies & Financial Mutuals, London.

Association of British Insurers (2018), How our industry is regulated, https://www.abi.org.uk/data-and-resources/tools-and-resources/regulation/, retrieval: 03.03.2019.

Bank of England (2018), Bank of England Annual Report and Accounts.

Bank of England, "Passporting", https://www.bankofengland.co.uk/prudential-regulation/authorisations/passporting, retrieval: 05.03.2019.

Beveridge, W. (1948), Voluntary action; a report on methods of social advance.

Board of Trade (1961), Insurance Companies Act, 1958: Summary of Statements of Insurance Business deposited with the Board of Trade, 1960, H.M. Stationery Office, London.

Board of Trade (1959), Insurance Companies Act, 1958: Summary of Statements of Insurance Business deposited with the Board of Trade, 1958, H.M. Stationery Office, London.

Board of Trade (1963), Insurance Companies Act, 1958: Summary of Statements of Insurance Business deposited with the Board of Trade, 1962, H.M. Stationery Office, London.

Board of Trade (1965), Insurance business: Summary of accounts and statements deposited with the Board of Trade under the Insurance Companies Act 1958 for accounting years ended on or after Dec. 31, 1963 and on or before Aug. 31, 1964, H.M. Stationery Office, London.

Board of Trade (1967), Insurance business: Summary of accounts and statements deposited with the Board of Trade under the Insurance Companies Act 1958 for accounting years ended on or after Sep. 30, 1964 and on or before Aug. 31, 1966, H.M. Stationery Office, London.

Board of Trade (1971), Insurance business, statistics, London.

Board of Trade (1972), Insurance business, statistics, London.

Booth, P., M. (2007), Freedom with Publicity – The Actuarial Profession and United Kingdom Insurance Regulation from 1844 to 1945, A.A.S., 2, I, 115-145.

Bridgewater, A. (1995), The modern mutual insurance company in Britain, in: *Peiner, W.* Grundlagen des Versicherungsvereins auf Gegenseitigkeit, Köln.

Business Statistics Office (1978), Insurance Business Statistics 1976, H.M. Stationery Office, London.

Business Statistics Office (1981), Insurance Business Statistics 1978-79, H.M. Stationery Office, London.

Business Statistics Office (1984), Insurance Business Statistics 1982, H.M. Stationery Office, London.

Carter, R., Falush, P. (2009), The British Insurance Industry Since 1900 – The Era of transformation, Palgrave MacMillan Studies in Banking and Financial Institutions.

Clark, G. (1997), Life insurance in the society and culture of London, 1700-75, in: Urban History, vol. 24, pt. 1 (May 1997).

Clayton, G. (1971), British insurance. London.

Cockerell, H.A.L.; *Green, E.* (1976), The British insurance business 1547-1970. An introduction and guide to historical records in the United Kingdom. London.

Cordery, S. (2003), British Friendly Societies, 1750-1914, Palgrave Macmillan.

Dreher, M. (2015), Harmonization of insurance supervisory law, in: *Dreher, M.* (2015), Treatises on Solvency II, chap. 1, Springer, Berlin, pp. 1-25.

FCA (2016a), Friendly societies: an introduction, https://www.fca.org.uk/firms/friendly-societies-introduction, retrieval: 03.03.2019.

FCA (2016b), Co-operative and Community Benefit Societies Act 2014, https://www.fca.org.uk/firms/registered-societies-introduction/co-operative-community-benefit-societies-act-2014, retrieval: 02.03.2019.

FCA (2016c), Registered societies: an introduction, https://www.fca.org.uk/firms/registered-societies-introduction, retrieval: 03.03.2019.

FCA (2016d), Building societies: an introduction, https://www.fca.org.uk/firms/building-societies-introduction, retrieval: 03.03.2019.

FCA (2018a), Reporting requirements: mutual societies, https://www.fca.org.uk/firms/reporting-requirements-mutual-societies, retrieval 02.03.2019.

FCA (2018b), About the FCA, https://www.fca.org.uk/about/the-fca, retrieval: 03.03.2019.

FCA (2019a), Register a mutual society, https://www.fca.org.uk/firms/register-mutual-society, retrieval: 03.03.2019.

FCA (2019b), Solvency II Directive, https://www.handbook.fca.org.uk/handbook/glossary/G2765.html, retrieval: 07.03.2019

Financial Services and Markets Act 2000.

Garrioch, D. (2016), 1666 and London's fire history: a re-evaluation. The Historical Journal 59(2).

Gosden, P. (1973), Self-Help: Voluntary associations in the 19th century.

Grijpstra et al. (2012), The role of mutual societies in the 21st century. European Parliament. Brusseles, Netherlands.

Gründl et al. (2016), Solvency II – Eine Einführung. Grundlagen der neuen Versicherungsaufsicht. Springer.

Haueter, N. V. (eds.), World insurance. The evolution of a global risk network. Oxford.

HM Treasury (2016): "Mutual deferred shares: consultation on technical policy details", OGL.

HM Treasury (2018): "Mutual deferred shares: response to the consultation on technical policy details", OGL.

https://heritage.aviva.com/our-history/companies/a/amicable-society/ retrieval: 07.03.2019.

https://tindallriley.co.uk/company-profile/, retrieval: 29.09.2019.

https://www.politics.co.uk/reference/national-insurance, retrieval:12.04.2019.

https://www.politics.co.uk/reference/national-insurance, retrieval: 12.04.2019.

https://www.britannica.com/event/South-Sea-Bubble, retrieved: 30.04.2019.

Humphry, D. (2017), Solvency II in the UK. Evolution Rather than revolution, in: *Pierpalo, Marano; Siri, Michele*, Insurance regulation in the European Union, 2017, ch.6, Palgrave Macmillan.

ICMIF (2009), Mutual Market Share 2006-2007 & Global 500, Cheshire.

ICMIF (2017), Market InSights 2016 – UK, Cheshire.

Ismay, P. (2010), Trust among strangers: Securing British Modernity `by way of friendly society,' 1780s-1870s; unpublished Dissertation University of California, Berkeley.

Ismay, P. (2018), Trust among strangers. Friendly Societies in Modern Britain.

Kingston, C. (2007), Marine insurance in Britain and America, 1720-1844: A comparative institutional analysis, in: Journal of Economic History, No. 67(2).

Kowaleski Wallace, E. (2000), The needs of strangers: Friendly Societies and insurance societies in late eighteenth-century England, in: Eighteenth century life 24.

Lobban, M. (2007), Slavery, insurance and the law, in: The Journal of Legal History 28(3).

MacLeod J. (2018), England and Scotland, in*: Hellwege, P.* (ed.). A comparative history of insurance law in Europe. A research agenda, Berlin.

Morrah, D. (1955) A History of Industrial Life Assurance. London, George Allen and Unwin, Ltd.

Mutuals' Deferred Shares Act 2015, http://www.legislation.gov.uk/ukpga/2015/13/contents/enacted, retrieval 30.04.2019

Neave, D. (1996), Friendly Societies in Great Britain, in: *Linden, M. van der* (ed.) (1996), Social security mutualism. The comparative history of mutual benefit societies.

O'Brian, C. (2006), The Downfall of Equitable Life in the United Kingdom: The Mismatch of Strategy and Risk Management, in: Risk Management and Insurance Review, Vol. 9, No. 2, 189-204.

O'Brien, C; Fenn, P. (2012), Mutual life insurers: Origins and performance in pre-1900 Britain. Business History, Vol. 54 (3).

Outreville, J. F. (1998), Theory and practice of insurance, Dordrecht.

Pearson, R. (1990), Thrift or dissipation? The business of life assurance in the early nineteenth century, in: Economic History Review, 2nd ser., XLIII, 2, pp. 236-254.

Pearson, R. (2002), Growth, crisis and change in the insurance industry: a retrospect. Accounting, in: Business and Financial History, 12(3), November 2002.

Pearson, R. (2002), Mutuality tested: The rise and fall of mutual fire insurance offices in eighteenth-century London, in: Business History, vol. 44, no. 4, October 2002.

Pearson, R. (2002): "Growth, crisis and change in the insurance industry: a retrospect", in: Accounting, Business & Financial History, 12(3), 487-504.

Pearson, R. (2004), Insuring the Industrial Revolution. Fire insurance in Great Britain, 1700-1850, Aldershot.

Pearson, R. (2012), United Kingdom: Pioneering insurance internationally, in: *Borscheid, P.*; *Haueter, N. V.* (eds.), World insurance. The evolution of a global risk network. Oxford.

Pearson, R. (2013): "Mergers and Concentration in the UK Insurance Industry", Enterprises et Histoire, No. 72, 7-20.

Pearson, R.; Doe, H. (2015), Organizational choice in UK marine insurance, in: *Pearson, R.; Yoneyama, T.* (2015), Corporate forms and organizational choice in international insurance. Oxford.

Penrose (2004), Equitable Life.

PRA (2015), Glossary – non-directive friendly society, http://www.prarulebook.co.uk/rulebook/Glossary/FullDefinition/53219/25-08-2015, retrieval: 08.03.2019.

PRA (2016). Rulebook, Bank of England, version: 9th of December 2016.

Raven, J. (2014), Publishing business in eighteenth-century England.

Raynes, H. (1948), A History of British Insurance, London, Sir Isaac Pitman & Sons, Ltd.

Relton, F. B. (1893), An account of the fire insurance companies. Associations, institutions, projects, and schemes.

Rupprecht, A. (2007), A very uncommon case: Representations of the Zong and the British campaign to abolish the slave trade, in: The Journal of Legal History 28(3).

Shaw et al. (2012), Country study on the current situation and prospects of mutuals. Country Studies: United Kingdom, pp. 325-342.

South Sea Bubble, https://www.britannica.com/event/South-Sea-Bubble, retrieval 30.04.2019.

Swiss Re (2009), World Insurance in 2008: life premiums fall in the industrialised countries- strong growth in the emerging economies, in: sigma, No 3/2009, Zurich.

Swiss Re (2018): World insurance in 2017: solid, but mature life markets weigh on growth, in: sigma, No 3/2018, Zurich.
The charters, acts of Parliament, and by-laws of the corporation of the Amicable Society for a Perpetual Assurance Office, London 1854.
The insurance register. Containing, with other information, a record of the yearly progress and the present financial position of British insurance Associations, several volumes from 1876 to 1905.
Walford, C. (1886), History of Life Assurance in the United Kingdom (conclusion), in: JIA 26 (1886-1887).
Walford, C. (1887), History of Life Assurance in the United Kingdom, in: JIA, 26, 436-465.
White, W. (1876), The Insurance Register – Yearly Progress and the Present Financial Position of British Insurance Associations, London, *Charles and Edwin Layton.*
White, W. (1878), The Insurance Register – Yearly Progress and the Present Financial Position of British Insurance Associations", London, *Charles and Edwin Layton.*
White, W. (1882), The Insurance Register – Yearly Progress and the Present Financial Position of British Insurance Associations, London, *Charles and Edwin Layton.*
White, W. (1887), The Insurance Register – Yearly Progress and the Present Financial Position of British Insurance Associations, London, *Charles and Edwin Layton.*
White, W. (1890), The Insurance Register – Yearly Progress and the Present Financial Position of British Insurance Associations", London, *Charles and Edwin Layton.*
White, W. (1899), The Insurance Register – Yearly Progress and the Present Financial Position of British Insurance Associations, London, *Charles and Edwin Layton.*
Whiteside, N. (1999), Private Provision and Public Welfare: Health Insurance Between the Wars, in: Before Beveridge: Welfare Before the Welfare State, Civitas, London, 26-42.
Wyndham, A. (1905): "The Insurance Register – Yearly Progress and the Present Financial Position of British Insurance Associations", London, *Charles and Edwin Layton.*

Historical Development, Structural Change and Perspectives of Mutual Insurance Societies in Germany

Richard Lorenz, Johann Brazda

1. Introduction

The origins of the insurance business in today's Germany can be traced back to an ancient past. It seems that in the event of emergencies some kind of mutual support was always available.[1] *Büchner* calls the common obligation of mutual neighborly help and support "natural risk-bearing community".[2]

It can be said that the insurance business developed based on three cooperative roots, self-help, governmental initiatives, and commercial roots.[3] These three original roots are still discernible in today's German insurance industry with mutual insurance societies, public companies, and insurance joint stock companies.

First traces of connections of cooperative solidarity can be found in the time of the Carolingian kingdom.[4] In the early Middle Ages, the first prototypes of life insurances developed for guilds of craftsmen and other professional groups and the first non-life insurances among the guilds of merchants.[5] During the 16th century, specialised institutions of risk-sharing developed, e.g. fire guilds, livestock, hail, and storm guilds in the countryside.[6] During the 17th century, these institutions became

---

1 Cf. *Koch, P.* (2012): Geschichte der Versicherungswirtschaft in Deutschland, Karlsruhe, p. 1.

2 Cf. *Büchner, F.* (1957): Zur Geschichte der Versicherung, in VersWissArch, 46. vol. p. 1.

3 Cf. *Koch, P.* (2012): Geschichte der Versicherungswirtschaft in Deutschland, Karlsruhe, p. 5.

4 Cf. *Koch, P.* (1988): Versicherungsgeschichte in Stichworten, Verein zur Förderung der Versicherungswissenschaft in München e.V., Number 32, Munich, p. 4.

5 Cf. *Farny, D.* (1977): Die Entwicklung der Versicherung auf Gegenseitigkeit von der Spezial- zur Generalversicherung, in Mutualité, H.1, pp. 78-98, p. 83.

6 Cf. *Koch, P.* (1995): Die historische Entwicklung des Versicherungsvereins auf Gegenseitigkeit, in *Peiner, W.* (ed.): Grundlagen des Versicherungsvereins auf Gegenseitigkeit. Verfaßt und veröffentlicht aus Anlaß des 175jährigen Bestehens der Gothaer Versicherungsbank VVag, Karlsruhe, pp. 13-26, p. 15.

independent and continued as Friendly Societies.[7] Until the end of the 18th century, small mutual insurance societies and public companies developed in regional limited areas, because companies working across borders were restricted and Germany consisted then of many very small states.[8]

At the beginning of the 19th century, the first big mutual societies developed. This was possible because of new methods in mathematics and statistics that made insured risks predictable. Moreover, thriving industrial development necessitated insurances and the territories of the German Confederation needed domestic insurance companies on a larger scale due to the increasing nationalism developing after Napoleon's defeat.[9]

Mutual insurance societies developed originally from daily practice without any specific legal regulations. With the introduction of the Insurance Supervision Act and the Insurance Contract Law at the beginning of the 20th century, mutual insurance societies got a uniform legal regulation.[10]

Since this time, mutual insurance societies developed further. Actuarial practice was refined, insurance protection adapted, the increasing business for the mass market was managed by economization and automation and the insurance protection was improved by legislation and jurisdiction (see Figure 1).[11]

2. Historical development

In § 171 of the Insurance Supervision Act 2016 (ISA 2016), a mutual insurance society is defined as an association which offers insurances for its members based on mutuality. Mutual societies exist for many generations and support essentially the economic development of Germany. Therefore, it is important to investigate the historical development of mutual insurance societies in some detail.

---

7 Ibid. pp. 13-26, p. 18.

8 Cf. *Koch, P.* (2012): Geschichte der Versicherungswirtschaft in Deutschland, Karlsruhe, p. 10.

9 Ibid.

10 Cf. *Benkel, G. A.* (2002): Der Versicherungsverein auf Gegenseitigkeit – Das Gesellschaftsrecht der großen konzernfreien VVaG, Munich, p. 24.

11 Cf. *Koch, P.* (2012): Geschichte der Versicherungswirtschaft in Deutschland, Karlsruhe, p. 10.

2.1 The situation until the beginning of the 19th century

Long before insurances existed, the obligation for mutual help and support was regarded as a natural obligation in Germanic families, clans, and tribes.[12] In the Early Middle Ages, the clans and tribes were replaced by guilds and crafts, which supported via special risk coverage, the further development of trade, craft, and agriculture.[13]

2.1.1 Guilds in Northern Germany

The first traditional legal source about the existence of guilds can be found in the capitulars of *Carl the Great* (742-814) from March 779.[14] In the first half of the 16th century, the first fire guilds developed in Schleswig-Holstein, at first in the countryside and later in towns. The first fire guild was established 1537 in Süderauerdorf, followed by several other foundations along the West coast of Schleswig-Holstein. In 1543, the Itzehoer Lieb-Frauen-Guild was established as the first urban fire guild.[15] Guilds also established the first steps for livestock, storm, and hail insurances which should protect the economic goods. Moreover, "death and bones guilds" developed which were the forerunners of today's accident and liability insurances.[16] Gradually, these fire guilds developed to sole mutual insurance societies. In 1591, the Hamburger building owners established the first Hamburger fire contract on voluntary basis for the mutual protection in the event of fire.[17]

The number of guilds increased continuously and although several of them were liquidated or taken over, some guilds received the status of large mutual insurance societies and expanded their business to entire Germany such as the in 1691 established mutual insurance society Itzehoer insurance/fire guild.

---

12 Cf. *Büchner, F* (1957): Zur Geschichte der Versicherung, in VersWissArch, 46. vol. pp. 1-19, p. 1.

13 Cf. *Völker, G.* (1995): Die wirtschaftliche Bedeutung des deutschen Versicherungsvereins auf Gegenseitigkeit, in Peiner, W. (ed.): Grundlagen des Versicherungsvereins auf Gegenseitigkeit. Verfaßt und veröffentlicht aus Anlaß des 175jährigen Bestehens der Gothaer Versicherungsbank VVag, Karlsruhe, pp. 89-106, p. 89.

14 Cf. *Koch, P.* (2012): Geschichte der Versicherungswirtschaft in Deutschland, Karlsruhe, p. 15.

15 Cf. *Koch, P.* (1995): Die historische Entwicklung des Versicherungsvereins auf Gegenseitigkeit, in Peiner, W. (Hrsg.): Grundlagen des Versicherungsvereins auf Gegenseitigkeit. Verfaßt und veröffentlicht aus Anlaß des 175jährigen Bestehens der Gothaer Versicherungsbank VVag, Karlsruhe, pp. 13-26, p. 15.

16 Cf. *Koch, P.* (2012): Geschichte der Versicherungswirtschaft in Deutschland, Karlsruhe, p. 15.

17 Cf. *Koch, P.* (1988): Versicherungsgeschichte in Stichworten, Verein zur Förderung der Versicherungswissenschaft in München e.V., Number 32, Munich, p. 6.

Figure 1: Trends of the historical insurance business in Germany

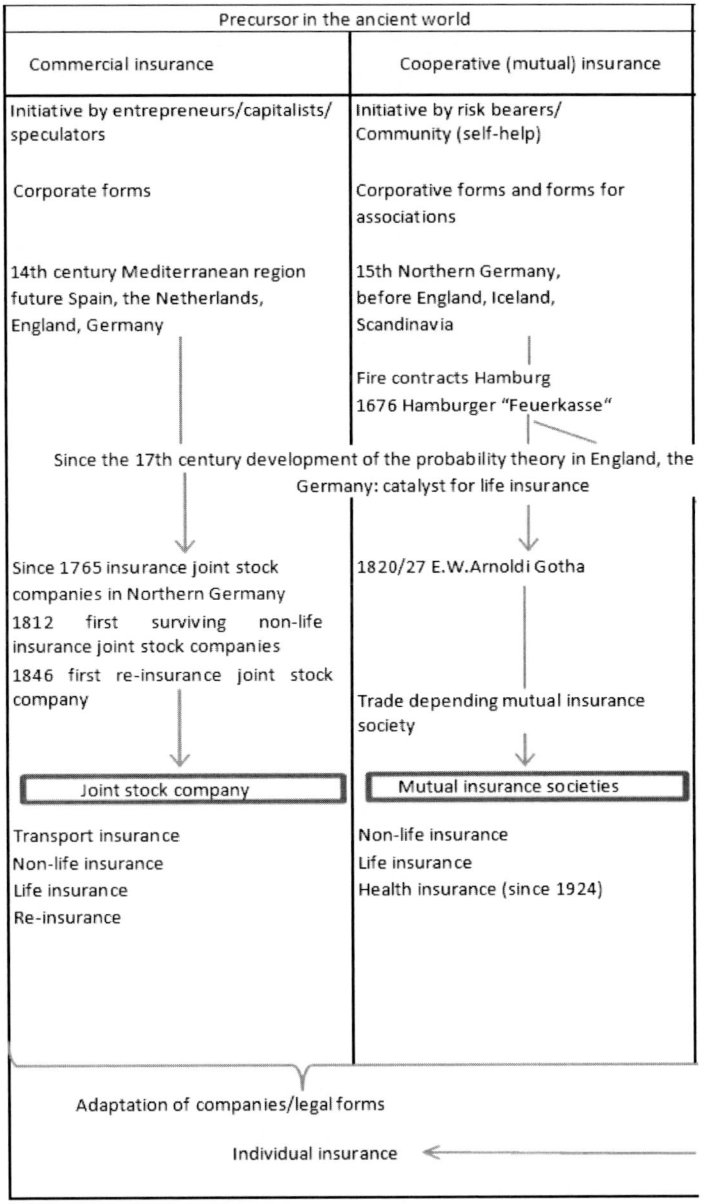

Quelle: *Farny, D.* (1980): Entwicklungslinien, Stand und Wirtschaftliche Bedeutung des Versicherungswesens in Deutschland, in *Henning, F.W.* (ed.): Entwicklung und Aufgaben von Versicherungen und Banken in der Industrialisierung, Schriften des Vereins für Socialpolitik, vol. 105, Berlin, p. 10.

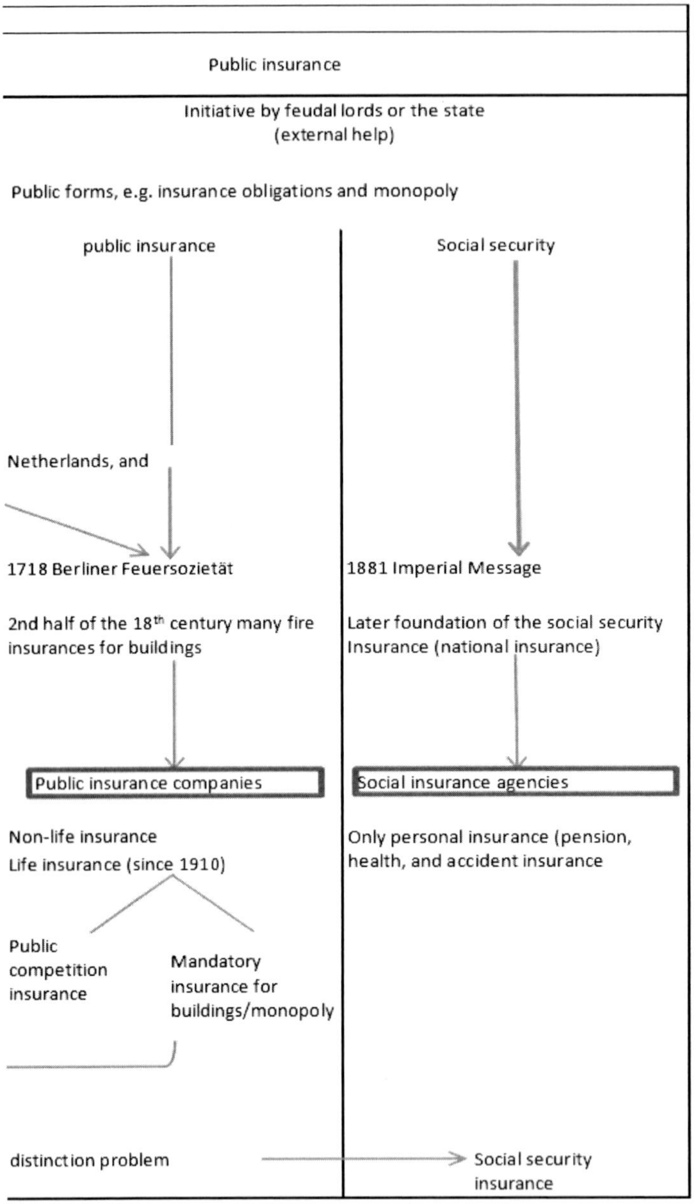
Public insurance
Initiative by feudal lords or the state
(external help)
Public forms, e.g. insurance obligations and monopoly
public insurance
Social security
Netherlands, and
1718 Berliner Feuersozietät
1881 Imperial Message
2nd half of the 18th century many fire
insurances for buildings
Later foundation of the social security
Insurance (national insurance)
Public insurance companies
Social insurance agencies
Non-life insurance
Life insurance (since 1910)
Only personal insurance (pension,
health, and accident insurance
Public
competition
insurance
Mandatory
insurance for
buildings/monopoly
distinction problem
Social security
insurance

The major fires in Hamburg in 1606, 1626, and 1676 showed the inadequacy of the insurance situation; therefore, the Hamburger City Council founded in 1676 the Hamburger fire insurance fund (Feuerkasse),[18] which replaced the fire contracts and transferred the assets of all existing contracts by February 1677.[19] The "Hamburger Feuerkasse" is the oldest still existing insurance company in the world and at the same time the first public insurance company.[20]

During the historical period of absolutism, several societies modelled after the Hamburger Feuerkasse developed in all parts of Germany. However, they were rather small businesses and did not work across borders yet.[21]

2.1.2 Crafts

In Germany, guilds of craftsmen can be found since 1150. They can be regarded as the origin of the German mutual life insurances. They supported their members in case of illness, disabilities, and old age.[22]

With the decline of the crafts during the 17th century, guilds based on mutual support became independent and developed to Friendly Societies that covered funeral expenses, provide funds for widows and orphans as well as marriage and endowment funds.[23] These Friendly Societies can already be regarded as small mutual insurance societies.[24]

The oldest of these societies is the parish-widow-society for Braunschweig-Lüneburg from 1636.[25] Additional societies developed in several parts of Germany, and in the second half of the 18th century, societies with unlimited business areas were established. The state started to be interested in this topic and in 1775 *Frederick the Great*, King of Prussia (1712-1786), established the Royal-Prussian general Widow-Support society ("Königlich-Preußische allgemeine Witwen-Verpflegungs-Anstalt") in Berlin. The term "pension", which was used for the widows' benefits,

---

18 Cf. *Niermann, U.* (1990): Geschichte und Organisationsstruktur öffentlich-rechtlicher Versicherer in Nordrhein-Westfalen, Frankfurt am Main, p. 24.

19 Cf. *Koch, P.* (2012): Geschichte der Versicherungswirtschaft in Deutschland, Karlsruhe, p. 30.

20 Cf. *Schneider, H.* (1963): die Verfassungsentwicklung der Versicherungsvereine auf Gegenseitigkeit im 19.Jahrhundert, Göttingen, p. 7.

21 Cf. *Niermann, U.* (1990): Geschichte und Organisationsstruktur öffentlich-rechtlicher Versicherer in Nordrhein-Westfalen, Frankfurt am Main, p. 35.

22 Cf. *Koch, P.* (1995): Die historische Entwicklung des Versicherungsvereins auf Gegenseitigkeit, in *Peiner, W.* (ed.): Grundlagen des Versicherungsvereins auf Gegenseitigkeit. Verfaßt und veröffentlicht aus Anlaß des 175jährigen Bestehens der Gothaer Versicherungsbank VVag, Karlsruhe, pp. 13-26, p. 16.

23 Ibid. pp. 13-26, p. 18.

24 Cf. *Koch, P.* (2012): Geschichte der Versicherungswirtschaft in Deutschland, Karlsruhe, p. 19.

25 Vgl. *Schmitt-Lermann, H.* (1954): Der Versicherungsgedanke im deutschen Geistesleben des Barock und der Aufklärung, Munich, p. 30.

became the modern term "pension fund /occupational provision funds". The main bank in Berlin took over the guarantee for these funds.[26]

2.1.3 Criticism and government supervision

The different societies were not based on solid mathematical-statistical foundations, but on apportionment procedure with all its disadvantages and shortcomings, which eventually led to massive problems. However, in 1693, the English astronomer *Edmond Halley* developed the first scientific mortality table, based on the statistical data of the German priest *Caspar Neumann* from Breslau and this opened the way for life insurances.[27]

Due to the cameralistic goals of the government, the state started to be interested in these scientific developments and established public Friendly Societies. With the Prussian regulation from 1781 about endowment, funeral, and other societies connected with money collections ("Aussteuer-, Begräbnis-, und andere Gesellschaften, zu welchen Geldsammlungen geschehen"), the first governmental supervision of mutual insurance societies was initiated, and in 1786 the City Council of Nuremburg followed.[28]

2.2 The development of mutual societies in the 19th century

At the end of the 18th and the beginning of the 19th century, several new societies based on mutuality were established. They showed the first steps towards modern actuarial practice and nationwide business, in contrast to most of the small associations. In 1797, the "Mecklenburgische Versicherungs-Gesellschaft a.G./Hagelschaden-Asssekuranz-Gesellschaft" (society for hail damage) was established and well known among the societies for agricultural risk coverage. It is today's oldest still existing mutual insurance society of this size in Germany.[29]

At the end of the 18th century, mostly private mutual insurance societies were successful, while public companies increasingly lost

---

[26] Cf. *Koch, P.* (2012): Geschichte der Versicherungswirtschaft in Deutschland, Karlsruhe, p. 24.

[27] Cf. *Koch, P.* (1998): Geschichte der Versicherungswissenschaft in Deutschland; Hrsg. Vom Deutschen Verein für Versicherungswissenschaften e.V. aus Anlaß seines 100jährigen Bestehens, Karlsruhe, p. 30.

[28] Cf. *Koch, P.* (1995): Die historische Entwicklung des Versicherungsvereins auf Gegenseitigkeit, in *Peiner, W.* (ed.): Grundlagen des Versicherungsvereins auf Gegenseitigkeit. Verfaßt und veröffentlicht aus Anlaß des 175jährigen Bestehens der Gothaer Versicherungsbank VVag, Karlsruhe, pp. 13-26, p. 19.

[29] Ibid. p. 20f.

their importance.[30] The mutual insurance societies were part of the economic and social changes at the beginning of the 19th century that were triggered by the increasing industrialization.[31] In this period, the first large mutual societies were established based on the findings in mathematics and statistics, which made the to-be insured risks more or less calculable.[32]

The establishment of the "Gothaer societies" was in particular important. *Ernst Wilhelm Arnoldi* (1778-1841) founded in 1821 and 1827 today's still existing Gothaer insurance banks for fire and life insurances. With these establishments, he constituted the type of the modern mutual insurance society.[33] He had the goal to break the foreign monopoly of the English joint stock companies and to offer members low-priced insurances.[34]

Three factors played an important role: the previous development of mutual insurance societies, the personality of the initiator *Arnoldi*, and the specific political and economic situation in Germany.[35] An essential point was the nationwide business and the actuarial, financial, and organizations imitation of insurance joint stock companies.[36]

Arnoldi transferred the mutuality principle from small local insurance societies with social background to large nationwide mutual insurers with economic orientation and combined the ideas of mutual insurance societies with those of joint stock companies.[37] This connection can also be found in the Insurance Supervision Act of 1901, in which the internal organization of large mutual insurance societies

---

30 Cf. *Niermann, U.* (1990): Geschichte und Organisationsstruktur öffentlich-rechtlicher Versicherer in Nordrhein-Westfalen, Frankfurt am Main, p. 39.

31 Cf. *Völker, G.* (1995): Die wirtschaftliche Bedeutung des deutschen Versicherungsvereins auf Gegenseitigkeit, in *Peiner, W.* (ed.): Grundlagen des Versicherungsvereins auf Gegenseitigkeit. Verfaßt und veröffentlicht aus Anlaß des 175jährigen Bestehens der Gothaer Versicherungsbank VVag, Karlsruhe, pp. 89-106, p. 90.

32 Cf. *Koch, P.* (2012): Geschichte der Versicherungswirtschaft in Deutschland, Karlsruhe, p. 10.

33 Cf. *Koch, P.* (1988): Versicherungsgeschichte in Stichworten, Verein zur Förderung der Versicherungswissenschaft in München e.V., n´Number 32, Munich, p. 11.

34 Cf. *Lorenz, E.* (1988): Versicherungsverein auf Gegenseitigkeit, in: *Farny D.* (ed.): Handwörterbuch der Versicherung (HdV), Karlsruhe, pp. 1147-1158, p. 1148.

35 Cf. *Koch, P.* (1995): Die historische Entwicklung des Versicherungsvereins auf Gegenseitigkeit, in *Peiner, W.* (ed.): Grundlagen des Versicherungsvereins auf Gegenseitigkeit. Verfaßt und veröffentlicht aus Anlaß des 175jährigen Bestehens der Gothaer Versicherungsbank VVag, Karlsruhe, pp. 13-26, p. 22.

36 Cf. *Peiner, W.* (2000): Die Zukunftschancen der Versicherungsvereine auf Gegenseitigkeit, in: *Koch, G. / Wagner, F.* (ed.): Aktuelle Fragen in der Versicherungswirtschaft, Band 1, Karlsruhe, pp. 129-145, p. 131.

37 Cf. *Martiensen, H. P.* (2006): Fusionen von Versicherungsvereinen auf Gegenseitigkeit: Verschmelzung gem. §§ 109 ff. UmwG und Gleichordnung gem. § 18 Abs. 2 AktG, Hamburger Reihe, Reihe A Rechtswissenschaft, Karlsruhe, p. 34.

is based on regulations of the Companies Act, while for small mutual insurance societies, according to § 210, association law, Civil Code, and cooperative law apply.[38]

Because of a strong nationalism, the "Gothaer" insurances developed rapidly. New nationwide mutual insurance societies were established due to the popularity of their program. For example, in 1830 the "Alte Leipziger Lebensversicherungsgesellschaft auf Gegenseitigkeit" was established after the model of the Gothaer insurance society.[39]

In a second wave of foundations in 1874, mutual life and health insurance societies were established, such as the "Hannoversche Lebensversicherung a.G." (1875) and the "Continentale Lebensversicherung a.G." (1892).[40]

In 1895, *Viktor Ehrenberg* and *Wilhelm Lexis* established the first insurance scientific seminar at the University of Göttingen and in 1899, the German association for insurance science ("Deutscher Verein für Versicherungs-Wissenschaft") was founded in Berlin.[41]

2.3 The 20th century

At the beginning of the 20th century, Germany's insurance industry was regulated by the Insurance Supervision Act (Versicherungsaufsichtsgesetz VAG 1901) and the insurance contract law (Versicherungsvertragsgesetz VVG 1908).[42] The economic development and the increasing risk awareness led to a fast growth of the entire insurance industry. Mutual insurance societies were important for this development, because they had sufficient experience and the willingness for innovations,[43] which resulted in numerous foundations.[44] In 1923, the inflation reached its peak. This was the most difficult period in the

---

38 Cf. *Hax, K.* (1969): Ist der Versicherungsverein auf Gegenseitigkeit noch eine geeignete Rechtsform für die große Versicherungsunternehmung?; in: *Farny, D.* (ed.): Wirtschaft und Recht der Versicherung: Paul Braeß zum 66. Geburtstag, Karlsruhe, pp. 139-164, p. 146.

39 Cf. *Brenzel, J.* (1973): Unternehmen und Organisation des Versicherungsvereins auf Gegenseitigkeit. Ein Beitrag zur Reformdiskussion, Göttingen, p. 10.

40 Cf. *Benkel, G. A.* (2002): Der Versicherungsverein auf Gegenseitigkeit – Das Gesellschaftsrecht der großen konzernfreien VVaG, Munich, p. 22.

41 Cf. *Koch, P.* (1988): Versicherungsgeschichte in Stichworten, Verein zur Förderung der Versicherungswissenschaft in München e.V., Number 32, Munich, p. 11.

42 Cf. *Völker, G.* (1995) Die wirtschaftliche Bedeutung des deutschen Versicherungsvereins auf Gegenseitigkeit, in *Peiner, W.* (ed.): Grundlagen des Versicherungsvereins auf Gegenseitigkeit. Verfaßt und veröffentlicht aus Anlaß des 175jährigen Bestehens der Gothaer Versicherungsbank VVag, Karlsruhe, pp. 89-106, p. 90.

43 Ibid. pp. 89-106, p. 90.

44 Cf. *Benkel, G. A.* (2002): Der Versicherungsverein auf Gegenseitigkeit – Das Gesellschaftsrecht der großen konzernfreien VVaG, Munich, p. 23.

history of the German insurance industry so far. Numerous mergers occurred and the share of mutual insurance societies decreased despite several new foundations.[45] In the time between 1933 and 1945, the entire German insurance industry was under the influence of the National Socialist Party. However, it stayed an economic branch of its own, but had major losses, like the rest of Germany, because of the Second World War and the fall of the Third Reich.[46] In 1945, the traditional insurance companies were not allowed to function any longer in the Russian occupation zone.[47] On the other hand, in other occupation zones insurance companies were organized to rebuild the economy.[48] The economic upswing required the economisation of the insurance industry and the use of punch cards for data processing was introduced again after the first time in the 1920s.[49]

In the 1970s and 1980s, several reforms were initiated and with the fall of the Berlin Wall in 1989, the German reunification started for the insurance companies too.[50] The realization of the European Common Market in 1995 brought the opening of the markets and deregulation. This was an important step in the younger history of the German insurance industry.[51] This period was shaped by increasing competition, take-overs, and mergers of companies to horizontal and subordinated groups.[52] For example, in 2001, the Gothaer insurance bank (mutual) was established in the form of a horizontal group[53] and in 2003, the umbrella company of the VHV "Vereinigte Hannoversche Versicherungen a.G." comprised the traditional Hannoversche life insurance society ("Hannoversche Lebensversicherung a.G.").[54]

The following table shows the decrease of the number of insurance companies in more than 55 years, but at the same time, it presents the continuous increase of employees. It also shows a rapid increase of the gross premium income of more than 50 times, which is a clear sign of the high productivity and efficient cost structure of the insurance sector.[55]

---

[45] Cf. *Koch, P.* (2012): Geschichte der Versicherungswirtschaft in Deutschland, Karlsruhe, p. 216.

[46] Cf. *Ibid.* p. 280.

[47] Cf. *Koch, P.* (1988): Versicherungsgeschichte in Stichworten, Verein zur Förderung der Versicherungswissenschaft in München e.V., Number 32, Munich, p. 14.

[48] Ibid. p. 339.

[49] Ibid. p. 378.

[50] Ibid. p. 417.

[51] Ibid. p. 474.

[52] Ibid.

[53] Ibid. p. 496.

[54] Ibid. p. 498.

[55] Ibid. p. 518.

Table 1: Key figures of the German insurance business

Year	Number of insurance companies under federal and state (regional) supervision	Premiums in billion Euro	Employees in insurance companies (in 100,000)
1960	9,853	4,501	116.2
1970	7,390	13,676	189.5
1980	3,343	36,000	202.3
1990	2,659	69,858	233.2
2000	1,882	131,335	240.2
2009	1,486	178,898	216.4
2016	1,293	260,967	295.8

Source: *Koch, P.* (2012): Geschichte der Versicherungswirtschaft in Deutschland, Karlsruhe, p. 518 ; BaFin (2018) Statistik der Bundesanstalt für Finanzdienstleistungsaufsicht – Erstversicherungsunternehmen und Pensionsfonds, p. 6.

2.4 Germany and the Austrian insurance business

Austria and Germany influenced each other mutually in numerous areas over time. Therefore, it does not surprise that both countries cultivated knowledge exchange regarding insurance business, which continues until today.[56]

2.4.1 Bavarian roots of the Austrian fire insurance

In the battle of Austerlitz 1805, *Napoleon* defeated Russia and Austria. Therefore, in the peace treaty of Bratislava the new established kingdom of Bavaria received Salzburg, Tyrol, and Vorarlberg as reparation.[57] The new territorial organisation had consequences for the insurance market.

In Austria, fire insurances in the form of farmer insurances (Bauernassekuranzen) have a long tradition. While in several parts of Austria, regional limited insurance companies had already existed, in other

[56] Cf. *Koch, P.* (2005): Historische Wechselwirkungen zwischen österreichsicher und deutscher Assekuranz, in: Versicherungswirtschaft, Beiträge zur Geschichte des Deutschen Versicherungswesens, Band II, Karlsruhe, p. 54.

[57] Cf. Haus der Bayerischen Geschichte, Königreich Bayern 1806-1918, https://www.hdbg.eu/koenigreich/web/index.php/objekte/index/herrscher_id/1/id/256, 22.06.2018.

parts they did not exist at all. An important impulse for the development of modern insurance business in Austria came e.g. from Bavaria.[58]

King *Maximilian* I of Bavaria was interested in fire insurance companies since 1806 and urged for the unification of the different legal forms in the course of an administration reform, which happened in the different parts of the kingdom.[59] In 1811, the public Bavarian country fire insurance company ("Königlich-baierische Landes-Brandversicherungsanstalt") was established which had the monopoly regarding building insurances.[60] The business activities of this company included the entire Habsburg Empire, including the territories that returned to the Monarchy after the Congress of Vienna.[61]

After the territories had returned to Austria, the new insurance companies of Salzburg and Upper Austria became the "Wechselseitige Brand-Assekuranz in Salzburg-Oberösterreich", a mutual insurance company for Salzburg and Upper Austria. The estates of the Tyrolian country established the "Tirolisch-Vorarlberg'sche Feuer-Versicherungs-Anstalt", a fire insurance company that still exists today in the form of two separate companies.[62]

2.4.2 Saxon roots of the Austrian fire insurance

In Saxony, fire insurances were widely known around 1800. In Dresden, the Austrian officer Major Georg Ritter von *Högelmüller* learned about the fire insurances in Saxony, i.e. societies with mandatory admission. After his return to Austria, he leaded for the foundation of a similar company in 1803.[63] *Högelmüller's* proposal from 1817 for the foundation of a mutual fire insurance society with mandatory membership was declined due to the resolution of the Emperor from 1819, which only allowed the foundation of private companies. In 1822,

[58] Cf. *Koch, P.* (2005): Historische Wechselwirkungen zwischen österreichsicher und deutscher Assekuranz, in: Versicherungswirtschaft, Beiträge zur Geschichte des Deutschen Versicherungswesens, Band II, Karlsruhe, p. 54.

[59] Cf. *Koch, P.* (2012): Geschichte der Versicherungswirtschaft in Deutschland, Karlsruhe, p. 100.

[60] Cf. *Koch, P.* (1988): Versicherungsgeschichte in Stichworten, Verein zur Förderung der Versicherungswissenschaft in München e.V., Number 32, Munich, p. 9.

[61] Cf. *Rohrbach, W.* (1988): Von den Anfängen bis zum Börsenkrach, in: Versicherungsgeschichte Österreichs, Band 1, Vienna, p. 208.

[62] Cf. *Koch, P.* (2005): Historische Wechselwirkungen zwischen österreichsicher und deutscher Assekuranz, in: Versicherungswirtschaft, Beiträge zur Geschichte des Deutschen Versicherungswesens, Band II, Karlsruhe, p. 54.

[63] Cf. *Lehner, U.* (1988): Der Konzern der Wiener Städtischen, in: Rohrbach W.: Das Zeitalter des modernen Versicherungswesens, vol. 3, Holzhausen/Vienna, p. 1014.

however, *Högelmüller's* proposal for the foundation of a mutual private company under governmental protection was accepted.[64]

On August 25th, 1824, Emperor *Francis* I. approved the foundation of the "k.k. privilegierte wechselseitige Brandschaden-Versicherungs-Anstalt" ("Wechselseitige Brandschaden") which came into effect on January 1st, 1825. This mutual insurance society was the first modern company in Austria and still exists under the name "Wiener Städtische Versicherung", belonging to the "Vienna Insurance Group".[65]

3. Today's mutual insurance societies

Insurance companies can only have certain legal forms, according to § 8 (ISA 2016). The mutual insurance company is one of the possible private legal forms for insurance companies.[66] § 171 (ISA 2016) states that an association, which insures its members according to the mutuality principles, becomes legal when the supervision authority permits the association to do business as a mutual insurance society. The principle of mutuality, however, is not defined legally. This generated numerous theories and interpretations. Some of them are the following.[67]

Manes defines the term mutuality in a very striking way: "One for all, and all for one"[68].

---

[64] Cf. *Brazda, J. / Hoppichler, F.* (2015): Versicherungsvereine auf Gegenseitigkeit versus Versicherungsaktiengesellschaften – Eine historische Betrachtung, in: *Brazda, J.* et.al. (Hrsg.): Perspektiven für die Genossenschaftsidee: Festschrift zum 65. Geburtstag von Verbandsanwalt Professor DDr. Hans Hofinger, p. 198-209, p. 205.

[65] Cf. *Lehner, U.* (1997): Abschied von der Gegenseitigkeit? Sympathieerklärung für eine im Verschwinden begriffene Rechtsform, in *Rohrbach, W.*: Assekuranzmosaik des ausgehenden 20. Jahrhunderts, Band 4, Holzhausen/Vienna, p. 1116.

[66] Cf. *Heidelbach, A.* (1994): Der kleinere Versicherungsverein auf Gegenseitigkeit unter besonderer Berücksichtigung der gesellschaftsrechtlichen Probleme, Versicherungsrechtliche Studien, Band 30, Diss., Frankfurt am Main, p. 23.

[67] Cf. *Benkel, G. A.* (2002): Der Versicherungsverein auf Gegenseitigkeit – Das Gesellschaftsrecht der großen konzernfreien VVaG, Munich, p. 42.

[68] *Manes, A.* (1930): Versicherungswesen, Band I, 5. Aufl., Berlin, p. 2.

Grossfeld[69] explains the term as following:

- The insurance society insures its members. The membership relationship comprises an insurance relationship, the position of the members, and the policyholders.
- The members raise the means for the insurance business and carry commonly the profits and the losses.
- The members have the control about the management in the supreme representation (§ 191 ISA 2016). They have the final decision-making power about the principles of the business policy.

Farny[70] states that equating the mutuality principle with the insurance principle is obsolete. He emphasizes the legal relationship between members and the mutual insurance society and argues that mutuality, as a feature of a mutual insurance society, should only be marked by the relationships between members, the legal entity, and the institutions of the society. The relationships are dual:

- as a membership relationship and
- as a legal contractual insurance and economic relationship, and, therefore, as a result of an autonomous market-based decision to transfer certain risks to the mutual insurance society in return for payment and to start a membership relationship.

Finally, *Benkel* uses the approach of the majority theory. This theory states that the mutual insurance society distinguishes between the contractual relationship, i.e. organization contract with its bylaws, and the relationship based on the law of obligations. This means that every policyholder has two different kinds of rights.[71] *Farny* also refers to the double relationship between members and the mutual insurance society. In theory, the membership relationships dominate the economic relationships; however, *Farny* argues that in reality the membership is used as a means to an end to take out an insurance policy at a mutual insurance society.[72]

It is important to note that, according to § 177 paragraph 2 (ISA 2016), non-member business activities are possible when the bylaws

69 *Grossfeld, B.* (1985): Der Versicherungsverein auf Gegenseitigkeit im System der Unternehmensformen, Tübingen, p. 4.

70 *Farny, D.* (2011): Versicherungsbetriebslehre, Karlsruhe, p. 208.

71 Cf. *Benkel, G. A.* (2002): Der Versicherungsverein auf Gegenseitigkeit – Das Gesellschaftsrecht der großen konzernfreien VVaG, Munich, p. 123f.

72 Cf. *Farny, D.* (2011): Versicherungsbetriebslehre, Karlsruhe, p. 208.

allow this explicitly.[73] However, this seems to be in conflict with the non-discrimination precept and, therefore, with the mutuality principle too, because in the event of financial difficulties non-members are not obligated to pay further capital. In case of insolvency, members have more disadvantages than non-members.[74] However, it is important to note that for including non-member business activities into the bylaws a decision of the supreme body is necessary. Additionally, the supervision body usually grants this possibility when it can be anticipated that non-member business activities are minor.[75]

3.1 Legal framework

The mutual insurance society is a special legal form of the insurance business. It comprises elements of business societies and cooperatives, but it has, in contrast to other company forms, no law of its own. Therefore, its legal basis is characterized by numerous references to other legal forms.[76]

The most important legal principles for mutual insurance societies can be found in the fourth section of the Insurance Supervision Act of 1 April 2015 – VAG 2015 (Versicherungsaufsichtsgesetz) in the Articles 171-210. Additionally, general regulations regarding the law of association of the Civil Code, regulations of the Company law, in particular regarding the bodies (management, supervision board, and supreme representation), and the Commercial Code regarding merchant status, accounting, and annual financial statement as well as the cooperative law are applicable.[77]

3.1.1 Criticism concerning the legal framework

The legal regulations for mutual insurance societies have been criticized very often.[78] The main criticism concerns the following three topics:[79]

---

[73] Cf. *Breuer, C.* (1999): Versicherungsverein auf Gegenseitigkeit versus Versicherungs-Aktiengesellschaft: Eine vergleichende Strukturanalyse der Rechtsformen, Köln, p. 4.

[74] Cf. *Nemson, J.* (2014): Geschäftsmodell VVaG: Rahmenbedingungen, Herausforderungen und Chancen, Karlsruhe, p. 77.

[75] Cf. *Müller, H.* (2000): Der Versicherungsverein auf Gegenseitigkeit. Chancen und Risiken aus der Sicht eines Versicherungsaufsehers, Karlsruhe, p. 21.

[76] Cf. *Farny, D.* (2011): Versicherungsbetriebslehre, Karlsruhe, p. 205.

[77] Cf. *Nemson, J.* (2014): Geschäftsmodell VVaG: Rahmenbedingungen, Herausforderungen und Chancen, Karlsruhe, p. 55.

[78] Cf. *Benkel, G. A.* (2002): Der Versicherungsverein auf Gegenseitigkeit – Das Gesellschaftsrecht der großen konzernfreien VVaG, Munich, p. 41.

[79] Cf. *Nemson, J.* (2014): Geschäftsmodell VVaG: Rahmenbedingungen, Herausforderungen und Chancen, Karlsruhe, p. 58.

- the legal method of reference
- the mutual insurance society has no law of its own
- up-to-date regulations are missing

In 1942, *Gierke*[80] takes the massive flood of legal references as the main problem. He sees the legal provisions as adequate but they are scattered over too many different locations.

Bühler (1959) and *Hax* (1969) demand special regulations for mutual insurance societies similar to those of joint stock companies, private limited companies, and cooperatives. In this way better clarity and independence could be reached.[81]

Bürkle states that the lawmaker usually forgets about mutual insurance societies when changing or readjusting legal regulations, which results in an outdated legal framework.[82]

Farny's[83] criticism is much broader. He sees: "the business law for a mutual insurance company, which is unchanged since 1901", in an urgent need of reforms. According to *Farny*, the basic notions regarding this insurance type and the terminology have to be adapted to the development of the business-management theories and practice as well as to other laws concerning economic matters (in particular Company law, Commercial Code, accounting regulations). A clear separation between private company regulations for mutual insurance societies and supervision regulations is also desirable.

According to *Benkel*, it would be sensible to treat the mutual insurance society in the context of the Insurance Supervision Act, because this would emphasise the special legal form for insurance transactions.[84] On the other hand, *Bürkle* argues that the lawmaker expands increasingly the applying area of mutual insurance societies and of the Insurance Supervision Act to non-insurance companies. The supervision based on the Insurance Supervision Act is expanded to other companies without insurance business or similar activities.[85]

---

[80] *Gierke, J.* (1942): Die Versicherungsvereine auf Gegenseitigkeit nach deutschem Recht, Stuttgart, p. 114.

[81] Cf. *Benkel, G. A.* (2002): Der Versicherungsverein auf Gegenseitigkeit – Das Gesellschaftsrecht der großen konzernfreien VVaG, Munich, p. 41.

[82] Cf. *Bürkle, J.* (2008): Verbesserte rechtliche Rahmenbedingungen für Versicherungsvereine auf Gegenseitigkeit, in *Bürkle, J.* (ed.): Rechtliche Rahmenbedingungen für Versicherungsvereine auf Gegenseitigkeit. Festschrift zum 100-jährigen Bestehen der Stuttgarter Lebensversicherung a.G., Karlsruhe, pp. 223-248, p. 235.

[83] *Farny, D.* (2011): Versicherungsbetriebslehre, Karlsruhe, p. 205.

[84] Cf. *Benkel, G. A.* (2002): Der Versicherungsverein auf Gegenseitigkeit – Das Gesellschaftsrecht der großen konzernfreien VVaG, Munich, p. 42.

[85] Cf. *Bürkle, J.* (2008): Verbesserte rechtliche Rahmenbedingungen für Versicherungsvereine auf Gegenseitigkeit, in *Bürkle, J.* (ed.): Rechtliche Rahmenbedingungen für Versicherungs-

3.1.2 The bylaws

The bylaws are part of the business plan and they are determined by the founders. The supervision authority gives its consent to the bylaws and grants the permission to engage in business operations, which makes the mutual insurance society to a legal entity.[86] Although the Insurance Supervision Act stipulates an extensive autonomy of the bylaws, there are must-, shall-, and can-regulations to consider.[87]

3.1.2.1 Must-regulations

The bylaws have to include the following issues:

- § 174 ISA (2015) – a name (company) which shows that it is a mutual insurance company and the place of business
- § 179 ISA (2015) – a foundation fund which is used for all foundation costs, guarantees, and business activities
- § 183 ISA (2015) – regulations about the contributions for covering all costs
- § 184 ISA (2015) – how notifications are passed
- § 29 ISA (2015) – how the bodies (management, supervision board, and supreme body) have to be constituted
- § 192 ISA (2015) – minority rights
- § 293 ISA (2015) – a reserve fund, building savings for covering special losses
- § 194 ISA (2015) – use of surpluses

These regulations are mandatory and have to be examined by the supervision authority. If granted bylaws violate mandatory regulations, the illegal regulation becomes invalid, while the legal capacity of the mutual insurance society stays intact, in contrast to a joint stock company.[88]

vereine auf Gegenseitigkeit. Festschrift zum 100-jährigen Bestehen der Stuttgarter Lebensversicherung a.G., Karlsruhe, pp. 223-248, p. 229.

86 Cf. *Farny, D.* (2011): Versicherungsbetriebslehre, Karlsruhe, p. 205.

87 Cf. *Benkel, G. A.* (2002): Der Versicherungsverein auf Gegenseitigkeit – Das Gesellschaftsrecht der großen konzernfreien VVaG, Munich, p. 70.

88 Cf. *Grosse, W.* (ed.) (1991): Gabler Versicherungsenzyklopädie, Band 3, Rechtslehre des Versicherungswesens, Wiesbaden, p. 525.

3.1.2.2 Shall- and can-regulations

The bylaws of an insurance company shall:

- § 187 ISA (2015) – determine the different insurance branches with their business activities and the principles for asset investments; the bylaws shall determine if the insurance business is conducted directly or indirectly (via reinsurance).
- § 176 ISA (2015) – include the regulations about the beginning of the membership
- § 178 ISA (2015) – include the regulations regarding the foundation fund of the association and how it can be liquidated. Moreover, they shall determine if and how many people who provided the fund are allowed to be part of the asset management.
- § 179 ISA (2015) – determine how and under what requirements further mandatory payments or contributions are allowed to be drawn-in.

The bylaws can:

- § 197 paragraph 1 (ISA 2015) – determine insurance terms and conditions (AVB) as part of the bylaws, but in this case changes have to be approved by the supreme representation.
- § 197 paragraph ISA (ISA 2015) – enable the management, with approval of the supervision board, to introduce or change general insurance conditions. When the management and the supervisory board are not empowered by the bylaws to change the general insurance conditions, then the supreme board can enable the supervisory board, in case of emergency, to change the general insurance terms and conditions temporarily. The changes have to be presented to the supreme board during the next meeting and, if demanded, to suspend them.

The can- and shall-regulations are non-mandatory norms, i.e. the law can be changed when the parties agree on them. This means they can diverge from the legal framework.[89]

3.1.3 Membership

A member can only be a person who constitutes an insurance agreement with the society. The membership ends with the omission of the insurance agreement (§ 176 ISA 2015). From the society's membership

[89] Cf. *Benkel, G. A.* (2002): Der Versicherungsverein auf Gegenseitigkeit – Das Gesellschaftsrecht der großen konzernfreien VVaG, Munich, p. 71.

results rights and duties for the member/policyholder regarding administrative and proprietary issues.[90]

Part of the policyholder's duties is the payment of insurance premiums, including possible additional payments. The rights of the policyholder include insurance protection according to the agreed insurance benefits, the share in periodical profits and in liquidation surpluses, and participation in the bodies of the mutual insurance society.[91]

3.1.4 The bodies

The three legal mandatory bodies of a mutual insurance society are the management as the executive body, the supervisory board as control body for the management as well as the supreme representation as the supreme body (§ 191 ISA 2015). The supreme body can be, depending on the bylaws of the particular mutual insurance society, either a general meeting of all members or a meeting of the members' representatives.[92] The members have the right, based on the mutuality principle, to participate in the society's administration via the bodies (see Figure 2).[93]

3.1.4.1 Supreme body

The members have influence via the supreme body and can thus protect their interests. The supreme body is responsible for the following tasks:

- the appointment of the board members of the supervisory board
- the dismissal of the members of the supervisory and management board
- the appointment of the annual auditor
- the use of the net profit
- the change of the bylaws
- the emission of the profit participation rights
- the transfer of portfolios
- the liquidation of the mutual insurance society.[94]

---

90 Cf. *Müller-Wiedenhorn, A.* (1993): Versicherungsvereine auf Gegenseitigkeit im Unternehmensverbund: Ein Untersuchung zum Recht und zu konzentrationsrechtlichen Fragen des Versicherungsvereins auf Gegenseitigkeit, Beiträge zum Privat- und Wirtschaftsrecht, Diss., Karlsruhe, p. 21.

91 Cf. *Farny, D.* (2011): Versicherungsbetriebslehre, Karlsruhe, p. 209.

92 *Wagner, F.* (ed.) (2011): Gabler Versicherungslexikon, Wiesbaden, p. 732.

93 Cf. *Müller-Wiedenhorn, A.* (1993): Versicherungsvereine auf Gegenseitigkeit im Unternehmensverbund: Eine Untersuchung zum Recht und zu konzentrationsrechtlichen Fragen des Versicherungsvereins auf Gegenseitigkeit, Beiträge zum Privat- und Wirtschaftsrecht, Diss., Karlsruhe, p. 44.

94 Cf. *Farny, D.* (2011): Versicherungsbetriebslehre, Karlsruhe, p. 214.

Figure 2: Bodies of the mutual insurance society

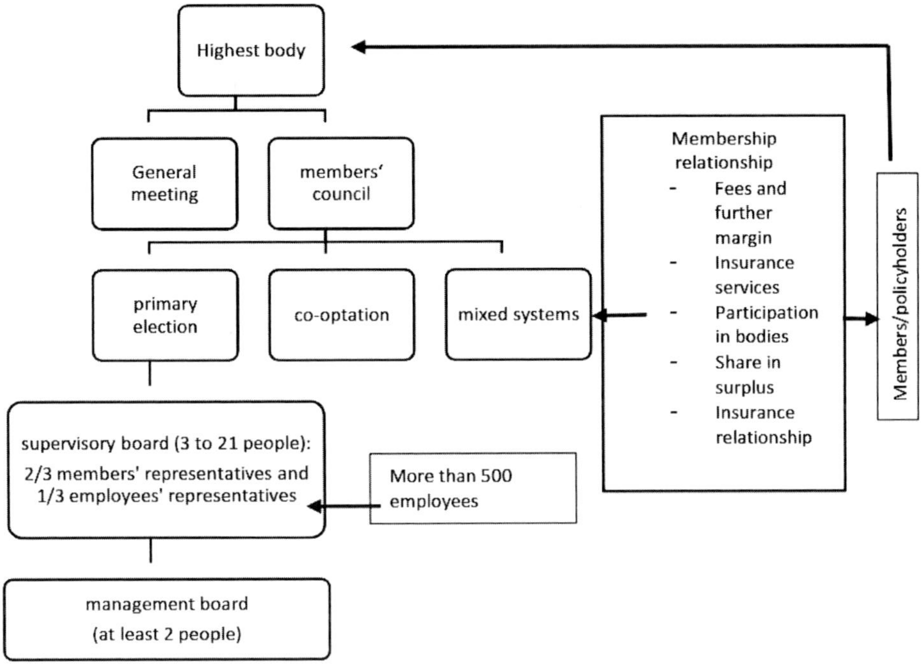

Source: *Farny, D.* (2011): Versicherungsbetriebslehre, 5. vol., Karlsruhe, p. 212

The bylaws determine how the supreme body has to be constituted (§ 184 ISA 2015). This is possible in the form of a general meeting of all members or as a meeting of the members' representatives.[95] Both forms have their advantages and disadvantages, but the three basic goals of the supreme body are difficult to comprise, therefore, they are more a compromise.[96] The goals are:

- the representative participation of the members
- high decision-making quality
- to be operational and economical.

[95] Cf. *Grossfeld, B.* (1985): Der Versicherungsverein auf Gegenseitigkeit im System der Unternehmensformen, Tübingen, p. 55.

[96] Cf. *Nguyen, T. / Romeike, F.* (2013): Versicherungswirtschaftslehre: Grundlagen für Studium und Praxis, Wiesbaden, p. 395.

According to *Bischoff*, small mutual insurance societies can have a general meeting of all members as their supreme body,[97] but usually the members use these meetings to protect their interests.[98] In contrast, large mutual insurance companies usually use the representative members' meeting, although some of them still use the form of a general meeting for all members.[99]

In health insurance societies, the general meeting is not used anymore, while in life insurance societies only the "Hannoversche Lebensversicherung a.G." uses this form of decision-making.[100] A third of the large non-life and accident insurance companies have still the general meeting as a supreme body[101], for example, the "LVM-Landwirtschaftliche Versicherungsverein Münster a.G." and the "VHV-Vereinigte Haftpflichtversicherung V.a.G.", both societies with a large number of members.[102]

a. General meeting of all members

The general meeting displays best the democratic idea of the representation of all members and self-administration.[103] However, according to *Grossfeld*, there are some problems:[104]

- the number of members attending is often very low
- the persons attending the meeting change, so their is no personal continuity
- It is possible that the members' interests are not in agreement with the persons attending.
- Special interests are followed.
- The administration may emphasise the attendance of members who have a positive attitude towards the administrative body.

---

97 Cf. *Bischoff, K.* (1961): Die oberste Vertretung beim kleineren Versicherungsverein auf Gegenseitigkeit – Möglichkeiten und Grenzen, VersR, p. 97.

98 Cf. *Heidelbach, A.* (1994): Der kleinere Versicherungsverein auf Gegenseitigkeit unter besonderer Berücksichtigung der gesellschaftsrechtlichen Probleme, Versicherungsrechtliche Studien, Band 30, Diss., Frankfurt am Main, p. 105.

99 Cf. *Grossfeld, B.* (1985): Der Versicherungsverein auf Gegenseitigkeit im System der Unternehmensformen, Tübingen, p. 55.

100 Cf. *Benkel, G. A.* (2002): Der Versicherungsverein auf Gegenseitigkeit – Das Gesellschaftsrecht der großen konzernfreien VVaG, Munich, p. 88.

101 Cf. *Nemson, J.* (2014): Geschäftsmodell VVaG: Rahmenbedingungen, Herausforderungen und Chancen, Karlsruhe, p. 72.

102 Cf. *Benkel, G. A.* (2002): Der Versicherungsverein auf Gegenseitigkeit – Das Gesellschaftsrecht der großen konzernfreien VVaG, Munich, p. 88.

103 Cf. *Hauth, H.* (1984): Unternehmensverfassungsrechtliche Probleme des Versicherungsvereins auf Gegenseitigkeit, Frankfurt am Main, p. 17.

104 Cf. *Grossfeld, B.* (1985): Der Versicherungsverein auf Gegenseitigkeit im System der Unternehmensformen, Tübingen, p. 55f.

- General meetings with a large number of members are difficult to execute for reasons of efficiency, costs (invitations, travel, accommodation, conference halls), and attendance control.

Therefore, in practice general meetings with all members are more common in small mutual insurance societies,[105] while in large societies they are rather rare.[106]

b. Members' representative meeting

When the supreme body is composed of members' representatives, then, according to *Farny*[107], the eligible passive and active voters as well as the voting procedures are as follows:

1. The active eligible voters
   1.1. All members are entitled to vote.
   1.2. Only the members' representatives of the supreme body are authorised to re-elect themselves or to co-opt another person (co-optation principle).
   1.3. Election combinations are established, for example election by direct vote in longer intervals and co-optation during the interim period.
2. The passive eligible voters and the nominations of candidates
   Usually all members (all natural persons) can be elected as members' representatives. The nomination of candidates is presented either by all members, a minimum number of members, a special election committee, by the supreme body or together with the supervisory board and the management.
3. Voting procedures
   3.1. The voting about the nominated candidates takes place either in written or oral form.
   3.2. The nomination of the candidates is accepted when there is no objection.

Before the ISA 1901 came into effect, the supporters of the general meeting criticized the possibility of a members' representative meeting. However, the lawmaker had already known about the practice regarding the members' representative meeting and its position did not

[105] Cf. *Farny, D.* (2011): Versicherungsbetriebslehre, Karlsruhe, p. 214.

[106] Cf. *Benkel, G. A.* (2002): Der Versicherungsverein auf Gegenseitigkeit – Das Gesellschaftsrecht der großen konzernfreien VVaG, Munich, p. 88.

[107] *Farny, D.* (2011): Versicherungsbetriebslehre, Karlsruhe, p. 215.

change over time. After the introduction of this election form, it was recognized as a useful solution.[108]

Grossfeld[109] states that the members' representative meeting has the opportunity to avoid the weaknesses of the general meeting. The quality of the decision-making process is higher, because an election based on expertise and personal qualification is possible. Moreover, this form guarantees a bigger consistence of the participants, who receive the possibility to expand their knowledge due to the work in the members' representatives meeting. The larger homogeneity of the group is the reason for the slight possibility of the administration to influence the decision-making process. The administrative costs are lower than of a general meeting. However, a representation is only guaranteed when the members' proxy are also members of the mutual insurance society. Moreover, the performance of official functions are only accepted unlimitedly when the composition of the members' council represents the interests of the insured to some extent.

Similar arguments can be found in other academic works.[110] *Grossfeld* detects problems when the members' representative meeting denies its responsibility and the relationship to the members or when the members' council becomes dependent on the administration. These problems can be restricted due to a proper nomination of candidates and appointing procedures. As a result, the following four appointment procedures of the members' representation meeting developed (election by direct vote, system of objection, co-optation as well as a mixed system).[111]

Figure 3 shows that large mutual insurance societies use co-optation most frequently. The mixed system is used frequently by health and life insurances, while the election by direct vote, which is similar to the general meeting, became very rare and the system of formal objection is almost insignificant.[112]

b.1 Election by direct vote

According to this system, all members elect the members' representatives in regular intervals. According to the bylaws, it is possible that

---

[108] Cf. *Benkel, G. A.* (2002): Der Versicherungsverein auf Gegenseitigkeit – Das Gesellschaftsrecht der großen konzernfreien VVaG, Munich, p. 91.

[109] *Grossfeld, B.* (1985): Der Versicherungsverein auf Gegenseitigkeit im System der Unternehmensformen, Tübingen, p. 57.

[110] Cf. *Benkel, G. A.* (2002): Der Versicherungsverein auf Gegenseitigkeit – Das Gesellschaftsrecht der großen konzernfreien VVaG, Munich, p. 94.

[111] Cf. *Grossfeld, B.* (1985): Der Versicherungsverein auf Gegenseitigkeit im System der Unternehmensformen, Tübingen, p. 58.

[112] Cf. *Nemson, J.* (2014): Geschäftsmodell VVaG: Rahmenbedingungen, Herausforderungen und Chancen, Karlsruhe, p. 74.

Figure 3: Election system for the members' representation meeting in the different insurance branches

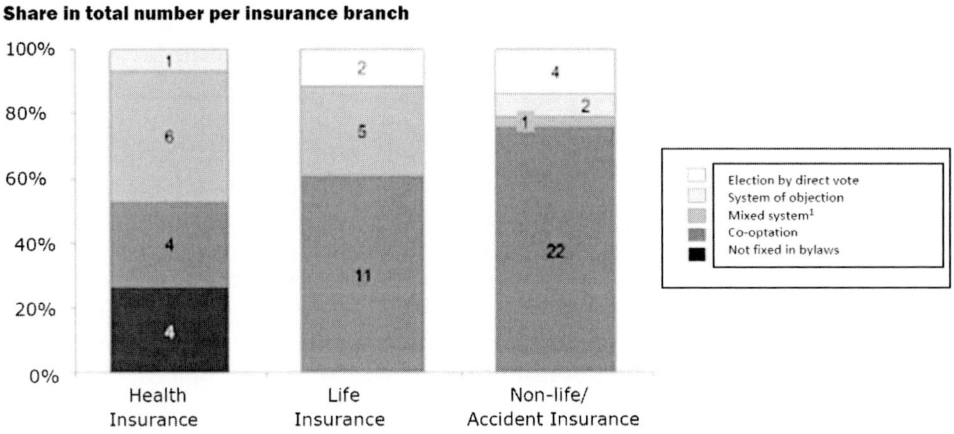

[1] Mixed system: election by direct vote-co-optation

Source: *Nemson, J.* (2014): Geschäftsmodell VVaG: Rahmenbedingungen, Herausforderungen und Chancen, Karlsruhe, p. 74.

the election committee can comprise constituencies and/or member groups.[113] In the process, similar problems can occur like in the members' representation meeting. The attendance is low, the costs are high, and the nomination of candidates of the management and the supervisory board are always accepted. As a result, the system becomes a covered co-optation system.[114]

b.2 System of formal objection

For this system, the election committee proposes competent members' representatives. If not a group of 5 to 10 percent of all members object to them, they are elected.[115] As a result, objections are very rare.[116] Moreover, the legitimation of the members' representatives is

[113] Cf. *Brenzel, J.* (1975): Der Versicherungsverein auf Gegenseitigkeit – Unternehmensform und Rechtsstruktur im Wandel, Karlsruhe, p. 30.

[114] Cf. *Benkel, G. A.* (2002): Der Versicherungsverein auf Gegenseitigkeit – Das Gesellschaftsrecht der großen konzernfreien VVaG, Munich, p. 95.

[115] Cf. *Brenzel, J.* (1975): Der Versicherungsverein auf Gegenseitigkeit – Unternehmensform und Rechtsstruktur im Wandel, Karlsruhe, p. 31.

[116] Cf. *Benkel, G. A.* (2002): Der Versicherungsverein auf Gegenseitigkeit – Das Gesellschaftsrecht der großen konzernfreien VVaG, Munich, p. 96.

questionable and the system may lead to a dominance of the management.[117]

b.3 Co-optation procedure

The co-optation system tries to solve problems by electing the general meeting via direct vote and then new members' representatives are co-opted by the current representatives.[118]

Critical voices argue that the democratic rights of the members are eliminated, the representative participation of members is permanently excluded, and only a low number of members are part of the administration. Some critics argue that the co-optation system is legally inadmissible.[119]

The majority of the literature, however, does not follow this opinion. The co-optation system was used before the Insurance Supervision Act of 1901 and is largely legally admissible.[120] Even in 1901, the lawmaker considered the co-optation procedure as admissible and stated in the Insurance Supervision Act as following:

The older bylaws do not include general meetings, but transferred the members' rights to a proxy body, which members receive permanently the right for co-optation via the bylaws or were elected by the policyholders or certain groups. Therefore, the different systems should be kept in the future.[121]

In 1964/65, *Raiser's* results of his analysis stated that the co-optation procedure is legal and should be re-approved in future legal revisions. He argues, however, that members should receive different rights in the bylaws, so that they are able to influence the business of the society.[122]

In 2007, a court decided about the legitimacy of the co-optation procedure for the first time. The judges of the regional court Cologne decided that the co-optation procedure is in practice and theory accept-

---

[117] Cf. *Müller-Wiedenhorn, A.* (1993): Versicherungsvereine auf Gegenseitigkeit im Unternehmensverbund: Eine Untersuchung zum Recht und zu konzentrationsrechtlichen Fragen des Versicherungsvereins auf Gegenseitigkeit, Beiträge zum Privat- und Wirtschaftsrecht, Diss., Karlsruhe, p. 49.

[118] Cf. *Grossfeld, B.* (1985): Der Versicherungsverein auf Gegenseitigkeit im System der Unternehmensformen, Tübingen, p. 61.

[119] Cf. *Benkel, G. A.* (2002): Der Versicherungsverein auf Gegenseitigkeit – Das Gesellschaftsrecht der großen konzernfreien VVaG, Munich, p. 98.

[120] Cf. *Benkel, G. A.* (2002): Der Versicherungsverein auf Gegenseitigkeit – Das Gesellschaftsrecht der großen konzernfreien VVaG, Munich, p. 97.

[121] Bundesaufsichtsamt für das Versicherungs- und Bausparwesen (ed.) (1963): Motive zum Versicherungsaufsichtsgesetz, Nachdruck, Berlin, p. 42.

[122] Cf. *Raiser, L.* (1965): Die Zulässigkeit des Kooptationssystems bei der Bildung von Mitgliedervertretungen großer Versicherungsverein auf Gegenseitigkeit, ZVersWiss., 54. Band, pp. 465-485, p. 485.

able and confirmed its legitimacy.[123] The judges of the regional court of Cologne justified their decision that in literature the typical organization structure of a mutual insurance society has been criticized, but the representation of the members via a proxy body is legally acceptable in case of large mutual insurance societies. The broad freedom of scope of mutual insurance societies is not exceeded by the co-optation system and the bylaws of the defendants complied with the Insurance Supervision Act. According to the resume of the *BaFin* from November 27th, 2006, the co-optation procedure is in general successful, it is part of many bylaws, and matches the intention of the lawmaker to keep the co-optation procedure as part of the bylaw autonomy. The membership is not mandatory for members and therefore they can still perform their interests in another way. The judges of the court in Cologne stated that it is not the court's function to restore additional influence and control in a mutual insurance society to its members by interpreting § 242 BGB further.[124]

The supervision authority has always considered the co-optation procedure as legitimate and has become established in the bylaws by continuously use. Now it is a feature of this legal form and therefore admissible.[125] *Farny* states that currently the co-optation system is acknowledged, but its evaluation is still difficult. He argues that the advantages and disadvantages of this procedure are based on the participants' actions and less on the system itself.[126]

b.4 Mixed system

In a mixed system, the election by direct votes occurs in longer intervals. Members' representatives who withdraw from their position between the elections were co-opted by the other representatives.[127] The mixed system appears to be advantageous, because the leaving representatives can be replaced very quickly using co-optation. Moreover, the intention of all members can be integrated occasionally into the supreme body due to a direct vote election.[128]

---

[123] Cf. *Fahl, H.* (2008): Demokratie im Versicherungsverein – Anmerkung zum Urteil des Landesgerichts Köln vom 24. August 2007 (AZ. 82 O 212/06), Versicherungswirtschaft, 63. vol., Number 14, p. 1165.

[124] Cf. OpenJur, LG Köln, verdict 24. August 2007 Az.82O212/06, https://openjur.de/u/127703.html, 20.06.2018.

[125] Cf. *Benkel, G. A.* (2002): Der Versicherungsverein auf Gegenseitigkeit – Das Gesellschaftsrecht der großen konzernfreien VVaG, Munich, p. 104.

[126] Cf. *Farny, D.* (2011): Versicherungsbetriebslehre, Karlsruhe, p. 215.

[127] Cf. *Grossfeld, B.* (1985): Der Versicherungsverein auf Gegenseitigkeit im System der Unternehmensformen, Tübingen, p. 58.

[128] Cf. *Müller-Wiedenhorn, A.* (1993): Versicherungsvereine auf Gegenseitigkeit im Unternehmensverbund: Eine Untersuchung zum Recht und zu konzentrationsrechtlichen Fragen des

3.1.4.2 Supervisory board

The supervisory board comprises between 3 and 21 members, while the number has always to be divisible by three.[129] The supervisory board comprises members elected by the supreme body as well as elected by employees. This is applicable to societies to which the One-third Participation Act applies (§ 1 paragraph 1 No 4). The supervision board appoints the management board and controls its activities. Moreover, it authorised the annual accountant, examines the annual financial report, helps with the use of the surpluses, and represents the mutual insurance society to the members of the management.[130]

3.1.4.3 Management

The management comprises at least two people and is appointed by the supervision board for not more than five years. The earliest possible extension is one year before the end of the term and members of the management can be recalled due to important reasons.[131] The management conducts the mutual insurance society self-dependently, represents the society in public and towards the members, and reports to the supervision board and the supreme body.[132]

3.1.5 Supervision by the Federal Government and the Regional Government

The supervision of the Federal Government is realised by the "German federal financial supervisory agency" (Bundesanstalt für Finanzdienstleistungsaufsicht) and the supervision of the regional government by the particular regional ministry.[133]

The first supervises private insurance companies with their head office or branch in Germany (§ 320 ISA 2015) and can advice the Federal Ministry of Finance to transfer the supervision of economically less important insurance companies to the regional government. The latter has to agree to the supervision transfer (§ 321 ISA 2015).

Versicherungsvereins auf Gegenseitigkeit, Beiträge zum Privat- und Wirtschaftsrecht, Diss., Karlsruhe, p. 53.

[129] Cf. *Arens, W./Tepper, F.* (eds.) (2013): Praxisformularbuch Gesellschaftsrecht: Schriftsätze – Verträge – Erläuterungen, Nördlingen, p. 772.

[130] Cf. *Farny, D.* (2011): Versicherungsbetriebslehre, Karlsruhe, p. 215.

[131] Cf. *Müller-Wiedenhorn, A.* (1993): Versicherungsvereine auf Gegenseitigkeit im Unternehmensverbund: Eine Untersuchung zum Recht und zu konzentrationsrechtlichen Fragen des Versicherungsvereins auf Gegenseitigkeit, Beiträge zum Privat- und Wirtschaftsrecht, Diss., Karlsruhe, p. 54.

[132] Cf. *Farny, D.* (2011): Versicherungsbetriebslehre, Karlsruhe, p. 216.

[133] *Wagner, F.* (ed.) (2011): Gabler Versicherungslexikon,1st edition, Wiesbaden, p. 53.

According to the old ISA, the main task of the federal government supervision in the traditional system was the substantive state supervision of the entire insurance business.[134] Since the realization of the third guideline in 1994, the main goals of the insurance supervision have been the protection of the interests of the insured and the safeguarding of the fulfilment of the insurance contracts.[135]

At first, the general legal supervision was repressed by the abolishment of the prior checking of insurance terms and conditions, the observance of the subsidiarity and proportionality principles, and the restriction of the ongoing supervision to a legality control, but since Solvency II (January 2016) a concentration of regulations has started.[136]

The insurance guideline of the European Community distinguishes regarding the place of business between insurance companies with their head office in Germany and foreign companies with business activities in Germany. The home country control comprises financial and general legal supervision, while the supervision of business activities is limited to a general legal supervision of regulations concerning general interests, because the basic supervision (general and financial) of foreign insurance companies lies in the home member state.[137]

The ISA was revised regarding both kinds of supervision. The supervision of business activities is limited to control the legality. Representatives of the supervision authority take the view that the control of deficits still applies even after the deregulation.[138] Nevertheless, the German insurance industry only accepts the control of legality.[139]

3.1.6 Solvency

The German insurance business had already been regulated intensively since the introduction of the Insurance Supervision Act in 1901.[140] The main goals of the insurance supervision are the protection

---

[134] Cf. *Rittner, F./Dreher, M.* (2008): Europäisches und deutsches Wirtschaftsrecht – Eine systematische Darstellung, Heidelberg, p. 816.

[135] Cf. BaFin, Versicherungsaufsicht in Deutschland, https://www.bafin.de/EN/DieBaFin/AufgabenGeschichte/Versicherungsaufsicht/versicherungsaufsicht_node_en.html 20.06.2018

[136] Cf. *Winter, G.* (2007): Versicherungsaufsichtsrecht – Kritische Betrachtung, Karlsruhe, p. 773.

[137] Cf. *Rittner, F. / Dreher, M.* (2008): Europäisches und deutsches Wirtschaftsrecht – Eine systematische Darstellung, Heidelberg, p. 817.

[138] Cf. *Müller, H.* (2001): Materielle Versicherungsaufsicht – Eine Standortbestimmung, in Müller, H. et.al. (ed.): 100 Jahre materielle Versicherungsaufsicht in Deutschland, 1901-2001, Bonn, p. 158.

[139] Cf. *Rabe, T.* (1995): Liberalisierung und Deregulierung im Europäischen Binnenmarkt für Versicherungen,Schriftenreihe des Instituts für Versicherungswissenschaft an der Universität zu Köln, Berlin, p. 204.

[140] Cf. *Wagner, F./Luo, J.* (2012): Solvency II: Ein neues aufsichtsrechtliches Regime und dessen Konsequenzen für Versicherungsunternehmen, in *Beckmann, R. M.* (ed.): Weitsicht in Ver-

of the policyholders' interests, the supervision of the system stability, and the stabilization of the entire economy.[141]

An essential part of the supervisory control is the Solvency system for the protection of the fulfilment of all policyholders' claims.[142] The foundation of solvency (capital requirements) is to show the overall risk of an insurance company based on certain regularly measured features and mirrored by the risk carrying capacity of the solvency funds. If insurance companies fall below the limit, supervisory sanctions are the results.[143]

3.1.6.1 Solvency II

The new system regulates quantitative and qualitative requirements, the obligation of insurance companies of notification and disclosure towards supervision authorities. It is usually presented as a three-pillar structure (see Figure 4).[144]

With Solvency II, the current insurance industry should be improved. Risk-based capital requirements: The directive requires insurance companies to hold capital in relation to their risk profiles to guarantee that they have enough financial resources to withstand financial difficulties. The Governance and risk management requirements state that insurance companies have to

- put in place an adequate and transparent governance system
- conduct their own risk and solvency assessment on a regular basis

sicherung und Wirtschaft. Gedächtnisschrift für Ulrich Hübner, Heidelberg (et.al.), pp. 319-340, p. 319.

[141] Cf. *Farny, D.* (2011): Versicherungsbetriebslehre, Karlsruhe, p. 108.

[142] *Wagner, F./Luo, J.* (2012): Solvency II: Ein neues aufsichtsrechtliches Regime und dessen Konsequenzen für Versicherungsunternehmen, in *Beckmann, R. M.* (ed.): Weitsicht in Versicherung und Wirtschaft. Gedächtnisschrift für Ulrich Hübner, Heidelberg (et.al.), pp. 319-340, p. 319.

[143] Cf. *Wagner, F.*: Beitrag auf Gabler Wirtschaftslexikon, Solvabilität, http://wirtschaftslexikon.gabler.de/Definition/solvabilitaet.html, 20.06.2018.

[144] Cf. http://www.solvency-ii-kompakt.de/.20.06.2018.

Figure 4: The solvency II three pillar structure

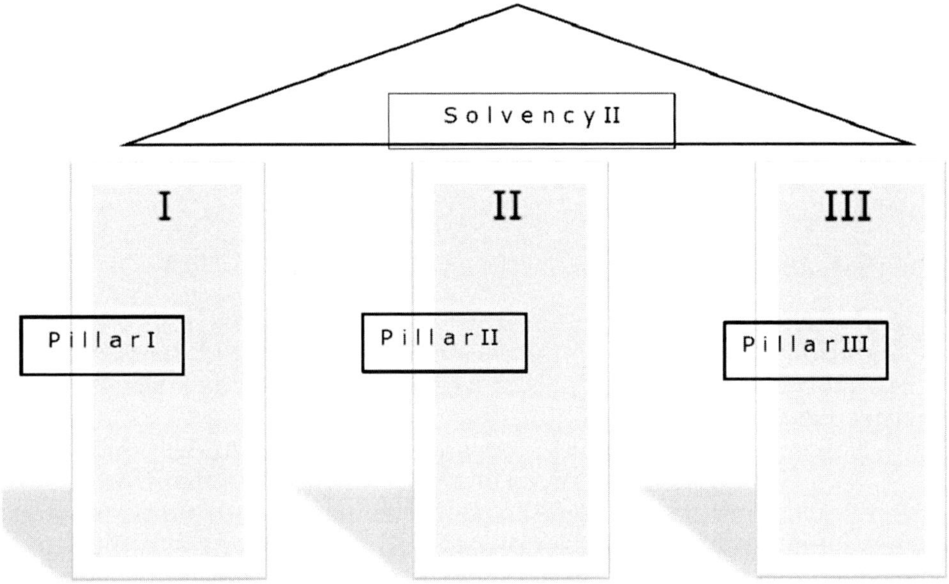

Source: Solvency II Kompakt, Säule I, http://www.solvency-ii-kompakt.de/content/uebersicht-ueber-saeule-i, 12.06.2018.

With regard to the Supervisory reporting and public disclosure, the directive

- enables supervisors to review and evaluate whether insurance companies comply with the rules
- requires these companies to report to supervisory authorities and disclose information publicly.[145]

Pillar 1: comprises the quantitative (solvency) requirements:[146]

- Own funds requirements
- The rules for calculating the technical provisions
- Review of the calculation approaches

[145] Cf.https://ec.europa.eu/info/business-economy-euro/banking-and-finance/insurance-and-pensions/risk-management-and-supervision-insurance-companies-solvency-2_en.html 20.06.2018.

[146] Cf. BaFin, Solvency II: https://www.bafin.de/EN/Aufsicht/VersichererPensionsfonds/Aufsichtsregime/SolvencyII/solvency_II_node_en 20.06.2018.

The evaluations should be carried out market consistently with the goal that the companies have sufficient equity capital at all times.

Figure 5: Solvency II – Overview of pillar I

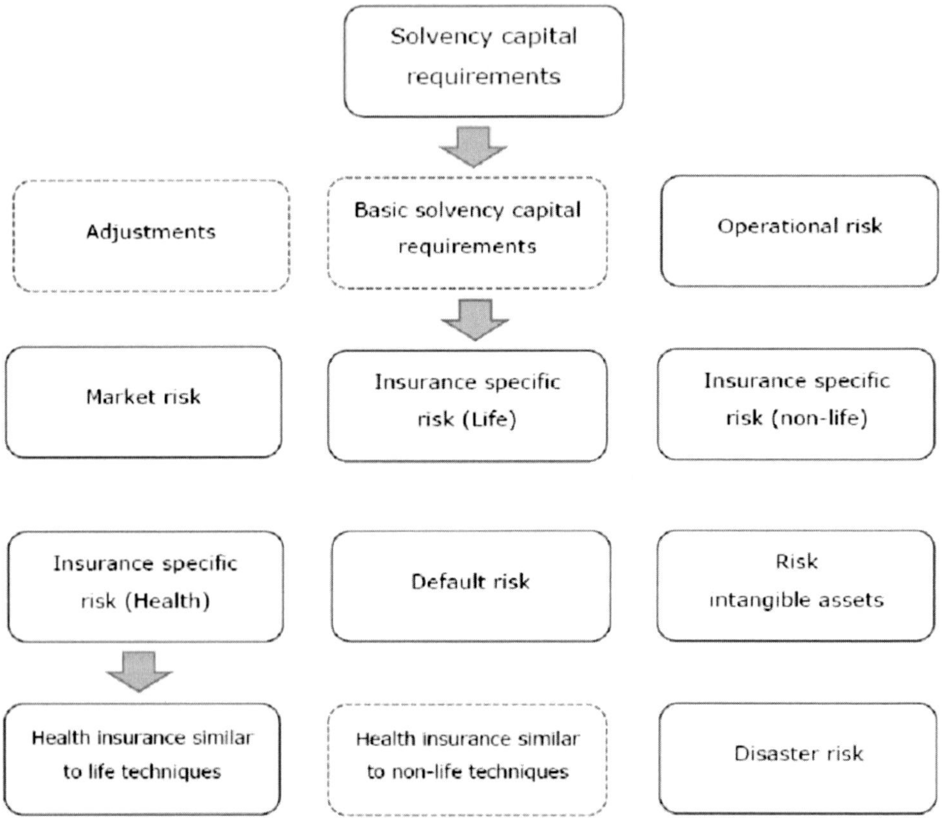

Source: Solvency II Kompakt, Säule I, http://www.solvency-ii-kompakt.de/content/uebersicht-ueber-saeule-i, 12.06.2018.

Pillar II: comprises the qualitative requirements for the governance system:[147]

- Principles and methods of supervision
- Qualitative requirements for engaging in insurance activities

[147] Cf. BaFin, Solvency II: https://www.bafin.de/EN/Aufsicht/VersichererPensionsfonds/Aufsichtsregime/SolvencyII/solvency_II_node_en.html 20.06.2018.

In terms of the supervisory rules, special attention is given to the Supervisory Review Process used by the supervisory authorities to review and assess compliance with the quantitative and qualitative requirements. Pillar II also deals with the individual aspects of governance, including in particular, the fit and proper requirements, risk management, the own risk and solvency assessment (ORSA), internal controls, the internal audit function, the actuarial function and the framework conditions for outsourcing.

Figure 6: Solvency II – Overview of pillar II

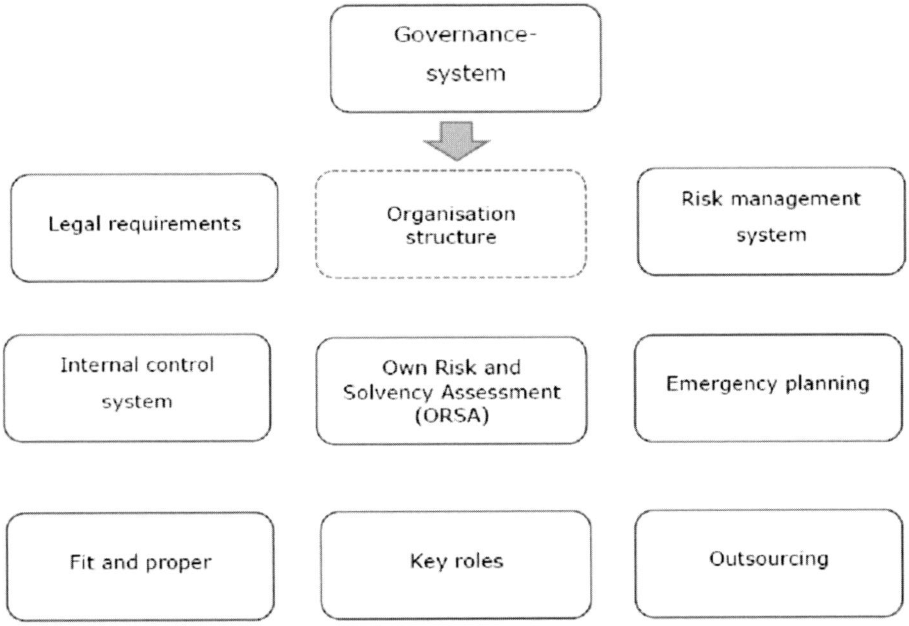

Source: Solvency II Kompakt, Säule II, http://www.solvency-ii-kompakt.de/content/uebersicht-ueber-saeule-ii (12.06.2018).

Pillar III deals with market discipline, transparency and disclosure obligations along with reporting to the supervisory authorities.[148]

[148] https://www.bafin.de/EN/Aufsicht/VersichererPensionsfonds/Aufsichtsregime/SolvencyII/solvency_II_node_en.html 20.06.2018; *Wagner, F./Luo, J.* (2012): Solvency II: Ein neues aufsichtsrechtliches Regime und dessen Konsequenzen für Versicherungsunternehmen, in *Beckmann, R. M.* (ed.): Weitsicht in Versicherung und Wirtschaft. Gedächtnisschrift für Ulrich Hübner, Heidelberg (et.al.), pp. 319-340, p. 331.

Figure 7: Solvency II – Overview of pillar III

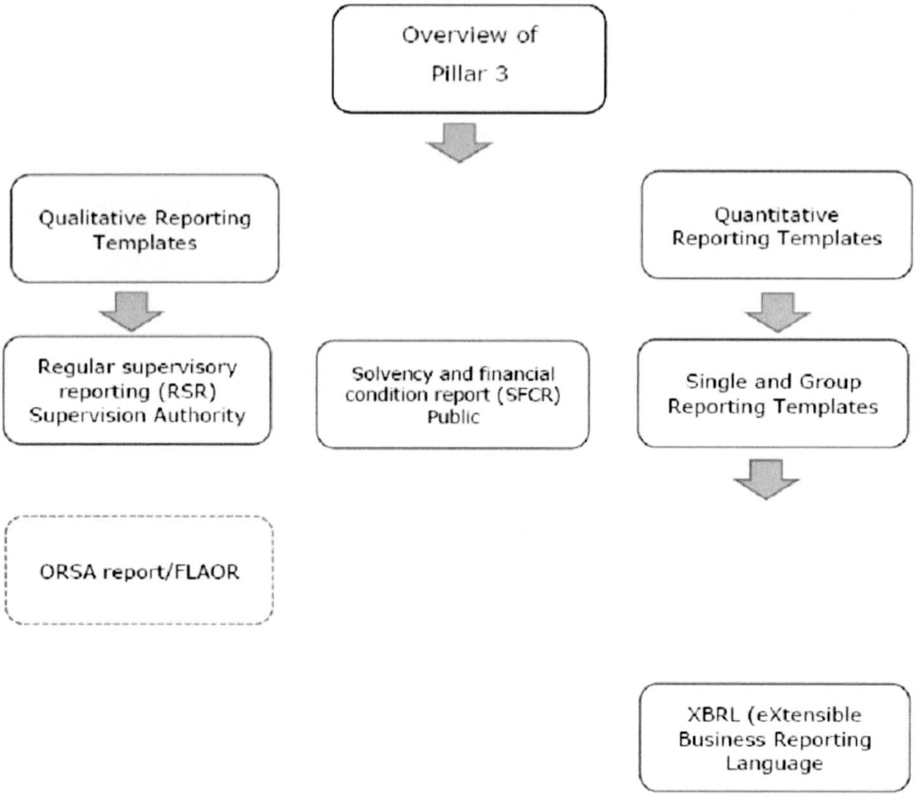

Source: Solvency II Kompakt, Säule III, http://www.solvency-ii-kompakt.de/content/saeule-iii, 12.06.2018; XBRL:eXtensible Business Reporting Language Solvency and Financial Condition Report; FLAOR: Final Guidelines on Own Risk and Solvency Assessment Own Risk and Solvency Assessment.

- The regular supervisory reporting (RSR) is used to report to the supervision authority;
- The solvency and financial condition report (SFCR) is used for publishing the solvency and financial situation of a company.
- Quantitative reporting templates are part of the annual report to the supervision authority and the public.

It is a new form of reporting which can be used only indirectly for market transparency and market discipline.[149] It comprises the obligation to notify the supervision authority and the public, which led to a revision of the current way of reporting to avoid future overlaps (see Figure 7).

[149] Cf. *Farny, D.* (2011): Versicherungsbetriebslehre, Karlsruhe, p. 809.

3.2 Economic importance

Today's situation of mutual insurance societies in Germany cannot be described easily. On the one hand, large mutual insurance societies offering all types of insurances, usually organized as holding enterprises, exist, on the other hand, many small mutuals exist, which have limited markets and offer highly specialised products. The latter are not part of the general market business. These include companies offering pension funds and death benefits funds. There are captive-insurers offering company retirement schemes for major companies as well as animal and hail insurance societies.[150]

The following tables show that with 879[151] (2016) small insurance societies are the majority of insurance companies. However, with a share of 1 percent in the generated gross premiums their economic importance is quite low. Nevertheless, this companies have social value, because they are specialised and able to operate flexibly on the market due to their size. Moreover, they introduced new and innovative products on the insurance market. Due to their limited market importance they are not analyzed in this study further.

The total premium volume of 266 Billion Euro on the German primary insurance market 2016 comprises 570 direct insurance undertakings under federal supervision.[152] Life insurance premiums are generated by life insurance companies, occupational provision funds (Pensionskassen), death benefit funds and pension funds. The latter are not insurance companies in the stricter sense, but they are presented here to give a better understanding. Additionally, health, non-life and re-insurance companies are large players on the market.

In Germany, companies with any kind of legal form that allows insurance business can be found on the insurance market and its sub markets. From the above mentioned 570 companies under federal supervision, 300 are joint stock companies (52%), 84 are large mutual insurance societies (15%), 163 small mutual insurance societies (29%), 18 public law entities (3%), and 7 have other legal forms (as subsidiaries of foreign insurers) (0.5%). In 2016, 300 joint stock companies achieved 84% of the total gross premium volume. Although the total number of the 84 large and 163 small mutual insurance societies is almost as high as the number of joint stock companies, their gross premium income accounts for only 14% of the market. The public insurers and companies

[150] Cf. *Farny, D.* (2012): Zustand und Perspektiven der Gegenseitigkeitsversicherung in Deutschland, in *Beckmann, R. M.* (ed.): Weitsicht in Versicherung und Wirtschaft. Gedächtnisschrift für Ulrich Hübner, Heidelberg (et.al.), pp. 77-88, p. 80.

[151] 716 under regional supervision and 163 under federal supervision.

[152] Cf. BaFin (2018): Statistik der Bundesanstalt für Finanzdienstleistungsaufsicht – Erstversicherungsunternehmen und Pensionsfonds –, Bonn.

Table 2: Number and gross premiums of insurance companies under regional governmental supervision, sorted according to provinces and type of companies in the business years 2015 and 2016

Country	BY	Occupational provision funds (Pensionskassen)		Death benefit fund		Health insurance associations		Non-life insurance associations		Animal insurance associations		Total	
		Number	Premium per 1,000 Euro	Number	Premium per 1,000 Euro	Number	Premium per 1,000 Euro	Number	Premium per 1,000 Euro	Number	Premium per 1,000 Euro	Number	Premium per 1,000 Euro
a	b	1	2	3	4	5	6	7	8	9	10	11	12
1. Baden-Württemberg	2016	5	687.2	7	489.2	0	0	2	140.0	6	145.2	20	1,461.6
	2015	5	670.2	7	506.3	0	0	2	137.5	6	141.8	20	1,455.8
2. Bayern	2016	4	9.0	86	1,522.0	6	11.0	43	2,475,0	0	0.0	139	4,017.0
	2015	4	10.0	86	1.642.0	6	12.0	44	2,530.0	0	0.0	140	4,194.0
3. Bremen	2016	0	0.0	8	128.3	3	174.4	1	106.0	0	0.0	12	408.7
	2015	0	0.0	8	124.4	3	156.8	1	116.1	0	0.0	12	397.3
4. Hessen	2016	2	0.5	16	1,520.6	3	99.7	2	511.8	2	39.9	25	2,172.5
	2015	2	0.5	16	1,582.4	3	104.2	2	515.6	3	69.5	26	2,272.2
5. Niedersachsen	2016	0	0.0	68	1,736.0	1	32.5	43	6,155.5	39	275.5	151	8,199.5
	2015	0	0.0	68	1,696.6	1	33.8	46	6,025.5	39	271.3	154	8,027.2
6. NRW	2016	3	346.5	202	13,819.2	3	97.9	19	2,381.6	0	0	227	16,645.2
	2015	3	418.4	209	15,342.1	3	94.2	19	2,226.0	0	0	234	18,080.7
7. Rheinland-Pfalz	2016	0	0.0	8	754.3	0	0.0	1	65.1	0	0.0	9	819.4
	2015	1	0.0	8	778.7	0	0.0	1	66.4	0	0.0	10	845.1
8. Saarland	2016	0	0.0	42	1,924.5	1	111.7	0	0.0	0	0.0	43	2,036.2
	2015	0	0.0	42	1,859.1	1	98.0	0	0.0	0	0.0	43	1,957.1
9. Schleswig-Holstein	2016	0	0.0	20	1,067.5	0	0.0	70	6,610.5	0	0	90	7,678.0
	2015	0	0.0	20	1,069.1	0	0.0	70	6,255.1	0	0	90	7,324.2
Sum	**2016**	**14**	**1,043.2**	**457**	**22,961.6**	**17**	**527.2**	**181**	**18,445.5**	**47**	**460.6**	**716**	**43,438.1**
	2015	**15**	**1,099.1**	**464**	**24,600.7**	**17**	**499.0**	**185**	**17,872.2**	**48**	**482.6**	**729**	**44,553.6**

Source: BaFin (2018): Statistik der Bundesanstalt für Finanzdienstleistungsaufsicht – Erstversicherungsunternehmen und Pensionsfonds –, Bonn, p. 12.

Table 3: Number and gross premiums earned (in thousand €) of insurance companies under federal and governmental supervision

Type of company		BY	Joint stock company	Mutual insurance society	Small mutual insurance society	Public insurance company	Other legal forms	Number and earned gross premiums of the companies	From them under federal supervision	From them under state supervision
Life insurance	number	2016	65	16	-	4	2	87	84	3
	gross premiums earned		71.800,397	12.179,691	-	993,916	1.193,626	86.167,630	85.926,282	241,349
	number	2015	64	17	-	4	2	87	84	3
	gross premiums earned		73.022,773	12.193,733	-	1.102,532	1.247.376	87.566,414	87.181,682	384,732
Occupational provision funds (Pensionskassen)	number	2016	22	6	109	1	-	138	138	-
	gross premiums earned		3.335,786	872,015	2.473,966	203,721	-	6.885,488	6.885,488	-
	number	2015	22	6	111	1	-	140	140	-
	gross premiums earned		3.160,083	791,336	2.454,673	205,775	-	6.611,868	6.611,868	-
Pension fund	number	2016	28	-	-	-	1	29	29	-
	gross premiums earned		2.366,293	-	-	-	40.386	2.406,679	2.406,679	-
	number	2015	30	-	-	-	1	31	31	-
	gross premiums earned		2.853,361	-	-	-	40.278	2.893,639	2.893,639	-
Death benefit insurance	number	2016	1	2	32	-	-	35	35	-
	gross premiums earned		14,680	3,882	51,512	-	-	70,075	70,075	-
	number	2015	1	2	32	-	-	35	35	-
	gross premiums earned		15,575	3,920	50,895	-	-	70,390	70,390	-
Health insurance	number	2016	24	15	7	-	-	46	46	-
	gross premiums earned		21.908,251	15.241,349	26,847	-	-	37.176,446	37.176,446	-

	number	2015	24	16	7	-	-	47	47	-
	gross premiums earned		21.001,805	15.655,950	25,962	-	-	36.683,718	36.683,718	-
Non-life/accident insurance	number	2016	136	44	15	11	2	208	201	7
	gross premiums earned		66.358,323	7.004,276	23,882	2.235,95	527.775	76.149,650	75.388,166	761,484
	number	2015	140	43	15	11	3	212	205	7
	gross premiums earned		64.785.356	7.543,157	24,232	2.134,842	521,154	75.008,740	74.303,037	705,704
Re-insurance [1]	number	2016	24	1	-	2	1	28	28	-
	gross premiums earned		57.757.008	29,793	-	457,548	36.204	58.280,554	58.280,554	-
	number	2015	24	1	-	2	1	28	28	-
	gross premiums earned		51.629.370	30,050	-	412,244	60.840	52.132,505	52.132,505	-
Insurance companies total	number	**2016**	**300**	**84**	**163**	**18**	**6**	**571**	**561**	**10**
	gross premiums earned		**223.540,737**	**35.331,007**	**2.576,207**	**3.890,580**	**1.797,992**	**267.136,522**	**266.133,690**	**1.002,833**
	number	**2015**	**305**	**85**	**165**	**18**	**7**	**580**	**570**	**10**
	gross premiums earned		**216.468,324**	**36.218,146**	**2.555,762**	**3.855,393**	**1.869,648**	**260.967,274**	**259.876,839**	**1.090,436**

[1] Balance sheets are from September and December of the previous year as well as June of the reporting year.

Source: BaFin (2018): Statistik der Bundesanstalt für Finanzdienstleistungsaufsicht – Erstversicherungsunternehmen und Pensionsfonds –, Bonn, p. 104.

Table 4: Comparison of the development of insurance joint stock companies with mutual insurance societies (without pension funds)

Year	Joint stock company	Mutual insurance society
1954	110	684
1960	125	646
1970	140	527
1980	196	406
1990	281	352
1995	319	322
2000	317	287
2001	302	273
2002	323	271
2003	329	269
2004	328	270
2005	321	267
2006	315	267
2007	321	267
2008	307	268
2009	313	267
2010	301	267
2011	300	261
2012	295	259
2013	291	254
2014	278	254
2015	275	250
2016	272	247

Source: GDV (2017) Statistisches Taschenbuch der Versicherungswirtschaft, Karlsruhe, p. 14 und BaFin.

Figure 8: Comparison of the development of market shares of insurance joint stock companies vs. mutual insurance societies in percent

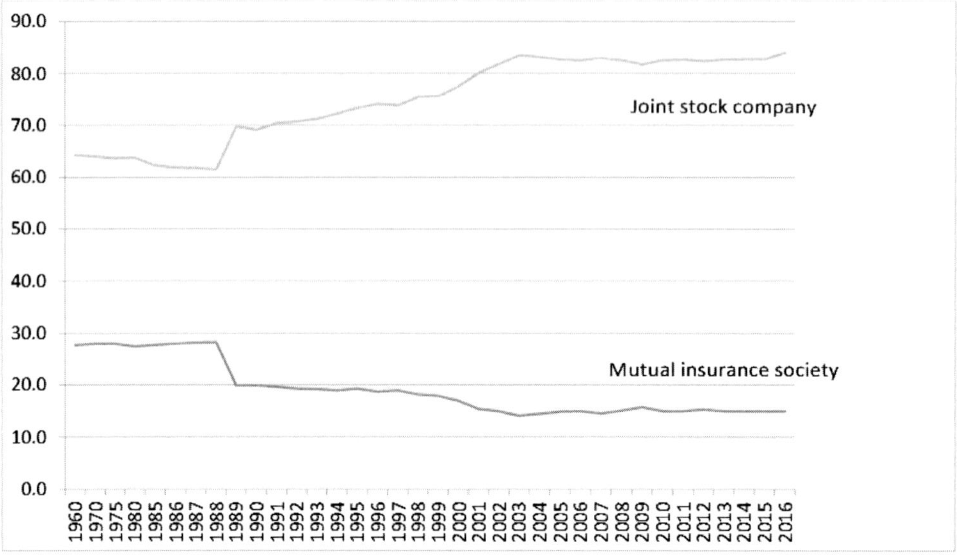

Source: GDV (2017) Statistisches Taschenbuch der Versicherungswirtschaft, Karlsruhe, p. 3 und BaFin, own calculation.

Table 5: Comparison of joint stock companies vs. mutual insurance societies regarding insurance branches

	Joint stock companies	Gross premiums written %	Mutual insurance societies	Gross premiums written %
Life insurance	65	83%	16	14%
Occupational provision funds (Pensionskassen)	22	48%	115	49%
Death benefit insurance	1	21%	34	79%
Health insurance	24	59%	22	41%
Non-life and accident insurance	136	87%	59	9%
Re-insurance	24	99%	1	0.05%
Insurance companies total 2016	**272**	**82.8%**	**247**	**14.2%**

Source: BaFin (2018): Statistik der Bundesanstalt für Finanzdienstleistungsaufsicht – Erstversicherungsunternehmen und Pensionsfonds –, Bonn, p. 104.

with other legal forms have only 1.5% of the earned gross premiums of the total market, when categorizing the companies according to their own legal form.

When comparing the mutual insurance societies under federal supervision with joint stock companies (without pension funds) we can notice that the market share and numbers of mutuals decrease since the end of WWII due to various reasons. These reasons are demutualization, change of legal form from mutual insurance society to joint stock company – in Germany, however, partial demutualization is dominant, in which case the society continues to exist with a small rest portfolio[153] – and mergers, e. g. a mutual society takes over another mutual society and intergrates its portfolio before the society is dissolved. Additionally, other dissolutions of mutual insurance societies occurred, which influenced the development of the market share slightly. These were occupational provision funds (Pensionskassen), death benefit funds and small mutual insurance societies. As a result, the numbers decreased since 1954 to 2015 (65%). This number has stabilized during the last years. The number of joint stock companies, on the other hand, increased until 2002/2003 and dropped sharply in 2009, the year of the global economic crisis (see Table 4).

Figure 8 shows a similar developed regarding the market share. In 1951, the market share of mutual insurance societies was almost 30 percent, while today it has decreased to 14.2 percent. It is important to notice that the drop in 1989 resulted from a changed systematic. Table 5 shows the market share in 2016 comparing insurance joint stock companies and mutual insurance societies regarding the insurance branches.

There are also effects that contradict the picture of the dying of mutual insurance societies[154]: Firstly, within mutual insurance enterprises restructuring processes occur and the operative business of the mutual insurance society is transferred to the subordinated joint stock company. The parent companies are still societies, but the official statistics regard the operative insurance business as business of a joint stock company. Therefore, the market share of mutuals decreases, while the number of joint stock companies increases. This development is not positive for mutuals and public insurers regarding their market share, although the company itself changes regarding to its business orientation. Additionally, new business is usually initiated in form of joint stock companies.

---

153 Cf. *Nemson, J.* (2014): Geschäftsmodell VVaG: Rahmenbedingungen, Herausforderungen und Chancen, Karlsruhe, p. 89.

154 Cf. *Beenken, M.* (2009): Das leise Sterben der Versicherungsvereine, in: VersicherungsJournal, 03.09.2009.

The mutual insurance societies under federal supervision are not a homogenous group, they are differentiated according to size, customer focus, and their integration into the enterprise.[155]

- Life and health insurance mutuals are integrated into horizontal or subordinated companies, while more than half of the 44 large non-life and accident insurances are single companies without subordinated companies or enterprises.
- With respect to size, there are differences between large mutuals. The mutual Debeka health insurance company had 5.5 billion Euro premium, while the mutual Vereinigte Postversicherung had only 7,300 € premium volume.
- The market is divided into large mutuals (holdings) offering all insurance branches and small insurance societies offering only some insurance branches. The latter are specialised small mutuals, limited to regions, customer groups, products or a combination of these features. Their economic relevance is important as a market niche offering products other insurers do not, with a high customer understanding regarding special needs, and high flexibility.

The different insurance branches are diverse regarding the number of joint stock companies and mutuals. The largest shares have occupational provision funds (Pensionskassen) and death benefit funds. In 2016, 34 mutuals were death benefit fund companies, from them 32 were small mutual insurance societies and 115 were occupational provision funds (Pensionskassen) offering company pension schemes. One of the most important institutions offering data today is the KIVI GmbH Kölner Institut für Versicherungsinformation und Wirtschaftsdienste[156], but unfortunately, they do not include small mutual insurance societies into their statistics due to their small economic importance on the market. Although occupational provision funds (Pensionskassen) and funeral expenses funds have large shares. Currently, KIVI divides its reports only into the submarkets non-life, life, and health insurance. Also *Farny* excluded them from his analysis of the German market, because of their limited market importance.[157]

Further *Farny* argues that the mutuality principle is not only a constituent feature of mutual insurance societies, but also influences partially or completely the insurance business of joint stock companies and

155 Cf. *Nemson, J.* (2014): Geschäftsmodell VVaG: Rahmenbedingungen, Herausforderungen und Chancen, Karlsruhe, p. 93.

156 Cf. http://www.kivi-online.de

157 Cf. *Farny, D.* (2012): Zustand und Perspektiven der Gegenseitigkeitsversicherung in Deutschland, in Beckmann, R. M. (ed.): Weitsicht in Versicherung und Wirtschaft. Gedächtnisschrift für Ulrich Hübner, Heidelberg (et.al.), pp. 77-88, p. 80.

public insurers.[158] He criticizes that the federal financial supervisory agency distinguishes between different legal forms without considering group and holding structures. So the Register of Companies does not take into account the legal form of the group or enterprise, therefore a joint stock company, which is a 100% subsidiary of a mutual insurance society, is regarded as a joint stock company. Therefore, it is not sensible to divide the companies regarding their legal forms like in public statistics (e.g. BaFin), in which each company is regarded as the legal form that is found in the Register of Companies.[159] *Farny* shows that the figures of the Federal Financial Supervisory Agency are misleading and have no connection with reality.[160] He stands for the concept that in a group with a mutual insurance society at the top, the operative insurance business of its subsidiaries has to be included, regardless of their legal form.

In 2016, mutual insurance societies comprised 127 insurance companies. From them 48 had the legal form of mutuals, while 80 were joint stock companies. The market share of mutuals was 34.78% and therefore twice as high as according to the BaFin data. This difference increases continuously due to the restructuring of mutual insurance enterprises, which do the operative insurance business by subordinated joint stock companies (see Table 6).[161]

Table 7 presents the results of comparing the total market share as well as the market shares of the health, non-life, and life insurance sector according to legal form from 2000 to 2015. It shows a continuous increase of the mutuals' total market share from 27.25% to 34.73%%. Joint stock companies, however, lost market share from 61.22% in 2000 to 53.96% in 2015. These trends can be explained due to the restructuring and partial demutualization of mutual insurance societies and the view to regard all joint stock companies as subsidiaries or in a corporation with a mutual insurance society at the top as mutuals. The market share of public insurers, on the other hand, maintained stable with 10.61% in 2000 and 11.23% in 2015. While by 2015, the market share of joint stock companies was more dominant in the life insurance market (60.55%), mutuals were more dominant in the health insurance sector (53.47%).[162]

---

[158] Ibid. p. 77

[159] Ibid. p. 80.

[160] Cf. *Farny, D.* (2012): Zustand und Perspektiven der Gegenseitigkeitsversicherung in Deutschland, in *Beckmann, R. M.* (ed.): Weitsicht in Versicherung und Wirtschaft. Gedächtnisschrift für Ulrich Hübner, Heidelberg (et.al.), pp. 77-88, p. 80.

[161] Cf. *Farny, D.* (2012): Zustand und Perspektiven der Gegenseitigkeitsversicherung in Deutschland, in *Beckmann, R. M.* (ed.): Weitsicht in Versicherung und Wirtschaft. Gedächtnisschrift für Ulrich Hübner, Heidelberg (et.al.), pp. 77-88, p. 80.

[162] Ibid. pp. 77-88, p. 81.

Table 6: Number of insurance companies and market share according to legal form in 2016

Legal form	Number[1]	From them Joint stock companies	Mutual insurance societies	Public insurances	Market share 2016 in percent Non-life	Life	Health	Total
Joint stock company	102	99	3[2]	-	51.79	61.54	39.51	53.95
Mutual insurance society	128	80	48	-	34.88	27.07	53.54	34.78
Public insurance	44	29	1	14	13.33	11.39	6.95	11.27
Total	274	208	52	14	100	100	100	100

[1] Without occupational provision funds (Pensionskassen), pension funds (Pensionsfonds), death benefit funds, without insurance companies/ groups with premiums below 50 Mio. Euro

[2] R+V Company

Source: KIVI: Die Marktanteile der Anbieter auf dem deutschen Versicherungsmarkt 2016, the data was made available by *Michael Thiemermann*.

Table 7: Development of the market shares in premiums according to legal forms: joint stock companies vs. mutual insurance societies (2000-2015)

Legal form	Year	Non-life	Life	Health	Total
Joint stock company	2000	61.16	67.07	44.19	61.22
	2005	55.35	63.46	43.46	57.00
	2010	55.97	62.66	41.00	56.46
	2015	52.27	60.55	39.55	53.96
Mutual insurance society	2000	24.72	21.91	49.40	27.25
	2005	30.08	26.24	50.41	32.52
	2010	30.20	25.54	51.95	32.03
	2015	34.55	27.97	53.47	34.73
Public insurance	2000	12.18	10.79	6.09	10.61
	2005	12.37	10.30	6.13	10.36
	2010	13.16	11.59	6.86	11.22
	2015	13.18	11.48	6.92	11.23

Source: The table is based on *Farny D.* (2012): Zustand und Perspektiven der Gegenseitigkeitsversicherung in Deutschland, in *Beckmann, R. M.* (ed.): Weitsicht in Versicherung und Wirtschaft. Gedächtnisschrift für Ulrich Hübner, Heidelberg (et.al.), pp. 77-88, p. 82, while the data for 2015 is drawn from KIVI: Die Marktanteile der Anbieter auf dem deutschen Versicherungsmarkt 2015 and was made available by *Michael Thiemermann.*

Besides the here presented table, data for the market share of mutual insurers in Germany can be found under following reference: ICMIF (2018): "Facts and figures – Mutual and cooperative insurance in Europe", *AMICE aisbl & ICMIF*, Vol 2. In this publication, the market share held by the "mutual insurance sector" was estimated to be 47% for the year 2015. The major reason for the obvious discrepancy can be easily explained by the fact that, contrary to the authors of this chapter, the ICMIF accounted public companies as part of the mutual sector.

In conclusion, the current situation based on present ideas and numbers can be evaluated positively. The mutual insurance societies are still of great importance within the insurance business and are able to assert themself on the market due to flexibility, member loyalty, and its stability against takeovers.[163]

3.3 Concentration of mutual insurance societies

Mutual insurance societies are in particular stable from a macroeconomic point of view.[164] *Grossfeld* emphasizes their takeover stability, which is responsible for the lower concentration degree in the German insurance industry.[165]
The reasons for concentration depend on the legal regulations, the different insurance branches, and the development of the market. This comprises also the principle of specialization, the reorganization, the competition, economic reasons, equity formation and legal restrictions.[166]

3.3.1 Principle of specialization

The principle of specialization is regarded as the main reason for the development of insurance holding companies.[167] Due to this principle, not every insurance company is allowed to practise any insurance type in a legal entity, but needs for offering all insurance branches several legal independent service enterprises.[168] According to § 8 No. 4 ISA (2015), life and health insurance companies have to be legally independent, a regulation which also included legal costs insurance, guaranty and credit insurance until 1990. The other insurance

---

[163] Cf. *Sieger, J.*; *Bank, S.* (2012): Probleme bei der Kooperation von Versicherungsvereinen auf Gegenseitigkeit, in: VersR, 63. vol., H. 7, pp. 270-278, p. 270.

[164] Cf. *Grossfeld, B.* (1985): Der Versicherungsverein auf Gegenseitigkeit im System der Unternehmensformen, Tübingen, p. 87.

[165] Ibid., p. 30.

[166] Cf. *Müller-Wiedenhorn, A.* (1993): Versicherungsvereine auf Gegenseitigkeit im Unternehmensverbund: Eine Untersuchung zum Recht und zu konzentrationsrechtlichen Fragen des Versicherungsvereins auf Gegenseitigkeit, Beiträge zum Privat- und Wirtschaftsrecht, Diss., Karlsruhe, p. 68.

[167] Cf. *Doerry, A.* (1988): Versicherungskonzerne, in *Farny, D.*/et.al. (ed.): Handwörterbuch der Versicherung HdV, Karlsruhe, pp. 1035-1042, p. 1035.

[168] Cf. *Farny, D.* (1980): Entwicklungslinien, Stand und Wirtschaftliche Bedeutung des Versicherungswesens in Deutschland, in *Henning, F.W.* (ed.): Entwicklung und Aufgaben von Versicherungen und Banken in der Industrialisierung, Schriften des Vereins für Socialpolitik, Band 105, Berlin, pp. 7-28, p. 20.

Figure 9: Structure of an insurance holding company

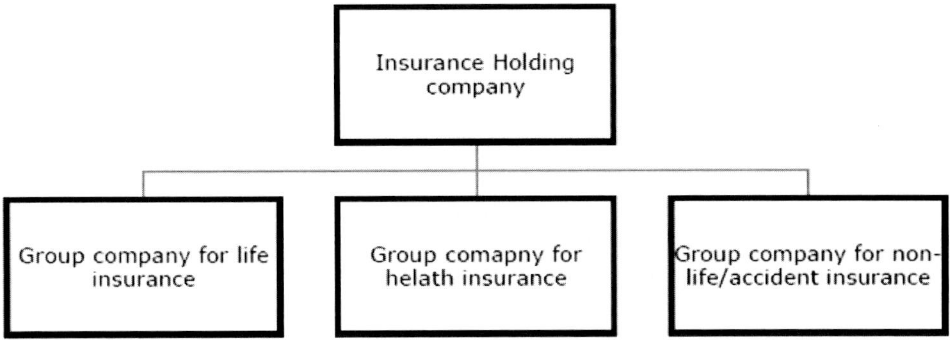

Source: *Nguyen, T. / Romeike, F.* (2013): Versicherungswirtschaftslehre: Grundlagen für Studium und Praxis, Wiesbaden, p. 172.

branches of the non-life and accident insurance can be practised together as composite insurer.[169]

The goal of the principle of specialization is to prevent cross-subsidisation. This concept aims to protect the policyholder. The principle of specialization makes the offer of all insurance branches by one insurance company impossible. However, holding companies are offering all branches by legally independent companies.[170]

3.3.2 Restructuring

When the equity capitalization of a company is not sufficient, restructuring has to take place. In this way, the interests of the policyholders can be protected. These types of takeovers often include the transfer of assets or a merger.[171]

However, such actions usually occur during times of crises such as under the pressure of inflation and economic crises.[172] Many restructur-

[169] Cf. *Farny, D.* (2011): Versicherungsbetriebslehre, Karlsruhe, p. 120.

[170] Cf. *Nguyen, T. / Romeike, F.* (2013): Versicherungswirtschaftslehre: Grundlagen für Studium und Praxis, Wiesbaden, p. 171.

[171] *Doerry, A.* (1988): Versicherungskonzerne, in *Farny, D.* et.al. (ed.): Handwörterbuch der Versicherung HdV, Karlsruhe, pp. 1035-1042, p. 1035.

[172] Cf. *Braeß, P.* (1971): Konzentration in der Versicherungswirtschaft, in *Arndt, H.* (ed.), Die Konzentration in der Wirtschaft – On Economic Concentration, Schriften des Vereins für Socialpolitik, 2. Band, 2. Aufl., Berlin, pp. 463-482, p. 472.

ings happened during the interwar period[173], while today the reforms are focused on the financial reconstruction.[174]

3.3.3 The competition and the competitors

Insurance companies are permitted to practise additional businesses if they are connected with their insurance transactions (§ 15 paragraph 1 ISA 2015). However, in reality the boundaries are blurred and open for different interpretations in particular regarding financial services and banking transactions.[175] Insurance companies often do business under the term “Allfinanz”, which includes transactions in areas such as capital formation, financial investments and administration, funding as well as commissions and insurances within the company’s group for individual customer service.[176]

3.3.4 Economic reasons

The merger to a holding company improves the competitive position and strengthens the market power. The concentration enables to distribute and balance the economic risk better, to implement economisation measures, and to use synergetic effects.[177] Moreover, all insurance branches are combined in one holding company that can offer all the different types of insurances.[178]

3.3.5 Equity capital formation

Mutual insurance societies are disadvantaged and restricted regarding equity capital formation in several ways due to their structural

---

[173] Cf. *Doerry, A.* (1988): Versicherungskonzerne, in *Farny, D.* et.al. (ed.): Handwörterbuch der Versicherung HdV, Karlsruhe, pp. 1035-1042, p. 1035.

[174] Cf. *Müller-Wiedenhorn, A.* (1993): Versicherungsvereine auf Gegenseitigkeit im Unternehmensverbund: Eine Untersuchung zum Recht und zu konzentrationsrechtlichen Fragen des Versicherungsvereins auf Gegenseitigkeit, Beiträge zum Privat- und Wirtschaftsrecht, Diss., Karlsruhe, p. 71.

[175] Cf. *Farny, D.* (2011): Versicherungsbetriebslehre, Karlsruhe, p. 121.

[176] Cf. *Müller-Wiedenhorn, A.* (1993): Versicherungsvereine auf Gegenseitigkeit im Unternehmensverbund: Eine Untersuchung zum Recht und zu konzentrationsrechtlichen Fragen des Versicherungsvereins auf Gegenseitigkeit, Beiträge zum Privat- und Wirtschaftsrecht, Diss., Karlsruhe, p. 71

[177] Cf. Beitrag auf Wissen Digital, Konzern, http://www.wissen-digital.de/Konzern, 20.06.2018.

[178] Cf. *Müller-Wiedenhorn, A.* (1993): Versicherungsvereine auf Gegenseitigkeit im Unternehmensverbund: Eine Untersuchung zum Recht und zu konzentrationsrechtlichen Fragen des Versicherungsvereins auf Gegenseitigkeit, Beiträge zum Privat- und Wirtschaftsrecht, Diss., Karlsruhe, p. 73.

peculiarity.[179] Only during the foundation process and first business period they are permitted to procure equity capital external after the manner of equity financing and to build an initial fund.[180] Additional equity capital comes from withholding of surpluses, which are, like profits, liable for corporation tax and become part of the reserve fund.[181]

Other possibilities to raise capital to improve the necessary solvency are limited to issue bonus shares and use subordinated obligations (§ 214 ISA 2015 VAG). However, the recognition as equity capital is linked to certain requirements and limits.[182]

In fact, however, mutual insurance societies allocate their profits to the equity capital on a larger scale compared to joint stock companies. The reason is that mutuals have to earn the necessary security capital to be protected from the fluctuations of the insurance business. Mutual insurance societies hold continuously very high security capital that is build up systematically; the policyholders only receive the remaining capital. The growth of the security capital has to be balanced with the growth of the business and as a result, mutuals are restricted by the economic growth. In the non-life/accident insurance, mutuals fulfil the solvability requirements easily with a coverage ratio between 250% and 450%. In the life insurance sector, the ratio is between 150% and 200%, while in health insurance it is between 220% and 300%. Joint stock companies have to pay high dividends for capital taken-up on the capital market, while mutual insurance societies have no expenses for their high capital reserves.

3.3.6 Legal restrictions

Legal restrictions such as the prohibition of non-insurance businesses and the limitation of shareholding in other companies with non-insurance businesses lead to increasing concentration attempts.[183]

---

179 Cf. *Martiensen, H. P.* (2006): Fusionen von Versicherungsvereinen auf Gegenseitigkeit: Verschmelzung gem. §§ 109 ff. UmwG und Gleichordnung gem. § 18 Abs. 2 AktG, Hamburger Reihe, Reihe A Rechtswissenschaft, Karlsruhe, p. 102.

180 Cf. *Farny, D.* (2011): Versicherungsbetriebslehre, Karlsruhe, p. 216.

181 Cf. *Müller-Wiedenhorn, A.* (1993): Versicherungsvereine auf Gegenseitigkeit im Unternehmensverbund: Eine Untersuchung zum Recht und zu konzentrationsrechtlichen Fragen des Versicherungsvereins auf Gegenseitigkeit, Beiträge zum Privat- und Wirtschaftsrecht, Diss., Karlsruhe, p. 73.

182 Cf. *Farny, D.* (2011): Versicherungsbetriebslehre, Karlsruhe, p. 216.

183 Cf. *Müller-Wiedenhorn, A.* (1993): Versicherungsvereine auf Gegenseitigkeit im Unternehmensverbund: Eine Untersuchung zum Recht und zu konzentrationsrechtlichen Fragen des Versicherungsvereins auf Gegenseitigkeit, Beiträge zum Privat- und Wirtschaftsrecht, Diss., Karlsruhe, p. 73.

3.4 Demutualization

For some time now, we can observe a discussion regarding the legal form of mutual insurance societies. A turning away from the mutuality principle has been observable. The legal and economic points of discussions are numerous.[184] In particular, the following topics are important:[185]

- Financing on the capital market: mutual insurance societies have only limited possibilities for financing on the capital market;
- Design of insurance corporations (groups). According to the Company law and the law relating to groups, groups can be either vertical (§ 18 paragraph 1, company law), i.e. one or several depending companies under the same management of a dominant company, or horizontal (§ 18 paragraph 2 company law), i.e. legally independent companies under the same management. It is complicated and difficult, legally and actually, to integrate a mutual insurance society into a holding;
- The distribution of responsibilities regarding corporate governance is difficult, because it is questionable if the interests of members/ customers and corporate governance is adequately balanced.

This argumentation is in particular presented by investment bankers, analysts, and law firms, which want to make demutualization to a fashionable topic to generate demand. They would also be the beneficiaries of the complex and expensive process of demutualization.[186] In general, demutualization can be observed in the following forms:

1. The mutual insurance society remains, its structural features are changed insofar that the responsibility of the members and owners as well as of the participating investors are mixed. The mutual insurance society has a position between a personal business association and a corporation, for example by splitting the mutual insurance societies into a business association with members as parent company and into an operative insurance joint stock company owned by the business association with the majority.[187] However, such legal constructions are hard to realize with the current German Company law.

[184] Cf. *Farny, D.* (2012): Zustand und Perspektiven der Gegenseitigkeitsversicherung in Deutschland, in *Beckmann R. M.* (ed.): Weitsicht in Versicherung und Wirtschaft. Gedächtnisschrift für Ulrich Hübner, Heidelberg (et.al.), pp. 77-88, p. 88.

[185] Cf. *Farny, D.* (2011): Versicherungsbetriebslehre, Karlsruhe, p. 212.

[186] Cf. http://www.arge-vvag.de/fsets/fthemen.htm, 25.07.2018.

[187] One example is the "Austrian model" (cf. later on).

2. A partial demutualization can be done within an insurance group when the group is structured in a particular form. A mutual insurance society, usually with a small insurance business, is the parent company of a vertical insurance group. The mutual is the owner of an intermediate holding company in the legal form of a joint stock company.[188] The latter has shares in the operative insurance joint stock company, which had taken over the insurance portfolio of the former mutual insurance society.
3. In case of a complete demutualization, the mutual insurance society is replaced by an insurance joint stock company. There a several legal possibilities for the change of this legal form. The legal foundations are the Conversion Law (Umwandlungsgesetz, UmwG) and the Insurance Supervision Act (ISA). The Conversion Law from 1995 gives the mutual insurance society four options:[189]
   - the modifying conversion of the mutual insurance society into a joint stock company (§ 291 UmwG)
   - during the merger of mutuals, the society can be absorbed by a joint stock company (§ 109, sentence 2 UmwG),
   - the splitting or separation of a mutual and the inclusion into a joint stock company (§ 123 I and II UmwG),
   - the transfer of the assets of a mutual to a joint stock company (§ 174 UmwG).

The Conversion Law effects only enterprises with their head office in Germany.

- As an alternative to these four options, a transfer of the portfolio is, according to § 13 ISA 2016, possible.[190]

Figure 10 presents the different transformation options according to the Conversion Law and the ISA.

The forms of a partial or full demutualization raise the questions what kind of compensation the members of a mutual insurance society receive for losing their membership completely or partially, the right

[188] Originally, mutual insurance societies, which are organized co-operatively, used the French model of the *Credit Agricole* due to the easier way to gain more equity capital. However, today mutual insurance societies use in the way of partial demutualization intermediate holding companies or/and joint stock companies as subsidiaries to rise their equity capital. Cf. *Braouet, C.* (2017). Ungleiche "Genossen" in Deutschland und Frankreich, in: Deutsch-Französisches Institut (ed.): Frankreich Jahrbuch 2016. Sozialwirtschaft in Frankreich und Europa, Wiesbaden, p. 112.

[189] Cf. *Wirsing, K.* (2007): Demutualisierung am Beispiel der Standard Life Versicherung, München, p. 40.

[190] Cf. Ibid.

Figure 10: Conversion options according to the Conversion Law the Insurance Supervision Act

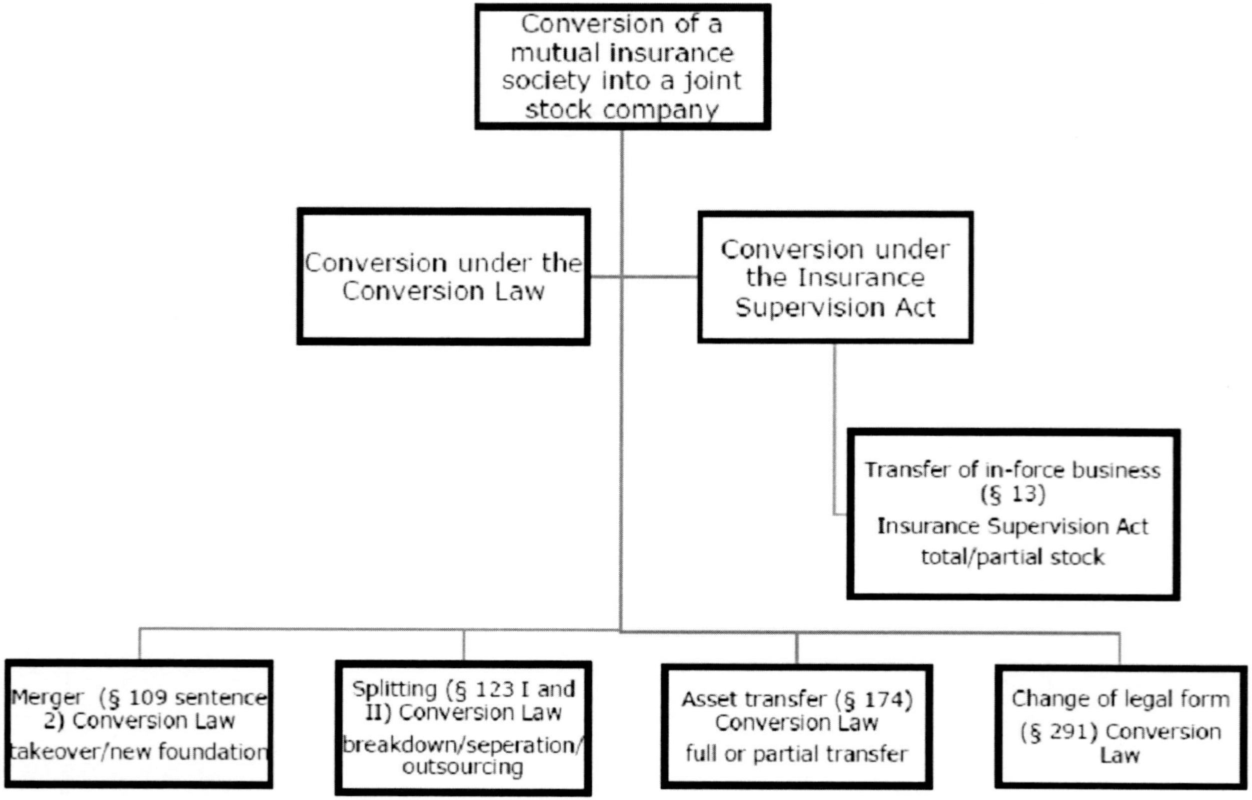

Source: *Wirsing, K.* (2007): Demutualisierung am Beispiel der Standard Life Versicherung, München, p. 41.

to participate in the bodies of the society as well as to have shares in profits and winding-up surpluses. Depending on the type of demutualization process, the former members of the society become shareholders of the joint stock company or they lose their membership completely or partially and receive monetary compensation.

In Germany, the transfer of the insurance portfolio of a mutual insurance society to an insurance joint stock company is most common. If the membership gets lost completely than the members have a legal entitlement for a fair money compensation (§ 201 ISA 2016). As a result, the policyholder of the transferred stays members of the remaining mutual.

3.4.1 Change of legal form

By changing the legal form, members become shareholders.[191] In this event, the mutual insurance society keeps its legal identity and changes only its legal form[192]; therefore, its independence is preserved for the moment. However, the functions of an insured and a shareholder are now separated and the members receive an offer for indemnity.[193]

3.4.2 Merger

In the event of a merger, the entire assets of a mutual insurance society are transferred to a joint stock company and the society is liquidated. The members become shareholders and policyholders of the insurance joint stock company.[194] In case the members object to the merger resolution, the joint stock company is obligated to offer the members compensation in the form of cash settlement, i.e. "windfall" pay-out.[195]

---

[191] Cf. *Führer, C.*: Demutualisierung von Versicherungsvereinen auf Gegenseitigkeit, Beitrag auf Hochschule Bochum, http://www.hochschule-bochum.de/fileadmin/media/fb_w/Kaiser/praxis/demutuFuehrer.pdf, 20.06.2018, p. 10.

[192] Cf. *Gerner, C.* (2003): Demutualisierung eines VVaG: Die Umwandlung eines Versicherungsvereins auf Gegenseitigkeit in eine Aktiengesellschaft, Diss., Frankfurt am Main, p. 125.

[193] Cf. *Führer, C.*: Demutualisierung von Versicherungsvereinen auf Gegenseitigkeit, Beitrag auf Hochschule Bochum, http://www.hochschule-bochum.de/fileadmin/media/fb_w/Kaiser/praxis/demutuFuehrer.pdf, 20.06.2018, p. 10.

[194] Cf. Ibid. p. 11

[195] Cf. *Gerner, C.* (2003): Demutualisierung eines VVaG: Die Umwandlung eines Versicherungsvereins auf Gegenseitigkeit in eine Aktiengesellschaft, Diss., Frankfurt am Main, p. 61

3.4.3 Splitting

The splitting can be divided into dissociation, separation, and demerger.[196] In that event, the entire asset or parts including the obligations are transferred to one or several legal entities.[197] The members have the option to make demands on cash settlement like in case of merger.[198]

3.4.4 Transfer of assets

A mutual insurance society transfers first the assets and then the liabilities to an existing company and afterwards dissolves the society. The members become policyholders and receive a financial compensation ("windfall" pay-out).[199] Assets can be transferred either entirely or partially with regard to the legal succession.[200]

3.4.5 Transfer of portfolio

The mutual insurance society transfers its entire portfolio (liabilities side) to an insurance joint stock company and the mutual insurance society becomes an empty torso after the assets are transferred too. As a result, the society dissolves itself. The society members are financially compensated and the policyholders become shareholders of the insurance joint stock company. In this context, a partial demutualization is possible.[201]

3.4.6 The reasons against a full demutualization in Germany

In Germany, in contrast to other countries with a large market share of mutuals, no mutual insurance society has been completely demutualized yet.[202] The reason is a negative stance of the mutuals' managers towards a full demutualization. The decision regarding demutualisa-

---

196 Cf. *Wirsing, K.* (2007): Demutualisierung am Beispiel der Standard Life Versicherung, Munich, p. 48.

197 Vgl. *Gerner, C.* (2003): Demutualisierung eines VVaG: Die Umwandlung eines Versicherungsvereins auf Gegenseitigkeit in eine Aktiengesellschaft, Diss., Frankfurt am Main, p. 68.

198 Ibid. p. 71.

199 Cf. *Führer, C.*: Demutualisierung von Versicherungsvereinen auf Gegenseitigkeit, Beitrag auf Hochschule Bochum, http://www.hochschule-bochum.de/fileadmin/media/fb_w/Kaiser/praxis/demutuFuehrer.pdf, 20.06.2018, p. 12.

200 Cf. *Gerner, C.* (2003): Demutualisierung eines VVaG: Die Umwandlung eines Versicherungsvereins auf Gegenseitigkeit in eine Aktiengesellschaft, Diss., Frankfurt am Main, p. 103.

201 Ibid. p. 13.

202 Cf. *Wackerbeck, P.* (2002). Strategische Optionen für Versicherungsvereine auf Gegenseitigkeit, Berlin, p. 86ff.

tion lies by the members, who depending on the legal regulations of the respective country have to reach a majority decision in favour of a demutualization. An analysis of the demutualization process of large mutuals in foreign countries shows that the members' polls have very high approving ratings when the management advertised actively the demutualization and emphasised its advantages for the members and the company.[203]

In contrast to other countries, the highest decision-making body is consulted and not the members. In large German mutuals, the members' representation is dominant, in particular in case of co-optation. Therefore, a decision of this body against the view of the management is not likely. Moreover, a decision for a full demutualization depends on the fact if the management considers it as a better alternative for solving the specific problems of mutuals compared to the models regarding the partial demutualization. However, this is not true in reality, because the partial demutualization is clearly favoured.

3.4.7 Partial demutualization by insurance corporations

Farny states the following principles for the restructuring of corporations:[204]

- A mutual insurance society is the parent company in the corporation, which still has members. The operative insurance business is done, however, only on a small scale or in a particular form, with the aim to maintain the status as an insurance company licenced by the Insurance Supervision Authority. The real function, however, is as the owner of all other companies of the corporation. Therefore, it is called "holding-mutual insurance society".
- The holding insurance society is the sole proprietor or co-owner of an intermediate holding company in the legal form of a joint stock company.
- The intermediate holding company is the owner of the operative insurance joint stock company and in some cases of other corporation companies.
- Connected with the restructuring is the transfer of the insurance portfolio of the parent company to the operative insurance joint stock companies, except small and special remaining stocks, which are necessary to maintain the status of the parent company as an insurance company.

With modifications and simplifications of the general corporation model (see Figure 11) for corporations with mutuals the following

[203] Ibid., p. 92.

[204] Cf. *Farny, D.* (2011): Versicherungsbetriebslehre, 5th edition, Karlsruhe, p. 289ff.

situation can be observed. The holding mutual insurance society is basically restricted to the function as owner of the intermediate holding company. Additionally, it is the connection to the remaining memberships of the policyholders. The intermediate holding company has the unified management legitimated by the holding mutual insurance society as sole or co-owner as well as by the members of the holding mutual insurance society. The intermediate holding company makes control agreements and/or profit transfer agreements with the subordinated operative insurance companies. The society has under certain conditions access to the capital market. With this possibility, equity capital can be procured in the way that shares are issued and the company expands. Usually this goal can be reached when other insurance companies or non-insurance companies participate in the intermediate holding company and eventually in the entire corporation.

Farny suggests the following new types of existing insurance corporations with mutual insurance societies:[205]

- *The insurance corporation with a holding insurance society, intermediate joint stock company and several operative insurance joint stock companies.*
  This is the modern type of the medium and large insurance corporations with a mutual insurance society at the top and with a predominant holding function and with a small remaining insurance business; under that is an intermediate holding company (sometimes several), below that there are the operative insurers. In this structure the mutuality principle is reduced, in particular when the intermediate holding company procures capital for financing the operative area on the capital market, for example by issuing shares or taking on hybrid capital; this is similar as when individual operative subsidiaries issue shares. So a model is produced which can be called "capital market orientated mutual insurance society"[206]. As a result, the influence of the members on the business of these insurance companies decreases and the membership weakens.[207]
- *An insurance corporation with one or several operative mutual insurance societies at the top, an intermediate holding company,*

[205] Ibid., p. 294ff.

[206] The Talanx Corpoaration is a good example for the sale of shares of a subordinated subsidiary, which was previously in the sole ownership of the parent mutual insurance society, during a stock market launch. The Talanx Corporation is owned in majority by the "HDI Haftpflichtverband der Deutschen Industrie V. a.G." At the end of 2017, the HDI V.a.G. held a share of 79.04% in the corporation insurance holding company, i.e. the Talanx AG", while the rest of the shares were in free float. The majority shares of the connected insurance companies of the existing Talanx corporation are exclusively concentrated in respective holding company (Cf. *HDI Lebensversicherung AG* (2017): Bericht über die Solvabilität und Finanzlage 2017, p. 5f.).

[207] Cf. *Dreher, M.* (2008). Der VVaG Konzern, in *Bürkler. J* (ed.): Rechtliche Rahmenbedingungen für Versicherungsvereine auf Gegenseitigkeit, Karlsruhe, p. 142.

Figure 11: Insurance corporations with a mutual insurance society

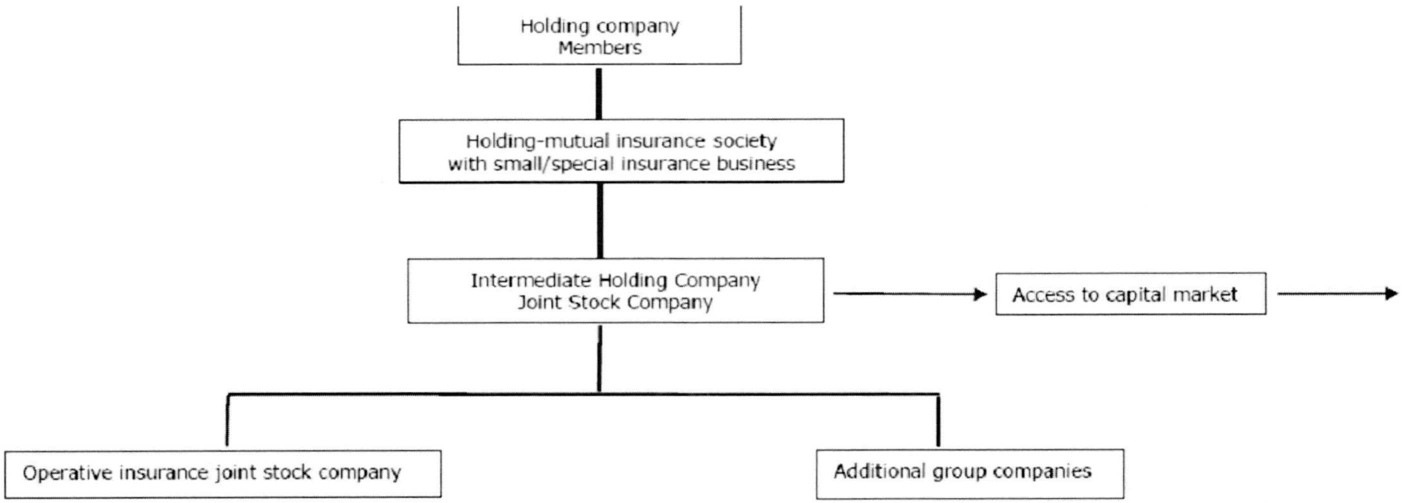

Source: *Farny, D.* (2011): Versicherungsbetriebslehre, Karlsruhe, p. 291.

a joint stock company and several other operative insurance joint stock companies.
This type of corporation is also common. Maintaining the mutuality principle depends on the fact, if the members of the mutual insurance society at the top have participatory rights and profit share rights also for the business of the operative joint stock companies or not. This type of corporation may have the risk that profits of the operative insurance joint stock company stay in the intermediate holding company and the mutual or the highest mutual receive only the capital appreciation from the share in the intermediate holding, on which the members have no direct participation. In this case, a certain capital orientation of the intermediate holding company can arise.

- *An insurance corporation with one or several operative mutual insurance societies at the top, without an intermediate holding company, with direct subsidiary operative insurance joint stock companies.*
This type is the obsolete form of a mutual insurance society corporation that has established or bought operative insurance joint stock companies to do several kinds of insurance branches. In this case, the mutuality principle is endangered least of all, in particular when the operative subsidiaries are led by the idea of the mutual insurances and give their profits to the parent mutual insurance company or companies. Usually there is no capital orientation.

Dreher has the opinion that such formation of insurance corporations with a mutual insurance society is questionable from the members' point of view. He argues that mutual insurance societies in which the members' representation assembly is comprised according to the co-optation principle, can lead to the fact that the information of the members' representation assembly and its decisions are no sufficient legal basis for such restructuring processes. The reason is that this is a double promulgation of the administration rights of the members that drains the membership completely. Such established restriction of the membership rights has a considerable practical importance.

- Currently, a new insurance corporation with a mutual insurance society develops, however, this time in reversed form and transnational. At the end of 2017, the Allianz Group, Europe's largest insurer, has initiated a merger to take-over the majority of the non-life and accident insurance portfolios of the well-established Liverpool Victoria Friendly Society, a company that has more than 6,000 employees and more than 5.8 million customers (from them 1.1 million members). The merger is the basis of a joint venture (Liverpool Victoria General Insurance Group Limited") with the brand name "LV=") that results in the third largest private insurer in the Uni-

ted Kingdom with an annual premium income of more than 1.7 billion Pounds.
The Allianz group regards the "LV=" as model and plans to form similar alliances with such competitors. The future idea of the Allianz group is that the borders will be dissolved. The company prescribes the corporation as cultural transformation including a turn to the legal form of mutual insurance societies.[208]

3.4.8 Advantages and disadvantages of demutualization

Demutualization has both advantages and disadvantages. The advantages are for example a better equity capital procurement, facilitations regarding consolidation, better chances for corporate governance, and an alternative to a mutual insurance society. Disadvantages are the possible loss of independence, a higher risk of an "unfriendly takeover", a chance of the business culture, and the loss of the members' interests.[209]

According to *Farny*, it is not possible to make a unified judgement about demutualization in Germany, because each case differs. The following Figure presents the current explanatory models derived from the Agency Theory (see Figure 12).[210]

This theory analyses the interests of the owners, policyholders, and the management. It is assumed that in mutual insurance societies no or less conflicts occur. The reason is that only the interests of two main groups have to be considered, i.e. managers vs. policyholders, while in insurance joint stock companies three main groups (managers – shareholders – policyholders) are concerned. As a result, the potential for conflicts is higher, which, on the other hand, has also some advantages. In general, it appears that in Germany the partial demutualization is by trend higher in large mutual insurance societies compared to small societies.[211]

---

[208] Cf. https://www.ovb-online.de/wirtschaft/allianz-kauft-grossbritannien-8571340.html 30.07.2018.

[209] Cf. *Wackerbeck, P.* (2002). Strategische Optionen für Versicherungsvereine auf Gegenseitigkeit, Berlin, p. 26.

[210] Cf. *Farny, D.* (2011): Versicherungsbetriebslehre, Karlsruhe, p. 214.

[211] Cf. *Ibid.* p. 214f.

Figure 12: Agency-conflicts in insurance joint stock companies vs. mutual insurance societies

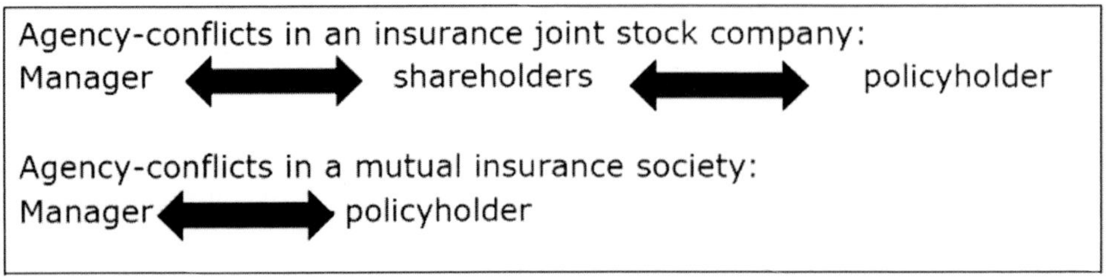

Source: *Führer, C.:* Demutualisierung von Versicherungsvereinen auf Gegenseitigkeit, Beitrag auf Hochschule Bochum, http://www.hochschule-bochum.de/fileadmin/media/fb_w/Kaiser/praxis/demutuFuehrer.pdf, 20.06.2018, p. 29.

Führer[212] summarises demutualization as the following: It is...

- not a strategy of a company
- sometimes helpful (equity capital, consolidation)
- sometimes necessary (equity capital)
- sometimes unnecessary

3.4.9 The formation of a mutual insurance society group

During the first phase of the formation from the 1990s onwards, the horizontal group was considered the best way, because in a vertical group companies with this legal form were only able to be a ruling company not a controlled company. Due to the lack of a fixed equity capital of mutual insurance societies, ruling based on capital share is not possible. The prevailing opinion is that such contract conclusion is not admissible, because mutual insurance societies are based on the mutuality principle and therefore on the procurement of a reasonable insurance coverage for the members. This is true for the conclusion of a controlling agreement with a mutual insurance society as the subordinated company.[213]

The formation of horizontal groups of mutual insurance societies was of a short duration. The supervision was extremely problematic, in particular regarding the missing authority to issue instructions of

[212] Cf. *Führer, C.:* Demutualisierung von Versicherungsvereinen auf Gegenseitigkeit, Beitrag auf Hochschule Bochum, http://www.hochschule-bochum.de/fileadmin/media/fb_w/Kaiser/praxis/demutuFuehrer.pdf 20.06.2018, p. 31.

[213] Cf. *Dreher, M.* (2008). Der VVaG Konzern, in *Bürkler. J* (ed.): Rechtliche Rahmenbedingungen für Versicherungsvereine auf Gegenseitigkeit, Karlsruhe, p. 140.

the group management in the event of conflict of interests between the involved companies. A further disadvantage was the higher organisation costs.[214]

As can be seen in Table 8[215], at the end of 2016, 30 mutual insurance groups with an annual premium income of above 50 million Euro existed, with 3 of those being horizontal groups, 15 of those being vertical groups without a holding company, and 12 of those being vertical groups with a holding company. The groups with and without a holding structure represent the two dominant types of mutual company groups, operating an approximate 97% of total business of German mutual insurers. At the same time, in 2016, 27 mutual vertical groups held a share of 33.57% of the total German insurance market, composed out of life, non-life as well as health insurance. As the major difference between the two dominant types of mutual company groups, it can be stated that groups with holding companies on average are composed out of a larger number of insurance companies (excluding the holding company and companies operating secondary business) than vertical company groups without a holding structure.

Table 9 presents the advantages and disadvantages of a full demutualisation vs. a mutual holding company.

3.4.10 The situation in Austria

In 1991, the Austrian lawmaker revised the Insurance Supervision Act to the effect that one or several mutual insurance societies can become part of a joint stock company in the form of a universal succession. In this scenario, the society is a shareholder of the company and its work is limited to the administration of the assets.[216] The mutual insurance society exists as long as it has 26 percent of the subsidiary's shares entitled to vote.[217]

---

[214] *Wackerbeck, P.* (2002). Strategische Optionen für Versicherungsvereine auf Gegenseitigkeit, Berlin, p. 44. An example for a dissolution is the horizontal group Parion, formed in 1997, between the Gothaer Versicherungsbank VVaG, the Gothaer Lebensversicherung a.G., the Berlin-Kölnische Krankenversicherung a.G., and the Berlin-Kölnische Lebensversicherung a.G. that merged as the parent company with the Gothaer Versicherungsbank VVaG.

[215] Data is drawn from KIVI: Die Marktanteile der Anbieter auf dem deutschen Versicherungsmarkt 2016 and was made available by *Michael Thiemermann*.

[216] Cf. *Weigele, H.J.* (1995): Eigenkapitalbildung von Versicherungsverein auf Gegenseitigkeit, in Peiner, W. (Hrsg.): Grundlagen des Versicherungsvereins auf Gegenseitigkeit. Verfaßt und veröffentlicht aus Anlaß des 175jährigen Bestehens der Gothaer Versicherungsbank VVag, Karlsruhe, p. 141-157, p. 145.

[217] Cf. *Fahl, H.* (2005): Corporate Governance im Versicherungsverein a.G.: Die Auswirkungen der Aktienrechtsreformen auf das System der Unternehmensführung und –kontrolle im VVaG, VersR-Schriften 30, Karlsruhe, p. 51.

Table 8: Group structures of mutual insurance societies 2016

	Horizontal Group	Vertical Group without a holding construction	Vertical Group with a holding construction	Total
Number of mutual insurance groups	3	15	12	30
Total number of mutual insurance societies in mutual groups	7	21	17	45
Total number of insurance joint stock companies in mutual groups	0	28	52	80
Average number of insurance companies per mutual group	2.3	3.3	5.8	4.2
Total premium income (Mio. €)	€ 1,862	€ 28,629	€ 36,576	€ 67,067
Share in the mutual insurance society market	2.78%	42.69%	54.54%	100%
Share in total insurance market	0.96%	14.70%	18.78%	34.4%

Source: KIVI: Die Marktanteile der Anbieter auf dem deutschen Versicherungsmarkt 2016 and was made available by *Michael Thiemermann*.

The Austrian solution is regarded controversially in Germany. *Müller-Wiedenhorn* sees in it a challenge for the German lawmaker,[218] while *Fahl* emphasizes that the German insurance societies regard this model critically. However, he argues that some mutual insurance societies have already announced to go public in the medium-term and in this way they undermine the current German legal system. Therefore, it is necessary to rethink the Austrian model and tolerate it.[219]

218 Cf. *Müller-Wiedenhorn, A.* (1993): Versicherungsvereine auf Gegenseitigkeit im Unternehmensverbund: Eine Untersuchung zum Recht und zu konzentrationsrechtlichen Fragen des Versicherungsvereins auf Gegenseitigkeit, Beiträge zum Privat- und Wirtschaftsrecht, Diss., Karlsruhe, p. 247.

219 Cf. *Fahl, H.* (2005): Corporate Governance im Versicherungsverein a.G.: Die Auswirkungen der Aktienrechtsreformen auf das System der Unternehmensführung und -kontrolle im VVaG, VersR-Schriften 30, Karlsruhe, p. 52.

Table 9: Advantages and disadvantages of restructuring possibilities of a mutual insurance society regarding a full and partial demutualisation

	Advantages	**Disadvantages**
Full demutualisation	* All advantages regarding capital raising and takeovers of a joint stock company are available	* cost-intensive
	* Clear distinction between owners and policyholders	* time consuming in particular regarding stock market launch
	* Realisation of the assets of membership rights	* corporate governance is transferred to shareholders
Partial demutualisation	*Faster and cost-efficient realisation compared to a full demutualisation	* Only limited possibility to raise equity money, because only up to 49 percent of the sub-companies are permitted to sell (members have to keep control)
	*Restricted access to the capital markets	* Conflict between different owner groups: members and independent shareholders
		* Probably more cost-intensive regarding a later demutualisation
		* No realisation of the assets of membership rights

Source: *Auchinleck, B.* u.a. (2002): Optionen für Versicherungsvereine: Demutualisieren oder restrukturieren?, in Versicherungswirtschaft 7/2002, p. 456.

Figure 13: Reason for the harmonisation of legal forms

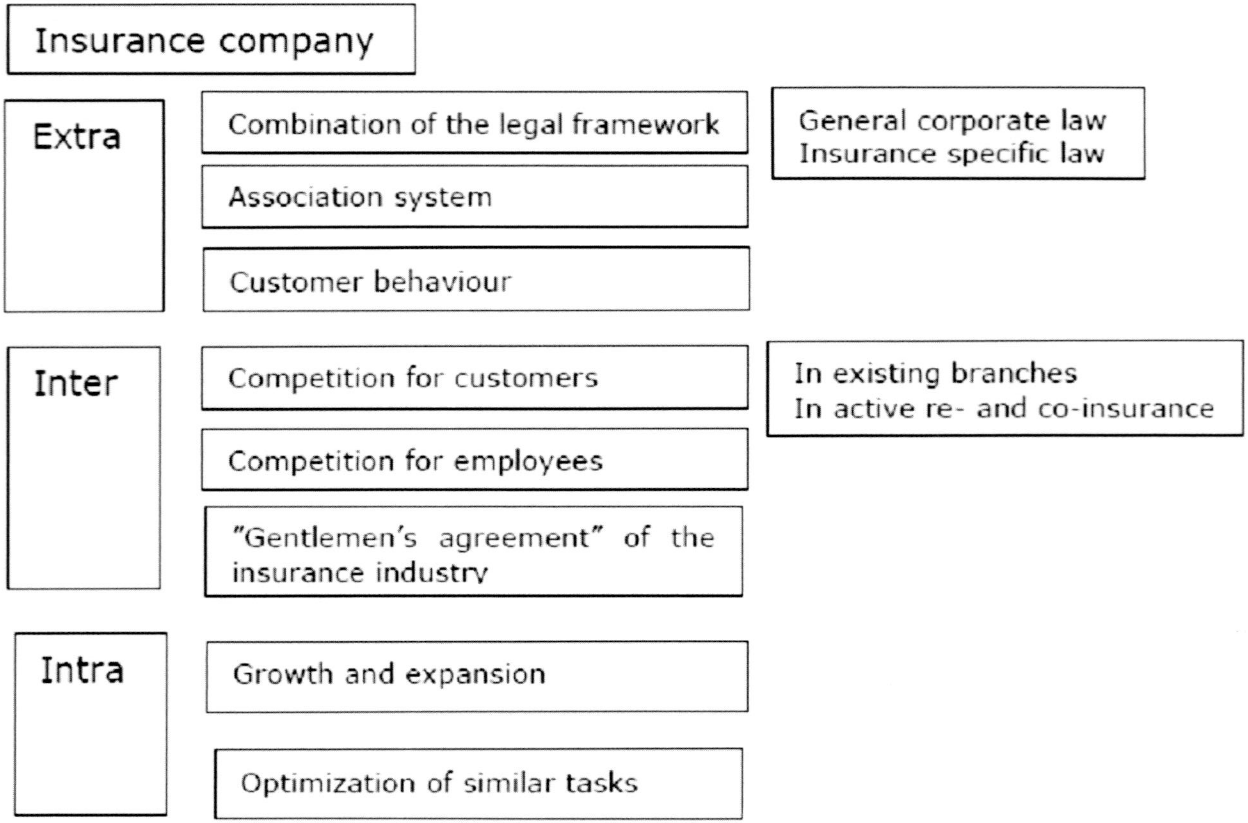

Source: *Nemson, J.* (2014): Geschäftsmodell VVaG: Rahmenbedingungen, Herausforderungen und Chancen, Karlsruhe, p. 34.

Weigele strongly argues against the Austrian model and states that the mutual insurance society loses its function completely. The society becomes a shareholder of an insurance joint stock company that is organized in the form of a membership. Therefore, the Austrian model is not suitable to preserve the mutual insurance society as a legal form for insurance companies.[220]

3.5 Harmonization tendencies

Until the foundation of the German Empire in 1871, mutual insurance societies were structured very differently and diverged from joint stock companies regarding their organization form.[221] Nevertheless, it can be stated that a harmonization tendency has always existed between the different legal forms of a company. *Nemson* investigates the reasons for this harmonization and elaborates three categories for insurance companies (extra, inter, and intra reasons) (see Figure 14).

- extra-reasons: comprise external framework such as insurance and general corporate law as well as interest group system and customer behaviour.[222] An interesting way of harmonisation can be found in the Insurance Supervision Act that refers in particular to company law regarding regulatory framework of mutual insurance societies. For example, there are no main differences concerning the bodies and competence.[223] Both the mutual insurance society and the insurance joint stock company are subject to the Insurance Supervision Act, the Insurance Contract Law, and the Insurance Intermediation Law. Additionally, the General Company Law of commercial, labour, tax, competition, and Economic order Law, which are mostly neutral concerning the legal form, apply.[224]
  Moreover, the interest group system also leads to harmonisation effects, because current topics and challenges of the sector are discussed commonly and solutions for e.g. general policy conditions-

[220] Cf. *Weigele, H.J.* (1995): Eigenkapitalbildung von Versicherungsverein auf Gegenseitigkeit, in *Peiner, W.* (ed.): Grundlagen des Versicherungsvereins auf Gegenseitigkeit. Verfaßt und veröffentlicht aus Anlaß des 175jährigen Bestehens der Gothaer Versicherungsbank VVag, Karlsruhe, p. 141-157, p. 146.

[221] Cf. *Brenzel, J.* (1975): Der Versicherungsverein auf Gegenseitigkeit – Unternehmensform und Rechtsstruktur im Wandel, Karlsruhe, p. 9.

[222] Cf. *Nemson, J.* (2014): Geschäftsmodell VVaG: Rahmenbedingungen, Herausforderungen und Chancen, Karlsruhe, p. 34.

[223] Cf. *Grossfeld, B.* (1985): Der Versicherungsverein auf Gegenseitigkeit im System der Unternehmensformen, Tübingen, p. 7.

[224] Cf. *Farny, D.* (2011): Versicherungsbetriebslehre, Karlsruhe, p. 234.

model, corporate statistics, and information service have to be found together.[225]

Farny states that the behaviour of customers has an essential influence on harmonisation, because the German policyholder has mostly no awareness regarding the three different legal forms. The only exception is the small mutual insurance society.[226]

- Inter-reasons: these are reasons that arise by the competition of insurance companies about customers and employees. The main effects are that mutual insurance societies calculate more carefully the premiums and limit or exclude mandatory additional payments. Insurance joint stock companies distribute profits, similar to mutual insurance societies, in the form of profit sharing and refunds to the policyholders.[227]
- Intra-reasons: they show internal harmonisation tendencies and concern in particular increase and extent of business areas and optimising of processes. With regard to structure and processes, large mutual insurance societies are already similar to insurance joint companies due to increasing memberships and the amount of contribution as well as the extant of business areas.[228]

  In large mutual insurance societies, the members' representatives meetings are more common than general meetings of members due to the size and nationwide businesses. Moreover, ongoing programs for process optimising, the increase of efficiency and sufficient equity capital as well as the offer of all insurance branches lead to harmonisation between specialised mutual insurance societies and insurance joint stock companies with a broad range of business areas.[229]

In contrast, *Martiensen* explains the results of legal harmonization and locates several harmonization tendencies in the following areas:[230]

- Organisation and market behaviour: Many new risks developed during the industrialisation of Germany. Only joint stock companies offered the advantageous mass-insurance business at first.[231] Mutual insurance societies with nationwide mass business had to

[225] Cf. *Nemson, J.* (2014): Geschäftsmodell VVaG: Rahmenbedingungen, Herausforderungen und Chancen, Karlsruhe, p. 36.

[226] Cf. *Farny, D.* (2011): Versicherungsbetriebslehre, Karlsruhe, p. 234.

[227] Cf. *Nemson, J.* (2014): Geschäftsmodell VVaG: Rahmenbedingungen, Herausforderungen und Chancen, Karlsruhe, p. 38.

[228] Ibid., p. 41.

[229] Ibid.

[230] Cf. *Martiensen, H. P.* (2006): Fusionen von Versicherungsvereinen auf Gegenseitigkeit: Verschmelzung gem. §§ 109 ff. UmwG und Gleichordnung gem. § 18 Abs. 2 AktG, Hamburger Reihe, Reihe A Rechtswissenschaft, Karlsruhe, p. 38.

[231] Ibid. p. 40.

meet the same challenges as insurance joint stock companies.[232] At the end of the 19th century, mutual insurance societies and joint stock companies were harmonised. As a result, the Insurance Supervision Act of 1901[233] used the present situation and referred to the Company Law regarding mutual insurance societies.[234]

- The system of fixed contributions: Mutual insurance societies had to limit mandatory additional contributions with the help of special insurances or even eliminate them in mid-19th century due to the competition with joint stock companies.[235]
- Distribution of surpluses: Insurance joint stock companies distribute their surpluses, similar to mutual insurance societies, in the form of profit shares and refunds among the policyholders due to competitive reasons.[236]
- Premium amount: Harmonisation tendencies are in particular important regarding the calculation of premiums. Although the profit margin and dividends of joint stock companies are higher compared to mutual insurance societies, the policyholders' premium payments are lower due to the competition on the market.[237]
- Equality principle: The equality principle applies to these insurance classes as well as to life insurance, health insurance as a type of life insurance (private health insurance), private nursing insurance and accident insurance with guaranteed premium refund (§§ 138 paragraph 2, 146 paragraph 2 No 1, 147, 148, 161 paragraph 1 ISA 2016). Another feature of the equality principle is that the premiums for a new private health insurances policy are not allowed to be lower compared to premiums of current policyholders at the same age and without considering ageing provisions (§ 146 paragraph 2 No 2 ISA 2016).

In conclusion, the harmonization tendencies apply only to certain areas such as premium calculation, profit distribution, organization structure, and administrative procedures.[238] Positive elements for the

---

232 Cf. *Brenzel, J.* (1975): Der Versicherungsverein auf Gegenseitigkeit – Unternehmensform und Rechtsstruktur im Wandel, Karlsruhe, p. 9.

233 RGBl_I_1901

234 Cf. *Brenzel, J.* (1975): Der Versicherungsverein auf Gegenseitigkeit – Unternehmensform und Rechtsstruktur im Wandel, Karlsruhe, p. 9.

235 Ibid., p 14.

236 Cf. *Grossfeld, B.* (1985): Der Versicherungsverein auf Gegenseitigkeit im System der Unternehmensformen, Tübingen, p. 54.

237 Cf. *Martiensen, H. P.* (2006): Fusionen von Versicherungsvereinen auf Gegenseitigkeit: Verschmelzung gem. §§ 109 ff. UmwG und Gleichordnung gem. § 18 Abs. 2 AktG, Hamburger Reihe, Reihe A Rechtswissenschaft, Karlsruhe, p. 46.

238 Cf. *Nemson, J.* (2014): Geschäftsmodell VVaG: Rahmenbedingungen, Herausforderungen und Chancen, Karlsruhe, p. 44.

policyholders were taken over by each legal form, while negative features were softened or eliminated. As a result, the differences between the legal forms were harmonised due to competition reasons that led to mutual development.[239] According to *Grossfeld*, the harmonisation theory is correct,[240] but the mutual insurance societies are considerably different from the insurance joint stock companies.[241]

4. Life insurances in different legal forms

In Germany, the life insurance sector is under pressure. The reason is the continuingly low interest rate that makes it difficult for companies to make profits for dividend payments. Some insurance joint stock companies such as the Heidelberger Lebensversicherung (2014), the Skandia Leben (2014), the Protektor Lebensversicherung (former Mannheimer Lebensversicherung) (2017), and the Generali Leben (2018) have already transferred their life insurance portfolios via run-offs.[242] The Ergo had prepared for a run-off, but decided against it in fear of damaging its public image.[243] *Weinmann's* study of the 12 largest life insurance companies and top 12 mutual life insurance societies of the business year 2017 offers a basis for comparing the economic performance of mutuals and joint stock companies in the German insurance industry.

Furthermore, *Weinmann* expanded his study from the top 8 to the top 12 largest mutual life insurance societies in comparison to previous

[239] Cf *Martiensen, H. P.* (2006): Fusionen von Versicherungsvereinen auf Gegenseitigkeit: Verschmelzung gem. §§ 109 ff. UmwG und Gleichordnung gem. § 18 Abs. 2 AktG, Hamburger Reihe, Reihe A Rechtswissenschaft, Karlsruhe, p. 53.

[240] Cf. *Grossfeld, B.* (1985): Der Versicherungsverein auf Gegenseitigkeit im System der Unternehmensformen, Tübingen, p. 7.

[241] Ibid., p. 33.

[242] Cf. *Seith, A.* Verkauf von vier Millionen Lebensversicherungen: Der langsame Zerfall der privaten Altersvorsorge, in: Spiegel Online. http://www.spiegel.de/wirtschaft/service/generali-verkauft-lebensversicherungen-der-zerfall-der-privaten-altersvorsorge-a-1216920.html (06.02.2019)

[243] *Wenig, M.* Ergo fürchtete massiven Imageschaden durch Verkauf der Leben-Töchter (07.02.2018) https://www.versicherungsbote.de/id/4863514/Ergo-fuerchtete-Imageschaden-Verkauf-Leben-Toechter/ (06.02.2019)

years.[244] He scrutinizes all companies in terms of gross premiums as well as based upon a self-developed model, as the researcher considers gross premiums of a company alone as being insufficient to evaluate economic performance. However, when evaluating the economic performance based upon a comparison of the increase/decrease of gross premium rates collected by the companies from 2008 to 2017, the mutual life insurance company Alte Leipziger Leben was the best with an increase of 7.3% (see Table 10). The company had the highest increase in terms of annual gross premium payments within the last 10 years. On the other hand, the joint stock company Allianz Lebensversicherungs-AG with the highest annual gross premium (20,113 Mio. Euro) has increased by 5% during the last ten years. At the same time, insurers such as the Debeka Lebensversicherungsverein a.G., with a plus of 1.9%, and the Alte Leipziger Lebensversicherung a.G. have kept their life insurance portfolios[245], the latter even increased its gross premiums immensely during the last ten years.

The general idea of *Weinmann's* study is that not the product "life insurance" is the basis for deciding for or against a particular life insurer as a customer, but a comparison of the life insurance companies. The main hypothesis is that customers of a mutual insurance society have advantages compared to customers of joint stock companies if the mutuality principle is realized by the management. The reason is that mutual insurance societies, like co-operatives, are owned by their policyholders and profits must not be shared with shareholders who are particularly interested in their return on investment. In another study about the total life insurance market, it is stated that during the last couple of years, mutual life insurance societies were able to increase their market shares compared to joint stock companies. The market share held in terms of gross premiums by joint stock companies decreased between 2007 and 2016 from 55.3% to 51.9%, while mutual life insurance societies increased their market share from 33.2% to 36.1%.[246]

Nevertheless, the question to be asked is, whether or not the hypothesis a potential superiority of mutual insurance societies and therefore of respective legal form can be made simply based upon the development of market share results. Trying to provide a much more solid analysis with respect to prior stated question, *Weinmann's* analysis model, which he has used for a couple of years, evaluates the economic performance of the twelve largest life insurance companies based upon

[244] Cf. *Weinmann, H.* (2017): Was machen die Lebensversicherer mit dem Geld ihrer Kunden?, Zeitschrift für Versicherungswesen 24/2017, Ludwigshafen, p. 772f.

[245] *Weinmann, H.* (2018): Was machen die Lebensversicherer mit dem Geld ihrer Kunden?, Zeitschrift für Versicherungswesen 18/2018, Ludwigshafen, p. 536.

[246] Cf. *Herz, C.* Große Kluft beim Thema Lebensversicherung. Handelsblatt from 16.12.2017

Table 10: Gross premiums in the business year 2017 and its development from 2008 to 2017

Top 12 life insurance companies			
Place	Company	Gross Premium (in Mio. Euro)	Increase/decrease of the gross premiums between 2008 and 2017 in percent
1.	Allianz Lebensversicherungs-AG	20,113	5.0
2.	R+V Lebensversicherung AG	4,975	3.2
3.	AachenMünchener Lebensversicherung AG	4,896	2.0
4.	Debeka Lebensversicherungsverein a. G	3,474	1.9
5.	Zürich Deutscher Herold Lebensversicherung AG	3,235	-1.3
6.	Generali Lebensversicherung AG	2,877	-2.4
7.	Bayern-Versicherung Lebensversicherung AG	2,722	3.4
8.	Axa Lebensversicherung AG	2,632	-2.2
9.	Ergo Lebensversicherung AG	2,458	-1.7
10.	Alte Leipziger Lebensversicherung a.G.	2,426	7.3
11.	Nürnberger Lebensversicherung AG	2,276	1.2
12.	HDI Leben	1,837	-0.7

Source: *Weinmann, H.* (2018): Was machen die Lebensversicherer mit dem Geld ihrer Kunden?, Zeitschrift für Versicherungswesen 18/2018, Ludwigshafen, p. 537f.

economic key-figures of the past (revenues, costs, and risk results) and the future (valuation and surplus reserves). Furthermore, the model includes an evaluation regarding consumer participation in the company's result as well as the company's solvability. Combined with above described economic evaluation, *Weinmann* ranks each of the examined insurance company from “very strong” to “weak”. The analysis is based upon public information of the companies, i.e. the company report, the annual report, and the report of the current situation as well as the sources of income according to § 15 of the Minimum allocation regulation (Mindeszuführungsverordnung/MindZV). Additionally, the solvability and financial reports of Solvency II (§ 40 ISA 2016) were used for the business year 2017.

The results of *Weinmann's* study show the top 12 life companies regarding their economic evaluation and their consumer grade (Table 11).

According to the study, the gap between the 12 analyzed life insurance companies is considerable and has increased continuously

Table 11: Total results of the top 12 insurance societies 2018 for the business year 2017

Place	Company	Economic evaluation	Consumer grade
1.	Allianz Lebensversicherungs-AG	Very strong	Very good (1.3)
2.	R+V Lebensversicherung AG	Strong	Good (2.0)
3.	Zürich Deutscher Herold Lebensversicherung AG	Strong	Good minus (2.3)
4.	Bayern-Versicherung Lebensversicherung AG	Improvable	Satisfactory plus(2.7)
5.	Nürnberger Lebensversicherung AG	Improvable	Satisfactory plus(2.7)
6.	Alte Leipziger Lebensversicherung a.G.	Improvable	Satisfactory plus(2.7)
7.	AachenMünchener Lebensversicherung AG	Improvable	Satisfactory (3.0)
8.	Axa Lebensversicherung AG	Improvable	Satisfactory (3.0)
9.	Ergo Lebensversicherung AG	Improvable	Satisfactory minus (3.3)
10.	Debeka Lebensversicherungsverein a. G.	Improvable	Satisfactory minus (3.3)
11.	Generali Lebensversicherung AG	Relatively weak	Sufficient plus (3.7)
12.	HDI Leben	Improvable	Sufficient (4.0)

Source: *Weinmann, H.* (2018): Was machen die Lebensversicherer mit dem Geld ihrer Kunden?, Zeitschrift für Versicherungswesen 18/2018, Ludwigshafen, p. 536f.

during recent times. With regard to economic efficiency (capital and costs), the Allianz Lebensversicherungs-AG is the best company by a long way, thus defending its first place and maintaining its strong economic performance of past years. On the second place comes the R+V Lebensversicherung AG with a strong economic performance. The results and assessments of the other companies show considerable differences and in some categories, the necessity for major catch-ups (see Table 11). Among the 12 largest life insurance companies in Germany, which were analyzed by *Weinmann*, two mutual insurance societies the Debeka Lebensversicherungsverein a.G. and the Alte Leipziger Lebensversicherungs a.G. can be found. The Debeka Lebensversicherungsverein a.G. is on the fourth place, while the Alte Leipziger Lebensversicherungs a.G. rank on the tenth place. At the end of the scale, the joint stock company HDI Leben is on the 12th place with "improvable" regarding its economic evaluation and "sufficient" in terms of its consumer grade, a result mainly caused by reductions in its solvency.[247]

Besides the evaluation and comparison of Germany's top twelve life insurance companies, *Weinmann* also applies the same model of analysis upon the country's largest twelve mutual insurance societies. Of these twelve mutual insurance societies, seven are "real" mutual societies[248], while the remaining five are joint stock companies and majority

247 *Weinmann, H.* (2018): Was machen die Lebensversicherer mit dem Geld ihrer Kunden?, Zeitschrift für Versicherungswesen 19/2018, Ludwigshafen, p. 593.

248 Lebensversicherung von 1871 (LV von 1871), Alte Leipziger Lebensversicherung, Stuttgar-

owned by mutual society horizontal groups. Similar to the above-depicted analysis, Germany's top twelve life insurers' results show large gaps in terms of economic performance and consumer benefits among the twelve scrutinized insurance societies, i.e. the differences between them are very big. In the business year 2017, the Hannoversche Lebensversicherung received the economic evaluation "very strong" as well as the grade "very good" in the category consumer benefits, followed by the Lebensversicherung von 1871 (LV von 1871) with a very strong economic result and a consumer grade of 2.0. This company as well as the HUK-Coburg-Leben are life insurance companies that have been added newly to *Weinmann's* analysis, meaning that they had not been part of the researchers analysis of prior years. The latter had a strong economic performance and a good consumer grade and can be found on the fourth place. Compared with last year's results, the Volkswohl Bund Lebensversicherung became economically weak and its consumer grade was only sufficient. The reason is that the company had to undergo structural changes to secure its future (see Table 12).[249]

Despite the good economic performance and grades of several mutual life insurers, *Weinmann* states that the results of his analysis show that mutual life insurance societies do not appear to be superior, but rather to be similarly in terms of economic performance and consumers' benefits provided. Therefore, the hypothesis that mutual insurance societies are the superior legal form as they and their capital belong to their policyholders and not to any type of shareholder cannot be concluded a priori. One potential reason delivered by *Weinmann* for this situation is that the requirements regarding the retention of profits diminish the historically existent competitive advantages of mutual insurance societies over their stock company competitors. As a result, mutual insurance societies work in a similar way than joint stock companies, the insurance sector in general and mutual insurance societies in particular became opaque.[250] The insurance sector declines legal regulation and, according to *Weinmann*, the sector harms itself by its questionable product and service practice.[251]

Apart from the life insurance segment, private health insurances is an important part of the insurance business (see Table 5). Therefore,

---

ter Lebensversicherung, Debeka Lebensversicherung, Iduna Vereinigte Lebensversicherung, WWK Lebensversicherung, Volkswohl Bund Lebensversicherung

249 *Weinmann, H.* (2018): Was machen die Lebensversicherer mit dem Geld ihrer Kunden?, Zeitschrift für Versicherungswesen 23/2018, Ludwigshafen, p. 724.

250 In one of his last articles, *Farny* criticised the opaque methods of insurance companies regarding direct credit notes and the annual accounts. Cf. *Weinmann, H.* (2018): Was machen die Lebensversicherer mit dem Geld ihrer Kunden?, Zeitschrift für Versicherungswesen 19/2018, Ludwigshafen, p. 586.

251 *Weinmann, H.* (2018): Was machen die Lebensversicherer mit dem Geld ihrer Kunden?, Zeitschrift für Versicherungswesen 24/2018, Ludwigshafen, p. 754.

Table 12: Total results of the top 12 mutual insurance societies 2018 for the business year 2017

Place	Mutual insurance company	Economic evaluation	Consumer grade
1.	Hannoversche Lebensversicherung	Very strong	Very good (1.3)
2.	Lebensversicherung von 1871 (LV von 1871)	Very strong	Good (2.0)
3.	Gothaer Lebensversicherung	Strong	Good (2.3)
4.	HUK-Coburg-Lebensversicherung	Strong	Good (2.3)
5.	Alte Leipziger Lebensversicherung	Improvable	Satisfactory plus (2.7)
6.	LVM Lebensversicherung	Improvable	Satisfactory (3.0)
7.	Stuttgarter Lebensversicherung	Improvable	Satisfactory (3.0)
8.	Continentale Lebensversicherung	Improvable	Satisfactory (3.3)
9.	Debeka Lebensversicherung	Improvable	Satisfactory (3.3)
10.	Iduna Vereinigte Lebensversicherung	Weak	Sufficient plus (3.7)
11.	WWK Lebensversicherung	Weak	Sufficient plus (3.7)
12.	Volkswohl Bund Lebensversicherung	Weak	Sufficient (4.0)

Source: *Weinmann, H.* (2018): Was machen die Lebensversicherer mit dem Geld ihrer Kunden?, Zeitschrift für Versicherungswesen 23/2018, Ludwigshafen, p. 724.

the *German Finance service institute (Deutsches Finanz-Service Institut, DFSI)* in Cologne evaluated and ranked 33 private health insurers by analyzing them in terms of capital, product quality, and service performance (Substanzkraft, Produktivität, Service). Doing so, the above mentioned three areas were first evaluated separately for each insurer, then weighted, and finally put together into a single grading system.[252] With regard to the ranking[253], the joint stock company Allianz receives 90.28 points in the category "corporate quality", i.e. the total result, and therefore the grade "very good". It was followed by the two mutual insurers namely Signal Iduna and Barmenia with 87.61 respectively 85.88 points. It is important to note that from the 33 analyzed insurers 18 are mutual insurance companies[254], from which 4[255] received the grade "very good", 12[256] the grade "good", and 2[257] the grade "satisfactory" (see Table 13).

[252] Cf. *Schulte, A.* Gesundheits-Check für Versicherer. Eine Analyse des Deutschen Finanz-Service-Instituts gibt Einblick in die Qualität der privaten Krankenversicherungen. Handelsblatt from the 15th of October 2018, No. 198, p. 50f.

[253] The companies in grey are mutual insurance societies.

[254] This includes joint stock companies in mutual society horizontal groups, which are indicated in the table 13 with *.

[255] Signal Iduna, Barmenia, Hanse Merkur, Inter.

[256] Debeka, Hallesche, LVM, Münchner Verein, Gothaer, Süddeutsche, Pax Familienfürsorge, Universa, DEVK, Concordia, Huk-Coburg, Continentale

[257] Landeskrankenhilfe, Vigo

Table 13: The ranking of private health insurance companies 2018

Company	Corporate quality		Capital		Product quality		Service	
	Points	Grade	Points	Grade	Points	Grade	Points	Grade
1. Allianz	90.28	Very good	80.40	Very good	95.32	Very good	99.95	Very good
2. Signal Iduna	87.61	Very good	94.64	Very good	85.85	Very good	77.08	Good
3. Barmenia	85.88	Very good	74.34	Good	92.10	Very good	96.50	Very good
4. Arag	83.43	Very good	84.95	Very good	82.78	Very good	81.68	Very good
5. Hanse Merkur*	81.01	Very good	83.17	Very good	75.42	Good	87.86	Very good
6. R+V	80.55	Very good	77.62	Good	91.82	Very good	63.87	Good
7. Axa	80.27	Very good	68.83	Good	92.29	Very good	79.09	Good
8. Inter*	80.09	Very good	83.33	Very good	76.50	Good	80.79	Very good
9. DKV	80.08	Very good	66.19	Good	87.29	Very good	93.46	Very good
10. Debeka	76.89	Good	63.83	Good	87.99	Very good	80.82	Very good
11. Hallesche	75.23	Good	74.72	Good	77.77	Good	71.15	Good
12. Central	73.87	Good	69.95	Good	74.85	Good	79.75	Good
13. LVM*	71,65	Good	73.86	Good	79.76	Good	51.00	Satisfactory
14. Münchener Verein	70.98	Good	73.99	Good	78.16	Good	50.61	Satisfactory
15. Gothaer*	70.34	Good	61.09	Good	76.65	Good	76.23	Good
16. Alte Oldenburger	69.91	Good	79.33	Good	69.96	Good	51.00	Satisfactory
17. Provinzial	69.64	Good	80.95	Very good	67.64	Good	51.00	Satisfactory
18. Bay. Beamten-KK	69.34	Good	72.72	Good	74.28	Good	52.72	Satisfactory
19. Süddeutsche	68.50	Good	61.21	Good	83.62	Very good	52.82	Satisfactory
20. Union	68.48	Good	64.62	Good	80.37	Very good	52.44	Satisfactory
21. Pax-Familienfürsorge*	67.73	Good	66.85	Good	60.48	Good	83.98	Very good
22. Universa	67.55	Good	76.54	Good	66.04	Good	52.59	Satisfactory
23. Ergo Direkt	67.28	Good	84.60	Very good	58.10	Satisfactory	51.00	Satisfactory
24. Württembergische	66.66	Good	73.66	Good	67.48	Good	51.00	Satisfactory
25. DEVK*	66.38	Good	85.80	Very good	54.65	Satisfactory	51.00	Satisfactory
26. Concordia*	66.10	Good	72.54	Good	67.20	Good	51.00	Satisfactory
27. Envivas	65.47	Good	83.87	Very good	54.31	Satisfactory	51.00	Satisfactory
28. Huk-Coburg*	61.84	Good	49.58	Satisfactory	60.73	Good	88.60	Very good
29. Continentale	60.18	Good	64.55	Good	60.78	Good	50.26	Satisfactory
30. DFV	59.44	Satisfactory	68.10	Good	55.00	Satisfactory	51.00	Satisfactory
31. Nürnberger	59.01	Satisfactory	72.23	Good	49.80	Satisfactory	51.00	Satisfactory
32. Landeskrankenhilfe	58.79	Satisfactory	76.00	Good	51.38	Satisfactory	39.19	Sufficient
33. Vigo	58.01	Satisfactory	72.09	Good	47.42	Satisfactory	51.00	Satisfactory

*insurers of the stock company form but owned by a mutual insurance company

Source: *Schulte, A.* Gesundheits-Check für Versicherer. Eine Analyse des Deutschen Finanz-Service-Instituts gibt Einblick in die Qualität der privaten Krankenversicherungen. Handelsblatt from the 15th of October 2018, No. 198, p. 51.

While *Weinmann* focuses onto the performance of German life insurance companies and the *German Finance service institute* on private health insurers, *Franke and Bornberg Ltd*[258] created a ranking of German insurance companies that offered insurances in the event of fire, water damage, break-in, theft, or storms for private households. In the analysis, *Franke and Bornberg Ltd* considered the conditions and premiums in the highest protection category, while the evaluation of cus-

[258] Cf. *Schmidt, L.* Alltagsrisiken im Griff. Handelsblatt from the 10th of December 2018, No. 238, p. 42

tomer services and information in which way the companies handled the damage in the practice were excluded (see Table 14).

Table 14 Ranking of the best household insurances offered by insurance companies 2017[259]

Company	Total number of points	Grade
Medien-Versicherung Karlsruhe	100	Very good
Basler	100	Very good
WGV*	100	Very good
HDI	100	Very good
Interrisk	97	Very good
Ammerländer	97	Very good
Öffentliche Sachvers. Braunschweig	97	Very good
Domcura	97	Very good
Häger Versicherungsverein	97	Very good
NV-Versicherungen	94	Very good
Huk-Coburg*	94	Very good
Barmenia*	94	Very good
Die Haftpflichtkasse	94	Very good
Janitos	91	Very good
Alte Leipziger*	91	Very good
DEVK*	91	Very good
Signal Iduna*	88	Good
S.L.P. Vertriebsservice	88	Good
SV Sparkassenversicherung	85	Good
Axa	85	Good
Cosmos	83	Good
VHV*	83	Good
Europa*	83	Good
BGV	82	Good
Rhion	82	Good
Concordia	80	Good
Nürnberger	79	Satisfactory
Debeka*	79	Satisfactory
Rheinland	76	Satisfactory
Ergo	76	Satisfactory
Stuttgarter*	73	Satisfactory
GVV*	72	Satisfactory
Prokundo*	72	Satisfactory
Gothaer*	57	Sufficient
Arag	51	Sufficient
WWK*	42	Sufficient
VGH	42	Sufficient

Source: *Schmidt, L.* Alltagsrisiken im Griff. Handelsblatt from the 10th of December 2018,

[259] Mutual insurance companies are indicated in grey. No. 238, p.42f.The table includes joint stock companies in mutual society horizontal groups, which are indicated in the table with *.

The results show that the customers' tariffs differ immensely between the companies. The winner in their analysis is the mutual insurance society *Medien-Versicherung* due to their insurance products' good contract conditions and reasonable price-performance ratio. In general, the analysis concluded that the premiums of the different companies vary and depend in particular on the situation of each customer. For example, customers who live in areas with a higher theft rate have higher premium rates compared to customers living in more secure parts of a city. Overall, 16 out of 37 analyzed companies (20[260] are mutuals) received the grade "very good", of which 10 are mutual insurance societies. This indicates that the majority of mutual insurance societies offer their customers fair conditions and prices, but, nevertheless, did not particularly outperform their stock company counterparts. Four mutual companies were graded with "good", 4 with "satisfactory", and 2 received the grade "sufficient".[261]

5. Perspectives of the mutual insurance societies

From an international point of view, mutual insurance societies experience a revival. In particular, during the peak of the financial crisis in 2008/2009 the number of policyholders increased above the average of the insurance market and increases now similar to the total market. After years and even decades of decline the turnovers increased stronger compared to the total market. The share in the global insurance market increased from 24 percent (2007) to 26 percent in 2015.[262] Table 15 shows that the mutual insurance societies in Germany had a similar positive development in 2008/2009. Their market share in Germany has been stabilized at about 15 percent in accordance to the GDV.[263]

Apart from Germany, the United States, Japan, France, and the Netherlands are the leading mutual insurance society markets. While the share in non-life insurance sector is rather small in Germany, the share in the life insurance sector is larger and solid (see Figure 15).

---

260 This includes joint stock companies in mutual society horizontal groups, which are indicated in the table with *.

261 Cf. *Schmidt, L.* Alltagsrisiken im Griff. Handelsblatt from the 10th of December 2018, No. 238, p. 42f.

262 Cf. Sigma (2016): Versicherung auf Gegenseitigkeit im 21. Jahrhundert: Zurück in die Zukunft? Nr. 4/2016, Swiss Re AG (Hrsg.), Zürich, p. 8.

263 Cf. GDV (2018) Statistisches Taschenbuch der Versicherungswirtschaft, Karlsruhe, p. 22

Table 15: The change of market shares regarding insurance premiums

Year	Joint stock companies	Mutual insurance societies	Public insurance companies	Other insurance companies
		Market share in percent		
1951	61.1	31.6	4.5	2.8
1960	64.3	27.8	3.8	4.1
1970	64.0	28.0	4.2	3.8
1975[4]	63,7	28.0	4.5	3.8
1980	63.8	27.5	4.8	3.9
1985	62.3	27.8	5.9	4.0
1990[4]	69.1	19.9	8.3	2.6
1991	70.4	19.6	7.5	2.6
1992	70.7	19.3	7.5	2.5
1993	71.2	19.2	7.6	2.1
1994	72.2	18.9	7.0	1.9
1995	73.3	19.3	5.9	1.5
1996	74.1	18.7	6.0	1.2
1997	73.8	18.9	6.0	1.3
1998	75.4	18.2	5.0	1.3
1999	75.6	17.9	5.1	1.3
2000	77.5	17.0	4.4	1.0
2001	80.2	15.4	3.3	1.1
2002	81.9	15.0	2.0	1.1
2003	83.5	14.1	1.5	0.9
2004	83.2	14.5	1.5	0.9
2005	82.7	14.9	1.5	0.9
2006	82.6	15.0	1.5	0.9
2007	83.0	14.6	1.4	0.9
2008	82.6	15.1	1.5	0.8
2009	81.8	15.8	1.5	0.9
2010	82.6	15.0	1.5	0.9
2011	82.5	15.2	1.4	0.8
2012	82.3	15.4	1.5	0.8
2013	82.7	15.0	1.5	0.8
2014	82.8	15.0	1.5	0.7
2015	82.8	15.0	1.5	0.7
2016	82.8	15.0	1.5	0.7

Source: GDV (2018) Statistisches Taschenbuch der Versicherungswirtschaft, Karlsruhe, p. 22.

Figure 15: Share of mutual insurance societies in the life and non-life insurance sector in the five largest insurance markets for mutual insurance societies.

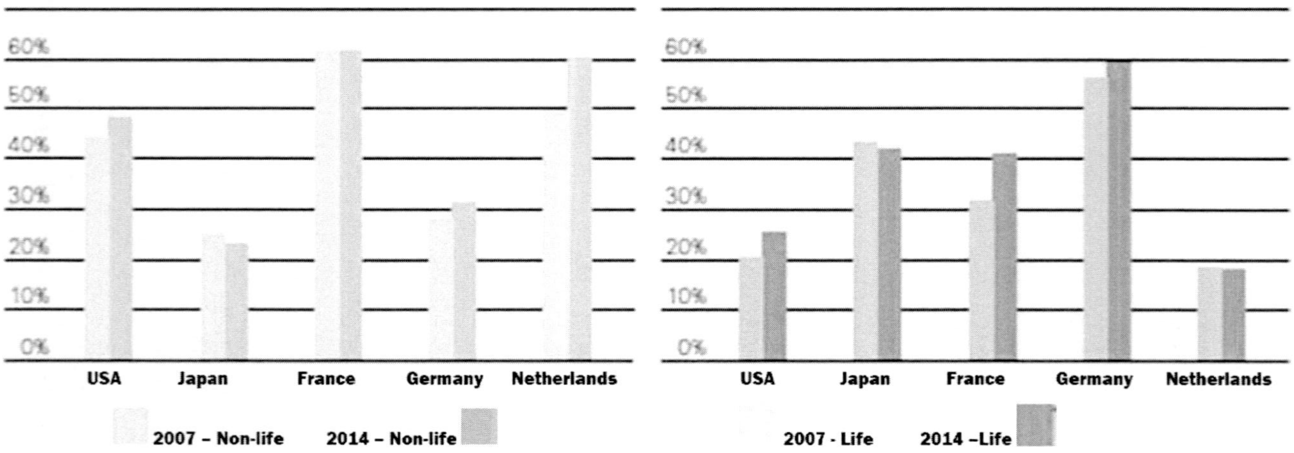

For the calculation of the market share of mutual insurance societies, the following steps were taken: in France, the total number of the sector was adjusted to be able to consider optional health insurance premiums (e.g. of "mutuelles 45", "institutions de prévoyance" and other insurer. In Japan, the written premiums of small co-operative non-life insurers were included into the calculation. In the USA, premiums of otherwise not considered mutual insurance societies were included as well as adjustments of accident- and health insurers and premiums for investments and their contribution to the total number were made.

Source: ICMIF, Swiss Re Economic Research & Consulting, Sigma (2016): Versicherung auf Gegenseitigkeit im 21. Jahrhundert: Zurück in die Zukunft? No. 4/2016, Swiss Re AG (eds.), Zürich, p. 9.

Are these results sufficient to make a prediction for the future for mutual insurance societies in Germany? The predictions depend on the developments in the different insurance branches, and therefore, on the mix of insurance branches of the mutual insurance societies. In the health insurance sector they exist above average, in the non-life insurance sector they are average and in life insurance below average. As a result, the total market share of mutuals depend on the development of the three major insurance branches:[264]

- The existence of the private health insurance is at risk due to the introduction of the citizens' insurance, which was regarded as a crucial requirement of the grand coalition ("Große Koalition"). However, the large political parties SPD and CDU/CSU agreed on, during their exploratory talks in 2018, that private and public health insurance will remain for the moment the same. The citizens' insurance is still a possible alternative.
- Such negative scenarios do not concern non-life insurance branches. However, the results depend very much on the loss ratios in car insurance and insurances that cover elementary risks that are changeable.
- In the life insurance branch the prediction for biometric risks are positive for insurances, while for short and medium term retirement provisions the predictions are moderate due to the dependence on the financial market. Exact predictions are not possible.

The future development of mutual insurance societies are influenced by reforms of the health system and the health insurance system.

Farny regards the legal development of mutuals in Germany as problematic.[265] The corporate law regarding mutuals in Germany can be found in the Insurance Supervision Act, which is however regarding terminology and topics partly obsolete; a reform, for example by a special law for mutual insurance societies, is not in the near future. The Corporation Law and the new regulations of Solvency II do not take the special features of mutuals into considerations.

Until today, the theoretical evidence is missing that size leads to economic advantages, because the system concerning the advantages and disadvantages of size is complex. It is possible to assume that size has advantages regarding risk balance in large insurance portfolios and a smaller need of security capital is evident in smaller portfolios. Nonetheless, a smaller business has advantages such as less complex-

[264] *Farny, D.* (2012): Zustand und Perspektiven der Gegenseitigkeitsversicherung in Deutschland, in *Beckmann R. M.* (ed.): Weitsicht in Versicherung und Wirtschaft. Gedächtnisschrift für Ulrich Hübner, Heidelberg (et.al.), pp. 77-88, p. 84.

[265] Ibid., p. 85.

ity and a better overview, better resistance and smaller organization structures. Only very small insurers have more problems to provide the necessary expertise of their business.

Mutual insurance societies have a better starting point regarding the choice of strategy. Due to their unity of members and customers and non-existence of owners and equity providers, they are suited for customer-oriented strategies. Today, a strong customer orientation is crucial in the insurance industry. In mutual insurance societies, customer orientation is in particular intensive when specializing the business regarding certain customer groups, insurance branches, or business areas.

A responsible management has to reconcile conflicts of interests. Important shareholders of an insurance company are the owners, the management, and the customers. In mutuals, the members and customers are identical, conflicts between the interests of the owners and customers do not exist. Nevertheless, conflicts between members/ customers and the management are possible, when the interests of members are not sufficiently looked after. The solution of such conflicts depends how the bodies (highest body, supervisory body, and the board of management) are defined in the bylaws and how the organization works in reality. In every scenario, a special quality of the decision-maker is crucial.

Mutual insurance societies have no share capital. The members' relationship to the society is established by capital contribution and not by taking out an insurance contract. Mutuals depend, therefore, on building up equity capital, i.e. a large part of the solvability funds, by profit and retaining profit. This however means that profits were made. In general, it can be assumed that self-financing of the equity capital will be successful.

Due to the principle of differentiating the insurance branches and the outsourcing of economic areas to independent service companies, the modern insurer is a holding enterprise with many operative companies. If the operative insurers keep the legal form of a mutual insurance society, then a horizontal group can be established that does not depend on capital investment. The subordinated group, that can be well controlled and organized firmly, with a parent company as owner requires that their subordinated companies are joint stock companies. In holding enterprises with a mutual insurance society at the top, restructurings are in motions to keep a balance between the mutuality principle and the economic necessities. Such restructurings are an important perspective for the future.

The harshest form of demutualization, i.e. the change of the legal form from a mutual insurance society to a joint stock company, was not used in Germany so far. However, during restructuring many insurance portfolios were transferred from mutuals to joint stock companies,

which is de facto a change of the legal form. Therefore, the modern form of mutual insurance holding enterprises means a partial demutualization.

6. Conclusion

In summary, it can be stated that the current situation of mutual insurance societies in Germany is not homogenous but has followed a positive development throughout recent times. The increase and profits are higher compared to other business areas and better than expected, which means above average. Moreover, mutuals are able to make sensible provisions of the security capital compared to the actions of joint stock companies. It appears that mutual societies were better prepared for Solvency II, although some small-specialised mutual insurance societies may get into difficulties due to increasing regulations and therefore resulting costs. However, new capital solutions are able to offer mutual insurance societies more financial flexibility.

The above-mentioned harmonization tendencies have become stronger and, therefore, mutuals adjust continuously to joint stock companies. This trend is also shown by the three studies regarding life insurances, private health insurances, and household insurances. Although these studies show that mutual insurance societies are successful in various insurance segments, it is not possible to find evidence of a superiority of the mutuality principle from the results. One reason is, as *Weinmann* points out, that mutuals have already adapted their business methods to those of joint stock companies. This fact may be also true for the good performance of mutuals offering private health insurance, which is shown by the *German Finance service institute's* analysis and the evaluated results presented by *Franke and Bornberg Ltd's* regarding household insurance. However, as *Weinmann* points out, mutuals have already adapted their business methods to those of joint stock companies. As a result, the insurance sector and mutual insurance societies in particular became opaque. Nevertheless, mutual insurance societies still play an important role in the German insurance business. They are able to assert their position on the market due to resistance against take-overs, member loyalty, and flexibility. The use of new digital technologies can initiate new impulses for mutual insurance societies but also for the entire insurance market.

However, in this context two developments should be presented to think about the current situation of the insurance market. On the one hand, the Allianz bought the mutual insurance company Liverpool

Victoria in 2017 and, as Allianz CEO *Oliver Bäte* stated, this acquisition should be used as a model for the future. His intention is to make an alliance with former competitors, because, according to *Bäte*, the border between mutuals and joint stock companies has already become fuzzy. *Bäte* signifies with this action that the Allianz is ready to change the company's policy and connect with mutual insurance societies and their tradition.[266] On the other hand, *Robert Glasser* from the Munich Re suggests that insurance schemes under the mutual form could be a solution for covering insurance necessities in underdeveloped countries, in which the risks of natural disasters are much higher and the risks for insurance companies to operate profitable are problematic. He states that insurance societies under the mutual form can develop suitable products to cover particular groups of the population against specified risks, implying that risks faced in respective countries can be covered through domestic self-organization of the developing nations' population.[267]

[266] *Magenheim-Hörmann, T.* Allianz kauft in Großbritannien zu. OVB online (05.08.2017) https://www.ovb-online.de/weltspiegel/wirtschaft/allianz-kauft-grossbritannien-8571340.html (06.02.2019)

[267] Cf. *Munich Re* (ed.): Corporate Responsibility Bericht 2017/2018, p. 89.

References

Arens, W./Tepper, F. (eds.) (2013): Praxisformularbuch Gesellschaftsrecht: Schriftsätze – Verträge – Erläuterungen, Nördlingen.

Auchinleck, B. et.al. (2002): Optionen für Versicherungsvereine: Demutualisieren oder restrukturieren?, in Versicherungswirtschaft 7/2002.

BaFin (2018) Statistik der Bundesanstalt für Finanzdienstleistungsaufsicht – Erstversicherungsunternehmen und Pensionsfonds.

Beenken, M. (2009): Das leise Sterben der Versicherungsvereine, in: VersicherungsJournal, 03.09.2009.

Beitrag auf BaFin, Solvency II: https://www.bafin.de/EN/Aufsicht/VersichererPensionsfonds/Aufsichtsregime/SolvencyII/solvencyII_node_en.html 20.06.2018.

Beitrag auf BaFin, Solvency II: https://www.bafin.de/EN/Aufsicht/Versicherer-Pensionsfonds/Aufsichtsregime/SolvencyII/solvencyII_node_en 20.06.2018.

Beitrag auf BaFin, Versicherungsaufsicht in Deutschland, https://www.bafin.de/EN/DieBaFin/AufgabenGeschichte/Versicherungsaufsicht/versicherungsaufsicht_node_en.html 20.06.2018.

Beitrag auf Haus der Bayerischen Geschichte, Königreich Bayern 1806-1918, https://www.hdbg.eu/koenigreich/web/index.php/objekte/index/herrscher_id/1/id/256, 22.06.2018.

Beitrag auf openJur, LG Köln, verdict 24.08.2007 Az.82O212/06, https://openjur.de/u/127703.html, 20.06.2018.

Beitrag auf Wissen Digital, Konzern, http://www.wissen-digital.de/Konzern, 20.06.2018.

Benkel, G. A. (2002): Der auf Gegenseitigkeit – Das Gesellschaftsrecht der großen konzernfreien VVaG, Munich.

Bischoff, K. (1961): Die oberste Vertretung beim kleineren Versicherungsverein auf Gegenseitigkeit – Möglichkeiten und Grenzen, VersR.

Braeß, P. (1971): Konzentration in der Versicherungswirtschaft, in *Arndt, H.* (ed.), Die Konzentration in der Wirtschaft – On Economic Concentration, Schriften des Vereins für Socialpolitik, vol., Berlin, pp. 463-482.

Brazda, J. / Hoppichler, F. (2015): Versicherungsvereine auf Gegenseitigkeit versus Versicherungsaktiengesellschaften – Eine historische Betrachtung, in: *Brazda, J.* et.al. (eds.): Perspektiven für die Genossenschaftsidee: Festschrift zum 65. Geburtstag von Verbandsanwalt Professor DDr. Hans Hofinger, pp. 198-209.

Braouet, C. (2017). Ungleiche "Genossen" in Deutschland und Frankreich, in: Deutsch-Französisches Institut (ed.): Frankreich Jahrbuch 2016. Sozialwirtschaft in Frankreich und Europa, Wiesbaden, pp. 107-121.

Brenzel, J. (1973): Unternehmen und Organisation des Versicherungsvereins auf Gegenseitigkeit. Ein Beitrag zur Reformdiskussion, Göttingen.

Breuer, C. (1999): Versicherungsverein auf Gegenseitigkeit versus Versicherungs-Aktiengesellschaft: Eine vergleichende Strukturanalyse der Rechtsformen, Köln.

Büchner, F (1957): Zur Geschichte der Versicherung, in VersWissArch, 46. vol. pp. 1-19.

Bundesaufsichtsamt für das Versicherungs- und Bausparwesen (ed.) (1963): Motive zum Versicherungsaufsichtsgesetz, Nachdruck, Berlin.

Bürkle, J. (2008): Verbesserte rechtliche Rahmenbedingungen für Versicherungsvereine auf Gegenseitigkeit, in *Bürkle, J.* (ed.): Rechtliche Rahmenbedingungen für Versicherungsvereine auf Gegenseitigkeit. Festschrift zum 100-jährigen Bestehen der Stuttgarter Lebensversicherung a.G., Karlsruhe, pp. 223-248.

Doerry, A. (1988): Versicherungskonzerne, in *Farny, D.* et.al. (ed.): Handwörterbuch der Versicherung HdV, Karlsruhe, pp. 1035-1042.

Dreher, M. (2008). Der VVaG Konzern, in *Bürkler. J* (ed.): Rechtliche Rahmenbedingungen für Versicherungsvereine auf Gegenseitigkeit. Festschrift zum 100-jährigen Bestehen der Stuttgarter Lebensversicherung a.G., Karlsruhe, pp 139-154.

Dreher, M. (2014): Stellungnahme für den Finanzausschuss des Deutschen Bundestags zu der öffentlichen Anhörung zu dem Gesetzesentwurf der Bundesregierung Entwurf eines Gesetzes zur Modernisierung der Finanzaufsicht über Versicherungen (Solvency II) BT-Drucks. 18/2956.

Fahl, H. (2005): Corporate Governance im Versicherungsverein a.G.: Die Auswirkungen der Aktienrechtsreformen auf das System der Unternehmensführung und -kontrolle im VVaG, VersR-Schriften 30, Karlsruhe.

Fahl, H. (2008): Demokratie im Versicherungsverein – Anmerkung zum Urteil des Landesgerichts Köln vom 24. August 2007 (AZ. 82 O 212/06), Versicherungswirtschaft, 63. vol., No. 14.

Farny, D. (1977): Die Entwicklung der Versicherung auf Gegenseitigkeit von der Spezial- zur Generalversicherung, in Mutualité, H.1, pp. 78-98.

Farny, D. (1980): Entwicklungslinien, Stand und Wirtschaftliche Bedeutung des Versicherungswesens in Deutschland, in *Henning, F.W.* (ed.): Entwicklung und Aufgaben von Versicherungen und Banken in der Industrialisierung, Schriften des Vereins für Socialpolitik, vol. 105, Berlin, pp. 7-28.

Farny, D. (2011): Versicherungsbetriebslehre, Karlsruhe.

Farny, D. (2012): Zustand und Perspektiven der Gegenseitigkeitsversicherung in Deutschland, in *Beckmann, R. M.* (ed.): Weitsicht in Versicherung und Wirtschaft. Gedächtnisschrift für Ulrich Hübner, Heidelberg (et.al.), pp. 77-88.

Führer, C.: Demutualisierung von Versicherungsvereinen auf Gegenseitigkeit, Beitrag auf Hochschule Bochum, http://www.hochschule-bochum.de/fileadmin/media/fbw/Kaiser/praxis/demutuFuehrer.pdf, 20.06.2018.

GDV (2018) Statistisches Taschenbuch der Versicherungswirtschaft, Karlsruhe.

Gerner, C. (2003): Demutualisierung eines VVaG: Die Umwandlung eines Versicherungsvereins auf Gegenseitigkeit in eine Aktiengesellschaft, Diss., Frankfurt am Main.

Gesetz über die Beaufsichtigung der Versicherungsunternehmen (Versicherungsaufsichtsgesetz - VAG), Versicherungsaufsichtsgesetz in der Fassung der Bekanntmachung vom 17. Dezember 1992 (BGBl. 1993 I p. 2), das zuletzt durch Artikel 2 Absatz 7 des Gesetzes vom 12. Juni 2015 (BGBl. I p. 926) geändert worden ist.

Gierke, J. (1942): Die Versicherungsvereine auf Gegenseitigkeit nach deutschem Recht, Stuttgart.

Görg, W. (2005): VVag-spezifische Besonderheiten bei Umsetzung von Solvency II, in *Gründl, H. / Perlet, H.* (ed.): Solvency II & Risikomanagement: Umbruch in der Versicherungswirtschaft, Wiesbaden, pp. 367-380.

Grosse, W. (ed.) (1991): Gabler Versicherungsenzyklopädie, vol. 3, Rechtslehre des Versicherungswesens, Wiesbaden.

Grossfeld, B. (1985): Der Versicherungsverein auf Gegenseitigkeit im System der Unternehmensformen, Tübingen.

Handelsblatt 16.12.2017.

Hauth, H. (1984): Unternehmensverfassungsrechtliche Probleme des Versicherungsvereins auf Gegenseitigkeit, Frankfurt am Main.

Hax, K. (1969): Ist der Versicherungsverein auf Gegenseitigkeit noch eine geeignete Rechtsform für die große Versicherungsunternehmung?; in: *Farny, D.* (ed.): Wirtschaft und Recht der Versicherung: Paul Braeß zum 66. Geburtstag, Karlsruhe, pp. 139-164.

Heidelbach, A. (1994): Der kleinere Versicherungsverein auf Gegenseitigkeit unter besonderer Berücksichtigung der gesellschaftsrechtlichen Probleme, Versicherungsrechtliche Studien, vol. 30, Diss., Frankfurt am Main.

http://www.arge-vvag.de/fsets/fthemen.htm, 25.07.2018.

https://ec.europa.eu/info/business-economy-euro/banking-and-finance/insurance-andpensions/risk-management-and-supervision-insurance-companies-solvency-2_en.html 20.06.2018.

https://www.bafin.de/EN/Aufsicht/VersichererPensionsfonds/Aufsichtsregime/SolvencyII/solvency_II_node_en.html 20.06.2018.

https://www.ovb-online.de/wirtschaft/allianz-kauft-grossbritannien-8571340.html, 30.07. 2018.

https://www.solvency-ii-kompakt.de/20.06.2018.

ICMIF (2018): Facts and figures – Mutual and cooperative insurance in Europe, AMICE aisbl & ICMIF, Vol 2.

KIVI GmbH, Kölner Institut für Versicherungsinformation und Wirtschaftsdienste, http://www.kivi-online.de.

Koch, P. (1988): Versicherungsgeschichte in Stichworten, Verein zur Förderung der Versicherungswissenschaft in München e.V., No. 32, Munich.

Koch, P. (1995): Die historische Entwicklung des Versicherungsvereins auf Gegenseitigkeit, in *Peiner, W.* (ed.): Grundlagen des Versicherungsvereins auf Gegenseitigkeit. Verfaßt und veröffentlicht aus Anlaß des 175jährigen Bestehens der Gothaer Versicherungsbank VVag, Karlsruhe, pp. 13-26.

Koch, P. (1998): Geschichte der Versicherungswissenschaft in Deutschland; Edit by Deutschen Verein für Versicherungswissenschaften e.V. aus Anlaß seines 100jährigen Bestehens, Karlsruhe.

Koch, P. (2005): Historische Wechselwirkungen zwischen österreichischer und deutscher Assekuranz, in: Versicherungswirtschaft, Beiträge zur Geschichte des Deutschen Versicherungswesens, vol. II, Karlsruhe.

Köstlin, M.: Reguliert Solvency II kleine VVaG aus dem deutschen Markt?, Vortrag Verband der Versicherungsvereine a.G.e.V., Beitrag auf BaFin, http://www.bafin.de/SharedDocs/Downloads/DE/Rede_Vortrag/dl_131114_solvency2_vortrag_koestlin.pdf?__blob=publicationFile&v=2, 20.06.2018.

Lehner, U. (1988): Der Konzern der Wiener Städtischen, in: Rohrbach W.: Das Zeitalter des modernen Versicherungswesens, vol. 3, Holzhausen/Vienna.

Lorenz, E. (1988): Versicherungsverein auf Gegenseitigkeit, in: *Farny D.* (ed.): Handwörterbuch der Versicherung (HdV), Karlsruhe, pp. 1147-1158.

Manes, A. (1930): Versicherungswesen, vol. I, 5, Berlin.

Martiensen, H. P. (2006): Fusionen von Versicherungsvereinen auf Gegenseitigkeit: Verschmelzung gem. §§ 109 ff. UmwG und Gleichordnung gem. § 18 Abs. 2 AktG, Hamburger Reihe, Reihe A Rechtswissenschaft, Karlsruhe.

Müller, H. (2000): Der Versicherungsverein auf Gegenseitigkeit. Chancen und Risiken aus der Sicht eines Versicherungsaufsehers, Karlsruhe.

Müller, H. (2001): Materielle Versicherungsaufsicht – Eine Standortbestimmung, in Müller, H. et.al. (ed.): 100 Jahre materielle Versicherungsaufsicht in Deutschland, 1901-2001, Bonn.

Müller-Wiedenhorn, A. (1993): Versicherungsvereine auf Gegenseitigkeit im Unternehmensverbund: Eine Untersuchung zum Recht und zu konzentrationsrechtlichen Fragen des Versicherungsvereins auf Gegenseitigkeit, Beiträge zum Privat- und Wirtschaftsrecht, Diss., Karlsruhe.

Munich Re (ed.): Corporate Responsibility Bericht 2017/2018.

Nemson, J. (2014): Geschäftsmodell VVaG: Rahmenbedingungen, Herausforderungen und Chancen, Karlsruhe.

Nguyen, T. / Romeike, F. (2013): Versicherungswirtschaftslehre: Grundlagen für Studium und Praxis, Wiesbaden.

Niermann, U. (1990): Geschichte und Organisationsstruktur öffentlich-rechtlicher Versicherer in Nordrhein-Westfalen, Frankfurt am Main.

Peiner, W. (2000): Die Zukunftschancen der Versicherungsvereine auf Gegenseitigkeit, in: *Koch, G. / Wagner, F.* (ed.): Aktuelle Fragen in der Versicherungswirtschaft, vol. 1, Karlsruhe, pp. 129-145.

Pfeifer, D.: Solvency II: Quo vadis VVag?, Beitrag auf Solvency II Kompakt, http://www.solvency-ii-kompakt.de/content/solvency-ii-quo-vadis-vvag, 20.06.2018.

Rabe, T. (1995): Liberalisierung und Deregulierung im Europäischen Binnenmarkt für Versicherungen, Schriftenreihe des Instituts für Versicherungswissenschaft an der Universität zu Köln, Berlin.

Raiser, L. (1965): Die Zulässigkeit des Kooptationssystems bei der Bildung von Mitgliedervertretungen großer Versicherungsverein auf Gegenseitigkeit, ZVersWiss., 54. vol., pp. 465-485.

Rittner, F. / Dreher, M. (2008): Europäisches und deutsches Wirtschaftsrecht – Eine systematische Darstellung, Heidelberg.

Rohrbach, W. (1988): Von den Anfängen bis zum Börsenkrach, in: Versicherungsgeschichte Österreichs, vol. 1, Vienna.

Schmidt, L. (2018): *Alltagsrisiken im Griff. Handelsblatt from the 10th of December 2018, No. 238, p. 42.*

Schmitt-Lermann, H. (1954): Der Versicherungsgedanke im deutschen Geistesleben des Barock und der Aufklärung, Munich.

Schneider, H. (1963): die Verfassungsentwicklung der Versicherungsvereine auf Gegenseitigkeit im 19.Jahrhundert, Göttingen.

Schulte, A. (2018): Gesundheits-Check für Versicherer. Eine Analyse des Deutschen Finanz-Service-Instituts gibt Einblick in die Qualität der privaten Krankenversicherungen. Handelsblatt from the 15th of October 2018, No. 198, p. 51.

Sieger, J.; *Bank, S.* (2012): Probleme bei der Kooperation von Versicherungsvereinen auf Gegenseitigkeit, in: VersR, 63. vol., H. 7, pp. 270-278.

Sigma (2016): Versicherung auf Gegenseitigkeit im 21. Jahrhundert: Zurück in die Zukunft? Nr. 4/2016, Swiss Re AG (ed.), Zürich.

Völker, G. (1995) Die wirtschaftliche Bedeutung des deutschen Versicherungsvereins auf Gegenseitigkeit, in *Peiner, W.* (ed.): Grundlagen des Versicherungsvereins auf Gegenseitigkeit. Verfaßt und veröffentlicht aus Anlaß des 175jährigen Bestehens der Gothaer Versicherungsbank VVag, Karlsruhe, pp. 89-106.

Wackerbeck, P. (2003): Neue Geschäftsfelder gesucht: Die Demutualisierung von Versicherungsvereinen auf Gegenseitigkeit, in M&A Review 2/2003.

Wagner, F. (ed.) (2011): Gabler Versicherungslexikon, Wiesbaden.

Wagner, F./Luo, J. (2012): Solvency II: Ein neues aufsichtsrechtliches Regime und dessen Konsequenzen für Versicherungsunternehmen, in *Beckmann, R. M.* (ed.): Weitsicht in Versicherung und Wirtschaft. Gedächtnisschrift für Ulrich Hübner, Heidelberg (et.al.), pp. 319-340.

Wagner, F./Luo, J. (2012): Solvency II: Ein neues aufsichtsrechtliches Regime und dessen Konsequenzen für Versicherungsunternehmen, in *Beckmann, R. M.* (ed.): Weitsicht in Versicherung und Wirtschaft. Gedächtnisschrift für Ulrich Hübner, Heidelberg (et.al.), pp. 319-340.

Wagner, F.: Beitrag auf Gabler Wirtschaftslexikon, Solvency I, http://wirtschaftslexikon.gabler.de/Definition/solvency-i.html, 20.06.2018.

Weigele, H.J. (1995): Eigenkapitalbildung von Versicherungsverein auf Gegenseitigkeit, in Peiner, W. (ed.): Grundlagen des Versicherungsvereins auf Gegenseitigkeit. Verfaßt und veröffentlicht aus Anlaß des 175jährigen Bestehens der Gothaer Versicherungsbank VVaG, Karlsruhe, pp. 141-157.

Weinmann, H. (2017): Was machen die Lebensversicherer mit dem Geld ihrer Kunden?, Zeitschrift für Versicherungswesen 24/2017, Ludwigshafen, pp. 772-776.

Weinmann, H. (2018): Was machen die Lebensversicherer mit dem Geld ihrer Kunden?, Zeitschrift für Versicherungswesen 1/2018, Ludwigshafen, pp. 18-22.

Weinmann, H. (2018): Was machen die Lebensversicherer mit dem Geld ihrer Kunden?, Zeitschrift für Versicherungswesen 18/2018, Ludwigshafen, pp. 536-543; 19/2018, pp. 586-594

Weinmann, H. (2018): Was machen die Lebensversicherer mit dem Geld ihrer Kunden?, Zeitschrift für Versicherungswesen 19/2018, Ludwigshafen, pp. 586-594

Weinmann, H. (2018): Was machen die Lebensversicherer mit dem Geld ihrer Kunden?, Zeitschrift für Versicherungswesen 23/2018, Ludwigshafen, pp. 724-730.

Weinmann, H. (2018): Was machen die Lebensversicherer mit dem Geld ihrer Kunden?, Zeitschrift für Versicherungswesen 24/2018, Ludwigshafen, pp. 749-753.

Winter, G. (2007): Versicherungsaufsichtsrecht – Kritische Betrachtung, Karlsruhe.

Wirsing, K. (2007): Demutualisierung am Beispiel der Standard Life Versicherung, Munich.

Appendix

Mutual insurance society horizontal groups			
Name of the group	Name of the member companies	Premium income 2016 (Mio. €)	Owner structure 2017
AGRORISK	Gartenbau-Versicherung VVaG	221,26	horizontal group
	Vereinigte Hagelversicherung VVaG		horizontal group
LKH	Landeskrankenhilfe VVaG	828,37	horizontal group
	Landeslebenshilfe VVaG		horizontal group
Süd-Deutsche Krankenversicherung	Süddeutsche Allgemeine Versicherung a.G.	812,64	horizontal group
	Süddeutsche Krankenversicherung a.G.		horizontal group
	Süddeutsche Lebensversicherung a.G.		horizontal group
Mutual insurance society without a holding structure			
Barmenia	Barmenia Allgemeine Versicherungs-AG	1.994,62	100% owned by der Barmenia KV a.G.
	Barmenia Krankenversicherung a.G.		-
	Barmenia Lebensversicherung a.G.		-
Continentale/Europa	Continentale Krankenversicherung a.G.	3.671,49	-
	Continentale Lebensversicherung AG		100% owned by the mutual insurance society
	Continentale Sachversicherung AG		100% owned by the mutual insurance society
	EUROPA Lebensversicherung AG		100% owned by the mutual insurance society
	EUROPA Versicherung AG		100% owned by the mutual insurance society
	Mannheimer Krankenversicherung AG		100% owned by the mutual insurance society
	Mannheimer Versicherung AG		100% owned by the mutual insurance society
Debeka	Debeka Allgemeine Versicherung AG	9.722,12	100% owned by Debeka Kranken-VVaGs
	Debeka Krankenversicherungsverein a. G.		-
	Debeka Lebensversicherungsverein a. G.		-
DEVK	DEVK Allgemeine Lebensversicherungs-AG	2.703,52	100% owned by DEVK-B AG
	DEVK Allgemeine Versicherungs-AG		100% owned by DEVK-B AG
	DEVK Deutsche Eisenbahn Vers. Lebensvers.Verein a.G.		-
	DEVK Deutsche Eisenbahn Versicherung Sach- und HUK-VVaG		-
	DEVK Krankenversicherungs-AG		100% owned by DEVK-

			B AG
	DEVK Rechtsschutz-Versicherungs-AG		100% owned by DEVK-B AG
	DEVK-B Rückversicherungs- und Beteiligungs-AG		100% owned by DEVK Deutsche Eisenbahn Vers. Lebensvers. Verein a.G.
	German Assistance Versicherung AG		100% owned by DEVK-B AG
GVV	GVV-Kommunalversicherung VVaG	213,09	-
	GVV-Privatversicherung AG		100% owned by the mutual insurance society
IDEAL	Ideal Lebensversicherung a.G.	370,63	-
	IDEAL Versicherung AG		100% owned by the mutual insurance society
INTER	Freie Arzt- und Medizinkasse VVaG	864,64	-
	INTER Allgemeine Versicherung AG		100% owned by INTER K.V. aG
	INTER Krankenversicherung aG		-
	INTER Lebensversicherung AG		100% owned by INTER K.V. aG
Itzehoer/Brandgilde	Itzehoer Lebensversicherungs-AG	437,75	100% owned by the mutual insurance society
	Itzehoer Versicherung/Brandgilde von 1691 VVaG		-
LV 1871	Delta Direkt Lebensversicherung AG	671,80	100% owned by the mutual insurance societies
	Lebensversicherung von 1871 a.G. München		-
	TRIAS Versicherung AG		100% owned by the mutual insurance society
LVM	LVM Krankenversicherungs-AG	3.366,90	100% owned by the mutual insurance society
	LVM Landwirtschaftlicher Versicherungsverein Münster a.G.		-
	LVM Lebensversicherungs-AG		100% owned by the mutual insurance society
Mecklenburgische	Mecklenburgische Krankenversicherungs-AG	539,59	100% owned by the mutual insurance society
	Mecklenburgische Lebensversicherungs-AG		100% owned by the mutual insurance society
	Mecklenburgische Versicherungs-Gesellschaft a. G.		-

Münchener Verein	MÜNCHENER VEREIN Allgemeine Versicherungs-AG	702,91	100% owned by MV K.V. a.G.
	MÜNCHENER VEREIN Krankenversicherung a.G.		-
	MÜNCHENER VEREIN Lebensversicherung a.G.		-
Universa	uniVersa Allgemeine Versicherung AG	696,41	100% owned by uniVersa KV a.G.
	uniVersa Krankenversicherung a.G.		-
	uniVersa Lebensversicherung a.G.		-
Volkswohl-Bund	Volkswohl-Bund Lebensversicherung a.G.	1521,43	-
	VOLKSWOHL-BUND SACHVERSICHERUNG AG		100% owned by the mutual insurance society
WWK	WWK Allgemeine Versicherung AG	1151,89	100% owned by the mutual insurance society (94% direct, 6% indirect ownership)
	WWK Lebensversicherung a.G.		-
Mutual insurance group with a holding structure			
Alte Leipziger-Hallesche	ALTE LEIPZIGER Lebensversicherung a.G.	3940,89	100% share in holding
	Alte Leipziger Versicherung AG		100% ownership of the holding
	HALLESCHE Krankenversicherung a.G.		100% ownership of the holding
Concordia	Concordia Krankenversicherungs-AG	748,58	100% ownership of the holding
	Concordia oeco Lebensversicherungs-AG		100% ownership of the holding
	Concordia Rechtsschutz-Versicherungs-AG		100% ownership of the holding
	Concordia Versicherungs-Gesellschaft a. G.		100% share in holding
Die Bayerische	Bayerische Beamten Lebensversicherung a.G.	446,7	100% share in holding
	BAYERISCHE BEAMTEN VERSICHERUNG AG		100% ownership of the holding
	Neue Bayerische Beamten Lebensversicherung AG		100% ownership of the holding
Gothaer	ASSTEL Sachversicherung AG	3958,52	100% ownership of the holding
	CG Car-Garantie Versicherungs-AG (1)		100% ownership of the holding
	Gothaer Allgemeine Versicherung AG		100% ownership of the holding
	Gothaer Krankenversicherung AG		100% ownership of the holding
	Gothaer Lebensversicherung AG		100% ownership of the holding
	Gothaer Versicherungsbank VVaG		100% share in holding

	GVO Gegenseitigkeit Versicherung Oldenburg VVaG		-
	Janitos Versicherung AG		100% ownership of the holding
	BD24 Berlin Direkt Versicherung AG		100% ownership of the holding
	HanseMerkur Allgemeine Versicherung AG		100% ownership of the holding
	HanseMerkur Krankenversicherung a.G.		100% share in holding
	HanseMerkur Krankenversicherung AG		100% ownership of the holding
HanseMerkur	HanseMerkur Lebensversicherung AG	1808,54	100% ownership of the holding
	HanseMerkur Reiseversicherung AG		100% ownership of the holding
	HanseMerkur Speziale Krankenversicherung AG		100% ownership of the holding
	HanseMerkur24 Lebensversicherung AG		100% ownership of the holding
	HDI Haftpflichtverband der Deutschen Industrie VVaG		79% share in holding (Talanx AG)
	HDI Lebensversicherung AG		Holding (Talanx AG) holds 94.9% of the shares
	HDI Versicherung AG		Holding (Talanx AG) holds 100% of the shares
	HDI-Global SE		Holding (Talanx AG) holds 100% of the shares
	Lifestyle Protection Lebensversicherung AG		Holding (Talanx AG) holds 100% of the shares
HDI-Gerling/Talanx	neue leben Lebensversicherung AG	8835,07	with 67.5% minus 1 share in indirect ownership of the Talanx AG
	neue leben Unfallversicherung AG		with 67.5% minus 1 share in indirect ownership of the Talanx AG
	PB Lebensversicherung AG		Holding (Talanx AG) holds 100% of the shares
	PB Versicherung AG		Holding (Talanx AG) holds 100% of the shares
	TARGO Lebensversicherung AG		Holding (Talanx AG) holds indirectly 100% of the shares
	TARGO Versicherung AG		Holding (Talanx AG) holds indirectly 100% of the shares
	Bruderhilfe Sachversicherung AG im Raum der Kirchen 1		with 72.5% in the indirect ownership of the HUK-Coburg-Holding AG
HUK Coburg	Familienfürsorge Lebensversicherung AG im Raum der Kirchen	6936,84	with 72.5% in the indirect ownership of the HUK-Coburg-Holding AG
	HUK24 AG		100% im Besitz der HUK-C-Holding

	HUK-COBURG Haftpflicht-Unterstützungs-Kasse kraftf. Beamter VVaG		The mutual insurance society holds 100% shares in the HUK Coburg-Holding AG
	HUK-COBURG Lebensversicherung AG		100% owned by HUK-C-Holding
	HUK-COBURG-Allgemeine Versicherung AG		100% owned by HUK-C-Holding
	HUK-COBURG-Krankenversicherung AG		100% owned by HUK-C-Holding
	HUK-COBURG-Rechtsschutzversicherung AG		100% owned by HUK-C-Holding
	PAX-FAMILIENFÜRSORGE Krankenversicherung AG		with 72.5% in the indirect ownership of the HUK-Coburg-Holding AG
	VRK VVaG im Raum der Kirchen		-

SIGNAL/Iduna	ADLER Versicherung AG	5245,5	100% in the indirect ownership of the holding
	DEURAG Deutsche Rechtsschutz-Versicherung AG		100% in the indirect ownership of the holding
	DEUTSCHER RING Krankenversicherungsverein a.G.		-
	IDUNA Vereinigte Lebensversicherung aG		holds 51% of the holding
	PVAG Polizeiversicherungs-AG		51% owned by the holding
	SIGNAL IDUNA Allgemeine Versicherung AG		100% owned by the holding
	SIGNAL Krankenversicherung a.G.		holds 46.93% of the holding
	SIGNAL Unfallversicherung a.G.		holds 2.07% of the holding

Stuttgarter	Direkte Leben Versicherung AG	762,65	100% ownership of the holding
	PLUS Lebensversicherungs AG		100% ownership of the holding
	Stuttgarter Lebensversicherung a.G.		100% shares in the holding
	Stuttgarter Versicherung AG		100% ownership of the holding

VHV	Hannoversche Direktversicherung AG	2758,01	100% ownership of the holding
	Hannoversche Lebensversicherung AG (1)		100% ownership of the holding
	VHV Allgemeine Versicherung AG		100% ownership of the holding
	VHV Vereinigte Hannoversche Versicherung a.G.		100% shares in the holding

VPV	VEREINIGTE POSTVERSICHERUNG VVaG	456,74	100% shares in the holding
	VPV Allgemeine Versicherungs-AG		100% ownership of the holding
	VPV Lebensversicherungs-AG		100% ownership of the holding

WGV	WGV-Lebensversicherung AG	677,87	100% ownership of the holding

	WGV-Versicherung AG		100% ownership of the holding
	Württembergische Gemeinde-Versicherung a.G.		100% shares in the holding

Source: Data is drawn from KIVI: Die Marktanteile der Anbieter auf dem deutschen Versicherungsmarkt 2016 and was made available by *Michael Thiemermann*. Additionally, see the solvency reports (2017) of the individual companies. The tables were compiled by *Stefan Preiner*, BSc., MSc.

Part II.
Mutual Insurance Organizations and Social Economy

Mutual Associations in the Finnish Insurance System

Juhani Laurinkari

1. Introduction

In this text, the social economy is structured around cooperatives, associations with commercial activities, foundations, and mutual societies. With regard to mutual societies, the focus lies on persons, non-life, and social security insurances. According to *Pekka Pättiniemi*, i.e. from a Finnish point of view, social economy can be characterized by distribution of the production results, the minimisation of the public influence concerning the organization of products and consumption by the citizens as well as the support of citizens' initiative. The core element is the cooperation between the producer and the customer, which should help to correct or prevent market disturbances and the failure of state intervention.[1] *Tapani Köppä* states that equality and the economic participation of the citizens have to be increased by social economy. In the traditional capitalistic private economy, the aim of joint stock companies is profit maximization.[2] In contrast, mutual associations, cooperatives, and (private) foundations focus on social goals.

Another key element of social economy is the participation of the citizens in the decision-making process concerning production and the distribution of products and services they provide. In general, the social economy has a stabilizing social-political function. This is obvious by the production goal of the products and services, but also by other goals such as employment. Compared to other business areas, social economy enterprises focus more on social security than on productivity and the

[1] Cf. *Pättiniemi, Pekka* (2004). Mitä on yhteisötalous? In: *Grönberg, Ville* (ed.). Yhteisötalous ja sosiaalinen yrittäjyys. Sosiaalisten yritysten kansallinen teematyö. Euroopan sosiaalirahasto ESR. Sosiaali – ja terveysalan tutkimus – ja kehittämiskeskus STAKES: Helsinki.

[2] Cf. *Köppä, Tapani* (2006). Kilpailutalous: Kehitysoptimismissa perikadon ainekset. In: *Pauli Niemelä & Terho Pursiainen* (eds.). Hyvinvointi yhteiskuntapoliittisena tavoitteena. Professori Juhani Laurinkarin juhlakirja. Sosiaalipoliittisen yhdistyksen tutkimuksia nro 62. Kuopion yliopisto, 156.

increase of assets.[3] For example, along *Panu Kalmi* there are differences between mutual companies and corporations regarding allocation and management of surpluses. In mutual companies, the surplus is divided according to customer relationships: customers receive part of the surplus, for example, in form of payment discounts. In corporations, surpluses are distributed as dividends in proportion to the shareholding.[4] In both mutual societies and corporations, the owners have the highest decision making power. It is exercised in the general meeting and by electing the key institutions. Mutual companies generally have a two-stage management system, whereby the general meeting appoints the board of directors, which in turn appoints the Board.[5]

Companies usually use a one-stage management model, in which the general meeting appoints the board. There are significant differences between a mutual company and a limited liability company regarding the distribution of voting rights at the annual general meeting. There is a voting power in limited liability companies and the proportion of the shareholding. In mutual companies, the shareholder's voting rights are weighted according to membership and premiums.[6]

In Finland, the term social economy comprises different company types and forms of production, in which the corporate governance is realized very differently. The pertinent research literature deals with the different forms of social economy in various ways. During the last years, cooperatives and associations (but also social enterprises) have received the highest attention in Finland, a trend that is connected with the expectation that these types of organizations can contribute to the employment. In contrast, mutual societies and foundations have not received much attention. *Arja Suomi* refers to this development in so far that he states that no general surveys for mutual associations are available in Finnish.[7]

In the Finnish social-political literature, social economy is rarely dealt with and plays along the general opinion just a marginal role in social policy compared to the topic of the social welfare state. This can also be observed regarding the definition of certain terms. Even at the beginning of the 21st century, there was a terminology gap, social eco-no-

---

3 Cf. *Laurinkari, Juhani* (2010). Hyvinvointipolitiikan talous. In: *Pauli Niemelä* (ed.) Hyvinvointipolitiikka. WSOYPro: Helsinki, 85-89.

4 *Kalmi, Panu* (2007). Keskinäisyys yritysmuotona. In: *Arja Suomi* (ed.) Keskinäisyys. Näkökulmia omistaja-asiakkuuteen. Edita Publishing: Helsinki, 37.

5 Ibid.

6 Ibid.

7 Cf. *Suomi, Arja* (toim.) (2007). Keskinäisyys. Näkökulmia omistaja-asiakkuuteen. Edita Publishing: Helsinki; *Pättiniemi, Pekka* (2004). Mitä on yhteisötalous? In: *Grönberg, Ville* (ed.) 2004. Yhteisötalous ja sosiaalinen yrittäjyys. Sosiaalisten yritysten kansallinen teematyö. Euroopan sosiaalirahasto ESR. Sosiaali – ja terveysalan tutkimus – ja kehittämiskeskus STAKES: Helsinki, 28.

my dealt with different economic questions concerning the public social politics compared to the central European practice.[8] Only a couple of years later, a pan-European definition of social economy was developed.

However, in a more detailed analysis, the situation may be slightly different. Based only on the number of estimations, social economy is in many ways an important business form. Its most important area concerns the cooperative activity. In 2015, 5,051 cooperatives[9], 37 mutual enterprises[10], and 140,700 entities belonging to the sector of associations, foundations and other non-profit and civil society and voluntary organizations that produce and sell goods and services can be found in Finland. Among this group of 140,700 entities, there are also 12,000 social and health entities as well as 28,000 culture entities. According to Finance Finland (2016), 417 non-profit associations and 37 foundations existed 2015 in Finland.

Mutual companies carry out insurance business in Finland. A large share of the companies are general insurance companies, the rest are pension companies and thus very important players in the Finnish social security system and in the welfare state as a whole. According to the Finnish Patent and Registration Office, their market share is 32% in insurance business. In the Finnish pension policy, their importance is much greater than the market share shows.

It is difficult to estimate accurately the impact of social economy for providing employment within the Finnish labour market. Generally, the impact is not as remarkable as in other Nordic countries or compared to economic powerful countries such as Germany, France, and Spain. At the time of writing this article, the social economy generates nearly 10% of the employment of Finnish society. Precise estimates are impossible to present due to various reasons. For example, cooperatives are key employers but often small and located in different parts of Finland and they do not constitute a special category in employment statistics. There is also scantily research available on the importance of cooperatives in this sense. Even though mutual societies are an important part of social economy they have not been studied sufficiently in Finland so far. According to *Antti Talonen*, insurance is a central aspect of social economy, because in case of a mutual contract the damage is taken care of by the associates.[11] This kind of insurance principle can be found in the Finnish national economy up to this day.

---

[8] Cf. *Poutanen, J., Veli-Matti* (2007). Sosiaalitaloudesta yhteisötalouteen?: *Laurinkari, J., Brazda, J., Kramer, J., Schediwy, R.*, Yhteisötalous. Johdatus perusteisiin.Palmenia. Palmenia-sarja.

[9] Cf. Cooperative Europe Key figures 2014-15.

[10] Cf. ICMIF Figures for 2015, Global Mutual Market Share 2015.

[11] Cf. *Talonen, Antti* (2015).

According to *Talonen*, the major competitive advantage of mutual associations lies in the identity between the client and the owner. This identity meets the difference between cooperatives and other types of corporate organizations and, as a result, mutuality should also receive a competitive advantage. The asset of the client relationship is in particular important. This should provide advantages with regard to the creation of values, perception, and facilitation.[12]

Mutual societies do not provide a high amount of employment. Their number of employees is approximately 6,000; however, in Finland its economic importance in the insurance industry is significant. The companies have prospered during the last couple of years. They furnished sizeable compensation to the gross national product, like associations, and equated with cooperatives. It is important to note that cooperatives are not allowed to operate insurance enterprises, but in Finland, a mutual society is allowed to operate like a cooperative.

The aim of this study is to investigate how far the established insurance industry is based on mutuality activities, the historical roots, and how it works in the area of social policy as a provider of services, employer and as a provider of non-life and life insurances. Moreover, possible future developments and challenges will be examined, in particular regarding life, non-life and social security insurances, i.e. the insurance branches which mutual associations are allowed to provide.

2. The insurance market in Finland

With regard to the type of corporate organization, insurance companies can be either a private or public joint stock insurance company, or a mutual insurance company in Finland. The latter can be private or public. A public joint stock insurance company is a joint stock company which trades its shares publicly owned. It is legally prohibited to trade the shares of a private joint stock company publicly owned. A public mutual insurance company is a creation of the most recent legislation, but it has not been defined by law or any preparative documents yet. It is suggested that the notion of public relates to merchantability of guarantee capital invested in the company. This company form does not exist in practice. As well as the other countries of the EU an insurance company in Finland can have the legal form of a European Company (Eurooppayhtiö/Societas Europaea) as well.[13]

[12] Ibid.

[13] Cf. AMICE (ed.), Facts and Figures. Mutual and cooperative insurance in Europe Vol. 2, http://www.amice-eu.org/publications/studies_reports.aspx.

Insurers with a cooperative legal form are not foreseen in Finland and thus there are no cooperative insurance companies. A life insurance undertaking can also carry out the non-life classes of accident and health insurance. Similarly, non-life undertakings that carry out only accident and health insurance can provide life insurance.

Companies which are joint stock companies belong to shareholders, while mutual societies belong to stakeholders. In Finland only insurance companies can operate on a mutual basis.[14] Joint stock companies working in the insurance industry have a different historical background than mutual associations, but both work in a similar way. The main differences are in the corporate governance, regarding the distribution of profits as well as solidity.[15]

The Finnish insurance market is characterized by a stable ownership with only minor changes. A change in the distribution of shares occurred in 2014, but this rare event took place only between legal forms.[16] Despite this stability, the insurance sector has changed noticeably in the last decades. For example, some companies merged, assets were transferred, and some companies had to declare bankruptcy.

Insurance associations (small mutual insurers) which are mutual insurance clubs, and regulated by the Act on Insurance Associations (1250/1987) also can offer insurances. They are regionally established and can be active in 40 municipalities at maximum. This restriction does not apply to fishing insurance associations. The bylaws of the association are ratified by the Ministry of Social Affairs and Health and the association is entered into the Trade Register. According to the Act on Insurance Associations, an insurance association is an insurance company based on the members' mutual liability.[17]

Apart from the insurance associations, there are a number of "independent associations". However, the number of insurance associations tends to decrease. They are merging to form mutual financial groups as in the case of the merger of Tapiola and Local Insurance in 2014 to form one mutual financial group. The new group is owned by its members/policyholders, established by merging the Local Insurance Mutual Company and the Tapiola General Mutual Insurance Company to form the group's central company. The financial ties between the

[14] Cf. *Suomi, Arja* (toim.) (2007). Keskinäisyys. Näkökulmia omistaja-asiakkuuteen. Edita Publishing: Helsinki, 31.

[15] ibid., 36.

[16] Non-life insurer Pohjola completed a process of re-mutualization, which transformed it from a stock-owned insurer back to its original structure of a member-owned insurer. As a result, the mutual market share figures in Finland reached a record level of 37.5%. (ICMIF (ed.) (2016). Market InSights: Europe 2014. Cheshire, 7.)

[17] http://www.finlex.fi/fi/laki/ajantasa/1987/19871250.

group-members are established via guarantee capital.[18] The main reason for the merger is to strengthen the mutual sector against the large bank-insurer-conglomerates operating in the Finnish market. Although there is not a direct pressure from Solvency II, it relieves pressure on the insurance associations to potentially implement it for their small mutual association.[19]

The insurance companies in Finland are distinguished according to their business activities, i.e. non-life, life insurance and statutory pension insurance. The particular companies function as a single corporate group or in cooperation with each other. These insurance groups (conglomerates of limited companies and banks) which offer comprehensive insurance products through specialised companies, in particular insurance fields, dominate the insurance market. Increasingly, banks have formed business partnerships with insurance groups to form "financial department stores" offering a wide range of financial services.[20]

The special pension insurance companies are an important feature of the Finnish insurance market groups. Employers obtain pension insurance for their employees from one of the private insurance firms (which in many cases are a part of insurance groups). Finland maintains a system, which requires establishment in Finland in order to offer pension insurance in Finland. These insurances are for example capacity pension insurances, which belong to the Finnish social protection, and the statutory accident insurance. This system is allowed by the EU through non-treaty derogation, although no prospect of remo-ving this derogation is pending since little competition is expected due to different pension systems in other Member States.[21]

The Finnish insurance markets are well developed and traditionally quite centralised. At the end of 2017, there were 50 licensed insurance undertakings in Finland, with a total premium of 23 billion Euros. These 50 companies included 35 specializing in non-life business and reinsurance, nine in life insurance, and six in statutory employee pen-

---

18 Policyholders/owners who invest funds create guarantee capital. They receive an interest of 5-6% on the invested funds. If the funds are returned to the investors, they only receive back their own investments and not any share of the capital. Guarantee capital is therefore different from share capital as the owner will not receive a return on investment (i.e. no capital gains). Policyholders/owners that provide the guarantee capital have voting rights on how the capital will be invested. Through the guarantee capital, mutual companies (e.g. the Tapiola life, non-life and pension fund mutuals) can have financial ties as they can cross own each other's' guarantee fund. The Financial Supervisory Authority supervises the guarantee capital.

19 Cf. Study on the current situation and prospects of mutuals in Europe. Final report. Country studies (2012), Zoetermeer 116.

20 http://crossborder.practicallaw.com/7-504-6240?source=relatedcontent.

21 Ibid.

sion insurance.[22] Total Finnish premiums in 2017 were split 20% in life insurance, 20% in non-life insurance, and 60% in statutory pension insurance. Insurance companies employed about 9,600 persons in total.

Finland is a good example of cross-border cooperation in the field of insurance. In the Nordic Countries, Tapiola, a Finnish company, engages in project based and information exchange cooperation with Länsförsäkringar Ab in Sweden, Gjensidige NOR in Norway and Topdanmark in Denmark. In Denmark Tapiola also cooperates with International Health Insurance Danmark.[23]

18 branches of foreign insurance companies offer insurances and, in addition, 730 foreign companies had notified the Financial Supervisory Authority that they provided cross-border insurance services. The Insurance Brokers Register (maintained by FIN-FSA) included 88 insurance broker businesses. A typical feature in the breakdown of Finnish insurance is that statutory lines generate a major share of premiums written. In 2017, two thirds of all premiums written came from statutory insurance, i.e. employee pension, workers' compensation, motor liability insurances, patient insurance and insurance for environment liabilities. Another typical feature of the Finnish insurance market is high concentration. The four largest life and non-life insurer companies and groups write 84% of all premiums. Statutory employee pension insurance is also highly concentrated: combined, the three largest companies hold over 90%.[24] In the last couple of years, several new companies were established, in particular in the life insurance sector due to an initiative of banks. However, their market share is still low.

There are numerous national and local insurance companies in Finland, of which the largest are: If, Pohjola, Fennia, Tapiola, Lähivakuutus, Nordea, Kaleva, Varma and Pohjantähti. Among them, the largest mutual insurance companies include the LähiTapiola, Fennia, Turva, Pohjantähti and the pension insurance companies Ilmarinen, Varma and Etera.

There are two most important acts which regulate the business activities of insurance companies. The Insurance Companies Act ("vakuutusyhtiölaki/försäkringsbolagslag 18.7.2008/521") regulates the carrying out of direct insurance business outside pension insurance and the Insurance Contract Act ("vakuutussopimuslaki/lag om försäkringsavtal 1994/543") covers all contracts of primary insurance.

---

22 Finance Finland (FFI) (ed.) (2018): Finnish Insurance in 2017, Helsinki 5.

23 Cf. Study on the current situation and prospects of mutuals in Europe. Final report. Country studies (2012), Zoetermeer 119.

24 Ibid. The main event in 2017 was the merger of If P&C Insurance Ltd, in charge of If's Finnish operations, with its Swedish parent company If P&C Insurance Plc. If's operations in Finland now fall under If Skadeförsäkring AB's branch in Finland. More than one-fifth of the sector's premiums written thus became cross-border.

The business activities of insurance companies are supervised by the Financial Market Authority. The insurance market in Finland has developed and insurances claims have become common. In 2017, insurance premiums written in Finland increased by 2% to a total of Euros 23 billion. Life insurers' premium income fell by 1%. Non-life insurers' premium income decreased by 2%. Premiums written in statutory employee pension insurance grew by 4%. Finnish insurers paid claims and pension benefits for nearly 22 billion Euros, which is 2% more than the year before.[25] Most private households (95%) have household contents insurances.

In Finland, there are no legal-form specific barriers for creating mutual-type organizations. The only limitation would be the method how the initial fund is gathered, i.e. not using share capital. In relation to limited companies, however, mutual societies of all types do have the disadvantage not to be able to issue shares and hence easily raise capital levels. Through this disadvantage, they need to be able to maintain capital levels continuously above the solvency requirements, which prevent them from conducting short-term investments.[26]

An insurance association foundation capital (authorized capital) must be at least a total of 42,000 Euros. If the association's activities include personal insurance, or its business scope covers more than 25 municipalities, the foundation capital must be at least 84,000 Euros.[27]

3. The history of the mutual insurance industry

According to *Michel Albertin*, the insurance business is based on two ideologically different principles, the common principle of the continent and the British business tradition. Both trends have their beginning in the Middle Ages.[28]

- The business tradition was strengthened by merchant shipping and the development of probability calculation in Great Britain. This tradition is based on the need to be protected collectively against the risks of shipping, for example against shipwreck and high costs due to piracy.

---

[25] Ibid.

[26] Study on the current situation and prospects of mutuals in Europe. Final report. Country studies (2012), Zoetermeer, 117.

[27] Article 5 of the Act on Insurance Associations.

[28] Cf. *Albertin, Michel* (2004). Vakuutuksen taloudellinen ja yhteiskunnalinen tehtävä. In: *Katri Hellsten* ja *Tuula Helne* (eds.). Vakuuttava sosiaalivakuutus? Kelan tutkimusosasto. Helsinki, 24-25.

Risk management, as part of the insurance industry, calculates the risk probability and is necessary for the business principle. The risk probability for the policyholder has to be estimated in a reliable way in order that a collective insurance business can function probably. This is important because it is unknown which policyholder will have damage. In general, all unpredictable risks can be objects of insurances; however, the main goal is to achieve profit.

- On the continent, insurances are based on the mutuality principle and on solidarity. This principle is rooted in the craftsmen guilds of the Middle Ages and is in its nature more than a business principle. The main goal is to protect the community. Members shall work together and take over responsibilities in case friends, neighbours, colleagues or other fellow men are in need. Mutuality was at that time and still is connected with the social security of a society. The main principle is not to gain profit, but economic security, solidarity among the members of the society, and to secure life.

While both principles can be found in the Finnish insurance business, the mutuality principle was very common in particular at the beginning of the development of insurances until World War II and to some extent even later. The Finnish insurance business is still composed collectively in several ways, for example regarding organization or ideology. This is noticeable for example in the marketing strategies of insurances.[29]

In Finland, mutual insurance societies developed due to the need of protecting assets. In agricultural societies, the village community was able to pay compensation to members for property damage. This principle was used for fire insurances in the early years of the Finnish insurance business.

The tradition of fire insurances in the Nordic states, for example in the Swedish speaking part of Finland, can be traced back to the Middle Ages. A common accountability for fire damage developed among the rural population in the Middle Ages and has been used in Sweden since the 14th century and in Finland since the 17th century. A resident of a village who had lost property, e.g. a house during a fire, was allowed to claim compensations at the local court. A jury confirmed the event and six controllers evaluated the amount of the fire damage. The residents of a village paid together the costs.[30] According to *Henttinen*, if a timber house or parts of a farmyard are burned down, this usually means for the owner losing the entire farmyard and the livelihood. To prevent such an outcome, residents pay into a common fund from which the

29 Cf. *Liukko, Jyri* (2007). Henkivakuutus ja solidaarisuuden kehät. Vakuutusmainonta vastuuajattelun muokkaajana Suomessa 1945-1990. In: Janus 15 (1).

30 Cf. *Henttinen, Annastiina* (2007). Keskinäisyyden alkulähteillä. In: *Arja Suomi* (ed.) Keskinäisyys. Näkökulmia omistaja-asiakkuuteen. Edita Publishing: Helsinki.

injured person received money. Even today, the business of mutual insurance societies is based on the same principle. Money is collected via insurance premiums and everyone who has deposited money has the right of compensations according to the insurance regulations.
Mutual insurance societies developed in several steps of changes.

- The first change in the tradition of mutual fire insurance took place at the end of the 19th century during the Industrial Revolution. In that time, the insurance business was expanded and included new classes of population and the economic nature of the business was intensified. At the same time, the first two Finnish insurance joint stock companies for fire damage, Fennia (1881) and Pohjola (1891), were established. Apart from these and statuary mutual insurance companies, associations were established which concentrated their business either on a specific region or on the entire country, on different professional guilds, society classes, or risk groups.
- However, these new companies usually did not include the majority of the rural population. As a result, this part of the population handled the problem of fire damage on their own. It is important to note that the rural population also started to change their insurance claims when they began to improve their homes and new farming machines were used. With the rising of the Industrial Revolution, the number of the warehouses grew and new kind of property, which was not insured, needed protection. With the expansion of the insurance business a strong national identification started to develop, connected with new national ideals and the beginning of a national state.[31]
  Although by the beginning of the 20th century fire insurance was the main insurance type of mutual insurance associations especially in the rural society, new developments and the expansion of the insurance business started to take place. For example, new insurance branches were introduced and insurance companies work nationwide. In 1908, the first statuary general mutual insurance company, Sampo in Turku, was established, offering a wide range of different kinds of insurances. The company decided to base its business on mutuality, because at this time the cooperation principle, which is connected with mutuality, dominated in Finland. The mutual responsibility was restricted to different types of insurances.
- In the time between the First and Second World War, new tensions developed in the insurance business, i.e. the class fight between workers and citizens and the ideological differences within the insurance market. The mutual insurance business reacted structurally to these changes and new insurance companies for different social classes were established. For example, the insurance company Pohja offered insurances for the bourgeoisie while Kansa protected the insurance rights of workers.

---

[31] Ibid.

This kind of tension also arose regarding the social security between the farmers, workers, and the parties they were represented of. This tension influenced and dominated the various reforms in this time. The workers fought with their groups of interests for a social security system based on salary and the rural population and their lobbies demanded a system which distributed tax advantages equally. As recently as the 1960s, Finland chose the Nordic system based on salary. This change was initiated by a left wing Parliamentary majority and the use of unemployment, health, and retirement pension insurance.[32]

- After the Second World War, the main goal of the Finnish economic policy was to use the welfare state to build up the society for the general good.[33] An important way to achieve this goal was to use the bank and insurance branches of the citizens. According to *Jyri Liukko*, the 1950s' insurance marketing emphasized that the insurance business is part of the economic and social activities. The money of the insurance companies supported, for example, industry, agriculture, maritime trade, the work of hospitals, electric power stations, schools, or railways and helped to build up Finland.[34]
  Finland became an industrial free-market economy after the Second World War when both insurance business and social security system disconnected from the tradition collective principle. This happened, compared to other Nordic states, late. During the development of the Finnish social security system and until the 1960s, a conflict was apparent between different social security models for farmers and models supported by lobbies of industrial workers and economic groups. The farmers' lobbies supported systems based on mutual help.[35]
  In the Finnish rural society, the principle of mutuality dominated compared to other European countries. The boundaries between insurance business and the system of mutual help of e.g. guilds, farmers, or craftsmen were fuzzy. The members of the village community were responsible to take care of typical risks occurring in their community.
  According to this tradition, insurance was regarded as a collective help of a member and not as a claim of a policyholder. Today's mutual insurance associations differ very much from these insurance communities, although both are based on a similar ideological foundation, e.g. cooperative companies. Within the last couple of years, the number of companies which emphasise ethical values and sustainable activities has increased.[36]

---

32 Ibid.

33 Cf. *Pantzar* (2000), 67.

34 Cf. *Fennia-Patria* (1952).

35 Cf. *Niemelä, Heikki & Salminen, Kari* (2009). Kansallisten eläkestrategioiden muotoutuminen ja Euroopan Unionin avoin koordinaatiomenetelmä. Sosiaali - ja terveysturvan tutkimuksia 104. Kela: Helsinki, 114-136.

36 Cf. www.yle.fi (2014).

- Cooperatives focus on efficient business activities with the community as its core element. After the Second World War, a new industrialization era began in Finland and statuary social security systems developed. Industrialization meant in this time in particular timber industry producing products with a low value-added grade. This industry was closely connected with agricultural businesses which provided timber for the production of paper and cellulose. The agricultural businesses worked together with cooperatives.
- A major change from the social security tradition happened in the 1960s when the pension, health, and unemployment insurances were transferred to cooperative companies. For example, the legally obligatory pension fund system is now managed by private companies and influenced by trade unions.[37] However, the Finnish insurance business is still influenced by the two traditions. This is true for the non-health and life insurances, e.g. social security. Several important insurance companies, which offer life, health, and personal accident insurance, are mutual associations regarding their organizational structure.
  The beginning of the Finnish insurance business was dominated by communality, while the economic point of view has been emphasized by all insurance companies since a couple of years. The new Finnish insurance business is a mixed system of the traditional continental and the British business principles, combining ideological key elements as well as organizational structures.
- The insurance business of the last couple of decades was confronted by new conflicts due to global economic markets and corporations. The importance of the economic point of view increased in the 1970s. Conflicts between profit seeking and key elements of social economy arose when customers and managers of mutual societies were interested more in higher profits than in the ideals and roots of the mutuality movement.
  The number of mergers during the 1970s increased and insurance companies which offered all types of insurances became more successful while at the same time the foundation of mutuality became weaker.

  The size of the companies changed and the conflict between business and community principle increased in particular in large companies.[38]
- The classification of companies into large, medium-sized, and small has become common in the last couple of years. The large companies increased their size and ended the cooperation with others in this business area. As a result, small companies approached each other. For example, in the 1970s the Aurayhtiöt and the Pohja enterprise started to work together

---

37 Cf. *Niemelä, Heikki & Salminen, Kari* (2009). Kansallisten eläkestrategioiden muotoutuminen ja Euroopan Unionin avoin koordinaatiomenetelmä. Sosiaali - ja terveysturvan tutkimuksia 104. Kela: Helsinki.

38 Cf. *Henttinen, Annastiina* (2007). Keskinäisyyden alkulähteillä. In: *Arja Suomi* (ed.). Keskinäisyys. Näkökulmia omistaja-asiakkuuteen. Edita Publishing: Helsinki, 26.

concerning data information and they merged into the Tapiola-enterprise (1982 to 1984).

- After the financial deregulation was carried out in the 1980s, the limited company form gained popularity, especially because it was considered to facilitate the access to capital and also because of efficiency reasons. Nevertheless, mutuality played an important role in the changing market. Core elements of mutuality were the cause that mutual associations were able to balance the Finnish banking crisis, in particular in the 1980s and 1990s.[39]
- In the last decades, there were significant restructuring arrangements in the Finnish insurance sector both externally and internally. Developments in the OP-Pohjola Group, for example, have been carried out in many different ways and for a long time. OP-Pohjola was formed in 2005, when it became Pohjola Group plc's largest shareholder. Pohjola, which OP-Pohjola acquired in 2005, started its operations under the corporate name of Palovakuutus-Osakeyhtiö Pohjola (fire insurance company) in 1891.[40] It was a striking combination of banking, investment and insurance services within the same organization group.
  Another large restructuring took place in the insurance industry in 2002, when Sampo became a shareholder of the Nordic insurance company If. Two years later, Sampo bought out the Norwegian company Storebrand, the Swedish-owned Skandia, and the Finnish insurance company Varma, making itself the sole owner of If .[41] Today, Sampo's business consists of four parts: If P&C Insurance is the largest non-life insurance company in the Nordic region, Mandatum Life is in charge of the life insurance business and also offers financial management services, Topdanmark is Denmark's second largest insurance company. In addition, Sampo owns over 20 per cent of Nordea Bank AB, the biggest bank in the Nordic countries. The structure of the insurance industry continues to change. The merger announced by the Local Insurance Group and the Tapiola Group in February 2012 is not the most recent structural change in the field, since the insurance business of the company If was purchasing Tryg insurance company as well in 2012.[42]
  Newly, The Finnish Competition and Consumer Authority (FCCA) approved OP Life Assurance Company Ltd's acquisition of the individual life insurance portfolio of Suomi Mutual Life Insurance Company on 31

[39] Cf. *Larsson, M., Lönnborg, M.* (2007). Keskinäinen vakuutustoiminta Ruotsin vakuutusmallissa, in: Suomi.A. (ed.): Keskinäisyys näkökulmia omistaja-asiakkuuteen, Edita Publishing Oy: Helsinki, 242.

[40] OP-Pohjola, OP-Pohjola Group Annual Report (2011). Great Finnish success story. Online. available here: http://www.op-pohjola-annualreport.fi/OP-Pohjola2011/en/year-2011/op-pohjola-group/history; OP Financial Group (2018). Corporate History. Online available here: https://uusi.op.fi/op-financial-group/about-us/op-financial-group-in-brief/history.

[41] Cf. *Sihvonen-Hovila, P.* (2013). Kahden keskinäisen vakuutusyhtiön fuusio: Lähi Tapiola Keskinäinen Vakuutusyhtiö 19.

[42] Ibid., 18.

March 2016. According to the press release, OP has already been managing Suomi Mutual‘s individual life insurance portfolio for 10 years, and the acquisition does not have a material negative impact on competition in the insurance market.[43]

The boundaries between mutual societies and other kinds of companies are closely connected with the development of the companies and their position from a historical point of view. In the last couple of years, conflicts have arisen about how risks should be managed with regard to business goals and social security. Additionally, the striving for power of the different groups has become more important. The most important change in the 1990s was Finland's decision to join the European Union (1995). As a result, the Finnish insurances law became part of the EU law. Even more important was the introduction of the Euro. The transition to the euro revolutionized the investment market by releasing insurance companies from the chains of the inflation-sensitive and unstable national currency. This was reflected in the strong growth of foreign investment. Nevertheless, during this period, both types of companies were able to quickly change the structure of their investment portfolios to meet the new requirements of international investment activity. At the same time, capital investments became global. According to *Olli-Pekka Ruuskanen*, in 2004 every third investment of insurance companies was not made in Finland.[44]

4. Mutual societies as a type of corporate organization

Insurance can be seen as a distribution of responsibility between the insured persons. As a result, mutual societies represent the original form of insurances, because the origin lies in mutual responsibility and not in gaining profits. Eventually companies with other organization forms, such as insurance joint stock companies, are based on similar principles. Traditionally, mutuality is based on the members' obligation to bear mutually the compensation on the insured asset of a contractual partner. In Northern Europe, the insurance principle developed in the Middle Ages in the form of mutuality.[45]

---

[43] KKV (2016)."FCCA approves acquisition between OP Life assurance company Ltd and Suomi mutual life insurance company".

[44] Cf. *Ruuskanen, Olli-Pekka* (2007). Suomen keskinäiset vakuutusyhtiöt. Kehitys 1994-2004. *Teoksessa, Arja Suomi* (ed.). Keskinäisyys. Näkökulmia omistaja-asiakkuuteen. Edita Publishing: Helsinki, 67.

[45] Cf. *Henttinen, Annastiina* (2007). Keskinäisyyden alkulähteillä. In: *Arja Suomi* (ed.). Keskinäisyys. Näkökulmia omistaja-asiakkuuteen. Edita Publishing: Helsinki, 26-27.

In contrast to joint stock companies, clients of mutual societies who bought insurances are owners of the association. They have the right to supervise business activities and participate in resolutions via the general meeting. Every deposited Euro/year gives the owner one vote. Mutual associations diverge from the cooperative principle "one man, one vote", because the voting right influences the collected insurance premium and the saving share.[46] The voting right is based on the clients and not on the capital (share ownership); therefore, the mutual association cannot be taken over. This and other core elements of mutuality were the cause that mutual associations were able to balance the Finnish Casino economy, in particular in the 1980s and 1990s.[47]

The owners or co-partners of mutual societies are the policyholders, i.e. the users of the services. These services concern the need of protection, the received services, and the reputation of the company. It is possible that shareholders live on different continents, only connected by their share in the company from which they receive profits.[48] With regard to mutual associations, ownership cannot be bought via shares nor sold to potential investors. The ownership ends with the end of the insurance contract. The voting right of the owners concerning the guarantee capital is limited to a fifth of the votes represented in the general meeting.

The main characteristics of mutual societies can be described as follows: A mutual society is a company with a licence for insurance activities. The associates are policyholders and possible owners of a guarantee share. The goal is to provide services, profits and other economic advantages for the copartner.[49] One of the features of mutual insurance societies is the responsibility towards other policyholders. In the insurance business, the risk is distributed among the policyholders. In general, the damages are paid from the money raised by the insurance premiums to those members who have claimed compensation. If the original capital of an insurance mutual society is not sufficient to assure stable assets after its establishment, which is necessary for the development of the business, then a regulation in the articles of association can order additional contributions provided by the members.[50]

---

[46] Cf. *Kalmi, Panu* (2007). Keskinäisyys yritysmuotona. In: *Arja Suomi* (ed.) Keskinäisyys. Näkökulmia omistaja-asiakkuuteen. Edita Publishing: Helsinki, 40.

[47] Ibid., *Henttinen, Annastiina* (2007). Keskinäisyyden alkulähteillä. In: *Arja Suomi* (ed.) Keskinäisyys. Näkökulmia omistaja-asiakkuuteen. Edita Publishing: Helsinki, 26-27.

[48] Cf. *Suomi, Arja* (toim.) (2007). Keskinäisyys. Näkökulmia omistaja-asiakkuuteen. Edita Publishing: Helsinki, 53.

[49] Ibid.

[50] Ibid., 51.

4.1 Types of mutual societies

There are three types of mutual societies in Finland, two in insurance and one in statutory pension insurance. All mutual societies have fixed premiums, variable premiums are not allowed.

- Mutual insurance companies fall under the Insurance Companies Act[51] (Vakuutusyhtiölaki), which includes special regulations for mutual insurance companies regarding establishment, organisation, financing, mergers, demutualization, and winding up. According to the Insurance Companies Act, the purpose of mutual insurance companies is to provide profit or other economic benefits to members, unless otherwise prescribed by the bylaws. These mutual insurance companies can be active in life insurance, non-life insurance, and reinsurance. Policyholders of mutual insurance companies are also members.[52]
- The insurance associations (small mutual insurers) are as mentioned above covered by the Act on Insurance Associations of 31 December 1987/1250, which includes regulations on establishment, financing, organisation, mergers, winding up, and inspection of this type of mutual societies. An insurance association is an insurance company based on the members' mutual liability, which operates in no more than 40 municipalities within a single area or is exclusively engaged in insurance of fishing equipment. These insurance associations may only underwrite voluntary non-life insurance. The *Act on Insurance Association* follows the exclusion regime of Solvency II in the sense that if an insurance association exceeds the amounts stipulated in Article 4(1) of Solvency II then the association meeting shall take a decision to change the insurance association to a mutual insurance company.
- According to the Act on Pension Insurance Companies ("laki työeläkevakuutusyhtiöistä/lag om arbetspensionsförsäkringsbolag 354/1997")[53], the owners of a mutual insurance company are the policyholders, i.e. the employers and the insured, i.e. the employees, as well as any holders of guarantee shares. Four of the six statutory pension companies in Finland are mutuals.

[51] The Insurance Companies act was amended in order to transpose the Solvency II Directive into national law. The amendments entered into force on 1 January 2016.

[52] http://www.finlex.fi/sv/laki/ajantasa/2008/20080521.

[53] http://www.finlex.fi/sv/laki/alkup/1997/19970354; and: http://www.etk.fi/en/service/pension_insurance_companies/1492/pension_insurance_companies.

Table 1: Overview main legislative texts related to the different mutual-type organisations

Legal types	Main Legal texts applicable to the mutual-type organisation
mutual insurance companies	Insurance Companies Act, (Vakuutusyhtiölaki/Försäkringsbolagslag 18.7.2008/521)[54]
insurance association	Law on Insurance Associations (Vakuutusyhdistyslaki/Lag om försäkringsföreningar 31.12.1987/1250)[55]
Pension Insurance Companies	Act on Pension Insurance Companies(Laki työeläkevakuutusyhtiöistä/Lag om arbetspensionsförsäkringsbolag 354/1997)[56]

In Finland, the characteristics of mutual societies are stipulated in the Act of insurance companies. This act applies to mutual insurance societies as well as insurance joint stock companies. The act presents various regulations concerning insurance activities and insurance companies which apply to both kinds of companies. The regulations regarding administrative bodies are similar for both kinds. Both mutual associations and insurance joint stock companies have copartners but the main difference is how the participating has been established.[57]

When addressing the change of the company form in the Finnish legal framework, the Insurance Companies Act is the fundamental legal act. According to chapter 22, which is called "Changing the company form" (in Finnish: Yhtiömuodon muuttaminen), the joint stock insurance company may become a mutual insurance company and the mutual insurance company may become a joint stock insurance company without specifying a clear procedure. If the form of a mutual insurance company is converted into a joint stock company, the members of the mutual insurance company will receive all the shares in the insurance company as a compensation for modifying the company form. Compensation can also be money, other assets and commitments. Also in case

54 http://www.finlex.fi/fi/laki/ajantasa/2008/20080521.

55 http://www.finlex.fi/fi/laki/ajantasa/1987/19871250.

56 http://www.finlex.fi/sv/laki/alkup/1997/19970354 and http://www.etk.fi/en/service/pension_insurance_companies/1492/pension_insurance_companies.

57 Cf. *Suomi, Arja* (toim.) (2007). Keskinäisyys. Näkökulmia omistaja-asiakkuuteen. Edita Publishing: Helsinki, 49-50.

of a vice-versa change of the organization form, any other providedcompensation shall be stated in the amendment plan.[58]

The changing insurance company must prepare a change plan regarding the modification of the company's form. The annual general meeting decides on the modification of the company's form. The decision of the annual general meeting to change the stock insurance company to a mutual company or vice-versa shall be made by a qualified majority. A mutual insurance company becomes a stock company and vice-versa when the Insurance Supervisory Authority has given its consent to change the form of the company and when the change in the articles of association concerning the change in the company form is registered in the trade register. Unless consent has been given, the change in the form of the company failed.

4.2 To establish a new mutual insurance

4.2.1 Mutual insurance company

To establish a new insurance company (including a mutual insurance company) in Finland generally the Company law ("osakeyhtiölaki/ Aktiebolagslag 21.7.2006/624") applies. To obtain a licence from the Financial Supervisory Authority, the application must, according to the Insurance Companies Act ("vakuutusyhtiölaki/försäkringsbolagslag 18.7.2008/521"), article 3:[59]

- Refer to the particular insurance classes to be provided.
- Be accompanied with documentation, including:
  - an action plan, with details on the intended business;
  - estimated premium income;
  - administrative structure and its costs;
  - reinsurance strategy; and
  - other aspects possibly requested by the Financial Supervisory Authority (its guidelines and prerogatives may contain more details).
- documents providing information about the management of the company and its shareholders;
- evidence about payment of the initial (foundation) fund;
- an account of potential conflicts of interest.

The licence applies within the European Economic Area or, on the request of the applicant, beyond the European Economic Area depending on agreements entered into by the Finnish authorities with other

[58] Insurance Companies Act – translated from Finnish "Vakuutusyhtiölaki", chapter 22, §§ 2-4.
[59] http://crossborder.practicallaw.com/7-504-6240?source=relatedcontent.

states. The sum of required capital/assets is the same for mutual insurance companies and for incorporated insurance companies, being 1,000,000 Euros for reinsurance captives, 2,000,000 Euros for standard non-life insurers, 3,000,000 Euros for life insurers, non-captive reinsurers and certain non-life insurers (including transport and unspecified liability insurers, credit and surety insurers, unemployment and entrepreneurial risk insurers). For incorporated insurance companies these sums are for share capital, for mutual insurance companies they refer to the minimum initial (foundation) fund or guarantee capital. At least half of the amount specified above has to be paid in cash.[60] The law does not specify a minimum or maximum number of legal/natural persons needed to create a mutual insurance company.

The articles of association of insurance companies (i.e. not of insurance associations) must specify the following:

1) company name;
2) the municipality in Finland, which is the company's domicile,
3) the company's activities and the classes and class groups that the activity is intended to encompass
4) persons entitled to vote at the general meeting, and
5) the amount of a guarantee capital and/or initial (foundation) fund (in case of a mutual insurance company) or the share capital (in case of a limited company).

Figure 1: Mutual insurance companies

- Establishment under Company Law
- No minimum/maximum number of legal/natural persons needed

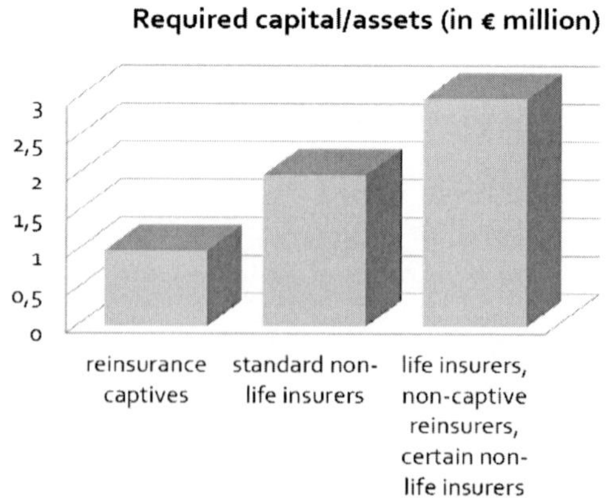

[60] Article 18, chapter 1 of the Insurance company Act.

The mutual insurance company's name needs to include the words "mutual", "insurance" and "company".

4.2.2 Mutual insurance association

The insurance association may be established by one or more natural or legal person ("vakuutusyhdistyslaki/lag om försäkringsföreningar 31.12.1987/1250"). The memorandum of association shall contain the bylaws of the association, specifications on the founding members, and specifications concerning the guarantee capital. The bylaws will include (article 3):

- the association's business, which must include the word "insurance association",
- the municipality in Finland, which is the association's home base,
- the classes of risks the association is about to cover,
- the amount of the association's guarantee capital and initial (foundation) capital or
- the value of the shares making up the guarantee capital,
- the conditions for interest on guarantee capital and the repayment of the guarantee capital,
- the policyholders' obligation to pay a surcharge to the association,
- the term for the Board of directors and deputies,
- the term of auditors and deputy auditors, and
- an indication how the remaining assets are to be shifted when the mutual insurance association is dissolved.

Figure 2: Mutual insurance association

- Establishment by one or more natural or legal persons
- Memorandum of Association

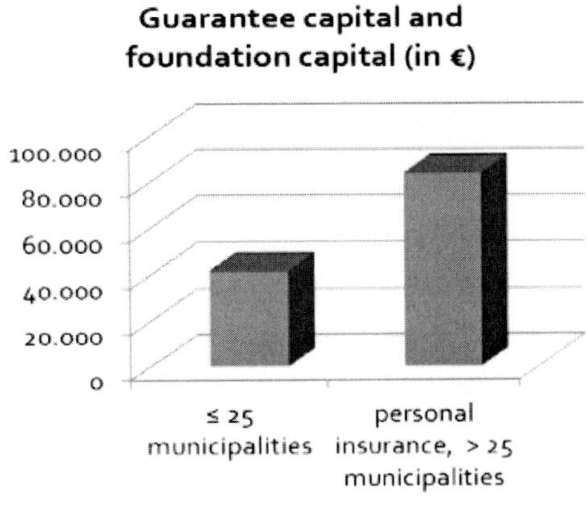

An insurance association guarantee capital and foundation capital (authorized capital) must total at least 42,000 Euros. If the association's activities include personal insurance, or its business scope covers more than 25 municipalities, the foundation capital must be at least 84,000 Euros ("vakuutusyhdistyslaki/lag om försäkringsföreningar 31.12.1987/1250, article 5").

4.2.3 Statutory pension mutual insurance company

Provisions on the nominal capital of insurance companies engaged in statutory pension insurance can be found in the Law on Pension Insurance Companies ("laki työeläkevakuutusyhtiöistä/lag om arbetspensionsförsäkringsbolag 354/1997"). The minimum basic capital (for joint stock companies share capital and for mutual insurance companies guarantee capital and initial (foundation) fund) required for a pension insurance company is 5 million Euros. In addition, a pension insurance company handling statutory earnings-related pension insurance is required to have a concession granted by the Council of State (cabinet). The Council of State may include conditions in its concession, necessary to safeguard the interests of the policyholders and the insured, to ensure the stable functioning of the company and to promote a healthy development of the earnings-related pension insurance business. Moreover, a pension insurance company's articles of association and any changes to them must be confirmed by the Insurance Supervisory Authority.[61]

A pension insurance company may not handle any other type of insurance activities than insurance under the Employee's Pensions Act and the Self-Employed Persons' Act and related reinsurance. The EU Life Insurance Directive is not applied to Finnish pension insurance companies, which is why statutory earnings-related pension insurance has to be kept legally separate from the group's other insurance activities. The assets of a pension insurance company have to be kept separate from the assets of companies that belong to the same group as the pension insurance company. The annual accounts of the pension insurance company may not be included in the consolidated accounts of another company.[62]

Moreover, the financial management and payments traffic of the pension insurance company must be arranged so that assets are not used for arranging the financial management or payments traffic of another company which belongs to the same group as the pension insurance company.

---

61 http://www.etk.fi/en/service/pension_insurance_companies/1492/pension_insurance_companies.

62 Ibid.

4.3 Statistical data concerning mutual insurance societies

In Finland, Sweden, and France mutual insurance societies play an important role. In Finland, the market share of mutual insurance societies was 37.5% (2014). This does not include mutual retirement insurances, but it has to be emphasized that the largest insurance companies offering retirement insurance are based on mutuality. The following table presents the distribution of Finnish insurance companies according to the company types.

Table 2: National mutual insurance companies and joint stock companies as well as foreign insurance companies in Finland

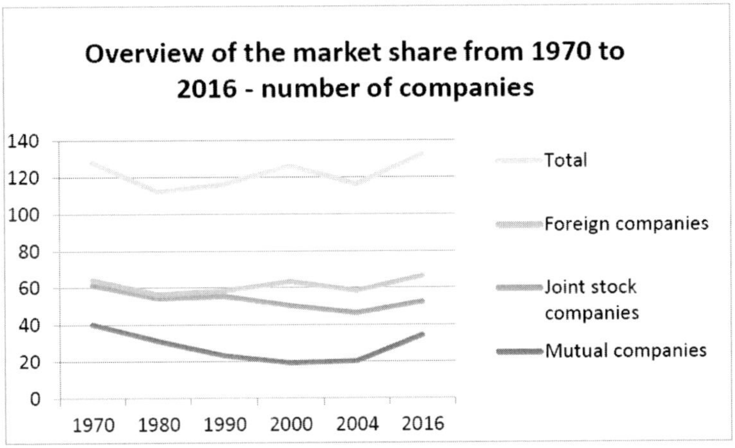

The numbers only show insurance companies which are members of the umbrella organization (cf. insurance yearbooks).

As the table shows, the number of mutual associations decreased according to the development of the Finnish social welfare state. The turning point lies between 1970 and 1980 when the Finnish insurance industry was centralised. However, the number of insurance companies has decreased since the 1950s.

The market share of mutual-type organizations in the Finnish insurance in the period 2011 to 2014 was as follows:[63]

[63] Statutory pension business is not included in the mutual market share figures. If it was included, the total market share in 2014 would be 69.7% (2013: 65.7%) and the life market share would be 69.5% (71.0%).

Table 3: Mutual market share

	Total mutual market share	Life	Nonlife
2011	30.7	14.5	44.7
2012	29.9	13.9	45.5
2013	26.8	123	43.4
2014	37.5[55]	11.8	70.6

Source: Finance Finland.

According to *Panu Kalmi*, the success of mutual societies at the Finnish market could be due to an information advantage and mutual control. Information advantage means that companies are better informed about the risks than their competitors and, therefore, they are able to save insurance costs.[65] *Kalmi* states, however, that in general there are no major differences between mutual societies, joint stock companies, and cooperatives.[66]

The European mutual sector wrote more than 400 billion Euros in insurance premiums for the first time in 2014, after a record growth of 7.2% from the previous year (2013: 380 billion Euros). Mutual insurers have consistently outperformed the total regional market since 2007, resulting in a significant boost in their collective share of the regional market, rising from 23.3% in 2007 to a record high of 31.2% in 2014, a proportional growth of more than a third. In five of the ten largest European markets, mutual societies held more than a third of the market, with record mutual market share levels again reported in 2014 in France (47.4%), Germany (44.4%), Spain (39.3%), and Sweden (49.5%), while in the Netherlands, mutual insurers represented more than 50% of the market (51.0%) for the first time in 2014. Norway (61.3%) had the highest penetration of mutual insurance in Europe in 2014, and these were the two largest mutual insurance markets in the world. Nine of the ten largest mutual markets in the world in 2014 were European.[67]

64 In 2014, non-life insurer Pohjola completed a process of re-mutualization, which transformed them from stock-owned insurers back to their original structure of member-owned insurers. As a result, the mutual market share figure reached record levels in 2014: 37.5%.

65 Cf. *Kalmi, Panu* (2007). Keskinäisyys yritysmuotona. In: *Arja Suomi* (ed.) Keskinäisyys. Näkökulmia omistaja-asiakkuuteen. Edita Publishing: Helsinki, 35.

66 Ibid., 44.

67 Cf. ICMIF (ed.). Global Mutual Market Share 2014, published March 2016, http://www.icmif.org/global-mutual-market-share-2014.

4.4 Voting and representation of members in general meetings

In Finland, the insured persons, who have also decision powers, own the mutual insurance society. This principle is similar to that of cooperatives which gives members voting rights ("one man, one vote") regarding company issues.

In Finland, with regard to the Insurance Companies Act, decisions in mutual insurance companies are taken by simple majority of votes cast, unless otherwise provided in the Act or the bylaws. In addition, all members of the insurance association have one vote, unless otherwise provided in the bylaws. The member exercises his/her right at the meeting personally or through representation. With regard to mutual insurance companies, the starting point is that all members are equal. Company rules (laid down in the statutes) may, however, alter the voting rights to be contribution based, so that each member receives an amount of votes in general meetings related to the size of her contribution to the mutual society. For instance, in Tapiola, every policyholder has at least one vote, with additional votes being conferred on the basis of insurance premiums (Tapiola General and Tapiola Pension) or life insurance savings (Tapiola Life).[68] Predominantly, the Nordic countries provide possibilities to have another organization of voting rights. In Finland, the voting rights can be altered to be contribution based instead of membership based.

In mutual insurance societies, each member has the right of compensation according to the insurance regulations. Communality means mutual responsibility, because all compensations are paid collectively. In case they cannot be paid due to weak economy, the necessary money can be collected according a regulation about additional contributions. This regulation allows an increase of the insurance premiums ex post. The owner's share in the successes is paid as customer's bonus and not as a dividend. This different use leads easily to wrong interpretations when mutual insurance societies and insurance joint stock companies are compared based on the correspondent ratios in the balance sheet.

Mutual societies realize social policy in particular, not only mutual insurance societies. They establish residential homes and working places for people with disabilities, homes for old, sick, or drug addicted people as well as meeting places for discriminated people. They help to prevent and reduce social isolation.[69]

---

[68] Cf. http://www.tapiola.fi/wwweng/Briefly/The+Tapiola+Group/Business+idea+and+values/Policyholders%E2%80%99+influence.htm.

[69] Cf. *Laurinkari* (2007).

4.5 Management and (corporate) governance

The management model of a mutual insurance society can be one- or two-tier. In case of a one-tier model, the society has no supervisory board, but a management board comprising independent members and deputies from the management. The two-tier management model has a supervisory board and a management board.[70] According to *Kalmi*, in large mutual companies the members' influence still exists, while small shareholders of joint stock companies have no influence due to the large numbers of shareholders.[71]

On the other hand, continental European countries, such as the Netherlands, Germany, and Finland, have adopted variants of the two-tier board model for corporations.

Two-tier governance model: Most, if not all mutual companies in Finland apply a two-tier governance structure, where the Board consists of knowledgeable persons from the company and where the supervisory board is composed of members or representatives of members. The requirements for board members are strict (and will under pressure of Solvency II even become stricter). The administrative structure of insurance associations resembles the administrative structure of mutual insurance companies.

4.6 Capitalization

It is possible to contribute capital to the mutual company, the so-called guarantee capital, which gives power to the owners. The client's ownership is a characteristic of mutual societies which is important for administrative issues but also for the distribution of profits and for a firm asset foundation.

The work of mutual societies depends on the principle of members' cooperation and management participation. Profits and surpluses are not distributed according to the capital, but used to improve services for the members. Moreover, the company's business is going to be developed, the deposits increased, or the surpluses distributed on a limited scale. Mutual insurance societies were one of the first types of companies using the so-called social financial statement. With the latter, the company's business activities and its effect on the environment and society can be shown and evaluated.[72]

---

70 *Suomi, Arja* (toim.) (2007). Keskinäisyys. Näkökulmia omistaja-asiakkuuteen. Edita Publishing: Helsinki, 54.

71 Cf. *Kalmi, Panu* (2007). Keskinäisyys yritysmuotona. In: *Arja Suomi* (ed.). Keskinäisyys. Näkökulmia omistaja-asiakkuuteen. Edita Publishing: Helsinki, 34.

72 Cf. *Laurinkari, Juhani* (2007).

Mutual societies differ from cooperatives in so far that a member of the latter does not invest initial capital. In case of mutual societies, the capital of the cooperative corresponds to the guarantee capital. Assets are accumulated and reserve funds are formed by profits. Investments into mutual societies can have higher risks than investments into insurance joint stock companies. However, this contradicts the principle of social economy. Mutual societies have no access to the stock market therefore raising money can be more difficult for them than for joint stock companies and the demands for stable finance are difficult to fulfil.

4.7 Non-member investor

In Finland, with regard to the mutual insurance companies, all policyholders of mutual insurance companies are members. Nevertheless, not all members are policyholders. There are also investor members.

Through the use of guarantee capital, non-member investors are possible in mutual insurance companies. Guarantee capital is constituted by policyholders/owners who invest funds, either during the foundation or throughout the life of the mutual insurance. Particular financial instruments to raise capital levels for mutual companies could be a:

- possibility to raise additional guarantee capital; and
- possibility to issue subordinated loans.

The bylaws determine the rights of non-member investors. The rights of the members are essentially those of owners of limited companies. According to article 21, chapter 1 of the Insurance Company Act, the shareholders exercise their power of decision at the general meeting. Decisions are taken by simple majority of votes cast, unless otherwise provided in the Act or the bylaws.

They receive an interest of 5 to 6% on the invested funds according to the bylaws of the society. If funds are returned to the investors, they only get back their own investments, i.e. book value and not the share of the capital. Guarantee capital is therefore different from share capital as the owner will not receive the return on investment. Just like the policyholders/members, the owners of the guarantee capital, have voting rights on how the capital will be invested.[73] Through the guarantee capital mutual companies (i.e. Tapiola, life, non-life and pension insurance) can have with each other financial ties as they can cross-own each other's guarantee fund. The guarantee capital is supervised

[73] This is similar to rules that apply to cooperatives.

by the Financial Supervisory Authority. Similar rules apply to the Finnish insurance association.

In many countries, non-member investors and external capital in the form of subordinated loans or guarantee capital (i.e. not share capital) is legally allowed for mutual-type organizations, i.e. in Denmark, Norway, Sweden, Finland, Germany, Austria, Poland, Slovenia, The Netherlands, United Kingdom, and France.

4.8 Protection of assets

The financial situation of mutual insurance societies is usually better compared to insurance joint stock companies. Nevertheless, the trend shows that societies transform more often into joint stock companies when their assets increase. This development is also noticeable in Finland.[74] The ratio between damages and contributions has to be higher for mutual associations than for joint stock companies.[75]

4.9 Auditing

With regard to disclosure, i.e. transparency and auditing, in Finland, the insurance society must submit annual accounts, key figures and analysis of insurance business to the Financial Supervisory Authority annually instead of four times a year (as is the case for mutual insurance companies.

4.10 Taxation

In the Finnish tax law there is no special treatment for mutual insurers, neither for insurance associations, nor for statutory pension mutual insurance companies.[76] Although there is no preferential treatment concerning particular company forms, there is some preferential treatment concerning specific lines of business. Insurance and reinsurance companies and other providers of insurance-related services are subject to tax on the company's income, based on the company's

---

[74] Cf. *Kalmi, Panu* (2007). Keskinäisyys yritysmuotona. In: *Arja Suomi* (ed.). Keskinäisyys. Näkökulmia omistaja-asiakkuuteen. Edita Publishing: Helsinki

[75] Cf. *Ruuskanen, Olli-Pekka* (2007). Suomen keskinäiset vakuutusyhtiöt. Kehitys 1994-2004. *Teoksessa, Arja Suomi* (ed.). Keskinäisyys. Näkökulmia omistaja-asiakkuuteen. Edita Publishing: Helsinki, 79.

[76] Cf. PWC (2011). International comparison of insurance taxation: http://www.pwc.com/at/de/publikationen/financial-services/international-comparison-of-insurance-taxation-2011/finland-insurance-taxation-2011.pdf.

Legal types	Protection of assets (What happens in case of dissolution?)
mutual insurance companies	In case of demutualisation of a mutual insurance company, the assets will be distributed amongst the shareholders (i.e. the policyholders).The same rules apply for mutual insurance companies as for incorporated company models
insurance association	In case of demutualisation, the assets will be distributed amongst the policyholders (i.e. the members).
Pension Insurance Companies	In case of demutualisation of a mutual insurance company, the assets will be distributed amongst the shareholders (i.e. the policyholders). The same rules apply for mutual insurance companies as for incorporated company models

financial results, at the flat rate of 20%. Different tax rules apply to different business forms, such as partnerships or limited partnerships. In Finland, an insurance premium tax of 24% is imposed on insurance premiums when the insured property is situated in Finland. Life insurance and pension insurance are not subject to insurance premium tax.[77] Insurance tax is a substitute for value added tax (Value Added Tax: VAT). However, it is separated from VAT, and therefore VAT deductions cannot be deducted from insurance tax (or vice versa).[78]

4.11 Merger

In Finland, in case of a merger of mutual societies, all debts and assets will be put together and policyholders/owners become the owners of the new company. In practice, for the policyholders/owners nothing changes as their positions are not changed. There are no legal barriers within a merger, but it might be more time consuming for mutual societies to merge as the owners need to be convinced of why they benefit from the merger. However, the same applies to incorporated companies.

77 Ibid.

78 https://uk.practicallaw.thomsonreuters.com/7-504-6240?__lrTS=20170411120239142&transitionType=Default&contextData=(sc.Default)&firstPage=true&bhcp=1.

By means of the use of guarantee capital, financial ties can be established between different mutual insurance companies and insurance associations

4.12 Re-mutualization

An example for a re-mutualization in Finland is the one between Tapiola and Local Insurance. This merger involved two types of mutual societies and more than 20 separate legal entities. The new company group, the LocalTapiola Group, which is owned by its customers, was established 2014 by emerging the Local Insurance Mutual Company[79] and the Tapiola General Mutual Insurance Company[80]. The number of owner-customers is nearly 1.6 million.[81]

Historically, there have been close links between the mutual companies and associations in Finland. On particular issues and topics, they already established joint platforms. In recent years, the market situation in the insurance business developed. Nowadays, stock listed companies and bank-driven groups are the major players which offer insurance policies as well.

The mutual companies that remain insurance-driven organizations facing increased competition from the bank-driven groups. Given this development, Tapiola, as insurance-driven mutual society in 2001 established an own asset management company and in 2004 formed its own bank. In 2010, the bank had, as a considerable, but minor player on the Finnish market, around 200,000 clients. Tapiola was one of the largest non-life insurers in Finland. It was the result of a merger in 1982 between Aura and Pohja.

Local Insurance consisted of more than 100 insurance associations. Through consolidation, this number has decreased to 52 insurance associations plus Local Insurance Mutual Company and the Federation of the Local Insurance Group. The Local Insurance Group was Finland's 5th largest non-life insurer in terms of premium income. Its market share was 9% of Finnish direct insurance income.

One of the key strategic aims of the merger was to strengthen the mutual sector against the large bank-insurer-conglomerates operating in the Finnish market. The LocalTapiola Group has become Finland's largest and most solvent non-life insurer. Although there is not a direct pressure from Solvency II, it relieves pressure on the insurance associations to potentially implement it for their small mutual association. The

79 https://www.lahitapiola.fi/henkilo.

80 Ibid.

81 https://www.lahitapiola.fi/en/information-on-localtapiola/localtapiola-group/information-on-localtapiola-group.

merging was finalized in 2014.[82] The merger consists of two phases: first in the beginning of 2013 and later in the beginning of 2014.

The new group LocalTapiola (in Finnish LähiTapiola) consists of 20 regional mutual insurance companies, as well as the national companies, LocalTapiola General, LocalTapiola Life, LocalTapiola Asset Management and LocalTapiola Real Estate Asset Management. The bank for LocalTapiola's customers is S-Bank, of which LocalTapiola owns 23.5%. A strategic partner for health and well-being is Pihlajalinna, of which LocalTapiola owns 23.4%. The group's statutory employee pension insurance partner is Elo.

LocalTapiola General is a leading non-life insurer offering both voluntary and statutory non-life insurances. Besides non-life companies the group consists of a mutual life insurance company and occupational pension insurance company plus the limited companies (bank, asset management and real estate). LocalTapiola Life is the fourth largest life insurance company in Finland. Alongside the central company, 19 regional mutual insurance companies are formed. Aside these 20 mutual insurance companies, one mutual insurance company, Turva,[83] has already been included in the group. The main reason why it has been decided to form a group of 21 mutual insurance companies instead of forming one overarching mutual insurance company is that the local insurance associations are well embedded in the regions and are valued for their vicinity to the members. Going from more than 50 associations to only one Helsinki-based company has been evaluated to have consequences for the policyholders and the service level they experience. In general, both new group models inherit components of both the Tapiola-model and the Lähi-model.

The argument about the legal status of insurance associations[84] regarding the question why a mutual insurance company statute[85] hasn't been obtained twofold:

- First of all, the larger companies do not fit well in the association statute as there are certain legal restrictions regarding the operations of associations;[86]
- secondly, as a group it is clearer and easier to adopt the same legal status for each of the companies.

---

[82] Cf. Local Insurance-Tapiola Press release 7 February 2012.

[83] http://www.turva.fi/.

[84] Covered by the Law on Insurance Associations (Lag om försäkringsföreningar 31.12.1987/1250). With the merger, the legal status of insurance association will not be used very often.

[85] Insurance Act (Försäkringsbolagslag 18.7.2008/521).

[86] According to the Law on Insurance Associations, an insurance association is an insurance company based on the members' mutual liability, which operates in not more than 40 municipalities within a single area or is exclusively engaged in insurance of fishing equipment. These insurance associations may only underwrite voluntary non-life insurance (Lag om försäkringsföreningar 31.12.1987/1250).

The LocalTapiola conglomerate is linked through guarantee capital[87]. The regional mutual insurance companies are for the larger part owned by the policyholders/members resident in the area it covers and for the remaining part (at most 35%) "owned" by the holders of the guarantee funds (which is the central company). In fact, the percentage demonstrates the maximum voting rights in the general meeting. The use of guarantee funds enables the mutual insurance companies to have internal cross ownership to tie the companies of the group together and to help each other out when needed. Although the Solvency II regulation applies to all 21 mutual insurance companies, the concept of the guarantee shares, which is a Nordic concept, allows the central company to have partial ownership of the regional companies. As determined by the statutes of the company, the holder of the guarantee fund (i.e. the central company) has voting rights and can nominate representatives in the board of the regional mutual insurance company. The guarantee fund counts as capitalization for the regional mutual insurance companies. The financial entanglement through the guarantee shares helps the group for some part of the Solvency II-requirements since the companies form a group according to a definition in the Solvency II directive 212.

A concept that needs to be further studied within the context of Solvency II is financial solidarity: How does financial solidarity of group members affect the solvency levels of the individual companies and how does it affect the solvability of the central company? Through the merger, the group estimated that it is more resilient to the competition of bank-driven conglomerates. In addition, it estimated that in the future it will be better equipped to strengthen and grow the own LocalTapiola Bank and to be able to profit from cross-selling (bank products and insurance products) in a better way. Also forming future alliances with other players in the banking market belongs to the possibilities. To arrive at this situation, a number of steps were taken:[88]

- Approval on the Annual General Meetings of Local Insurance Mutual Company and Tapiola General in spring 2012 was a prerequisite for the merger, as is obtaining consent from the Financial Supervisory Authority and as well as the Finnish Competition Authority.

[87] Policyholders/owners who invest funds create guarantee capital. They receive an interest of 5-6% over the invested funds. If the funds are returned to the investors, they only receive back their own investments and not the share of the capital. Guarantee capital is therefore different from share capital, as the owner will not receive the return on investment. As the policyholders/owners contribute the guarantee capital, they have voting rights on how the capital will be invested. Through the guarantee capital mutual companies (i.e. Tapiola, life, non-life and pension fund) can have financial ties as they can cross own each other's guarantee fund. The Financial Supervisory Authority supervises the guarantee capital.

[88] Cf. Local Insurance-Tapiola Press release 7 February 2012.

- By the end of 2012, LocalTapiola, a mutual company engaging in non-life insurance business, had been established. During 2012, 19 regional mutual insurance companies were set up. The transfers of insurance portfolios to regional companies were completed by the end of 2013. LocalTapiola Bank and S-Pankki announced merger of banking business. LocalTapiola Pension and Pension Fennia announced merger. The name of the new company is Elo.
- During 2012, the new name and visual look of LocalTapiola were decided. The total merger was completed in two years. 2012 the two central companies were merged. 2013 the 19 regional, so-called 'spearhead' associations were formed and transformed into mutual insurance companies. By the end of 2013, portfolios were transferred between Tapiola and the regional companies, i.e. the portfolios of members of Tapiola not residing in Helsinki were transferred to the regional companies. In addition to this, assets were transferred between the regional and central company.

The merger was examined by both the Financial Supervisory Authority (FSA)[89] and the Finnish Competition Authority[90]. Both organizations reacted positively to the negotiated merger. LocalTapiola strengthened 2015 its position as the second largest non-life insurer by increasing its market share to 25.4%.

The merger also involved strong suspicions about the improper transfer of accrued pension assets to general insurance operations, but no concrete evidence has been obtained. There was also an intense discussion about problems of the process in the public media. As a matter of principle, this merger also involves the question wether and to what extent social economy organizations are able to combine their citizen-based special quality with operation and appearance of cross-sectoral financial houses.

From January to June 2017, LocalTapiola Group's premium income from direct non-life insurance increased by 0.4% to 704.8 million Euros. LocalTapiola strengthened its position as the second largest non-life insurer by increasing its market share to 25.8%. Premium income from life insurance showed particularly strong development, with growth of 35.9%. The return on investment activities was good during the first half of the year. Customers were paid a total of 505.0 million Euros in compensation and 29.5 million Euros in technical interest. Approximately 34 million Euros were distributed to customers in the form of customer bonuses.[91]

---

89 http://www.fin-fsa.fi/en/About_us/Pages/Default.aspx.

90 http://www.kilpailuvirasto.fi/cgi-bin/english.cgi.

91 https://www.lahitapiola.fi/en/information-on-localtapiola/newsroom/news/news-and-press-releases/uutinen/1497554399275.

5. Profiles of mutual insurance societies

5.1 Non-life insurances

The following table shows a list of Finnish insurance companies offering compensation insurances. The market share of mutual societies regarding compensation insurances has been steady in the last couple of years.

Table 4: Non-life insurers' market shares in 2017[92]

Name of the company	Market share (in %)	Premiums earned (in €mil.)
OP Insurance Ltd	29,2	1,280
LocalTapiola Group	25,8	1,185
If P & C Insurance Company Ltd	22,3	961
Fennia Mutual Insurance Company	9,3	394
Turva Mutual Insurance Company	2,5	108
Pohjantähti Mutual Insurance Company	2,4	104
A-Insurance Ltd	2,2	93
Folksam Non-Life Insurance Company Ltd	1,8	76
Eurooppalainen Insurance Company Ltd	1,6	66
Försäkringsaktiebolaget Alandia	1,0	49
Finnish P&C Insurance Ltd	0,8	35
Aaland Mutual Insurance Company	0,5	26
Garantia Insurance Company Ltd.	0,4	15
Ins. Co. for Pharmaceutical Injury Indemnities	0,1	5
Valion Keskinäinen Vakuutusyhtiö	0,0	1

Source: Finanssiala Report 2018, Annex 1.

[92] Mutual insurance companies in grey.

Figure 3: Non-life insurance market share in % in 2017

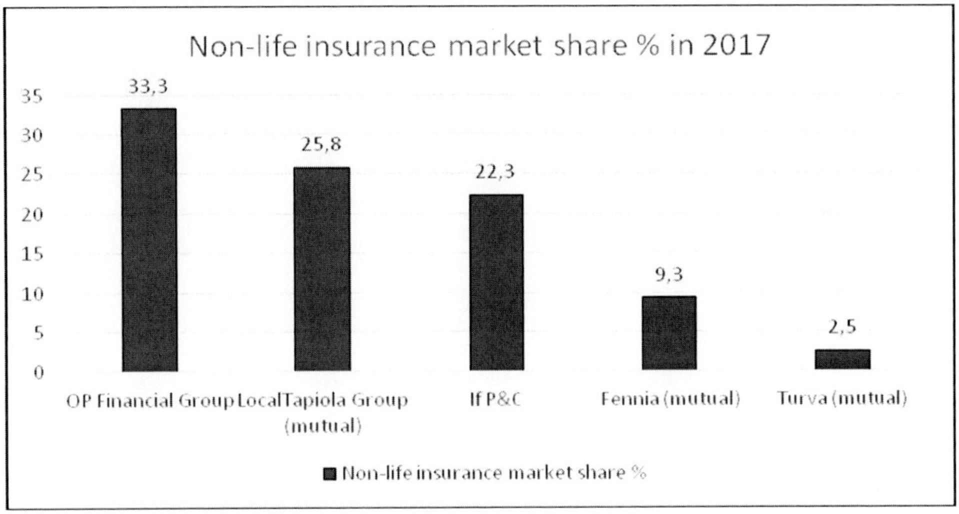

The contribution payments of insurance companies are collected in four different ways:

1. Insurances against fire and other property damage
2. motor vehicle
3. workers' compensation
4. motor liability

The five largest insurer groups commanded 89% of the market. Insurance against fire and other damage to property remained the largest non-life class. This group of insurance classes includes both business and personal property cover. A part of the income is based on statuary insurances. The insurance market is stabilized by these four large groups of income. The competition expenses in the insurance industry are low compared to other sectors. The companies sell the same product, and the possibilities for variations are low on the market. Mutuality gives the associations informative benefits for compensation insurances due to the members' ownership.

Up to the last decade, mutual societies dominated the market of non-life insurances compared to other types of companies, but within the last couple of years joint stock companies conquered the market and the position of mutual associations has been decreased slightly. In the

first decade of the 21st century, one third of the income was used for life insurances offered by mutual societies.[93]

5.2 Life insurances

The competition in the life insurance branch is stronger than in the non-life insurances due to more competitors and foreign companies. Personal pension saving insurances and personal pension insurances are the main products. Their income together comprises 80% of the insurances industry

Table 5: Life insurers' market shares in 2017[94]

Name of the company	Market share (in %)	Total premiums written (in €mil.)
Nordea Life Assurance Finland Ltd	30.7	1,377
OP Life Assurance Company Ltd	21.8	976
Mandatum Life Insurance Company Limited	21.3	957
LocalTapiola Mutual Life Insurance Company	11.5	516
Sb Life Insurance Ltd	3.8	170
Fennia Life Insurance Company Ltd	3.7	167
Aktia Life Insurance Ltd	2.8	126
Kaleva Mutual Insurance Company	1.3	60
Försäkringsaktiebolaget Liv-Alandia	0.1	6

Source: Finanssiala Report 2018, Annex 5.

[93] Cf. Finance Finland 2016.

[94] Mutual insurance companies in gray.

In life insurance, market share is measured on two variables: premium income and life insurance assets. Calculated either way, the three largest companies commanded the market. In 2017 their order was also the same, calculated either way: Nordea Life Assurance was the market leader, followed by OP Life Assurance and Financial Group Mandatum Life.[95]

Jyri Liukko investigates the identity of mutuality of Finnish life insurance companies. According to him, in the history of life insurances the connected common good was emphasized. On the Finnish market, mutuality is an essential part when advertising life insurances.[96]

In the Finnish life insurance business, the principle of mutuality had different key elements. Both mutuality and life insurances have the altruism principle in common. In the time between the 1950s and 1980s, the largest Finnish life insurance companies were based on mutuality, such as Kaleva, Suomi, Salama, Pohja, Tapiola, Kansa, and Aura as well as local insurance societies. Mutuality was an important element for the marketing strategies of life insurance companies in the 1950s and 1960s. In the beginning, mutual insurance societies and joint stock companies were regarded as two completely different things. However, in 1948 a commission which dealt with mutuality noted that in practice no differences can be found between mutual societies and joint stock companies.

In the 1960s, this topic was discussed again. In the 1960s, the principle of solidarity was emphasized in the marketing of life insurances, because mutuality was regarded as a value worth to support.[97] In the booklet of the company Salama from 1967, the collective basis of the insurance was used to present the "principle of the life insurance". The company used the image of the four musketeers with their swords and the motto "All for one and one for all" on the title page of the booklet. The Suomi Company explained in the booklet that the insurance foundations are for collective responsibility and the distribution of risks.

At the beginning of the 1960s, the group life insurance became more common.[98] In particular during the 1970s, trade unions and companies agreed on group life insurances which became the obvious product in advertising life insurances.

The group life insurance became an intermediate form between individual and statuary social security, because the regulations and

[95] Cf. Finance Finland (FFI) (ed.) (2017): Finnish Insurance in 2016. Helsinki, 9.

[96] *Liukko, Jyri* (2007). Henkivakuutus ja solidaarisuuden kehät. Vakuutusmainonta vastuuajattelun muokkaajana Suomessa 1945-1990. In: Janus 15 (1).

[97] Cf. *Sipilä, Jorma* (1985). Sosiaalipolitiikan tulevaisuus. Helsinki: Tammi, 62.

[98] Cf. *Näräkkä*, Aimo Y. (1992). Henkivakuutuksen kehityspiirteitä Suomessa. Teoksessa Suomen vakuutustarkastus 100 vuotta 1892–1992. Sosiaali - ja terveysministeriö, vakuutusosasto, 263.

advantages were negotiated and agreed on between the trade unions and the insurance companies, and the trade unions functioned as policyholders. The booklet emphasized the solidarity principle and noted that members of the trade union can have insurances even if they have problems to get an individual insurance due to health problems.[99]

The group life insurance was only for members of the trade unions and the policyholders were divided into classes according to statistical risk vulnerability due to their profession. In the accident insurance booklet of Kullervo[100], the policyholder was divided into nine groups according to their professions and the accident risks. The insurance premium was based on the kind of risk group. The first group comprised for example teachers, clerks, or managers, while the last group included divers, carpenters, butchers or workers dealing with explosive materials.

The classification was not only based on the kind of profession but also on the fact if members had dangerous hobbies. However, this classification questioned the solidarity principle of insurances, because it divided people in those who receive favourable insurances and in those who had to pay higher insurance premiums. Today such a type of classification is not used anymore regarding e.g. natural disasters, like a tsunami, an earthquake or a terror attack, which can concern anyone in a globalized world.

The boundaries of solidarity were drawn regarding the regulations of the terms of insurance: The Pohja-Company advertised that an accident insurance without any restrictions can only be offered to healthy and respectable people, who have a regular lifestyle and were in possession of their mental and physical health. They also should have on average weight and no physical disadvantages.[101] Advertising created a picture of respectable people and warned them at the same time to keep up their lifestyle or otherwise their right of an individual insurance could be curtailed. These kinds of exclusions present clearly the problem of solidarity of private insurances and at the same time it presents a moral compass: Act with low risk!

Since the 1980s at least, the emphasis on mutuality and the collective insurance principle decreased rapidly to a minimum. However, the idea of mutuality lived on. In 1989, the Suomi Compani published an advertisement against the mainstream.

[99] Cf. Kaleva. Annual report (1974; 1976).

[100] Cf. Kullervo. Annual report (1963; 1964).

[101] Cf. Pohja. Annual report (1965; 1966; 1968).

5.3 Statutory pension insurance

In the 1960s, Finland was affiliated into the group of Nordic welfare states and the central social security systems, based on salary, were established: unemployment, health, and retirement insurance. This transition also meant a transition to a salary-based type of insurance. Before that, the focus was on national insurances without transfer's connection to the labour market status of the policyholder. Even today this focus is important and has still applied to the large share of all insurances in the 21st century.[102] During the same period, the salary differences have increased and people with higher salaries and a longer professional career were favoured while the income position of people with small salaries, fixed-term contracts, and in particular unemployed people have deteriorated.

A pension insurance company is a strictly regulated company form (regulated by the Act on Pension Insurance Companies ("laki työeläkevakuutusyhtiöistä/lag om arbetspensionsförsäkringsbolag 354/1997"))[103]. A pension insurance company may be a limited liability insurance company (including a public one) or a mutual insurance society. The owners of a mutual insurance society are the policyholders, i.e. the employers and employees, as well as any holders of guarantee shares.[104] The business of statutory pension is not classified as life insurance and hence is not regulated by the EU life directive. The business is regulated by different laws. The private sector laws have been bundled into the TyEL-law starting January 1st, 2007[105]. Nevertheless, all these laws follow the same basic principles for private, public sector employment, and self-employed persons. The main law for private sector pensions is the Employees' Pension Act (known as TyEL), which covers three fourths of the insured in the private sector. In practice, almost all employed persons, irrespective of nationality, are covered by Finnish employment pension legislation.[106] Foreign pension insurance companies may not directly engage in statutory pension insurance in Finland, but a foreign corporation or natural person may establish a pension insurance company in Finland. The company shall be subject to the same restrictions regarding the line of industry and concessions as a pension insurance company established by Finns. So far, no foreign

---

[102] Cf. *Niemelä, Heikki & Salminen, Kari* (2006). Suomalainen sosiaaliturva. Kela: Helsinki.

[103] http://www.etk.fi/en/service/pension_insurance_companies/1492/pension_insurance_companies.

[104] Ibid.

[105] Cf. http://tyoelakelakipalvelu.etk.fi/fi/saados/en/20060395/?_navi=haku.

[106] IGP (2011). Summary of Social Security and Private Employee Benefits Finland. http://www.igpinfo.com/igpinfo/public_documents/ss_summaries/Finland.pdf.

insurance company has engaged in the earnings-related pension insurance business in Finland.

According to *Talonen*, companies which offer retirement insurances based on earnings differ from other insurance societies in which policyholders and insured people are not the same. A mutual insurance society based on earnings has two different customer-owner groups. Both groups have voting rights and owner rights, but only one group has the right to buy. It is interesting, according to *Talonen*, which effects occur when the policyholders are much more included. If it is possible to influence the policyholders, it may have a positive effect on the customer value and its structure as well as on customer satisfaction.[107]

The pension scheme based on earnings has developed into a system dominated by private companies and financed by corporations. Pension insurers' market shares underwent only slight changes which had no effect on the companies' relative positions. Reserve funds were established from the pension scheme system to pay the pension and additional funds were used to neutralise the cost pressure caused by an aging population. The value of the pension fund was 175 billion Euros in 2015. The assets are three times as high as the annual income and expenditure of Finland.

In Finland, there are not only many indications that mutual insurance societies which offer retirement funds are important, moreover they are among the largest companies. They are crucial for the national economy as well as for social protection tasks. For example, Nokia was a leading company in the last decade and 10% of its shareholders were Finnish. The largest single owners were mutual societies offering retirement insurances.

Table 5 presents Finnish work pension companies. The company with the largest capacity is Ilmarinen. With the exception of Veritas all other companies presented in the table are mutual societies.

It is important to notice that private pension companies manage the Finnish statutory work pensions, with the exception of the pensions of state and municipal employees. In Finland, the first pillar of the pension system is wider than in most other European Union member states. The pension systems for the public and private sector are nowadays coordinated with each other.

The market share of pension scheme companies hase been based legally on the branches of the employed people. The Finnish pension scheme system has no ceiling regarding pensions, although it was requested in several amendments over time.

These companies are self-financed by pension contributions and investments. The objectives of these investments may differ immensely

[107] Cf. *Talonen, Antti* (Interview 2015).

from the ones of company. The difference between mutual associations, joint stock companies, and public pension organisations are minor.

Table 6: Pension companies' market shares in 2017

Name of the company	**Market share in %**	**Total premium written (in €mil.)**
Varma Mutual Pension Insurance Company	34.6	4,867
Ilmarinen Mutual Pension Insurance Company	30.7	4,312
Elo Mutual Pension Insurance Company	25.0	3,511
Etera Mutual Pension Insurance Company	5.7	794
Veritas Pension Insurance Company Ltd	3.7	521
Försäkringsaktiebolaget Pensions-Alandia	0.3	46
Total/average 2017	**100.0**	**14,051**

Source: Finanssiala 2018, p. 19, Annex 8.

KEVA, which also constitutes reserve funds, is responsible for the pension of employees working in the public sector. The formation and distribution of insurance benefits are coordinated by the pension reform. The latest reform in 2005 reduced the differences between the pension systems in the public and private sector even more. According to *Liukko*, in Finland the private insurance industry has developed and is now under state control.[108] This is evident in the state control of the pension system based on salary as well as how the government dealt with voluntary pension funds managed by banks and life insurance companies.[109]

The life insurance companies have offered their customers voluntary retirement insurances, which complement the public pension funds,

[108] *Liukko, Jyri* (2013). Vakuutusyhteiskunta: François Ewald ja solidaarisuuden teknologiat. In: *Saari, Juho & Taipale, Sakari & Kainulainen, Sakari* (ed.) Hyvinvointivaltion moderneja klassikoita. DIAK, Helsinki 126.

[109] Ibid.

and belong to the European system of social security. However, the dealings between the government and the companies were problematic. While in the 1990s during the depression, the state supported such insurances, e.g. via tax incentives, in the 21st century the terms were changed retroactively and lost in practice their importance regarding pension funds security. In contrast to Liukko's view, the public authorities' goal to support the social task of private insurances in this insurance sector was not realised.

The missing ceiling of the pension system has the same effect as social insurances based on salaries. There has been no need for a system other than the working statuary pension funds system, because a recent arrangement brings up quite prestigious transfers for the majority. However, it is necessary to renew and amend the pension system. The last amendments were brought about in 2005 and in 2015. The economic crises and the deficit of the public finance have motivated reforms. It is an interesting question, if new models, based on the mutual insurance policy innovations, have better chances to handle the increasing cost pressure in the social security system than models based on corporations.

6. The future of the mutual insurance business

From an economic point of view, mutual insurance societies have been successful in Finland, even more successful than their competitors. However, the current economic recession influenced all kinds of insurance companies but their ability to adjust to the new market condition varies. There are main differences regarding profitability in the insurance industry. For example, Tapiola and Lähivakuutus differ from other companies in the sector due to their stable and well guided management.

With regard to investments, problems have arisen in the last couple of years. In particular mutual societies had problems to find profitable investments due to the fluctuation of the stock exchange prices and the value of gilt-edged security. The long term downswing of the stock exchange prices had a negative effect on the results of banks and insurance companies. According to *Markus Karjalainen*, this situation forced insurance companies to rethink their investment objectives and to develop risk management, i.e. experts have to be recruited to assess the risks via an evaluation procedure. It has become more common

between companies to work together or to merge. This development will continue.[110]

An example for a merger of companies is the one between Osuuspankkikonzerns with the mutual insurance societies Lähivakuutus and Fennia in 2001. This merger was done, because it helped to keep the costs for the customers low. The merger raises the questions about the basic values of the mutual insurance business and its consistency in a changed context. The above mentioned merger has also caused uproar. The fear was that profit seeking will become the main goal at the expense of other social goals.[111]

Criticism has also been raised by other insurance companies and concerns the problem that within the last decades any kind of individuality dominated over solidarity with regard to the development of voluntary insurance products. In general, the interests of investors have become stronger due to the globalization of the financial markets. Another concern is risk management with regard to the decentralisation strategies of insurance companies: How can they be applied in such a way that the owners/customers can still control the activities? In mixed companies based on mutuality, questions have arisen concerning the ideals of social economy, i.e. the owners'/customers' role. Are the activities transparent enough?

This was in particular evident regarding the above mentioned distribution of profits and about correct risk management among the policyholders and between policyholders and the insurance companies. According to *Asmo Kalpala*, the choice of risks dominates.[112] The insurance companies still decide about the correct extent of the statuary compensation insurances and the total costs have become the main efficiency scale in the public eye. Nevertheless, the different types of statuary compensation insurances and their generated investment results are still of great importance to Finland.

With the change of values in the insurance industry, the welfare state has shown increasing problems as the main element to balance the insurance risks are caused by the different kinds of population groups. The earlier polarization between industrial and developing countries has changed due to the globalization of the economy and has become a polarization within societies.

An unanswered question is, how far advanced is the process of the polarization in Finland. Also there is the question whether a private insurance industry is part of the solution or part of the problem. As earlier stated, competition was regarded as a way to develop the society between companies with the goal to support the interests of the market

---

110 *Karjalainen, Mauno-Markus* (Interview 2015).

111 Ibid.

112 Cf. *Kalpala, Asmo* (Interview 2015).

and the consumers. Competition was not regarded as a fight between several financial institutes about the capital and the interests of the people.

Today the Finnish insurance industry is fragmented. The retirement companies are separated, the bigger part of the life insurance companies has grown due to investments distributed by banks. The insurance company which had earlier a dominant market position has already reduced its activities and another company which is based on the traditional model works rarely.

The compensation insurances are stronger connected with the interests of banks and have to face great structural challenges. Nevertheless, basic knowledge is necessary in the insurance industry when relevant insurance solutions are discussed in society. The best forum to discuss the future role of the insurance industry is the Finnish Aktuar-association.

According to *Talonen*, a future challenge for mutual societies is the need to emphasise the value of customers and their various competition advantages. The latter is always based on the value the customers/owners perceive. Therefore, the customer decides about the competition advantages. In case the customer does not feel valued, the competition advantages are no advantages at all. It is important that the customers' assets are emphasized in the decision making process regardless of the customers' field of responsibility.[113]

The international competition and the economic crisis have opened new opportunities for mutual societies. It seems that the economy and solidarity of mutual societies function well. In a situation of international competition, the local element can be regarded as an advantage. Although mutual societies usually do not work on an international scale, they can benefit of cooperating with foreign mutual association regarding their efficiency and scale values. For example, ICMIF and EURAPCO are well working networks.[114]

The social-political importance of social economy and mutual societies are influenced by the way the challenges will be handled. Is it possible that the political importance of social economy can be increased even more? Is it possible that changes of activities can be considered in a better way than joint stock companies are able to do (globalization, privatization of district's and state's tasks, orientation according the market requirements and the technological development)?

Is the cultural character still preserved in large mutual societies (democratic decision making process, communality of the activities, activities on a smaller scale)? Is it possible to find a unified perception regarding the main goals and topics of social economy? The importance

---

[113] Cf. *TTalonen, Antti* (Interview 2015).

[114] Ibid.

of social economy and the mutuality principle are also influenced by how well those are connected to the academic research, teaching, and future developments. At the moment, mutuality is not a main topic of economic and social research, although studies and courses at universities and colleges of higher education have increased in the last couple of years.

According to *Tapani Köppä*, it is necessary for mutual societies and social economy to find a future profile between the field of private economy, which looks at the requirements of the market, and public economy.[115] Danger lies in a kind of marginalization between these two. According to *Köppä*, education, knowledge about the field in general and in particular critical social-political research can help to avoid marginalization.[116]

It is necessary to see if social economy is able to use empirical results of social politics and practical competitive solutions to solve social risks and problems of our time. A reform of social and health services of the public sector happens in Finland at the moment. The national economy has to deal with deficits and increasing debts. In the discussion, social economy is regarded as an alternative to public institutions, but a break-through is still missing.

According to *Köppä*, in Finland social-economic models are not regarded as useful tools for discussing the future of social and health politics. The reforms developed to polemic discussions between groups who support a strong national economy and others who favour the market forces.[117] The latter group consists of two political lobbies, one which represents the interests of the rural population and their communities and the other of large cities. The main topic is more about splitting the political power between the fighting groups than to find the boundaries regarding the terms of the market. It is evident that the insurance industry is able to provide alternatives, e.g. in the field of social security. To follow up these alternatives is, however, a political choice. The fact that Finland has followed the collective tradition for a long time may help citizens to find a new way to solve the economic problems on their own.

115 Cf. *Köppä, Tapani* (Interview 2015).

116 Ibid.

117 Ibid.

Bibliography

Albertin, Michel (2004). Vakuutuksen taloudellinen ja yhteiskunnalinen tehtävä. In: *Katri Hellsten* ja *Tuula Helne* (eds.). Vakuuttava sosiaalivakuutus? Kelan tutkimusosasto: Helsinki, 22-42.

Cooperative Europe Key figures 2014-15.

Ewald, Francois (2004). Vakuutusyhteiskunnan synty. In: *Katri Hellsten* ja *Tuula Helne* (eds.). Vakuuttava sosiaalivakuutus? Kelan tutkimusosasto: Helsinki, 44-66.

Henttinen, Annastiina (2007). Keskinäisyyden alkulähteillä. In: *Arja Suomi* (ed.) Keskinäisyys. Näkökulmia omistaja-asiakkuuteen. Edita Publishing: Helsinki, 9-30.

Federation of Finnish Financial Services (ed.): Finnish Insurance in 2015, Helsinki 2016.

http://blogs.helsinki.fi/jliukko/files/2008/04/henkivakuutus-ja-solidaarisuuden-kehat-janus07.pdf.

http://crossborder.practicallaw.com/7-504-6240?source=relatedcontent.

http://tyoelakelakipalvelu.etk.fi/fi/saados/en/20060395/?_navi=haku.

http://www.diak.fi/tyoelama/Julkaisut/Sivut/A-tutkimuksia.aspx.

http://www.etk.fi/en/service/pension_insurance_companies/1492/pension_insurance_companies.

http://www.fin-fsa.fi/en/About_us/Pages/Default.aspx.

http://www.finlex.fi/fi/laki/ajantasa/1987/19871250.

http://www.finlex.fi/sv/laki/alkup/1997/19970354.

http://www.finlex.fi/fi/laki/ajantasa/2008/20080521.

http://www.icmif.org/global-mutual-market-share-2014.

http://www.igpinfo.com/igpinfo/public_documents/ss_summaries/Finland.pdf.

http://www.kilpailuvirasto.fi/cgi-bin/english.cgi.

http://www.pwc.com/at/de/publikationen/financial-services/international-comparison-of-insurance-taxation-2011/finland-insurance-taxation-2011.pdf.

http://www.sosiaalipoliittinenyhdistys.fi/janus/Sisallys%200210.htm.

http://www.tapiola.fi/wwweng/Briefly/The+Tapiola+Group/Business+idea+and+values/Policyholders%E2%80%99+influence.htm.

http://www.turva.fi.

https://uk.practicallaw.thomsonreuters.com/7-504-6240?__lrTS=20170411120239142&transitionType=Default&contextData=(sc.Default)&firstPage=true&bhcp=1.

https://www.lahitapiola.fi/henkilo.

ICMIF (ed.). Global Mutual Market Share 2014, published March 2016,

ICMIF (ed.). Figures for 2015, Global Mutual Market Share. Cheshire.

ICMIF (ed.). Market InSights: Europe 2014 (2016). Cheshire.

IGP (2011). Summary of Social Security and Private Employee Benefits Finland 2011.

Immonen, Niina (2006). Yhteisötalous Suomessa. Sisäpiirin slangia vai uutta yhteistyön taloutta? Tampereen seudun osuustoiminnan kehittämisyhdistys: Tampere. Akateeminen väitöskirja.

Kalmi, Panu (2007). Keskinäisyys yritysmuotona. In: *Arja Suomi* (ed.). Keskinäisyys. Näkökulmia omistaja-asiakkuuteen. Edita Publishing: Helsinki, 31-46.

Köppä, Tapani (2006). Kilpailutalous: Kehitysoptimismissa perikadon ainekset. In: *Pauli Niemelä & Terho Pursiainen* (eds.). Hyvinvointi yhteiskuntapoliittisena tavoitteena. Professori Juhani Laurinkarin juhlakirja. Sosiaalipoliittisen yhdistyksen tutkimuksia nro 62. Kuopion yliopisto.

Laurinkari, Juhani (2010). Hyvinvointipolitiikan talous. In: *Pauli Niemelä* (ed.) Hyvinvointipolitiikka. WSOYPro, Helsinki.

Lehtonen, Turo-Kimmo & Liukko, Jyri (2010). Vakuutussolidaarisuuden muodot ja rajat. In: Janus 18 (2), 121-136.

Liukko, Jyri (2007). Henkivakuutus ja solidaarisuuden kehät. Vakuutusmainonta vastuuajattelun muokkaajana Suomessa 1945-1990. In: Janus 15 (1), 3-18.

Liukko, Jyri (2013). Vakuutusyhteiskunta: François Ewald ja solidaarisuuden teknologiat. In: *Saari, Juho & Taipale, Sakari & Kainulainen, Sakari* (eds.) Hyvinvointivaltion moderneja klassikoita. DIAK, Helsinki:

Local Insurance-Tap. http://www.diak.fi/tyoelama/Julkaisut/Sivut/A-tutkimuksia.aspx.iola. Press release 7 February 2012.

Niemelä, Heikki & Salminen, Kari (2006). Suomalainen sosiaaliturva. Kela: Helsinki.

Niemelä, Heikki & Salminen, Kari (2009). Kansallisten eläkestrategioiden muotoutuminen ja Euroopan Unionin avoin koordinaatiomenetelmä. Sosiaali- ja terveysturvan tutkimuksia 104. Kela: Helsinki.

Pättiniemi, Pekka (2004). Mitä on yhteisötalous? In: *Grönberg, Ville* (ed.). Yhteisötalous ja sosiaalinen yrittäjyys. Sosiaalisten yritysten kansallinen teematyö. Euroopan sosiaalirahasto ESR. Sosiaali – ja terveysalan tutkimus – ja kehittämiskeskus Stakes: Helsinki, 23-29.

Poutanen Veli-Matti (2007). Sosiaalitaloudesta yhteisötalouteen?. In: *Laurinkari, J; Brazda. J; Kramer, J,; Schediwy, R*; Yhteisötalous. Johdatus perusteisiin.Palmenia. Palmenia-sarja, 67-91.

PWC (2011), International comparison of insurance taxation: http://www.pwc.com/at/de/publikationen/financial-services/international-comparison-of-insurance-taxation-2011/finland-insurance-taxation-2011.pdf.

Ruuskanen, Olli-Pekka (2007). Suomen keskinäiset vakuutusyhtiöt. Kehitys 1994-2004. *Teoksessa, Arja Suomi* (ed.). Keskinäisyys. Näkökulmia omistaja-asiakkuuteen. Edita Publishing: Helsinki, 71-91.

Study on the current situation and prospects of mutuals in Europe. Final report. Country studies. Zoetermeer 2012.

Suomi, Arja (toim.) (2007). Keskinäisyys. Näkökulmia omistaja-asiakkuuteen. Edita Publishing: Helsinki.

Mutual Insurance and Limited Companies in the Norwegian Insurance Industry

Balázs Lovescher

1. Introduction

The Kommunal Landspensjonskasse (KLP) was 2017 again the largest life insurance company in Norway with approximately 450,000 members, 280,000 pensioners and 215,000 members who have pension entitlements with KLP deriving from previous employment. The mutual insurance company was able to regain a large part of the repurchase agreement in 2014, which was lost in the 1990s due to the increase of competition in the public law pension market. At the same time, several Norwegian communities with pension funds managed by the KLP switched to other commercial suppliers such as Storebrand and DNB Livsforsikring. The latter decided to leave the public law pension market and their market share of 3 to 5 percent were regained by KLP. With the exit of these private limited companies, KLP has won approximately 150,000 new members (58 parishes and 200 companies). In 2017, most of the country's municipalities and county councils have their pension schemes with KLP. Several of these municipalities have decided to merge with municipalities that have their own pension fund. Such mergers can also make new municipalities big enough to allow some of them to consider establishing their own pension funds. These factors may affect the market in for public-sector occupational pensions.

In June 2003, DNB Livsforskring announced to leave the public pension sector due to more strict regulations in the bank and insurance sector as well as increasing competition, which have made the market situation too difficult for them. Additionally, the company claimed that the public pension sector is only accessible to some extent.[1, 2] In December 2012, the life insurer Storebrand left the market, too. The management had to make this decision because future investments would have been necessary to continue the business. However, such

[1] Cf. Investment & Pensions Europe (2014a).

[2] DNB Group Annual Report (2013), p. 19-21.

high investments are opposed to a low amount of customers.[3, 4] Moreover, the Financial Market Authority (Finanstilsynet) warned that within the next couple of years the Norwegian pension funds and life insurance companies are going to face great challenges. Finanstilsynet referred to the obligations of life insurance companies, which usually comprised contracts with an annual profit. Today's low global interest policy hinders to secure the guaranteed minimum rates. Finanstilsynet also puts the attention to other factors such as the increasing life span of policyholders and Solvency II. With Solvency II, which has come into effect in the European Union on January 1st, 2016, much higher capital requirements for insurance companies are obligatory.[5] This change means for Norwegian insurance companies[6] that the insurance reserves provisions are estimated by the current risk-free interest rate and not as before by the guarantee interest rate. As a result, the provisions are influenced by the market interest rate change and the capital requirement for interest rate risk is influenced by the interest rate sensitivity. Therefore, life insurance companies with long-term pension liabilities have to invest in investment bonds, which have the same duration as the other obligations to hedge the capital requirements of Solvency II. However, such long-term investments are very difficult to fulfil in the current financial situation, because they have to use short-term investments to generate the necessary guaranteed interest rate.[7]

Today's events show that the Norwegian insurance business is dynamic. Four legal forms have been established: public limited companies, private limited companies, mutual companies and pension funds. At the end of 2017, 76 insurance companies: 58 non-life insurers (including 15 fire insurers) and six marine insurance associations were licensed to operate in Norway. A further 13 branches of Norwegian insurers were operating abroad (in the EEA area) and 29 branches of foreign insurers in Norway.[8] Mutual companies have a strong business in the pension funds sector, e.g. like KLP, as well as in other insurance branches such as in the fire, life, maritime, or non-life sector. The question is on what the mutual insurance companies' success is based on and why they are so strongly represented in the market. Are the reasons based on historical, legal or other facts, which are responsible for their success?

---

3 Cf. Investment & Pensions Europe (2014a).

4 Cf. Storebrand Annual Report (2012), p. 8, 11.

5 Cf. Investment & Pensions Europe (2014c).

6 Norway is not a member of the EU, but the regulations of Solvency II apply to members of the EWRs, which includes Norway too.

7 Cf. *Carlén* (2013), p. 30.

8 Cf. Finanstilsynet (2018), Annual Report 2017, p. 40.

2. Ideas and principles of mutual insurance companies

The basic and most simple form of insurance is the mutual adoption of risks in terms of distributing risks among a homogenous group of people.[9] The ideology of mutual risk distribution is regarded as a special form of solidarity in the community.[10] The principle of insurance has a long history and is an efficient instrument to protect individuals.[11] In the past, rural and urban guilds and crafts established voluntary and regional interest groups and combined the insurance offer with other social and religious help offers, also based on the principle of mutuality.[12] In most of the European countries, mutual insurance companies were the cornerstones of the public and social security system, which were based on social redistribution and organized as non-profit companies. They offered employees social security.[13] Therefore, mutual insurance companies have contributed highly to the creation of economic and social values.[14]

Mutual insurance companies are based on similar principles as e.g. cooperatives in the social economy. They are voluntary societies of natural persons or legal entities with the goal to fulfil the members' needs and not to focus on the return of investments. This kind of companies follows the solidarity principle when fulfilling the needs of their members. The profits and surpluses are not distributed among the shareholders, but reinvested to improve the service for members, to create and finance new offers, and to increase the company's own funds. With this action, the reserves are distributed among the members. In contrast to cooperatives, the shares of mutual insurance companies lie inseparably in the mutual possession and management of all members. As a result, the admission fees of new members are low, because they only contribute to the costs of services and do not purchase shares in the original capital. A resignation has no influence on the capital, because members have no owners' rights on the capital.[15] The European Commission's goal is to create a European mutual insurance company. The general principles of mutual insurance companies are according to the European Commission as the follows:

---

9 Cf. *Broek* et al. (2012a), p. 10.

10 Cf. *Greve* (2006), p. 5.

11 Cf. *Broek* et al. (2012a), p. 10.

12 Cf. *Greve* (2006), p. 5.

13 Cf. European Commission (2003), p. 8.

14 Cf. *Broek* et al. (2012a), p. 10.

15 Cf. European Commission (2003), p. 5-6.

Voluntary membership

Mutual insurance companies are a union of people and not of resources[16] and accessible for all who fulfil the regulations of the contract and obey the principles of the society. There are two kinds of mutual insurance companies: unrestricted and restricted. While the membership of unrestricted mutual insurance companies has no certain restrictions, the membership of restricted mutual insurance companies is connected with geographic or profession related regulations of the contract.[17]

Non-existence of shares

Mutual insurance companies do not consist of shares or stocks, which generate yields for their shareholders. They are based on an opening capital or own funds funded by members or via loan. This fund is the collective-indivisible asset of the society.[18]

Benefit to the public

The main goal is not profit but to fulfil the needs of the members or in some cases the interest of the public. Therefore, the focus lies on the people and not on the capital. Despite the missing profit seeking, the society has still to work economically and may generate surpluses. It is important that the society is able to be competitive. Mutual insurance companies are obligated to present their annual accounts. The main difference compared to other company forms lies in the profit use. The profits are used to reduce members' contributions or to reinvest to improve offers and services. They are also used to fund the business and to increase the capital adequacy.[19, 20]

Solidarity

The members of a mutual insurance company have the goal to fulfil individual expectations via collective action. In the process, they aim at the optimal allocation of resources and actions to fulfil all needs at its best.[21]

Democracy

Mutual insurance companies are democratic organizations with members participating actively in business activities. In general, each member has the same voting right (one-man-one-vote-principle) in the decision making process.[22]

---

16 *Ballester* (2013), p. 9.

17 Cf. European Commission (2003), p. 6.

18 Cf. ibid.

19 Cf. ibid.

20 Cf. *Ballester* (2013), p. 9.

21 Cf. European Commission (2003), p. 6.

22 Cf. European Commission (2003), p. 6-7.

Independence

Mutual insurance companies are independent companies without governmental control and vital subsidies.[23] [24]

3. Historical development of the Norwegian insurance industry

Norway has an eventful history, because it was ruled for centuries by its neighbours Denmark and Sweden. Originally, Sweden was a small country compared to the kingdom of Denmark. The latter included in addition to its present's area Greenland, Faroe Islands, Norway, Iceland, Schleswig-Holstein, and the southern part of today's Sweden. Over time, Denmark lost several areas, for example today's south Sweden (middle of the 17th century), Schleswig-Holstein (it went 1864 to Germany), Sweden (it went to Norway 1814 during the Napoleonic Wars), and Iceland that declared independence after the German occupation of the mainland in the Second World War.[25] The latter had, together with Sweden, considerable influence on the economic and social developments of Norway. Therefore, it is important to present the insurance industry in connection with these historical events in order to get a picture about the influences and developments in this sector.

After the death of King *Håkon VI.* Magnusson of Norway, his son *Olav IV.* became king in 1380. *Olav* was a ten-year-old-minor but ruled as king of Denmark since 1376. His mother, *Margarete Waldemarsdatter*, daughter of the Danish King *Waldemar IV. Atterdag*, initiated a personal union between Norway and Denmark.[26] The Danish royal dynasty aimed at the creation of a Nordic union, which became reality in 1389 after the victory over King *Albert of Sweden*. After her son's death in 1387, *Margarete* became Queen and established in 1397 the Kalmarer Union, i.e. the union between the Danish, Norwegian, and Swedish kingdoms. Although the interests of these kingdoms were divergent, the union existed up to 1523.[27] The personal union meant for Norway the beginning of its decline, in particular regarding culture. The Norwegian language and its literature were replaced by Danish,

---

23 Cf. European Commission (2003), p. 7.

24 Cf. *Ballester* (2013), p. 9.

25 Cf. *Klausen* and *Selle* (1996), p. 101.

26 Cf. *Petrick* (2002), p. 70-73.

27 Cf. *Johnsen* (1939), p. 129-131.

the construction of new and large buildings stopped, and territorial losses occurred.[28] From the end of the 14th to the middle of the 15th century, several pest epidemics reduced the peasant population by almost 90 percent. The entire population decreased until 1500 from 500,000 to 200,000 people.[29] Norway lost most of its sovereignty, which was restored not until 1905. Norway was perceived for more than 200 years as a Danish colony, without its own capital, oppressed and exploited.[30] From the middle of the 17th century on, however, Norway experienced a boom. Its population increased to 500,000 people and resulted in the development of a strong middle class. In this time, an economic expansion started, fishery, coal mining, craft, and trade flourished. Norway became the largest exporter of timber in Europe.[31] In 1665, Norway received its first national constitution, which was the only constitution in the absolutistic Europe.[32] In the following decades, several Nordic wars occurred and on January 14th, 1814, after 430 years, the time of the Danish occupation ended. Denmark had to give Norway to Sweden according to its defeat in the Napoleonic War and regarding the decision of the Peace of Kiel.[33] On May 17th, 1814, Norway got its first modern constitution, which stated Norway as a "free, independent, impartible and indefeasible realm, united with Sweden under one king."[34] The first couple of years in this new personal union was an era of economic reconstruction. This union brought a new constitution, the abolishment of the feudalism, and the beginning of a constitutional monarchy. In the 1820s, it initiated cultural, religious and social movements, which led to a renaissance of language and traditions, a support of a democratic government, economic self-help, and regional welfare. The following decades revived the third sector, too. As a result, voluntary organizations, such as consumers cooperative societies, sport and cultural societies, religious organizations and organizations for people with special needs, developed. In the Norwegian society, the idea of altruism as an independent mechanism was never deeply rooted due to aristocratic and mercantile traditions. It was not until the cooperation of local and central public authorities that the civil and member based organizations received their legitimacy. The local government usually supported financially the independent citizen initiatives. Additionally, local government workers were the head of civil organizations. In return, volunteer organizations did public services in collaboration with local public authorities. This close collaboration led to an important

28 Cf. *Petrick* (2002), p. 73, 83.

29 Cf. *Petrick* (2002), p. 80.

30 Cf. *Petrick* (2002), p. 73-75.

31 Cf. ibid, p. 92, 96.

32 Cf. ibid, p. 104.

33 Cf. ibid, p. 113.

34 Ibid, p. 119.

integration of public and private services.[35] However, this boom was contrasted by a huge capital scarcity and a large impoverished population, such as fishermen, peasants, and urban lower class people.[36] In 1806, *Napoleon's* Continental System disrupted Norway's exports, while British war vessels prevented the maritime trade and, as a result, the food supply for the population, in particular essential corn imports.[37] The Norwegian state pauperized and extended its authority regarding the economic life only gradually. Norway's first industrial intervention was the development of the transport infrastructure. The focus was the development of the railroad network, which needed all available resources and led to a neglect of other economic sectors. Therefore, the government had only a passive role in the development of the insurance industry.[38]

On June 7th, 1905, the Norwegian Parliament (Storting) decided to dissolve the personal union with Sweden. Sweden demanded verification by a referendum, which took place on August 13th, 1905. The decision was 368,208 yes-votes to 184 no-votes and resulted in the dissolution of the union. Norway became independent on October 13th 1905, the first time since 1380.[39]

The Norwegian insurance industry can be traced back to the 18th century. By 1840, the concentration of insurance companies was low and the few existing individual insurers were not well known. At this time, foreign insurance companies mostly concluded the insurance contracts. Within the next couple of years, many new insurance companies were founded which led to an establishment of the insurance industry. However, the economic and social conditions were still harsh in this period. The insurance industry comprised mutual insurance companies, dedicated to charitable work and economic self-help, and private limited companies with the aim to gain profit. Mutual insurance companies were managed by their members and able to create identity and homogeneity, which was helpful for collective actions. In contrast, private limited companies distinguished between owners and customers who had advantages regarding problems triggered by diversity and social inequality. In contrast to mutual insurance companies, private limited companies were able to expand their business to other insurance markets, because they were less confronted by the peculiarities of a community.[40]

---

[35] Cf. *Salamon* et al. (2004), p. 265-266.

[36] Cf. *Greve* (2006), p. 5.

[37] Cf. *Petrick* (2002), p. 112.

[38] Cf. *Færden*, (1967).

[39] Cf. *Petrick* (2002), p. 165.

[40] Cf. *Greve* (2006), p. 5.

The mutual organization form enabled in the insurance industry an expansion of the balance between risks and advantages in form of transportation insurances regarding merchant shipping and fishery as well as mutual help in local villages in case of fire. Mutual insurance companies were a development in two ways. Firstly, mutual insurance companies based on individual contracts and were established on a permanent base in merchant shipping. Secondly, they had formal regulations and the principle of prepayment of insurance premiums. Insurance as an instrument for risk sharing between members was one of the most important ideological elements of earlier mutual insurance companies. This ideology regards insurances as a special form of solidarity in the community, which minimizes the problem of copycats and leads to a natural restriction of membership. Restricted access for insurances can be useful because the meaning of trust increases when ceteris paribus the danger of carelessness and deception increases. Insurances were created in particular to solve problems regarding the collective assurance of help between people who trust each other. The step to restrict membership had the objective to enable a better organization and easier control of collective actions.[41]

In the beginning, only a few insurance companies were established to fulfil the need of fire and merchant shipping insurances. The organization forms were usually mutual societies, mutual insurance companies or private limited companies. The first group was distinguished in regional restricted and unrestricted forms.[42] Both forms wanted that the customer and the owner were unified in one person and had the ideology that profits have to be divided within the community. In contrast to the restricted form, the unrestricted form had no geographic restrictions and no additional terms of admission. This form followed not compulsorily the idea of common public interest and the overlapping of social and contractual obligations. Instead, general contractual and impersonal rights and obligations were agreed with the members. The unrestricted form aimed at an efficient management and the creation of a sufficient large risk pool to minimise extreme high losses due to major urban fires or heavy storms on sea. Therefore, the unrestricted form is midway on a scale between two very different ends, either the restricted and communal orientated mutual insurance company or the commercial limited company.[43] The Norwegian insurance industry expanded over the years, created more sub-segments without new organization forms.[44]

[41] Cf. *Greve* (2006), p. 6-7.

[42] Cf. ibid, p. 5-6.

[43] Cf. ibid, p. 9-10.

[44] Cf. ibid, p. 5-6.

Today's Norwegian Insurance Act states in Article 3 § 3-1 the acceptable society forms for insurances, i.e. mutual societies or limited companies. The following historical analysis is restricted to these legal forms.

3.1 History of private insurance companies

At the beginning of the 19th century, only a few private insurance companies[45] can be found in Norway. The reason was to some extent that most of the main organizations, such as commercial credit institutions, which were usually organized as private limited companies, remained in Denmark after the personal union between Norway and Denmark was dissolved. Therefore, the insurance companies were the pioneers regarding the foundation of private limited companies. The first Norwegian insurance private limited company was the merchant shipping insurer Det norske Søe Assurance Selskab[46], which was established in 1808 in Christiana, today's Oslo. Its aim was apart from profits the increase of food transports between Denmark and Norway via the English naval blockade. When Det norske Søe Assurance Selskab became insolvent in 1820 the only existing insurance private limited company disappeared[47] until the fire insurance company Det norske Brandassuranceselskab paa Varer og Effekter, later named Gamle Bergen, was founded in Bergen in 1838. The company offered contracts to insure provisions, household goods, furnishings, and clothes. Before that, such goods could only be insured via foreign insurers and with the help of policy dealers.[48] In 1900, Gamle Bergen was integrated into Vesta Brandforsikringsselskabet. The Norwegian business man and Politican *Frederik Georg Gade* founded Vesta in 1880 and Hygea, the so-called Vesta-Hygea, in 1884.[49] [50]

Vesta focused on fire insurances, while Hygea was specialised in life insurances. The company merged over time with other insurance companies, for example in 1966 with Æolus und Bergens Brand. A side effect of the merger was that Vesta became the majority shareholder of the life insurance company Norsk Kollektiv Pensjonskasse A/S (NKP), in which Bergens Brand and Æolus hold many shares. From that point on, an attempt for a reorganization via a merger of NPK and

---

45 The Norwegian law started to distinguish between Aksjeselskaper (AS – private limited liability companies /restricted company) and Allmennaksjeselskap (ASA – private limited companies) not before 1997. An overview on the definition of Norwegian company organisation forms can be found in the appendix.

46 Cf. *Espeli* (2011), p. 49.

47 Cf. *Greve* (2006), p. 9.

48 Cf. Den Norske Forsinkringsforening-Storebrand.

49 Cf. Vesta Forsinkring A/S.

50 Cf. *Bull* et al. (1929), p. 334-335.

Vesta-Hygea started. However, Vesta could not be restructured due to a special kind of voting right restriction, which resulted in a difficult relationship between these two life insurance companies. The merger could not be concluded before 1989 when the Vesta group was bought by the Swedish conglomerate Skandia. Skandia was able to restructure NKP and Hygea to the new company Vital Forsikring. Since the Vesta groups were founded, the name changed several times, for example in 1984 when the Norske Assuranceunion A/S was integrated. Forsikringsaktieselskapet Vesta became Vesta groups A/S and the compensation portfolios were given to the 100 percent sub-company Vesta Skade, which was established due to acquisition of Norske Assuranceunion A/S. Vesta Skade started an acquisition phase and expanded the company by buying Stavanger Forsikringsselskap A/S and the merchant shipping insurer Polaris Assuranse A/S. While the fist company was completely integrated into Vesta Skade, Polaris Assuranse A/S was sold to VVaG UNI Forsikring (up to 1987 named Norges Brannkasse), and became the object of demutualization and, as a result, part of Storebrand ASA.[51] In 1999, Skandia sold the Vesta groups, comprising Skadeselskapene Vesta Forsikring, Vesta Dial, Aktiv and Vesta Liv of danske Tryg-Baltica, which was part of the Danish financial syndicate Unidanmark. In 2002, the Unidanmark was integrated into the Nordea group and Vesta became with Tyrg Forsikring Denmark's largest compensation insurance company (TrygVesta group). Since 2010, its name is Tryg. In the process, the life insurance sector of Vesta was transferred to Nordea Liv.[52] [53]

In Christiania, the first fire limited company Christiania Almindelige Brandforsikrings-Selskap for Varer og Effekter was established in 1847. The idea for this foundation came from an article published in the Morgenbladet on March 17th, 1847 by the journalist and later lawyer of the High Court *Daniel Kildal*. He invited the readers to start with him an issue prospectus. *Kildal* had already the necessary knowledge for such a project, because one year before he was part of establishing the Christiania Bank og Kreditkasse. On April 8th, 1847, the issue prospectus was signed by two trading houses, Ths. Joh. Heftye & Søn and A. Grüning & Co., as well as by the representative of Gamle Bergen in Christiania, *Jacob Dybwad*, and other leading figures. The origin capital was 300,000 Specidaler created by issuance of 3,000 capital stocks, which were issued in the entire country. The foundation of the private limited company in Christiania, known as Storebrand, benefited from the 18 percent profit of the shares of Gamle Bergen the year before. In 1856, the business sector was restructured. As a start,

---

[51] Cf. Den Norske Forsinkringsforening-Vesta.

[52] Cf. Vesta Forsinkring AS.

[53] Cf. Tryg.

fire insurances were distinguished between different industrial sectors such as forestry, seafaring, or building construction. Later an additional classification of insurance objects into various risk classes followed. At the same time, Storebrand started with a systematic reinsurance strategy to diversify its risks. Storebrand benefited from this strategy, because despite several big fires, which destroyed parts of Christiania, the boroughs Moss, and Drammen within the next couple of years, the company was able to fulfil its obligations. As a result, Storebrand initiated a meeting with other insurance companies to determine a new rate for the cities. However, after a couple of months it became evident that other companies did not follow the new regulations and the price war between the companies increased. In 1861, Storebrand founded the Norwegian insurance company Idun in which it had a share of 72.7 percent and joint management. Originally, the idea was to establish life insurances in Storebrand as a sector of its own, but this idea could not been realized due to the opposition of the board. As a result, the life and compensation insurance were carried on separately. Doctor *Ole Jacob Brock*, a member of the board, was in particular opposed to the foundation of a life insurance within Storebrand. In 1847, he was the main initiator for the foundation of Christiania almindelige gjensidige Forsørgelsesesanstalt and had the belief that life and compensation insurances differed fundamentally. In his opinion, life insurances are based on social and philanthropic initiatives, while compensation insurances focused on profit. Therefore, both kinds of insurances should be offered separately.[54]

Storebrand expanded fast on the Norwegian insurance market as well as abroad. Since 1868 Storebrand offered insurance products in Stockholm, Göteborg, and Malmö, in the next year in Copenhagen, Flensburg, Hamburg, and Berlin and finally in 1870 Storebrand was represented in Finland. However, the business was not very successful although they were able to expand to foreign markets very quickly. As a result, the company withdrew from these markets, except in Sweden and Finland. In 1872, they cooperated with two British and two Austrian reinsurers, but the latter declared bankruptcy and Storebrand had to leave these markets with high losses. In 1880, the next expansion followed in cooperation with Norge and Bergens Brand via a branch for reinsurer in London. In this case, too, they were not successful due to fierce competition and three years with losses in a row. In 1886, the company had losses in the Swedish business without any hope of improvement. Storebrand accepted an offer of Skandia and exchanged their Swedish sales business for Skandia's Norwegian business. In the next year, the name Storebrand was used officially on a policy for the first time although only in combination with the name Christiania Al-

---

[54] Cf. Den Norske Forsinkringsforening-Storebrand.

mindelige Brandforsikrings-Selskab. The name "Storebrand" became the official designation not before 1915. Despite the failed expansion, Storebrand signed a deal with Vesta in 1902 regarding a common reinsurance business in Sweden and Denmark. Storebrand ended the cooperation in 1918 due to losses. During the next five decades, Storebrand expanded in various markets and acquired numerous companies, for example the largest Norwegian travel insurer Europeiske. In the 1960s, the largest private life insurance company Norden Livsforsikring A/S was established due to a merger of Livsforsikringsselskapet Brage with Det Norske Livsforsikringsselskap Fram, the new company became Storeband's strongest competitor. On August 11th, 1983, the government agreed on the merger of the two holding companies Norden Livsforsikring A/S and the Storebrand-Indun group. The new company with the name A/S Storebrand-Norden Livsforsikring had a market share of 20 percent of the entire insurance sector and became with assets of seven billion NOK the largest single enterprise in Norway. After the finance crisis of the 1970s, the life insurance market grew sharply. The driving force was the sale of single premium policy insurances, which was also offered by Storebrand-Norden Liv on a large scale. Storebrand started a marketing campaign with the slogan that "stupid sheep bring their money to bank while clever foxes contract insurance". This slogan led to a huge disapproval by the government and was one of the main points which led to the elimination of the deductibility of the premium subsidy when the individual taxable income base is determined.[55, 56] At the beginning of the year 1990, the holding company Storebrand A/S conducted negotiations with UNI Forsikring A/S regarding merger, although the latter did not exist yet. The reason was that both mutual insurance companies UNI Forsikring-gjensidig livsforsikringsselskap (former Norske Folk) and UNI Forsikring-gjensidig skadeforsikringsselskap (former Norges Brannkasse) were still in a progress of reorganisation to be demutualised into two private limited companies with UNI Forsikring A/S, a holding company, as an umbrella company. The official main purpose of the merger was capital procurement, although critics believed that the real purpose was to prevent other mergers. On November 30th, 1990, the holding company UNI Forsikring A/S was established and the operational business of both mutual insurance companies were transferred to the insurance company UNI Livsforsikring A/S and UNI Skadeforsikring A/S.[57] In 2005, Storebrand founded the Storebrand Folkepensjon. The reason was that it became obvious that the statuary obligation to a company pension scheme will be enacted

---

55 Cf. Den Norske Forsinkringsforening–Storebrand.

56 Cf. Den Norske Forsinkringsforening–Brage.

57 Cf. ibid.

by the Storting and come into effect on January 1st, 2006.[58, 59] In 2014, Storebrand and Gjensidige Forsikring were one of the largest insurance companies in Norway.[60]

In June 2010, the Financial Market Authority agreed to the demutualization and the following stock market launch of Gjensidige Forsikring BA, which became Gjensidige Forsikring ASA.[61] The insurance company had a long history beginning with the year 1689. At this time, a mutual fire society was established in the district Nes and was integrated with other mutual societies into an umbrella organization in 1922. At the beginning of the 1920s, approximately 260 fire insurance societies existed. The major part of these companies had no sufficient reinsurances in case of mass fires. In 1920, a commission and task force were established to prepare the foundation of a central reinsurance centre. On October 17, 1922, the Samtrygd-Norsk Gjensidig Forsikringsforening was established in Oslo. The umbrella organization was regarded sceptically by the mutual societies and only 23 out of 260 companies became part of Samtrygd. The major criticism was that different risk classes were put together. As a result, only three months later three sectors were created, i.e. reinsurance, urban insurances, and rural insurances. Later these sectors were reorganized in real estate and moveable property insurance. This reorganization contributed to the fact that Samtrygd had, at the end of 1926, 129 mutual companies as members.[62] As an umbrella organization, Samtrygd supported the creation of companies in other insurance branches. The director *Hjalmar Steenstrup* and the manager *Olav Hernæs* of Samtrygd were both key figures for the foundation of the first Norwegian mutual car society Norsk Bilforsikringsforening, Gjensidig (NBG) in 1928 and the mutual taxi society Drosjeforsikringen, Gjensidig in 1930.[63, 64] Until 1958, Samtrygd offered in particular fire and reinsurances, in June of the same year they received the licence for all kinds of insurance branches, except credit insurance. Afterwards they concluded cooperation contracts with the Norwegian farmers' society and in 1964 the livestock insurer Tyr and Odin were integrated. As a result, Samtrygd became the largest insurance company in the agriculture sector. In 1962, Samtrygd founded with several saving banks and fire insurance companies the credit insurance company Kredittforsikringsselskapet Samkredit. The latter merged in 1986 with Agder Assuranceselskap A/S, was taken over a year later by Gjensidige Norsk Skadeforsikring,

[58] Cf. Storebrand Annual Report (2012), p. 4.

[59] Cf. *Altinn* (2013).

[60] Cf. Forbes Global 2000.

[61] Cf. Regjeringen (2010).

[62] Cf. Den Norske Forsinkringsforening-Samtrygd.

[63] Cf. Den Norske Forsinkringsforening-NBG.

[64] Cf. Den Norske Forsinkringsforening-Drosjeforsikringen.

and renamed in Gjensidige Kredittforsikring AS. Between 1960 and 1970, the number of fire insurance companies decreased from 227 to 134 due to numerous mergers. Samtrygd merged with the mutual car company NBG in 1974 and became as Samtrygd-NBG, Norsk Skadeforsikring Gjensidig the largest car insurer of Norway. In the same year, Samtrygd concluded a cooperation contract with the life insurer Gjensidige Liv. From 1976 onwards, both companies, Gjensidige Norsk Skadeforsikring and Gjensidige Liv, used the name Gjensidige Forsikring due to market strategical reasons. In 1982, Gjensidige Norsk Skadeforsikring suggested a cooperation with Norges Brannkasse with the intention to strengthen the position of mutual companies on the market. At first, they conducted negotiations, but Norges Brannkasse ended the talks very quickly. The reason was Norges Brannkasse's intention to conduct a contract with NKP. However, this could not be realised and in 1982 Norges Brannkasse cooperated with Norske Folk Livs- og Pensjonforsikring. This company was established in 1917 as Livsforsikrings-Aktieselskapet Norske Folk, renamed Norske Folk Livsog Pensjonsforsikring A/S in 1939 and in 1979 demutualized in a mutual society. The remutualization was triggered by the concerns of the Norwegian insurance council Forsikringsrådet. This council criticized the regulations of the new private limited company Act (Lov om aksjeselskaper) from July 4th, 1976 and the possible loss of the independence of the companies due to the new regulations. The new law required a two-thirds voting and capital majority for any kind of changes regarding the articles of societies. The council emphasised a strengthening of the mutual societies' position. In addition to Forsikringsrådet, politicians and the media advocated the remutualization, which was carried out on March 3rd, 1979. In 1987, the companies were renamed Norges Brannkasse in UNI Forsikring-Gjensidig Skadeforsikringsselskap and Norske Folk Gjensidig Livsforsikringsselskap in UNI Forsikring-Gjensidig Livforsikringsselskap. In 1990, both companies were demutualised and merged to Holding UNI Forsikring A/S. The transformation and merger process ended in 1991 when UNI Skadeforsikring A/S and Storebrand Skadeforsikring A/S merged as well as when UNI Livforsikring A/S merged with A/S Storebrand Livforsikring. These mergers created the foundation for today's enterprise Storebrand ASA.[65, 66, 67, 68]

In the sector of maritime insurances, private limited companies were mainly specialised in cargo and transport insurances, in contrast to mutual insurance companies, which offered hull insurances. The first two maritime private limited insurance companies Det Berge-

[65] Cf. Den Norske Forsinkringsforening-NKP.

[66] Cf. Den Norske Forsinkringsforening-Brage.

[67] Cf. Den Norske Forsinkringsforening-Norske Folk.

[68] Cf. Den Norske Forsinkringsforening-Samtrygd.

ske Søassuranceselskab and Christiania Søforsikringsselskab were founded in Bergen in 1845 and in Christiana in 1847. Bergenske Sø offered transport insurances for the route North-Norway to Bergen, usually for goods such as dry fish and cod liver oil. Generally, the merchants in Bergen used the same regulations that they knew from their trade with Hamburg. These regulations were based on the Hamburger "Assekurantz and Haverey-Ordnung" (1731), the "Allgemeinen Plan hamburgischer See-Versicherung" (1847), and the "Hamburg-Bedingungen" (1867). By 1870, several Swedish, German, Austrian, and Swiss companies could be found on the Norwegian market usually in form of agents. The good economic situation in the early 1870s led to the foundation of new companies, for example Poseidon in Christiania, Union in Bergen, and Allianz in Stavanger, all established in 1871. Other companies followed in Arendal and Trondheim. In 1875, 16 Norwegian private limited companies, specialised in maritime insurances, can be found in Norway as well as numerous agents of foreign companies. The crisis of the 1890s was very hard for both mutual insurance companies and private limited companies. Nine out of 15 insurance private limited companies left the market and after 1897 only six remained: Christiania Sø and Poseidon in Christiania, Æolus and Union in Bergen, and Stavanger Sø and Arendals Sø.[69] In 1895, the private limited companies founded an association of the Norwegian maritime insurance companies, the Norske Sjøforsikringsselskabers Forening, initiated by *Hans C. Stephensen* of Poseidon and *Harald Hougen* of Christiania Sø. Both men became the leading men of the association. At the turn of the century, another network was established: the Den Norske Forsikringsforenings Transportforsikringsgroup. This was the Norwegian insurance association of the transport insurance companies, which represented companies and general agents of foreign companies. This association was intended more for personal public relations than business activities.[70] In 1910, *Hougen* initiated a meeting with the directors of five insurance companies and with 47 insurance agents to establish a central organization for the maritime insurance branch. The idea was to connect this organization with governmental organizations, stock exchange, trade associations, ship-owners, and shipping company owners to protect the interests of the maritime insurance branch. One of the main goals of this organization was the introduction of binding prices and regulations for insurances, which should not lead to any restrictions regarding free competition. In the first general meeting on August 15th, 1911, Sjøassurandørernes Centralforening i Kristiania was established, which became known under the acronym CEFOR.[71] In

[69] Cf. *Cefor* (2011), p. 18, 24.

[70] Cf. ibid, p. 26.

[71] Cf. ibid, p. 28-30.

2011, this company celebrated its 100th anniversary. Its goal is still the strengthening and development of the basic concept of the Norwegian maritime insurance economy and the coordination and unification of its members. The members of the organization are working in comprehensive insurance, cargo, and war insurance as well as in P&I, energy, and offshore insurance branches. Today members belong to mutual insurance companies and private limited companies.[72]

Demutualization – Transfer of a mutual insurance company into a private limited company.

A demutualization initiates a change of the legal form of an insurance company from a mutual insurance company into a private limited company.[73] The reasons for demutualization are numerous and can include improving the capital procurement, consolidation as well as obtaining new channels of distribution. However, the transfer has also possible side effects, such as the loss of the mutuality principle or the loss of the company's control to shareholders due to a decreasing interest for the welfare of the members.[74] In 2010, a big demutualization happened in Norway, when Gjensidige Forsikring BA was changed into a public limited company. At first, all shares were transferred to Gjensidigestiftelsen. With the begin of the trade of the shares at the Oslo stock exchange on December 10th, 2010, 38.3 percent of the shares were issued to more than 50,000 shareholders, while 61.7 percent remained with the foundation.[75] With the stock market launch, Gjensidige Forsikring earned 1.66 billion US-Dollar.[76] The company justified its action for remaining the main part of the shares at the foundation with its steady ownership structure, the stable investments, and the better prediction of the business.[77] However, these are exactly the reasons, which were regarded as the disadvantages of demutualization. The annual report of 2014 shows that Gjensidigestiftelsen's share increased at 0.5 percent to 62.2, while the remaining 38.8 percent were distributed among 34.000 shareholders.[78] The company pointed out that the foundation works primarily on behalf of the insurance customers and gives the dividend directly to the customers.[79] However, the foundation was changed from a regular to a financial foundation due to demutualization. Moreover, the foundation's benefit to the public was emphasized. The reason was that Norwegian foundations were not subjected to

---

72 Cf. Cefor–About Cefor.

73 Cf. Gabler Wirtschaftslexikon – Demutualisierung.

74 Cf. *Auchinleck, Komar* and *Mühlbauer* (2002), pp. 455-458.

75 Cf. Gjensidige – Annual Report 2010, p 46.

76 Cf. *Moen* (2010).

77 Cf. Gjensidige – Annual Report 2010, p. 46

78 Cf. Gjensidige – Annual Report 2014, p. 21.

79 Cf. Gjensidige – Annual Report 2010, p. 46.

income taxes when they are classified as non-profit organizations.[80, 81] Therefore, the exact motivation of Gjensidige Forsikring ASA's ownership structure is still unclear.

3.2 History of mutual insurance companies

At the time when mutual insurance companies became common, Norway was a young nation with a still developing political structure while traditions, professions, and religion were rooted deeply in civic life. Rural parishes were more unified than towns. They had different economic roles and a clear defined hierarchical structure consisting of landowners, tenants, and unemployed workers. Farmers had great interests in fire insurance offers, because they were most important to protect their agricultural facilities and personal assets. Therefore, the insurance companies offered fire insurances in particular in rural areas, but also to some extend additional insurances such as livestock insurances. Fishery was either the sole or the additional income of small farms. Parishes specialised in seamanlike professions needed higher economic protections due to the professional and geographical mobility as well as the higher risks for life and equipment. With regard to fishery, ships and equipment were essential and exposed to higher risks. Therefore, this kind of insurance was more important than fire insurances for housing. Owners of merchant vessels insured their ships and cargo, while sailors insured their property. Members of agricultural and marine districts were well aware of the economic dependence of urban goods and services; therefore, they appreciated the offer of regional mutual insurance companies in two ways: to reduce the dependence on towns and to guarantee the consistency of mutual help. These were the main reasons that the founders of mutual insurance companies reinforced the general ideology of communal self-supply and, at the same time, fulfilled the specific needs of the most common professions in a parish.[82]

In rural areas, the regional mutual fire insurance companies dominated the market for fire insurances despite the competition of state supported unrestricted mutual fire insurance companies, which were more successful in towns. The reason was that mutual insurance companies in rural parishes evaluated their risks better regarding fire damage and included their members into their on-site organization. As a result, the position of public mutual insurance companies was weak with farmers. Moreover, farmers were unwilling to contribute to the

80 Cf. Gjensidige Foundation.
81 Cf. Gjems-Onstad.
82 Cf. *Greve* (2006), p. 11-12.

higher fire risks in towns. Due to these higher risks, the premiums of public mutual insurance companies were much higher. The rural constructions of buildings, i.e. buildings were separated from each other, helped to control the spread of fires in a better way and, therefore, to contain fire damage. Rural mutual fire insurance companies insisted that their members had fire extinguishers and purchased water pumps to compensate for absent fire stations in the less populated areas. The governmental-funded unrestricted mutual insurance companies insured only such buildings, which were either too large or too risky to be insured by regional mutual insurance companies.[83]

The foundation of insurance companies in Norway was modelled after the Danish companies. After the big fire in Copenhagen in 1728, the city administration recognized the necessity of an insurance system for real estate. With the fast growing urban centres, the possibility and the extent of fire damage increased immensely and accelerated the establishment of a new insurance system. The main goal of this system was eventually the financial covering of rebuilding. As a result, the first Danish Fire Insurance Act was passed in 1731 and the first mutual fire insurance company, Brand-Cassen i Kjøbenhavn, was established.[84, 85] Two decades later, the regulations from 1731 were used as a model for a similar law in Christiana, today is Oslo. Based on a recommendation of the Christiana's city council, the Danish-Norwegian King *Frederik V.* established on December 24th, 1753 the first Norwegian fire insurance Christianiæ Byes Brand Assurance Casse. The insurance was a voluntary, independent, and private organization and insured building owners in and around Christiana. Christianiæ Byes ended its service in 1827 and was dissolved in 1860.[86]

The fire protection insurance act (Brandforsikringsanordningen for alle købstæder i Danmark) for all Danish towns (except Copenhagen) by *Christian VII* (son of *Frederik V*) from January 13th, 1761 influenced the development of Norwegian mutual insurance companies, too. At the same time, the mutual fire insurance company Kjøbstædernes almindelige Brandforsikring was established and was obligatory for all building owners in all 67 Danish provincial towns.[87, 88] Due to the efficiency of this law, the government started considerations for a similar law in Norway. In 1762, the Danish Board of Trade sent a draft bill to the Norwegian municipal authorities and asked for their opinion. However, these bills were controversial. Some towns worried that fire insurances were too expensive and rejected the proposition, while others believed

83 Cf. Ibid, p. 8.
84 Cf. *Thomsen* (1999).
85 Cf. Den Norske Forsinkringsforening – Norges Brannkasse.
86 Cf. ibid.
87 Cf. Danmark Historien.
88 Cf. *Thomsen* (1999).

that Norway and Denmark should split the costs. However, the Danish Board of Trade was worried that the insurance in Denmark would be discredited due to a higher fire danger in Norwegian towns. As a result, they rejected the proposition. The big fire in 1764 in the Norwegian town Fredrikstad destroyed 73 out of 133 buildings. This event increased the general interest in a fire insurance code and accelerated the process of law making.[89] On August 18th, 1767, the King enacted the Brand-Forsikkrings-anordning I Særdeleshed for Kiøbstæderne i Norge for Norwegian towns, an act similar to the Danish law on fire protection insurance. All owners of public and private buildings in towns had to join and calculate the value of their property every ten years. The valuation as basis for the assessment in case of damage was used for the payment of contributions to the injured party proportional to the assets.[90] Experts, who were appointed by the city council, did the evaluation of the real estate. Joining the mutual insurance company De norske kjøbstæders almindelige Brandforsikring, established when the law was introduced, was obligatory. Only Christiana was excluded from this regulation.[91] In 1767, the King signed the Act Forordning, Angaaende Brand-Væsenet for Kiøbstæderne i Norge, which provided the fire brigade with equipment. However, it took a long time until they were fully equipped.

Between 1760 and 1770, the business community, in particular the sugar producers in Copenhagen, insisted on the protection of their trading stocks and production facilities through fire insurance companies. However, these companies refused to insure goods in transit despite their own maritime trade with Norway, other European countries, and the Danish trade relations with China, India, Africa, and the Caribbean. Eventually, the politicians recognized the necessity of this kind of insurance, probably because the minister of finance *Heinrich Carl von Schimmelmann* owned a sugar refinery. On May 11th, 1778, *Christian VII.* signed the act for the foundation of Det Kongelige Octroierede Kjøbenhavnske Brand-Assurance-Compagnie Paa Varrer og Effecter, a mutual fire company for products and trading goods. However, the bylaws of this society excluded trades working with combustible goods, such as blacksmiths, bakers, breweries, and distilleries.[92]

From 1779 on, the buildings in Christiana had to be insured. Owners who did not want to join the private Christianiæ Byes Brand Assurance Casse had to be insured by a public insurance company. Real estate in rural areas had not to be insured by their owners; nonetheless, owners of buildings in specific areas outside the towns had the possibility to

[89] Cf. Mot alminneling brannforsikring.

[90] Cf. Den Norske Forsinkringsforening – Norges Brannkasse.

[91] Cf. *Amnéus* (1900), p. 257.

[92] Cf. *Thomsen* (1999).

join. The idea was based on the mutuality principle and the members received annually the unused capital. This procedure was time consuming and troublesome, therefore, from 1786 on, the paid-in capital was withheld and a fund was established. The fire insurance company Den Almindelige Brand-Forsikrings-Anstalt in Copenhagen managed the administration for Denmark and Norway. After the personal union with Denmark ended, the Norwegian part of the Forsikrings-Anstalt was relocated to Christiana on November 30th, 1814, had to report to the ministry of finance, and renamed Den Almindelige Brandforsikrings-Indretning for Bygninger (Norges Brandkasse from 1912 on, and Norges Brannkasse from 1938 on). At March 13th, 1819, an insurance department under the direction of *Ambrosius Flor Hofgaard* and as a part of the ministry of finance was established. The administration was small and consisted of two secretaries and one cashier, who functioned as treasurer and accountant of the widow pension fund ("Witwenversorgungskasse"). In 1821, the ministry of finance decided that the contributions of the fire insurance for rural buildings had to be half of the contributions for urban buildings.[93] This decision was justified by fire hazard and enacted on January 1st, 1847 with Lov angående den Almindelige Brandforsikrings-Indretning for Bygninger, i.e. a fire insurance Act for buildings. This Act led to the liberation of the general insurance obligation in the Brannkasse, which dominate the Norwegian insurance market by 1847 and promoted the development of new insurance companies. After several years of discussion, Norwegian and foreign fire insurance companies established Den norske Brand-Tarifforening in 1876. The founders consisted of seven Norwegian and 16 foreign companies. The goal was to establish a common standard rate and terms of insurance to ease the increasing competition pressure. At the end of the 19th century, the competition policy was well-balanced between mutual insurance companies and private limited companies with regard to unrestricted building insurance. The main reason was that private limited companies usually did not offer building insurance, in particular in towns dominated by Brannkasse.[94]

The relations between the insurance companies differed in the shipping industry from fire insurance companies. Geographically (restricted) mutual insurance companies competed against unrestricted mutual insurance companies and private limited companies for the insurance of the economically important merchant vessels. Geographic-restricted mutual insurance companies dominated other market segments, such as the insurance of small ships. Private limited companies offering seafaring insurance avoided this market due to the high risks for small vessels. The best catch areas were in highly dangerous wa-

[93] Cf. Den Norske Forsinkringsforening – Norges Brannkasse.

[94] Cf. Den Norske Forsinkringsforening – Storebrand.

ters and the transport of the catch to the central collecting points was dangerous for the overloaded ships.[95] Denmark had great influence on the development of mutual insurance companies for both fire insurance and the shipping industry. Denmark had global trade relations in seafaring and, therefore, also a leading role in this insurance branch. The first Danish seafaring insurance company, Det Kongelig Octroierede Søassurance Kompagni, was established in Copenhagen on April 20th, 1726.[96] This company had a monopoly and the Norwegian ship owners were insured almost exclusively in Copenhagen up to the end of the union.[97] Nonetheless, some insurance companies were established in Norway: For example on February 7th, 1806 the seafaring mutual insurance company Oxefiordens Gjensidige Søsassuranceforening was established on the island Borøya. The company had at first 29 founding members and by the end of the year, the number increased to 42. The company covered in the event of a total loss 4/5 of the insurance sum and half of the repair costs for a damage up to 1/6 of the value. However, in August 1807 the insurance ended its service due to the war of Denmark and Norway with Napoleon against England.[98] Due to the war, a new insurance branch developed between 1808 and 1814 to cover war damage. For example, in 1808, the private company Det Norske Sø-Assuranceselskab was established to uphold the corn transports between Denmark and Norway.[99]

In 1814, after the end of the war, the British market was blocked for timber trade via prohibitive tariff, which led to a limited market for the Norwegian trading houses. Although France became a new buyer market, the fleet had to be reduced. The turning point was 1826 when Norwegian ships were allowed to transport timber from Danish ports. The Swedish license opened the access to larger markets. The new timber trade in the Baltic Sea was the foundation for a prosperous seafaring community. It became a new and thriving industry and more than an additional income of export sales. The upswing of seafaring led, on a regional level, to an increasing demand for simple, low priced, and transparent insurance policies in the transport industry. In 1837, two mutual seafaring companies were established. In the two strongholds of seafaring Langesund Fjord, including Brevik, Skien, and Porsgrunn, and Arendal the companies Langesundsfjordens Assuranceforening and Skibsassuranceforeningen i Arendal were established. The latter had the largest fleet in the country during those days. Local ship owners within each seafaring community founded both companies. Most of

95 Cf. *Greve* (2006), pp. 8-9.

96 Cf. *Thomsen* (1999).

97 Cf. *Amnéus* (1900), p. 258.

98 Cf. Cefor (2011), p. 13.

99 Cf. Den Norske Forsikringsforening – Krigsforsikringen.

the decisions were made during general meetings and directed by the board of administration as well as by the committees responsible for the classification and evaluation of the tonnage. The guidelines of the companies made the control easy and provided a high degree of transparency between the members. Langesundsfjordens Assuranceforening was renamed Første Norske Assuranceforening (First Norwegian underwriting association) and the insurance period was changed into a twelve-month interval. The periods comprised then trading hours, between February 15th and September 30th, and closedown hours, between November 1st and January 31st in which the ships were in the Fjord of Langesund. It was possible to trade during the winter season but additional and higher premiums had to be paid. Skibsassuranceforening i Arendal changed its name several times, first to Den Vestsøndenfjeldske Skibsassuranceforening later to Skibsassuranceforeningen i Arendal and finally to Dampskibsassuranceforeningen i Arendal. While Første Norske admitted soon owners from outside the local community, Arendals kept its strict admission policy and only allowed owners to become members who lived in the region of the south coast. Both mutual insurance companies insured total loss, grounding, collision, and repairs up to 40 percent of the value of the vessel. Numerous companies were established soon after the first two mutual insurance companies were founded and in 1860, the entire Norwegian fleet was insured by mutual insurance societies. From the end of the 1860s onwards, foreign insurance companies entered the Norwegian insurance market with the help of insurance agents. While the market still grew, mutual insurance companies kept their main insurance business, but came under pressure by foreign competitors in other insurance branches such as cargo insurances. Most of the mutual insurance companies achieved considerable profits with the exception of two large catastrophes, which led to serious losses. The first happened in 1867 when dozens of vessels disappeared in the White Sea, and the second when a hurricane destroyed hundreds of vessel in the Baltic Seas in November 1872.[100]

From the start on mutual insurance companies had their own committees which evaluated and classified the vessels into insurance classes. For this purpose, they created and used their own quality criteria and classification systems. However, standardised classifications and common structure, created by experts, were introduced and became very soon the norm. In particular, the reinsurance branch needed a compatible classification system. By 1850, common regulations for trading vessels were introduced and in 1859, standardised building codes were established. On June 15th, 1864, Det Norske Veritas (DNV) Første was established as the official classification company in Christiania by the insurance companies Norske, Drammen, Bergens, Agder, Vestfold-

[100] Cf. Cefor (2011), p. 14, 18-19.

ske, and Det Norske Lloyd. Some of the important mutual insurance companies, such as Arendals, Fjære Sogn, Egersund and Stavanger, refused to participate at first, because DNV included vessels with steam engines into their insurance offers. The problem was that companies did not have sufficient experience with steam engines and the machines did not work reliably yet. Therefore, frequent damage and high losses were the results. Only after the DNV had published its building regulations for steam engines, more mutual insurance companies jointed the association. Another result was that new mutual insurance companies were founded, which specialised in steam-ships. In 1879, the two mutual insurance companies Dampskibsassuranceforeningen Nora and Bergens Dampskibsassuranceforeningen were established. All new vessels registered in the DNV had to be built according to the imposed regulations and assessed regularly. From 1871 on, the DNV certificates were acknowledged internationally and in 1884, the DNV became the legitimate successor of the seafaring insurance companies. At this time, the organization comprised 16 mutual insurance companies and seven private limited companies.[101, 102] On December 12th, 2013, the foundation DNV merged with Germanischer Lloyd SE in Hamburg to the DNV GL Group.[103]

Already in 1869, the idea of unified and general applicable insurance regulations in seafaring emerged, because by this time each company had its own rules. These regulations were based on the Hamburg principles of 1852 and under the patronage of the DNV. In 1871, the Norwegian marine insurance plan #8Norsk Sjøforsikringsplan) was passed. It was a codification of the pertinent laws and usual methods and became the pertinent basis of the Norwegian marine insurance. Within a short time, the Norsk Sjøforsikringsplan was a good addition for insurance companies on the international insurance market, because it was formulated in a less complicated way and easier to apply than regulations from other companies.[104]

From 1885 onwards, the insurance branch decreased economically. The cause of the crisis was the diminishing value of vessels as well as the excessive use of loss-sharing agreements that led to the financial collapse of the seafaring towns Arendal and Stavanger. Nevertheless, damage was a profitable business for some owners in a market with decreasing values such as in the middle of the 1880s, because at that time the compensation was usually substantially higher than the market value of a ship. For the insurer, however, increasing compensations of higher damage led to increased losses and to diminished profit

[101] Cf. Ibid, pp. 19-20.

[102] Cf. DNV GL.

[103] Cf. Börse Frankfurt (2013).

[104] Cf. ibid.

margin. The pool of insured vessels diminished and new entrants were usually used vessels. This development led to a further increase of insurance claims. This had an immediate effect on unrestricted insurers and therefore on mutual insurance companies. Several companies had financial problems that led to additional high premiums. After a brief upswing in 1889/90, the market crashed again. The crisis was of a structural nature and a large part of the traditional Norwegian sailing shipping communities vanished. The insurer had more and more difficulties to handle steam-engine vessels and sailing ships, even in separated business areas, because the industrial change from wooden sailing ships to iron steam vessels generated too many conflicts of interests. The crisis led to the dissolution of six companies and eventually to a union of several mutual insurance companies. The only positive aspect of this development was that the increase of steam vessels as insured objects generated half of the premium income in 1895. The larger part of the Norwegian steam ship fleet comprised smaller ships limited to the European trade. In the late 1880s, a specialised business sector developed by the mediation of ship agents. Norwegian steam ships established a strong position in trading bananas from Central America and the Caribbean to the United States. Inspired by this developed many ship owners from the Norwegian South Coast bought used iron and steel ships from British, German, and French merchants at attractive prices. Between 1898 and 1913, more than 550 ships were transferred in this way and eventually proved to be profitable investments. This new kind of trade opened new opportunities, in particular regarding transport insurances. Most ship owners at this time had established their business near large ports, such as Oslo, which decreased the importance of local and traditional mutual insurance companies. The new requirements regarding insurance protection led in 1897 and 1907 to the foundation of the Norwegian P&I Clubs (Protection and Indemnity) Skuld and Gard, based on mutuality.[105]

With the outbreak of World War I in 1914, it became evident that the major part of the Norwegian merchant fleet was not insured against war risks.[106] However, for Norway as maritime nation, which depended completely on imports/exports via the sea routes, it became crucial to have a reliable war insurance. On August 11th, 1914, the government convened a committee, including *J. Ludwig Mowinckel*, an important shipping company owner and member of the Norwegian Parliament, to find a solution for this problem. While the association of the Norwegian shipping company owners favoured voluntary membership, the committee around *Mowinckel* decided an obligatory membership of all Norwegian vessels participating in international trade. The more prominent

---

[105] Cf. Cefor (2011), pp. 21-24, 26.

[106] Cf. Norwegian Hull Club.

mutual insurance companies and the government promised temporary profit but without governmental liability. The plan was confirmed politically on August 21st, 1914 and the Krigsforsikringen for Norske Skib, the Norwegian war insurance company for shipping owners, was established.[107] The company was dissolved in 1923, but on October 30th, 1935 a new mutual insurance company, Den Norske Krigsforsikring for Skib, Gjensidig Forening, was founded due to political conflicts.[108]

After the end of World War I, the number of prominent mutual seafaring companies decreased from 16 to eight in particular due to the financial crisis of the 1920s. Some of the mutual insurance companies were dissolved, others were transferred to large societies, or new societies were established by merger. The remaining eight companies were Bergens Assuranceforening, Bergens Dampskibsassuranceforening, Christianssands Dampskibsassuranceforening, Dampskibsassuranceforeningen i Arendal, Dampskibsassuranceforeningen Nora, Skibsassuranceforeningen i Christiania, Dampskibsassuranceforeningen Skjold and Dampskibsassuranceforeningen Vidar.[109] The fierce competition between Norwegian and foreign insurers led to even more mergers, in particular after the end of World War II. The mutual insurance companies were not prepared for international competition, because of their small size and large number on the market. In the 1950s, the number of mutual insurance companies decreased to seven. In the 1960s, only four seafaring mutual insurance companies existed (Arendal & Christiania, Bergen Skibs, Christianssand, and Unitas), in particular due to US competition. This competition also led to a reduction of premiums and the start of individual pricing based on accident analysis and statistics. The discovery of North Sea oil in Norway in 1967 resulted in an economic upswing during the first years of the 1970s. The business expansion due to oil tankers resulted in strong economic years for mutual insurance companies. For example, Bergen Hull Club doubled its insurance policies between 1970 and 1973. The increase of the oil price and the following oil crisis in 1973 struck the seafaring industry hard. By 1977, the economy, in particular the seafaring industry, had bounced back to their numbers before the crisis. By the turn of the millennium, Unitas had taken over Christianssand (1996) and merged with Bergen Skibs to Norwegian Hull Club in 2001.[110]

---

[107] Cf. Cefor (2011), p. 33.

[108] Cf. DNK

[109] Cf. Cefor (2011), pp. 37-38.

[110] Cf. Norwegian Hull Club.

3.3 Empirical data for the historical analysis of the insurance industry

The analysis of the historical development of the Norwegian insurance business shows that in the beginning it was influenced strongly by Denmark and later by Sweden. The development is evident in both the first laws as well as in the foundation of the first insurance companies. However, this does not surprise when one considers the political implications. Nevertheless, Norwegian's own dynamism contributed to the increasing number of insurance companies.

Figure 1: The number of insurance companies and savings banks in Norway between 1820 and 1940[111]

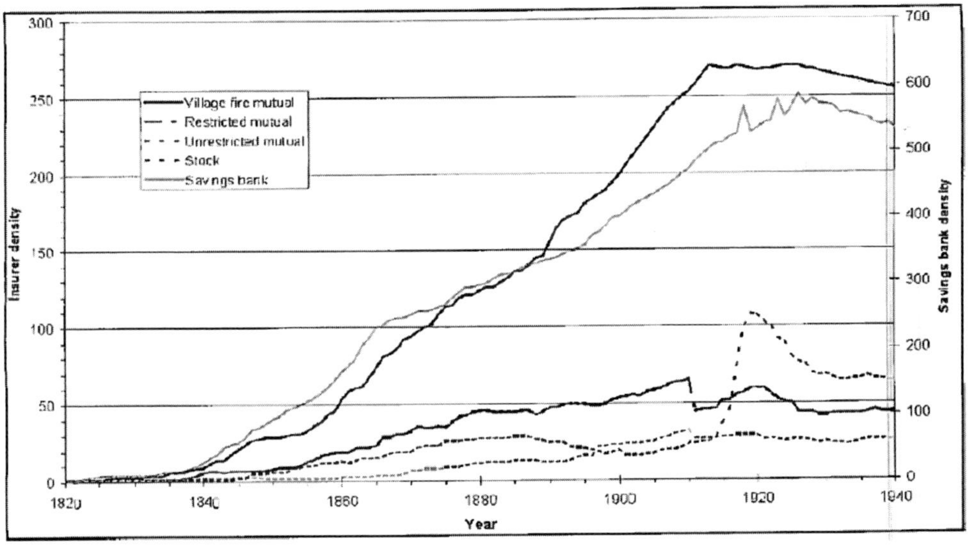

The foundation of new mutual fire companies benefitted from the act regarding fire insurances for buildings from January 1st, 1847. From the second half of the 1840s onwards, more mutual village fire companies were established and by 1900, 200 societies existed. Figure 1 presents this development. Table 1 shows a more detailed picture for the second half of the 19th century by presenting the number of mutual fire companies divided into administrative districts. In some districts,

[111] Cf. *Greve* (2006), p. 48.

the number of mutual fire companies is much higher compared to others due to several factors, e.g. in Sør and Nord Trøndelag, Rogaland and Møre og Romsdal. The geographic size, the number of communities as well as the development, concentration, and composition of the population in each district have to be evaluated. An analysis of selected factors can be found in chapter VI.

Table 1: The number of mutual fire companies according to Norwegian administrative districts between 1845 and 1895[112]

	1845	1850	1855	1860	1865	1875	1880	1885	1890	1895
Ostfold						3	4	6	7	6
Akershus	1					1	1	4	7	6
Hedmark	2	2	5	6	7	9	12	12	12	12
Oppland	3	4	4	6	12	14	14	13	13	16
Buskerud				3	3	4	4	3	6	7
Vestfold			1	1	1	2	2	2	1	1
Telemark						3	5	4	4	4
Aust-Agder						3	3	3	2	4
Vest-Agder					1	7	8	7	8	15
Rogaland			1	5	9	12	14	17	18	21
Hordaland				1	3	9	9	9	10	10
Sogn og Fiordane					1	4	4	4	4	11
Mare og Romsdal	2	3	3	11	12	12	16	17	19	18
SOr TrOndelag	5	8	8	9	8	11	13	16	21	23
Nord TrOndelag	12	12	11	14	14	15	16	19	20	18
Nordland										
Troms				1	1	1	1	1	1	1
Finnmark										
Sum	25	29	33	57	72	110	126	137	153	173

Similar and additional factors of influence can also be found regarding the development of mutual seafaring companies, which are usually organized as restricted societies.[113] Although Table 1 shows a drop between 1910 and 1915, this development cannot be related entirely to the mutual seafaring companies. At first, it seemed that the seafaring industry had profited from the supply deficit during the war, however, from 1915 on this led to inflation, which marked the beginning of the

[112] Adapted by *Espeli* (2001), p. 52.

[113] Cf. *Greve* (2006), p. 8.

financial crisis of the next decade. The Norwegian ship owners worked an active buying strategy of used ships from the Netherlands, the USA, and even China. This led to increased prices and monetary surpluses that increased the inflation even more. While a steam ship of 1.8 tons had a value of 350,000 NOK in 1914, the value increased by 1917 to two million NOK.[114] This meant higher premiums for higher values but at the same time in the event of damage higher insurance benefits. In times of increasing inflation, this led to economic problems, in particular when the premiums were paid in times with low inflation rates and the insurer had to compensate the damage in times with a higher inflation rate. This became reality in fall of 1916 when Germany expanded its war efforts to submarines and destroyed 1,169 Norwegian vessels by the end of the war. In addition to the war losses and the difficult economy, the Norwegian mutual insurance companies had to deal with the competition by foreign seafaring insurer. This new competition influenced the market share of the Norwegian seafaring societies that had decreased since the beginning of the 20th century. While they handled 90 percent of the tonnage in 1900, their share dropped to 45 percent by 1914, and decreased further to 17.5 percent by 1922. This development resulted in dissolutions, take-overs, and mergers and eventually in the mid 1920s only eight prominent mutual seafaring insurances had existed anymore.[115] When looking at Figure 1, the curve of restricted mutual insurances differs from the events after 1910, in particular when equating the curve to mutual seafaring companies. Therefore, it is not clear what data was included for representing restricted mutual insurance companies in Figure 1.

Figure 1 shows an abrupt rise of private limited companies between 1915 and 1920, followed by a sharp drop. In the belligerent countries, the prices increased rapidly between 1914 and 1918 caused by high demands and few offers. This also influenced neutral countries such as Norway. After World War I, a short economic upswing, caused by low prices, had a positive economic effect on neutral countries between 1919 and 1920. The inflation increased with different intensity in the various countries during 1919. In the mid 1920s, the upswing gave way to a downswing and this resulted in a collapse of the European banking sector. Norway was hit very hard due to a tough deflation policy to stabilise the currency and to introduce the gold standard.[116] As a result, the insurance companies were reconstructed via bankruptcies, voluntary dissolutions, or controlled mergers. While 234 private insurance companies were registered in 1920, the number decreased to 178

114 Cf. Cefor (2011), p. 34.

115 Cf. Cefor (2011), pp. 37-38.

116 Cf. *Feinstein* et al. (2008), pp. 39-46.

by 1940 and further to 131 by 1960.[117] Figure 2 presents the number of compensation insurance companies between 1914 and 1960 (Aksjeselskaper: private limited companies, Gjensidige selskaper: mutual insurance companies, Utenladske: foreign companies). However, the high number of foreign companies should be interpreted with caution, because most of these companies were very small and had no strong position in the Norwegian insurance sector. While they earned only 20 percent of the total premiums in 1914, their share decreased to fewer than 5 percent by 1960.[118]

Figure 2: The number of compensation insurance companies between 1914 and 1960 in Norway[119]

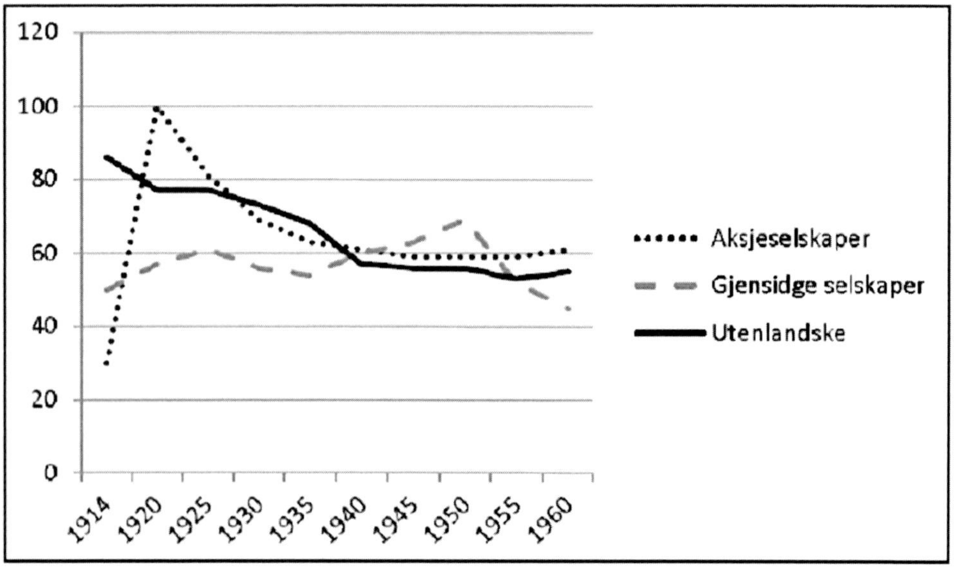

Figure 2 indicates that the absolute number of companies is not a suitable parameter to make a reliable statement regarding the success of a legal form, i.e. of a private limited company or a mutual company. To present a more comprehensive picture concerning the number of insurance companies, Table 2 and Figure 3 give a more detailed picture of the development of insurance companies between 1996 and 2016.

[117] Cf. *Ekberg* (2013), p. 3.

[118] Cf. ibid, p. 3.

[119] *Ekberg* (2013), p. 3.

Table 2: The number of insurance companies in selected insurance branches between 1996 and 2016 in Norway[120]

	1996	1997	1998	1999	2000	2001	2002	2003	2004	2005	2006	2007	2008	2009	2010	2011	2012	2013	2014	2015	2016
Life insurers	9	10	10	9	8	8	7	7	6	6	9	10	11	12	12	12	12	12	13	13	13
Non-life insurers, incl. local fire insurance associations	91	92	90	73	73	73	72	66	67	66	64	64	65	65	64	62	62	59	59	59	60
Local marine insurance associations	19	18	15	15	14	14	14	13	13	13	13	13	13	13	13	13	12	11	10	9	6
Norwegian insurer's branches abroad[1]	x	x	x	x	x	x	x	x	x	x	x	x	9	11	5	12	16	15	15	13	13
Foreign insurers' branches in Norway	18	13	17	21	29	29	29	39	30	39	41	46	37	41	43	37	36	34	31	32	29
Insurance intermediaries	44	40	41	41	44	49	50	50	49	56	73	91	103	97	98	99	96	97	102	102	107
Private pension funds	136	136	144	132	130	122	120	107	93	93	91	86	81	76	66	63	56	51	52	48	49
Municipal pension funds	31	29	28	26	30	29	29	30	31	29	28	29	30	31	31	32	32	33	38	39	39
Pension funds	114	104	96	84	80	70	65	50	30	22	19	17	15	9	8	7	5	5	4	4	4

[1] no statistical data before 2008 available

[120] Description is based on Finanstilsynet – Annual Reports 2000-2017.

Figure 3: Overview on life insurers, non-life insurers, and local marine insurance associations between 1996 and 2016[121]

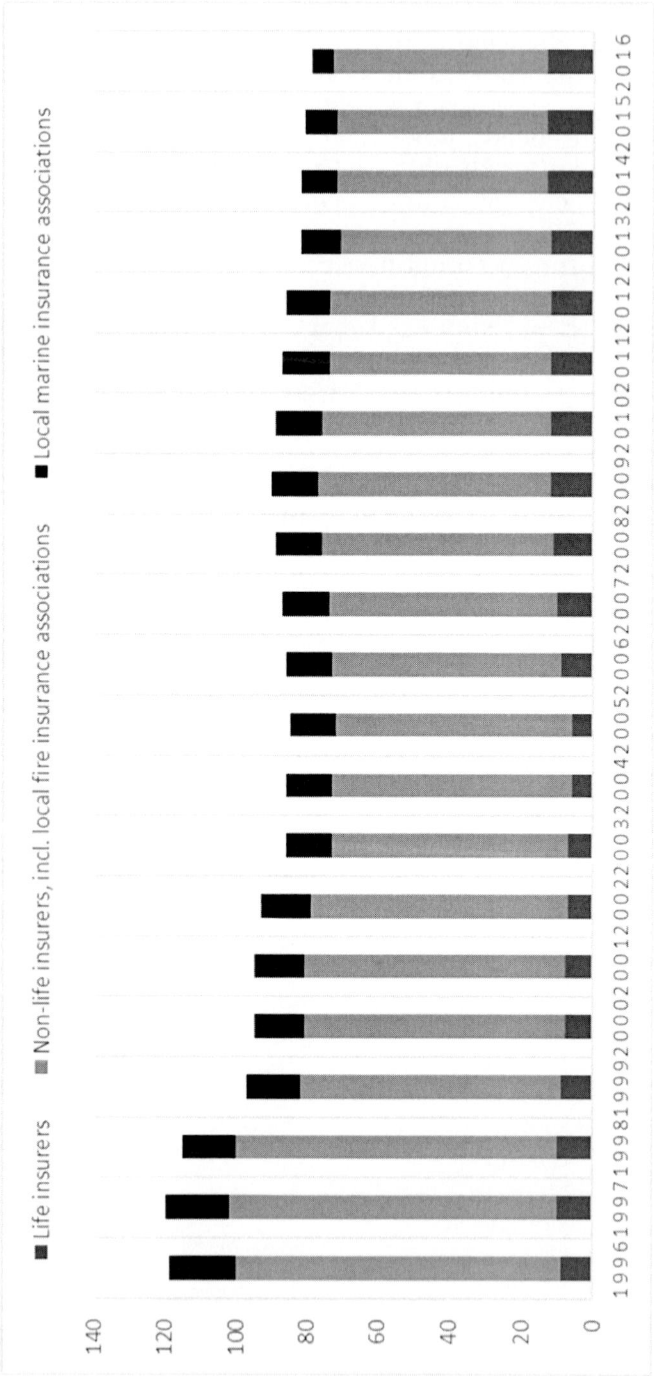

[121] Description is based on Finanstilsynet – Annual Reports 2000-2017

Interim conclusion

The analysis of the Norwegian insurance business shows a dynamic historical development. Many diverse insurers were confronted with several new start-ups, dissolutions, take-overs, or mergers. The insurance market was influenced by political and economic events, such as crises, wars, legislation, or threats due to foreign competitors as well as technical progress, e.g. the change from sailing ships to steamboats. These developments and events influenced both mutual insurance companies and private limited companies. Nonetheless, both legal forms were able to remain on the market. Another justification of both legal forms is provided by the coexistence theory, which will be explained further in chapter VI. With a theoretical point of view, the choice of legal forms by the insurance company is restricted. The insurance economics regards social insurances as organizing institution of cooperatives (accident insurance), private-law companies (company health insurance) or statuary bodies, which are established by a state of act.[122] Additionally, private, individual or market insurances (all three terms should be used as synonyms) are defined as private limited companies, mutual insurance companies or public law insurance corporations.[123] Other legal forms, such as a limited liability company, cannot guarantee the insurance company's obligation to pay contractual claims.[124]

122 Cf. *Schulenburg* (2005), p. 13.

123 Cf. Gabler Wirtschaftslexikon – öffentlich-rechtliche Versicherungsunternehmen.

124 Cf. *Schulenburg* (2005), p. 13.

4. The Norwegian legal foundation for insurance companies

In Norway, the legislation is performed by parliament (*Storting*) and supervised by the Ministry of Finances (*Finanstilsynet*). Insurance business can only be carried out by insurance undertakings and pension funds that are licensed under the Financial Institutions Act 2015 (*Lov om finansforetak og finanskonsern*), which entered into force on 1st January 2016, transposes the main elements of Solvency II into Norwegian law. The 2015 Act has special provisions in relation to mutual insurance undertakings regarding their articles of association (Section 7-8), the liability of members (Section 11-3), winding up (Section 12-8(4)) and the establishment of financial groups (Section 17-4).[125]

Insurance undertakings in Norway can be organised as:[126]

- public limited companies (*allmennaksjeselskap*),
- private limited companies (*aksjeselskap*),
- mutual companies (*gjensidig forsikringsselskap*),
- pension funds (*pensjonskasse*).

The legislation of mutual insurance companies can be found in Lov om forsikringsselskaper, pensjonsforetak og deres virksomhet mv. (forsikringsvirksomhetsloven)[127], i.e. Act on insurance companies, pension undertakings and their activities (Insurance Act).[128] It came into effect on July 1st, 2006 and replaced Act No. 39 from June 10th, 1988 regarding insurance activities.[129] [130] Other legal provisions are not obligatory for mutual insurance companies if not stated otherwise in the Insurance Act. Cooperative insurance is not legally foreseen in Norway.

---

[125] Act on financial institutions and financial groups 2015 (Financial Institutions Act 2015) 10 April 2015, No. 40.

[126] Cf. ICMIF (2018): Facts and figures – Mutual and cooperative insurance in Europe, AMICE aisbl & ICMIF, Vol 2, p. 144.

[127] Cf. Lov om forsikringsselskaper, pensjonsforetak og deres virksomhet mv. (forsikringsvirk somhetsloven)-2005-06-10-44.

[128] Cf. *Broek* et al. (2012a), p. 62.

[129] Cf. Finanstilsynet (1988).

[130] Cf. Finanstilsynet (2013), p. 54, § 17-1 and IA: (Lov-2005-06-10-44).

4.1 Regulations of the Norwegian Act on insurance companies (Act on insurance companies, pension undertakings and their activities etc.)

Part I – General provisions

Chapter 1 General provisions for insurance companies

The general provisions for insurance companies can be found in chapter 1 §§ 1-1. The introductive regulations § 1-2 define that insurance activities may only be engaged in by insurance companies and pension funds. The insurance classes are separate according §§ 1-3 into four insurance classes: life insurance, non-life insurance, credit insurance and reinsurance. Finanstilsynet shall decide in cases of doubt whether a class of insurance may or must be provided by life insurance, non-life insurance or credit insurance companies. Companies offering a specific insurance branch are not allowed to pursue another insurance branch without the approval of the Finanstilsynet. Reinsurance companies may only write reinsurance. Other articles of the first section comprise general provisions regarding pension funds, duty of confidentiality of employees in the insurance business, and the territorial extent of Norwegian insurance companies, a topic that will not be discussed here any further.

Part II – Insurance companies

The second part discusses in chapters 2 to 6 insurance companies in a more detailed way.

Chapter 2 – Licensing requirement

§§ 2-1 et seqq. comprises the provisions regarding the licensing requirements of insurance companies. According to § 2-1, no insurance company may carry on business without a licence from the King, who may set conditions for the licence. An insurance company shall have its registered office and head office in Norway. A licence shall be refused if any board member, the managing director or other person effectively in charge of the company

- is not presumed to have the necessary experience to discharge the position or office,
- has been convicted of a criminal offence, and the offence gives cause to presume that the person concerned will not be able to fulfil the position or office in a proper manner, or
- in his position or in his performance of other offices has demonstrated such behaviour as to give cause to presume that the person will not be able to discharge the post or office in a proper manner.

A licence shall otherwise be granted unless there is cause to presume

- that the company will not fulfil the requirements laid down in or pursuant to law,
- that the start-up capital is not in reasonable proportion to the planned activity, or
- that the granting of a licence will otherwise have detrimental effects for the policyholders or groups of policyholders.

A licence shall be granted for one or more classes of insurance, or for part of a class. In the case of insurance companies engaged in direct insurance business, a licence shall be granted for specified insurance classes. The licence may be limited to a specific geographic area, to specific customer groups or by other means.
The licensing requirement under this section does not apply to companies whose head office is in another state in the European Economic Area. (EEA). The following provisions (§§ 14 et seqq.) apply to the business activities of foreign insurance companies:
According to § 2-2, the King may revoke a licence or parts of it if

- the board of directors or other bodies of the insurance company are guilty of gross or repeated violation of their duties pursuant to law, regulations laid down pursuant to law,
- irregularities are present in the company's management, or other circumstances which give cause to fear conditions as mentioned in § 2-1 second subsection (a) and (c),
- the insurance company no longer has an adequate financial basis, or
- the insurance company no longer carries on active business in the class of insurance concerned.

The insurance company has to submit an operations plan for the company's first three years of operation (according to § 2-3 first subsection) to receive an insurance licence (according to § 2-1). The operations plan shall contain

- an overview of the insurances to be offered by the company,
- details of the company's capital,
- a budget for establishment and administration expenses,
- details of the principles to be applied for calculating premiums,
- details of the plan regarding reinsurance arrangements, and
- a forecast of financial position after three years' operation.

Additionally, the application shall be accompanied by the company's articles of association (according to § 2-3 second subsection), a certified copy of the company's memorandum of association and a certified copy of the minutes of the first general meeting.

Chapter 3 – General rules of company law

§ 3-1 states the permissible legal forms of business organization in Norway. They must be organized as private limited insurance companies, public limited insurance companies or mutual insurance companies. Except where otherwise provided in or pursuant to this Act, the rules of the Private Limited Companies Act and the Public Limited Companies Act respectively apply to private limited insurance companies and public limited insurance companies. According to § 3-1 third subsection, except where otherwise provided in or pursuant to this Act, the Private Limited Companies Act does not apply to mutual insurance companies. According to § 3-2, an insurance company's articles of association shall be approved by the King and may not be amended without the King's approval. § 3-3 states that an insurance company shall be registered with the Register of Business Enterprises no later than six months after the granting of a licence. The registrar shall verify that the company is licensed to carry on business pursuant to § 2-1, and that its articles of association are approved pursuant to § 3-2. § 3-3 third subsection refers furthermore to the application of § 2-20 of the company law for private limited insurance companies[131] to mutual insurance companies. The article comprises the rights and duties of mutual insurance companies before the registration into the Register of Business Enterprises. According to § 2-20 first subsection for private limited insurance companies, an unregistered company cannot claim rights concerning a third party or incur a liability stated in the bylaws or the articles of incorporation. In the event liabilities were incurred in the name of an unregistered company, the person or persons responsible for such actions are liable according to § 2-20 second subsection if not agreed on otherwise with the creditor. It is assumed that after the company's registration the liability is transferred automatically to the company. If an agreement has been made before the registration, it is not obligatory according to § 2-20 first subsection. The opposing party can disregard this agreement when either the company was not registered within three months since signing the articles of incorporation or the bylaws, or the registration was declined during this period. It is important to note that when the opposing party was not aware of the fact that the company was not registered, then the contract can be recanted until the company is registered. This provision can be abolished by an agreement between creditors and the company.

[131] Cf. Lov om aksjeselskaper-1997-06-13-44.

Chapter 4 – Company law rules applying specifically to mutual insurance companies

Chapter 4 comprises special company law provisions applying to mutual insurance companies, defined in §§ 4-1 to 4-10.

§ 4-1 Formation

According to § 4-1, a mutual insurance company may be formed by one or more founders. The founders shall draw up, date and sign a document containing draft articles of association and provisions of § 4-4. Additionally, at least half of the founders shall be resident in Norway and shall have lived here for the past two years, unless the King makes an exception in the individual case (§ 4-1 second subsection). The provision of the first sentence does not apply to citizens of states which are party to the European Economy Area (EEA) Agreement when they are resident in such a state. The regulation also does not apply to a legal entity founded by the legislation of a European Union (EU) member state or of a European Free Trade Association (EFTA) state, and whose registered office (as provided by its articles of association), main administration or main undertaking is within the territory of an EU or EFTA state. The state and Norwegian districts as well as Norwegian limited liability companies, cooperatives, associations, and foundations are equal under the law with a person with Norwegian residence.

§ 4-2 Guarantee fund

This Article was repealed by Lov om endringer i finansieringsvirksomhetsloven og enkelte andre lover (kapital- og organisasjonsformer i sparebanksektoren mv.)[132] – Law for the change of the Act about financial institutes and other laws (capital and organization forms in the saving banks sector) on June 19th, 2009. Chapter 4 § 4-2 of the Act No. 39 from June 10, 1988 regulates the guarantee fund. The guarantee can be a subordinate loan. A limited liability company, a private limited company, which was founded for this reason, another company, or another party, can grant this financial credit.[133]

§ 4-3 Articles of association

The articles of association of a Norwegian mutual insurance company are regulated in § 4-3 in connection with § 5-1 of the company law as well as in § 2-2 of the company law for private limited companies. The articles of association have to include

[132] Cf. Lov om endringer i finansieringsvirksomhetsloven og enkelte andre lover-2009-06-19-46.

[133] Cf. Finanstilsynet (1988), p. 9, § 4-2.

- the items specified in the Private Limited Companies Act § 2-2 first subsection nos. 1, 2, 3, 6 and 7.[134] The articles of association have to include the name (no. 1), the parish where the company has its main office (no. 2), and the area of business activities (no. 3),[135]
- the rules for membership, composition of the general meeting and voting rights at the general meeting,
- the number of insurance contracts and the total amount of insurance that needs to be written in order for the company to commence operations,
- the rules for the members' mutual liability,
- the rules for dissolving the company,
- the rules for application of the annual profit and for covering any deficit,
- the rules for when the general meeting shall be held,
- the rules for who shall convene the general meeting, and how this shall be done.

According to § 5-1 subsection 1, an insurance company shall have a board of directors of at least three members. The employees of the company shall be represented on the board of directors. The King may make further provision in this respect. A majority of the board of directors shall be persons who are not employed by the company or by companies in the same group. The chairperson shall be appointed from among this majority. The articles of association shall contain rules concerning alternates. The board of directors shall be elected by the supervisory board. If the company does not have a supervisory board, the board of directors shall be elected by the general meeting. The right of the supervisory board or the general meeting to elect may be transferred by the articles of association to others, but not to the board of directors or its members.

§ 4-4 Memorandum of association

According to § 4-4, the memorandum of association shall in addition state

- the types of insurances,
- when the statutory meeting must be held in order for writing of insurance contracts to be binding on the members,
- the size of the guarantee fund, if any,
- what portion of the guarantee fund shall, in the event, be paid up immediately and the rules for the guaranteeing company's obligation to make further payments to the guarantee fund,
- the rules for payment of interest on and repayment of the guarantee fund, if any,

[134] Cf. Lov om aksjeselskaper-1997-06-13-44.

[135] No. 6 and 7 are not included in the current version of the Act for private limited companies.

- rules, if any, to the effect that the guaranteeing company shall be entitled to exert influence on or oversee the insurance company,
- who shall pay the expenses of formation, and, in the event, remuneration to persons for work done in connection with the formation.

Provisions not set forth in the memorandum of association may not be invoked against the company.

§ 4-5 Invitation to take out insurance

According to § 4-5, the provision on the licensing requirement (§ 2-1) shall not prevent the enrolment of members where such enrolment is for forming a mutual insurance company. The company shall incur no insurance liability, nor may premiums be collected, until the company is duly registered.

§ 4-6 Notice of the statutory meeting

The founders shall summon the members to the statutory meeting which shall be held no later than six months after the memorandum of association has been signed. If this time-limit is exceeded, enrolment shall not be binding (§ 4-6).

§ 4-7 Statutory meeting

The decision to form the company shall be taken at the statutory meeting (§ 4-7). The enrolment list shall be made available to the enrolled members for at least one week before the statutory meeting at a location stated in the notice of the meeting. At the statutory meeting the founders shall present the memorandum of association and the list of enrolled members.

If the number of insurances and the amount of insurance written fall short of what is required by the memorandum of association, a decision to form the company may not be taken. In that case, the amounts that have been paid in shall be refunded without delay.

Before a decision to form the mutual insurance company can be taken, the statutory meeting shall have considered and decided any proposal that may have been put forward to amend the articles of association or the memorandum of association. The statutory meeting may nonetheless not adopt a decision that conflicts with the memorandum of association in cases as mentioned in § 4-3 b, c, d, and e as well as § 4-4 a, c, d, and e. A proposal to form the company is deemed to be adopted when it is supported by a majority of the votes cast and by at least two-thirds of the capital represented at the statutory meeting. In the absence of such majority, formation of the company cannot take place.

Once the company is formed, the general meeting shall appoint a control committee and, where required, a supervisory board or board of directors.

§ 4-8 Apportionment of profits and losses

Except where otherwise provided in the articles of association, profits and losses shall be apportioned on persons who were members in the same accounting period, in proportion to an estimated prepaid premium.

The articles of association of a life insurance company may provide that the members shall not be liable for the company's liabilities, but that losses shall instead be apportioned by means of a pro rata reduction of insurance claims.

§ 4-9 Liability towards third parties

Members' liability for a company's liabilities may only be invoked by the company. The company's claim for contributions from the members when apportioning losses may not be transferred, pledged as security or distrained on for debt.

§ 4-10 Cooperation

According to § 4-10, mutual insurance companies may by means of cooperation agreements form group entities based on common company bodies established in articles of association, and the articles of association may in such case deviate from the rules of this Act and of the Act on Financing Activities and Financial Institutions.

Chapter 5 – The company's bodies

Chapter 5 states the provisions regarding the company's bodies. In addition to the board of directors, which has to comprise at least three members (§ 5-1), a managing director (chief executive) is obligatory for an insurance company (§ 5-2). § 5-3 refers to §§ 6-1 to 6-3 and §§ 6-6 to 6-34 of the Private Limited Companies Act except as otherwise provided by the present Act. These Articles stipulate the requirements for the management board and the chairperson (§§ 6-1 to 6-11), the provisions regarding the administration and connected proceedings (§§ 6-13 to 6-33), and regulations regarding third parties (§§ 6-30 to 6-34). According to § 6-11, the director and at least half of the management board members have to reside in Norway if the King has not made an exception. Citizens of an EEA country or residing in an EEA country are excluded from this regulation. § 69 of Lov om samvirkeforetak (samvirkelova)[136], i.e. Cooperative Societies Act, is applicable to mutual insurance companies with more than 1,000 members at the time of the election of the board of directors. This article determines that both genders, in variable combinations depending on the size of the board, have to be part of the management board. § 69 of the Cooperative Societies Act is not applicable if one gender is represented less than 5 percent among the members.

[136] Cf. Lov om samvirkeforetak (samvirkelova)-2007-06-29-81.

If an insurance company has more than 50 employees, a supervisory board with twelve members or with a larger number divisible by three has to be elected by the general meeting.
According to § 5-4, at insurance companies with more than 50 employees a supervisory board shall be elected comprising twelve members or a higher number divisible by three which shall be fixed by the general meeting. Two-thirds of the members with alternates shall be elected by the general meeting. The elected members shall in aggregate reflect the company's interest groups, customer structure and social role. The articles of association shall contain further rules in this respect. The articles of association may transfer the right to elect to others. One third of the members with alternates shall be elected by and from among the employees in accordance with rules laid down by the King.
According to § 5-5, an insurance company shall have a control committee of at least three members and one alternate. Members and alternates shall be elected by the general meeting. One member of the committee shall satisfy the requirements set for judges under the Courts of Justice Act (of 13 August 1915 No. 5) § 54 second subsection. The election of this member shall be approved by Finanstilsynet. Finanstilsynet may grant dispensation from the provisions of the two previous sentences.
The members of the control committee may not be chairman or deputy chairman of the supervisory board, member of the board of directors, alternate to the board of directors, the company's auditor or employee of the insurance company, or be as closely related or related by marriage to any of these as mentioned in the Public Administration Act § 6.
The provisions of § 5-8 for cooperative companies regarding the annual general meeting are applicable like the ones of § 5-8 and § 5-12 (1, sentence 3) of the Act for private limited companies. The general meeting is held at the head office if not another location of the head office is stated in the bylaws.[137] The chairperson or another member of the management board opens the meeting. In the event the general meeting is called in by the local court, the latter names the person who opens the meeting.[138]
§ 5-9 regulates auditing. The supervisory board shall elect one or more registered or state authorised auditors, and shall approve the remuneration of the auditor(s). Additionally, §§ 7 et seqq. of the Act for private limited companies in combination with § 5-25 to 5-27 as well as Lov om revisjon og revisorer (revisorloven)[139], i.e. the Norwegian Act regarding accounting and accountants, are applicable for mutual insurance companies. The general meeting decides about the selection

[137] Cf. Lov om samvirkeforetak (samvirkelova)-2007-06-29-81 § 5-8.

[138] Cf. Lov om samvirkeforetak (samvirkelova)-2007-06-29-81 § 5-12 first and third subsection.

[139] Cf. Lov om revisjon og revisorer (revisorloven)-1999-01-15-2.

of the accountants (§ 7-1 in connection with § 7-3 Act for private limited companies) who have to submit a report of the previous fiscal year during the general meeting (§ 7-2 Act for private limited insurance companies) and to attend the same meeting (§ 7-4 Act for private limited insurance companies). The accountant report has to be submitted to the management board two weeks before the general meeting. The exemptions regarding the compilation of the report are stated in §§ 7-6 to 7-9 of the Act for private limited companies. The majority vote of the general meeting can change the bylaws of the company insofar that the management board can be empowered to decide if the accountant report is reviewed in agreement with the auditing law. This exception is only enforceable when the turnover of the company is less than five Mio. NOK (§ 7-6 (1)), the balance sheet total not over 20 Mio. NOK, and the average number of employees not exceed ten fulltime positions. According to §§ 7-7 to 7-9 of the Act for private limited companies in connection with §§ 5-25 to 5-27, a company must not conduct auditing if one share owner proposes a simplified auditing process during the general meeting.

Chapter 6 – The company's activities

According to § 6-3, first subsection, an insurance company shall have a capital ratio which at all times constitutes at least eight percent of the company's assets and the company's off-balance sheet commitments, calculated in accordance with risk-weighting principles. In addition, the King may prescribe § 6-3 second subsection

- a minimum amount of own funds,
- rules on the calculation of capital adequacy,
- what items are eligible for inclusion in own funds,
- a percentage other than that mentioned in the first subsection to bring Norwegian provisions into line with international standards.

According to § 6-4, an insurance company shall at all times have sufficient capital to cover the solvency margin in respect of the company's overall business. The King may issue regulations on the calculation of the solvency margin for, respectively, life insurance companies and non-life insurance companies, the capital that is eligible to fulfil the requirement and other factors with a bearing on the implementation of the solvency margin requirements.
According to § 6-5, Finanstilsynet oversees insurance companies' solvency. If a company no longer fulfils the requirements on capital adequacy or solvency margin, the King may order the company to cease writing new insurance policies. The King may also order the company to undertake specific dispositions with a view to fulfilling requirements on capital adequacy or solvency margin. The King may in special cases

and for a limited period authorise the company to maintain a capital adequacy or solvency margin that is lower than prescribed.

Part III – Pension undertakings

This section includes the provisions regarding pension funds (chapter 7) and defined contribution pension undertakings (chapter 8). In this case, no diverse provisions for the different corporate forms exist; therefore, this topic will not be investigated further.

Part IV – Life insurances

This section comprises regulations for group and individual life insurances (chapter 9), to municipal pension schemes (chapter 10), and for the transfer of pension institutions between insurance companies (chapter 11). In this case, no diverse provisions for the different corporate forms exist; therefore, this topic will not be investigated further.

Part V – General rules on non-life insurances

This section includes general provisions for non-life insurances (compensation insurances) (chapter 12). In this case, no diverse provisions for the different corporate forms exist; therefore, this topic will not be investigated further.

Part VI – Miscellaneous provisions

Chapter 13 – Liquidation

Should the insurance portfolio of a mutual insurance company (§ 13-2) fall below the level stipulated in the articles of association pursuant to § 4-3 c, the board of directors is obliged forthwith and with not more than 14 days' notice to call a meeting of the company body that is authorised to decide that the company shall be liquidated. If liquidation is not decided upon, and the portfolio is still too low three months after the company body held its meeting, the board of directors is obliged to initiate liquidation. Writing of new and renewal of older insurance contracts shall not take place once liquidation is decided or initiated. According to § 13-1, Finanstilsynet shall assume the role of the district court as regards application of the rules of the Private Limited Companies Act and the Public Limited Companies Act chapter 16. The Private Limited Companies Act chapter 16 applies to mutual companies.

According to § 13-5, a mutual insurance company may transfer assets, rights and obligations in their entirety to another mutual insurance company provided that the members become members of the acquiring company. Finanstilsynet has to approve the liquidation agreement or the transfer (§ 13-3). The provisions of § 13 et seqq. (company mergers), § 14 et seqq. (demerger), and § 4-26 (compulsive transfer of shares to sub-companies) of the Act for private limited companies are applicable

for mutual insurance societies, with the exception of the § 13-25 (cross-border company merger) and § 14-12 (cross-border demerger).

Chapter 14 – Foreign insurance companies' activities in Norway

According to § 2-4, foreign insurance companies can be granted a licence for the Norwegian market through a branch if the regulations of § 14 et seqq, are observed. For example, a foreign insurance company is allowed carrying on insurance activity in Norway through a branch (§ 14-1). This requires a licence for the insurance company in its home state and the proper supervision and control by the authorities in that state. Before an insurance company commences operations in Norway through a branch, adequate cooperation on supervision shall be established between the supervisory authorities in the insurance company's home state and Finanstilsynet.
The provisions of §§ 3-1 to 3-7, § 4 and 5, §§ 6-3 to 6-5 (and § 11-2) as well as § 13 shall not apply to branches of foreign companies. Nevertheless, other regulations have to be observed. According to § 14-2, the company shall designate an authorised agent (a general agent) to manage the Norwegian branch. The general agent represents the company in its external dealings, and is authorised to bind the company vis-à-vis third parties and to receive notices of legal action on behalf of the company. The general agent shall be resident in Norway.

Chapter 15 – Excepting provisions

The provisions of this Act shall not apply to schemes managed by the state. The King may nonetheless prescribe that this Act, or parts of it, shall apply to Norges Bank's pension fund. These are schemes managed by the state (§ 15-1), livestock insurer (§ 15-2), funeral funds and provident funds (§ 15-3), marine insurance associations (§ 15-5), companies whose activity is confined to reinsurance (§ 15-6), and insurance of war risk at sea (§ 15-7) as well as small mutual insurance companies (§ 15-4). In these cases, the King may grant small mutual insurance companies a full or partly exception from the provisions of this Act. Chapter 16 defines penal provisions when mutual insurance companies do not comply with this Act and chapter 17 illustrates commencement and transitional provisions.

4.2 Comparison of the Norwegian legislation for mutual insurance companies and private insurance limited companies

The Norwegian legislation does not include general definitions for mutual insurance companies. It only determines the legal company forms for insurances, i.e. private or public limited companies, or mu-

tual insurance companies. The only legitimate legal form for a mutual company is a mutual insurance company. According to § 15-4, small mutual insurance companies must not follow the regulations of the Insurance Act if the King had granted a licence. The law does not specify which characteristics.[140] A mutual insurance company has to have to be considered a small mutual society. Other companies, which operate according to mutual principles, e.g. Protection&Indemnity (P&I) clubs, or similar forms, were not perceived as mutual insurance companies.[141] For those companies the Norsk Sjøforsikringsplan, i.e. the Norwegian maritime insurance plan, has been used since 1871. This regulation is based on the "Allgemeiner Plan hamburgischer See-Versicherung", i.e. the general plan of the Hamburger marine insurance.[142]

Table 3 presents a comparison of the legal forms of companies regarding founder, bylaws, contingencies etc. between the three organisation forms of mutual insurance companies, private or public limited company. Additionally, a general differentiation regarding the organization form can be made. In general, monistic and dualistic systems can be differentiated. A monistic or one-level business management does not separate between supervisory board and management board. On the other hand, the dualistic or two-level system has an additional organization level that separates the management and the control level. While Anglo-Saxon countries (USA, Canada or the UK) have adapted the monistic system, the European Continental countries (Germany, Netherlands, or Finland) use the dualistic system.[143] In Norway, the insurance companies can decide on their own which system they want to use.[144] [145]

Intermediate result

In conclusion, the Norwegian legislation does not differ regarding the basic regulations between legal forms. The mutual life insurance companies have the big advantage that they have to have a much smaller capital fund for the foundation. This can be regarded as a legal advantage granted by the government.

---

140 The German Insurance Supervision Act defines in Article § 53 small and large mutual societies differently when the bylaws of the society differs regarding type of insurance, region, or group of people. Cf. *Theis* (2005), p. 30-31

141 Cf. *Broek* et al. (2012b), p. 219.

142 Cf. Cefor (2011), p. 20.

143 Cf. *Maassen* (2002), p. 15.

144 Cf. *Broek* et al. (2012a), p. 97.

145 The advantages and disadvantages of both systems will be discussed in chapter V. 2 using the principal-agent-theory.

Table 3: Comparison of legal forms permitted for insurances.[146]

Mutual insurance society
Founder
At least the founders (one or more) shall be resident in Norway and have to have lived there for the past two years
Board; members of the board
Different regulations when more than 1,000 members: Board has 2 or 3 board members; both genders have to represented Board has 4 or 5 board members; both genders have to represented two at the time Board has 6 to 8 board members, both genders have to represented three at the time Board has 9 board members; both genders have to represented at least four at the time if board members of both genders have at least 40%
Liability
No individual liability of the members; individual liability in the event of insolvency
Articles of association
1 Name of the company
2. Municipality of the registered company
3. Business sector
4. Membership regulations; composition of the general meeting and the right to vote in the general meeting
5. Number of insurance contracts and total amount and total amount of the insurance company during business activity
6. Regulations concerning mutual liability
7. Provisions concerning the dissolution of the company
8. Provisions concerning the use of the annual profit and covering of losses
9. Provisions regarding holding the general meeting
10. Provisions for convening the general meeting und the type of invitation
Articles of incorporation
The articles of incorporation have to include the following information (if available)
1. Type of insurance
2. Date of the inaugural meeting and the creation date of binding insurance contracts for the members
3. Size of the guarantee fund
4. Provisions which part of the guarantee fund has to be paid immediately and provisions regarding the obligation of the company that has taken over the guarantees for the payments of the guarantee fund.
5. Regulations regarding the payment of interests and repayment of the guarantee fund.
6. Provisions for the guaranteeing company regarding supervision and influence on the the insurance company
7. Cost unit of the foundation and remuneration
Capital upon new foundation
Non-life insurance: 2.5 Mio EUR, life insurance: 3.7 Mio. EUR

[146] AdaptedfromtheIA:Lov-2005-06-10-44,Lovomsamvirkeforetak(samvirkelova)-2007-06-29-81, Lov om aksjeselskaper-1997-06-13-44, Lov om allmennaksjeselskaper-1997-06-13-45.

Private limited insurance company (AS)
Founder
No requirements
Board; members of the board
No requirements
Liability
No individual liability of the shareholders
Articles of association
Minimum requirements of articles of association
1 Name of the company
2. Municipality of the registered company
3. Business sector
4. Total amount of the share capital
5. Face value
Articles of incorporation
The articles of incorporation have to include the following information (if available)
1. Name of the founder and the company, address, and identification number
2. Number of shares that are subscripted by each founder
3. The amount owing for the shares
4. Time of the formation of the share capital.
5. Members of the management
6. Auditor of the company
Capital upon new foundation
Non-life insurance: 2.5 Mio EUR, life insurance: 3.7 Mio. EUR

Insurance joint stock company (ASA)
Founder
No requirements
Board; members of the board
Different regulations:
Board has 2 or 3 board members; both genders have to represented
Board has 4 or 5 board members; both genders have to represented two at the time
Board has 6 to 8 board members, both genders have to represented three at the time
Board has 9 board members; both genders have to represented at least four at the time if board members of both genders have at least 40%
No individual liability of the shareholders
Articles of association
Minimum requirements of articles of association
1. Type of company: joint stock company
2. Name of the company
3. Municipality of the registered company
4. Business sector
5. Total amount of the share capital
6. Face value
7. Number of shares
8. Exact, minimum or maximum number of the managers
9. Optional: a company can have several managers/supervisory board members which work together in form of a collective body
10. Topics for discussion during the general meeting
II. Provisions regarding the allocation of the surplus if the rate of the return has not to be paid to the shareholders
Articles of incorporation
The articles of incorporation have to include the following information (if available)
1. Name of the founder and the company, address, and identification number
2. Number of shares that are subscripted by each founder
3. The amount owing for the shares
4. Time of the formation of the share capital.
5. Members of the management
6. Auditor of the company
Capital upon new foundation
Non-life insurance: 2.5 Mio EUR, life insurance: 3.7 Mio. EUR

5. Quantitative success parameters for the evaluation of Norwegian insurance companies

It has been said before that the number of insurance companies is not a reliable indicator to evaluate the success of a particular legal form (see chapter 2). Hypothetically, five insurance private limited companies can comprise 90 percent of the market share in a particular market while the remaining 10 percent are distributed among 50 mutual insurance companies. In absolute numbers, the mutual insurance companies can be ten times as numerous but in reality their share would only be a tenth of the total market. As a result, the success evaluation is more reliable based on the market share. However, the figures show different results based on the definition of the main unit. The International Cooperative and Mutual Insurance Federation (ICMIF) includes in the statistics for mutual insurance companies with the terms "mutual" and "cooperative" companies with values which reflect mutual and cooperative forms, i.e. companies possessed by their members and managed according their interests. This is, however, a broad definition even when the ICMIF compares globally mutual and cooperative companies without considering the legal definition and national particularities.[147] Based on the definition the market shares of Norwegian mutual and cooperative companies are as the following (Table 4). With regard to key parameters, they show increasing market shares since 2009 and therefore success.

The Association of Mutual Insurers and Insurance Cooperatives in Europe (AMICE) uses a different procedure to determine the market shares of mutual insurance companies. Although they use the ICMIF data, the methods of the AMICE differs in two different ways. Firstly, the definition of the ICMIF regarding mutual and cooperative insurance sectors is broader. AMICE excludes several mixed and hybrid mutual companies, when their main shareholder is a cooperative, a mutual or previous mutual foundation and additionally when the owner structure is open due to the issues of shares. Secondly, the figures of the national insurance markets of the ICMIF report are based on the figures of the World Insurance Reports of Swiss Re. In contrast, AMICE pursues the goal to generate the market volume data by using national sources and the bottom-up method. Therefore, small deviations arise between the results. According to AMICE, the total market share of mutual insurance companies in Norway has already been over 40 percent in 2008.[148]

[147] Cf. ICMIF (2014a).

[148] Cf. AMICE (2010), pp. 4-5, 8.

Table 4: Market shares of mutual and cooperative companies in Norway between 2008 and 2015[148]

	2008	2009	2010[1]	2011	2012	2013	2015
Market share	38.5%	36.3%	39.2%/40.2%	40.4%	42.5%	45.1%	46.7%
Life insurance market	40.4%	37.0%	37.6%/39.2%	38.8%	43.2%	47.3%	50.4%
Non-life insurance market	35.9%	35.4%	41.3%/41.5%	42.6%	41.4%	42.0%	41.5%

[1] The figures differ in the publications of the ICMIF of 2010 and 2012

[149] Presentation is based on ICMIF Global Mutual Market Share. 2010/2012/2013/2017.

A more detailed overview on the structure of the insurance markets presents Finans Norge (FNO), an organization which represents the 200 finance institutes operating on the Norwegian market.[150] Figure 4 presents the market share of life insurances and pensions as well as compensation insurances in 2013 based on the FNO publication.

The mutual company KLP has already dominated the life insurance and pension market in 2013 with 30.6 percent. This share has been increased since 2014 due to withdraw of DNB Liv and Storebrand from the public financial precaution market. In 2013, they had a market share of 19.1 percent (Storebrand) and 24.2 percent (DNB Liv). According to the FNO, the life insurance and pension market was divided with more than 80 percent between one mutual company and three private limited companies.

The market leaders for compensation insurances were the private limited companies Gjensidige (25.2 %) and If Skadeforsikring (23.9 %), followed by Tryg (14.3 %) and Sparebank 1 Forsikring (10.4 %). With four private limited companies and approximately 75 percent of the total market the question arises how a market share of approximately 40 percent of mutual insurance companies in non-life insurances is possible.

On behalf of the European Commission, a private Dutch market research institute determined the current situation of mutual insurance companies in Europe. With regard to this report, Norwegian mutual insurance companies and similar organizations (mutual-type organizations) had a total market share of 20 percent in 2008, 17 percent in 2009, and 18 percent in 2010. Moreover, Norwegian mutual insurance companies have a 30 percent share in the life insurance market, but only one percent regarding non-life insurances.[151] Although the authors of this report refer to the ICMIF data material, it is still unclear how these results were attained.

Therefore, it is necessary to use additional success parameters, but it is difficult to find additional market data. The Austrian Institute for Economic Research (WIFO) recommends using, for example, the premium income of insurance companies, because the income presents the base for the success evaluation of the sector and for the comparison of their assessment to the entire national economy.[152] The latter can be stated by the proportion of premiums to the gross domestic product

[150] Cf. FNO.

[151] Cf. *Broek* et al. (2012a), p. 49.

[152] *Url* (1996), p. 4.

Figure 4: Market shares of life insurances and pension as well as compensation insurances in Norway in 2013[156]

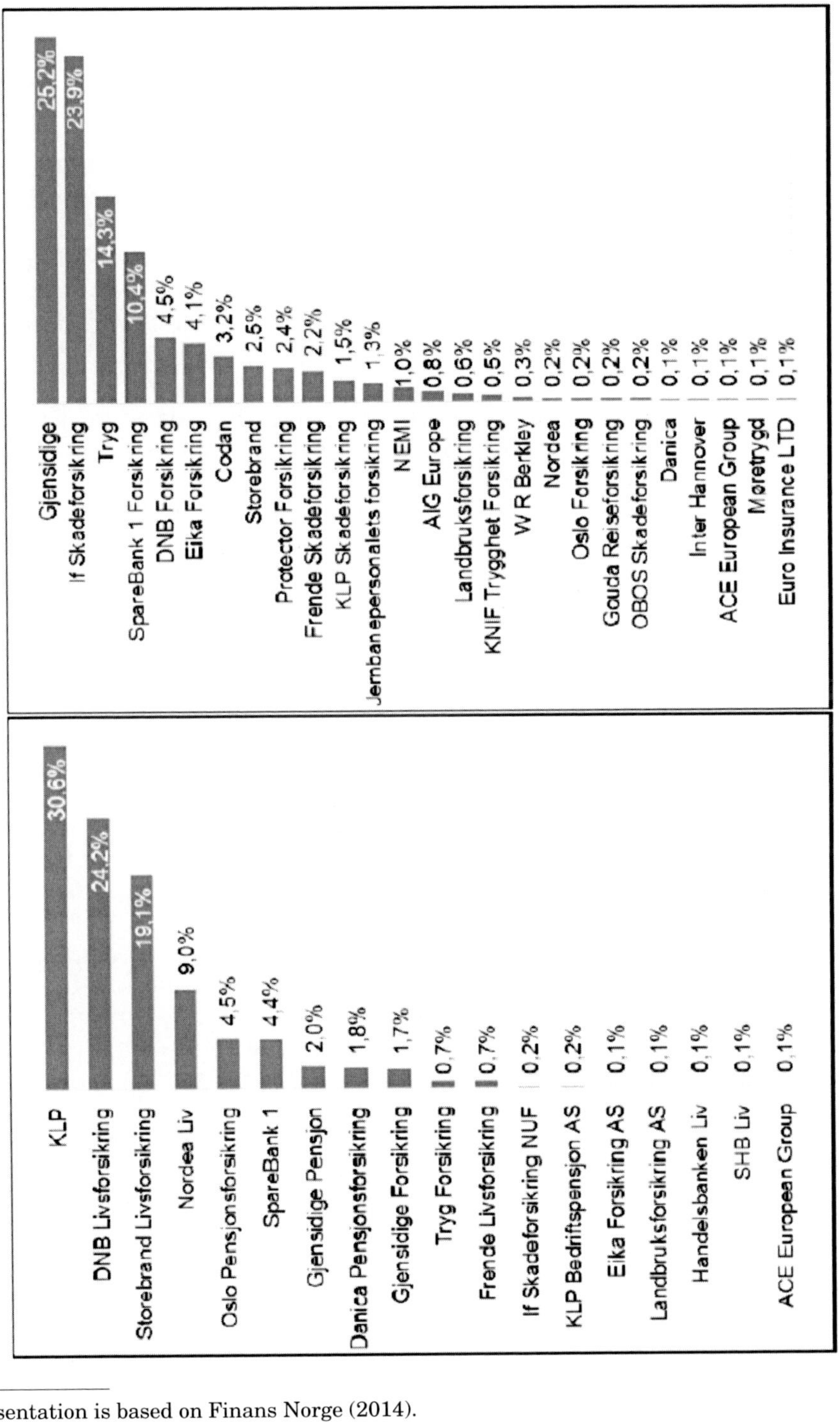

153 Presentation is based on Finans Norge (2014).

(GDP) and defined by the term rate of insurance. In the current example, the input of the insurance economy to the GDP should be established by using the rate of insurance and as a result the importance of these sectors. The performance of the mutual and cooperative companies is investigated more detailed, to make a statement regarding the overall economic performance. According to the Austrian Institute for Economic Research, additional conclusions can be made by using the rate of insurance. For example, it is possible to determine if the insurance economy of a country is a dynamic branch of economy. This is the case when the rate of growth of the GDP lies under the rate of insurance. The dissociation of premiums between domestic and foreign insurance companies can also be used to determine the extent of risk assumption and therefore the risk awareness in an international comparison.[154]

Table 5 presents data of various sources with the goal to verify the market share displayed by the ICMIF and to determine the rate of insurance for the total market of mutual and cooperative companies (mutuals). The results of the total market share based on own calculations are above the figures of the ICMIF, but differ in the life insurance sector for 2009 and 2012 only by 0.1 percent. For 2008, 2010, and 2011 the figures are the same. However, in the non-life insurance sector the difference lies by eight to ten percent and is therefore much higher. One reason is probably the diverge definition of non-life insurance between Insurance Europe and ICMIF. While Insurance Europe defines car insurance, compensation, health, accident, and third party liability insurance as non-life insurances, the ICMIF complements this kind of insurance with additional insurances: worker, maritime, aviation, transport, agriculture, reinsurance, and takaful insurance.[155] [156]

It is possible that the broader definition of the ICMIF is the reason that the calculation base for the total premiums in the non-life insurance market is higher and led to a lower value for the market shares. Moreover, it cannot be excluded that the differences originated from the currency conversion. For the determination of the market share, the gross premiums of mutual and cooperative companies were opposed to the gross premiums of the total insurance economy in both the life and non-life insurance sectors. Firstly, the values of the ICMIF were converted from USD into Euros to create a common basis. For this, the annual exchange rates of the historical average value of the European Central Bank were used. The figures of the own calculations based on data from several different source material are approximately the same as the data of the ICMIF, which leads to the conclusion that the results

[154] Cf. Ibid, p. 10.

[155] Cf. ICMIF (2014b), p. 20.

[156] Cf. Insurance Europe (2014), p. 22.

Table 5: Premiums, market shares, and rate of insurance in the Norwegian insurance sector between 2008 and 2013[160]

In Mio. EUR	2008	2009	2010[3]	2011	2012	2013
Turnover/Gross premiums total[1]	**12,711**	**11,846**	**13,784**	**15,221**	**17,489**	**15,219**
Life insurance market	7,973	7,140	8,382	9,249	11,027	9,722
Non-life insurance market	4,738	4,706	5,402	5,972	6,462	5,497
Turnover/Gross premiums mutual total[2] [5]	**5,360**	**4,693**	**5,846/5,996**	**6,576**	**7,973**	**8,197**
Life insurance market[5]	3,219	2,651	3,155/3,290	3,588	4,770	4,947
Non-life insurance market[5]	2,141	2,043	2,691/2,706	2,989	3,204	3,250
Market share total[1]	**42.2%**	**39.6%**	**42%/43%**	**43.2%**	**45.6%**	**53.6%**
Life insurance market	40.4%	37.1%	37.6%/39.3%	38.8%	43.3%	50.9%
Non-life insurance market	45.2%	43.4%	49.8%/50.1%	50%	49.6%	59.1%
Insurance density total[4]	**4%**	**4.3%**	**4.3%**	**4.2%**	**4.4%**	**3.9%**
Insurance density mutuals[4]	**1.7%**	**1.7%**	**1.8%/1.9%**	**1.8%**	**2.0%**	**2.1%**
GDP (market price)[6]	316.813	278.386	323.587	358.248	396.678	393.098
GDP (growth rate)[7]	0.03%	-1.39%	0.61%	1.06%	2.79%	0.76%

[1] Insurance Europe
[2] ICMIF
[3] different results in the publication of the ICMIF in 2010 and 2012
[4] own calculations
[5] original specification in USD, exchange to the historical average value of the EZB
[6] Eurostat
[7] Statista (1)

[157] Own presentation based on Insurance Europe (2014), pp. 41-46, Insurance Europe (2015), pp. 41-46, ICMIF Global Mutual Market Share (2010), p. 27, (2012), p. 34, EZB, Eurostat, and Statista (1).

of the private market research institute have to be examined critically, in particular the non-transparent method. Moreover, the calculated figures show that the Norwegian insurance economy is a dynamic market, because the rate of insurance is in the particular years higher than the GDP growth rate. It is important to note that almost half of the contribution comes from the mutual and cooperative companies.

The ICMIF publishes in their annual reports additional data, which can be interpreted as success indicators, such as the number of employees in cooperative companies. However, the absolute number of employees has to be interpreted critically, like the absolute number of companies discussed above, because in both cases these numbers are not a reliable indicator for a successful company or corporate structure. Although a high number of employees can be regarded as an economic success, at the same time, it can also be a sign of inefficiency when the same tasks are done by an increasing number of employees.

Employment rates are connected with macroeconomic factors.[158] Therefore, the changes of the last year were opposed to the Norwegian unemployment rate of the same year. When looking at the changes in employment with regard to the entire insurance business, it becomes evident that these are similar to the unemployment rate, although not proportional. For example, when the unemployment rate increased from 3.16 percent to 3.58 percent between 2009 and 2010, the employment decreased from 9,753 to 9,688 people at the same time. The changes were reversed between 2010 and 2011. While the unemployment rate decreased slightly, the employment increased from 9,688 to 9,921 people. In cooperative companies, the number of employees developed differently. While between 2009 and 2013 the average annual employment rate of cooperative companies decreased by 4.8 percent[159] and developed therefore highly negative, the employment increased annually in the insurance business on average by 0.50 percent at the same time. Therefore, it is not surprising that the portion of employees in cooperative societies, measured by the entire insurance sector, decreased from 52.2 percent (2009) to 42.2 percent (2013). However, it is still unclear, why the employment in mutual and cooperative companies is substantially higher than in the entire insurance sector.

[158] The here presented analysis is simplified. Important factors that are connected with the employment rates, e.g. natural fluctuation, birth rates, retirement, immigration and emigration, are not part of the analysis. The unemployment rate is opposed directly to employment.

[159] Calculation: (4.215/5.125)^(1/4)-1.

Table 6: Success indicator employment – Overview on employment in the Norwegian insurance sector[159]

	2008	2009	2010	2011	2012	2013	2014	2015
Number of employees total[1]	9,902	9,753	9,688	9,921	9,950	9,950	9,950	9,950
Change compared to year before[3]	-	-1.5%	-0.7%	2.4%	0.3%	0.0%	0.0%	0.0%
Number of employees mutuals[2]	-	5,125	4,568	3,885	3,961	4,215	4,394	4,394
Change compared to year before[3]	-	-	-10.9%	-15.0%	2.0%	6.4%	0.0%	0.0%
Share of mutuals of total[3]	-	52.2%	47.2%	39.2%	39.8%	42.4%	44.2%	44.2%
Unemployment in Norway[4]	2.6%	3.16%	3.58%	3.28%	3.22%	3.5%	4.3%	4.7%

[1] Insurance Europe

[2] ICMIF 2010/2013/2015

[3] own calculation

[4] Statista (2)

160 Own presentation based on Insurance Europe (2015), S. 63, ICMIF Global Mutual Market Share (2010), p. 31, (2013), p. 36 and Statista (2).

Table 7: Success indicator employment – Generated per capita premium and employment efficiency[160]

In Mio. EUR	2008	2009	2010[4]	2011	2012	2013	2014	2015
Turnover/Gross premiums total[1]	12,711	11,846	13,784	15,221	17,489	15,219	14,159[5]	13,441[5]
Number of employees total[1]	9,902	9,753	9,688	9,921	9,950	9,950	9,950	9,950
Premium per capita total[3] (Mio. EUR)	**1,28**	**1,21**	**1,42**	**1,53**	**1,76**	**1,53**		
Turnover/Gross premiums mutual total[2]	5,360	4,693	5,846/5,996	6,576	7,973	8,197	15,386(US Dollar)	9,285 (US Dollar)
Number of employees mutuals[2]	-	5,125	4,568	3,885	3,961	4,215	4,394	4,394
Premium per capita mutuals[3] (Mio. EUR)	-	**0,92**	**1,28/1,31**	**1,69**	**2,01**	**1,94**		

[1] Insurance Europe
[2] ICMIF 2010/2012/2013
[3] own calculations
[4] figures which differed from the publication of the ICMIF of 2010 and 2012
[5] figures (without reinsurance) taken EIOPA (European Insurance and Occupational Pension Authority) 2016

[161] Own presentation based on Insurance Europe (2014), p. 41-46, 63, Insurance Europe (2015), p. 41-46, 63, ICMIF Global Mutual Market Share (2010), p. 29, (2012), p. 32, (2013), p. 32.

The employment rates offer an additional analysis. By using the per capita premium a key parameter can be determined which can be interpreted as employee efficiency. The generated gross premium volume of a particular year is divided by the number of employees in the same time period. Tables 6 and 7 show that despite the stronger increase in employment, the pro capita premium in cooperative companies in 2012 (+2.0 %) and 2013 (+6.4 %) (2012: 2.01 Mio. Euro, 2013: 1.94 Mio. Euro) is higher than in the entire insurance sector (2012: 1.76 Mio. Euro, 2013: 1.53 Mio. Euro). This means a higher efficiency of employees regarding performance and can be regarded as a possible contribution to the overall success of the company.

Another important success indicator for insurance companies is the number of closed insurance contracts. Unfortunately, the ICMIF reports provide only limited information about this. While for 2012, Norway had 1.6 Mio. policyholders, 2013 increased the number to 1.7 Mio., i.e. an increase by 4.7 percent.[162] More data regarding the number of policyholders are not available by the ICMIF and additional research has not offered more results.

The last parameter for measuring success is the key parameter of total assets. This is the total amount comprising the overall gross investments, liquid assets, obligations and other assets in the balance sheet of a company.[163] The following Table 8 presents the total amount of assets and the change in percentage terms compared to the year before for mutual and cooperative companies in Norway. The figures are in USD to avoid distortion caused by currency conversion.

The data shows that the amount of total assets have increased since 2010 with a high in 2014 and a significant drop in 2015. However, a detailed composition of total assets is not available. This hinders the interpretation, because the change of different factors has different effects on the overall business performance of a company. For example, too many liquid assets of a company indicate bad cash management, because dead capital is inefficient and unprofitable. This is also true for a large portfolio of claims, which involves a general risk of payment. With an increasing number of debtors, the risk of non-payment increases, too. As a result, adjustments of the value have to be made, which lead to a diminution on the assets side of the balance sheet. Therefore, the significance of the total amount of assets has to be taken carefully into account and it is not a preferable success indicator to evaluate the performance of mutual insurance companies. However, this key parameter is used as a base for other kinds of key indicators and eventually to make evaluations about the investment and claim intensity as well as the assets and liabilities structure of a company.

[162] Cf. ICMIF Global Mutual Market Share (2013), p. 36.

[163] Cf. Businessdictionary – Total Assets.

Table 8: Total assets of Norwegian mutual and cooperative companies[163]

In Mio. USD	2008	2009	2010	2011	2012	2013	2014	2015
Total assets	50,432	49,933	56,193/56,253	64,439	69,462/69,579	77,621	85,042	72,152
Change compared to year before[3]		-1,0%	+12,5%+12,7%	+14,7%/14,6%	+7,8%/+8,0%	+11,7%/+11,6%	9,5%	-15%

[1] figures which differed from the publication of the ICMIF of 2010 and 2012
[2] figures which differed from the publication of the ICMIF of 2012 and 2013
[3] own calculations

[164] Own presentation based on ICMIF Global Mutual Market Share (2010), p. 32, (2012), p. 36, (2013), p. 36, (2015), p. 39.

Intermediate result

Different key parameters can be used to evaluate the success of mutual insurance companies. While key parameters such as the absolute number of companies on the market only give a limited reliable conclusion, others such as data about market shares or the rate of insurance provide more information. The most interesting parameter but also the least available is the number of concluded insurance contracts. Moreover, freely accessible market data or key parameters such as the amount of total assets have to be questioned critically regarding their elicitation, in particular the methodological process that was used, and the general significance.

6. Discussion of qualitative success indicators and the results of additional analyses for the evaluation of the success of Norwegian insurance companies

6.1 Effects of cultural and socio-structural parameters on mutual insurance companies

The analysis of the absolute number of insurance companies has shown that it depends to a larger part on the overall economic development. Nevertheless, in some Norwegian districts more mutual insurance companies have been founded than in others (cf. Table 1). In the following, factors that are able to influence the development of mutual insurance companies are presented and discussed. These parameters are based on the analysis of *Greve* and *Hayagreeva*. Then the correlation between culture, national wealth, and risks as well as gender quota, company structures, and economic success will be investigated.

6.1.1 Occupational, religious, and ethnic diversity as well as social inequality

The influence of occupational choice

Mutual forms of organizations have to have a unique identity, which is based on a strong ideological foundation. The identity of the organization must have a strong appeal, because the members are also owners. They are able to recruit new members more effectively, because they share the same values and principles and do not follow a regular profit motive. The founders of mutual insurance companies have the strong incentive to create their organization based on common self-help and on the specific needs of the most prevalent professions in the community. This view led at first to the assumption that mutual fire companies were more common in regions with agricultural professions and regional-limited maritime mutual insurance companies more often in areas with fishing. As a result, the spread of potential members in the district is a factor that influences the foundation rate. In the analysis, it is hypothesized (H1a and H1b) that the more farmers/fishers live in a district the higher the number of mutual fire companies/regional-limited mutual companies is. *Greve* and *Hayagreeva* have confirmed both hypotheses. As a result, the frequency of the professional identity is positively connected with the foundation rate of mutual insurance companies.[165]

The influence of occupational diversity

The second hypothesis investigates if occupational diversity of a district is positively connected with the number of mutual insurance companies. The assumption is that the dominance of a particular profession in the community is not sufficient for the foundation of an organization which identity is compatible with the particular profession. In fact, the latter should stand out among numerous other professions. The frequency of a particular occupation increases the probability that a certain amount of people can be reached who are prepared to cooperate and establish a mutual insurance company. However, it can be argued that organizations do not focus entirely on frequency but also on the members' preparedness and awareness to be part of a social group.[166] The awareness of the own identity can also be the result of the social structure of a society, because individuals are confronted with the daily decision of the chosen identity. Despite that, the selection of the identity is influenced by mutual reactions when individuals accept, ignore, or contrast the particular identity.[167] One consequence is that the aware-

[165] Cf. *Greve* (2006), pp. 12, 26-27.

[166] Cf. Ibid.

[167] Cf. *Ashforth* and *Johnston* (2001), p. 32.

ness for a particular identity increases when the individual faces a different identity.[168] For example, a farmer is not constantly reminded about his profession within a homogenous agricultural parish. However, when a farmer meets a group of construction workers in a town, he becomes aware about his professional identity. From this point of view, two additional hypotheses are devised: the larger the professional diversity of a parish, the higher the number of mutual fire companies/regional limited mutual companies. Both hypotheses were confirmed by the analysis due to a positive and significant correlation between the professional diversity and the frequency of the social group. Therefore, professional diversity increases the foundation rate of mutual insurance companies in a parish.[169]

The influence of religious and ethnic diversity

Another important factor for the foundation of mutual insurance companies is social diversity. Two additional assumptions were hypothesized (H3a and H3b): high levels of religious and ethnic diversity tend to decrease the number of mutual fire companies/regional limited mutual insurance companies. Mutual insurance companies are a mechanism for self-help and joint help. Therefore, the ability for an effective organization depends on the ability of the group members to recognise a common identity. This parameter depends on the members' ability to reduce the different characteristics of their community to a common denominator.[170] Hereby, two different kinds of differences are defined: differences regarding rank and non-rank differences. Rank differences e.g. of power or assets lead to inequalities and therefore to a vertical differentiation, while non-rank differences e.g. religion affiliation lead to diversity within the community and therefore to a horizontal differentiation.[171] Inequalities and diversity can reduce the organization potential of a community, because differences in social characteristics can weaken the cohesion of a community and therefore have the possibility for the foundation of competing organization.[172] Different groups are unable to produce collective goods due to their divergence regarding their interests.[173] The more heterogeneous the parts of a group are, the more difficult it is for activists to mobilise them and as a result, the less a success is probable.[174] Laboratory experiments have shown that players connect more easily with players with similar characteristics. Others with dissimilar characteristics are rejected. Therefore, inequality

[168] Cf. *Tajfel* and *Turner* (1979), p. 282.
[169] Cf. *Greve* (2006), pp. 12-13, 26-27.
[170] Cf. Ibid, p. 13.
[171] Cf. *Blau* (1977), p. 77 ff.
[172] Cf. *Greve* (2006), p. 14.
[173] Cf. *Olson* (1965), p. 173.
[174] Cf. *Tarrow* (1994), p. 16.

is the reason for weak integration.[175] Various types of differentiations produce several foundations for identification. This reduces the probability that a person maintain a stable identification with all identities.[176] While professional diversity promotes the foundation of mutual insurance companies, types of diversity such as religious affiliation or ethnic origin lead to a competing identification base. Therefore, it does not surprise that both ethnic and religious diversity receive a negative coefficient in the analysis. However, it is important to note that only religious diversity had a significant influence. This result offers only weak support regarding both hypotheses.[177]

The influence of social inequalities

While social diversity weakens the social cohesion, inequality decreases the pursuit of common interests. There are three reasons why inequality influences the common identity and the collective action. Firstly, socially higher-ranking people are hesitant to interact with socially lower ranking people in order to protect their social status and to prohibit being degraded. Secondly, inequality reduces the willingness that people engage in partnerships.[178] Thirdly, inequality can lead to higher negotiation costs and limits the best negotiation results.[179] Social inequality hinders the relation between people and lead to a reduced perception of interests. Therefore, it leads to lower economic self-help and reduces the foundation rate of mutual insurance companies. To analyze the latter, *Greve* and *Hayagreeva* hypothesized only one assumption, because only data regarding farmers were ascertainable due to different ownership classes, e.g. landowner, tenants and workers without land. It is hypothesized (H4) that inequality in a parish leads to a decrease of foundation rates of mutual insurance companies. The analysis shows a significant connection with a negative coefficient for the hypothesis.[180]

6.1.2 Culture, national wealth, and risk preference

Insurance via a mutual insurance company can lead to a reduction of insurance benefits or additional payment liabilities by the members due to bad financial results.[181] Although additional payment liability can be reduced by reinsurance or restricted to a maximum amount by an agreement in the bylaws, the policyholder carries the earning risk

[175] Cf. *O'Reilly* et al. (1989), p. 34.
[176] Cf. *Ashforth* and *Johnston* (2001), pp. 45-46.
[177] Cf. *Greve* (2006), pp. 14, 23-24.
[178] Cf. Ibid, p. 14-15.
[179] Cf. *Molm* et al. (1999), p. 880.
[180] Cf. *Greve* (2006), pp. 15, 27.
[181] *Breuer* and *Breuer* (2002), p. 5.

of the company. This can result in an actual additional payment and therefore in a higher financial disadvantage for the policyholder.[182, 183] With regard to health and life insurances, participating contracts can also be found for insurance private limited companies, but compensation and accident insurances are only possible for mutual insurance companies. An insurance private limited company can only participate in the earning risk of a company by acquiring a share. The policyholder of a mutual insurance company has a higher risk regarding compensation and accident insurance, because a differentiation in risk sharing is not possible unlike to an insurance private limited company.[184] Therefore, the question arises why policyholders should take a higher risk regarding compensation and accident insurances. A possible explanation is the connection between cultural origin and risk approach as well as between the wealth of a nation and its risk preference. *Rieger* et al. created the study "Risk preferences around the World" with the goal to analyze if international differences between risk preferences exist. If they do, the question is to what extent they correlate with economic and cultural factors. In the study, the risk preference is measured by two different kinds of lotteries: win and loss lotteries. With regard to win lotteries[185], the participants were asked how high their willingness to pay was, to participate in the lottery. With regard to loss lottery[186], the participants were asked how high their willingness to pay was, not to participate in the lottery. With the help of win lotteries the risk aversion should be determined and via the loss lottery the risk affinity. The risk affinity correlates with the conclusion of a contract, which should protect from losses. To strengthen the results, the relative risk premium was determined (RRP)[187] and two indexes were deduced from it: RRP for wins (= dimension for risk aversion) and RRP for losses (= dimension for risk affinity). The RRP is positive when the player is risk-averse and negative when the player is willing to take risks. The higher the absolute result is, the stronger the characteristic of the particular behavior is. For the determination of a value for a country, the median of the individual RRPs is used. The study shows a significant asset-price effect on risk preference regarding win lotteries at the nation level, in which participants from richer countries are more risk averse by trend. This means that the higher the monetary starting

[182] Cf. *Schierenbeck* (1994), p. 696.

[183] Cf. *Breuer* and *Breuer* (2002), p. 5.

[184] Cf. ibid.

[185] E.g. state the maximum amount to participate in the lottery: payment with 40% = 0, with 60% = 100$.

[186] E.g. state the maximum amount to not participate in the lottery: payment with 40% = -80$, with 60% = no loss, no win.

[187] RRP = (expectancy value of the lottery – individual security equivalent expectancy value of the lottery

position of a person is, the lower the security equivalent (SE) regarding the expectancy value (µ) is. With regard to risk perception and loss lotteries, participants from richer countries are more risk affine, when the cultural dimension is included into the regression.[188] This means the higher the monetary starting position is, the bigger the SE is, i.e. the indifference between the secure payment and the loss lottery. In reverse, this means that the higher the difference between a secure payment and an uncertain loss lottery is, the lower the willingness to take out insurance is.

Table 9 presents the results of the study. The SE can be determined with the help of the RRPs and the SE can be used to evaluate risk preference. For the chosen lotteries, both RRP factors show the expected risk preference of Norwegian. In case of win lottery, the SE is smaller as the expected value (15.60 < 60), which shows risk aversion. In case of loss lottery, the results are reversed, because the SE is higher than the expected value (-17.28 > -32), which shows risk affinity.[189]

Table 9: Win and loss lotteries – calculation example for Norway (= NO)[190]

Win lottery

Probability	40%	60%
Win	0	100
Expectancy value µ	0.4*0 +0.6*100 = 60	

RRP (win) NO	0.74
Security equivalent (SE) for NO	((0.74*I60I) -60)*-1 = 15.60
Risk aversion as long as SE< µ	

Loss lottery

Probability	40%	60%
Win	-80	0
Expectancy value µ	0.4*-80 +0.6*0 = -32	

RRP (loss) NO	-0.46
Security equivalent (SE) for NO	((-0.46*I32I)*-1) -32 = -17.28
Risk aversion as long as SE> µ	

$$RRP = \frac{\mu\,(lottery) - SE}{I\mu\,(lottery)I}$$

[188] Cf. *Rieger* et al. (2014), pp. 1-12.

[189] Cf. *Laux* et al. (2014), pp. 215-218.

[190] Own presentation.

The following analysis investigates if wealthy countries act in the particular lotteries risk averse or adventurous and therefore if the study presents reliable results. Table 9 compares the results of the study with the gross domestic product per capita, the market share of mutual non-life insurance companies, and with both lotteries from Table 9 in Norway and five randomly selected countries.

The results show that the higher the GDP per capita and therefore the financial situation of a country is, the more risk averse the player acts. When comparing Norway to the five selected countries, the latter should have a lower RRP (win) due to their lower GDP per capita. The SE of the five countries should be compared to Norway higher, because the higher the SE is, the risk adventurous the behavior is. Therefore, Norway should have the highest RRP (win) and the lowest SE. However, only Austria has a lower RRP (win) and a higher SE with a lower GDP per capita, while all other countries have a higher RRP (win) and a lower SE with a lower GDP per capita. Mexico has the highest RRP (win), although it has the lowest GDP per capita. Therefore, the results of the study are not confirmed by the selected examples.

Table 10: Economic factors and risk preference in selected countries[191]

	GDP per capita[1] (2012)	**Market share non-life mutual societies[2] (2012)**	**RRP[3] (win)**	**µ win lottery[4]**	**SE win lottery[4]**	**RRP[3] (loss)**	**µ loss lottery[4]**	**SE win lottery[4]**
Norway	99,249	41.4%	0.74	60	15.60	-0.46	-32	-17.28
USA	51,709	39.2%	0.78	60	13.20	-0.43	-32	-18.24
Austria	46,620	67.0%	0.65	60	21.00	-0.63	-32	-11.84
Germany	42,569	30.3%	0.80	60	12.00	-0.54	-32	-14.72
Slovenia	22,089	20.0%	0.83	60	10.20	-0.53	-32	-15.04
Mexico	10,111	7.8%	0.93	60	4.20	-0.72	-32	-8.96

[1] IWF, values in USD
[2] ICMIF
[3] Rieger et al. (2014), p. 5
[4] own calculations

[191] Own presentation based on ICMIF Global Mutual Market Share (2012), p. 34, IWF (2014) and *Rieger* et al. (2014), p. 5.

When considering the RRP (loss), the results are similar. In case a country has a higher GDP per capita, it should have a higher RRP (loss). The more negative the RRP (loss) value is, the more risk adventurous the player is. The SE should be all the higher, the higher the risk affinity and in this case the GDP per capita is. However, in this case the results of the study are not confirmed by the selected lotteries. Norway should have the highest RRP (loss), because of the highest GDP per capita. With the exception of the USA, all countries have a higher value. This is also true for the SE, which shows for Norway the second lowest result among all countries. Therefore, the question arises how far the results of this study endure. Therefore, it is not possible to determine a final connection between the wealth of a nation and its risk preference. Moreover, it is not possible to give an explanation regarding the amount of market shares of mutual non-life insurance companies, which have, as stated before, the highest risks for the policyholders. It is assumed that with an increasing risk affinity the willingness of taking out insurance decreases. As a result, the market share of mutual non-life insurance companies should decrease with an increasing RRP (loss). However, as Figure 5 shows, this assumption is not true for the selected countries.

In general, it is difficult to measure and quantify the cultural influence. However, in order to analyze the cultural influence on risk preference, the two dimensions of *Hofstede*, i.e. individualism and uncertainty avoidance, were used for the study.[192] Individualism mirrors how far an individual is able to integrate into a group.[193] Hereby two opposite hypotheses assume how individuality influences risk preference. On the one hand, personal achievements and single values are emphasized in an individualistic society, which can lead to an overestimation of one's own capabilities and to too much optimism.[194] As a result, a risk affine behavior can be supposed. On the other hand, countries with collectivistic culture have usually less financial risks and appear to be less risk-averse. This phenomenon is explained by the padding-hypothesis: the strong social networks in a collectivistic society work like a padding against financial catastrophes and induce a risk adventurous behavior.[195] The avoidance of uncertainty as a second cultural dimension is concerned with the amount how far an unclear or uncertain situation is tolerated in the society. From an intuitive point of view, one would assume that a risk adverse behavior is closely connected with the avoidance of uncertainty. However, the latter is not the same as risk

[192] Cf. *Rieger* et al. (2014), p. 2.

[193] Cf. *Hofstede* (2001), p. 209 ff.

[194] Cf. *Chui* et al. (2010), p. 364.

[195] Cf. *Hsee* and Weber (1999), p. 172.

Figure 5: Risk affinity and market share of mutual non-life insurance companies for selected countries[196]

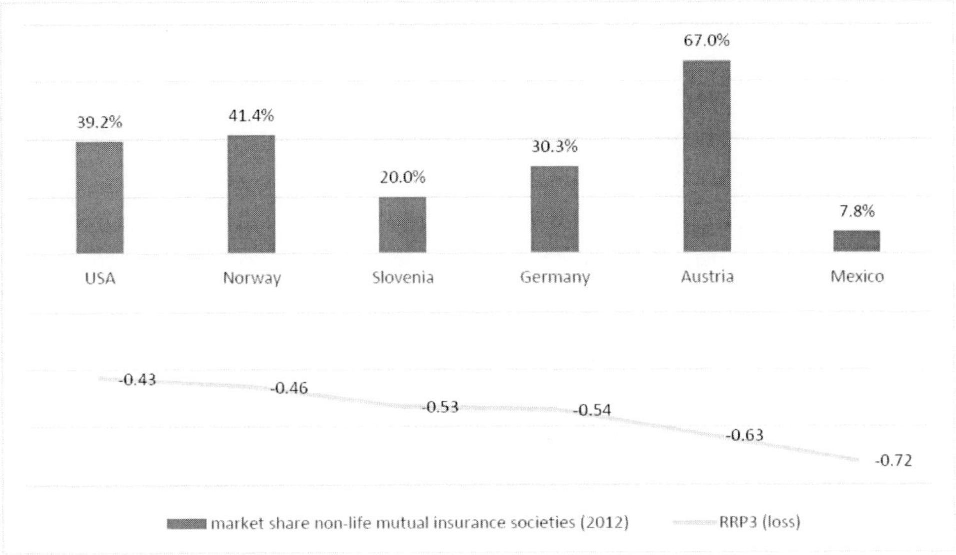

avoidance. It is suggested that civilizations with a high amount of uncertainty avoidance take more risks to reduce the ambiguity.[197, 198]

The results of *Rieger*'s et al. study show that nations with an individualistic society have a lower risk aversion in win lotteries and a lower risk affinity in loss lotteries. With regard to Hofstede's index of uncertainty avoidance, a strong and sturdy influence of culture can be asserted. In win lotteries, a high amount of uncertainty avoidance manifests in a higher degree of risk aversion while in loss lotteries it manifests in a higher risk affinity.[199]

---

196 On presentation based on ICMIF Global Mutual Market Share (2012), p. 34 and *Rieger* et al. (2014), p. 5

197 Cf. *Hofstede* (2001), p. 148.

198 Cf. *Rieger* et al. (2014), p. 2.

199 Cf. Ibhid., p. 7.

Table 11: Risk aversion and risk affinity based on individualism and uncertainty avoidance in selected countries[200]

<table>
<tr><th></th><th>Norway</th><th>USA</th><th>Austria</th><th>Germany</th><th>Slovenia</th><th>Mexico</th></tr>
<tr><td>Individualism</td><td>69</td><td>91</td><td>55</td><td>67</td><td>27</td><td>30</td></tr>
<tr><td>Win lottery</td><td colspan="4">Risk affine</td><td colspan="2">Risk averse</td></tr>
<tr><td>Loss lottery</td><td colspan="4">Risk averse</td><td colspan="2">Risk affine</td></tr>
<tr><td>Uncertainty avoidance</td><td>50</td><td>46</td><td>70</td><td>65</td><td>88</td><td>82</td></tr>
<tr><td>Win lottery</td><td rowspan="2">Risk neutral</td><td>Risk affine</td><td colspan="4">Risk averse</td></tr>
<tr><td>Loss lottery</td><td>Risk averse</td><td colspan="4">Risk affine</td></tr>
</table>

In the next step, a connection between cultural aspects and the willingness to take out insurance, based on the data of Table 11, will be investigated. With regard to individualisms and loss lottery, the market share of mutual non-life companies is higher in risk adverse nations than in risk affine nations. This dimension can help to explain why mutual insurance companies in some nations are stronger represented then in others. However, the previous hypothesis does not apply when the figures of the uncertainty avoidance are used for the loss lotteries. For example, Austria has an uncertainty avoidance index of 70, which is risk affine, because the limit lies at 50 (= neutrality). Nonetheless, Austria has with 67 percent the highest market share for mutual non-life insurances companies. The previous statement, however, has suggested that the risk affinity in the loss lottery is attended by a low willingness to take out insurance. As a result, it is difficult to find an explanation for the various connections even when using Hofstede's cultural dimension.

The study of *Rieger* et al. has to be examined critically due to three reasons. Firstly, the study was executed at universities which participants have usually a low average age (21.5 years) and therefore do not represent the social structure of a country. Secondly, the low number of interviewed people in the particular countries is not sufficient to make a conclusion about the entire nation. For example, only 190 students were part of the project in Norway. Thirdly, because no real payments were done at the lotteries, the decisions of the participants were only hypothetical and may have led to a distortion of the real risk preference.

200 Own presentation based on Hofstede Centre – Country Comparison and *Rieger* et al. (2014), p. 7.

6.1.3 Gender quota, company structure, and economic success

The legal comparison has shown that a fixed quota is obtained for the distribution between genders in mutual insurance companies (above 1,000 members) and public limited companies. Norway has here a pioneering role, because since 2003 it is the first country in the world, which has a fixed distribution of 40 percent between genders in the board of administration. From that time onwards, all private limited companies, public and local companies, and cooperatives are compelled to adhere the quota. Since January 1st, 2010, private limited companies and limited liability companies have to follow the gender quota, when parishes hold shares of more than three quarters. Otherwise private limited companies and limited liability companies are not obliged to follow the quota. As mentioned before, Norwegian companies have the choice between a monistic and a dualistic system regarding the organizational structure. The monistic system does not distinguish between supervisory and management board, but an administrative board is elected which bears the responsibility of the entire company. The administrative board consists of shareholders' agents and spokespersons for the employees. Additionally, a director is elected who is bounded by instructions of the administrative board. A chairperson of the administrative board is elected, but cannot be the director at the same time. Usually with the size of a company, the organization form changes from monistic to dualistic system. When a company with more than 30 employees does not have a supervisory board, the employees have the right that one administrative board member and an additional observer and proxy are elected from the employees' pool. As a result, a supervisory board develops, which is responsible for supervision, and works alongside the management board which is responsible for the management. The quota agreement refers to the administrative board in a monistic system and to the supervisory board in a dualistic system.[201]

One of the main arguments for advocacies was that a balanced proportion between men and women in the administrative board has a positive influence on the profitability of a company.[202] However, economic researchers do not agree on the actual influence of gender quota. Some studies uncover a connection, but do not refer to the causality of the results. Moreover, the quantification of the economic profitability of a company can be determined by various ratios, e.g. return on equity or return on total assets.[203] While some studies emphasise a positive[204]

---

[201] Cf. *Storvik* and *Teigen* (2010), pp. 3-5.

[202] Ibid., p. 7.

[203] Cf. Ibid (2010), pp. 11.

[204] Cf. *Terjesen* et al. (2009), *Smith* et al. (2006) and *Carter* et al. (2003).

connection between gender quota and company's success, other studies present a significant negative[205] connection. Therefore, a clear statement referring to an existing connection is not possible. The quota agreement had different impacts in Norway in the last years. At first, the legal quota was transacted gradually in the concerned companies. In 2002, the quota was at 6 percent and increased during the next years so that in 2004 it was at 9 percent, in 2005 at 12 percent, 2006 at 18 percent, in 2007 at 25 percent, in 2008 at 36 percent, and in 2009 at 40 percent. The limited successful realization of the quota was not carried out without sanctions, which could have meant beside fines also the compulsory liquidation of a company. After the 40-percentage rate was achieved, it usually was not exceeded further. Moreover, only 5 percent of women are chair of the administrative board, which mirrors the still existing gender hierarchy. Some companies have even changed their legal form from a public to a private limited company to avoid the quota agreement.[206]

Intermediate result

The study of *Greve* and *Hayagreeva* shows that parameters such as the size of a social group, its professional, religious, and ethnic diversity as well as social inequity in the society influence differently the foundation rate of mutual organizations. These results show the complex connections which influence the success of a legal form and therefore cannot be reduced to a few parameters, e.g. the overall development. Moreover, there are interesting interactions between culture, a nation's wealth, and the risk aversion of a society. The study of *Rieger* et al. is only one of many academic studies ana lysing risk behavior, most of them present different results. A connection between culture, a nation's prosperity and its risk attitude can be assumed but a clear connection between these parameters cannot be proven. This is also true for the connection between legal quota agreements and economic success. Norway has fixed quota agreements for particular legal forms that state the distribution between genders in administrative and supervisory boards. Nevertheless, studies show conflicting results, therefore, it is not possible to make a clear connection between gender quota and the success of a company.

[205] Cf. *Lee* and *James* (2007), *Ahern* and *Dittmar* (2009) and *Liable* (2013).

[206] Cf. *Storvik* and *Teigen* (2010), pp. 10-11.

6.2 Hypotheses regarding the legitimation of the coexistence of mutual insurance companies and private limited companies on insurance markets

The historical analysis has shown that mutual insurance companies as well as private limited companies are equally established as legal forms on the Norwegian insurance market. Both legal forms compete against each other although both have the same supply and business market as well as the same production processes[207]. Therefore, the question arises why both legal forms are able to coexist successfully.

6.2.1 Conflict of interests and efficiency

Various empirical studies have dealt with the question about the coexistence of both legal forms on the insurance market. For that matter, different influencing factors have been analyzed. The results have been controversial and have shown the advantages and disadvantages of each legal form. For example, *O'Hara* states that mutual insurance companies are less cost-effective and profitable and therefore give their owners less profit. He explains these results with the view that mutual insurance companies are non-profit companies, which have no instruments to operate efficiently and eventually exist on the market due to public control.[208] *Nicols* argues that the management enriches itself at the expense of the stakeholders due to the absence of profit-maximising shareholders and this generates great inefficiency.[209] *Spiller* states that the unequal economic productivity of insurance private limited companies and mutual insurance companies is based on different incentive structures within the management. Companies traded on the stock exchange are more under pressure by the capital market. Therefore, they are able to provide better incentive structures for the management.[210] The points of criticism show that mainly the owners' structures and the relation between the different entitlement groups in mutual insurance companies and private limited companies were ana lysed. In contrast to the mentioned disadvantages, the analysis of *Mayers* and *Smith* shows theoretical and empirical evidence which emphasizes the efficient distribution of ownership in mutual insurance companies. Moreover, it shows the elimination of the conflict between owners and policyholders as crucial advantage over insurance private limited companies. Based on this study, they conclude that the transformation of a

207 *Breuer* and *Breuer* (2002), p. 1.

208 Cf. *O'Hara* (1981), pp. 330-331.

209 Cf. *Nicols* (1967), pp. 341-345.

210 Cf. *Spiller* (1972), pp. 21-23.

private limited company into a mutual insurance company (demutualization) sometimes increase the efficiency. They ana lysed the relations between shareholders, policyholders, and management in the insurance sector and their different conflicts of interest. Therefore, the improvement of these relationships could lead to increased efficiency. Initially, there is a conflict between owners and policyholders. Policyholders pay premiums to receive a sum stipulated by contract but in this manner, they become debtors to the insurance company. Shareholders have the goal to maximise the value of the company, which usually goes at the expanse of the debtors. The price of insurance products is linked with a constant dividend payment, in the event of an unexpected increase of the dividends this can only be done by the reduction or transformation of assets. This transformation can be achieved, for example, by the substitution of low-risk and risk carrying assets, which decreases the value of the claim of the policyholder. This is in particular the case when owners take out risky insurance policies which disadvantages have to be carried by the existing policyholders. The policyholder can withdraw from the contract, but has to pay high costs for this action. Therefore, common assets are the most effective possibility to eliminate the costs of conflicts between owners and policyholders. In a mutual insurance company, owner and policyholder are combined in one person, a fact that eliminates divergent goals and conflicts. However, mutual insurance companies are not the only way to eliminate this conflict, because in private limited companies conflicts of interests can be avoided by participating contracts.[211] [212] However, as mentioned above, private limited companies cannot use these kinds of contracts in all insurance branches.

Another conflict lies between owners and the management of the company. Based on the principal-agent problem[213] [214], this conflict of interest exists due to asymmetries regarding information and incomplete contracts and concerns both mutual insurance companies and private limited companies. *Mayers* and *Smith* argue that the owner-manager

---

211 Cf. *Mayers* and *Smith* (1986), pp. 75-76.

212 Cf. *Breuer* and *Breuer* (2002), pp. 6-7.

213 Cf. *Jensen* and *Meckling* (1976), pp. 305-360.

214 An information asymmetry is between owners and policyholders. When these two roles are not unified in one person, a risk develops due to Moral Hazard, which is signified by an irresponsible behaviour of a policyholder after concluding a contract. Such misconduct can be solved differently. For example, in Norway in the 19th century, the challenges of such an information asymmetry were addressed by regional limited mutual societies. Only registered customers could become members within a clearly defined field. To achieve the highest transparency, local knowledge regarding the behaviour of fellow men and various forms of social control were most important. The general view had been that it was amoral or irresponsible to make newcomers to members due to joint and several liabilities. In universal mutual societies, the premiums were higher than in regional limited to avoid uncertainty and to compensate loss of control due to geographic expansion. Cf. *Espeli* (2001), p. 61.

problem can be solved for private limited companies by tender offers[215] or proxy fights[216]. Due to the take-over offers, the management can be put under pressure and, as a result, can be disciplined regarding its behavior. It is also possible that the management loses control by using proxy-voting powers and is replaced eventually.[217] Moreover, in case of companies listed on the stock exchange the decisions of the management are mirrored by the share price, which offers an additional supervision possibility for the shareholders. Mutual insurance companies have only limited management control systems, because they do not receive information via the capital market or obtain a takeover bid due to their ownership structure. *Mayers* and *Smith* assume that managers of mutual insurance companies have compared to managers of private limited companies more decision-making powers because of a less effective management control. According to *Mayers* and *Smith's* view, the appeal to act in their own interests is greater for managers of mutual insurance companies than for managers of private limited companies.[218] *Mayers* and *Smith's* managerial discretion hypothesis regarding mutual companies states that mutual insurance companies should act in branches of insurance in which only a discretionary scope of action for the management is required. These kinds of branches have few varieties regarding the overall distribution of claims or they have low pricing possibilities, because they can be well actuarially determined. Because of these two characteristics, the management only needs low competence that makes the control by the shareholders much easier. Moreover, a more specialised company has a smaller scope of action, which decreases the possibilities of enrichment by the management.[219] [220] Several empirical studies verify the managerial discretion hypothesis. A study of *Mayers* and *Smith's* states that the level of salary for managers in insurance private limited companies is higher compared to mutual insurance companies.[221] It is possible that these results indicate lower requirements for mutual insurance companies due to a restricted scope of action and a distinctive specialization.[222] Other studies have not determined clear results regarding cost differences based on dif-

215 Definition: Tender offer: A public offer to buy shares of a company above the market price with the intention to gain control. Cf. Finanz und Wirtschaft.

216 Definition: Proxy-Fight is the fight about the shareholders' vote – a take-over method by using proxy-voting powers or recruiting shareholders' votes with the goal to take control of the company without buying shares. Cf. Onpulson.de.

217 Cf. *Mayers* and *Smith* (1986), pp. 76-77.

218 Cf. *Lamm-Tennant* and *Starks* (1993), p. 31.

219 Cf. *Breuer* and *Breuer* (2002), pp. 9-10.

220 Cf. *Mayers* and *Smith* (1988), p. 353.

221 Cf. *Mayers* and *Smith* (1992), p. 68.

222 *Breuer* and *Breuer* (2002), p. 10.

ferent legal forms, which would have weakened *O'Hara's* argument regarding cost disadvantages of mutual insurance companies.[223]

6.2.2 Irrelevance of the legal form due to official supervision and competitive pressure

Insurance companies are classified in two different groups. While national insurance is obligatory and controlled by public corporations, the individual insurance is subject to private law and market-based organization. For that matter, the legal and economic relations between insurance companies and policyholders are based on autonomous decisions. Contracts can be concluded freely and independently. Official supervision and the Insurance Act are the only restrictions to the autonomy of insurance companies.[224] As long as the official supervision regarding the work of insurance companies is so strong that conflicts between owners and policyholders as well as owners and managers are levelled to the same degree then a balance between the legal forms in everyday economy life[225] is possible. Nevertheless, the primary goal of the government is the elimination of the owner-policyholder conflict and not the reduction of the opportunistic behavior of managers. Therefore, it is possible that the conflict of interests between policyholders and owners can be reduced; however, this does not mean a regulatory-induced irrelevance of the legal forms.[226]

The reduction of the opportunistic behavior of managers is only possible due to increasing competitive pressure on the market. Companies with higher costs, caused by different legal forms, cannot be competitive on a long-term basis, because they cannot transfer higher costs to the policyholders. As a result, they are economically unviable on the market. Competition is a possibility to restrict the enrichment of the management at the expense of the owners and to minimize the owner-management problem. This effect increases, the higher the price elasticity of the policyholders, the more transparent the entire insurance market, and the lower the costs for changing the insurance company for policyholders is. For this matter, competition can have a disciplinary effect and can lead to the suspension of the advantages and disadvantages caused by different legal forms. Nonetheless, when evaluating if an actual advantage is caused by the effect, it is necessary to investigate how strong the competitive pressure on the particular insurance market is.[227]

223 Cf. ibid (2002), p. 10.

224 Cf. *Möbius* and *Pallenberg* (2013), pp. 49-51.

225 *Breuer* and *Breuer* (2002), pp. 7-8.

226 Ibid (2002), p. 8.

227 Cf. ibid (2002), pp. 8-9.

Intermediate result

Both private limited companies as well as mutual insurance companies have their strengths, which emphasise their right to exist. While in private limited companies the possibility exists to minimize the owner-management conflict with the help of control instruments, in mutual insurance companies the owner-policyholder conflict can be eliminated completely. An irrelevance of the legal form only exists in case of a very distinctive competitive problem. In this case, various requirements such as high price elasticity of demand, transparency of the market, and low changing costs have to be fulfilled. Nevertheless, a regulation-driven irrelevance of the legal form cannot be assumed.

7. Conclusion and outlook

This paper has the goal to provide an overview on mutual insurance societies and joint stock companies in the Norwegian insurance sector. The historical analysis shows that the Norwegian insurance business was influenced by numerous political and economic events as well as by technological progress. Ongoing wars, economic crises, change of legal frameworks and innovations led to several foundations, liquidations, take-overs, and mergers of insurance companies. Both mutual insurance societies and joint stock companies were influenced by these changes to the same degree. It was possible to reconstruct partially the historical development for several companies due to the analysis of historical data. The analysis shows that both legal forms became firmly established on the market. During the 525 years of the Danish and Swedish occupation, the regulations for the insurance sector developed and created the legal basis in Norway that endures to this day. By comparing the legal regulations for mutual insurance societies and joint stock companies, it became obvious that no fundamental legal differences exist. However, mutual life insurance societies have the advantage of a smaller required capital equipment when they are founded. This fact gives rise to the suspicion that the legislator favours mutual insurance societies. Nevertheless, this is not a sufficient explanation for the success of mutual insurance societies in general.

Additionally, analyses of quantitative and qualitative parameters have been made to evaluate the success of both legal forms in Norway. The results of the analysis of the quantitative parameters suggest that the number of companies on the market and the ratio of total assets are not adequate parameters to evaluate success. As a result, other key figures have to be used. In contrast, data that include information

about market share and premium income provide better results when evaluating and comparing the success of joint stock companies and mutual insurance societies. Increasing market shares (2008: 38.5 %, 2015: 46.7 %) of mutual insurance societies combined with own calculations confirm the strong position of mutual insurance societies on the market. Additionally, with the help of the premium income the insurance density was calculated which signifies when comparing to the growth rates of the GDP a dynamic insurance market in Norway. At this point, the overall economic performance of mutual insurance societies has to be acknowledged due to their considerable contribution. Other ratios such as the pro-capita-premium, which is the result of comparing the number of employees to the gross premium, enables the evaluation of the efficiency of the employees. Between 2011 and 2013, the efficiency was higher for mutual insurance societies compared to the total insurance sector. This indicates, therefore, a more efficient performance of mutual insurance society employees'. This is also true for the insurance density as an indicator for the overall success of a company. However, in general all quantitative data has to be questioned critically regarding their meaning and methodical gathering. The study of *Greve* and *Hayagreeba* shows that socio-structural factors, such as the size of a social group, the choice of profession, religious and ethnic diversity as well as social disparities in society have different effects on the success of particular forms of society. While the size of the social group and the professional diversity has a positive connection with the success of mutual insurance societies, religious and ethnic diversity as well as social disparity have a negative influence on success. The correlation between cultural background, prosperity, and risk opinion of a nation may have influence on success of mutual insurance societies and joint stock companies, however, a clear connection cannot be established. Additionally, academic studies present conflicting results when the influence of the gender quota is connected to the success of a company. The results show in general that the interdependence of various factors leads to a high complexity. Therefore, the analyzed factors show no clear influence when comparing their effect on the success of a particular legal form.

Mutual societies have no access to capital markets and receive capital only by their members. As a result, mutual societies are not so prone to financial and credit crunches and, therefore, demonstrate higher potential for doing sustainable business. However, it is not possible to decide if mutual insurance societies work better or worse than joint stock companies do. Nevertheless, both legal forms have earned a right to exist on the market due to their strengths. While the owner-policyholder-problem has been resolved entirely in mutual insurance societies, the owner-management-conflict can be reduced to a minimum in joint stock companies with the help of control instruments. Therefore, neither a general irrelevance nor one imposed by regulations ex-

ist. However, the general irrelevance requires that no particular fierce competitive pressure, based on a high price elasticity of demand, high market transparency, and low exchange costs, exist. As a result, both legal forms coexist. The following paragraphs show developments and challenges for mutual insurance societies in the future.

Opportunities and risks for future developments

From the 1990's onwards, a European initiative proposed to establish a legal instrument that should help to establish European mutual societies with bylaws based on European foundations and cooperatives. In 1992, a draft for bylaws was presented to the European commission, but was withdrawn in 2006 due to the complexity of the business of mutual societies. The member states were given the freedom to decide about the types and work of mutual societies. In 2013, during the last plenary, the European Commission was asked by the European Parliament to give a legislative proposition regarding the creation of a European mutual society statute. Although a favorable opinion from the Commission on Employment and Social Affairs was made and the Commission of Legal Affairs expressed support to the adoption of a legislative text concerning the creation of such a bylaw, no further attempt has been made since this time.[228] Nonetheless, the European Parliament, the European Economic and Social Committee as well as the European Committee are willing to reinitiate this idea. A European bylaw would probably lead to more equality of opportunities for European mutual societies and offer international business activities.[229] [230] In times of globalization such measures are in particular necessary to maintain competitiveness of mutual societies. In return, mutual insurance societies have to follow the requirements of financial institutions and the regulations of Solvency II, which demands a higher solvability span and risk differentiation. The access to capital is limited for mutual societies, because they are mostly present on niche markets. This may lead to problems obeying Solvency II. The European regulations for insurance companies and financial institutions are based on the business concept of joint stock companies that makes the insurance market increasingly homogenous. In the course of such development, mutual societies may be forced to act like joint stock business and eventually demutualize.[231] With keeping this development in mind, the need of protection concerning mutual insurance societies has to be reconsidered and necessary measures have to be taken. Additionally, the adaptability of mutual societies in a changing business world is

228 Cf. http://www.ess-europe.eu/en/page/mutual-societies-top-eu-agenda; Report with recommendations to the Commission on the Statute for a European mutual society (2012/2039(INI)).

229 Cf. *Douwe* et al. (2011), p. 8

230 Cf. *Ballester* (2013), p. 6

231 Cf. *Douwe* et al. (2011), p. 8

most important. Mutual societies have two options: firstly, to give up service which are not directly connected with insurance business or, secondly, offer their services in companies with different legal forms. For example, a distinction can be made between insurance business and administration of health institutions or a distinction between optional and compulsory insurance. Moreover, mutual societies may expand their business activities to increase competitiveness by extending to new markets, offering new services to their members, organise their business more cost-efficiently, and use the economy of scale. This can be achieved by merging or cooperating with other mutual societies. Mutual insurance societies can use the business concepts of profit-orientated insurer, e.g. using an extended risk selection. This may help to improve the risk portfolio of the insurer, while using cost-efficient strategies can help to be competitive with joint stock companies. The use of profit-orientated business models has already been observed in connection with inter-generation versus intra-generation solidarity. With regard to optional health insurance, age is an important variable when calculating risks and the payment of dues, because older people have usually a higher need of health services. Therefore, insurers have to integrate in particular young people into their insurance portfolio. The more young people are part of an insurer's portfolio, the lower the insurance premiums are. However, when both mutual insurance societies and joint stock companies are on the market, the danger of cream skimming may occur. Joint stock companies focus more on young people and avoid risky customers (older, low-income) who are left to mutual insurance societies. As a result, mutual insurance societies develop to insurers focusing more on solidarity within generations and less on solidarity between generations. This means that risk diversification happens increasingly among similar policyholders. This leads to lower premiums for young people and higher premiums for older policyholders with a higher risk profile.[232]

The demographic change has been another challenge for mutual insurance societies. The increasing aging of the population has an important global effect on the social security system. While in the near future, age groups with higher birth rates will reach retirement age, the number of employees will drop significantly and, at the same time, the costs for pensions and health care will increase. The aging population has to be taken care of by the smaller group of the working population.[233] According to studies, the European average of the age quotient[234] will increase from 25.4 % to approximately 53.5 % in

[232] Cf. *Douwe* et al. (2011), p. 71-72

[233] Cf. *ibid.*, p. 66-67

[234] This is the number of people over 65 years old divided by the number of people between 14 and 65 years old.

2060. This means that in 2060 two people between the age of 14 and 65 have to secure the income of someone over the age of 65. In Norway, the numbers a lower compared to the EU-average (22.1 % in 2008 and 43.9 % in 2060).[235] The aging population increases the pressure on the national budget due to increasing costs for social security. It has been calculated that in most EU member states the national costs for health care are going to increase between 0.7 % and 3.8 % of the GDP (in Norway around 1.6 % of the GDP) between 2007 and 2060.[236] Higher costs for health care and pensions will influence future social security systems. Therefore, several nations have already started to change their social security systems. Changes comprise the retirement age, to move services taken care of at the present by obligatory and statutory systems to voluntary social and health care insurances, and the use of private pension schemes. It is not clear if in the future the national social security systems are able to offer sufficient security for all people or if additional regulations will be necessary. This question is in particular important for people with a low income, old people, and similar risk groups.[237]

While future challenges for social security systems can be estimated quite well, the flexibility of mutual societies towards changing business environments are harder to predict. Although mutual insurance societies have now a large market share, the current developments show that mutual insurance societies will work more profit-orientated in the future due to increasing competitions and legal standardization for insurance companies.

[235] Cf. *Giannakouris* (2008), p. 1

[236] Cf. *Przywara* (2010), pp. 45-46

[237] Cf. *Douwe* et al. (2011), p. 69

Appendix

Definitions of types of companies in Norway[238]

Aksjeselskap (AS) – private limited company / PLC

A corporate enterprise, registered in the commercial register, has to have a capital stock of at least 30.000 NOK[239]. The annual account has to be taken place seven months after the end of the business year at the latest. The company will be winded up, if the annual account is not available after 13 months after the end of the business year at the latest. In the event of a delayed annual account, a fee is imposed on the chairman of the supervision board.

Allmenn Aksjeselskap (ASA) – public limited company

A private limited company, registered in the commercial register, has to have a capital stock of at least one Mio NOK[240]. The shares of the company are traded publically. The annual account has to be taken place seven months after the end of the business year at the latest. The company will be winded up, if the annual account is not available after 13 months after the end of the business year at the latest. In the event of a delayed annual account, a fee is imposed on the chairman of the supervision board.

For trading the shares of the ASA at the stock exchange in Oslo, transparency requirements have to be fulfilled. These include among other things a market capitalization of 300 Mio. NOK, a minimum age of the company of 3 years, a nominal value of a share of at least 10 NOK as well as a minimum of 500 shareholders who each hold shares of not less than 10,000 NOK.[241]

Ansvarlig Norsk Selskap (ANS) – General commerical partnership

It is registered as general commercial partnership in the commercial register. The shareholders are personally liable for the joint and several obligations of the company. The annual account is not available publicly.

---

238 Cf. *Dan & Brandstreet*.

239 Cf. Lov om aksjeselskaper-1997-06-13-44) § 3-1 first sunsection.

240 Cf. Lov om allmennaksjeselskaper-1997-06-13-45) § 3-1 first sunsection.

241 Cf. *Oslo Børs* – Listing Requirements.

Delt Ansvar (DA) – Partnership limited by shares

It is registered as a partnership limited by shares in the commercial register. The shareholders are liable for the joint and several debts of the company. The annual account is not available publicly.

Enkeltmannsforetak (ENK) – Sole proprietor

This kind of company is registered as sole proprietor in the commercial register. The owner is liable for the joint and several debts of the company. The annual account is not available publicly.

Begrenset Ansvar (BA) – limited liability Company for cooperatives

It is registered as cooperative in the commercial register. The annual account is not available publicly.

Bibliography

Ahern, Kenneth R. / Dittmar, Amy K. (2009), „The Changing of the Boards: The Value Effect of a Massive Exogenous Shock", Working Paper University of Michigan, http://citeseerx.ist.psu.edu/viewdoc/download?doi=10.1.1.370.9925&rep=rep1&type=pdf (29.01.2015)

Altinn (2013), https://www.altinn.no/en/Start-and-Run-a-Business/Start-up-and-registration/Insurance-and-pensions/Mandatory-occupational-pensions/ (15.12.2014)

AMICE (2010), „The market share of Mutual and Cooperative Insurance in Europe 2008", http://www.amice-eu.org/Download.ashx?ID=17186 (08.01.2015)

Amnéus, G. (1900), „Noway. Official Publication for the Paris exhibition, 1900", Aktie-Bogtrkkeriet, Kristiania 1900

Ashforth, Blake E. / Johnston, Scott A. (2001), „Which hat to wear? The relative salience of multiple identities in organizational contexts" p. 31-48 in *Hogg, Michael A. / Terry, Deborah J.* (eds.): Social Identity Process in Organizational Contexts, Psychology Press, New York, 2012

Auchinleck / Bruce, Komar / Edmund, Mühlbauer / Eva (2002), „Optionen für Versicherungsveriene: Demutualisieren oder restrukturieren?" in Versicherungswirtschaft Heft 7, p. 455-458, Köln, 2002

Ballester, Blanca (2013), „Ein Statut der Europäischen Gegenseitigkeitsgesellschaft" in European Added Value Assessment 1/2013, Europäische Union, Brüssel

Blau, Peter M. (1977), „Inequality and Heterogenity", The Free Press, New York

Benkel, Gert Andreas (2002), „Der Versicherungsverein auf Gegenseitigkeit", 2. Auflage, C. H. Beck, München

Börse Frankfurt (2013), http://www.boerse-frankfurt.de/de/nachrichten/unternehmensnachrichten/roundup-fusionierte+pruefkonzern+dnv+gl+group+sieht+gute+wachstumschancen+5244171 (07.12.2014)

Breuer, Wolfgang / Breuer, Claudia (2002), „Versicherungsvereine auf Gegenseitigkeit und Versicherungsaktiengesellschaften" Arbeitspapiere der Betrieblichen Finanzwirtschaft, RWTH Aachen, http://www.bfw.rwth-aachen.de/kos/WNetz?art=File.download&id=173 (15.01.2015)

Broek, Simon / Buiskool, Bert-Jan / Horst, Rob van der / Vennekens, Alexandra (2012a), „Study on the current situation and prospects of mutuals in Europe", Final Report, European Comission Projectnumber: BA03954, http://ec.europa.eu/enterprise/policies/sme/files/mutuals/prospects_mutuals_fin_en.pdf (24.11.2014)

Broek, Simon / Buiskool, Bert-Jan / Horst, Rob van der / Vennekens, Alexandra (2012b), „Study on the current situation and prospects of mutuals in Europe", Final Report Country Studies, European Comission Projectnumber: BA03954, http://ec.europa.eu/enterprise/policies/sme/files/mutuals/prospects_mutuals_annex_en.pdf (24.11.2014)

Börse Frankfurt (2013), http://www.boerse-frankfurt.de/de/nachrichten/unternehmensnachrichten/

Bull, Edvard / Anker, Øyvind / Jansen, Jonas (1929), „Norsk biografisk Leksikon", Band 4., Aschehoug, Oslo

Businessdictionary – Total Assets, http://www.businessdictionary.com/definition/total-assets.html (12.04.2015)

Carlén, Martin (2013), „Financing infrastructure" in The Norwegian Financial Industry, Finance Norway, https://www.fno.no/pagefiles/11388/%28en%29download/the%20norwegian%20financial%20industry%202013.pdf (29.11.2014)

Carter, David A. / Simkins, Betty J. / Simpson, Gary W. (2003), „Corporate Governance, Board Diversity and Firm Value" in Financial Review, Vol. 38, No 1, p. 33-35

Cefor (2011), „100 years reflections", The Nordic Association of Marine Insurers 1911-2011 http://www.cefor.no/Documents/About%20Cefor/Cefor%20Centennial%20book.pdf (06.12.2014)

Cefor – About Cefor, http://www.cefor.no/About-Cefor/ (22.12.2014)

Chui, Andy C.W. / Titman, Sheridan / Wei, John K.C., (2010) „Individualism and momentum around the world" in Journal of Finance, Vol. 65, No. 1, p. 361–392.

Country Studies, European Comission Projectnumber: BA03954, http://ec.europa.eu/enterprise/policies/sme/files/mutuals/prospects_mutuals_annex_en.pdf (24.11.2014)

Danmark Historien, http://danmarkshistorien.dk/leksikon-og-kilder/vis/materiale/brand-forsikkrings-anordning-1761/ (01.12.2014)

Dan & Brandstreet, http://dbinteractive.dbsverige.se/England/Rad&tips/bolagsfo.htm#BolagsformeriNorge (17.12.2014)

Den Norske Forsikringsforening – Brage, http://www.forsikringsforeningen.no/brage-2/ (15.12.2014)

Den Norske Forsinkringsforening – Drosjeforsikringen, http://www.forsikringsforeningen.no/Drosjeforsikringen/ (17.12.2014)

Den Norske Forsikringsforeningen – Historikk, http://www.forsikringsforeningen.no/historikk-forsikringshistorisk-forum/ (21.12.2014)

Den Norske Forsikringsforening – Krigsforsikringen, http://www.forsikringsforeningen.no/krigsforsikringen/ (06.12.2014)

Den Norske Forsinkringsforening – NBG, http://www.forsikringsforeningen.no/nbg/ (17.12.2014)

Den Norske Forsinkringsforening – NKP, http://www.forsikringsforeningen.no/nkp/ (19.12.2014)

Den Norske Forsinkringsforening – Norges Brannkasse, http://www.forsikringsforeningen.no/brannkassen/ (24.11.2014)

Den Norske Forsinkringsforening – Samtrygd, http://www.forsikringsforeningen.no/Samtrygd/ (17.12.2014)

Den Norske Forsinkringsforening – Storebrand, http://www.forsikringsforeningen.no/storebrand/ (24.11.2014)

Den Norske Forsinkringsforening – Unitas, http://www.forsikringsforeningen.no/unitas/ (09.12.2014)

Den Norske Forsinkringsforening – Vesta, http://www.forsikringsforeningen.no/vesta/ (13.12.2014)

DNB Group Annual Report (2013), https://www.dnb.no/portalfront/nedlast/no/om-oss/resultater/2013/annual-report-dnb-group-2013.pdf (28.11.2014)

DNK, https://www.warrisk.no/about/history/ (08.12.2014)

DNV GL, http://www.dnvgl.com/about-dnvgl/history.aspx (07.12.2014)

Ekberg, Espen (2013), „Trygghet risiko og forsikring", Norske historiedager Sogndal 2-5 mai 2013, http://historiedagar2013.hisf.no/wp-content/uploads/2013/03/Ekberg-Spesialisering-i-norsk-forsikring-1914-.pdf (03.01.2015)

European Commission (2003), „Consultation Document – Mutual Societies in an enlarged Europe", http://ec.europa.eu/enterprise/policies/sme/files/mutuals/mutuals-consult-doc_en.pdf (25.11.2014)

Eurostat, Gross Capital Product at Market prices, http://ec.europa.eu/eurostat/tgm/refreshTableAction.do?tab=table&plugin=1&pcode=tec00001&language=en (09.01.2015)

Espeli, Harald (2011), „Fortropper for gjensidig skadeforsikring i Norge", http://historiedagar2013.hisf.no/wp-content/uploads/2013/03/Espeli-Fortropper-for-gjensidig-skadeforsikring-i-Norge.pdf (27.11.2014)

EZB, Historische Durchschnittswerte EUR / USD, https://www.ecb.europa.eu/stats/exchange/eurofxref/html/eurofxref-graph-usd.en.html (09.01.2015)

Færden, K. (1967), „Forsikringsvesenets Historie i Norge 1814-1914", Wesmanns Skandinaviske Forsikringsfond, Oslo

Fahl, Holger (2005), „Corporate Governance im Versicherungsverein a. G.", *Lorenz, Egon* (ed.), Verlag Versicherungswirtschaft GmbH, Karlsruhe

Feinstein, Charles H. / Temin, Peter / Toniolo, Gianni (2008), „The World Economony between the World Wars", Oxford University Press, New York

Finans Norge (2014), „Nøkkeltall for norsk forsikring", https://www.fno.no/pagefiles/650/n%C3%B8kkeltall%20i%20skadeforsikring/n%C3%B8kkeltall%20for%20norsk%20forsikring%202014%20-%20brosjyre.pdf (11.01.2015)

Finanstilsynet – Annual Reports 2000-2017

Annual Report 2000, p. 11, http://www.finanstilsynet.no/archive/Ekstra/vev03082001/aarsmeld2000/kredittilsynet2000.pdf (04.01.2015)

Annual Report 2001, p. 18, http://www.finanstilsynet.no/Global/English/Reports/Annual%20Reports/Annual_Report_2001.pdf (04.01.2015)

Annual Report 2002, p. 14, http://www.finanstilsynet.no/Global/English/Reports/Annual%20Reports/Annual_report_2002.pdf (04.01.2015)

Annual Report 2003, p. 16, http://www.finanstilsynet.no/Global/English/Reports/Annual%20Reports/Annual_rep03.pdf (04.01.2015)

Annual Report 2004, p. 22, http://www.finanstilsynet.no/archive/0sto/01/03/Aarsm070.pdf (04.01.2015)

Annual Report 2005, p. 18, http://www.finanstilsynet.no/archive/stab_pdf/01/02/Annua053.pdf (04.01.2015)

Annual Report 2006, p. 29, http://www.finanstilsynet.no/archive/stab_pdf/01/03/Annua069.pdf (04.01.2015)

Annual Report 2007, p. 23, http://www.finanstilsynet.no/archive/stab_pdf/01/05/KT080022.pdf (04.01.2015)

Annual Report 2008, p. 26, http://www.finanstilsynet.no/Global/English/Reports/Annual%20Reports/KT_Annual_Report_2008.pdf (04.01.2015)

Annual Report 2009, p. 31, http://www.finanstilsynet.no/Global/English/Reports/Annual%20Reports/Finanstilsynet_Annual_Report_2009.pdf (04.01.2015)

Annual Report 2010, p. 25, http://www.finanstilsynet.no/Global/English/Reports/Annual%20Reports/Finanstilsynet_Annual_Report_2010.pdf (04.01.2015)

Annual Report 2011, p. 20, http://www.finanstilsynet.no/Global/English/Reports/Annual%20Reports/Annual_Report_2011.pdf (04.01.2015)

Annual Report 2012, p. 22, http://www.finanstilsynet.no/Global/English/Reports/Annual%20Reports/Annual_Report_2012.pdf (04.01.2015)

Annual Report 2013, p. 22, http://www.finanstilsynet.no/Global/English/Reports/Annual%20Reports/Annual_Report_2013.pdf (04.01.2015)

Annual Report 2016, p. 12, https://www.finanstilsynet.no/contentassets/ff339532013445568 79eb1f2613e7a43/annual-report-2016.pdf (07.05.2018)

Annual Report 2017, p. 39, https://www.finanstilsynet.no/contentassets/fb9e3ec2b17f4c4c9772801ce08f184e/annual-report-2017.pdf (15.02.2019)

Finanstilsynet (1988), „Act on Insurance Activity“, http://www.finanstilsynet.no/Global/English/Laws_and_regulations/Insurance_Pensions/Act_Insurance_Activity.pdf (24.11.2014)

Finanstilsynet (2013), „Act on insurance companies, pension undertakings and their activities etc. (Insurance Act)“, The Financial Supervisory Authority of Norway, Translation as of June 2013 http://www.finanstilsynet.no/Global/English/Laws_and_regulations/Insurance_Pensions/Insurance_Act.pdf (24.11.2014)

Finanstilsynet Rundskriv (2013), http://www.finanstilsynet.no/no/Artikkelarkiv/Rundskriv/2013/1_kvartal/Regulering-i-samsvar-med--5-i-Forskrift-om-minstekrav-til-egenkapitalen-i-norske-forsikringsselskaper/ (24.11.2014)

Finanz und Wirtschaft, http://www.fuw.ch/term/ubernahmeangebot-tender-offer/ (09.02.2015)

FNO, Finanse Norge, https://www.fno.no/en/ (12.01.2015)

Forbes Global 2000, http://www.forbes.com/global2000/ (15.12.2014)
Gabler Wirtschaftslexikon – Demutualisierung, http://wirtschaftslexikon.gabler.de/Definition/demutualisierung.html (14.04.2015)
Gabler Wirtschaftslexikon – öffentlich-rechtliche Versicherungsunternehmen, http://wirtschaftslexikon.gabler.de/Definition/oeffentlich-rechtliche-versicherungsunternehmen.html (27.01.2015)
Gabler Wirtschaftslexikon –Versicherungsgesellschaft, http://wirtschaftslexikon.gabler.de/Definition/versicherungsgesellschaft.html (27.01.2015)
Gjensidige Annual Report 2010, https://www.gjensidige.no/group/investor-relations/corporate-governance/merger-with-the-wholly-owned-danish-subsidiary-gjensidiges-arbejdsskadeforsikring-a-s/_attachment/6478?_ts=13d87e6d177 (14.04.2015)
Gjensidige Annual Report 2014, http://feed.ne.cision.com/wpyfs/00/00/00/00/00/2C/3A/F6/wkr0010.pdf (14.04.2015)
Gjensidige Foundation, http://www.gjensidigestiftelsen.no/no/In+English (14.042015)
Gjens-Onstad, Ole, „Direct Taxation: Income and net wealth taxation", Norwegian School of Busines, University of Oslo, University of Stavanger, http://eatlp.org/uploads/public/Reports%20Rotterdam/National%20Report%20Norway.pdf
Greve, Heinrich R. / Hayagreeva, Rao (2006), „Mutual Consent: The Demography of Organizational Identity in the Insurance Industry in Norway", http://www.chicagobooth.edu/research/workshops/orgs-markets/archive/hgrevecommunity2006.pdf (24.11.2014)
Hofstede Geert (2001), „Culture's Consequences, Comparing Values, Behaviors, Institutions, and Organizations Across Nations", Sage Publications, Thousand Oaks
Hofstede Centre – Country Comparison, http://geert-hofstede.com/countries.html (23.01.2015)
Hsee, Christopher K. / Weber, Elke U. (2010), „Cross-National Differences in Risk Preference and Lay Predictions" in Journal of Behavioral Decision Making, Vol. 12, No 2, p. 165-179
ICMIF (2014a), http://www.icmif.org/news/mutual-and-cooperative-insurers-continue-outperform-rest-insurance-market-0 (07.01.2015)
ICMIF (2014b), http://bccm.coop/wp/wp-content/uploads/2014/07/BCCM_webinar_STarbuckICMIF.pdf, (11.01.2015)
ICMIF Global Mutual Market Share 2010/2012/2013/2017.
ICMIF (2018): Facts and figures – Mutual and cooperative insurance in Europe, AMICE aisbl & ICMIF, Vol 2,
Global Mutual Market Share 2010, http://www.icmif.org/2010-mutual-market-share-icmif-global-500-reports (07.01.2015)
Global Mutual Market Share 2012, http://www.icmif.org/2012-global-mutual-market-share (07.01.2015)

Global Mutual Market Share 2013, http://www.icmif.org/global-mutual-market-share-2013 (30.03.2015)

Investment & Pensions Europe (2014a), „Pension in Nordic Region: Still a competitive market", http://www.ipe.com/pensions/pensions-in/nordic-region/pensions-in-nordic-region-still-a-competitive-market/10004154.fullarticle (28.11.2014)

Investment & Pensions (2014b), „Norway's Kristiansund, Eide award pension schemes to KLP", http://www.ipe.com/countries/nordic-region/norways-kristiansund-eide-award-pension-schemes-to-klp/10003845.fullarticle (29.11.2014)

Investment & Pensions Europe (2014c), „Norwegian roundup: KLP, transfers, Finanstilsynet", http://www.ipe.com/countries/nordic-region/norwegian-roundup-klp-transfers-finanstilsynet/10004683.fullarticle (29.11.2014)

Insurance Europe (2014), European Insurance in Figures, Statistics N°48, http://www.insuranceeurope.eu/uploads/Modules/Publications/european-insurance-in-figures-2.pdf (09.01.2015)

Insurance Europe (2015), European Insurance in Figures, Statistics N°50, http://www.insuranceeurope.eu/facts-figures/statistical-publications/european-insurance-in-figures (30.03.2015)

IWF (2014), World Economic Outlook, http://www.imf.org/external/pubs/ft/weo/2014/01/weodata/download.aspx (21.01.2015)

Jannott, Horst K. (1974), „Eigenkapitalbedarf und Eigenkapitalausstattung der Rückversicherer" S. 185-218 in *Hauß, Fritz / Schmidt, Reimer* (eds): Festschrift für Ernst Klingmüller, Verlag Versicherungswirtschaft GmbH, Karlsruhe

Jensen, Michael C. / Meckling, William H. (1976), „Theory of the Firm: Managerial Behavior, Agency Costs and Ownership Structure" in Journal of Financial Economics, Vol. 3, No. 4, p. 305-360

Johnsen, Oscar Albert (1939), „Norwegische Wirtschaftsgeschichte", Verlag von Gustav Fischer, Jena

Klausen, Kurt Klaudi / Selle, Per (1996), „The third sector in Scandinavia", in Voluntas, Vol. 7, p. 99-122

KLP Annual Report (2013), https://www.klp.no/polopoly_fs/1.25280.1398330304!/menu/standard/file/KLP%20%C3%A5rsrapport%202013_engelsk_web.pdf (28.11.2014)

Lamm-Tennant, Joan / Starks, Laura T. (1993), „Stock Versus Mutual Ownership Structures: The Risk Implications" in The Journal of Business, Vol. 66, No. 1, p. 29-46

Laux, Helmut / Gillenkirch, Robert M. / Schenk-Mathes, Heike Y. (2014), „Entscheidungstheorie", 9. Auflage, Springer-Verlag, Berlin Heidelberg

Lee, Peggy M. / James, Erika Hayes (2007), „She'-e-os: Gender Effects and Investor Reactions to the Announcements of Top Executive Appointments" in Strategic Management Journal, Vol. 28, No 3, p. 227-241

Liable, Marie-Christine (2013), „Gender Diversity in Top Management and Firm Performance: An Analysis with the IAB-Establishment Panel“, Institute for Employment Research (IAB), CAED Conference Paper, Atlanta, http://www.frbatlanta.org/documents/news/conferences/13caed/g_1_laible.pdf (29.01.2015)

Lov om aksjeselskaper-*1997-06-13-44*, https://lovdata.no/dokument/NL/lov/1997-06-13-44 (30.12.2014)

Lov om allmennaksjeselskaper-*1997-06-13-45*, https://lovdata.no/dokument/NL/lov/1997-06-13-45 (30.12.2014)

Lov-1999-01-15-2, WiPrG, https://lovdata.no/dokument/NL/lov/1999-01-15-2 (24.11.2014)

Lov-2005-06-10-44, IA, https://lovdata.no/dokument/NL/lov/2005-06-10-44 (24.11.2014)

Lov-2007-06-29-81, GenG, https://lovdata.no/dokument/NL/lov/2007-06-29-81 (24.11.2014)

Lov-2009-06-19-46, Gesetz zur Änderung des Gesetzes über Finanzinstitute und anderer Gesetze, https://lovdata.no/dokument/LTI/lov/2009-06-19-46 (24.11.2014)

Maassen, Gregory Francesco (2002), „An International Comparison of Corporate Governance Models“, 3. edition, Spencer Stuart, Amsterdam

Mayers, David / Smith, Clifford W. Jr. (1986), „Ownership Structure and Control, The Mutualization of Stock Life Insurance Companies“ in Journal of Financial Economics, Vol. 16, No. 1, p. 73-98

Mayers, David / Smith, Clifford W. Jr. (1988), „Ownership Structure across Lines of Property-Casualty Insurance“ in Journal of Financial Economics, Vol. 31, No. 2, p. 351-378

Mayers, David / Smith, Clifford W. Jr. (1992), „Compensation in the Life Insurance Industry“ in Journal of Business, Vol. 65, No. 1, p. 51-74

Möbius, Christian / Pallenberg, Catherine (2013), „Risikomanagement in Versicherungsunternehmen“, *Kornmeier, Martin / Schneider, Willy* (eds), Springer Gabler Verlag, Heidelberg

Moen, Arild (10.12.2010), „Gjensidige Raises $1.66 Billion in IPO“, in The Wall Street Journal, http://www.wsj.com/articles/SB1000142405274870 4457604576010772801318608 (14.04.2015)

Mörsdorf, Roland (2012), „Die norwegische GmbH – Neueste Rechtsentwicklungen im Überblick“, in Recht der Internationalen Wirtschaft (RIW), Heft 4, 2012, p. 211-223

Molm, Linda D. / Peterson, Gretchen / Takahashi, Nobuyuki (1999), „Power in Negotiated and Reciprocal Exchange“ in American Sociological Review, Vol. 64, No. 6, p. 876-890

Mot alminnelig brannforsikring, http://digitalarkivet.uib.no/sat/1766brtxt/brannforsikring.htm (05.12.2014)

Nappdata.org, https://www.nappdata.org/napp/resources/excelfiles_maps/NorwayProvinces.jpg (02.01.2015)

Nicols, Alfred (1967), „Stock Versus Mutual Savings and Loan Associations: Some Evidence of Differences in Behavior“ in The American Economic Review, Vol. 57, No. 2, p. 337-346

Norwegian Hull Club, https://www.norclub.no/network/one-for-all-and-all-for-one/ (08.12.2014)

O'Hara, Maureen (1981), „Property Rights and the Financial Firm“ in Journal of Law and Economics, Vol. 24, No.2, p. 317-332

O'Reilly III, Charles A. / Caldwell, David F. / Barnett, William P. (1989), „Work group demography, social integration, and turnover“ in Administrative Science Quarterly, Vol. 34, No. 1, 1989, p. 21-37

Onpulson.de, http://www.onpulson.de/lexikon/proxy-fight/ (09.02.2015)

Orson, Mancur (1965), „The logic of collective action“, 20. Auflage, Harvard University Press, Cambridge

Oslo Børs – Listing requirements, http://www.oslobors.no/ob_eng/Oslo-Boers/Listing/Shares-equity-certificates-and-rights-to-shares/Listing-requirements (03.01.2015)

Petrick, Fritz (2002), „Norwegen: Von den Anfängen bis zur Gegenwart“, 1. Auflage, Friedrich Pustet Verlag, Regensburg

Regjeringen (2010), „Gjensidige Forsikring BA og Gjensidigestiftelsen gis tillatelse til omdanning“, https://www.regjeringen.no/nb/dokumenter/Gjensidige-Forsikring-BA-og-Gjensidigestiftelsen-gis-tillatelse-til-omdanning/id608973/ (17.12.2014)

Rieger, Marc Oliver / Wang, Mei / Hens, Thorsten (2014), „Risk preferences around the World“ in Management Science, Published online in Articles in Advance 21 Feb 2014 http://pubsonline.informs.org/doi/suppl/10.1287/mnsc.2013.1869 (21.01.2015)

Salamon, LesterM. / Sokolowski, S. Wojciech / and Associates (2004), „Global Civil Society: Dimensions of the Nonprofit Sector“, Vol. 2, Kumarian Press, Blommfield

Schierenbeck, Henner (ed) (1994), „Bank- und Versicherungslexikon“, 2. Auflage Oldenbourg Verlag, München Wien

Schulenburg, Graf von der, J.-Matthias (2005), „Versicherungsökonomik Ein Leitfaden für Studium und Praxis“ Verlag Versicherungswirtschaft GmbH, Karlsruhe

Smith, Nina / Smith, Valdemar / Verner, Mette (2006), „Do Women in Top Management affect Firm Performance? A Panel Study of 2500 Danish Firms“ in International Journal of Productivity and Performance Management, Vol. 55, No 7, p. 569–593

Spiller, Richard (1972) „Ownership and Performance: Stock and Mutual Life Insurance Companies“ in The Journal of Risk and Insurance, Vol. 39, No. 1, p. 17-25

Statista (1), Wachstum des realen Bruttoinlandproduktes (BIP) von 2003 bis 2013 (gegenüber Vorjahr), http://de.statista.com/statistik/daten/studie/14549/umfrage/wachstum-des-bruttoinlandsprodukts-bip-in-norwegen/ (30.03.2015)

Statista (2), Norwegen: Arbeitslosenquote von 2004 bis 2014, http://de.statista.com/statistik/daten/studie/17323/umfrage/arbeitslosenquote-in-norwegen/

Statistisk sentralbyrå Kommunekatalog, (Stand 01.01.2013), Kommunekatalog gjeldende fra 1. januar 2013, http://www.ssb.no/informasjon/kommunekatalog/kommunekatalogen (29.11.2014)

Storebrand Annual Report (2012), http://www.storebrand.no/site/stb.nsf/Get/get190fea5be79de07534000d6ec4c87c79/$FILE/Annual-Report-2012-full-english.pdf (28.11.2014)

Storvik, Aagoth / Teigen, Mari (2010), „Das norwegische Experiment – eine Frauenquote für Aufsichtsräte", Friedrich-Ebert-Stiftung http://www.astrid-online.it/Le-pari-op/Documenti/FES_Frauenquote_06_2010.pdf (27.01.2015)

Tajfel, Henri / Turner, John C. (1979), „The social identity theory of inter-group behavior", S. 276-293 in Jost, John T./Sidanius, Jim (Hrsg.): Political psychology: Key readings. Key readings in social psychology, Psychology Press, New York

Tarrow, Sidney G. (1994), „Power in Movement: Social Movements, Collective Action and Politics", Cambridge University Press, Cambridge

Theis, Alexander (2005), „Die Europäische Gegenseitigkeitsgesellschaft", Klingmüller, Ernst/Deutsch, *Erwin / Herber, Rolf / Hübner, Ulrich / Medicus, Dieter / Roth, Wulf-Henning / Schlechtriem, Peter* (eds), Verlag Versicherungswirtschaft GmbH, Karlsruhe

Terjesen, Siri / Sealy, Ruth / Singh, Val (2009), „Women Directors on Corporate Boards: A Review and Research Agenda", in Corporate Governance: An International Review, Vol. 17, No 3, p. 320–337

Thomsen, Allan Mylius (06.11.1999), „Kongelig brandforsikring", in Jyllands-Posten, http://jyllands-posten.dk/indland/kbh/ECE3276729/kongelig-brandforsikring/ (30.11.2014)

Tryg, http://tryg.com/en/about-tryg/history/index.html (13.12.2014)

Url, Thomas (1996), „Kennzahlen zur österreichischen Versicherungswirtschaft" Studie des Österreichischen Instituts für Wirtschaftsforschung im Auftrag des Verbandes der Versicherungsunternehmen Österreichs (VVÖ), Österreichisches Institut für Wirtschaftsforschung, Wien

Vesta Forsinkring AS, https://snl.no/Vesta_Forsikring_AS (24.11.2014) roundup+fusionierter+pruefkonzern+dnv+gl+group+sieht+gute+wach stumschancen+5244171 (07.12.2014)

Part III.
New Organizational Forms of Insurance Companies

The Legal Foundations of the Versicherungsvereins auf Gegenseitigkeit in Austria - Insurance Supervision Act – VAG 2016[1]

Johann Brazda

The European guideline of Solvency II put Austrian insurance supervision on a completely new legal basis. Solvency II was implemented in Austria via the Insurance Supervision Act of 2016, which became effective on January 1, 2016. However, the regulations of the VAG 1978 regarding the mutual insurance company remain in effect mostly unchanged.

1. Requirements for insurance undertakings in Austria

The VAG 2016 excludes from its scope pension companies, activities in insurance classes belonging to personal insurance by corporations under public law and assistance activities provided in the event of accident or motor vehicle breakdown. It determines that companies with their main office in Austria which pursue contractual insurance activities (§ 5 Z 1) or reinsurance activities (§ 5 Z 2) fall under the Insurance Supervision Act. This applies to all business activities of insurance companies with their main office in Austria, while it only applies to the Austrian business activities of companies with their main office not in Austria. – The main requirement for them is a valid licence by the Financial Market Authority of Austria - FMA (*Finanzmarktaufsicht Österreich*) for their insurance undertaking in Austria. – The management of the company of foreign subsidiaries has the same

[1] Federal Act on the operation and supervision of contractual insurance – VAG 2016 (Bundesgesetz über den Betrieb und die Beaufsichtigung der Vertragsversicherung, BGBl. I Nr. 34/2015)

rights and obligations as those applying to the legal representatives of an Austrian undertaking as specified in the Insurance Supervision Act. An insurance contract is considered to be concluded when persons are involved who have their permanent residence in Austria or when there is an involvement of a professional intermediary or consultant, irrespective of the form of involvement (§ 13 Abs. 3 VAG).

The Austrian Financial Market Authority determines whether an undertaking is subject to the provisions of the Insurance Supervision Act (§ 1 Abs. 4 VAG). Apart from regulations regarding Insurance Supervision Act, this law also comprises civil law regulations regarding the transfer of insurance activities, mutual insurance companies under company law, financial statement, bankruptcy, and legal sanctions. As mentioned above, the FMA conducts the insurance supervision. Its duties and organization are regulated in the Financial Market Authority Law (BGBL I 2001/97).[2]

However, Non-EU insurance companies with their main office in a country which is part of the European Economic Zone do not fall under the Insurance Supervision Act. They are supervised by the Financial Market Authority of their own country.[3] The Austrian Financial Market Authority supervises small insurance undertakings (§5 Z 4), insurance holding companies (§ 195 Abs. 1 Z 8), mutual insurance companies the object of which is limited to asset management (§ 63 Abs. 3), private foundations (§ 66 Abs. 1), and single/special purpose companies (§5 Z 33) with their main office in Austria.

2. The concept of branch separation

The Austrian insurance market has been characterized traditionally by the dominance of the so-called "composite insurance". These composite insurers are insurance companies that offer several insurance classes, such as life, health, non-life or casualty insurance.[4]

The concept of branch separation signifies that insurance companies are only allowed to offer particular insurance classes at the same time. This means that the licence for life insurance can only be combined with related fields except non-life insurance, health insurance, and reinsurance. The licence for re-insurance may be granted for non-life

---

2 Cf. *Baran, P.* (2016): Das Österreichische Versicherungsaufsichtsrecht, 3rd edition, Vienna, p. 25.

3 Cf. Ibid., p. 32.

4 Cf. FMA (ed.): Bericht über die Lage der Versicherungswirtschaft 2015, p. 33.

reinsurance activity, life reinsurance activity or all types of reinsurance activities (§7 Abs 3 VAG). However, a licence for health and casualty insurances as well as re-insurances can be granted to companies that offer indemnity insurances.[5]

The concept of branch separation was introduced into Austrian law with the adoption of EU law. However, insurance companies which had been licensed for several insurance branches before the 2nd of May 1992 (signing of the EWR treaty) were allowed to continue different insurance classes. This means that insurance companies which offered several insurance classes before the EWR treaty became law are not affected by this rule.[6]

The primary reason for this concept is that policyholders and beneficiaries of life assurances should not be influenced by disadvantageous results of other insurance classes. The balance sheet of insurance companies with composite undertakings have to show the effects on their own funds separately with regard to their various activities, i.e. life assurances, health insurances, and indemnity insurances (§ 141 Abs. 1 VAG). Surpluses may be transferred to another balance sheet group only as long as in accordance with Article 194, the theoretical life Minimum Capital Requirement and the theoretical non-life Minimum Capital Requirement are fulfilled.

Branches of insurance companies with their main office in other than EU member countries are not allowed to offer other than life assurances regardless of their licensed insurance branches in their country.[7]

3. Legal structures of insurance companies in Austria

Since the beginning of insurance supervision in 1880, two legal forms have been permitted for private insurance undertakings in Austria. The association act from 1852 had already stated that insurance companies needed an official permission for their formation. According to the insurance regulation of 1880, insurance companies had to be formed as a joint stock company or a mutual insurance company.[8] Both legal

---

5 Cf. *Baran, P.* (2016): Das Österreichische Versicherungsaufsichtsrecht, 3rd edition, Vienna, p. 41.

6 Cf. Ibid.

7 Cf. Ibid., p. 42.

8 Cf. *Korinek, S.* (2008): Der österreichische Versicherungsvereine auf Gegenseitigkeit; in: *Bürke, J.* (ed.): Rechtliche Rahmenbedingungen für Versicherungsvereine

forms still exist: according to §8 Abs. 1 VAG, insurance or re-insurance undertakings shall only be operated with the legal form of a joint stock company or a mutual insurance company. Since 2004, the legal form of a European Company (SE) is admissible to.[9]

Today all insurance undertakings are still supervised. § 1 VAG states that insurance undertakings, small insurance undertakings, small associations etc. "shall be subject to supervision in accordance with the provisions of this federal act". Moreover, mutual insurance companies are regulated by additional procedures and joint stock companies are subject to the Company Law. Although mutual insurance companies are similar to cooperatives, there are references to certain Company Law rules.

According to § 6 Abs. 1, the pursuit of contractual insurance activities in Austria requires a licence granted by the FMA, unless explicitly stated otherwise. The licence can be refused due to various reasons (cf. § 8 Abs. 2 VAG).

4. Mutual insurance companies

4.1 Organizational Standards

The organizational standards for mutual insurance companies are stated in the Insurance Supervision Act (2016). However, the literature covering this topic discusses this inclusion in a slightly controversial way. Some authors regarded it as somewhat out of place. Others emphasise the connection between supervision law and organizational law of mutual insurance companies. The latter opinion points to the fact that the formation of mutual insurance companies can only take place when based on a valid license. Additionally, the Insurance Supervision Act (2016) includes norms to safeguard the interests of their members. Although the second part of the Insurance Supervision Act (2016) seems not to fit into the supervisory purpose norm structure of the Insurance Supervision Act generally, an inclusion of the mutual

auf Gegenseitigkeit – Festschrift zum 100 jährigen Bestehen der Stuttgarter Lebensversicherung a.G., Karlsruhe, p. 157.

[9] Cf. *Baran, P.* (2016): Das Österreichische Versicherungsaufsichtsrecht, 3rd edition, Vienna, p. 4f.; Rechtsvorschrift für das Versicherungsaufsichtsgesetz (VAG); https://www.ris.bka.gv.at/GeltendeFassung.wxe?Abfrage=Bundesnormen&Gesetzesnummer=20009095 (05.05.2019).

insurance company's organizational law into the Insurance Supervision Act can be justified due to their close connection.[10]

The norms regarding mutual insurance companies are predominantly of a civil law type. They are either modelled after regulations pertinent to joint stock companies or simply copies of these. However, their different legal structures, in particular regarding the corporate bodies, have to be considered. Main principles from the joint stock companies' law cannot simply be cited by reference but repeated verbatim or in paraphrase. Here references are inserted only for less important matters. As a result, the corporate law norms regarding mutual insurance companies are evident from the Insurance Supervision Act. There are special norms for small mutual insurance companies.[11]

The structural differences between mutual insurance companies and joint stock companies are rather of a theoretical nature. Most policyholders are not able to tell if they are insured with a mutual insurance company or a joint stock company. Generally, the question about the importance of mutual insurance companies as a legal form of organization regarding insurance undertakings is a controversial topic. According to *Braumüller*, mutual insurers are useful in cases where they address a limited public, i.e. they deal with special branches of insurance business where the membership element is crucial.[12] *Baran* states that this is an important point for mutual insurance companies on the insurance market; therefore, it is the legislature's task to preserve the core element of this legal form. However, such mutual insurance companies which are in competition with large joint stock companies should have the option for necessary adaptations regarding their legal form.[13]

Article 35 defines a mutual insurance company as "an association that pursues insurance activities for its members based on the principle of mutuality (mutual insurance company)". The norm does not provide any further definition regarding the principle of mutuality, but the requirements can be found in several other regulations. It is a union of risk bearers, who share certain risks collectively. The concept of mutuality displays the special relationship between policyholders as members and mutual insurance company as a legal entity in this respect. The policyholders are members and owners of their mutual insurance company but they do not hold shares they can pass on. Because of this tie between their members they create an entity that

[10] Cf. *Braumüller, P.* (1999): Versicherungsaufsichtsrecht: internationale Standards, europäische Richtlinien und österreichisches Recht, 1st edition, Springer Verlag, Vienna, New York, p. 158.

[11] Cf. Ibid.

[12] Cf. Ibid., p. 159.

[13] Cf. *Baran, P.* (2016): Das Österreichische Versicherungsaufsichtsrecht, 3rd edition, Vienna, p. 44.

differs legally from its members. This corresponds to the basic idea of insurance, i.e. the creation of a risk community.[14]

With regard to their range of business, mutual insurance companies can be divided into large and small societies. Small mutual insurance companies are limited regarding territory, type of business, and group of people (§ 68 Abs.1 VAG). The FMA decides whether a mutual insurance company is to be considered a small mutual insurance company or not.

Mutual insurance companies can undertake their insurance activities exclusively for their members (the so-called "pure" societies) or for both members and non-members (the so-called "mixed" societies).[15]

4.2 Formation

A civil law act of formation is necessary to incorporate a mutual insurance company. The law does specify a minimum number of founders. According to the prevailing opinion, two people are necessary for the formation.[16] Additionally, a licence granted by the FMA is required for their insurance activities (§ 6 Abs. 1 VAG) as well as the entry into the company register (§ 42). According to § 2 UGB[17], a company is by law a legal form and has as a legal entity rights and obligates. Therefore, it has the capacity to sue and to be sued in court.

In the act of formation, the founders' intention to form a mutual insurance company has to be evident in the form of a notarial deed (§ 37 Abs. 1 VAG) and granted by the FMA. § 37 Abs. 2 VAG states the necessary elements of a founding charter as the following:

- the name and head office of the company;
- the object of the undertaking;
- the form of the association's disclosures;
- the beginning of membership;
- the initial fund;
- the manner of funding by the members;

---

[14] Cf. *Bartl, K* (2016): §§ 35-67, in: *Korinek, S. / Saria, G. / Saria, S.* (eds.): Versicherungsgesetz VAG, Vienna, p. 3.

[15] Cf. *Pressl, A.* (1993): Die Einbringung des Geschäftsbetriebes eines Versicherungsvereins auf Gegenseitigkeit in eine Aktiengesellschaft, Unpublished dissertation University Salzburg, p. 25.

[16] Cf. *Braumüller, P.* (1999): Versicherungsaufsichtsrecht: internationale Standards, europäische Richtlinien und österreichisches Recht, Springer Verlag, Vienna, New York, p. 159.

[17] The Unternehmensgesetzbuch (BGBl I 2005/120) replaced on 1.1.2007 the Handelsgesetzbuch (HGB).

- the contingency reserve;
- the appropriation of net income;
- the bodies of the company and their composition; and
- the number of members of the supreme body required for exercising minority rights.

The licence or the approval of an amendment to the bylaws have to be withheld from a mutual insurance company if the members' interests are not sufficiently safeguarded by the provisions of the bylaws (§ 37 Abs. 3 VAG). Any amendment to them requires a resolution by the supreme body (§ 54 Abs. 1), but, in contrast to the joint stock company law, the supreme body can transfer the power to make amendments that only concern the wording to the supervisory board. The FMA's administrative decision approving the amendment to the bylaws is necessary (§ 54 Abs. 3) and the amendment is valid only once it has been entered in the company register at the company's head office (§ 54 Abs. 5). In this case, different rulings are possible, because the company register court and the FMA pursue different goals and protective purposes.[18]

According to § 4 of the joint stock company law, the name of the company has to express the fact that mutual insurance activities are being pursued (§ 36 VAG) and the name has to be verified by the FMA during the process of granting the licence. For example, the company can use adjuncts such as "mutual" or "reciprocal". While insurance companies such as the "Wiener Städtische", the "Oberösterreichische" and the "Merkur" used this kind of amendment formerly, the Grazer Wechselseitige Versicherungsaktiengesellschaft still uses it. The Tiroler and Vorarlberger insurance companies added to their company names the abbreviation "V.a.G.", which seems to be sufficient. Ambiguous abbreviations such as "aG" are not approved due to a possible confusion with joint stock companies.[19]

Apart from contractual insurance, insurance or re-insurance undertakings may only pursue such activities which are directly related to contractual insurance. This may specifically include the mediation of home-purchase savings plans, leasing agreements, UCITS and the provision of services in the field of automated data processing as well as the distribution of credit cards (§ 6 Abs. 3 VAG).

---

[18] Cf. *Bartl, K.* (2016): §§ 35-67, in: *Korinek, S. / Saria, G. / Saria, S.* (eds.): Versicherungsgesetz VAG, Vienna, p. 43.

[19] Cf. *Korinek, S.* (2008): Der österreichische Versicherungsvereine auf Gegenseitigkeit; in: *Bürke, J.* (ed.): Rechtliche Rahmenbedingungen für Versicherungsvereine auf Gegenseitigkeit – Festschrift zum 100 jährigen Bestehen der Stuttgarter Lebensversicherung a.G., Karlsruhe, p. 157.

§ 41 Abs. 1 states that an initial fund has to be established to cover the costs of foundation and setting up the company, the organization costs as well as other expenses incurred through taking up the business activities. Business activities can only be started after the initial fund has been fully deposited in cash. If the bylaws of the company do not state otherwise, the fund may also be used to cover losses. The amount of the fund is based on the business activities. The fund covers the company's founding and its financial liability and assumes the function of the non-existing equity capital, which will be established by future surpluses. Additional financial payments of the insured parties can only be used to cover financial losses. Therefore, it is important to estimate the launching costs accurately, because the provision of fresh capital may be difficult at a later time. The financing function is related to cover the current expenditure after the business establishment.

The repayment or any other use of the initial fund has to be specified in the bylaws of the company. The initial fund may only be repaid out of the net income. If the mutual insurance company does not make any surpluses, no repayment has to be made. The repayment made in one year must not exceed the amount allocated to the contingency reserve (Article 45) in that year. According to the Insurance Supervision Act, the initial fund may be paid back, or used up by the current provisions for losses or allocated to the reserve fund.

Those persons who have made the initial fund available can be entitled to participate in the management of the company, or to receive an interest payment from the annual income, or to a part of the net income as shown by the financial statements if the bylaws may stipulate that (§ 41 Abs. 6 VAG).

On the basis of the principle of mutuality, members have to raise the means regarding the insurance activities based on the member's obligation, which means they receive the net income, but also have to cover the losses. The contingency reserve corresponds to the share capital of the joint stock company and it is, therefore, the main resource of the mutual insurance company.[20]

4.3 Legal form: self-responsibility, autonomy and equal treatment

The idea of protection and taking precautions was already been part of the Germanic communal life, long before the idea of today's insurance and policyholder developed. The acceptance of taking over economic risks within the community was assumed to be a duty in the

---

20 Cf. *Bartl, K.* (2016): §§ 35-67, in: *Korinek, S. / Saria, G. / Saria, S.* (eds.): Versicherungsgesetz VAG, Vienna, p. 7.

Germanic family, kin, and tribe. The idea of mutual help and support based on the social and religious sense of community was the starting point for mutual insurances, which defined the "natural risk community". From this kind of community developed fire-guilds and guild of craftsmen, whose purpose was at first mutual support to some extent, while later its sole. It dominated the goal to fulfil all the necessary needs and not the pursuit of profit.[21] Therefore damage as well as surpluses were distributed amongst all group members. This was the basis for today's mutual insurance companies which are highly specialized insurance companies for a homogenous group of people, because their business is restricted regarding the type of insurance, regional business, and group of people. This model applies in particular to small mutual insurance companies. However, members of large mutual insurance companies usually are not aware of what it means to be a member of a mutual insurance company.[22]

An important feature of mutual insurance companies is the membership (natural person or corporate entity), which requires the existence of an insurance contract (§ 40 Abs. 1 VAG). Additionally, any new member has to receive the bylaws by no later than obtaining the insurance policy. The company is also allowed to conclude insurance contracts without establishing a membership, provided that this is explicitly specified in the bylaws (§ 40 Abs. 2 VAG). In such a case, the bylaws must specify in which insurance classes and to what extent insurance contracts are permitted to be concluded without establishing a membership, while considering that insurance contracts without a membership must not represent the majority. This regulation has also to be considered when the permission for changing the bylaws is granted (§ 11 Abs. 1 VAG).

The membership ends with the expiration of the contract, i.e. an insurance relationship without membership is possible, but not a membership without such a relationship.[23] The member has no right to compensation.

Mutual insurance companies focus on the interests of their members. Insurance contracts without a membership are only allowed to be the secondary aim of mutual insurance companies, because this kind of contract is an exception of the mutuality principle, which is based on membership. According to standard practice, mutual insurance compa-

[21] Cf. *Büchner, F.* (1957): Zur Geschichte der Versicherung, in: Versicherungswissenschaftliches Archiv, p. 1.

[22] Cf. *Bartl, K.* (2016): §§ 35-67, in: *Korinek, S. / Saria, G. / Saria, S.* (eds.): Versicherungsgesetz VAG, Vienna, p. 4.

[23] Cf. Ibid., p. 3.

nies are allowed to have non-membership contracts to the extent of 10 percent of their premium income.[24]

Different theoretical approaches investigate the still difficult relations between the insurance contract and membership. According to the membership or entity theory, the legal relationship between the member and the mutual insurance company is an entity, while the insurance or insurance contract theory focuses on the legal insurance contract. The latter is commonly used by big mutual insurance companies. According to the combination theory, all legal relationships between the association and its members as well as the insurant form an entity, i.e. legal consequences derive from considerations regarding the functional requirements. The majority or separation theory differs regarding legal relationships between insurance contract and membership, i.e. both a partnership agreement and an insurance contract have to be made.[25]

According to *Braumüller*, supervision by the FMA is the solution regarding the problem of complete and distinct differentiation between the insurance relationship and membership. Therefore, issues which connect inseparably aspects of both membership and insurance contracts have to be under the supervision of the FMA. The more the membership components predominate regarding a certain issue and the more the aspect of insurance contract subordinate, the less the supervision has to be. As a result, general instruments for protecting the interests can be given greater priority.[26]

From a business point of view, the mutual insurance company's membership is established on the basis of a sales process in contrast to the joint stock company's investment financing.[27] This special sales process creates at the same time the unity of member and policyholder. The new member is part of the mutual insurance company and shares its profits and losses. The permanent and inseparable linkage between the role of a member and policyholder is the reason for the fact that the mutual insurance company emphasizes the interest of the policyholder[28], which is ensured due to the principle of self-responsibility (rights and obligations regarding the capital), autonomy (cooperation) and equal treatment of the policyholder.[29]

---

[24] Cf. *Braumüller, P.* (1999): Versicherungsaufsichtsrecht: internationale Standards, europäische Richtlinien und österreichisches Recht, Springer Verlag, Vienna, New York, p. 163.

[25] Cf. Ibid., p. 165.

[26] Cf. Ibid..

[27] Cf. *Farny*, D. (2000): Versicherungsbetriebslehre, 3rd edition, p. 209.

[28] Cf. *Großfeld, B.* (1985): Der Versicherungsverein auf Gegenseitigkeit im System der Unternehmensformen, Tübingen, p. 16.

[29] Cf. *Nemson, J.* (2014): Geschäftsmodell VVaG: Rahmenbedingungen, Herausforderungen und Chancen. Band 18, Leipziger Schriften zur Versicherungswissen-

Figure 1: Structure of the legal features of large mutual insurance companies

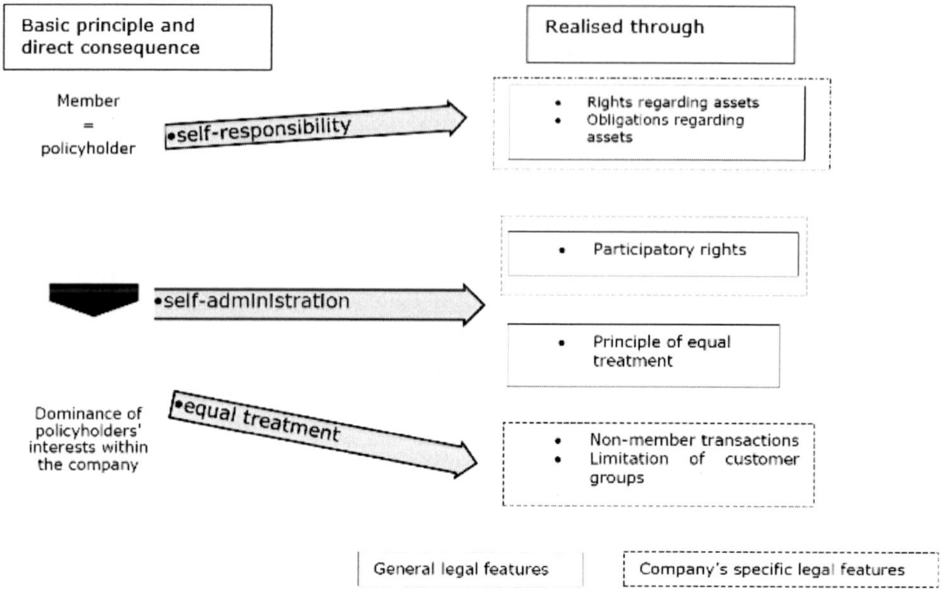

Source: *Nemson, J.* (2014): Geschäftsmodell VVaG: Rahmenbedingungen, Herausforderungen und Chancen, Karlsruhe, p. 53.

4.4 Self-responsibility (general rights and obligations regarding the capital)

The members' own self-responsibility is expressed in their rights and obligations with regard to their assets, because they are the results of the association's business activities. The members are not liable towards the association's creditors (§ 40 Abs. 3 VAG), while shareholders of joint stock companies bear the risks of the company. The focus of mutual insurance companies lies on the members' interests. Therefore conflicts with the business owners, in contrast to joint stock companies are prevented. However, conflicts with insured non-members are possible.[30]

schaft, VVW, Karlsruhe, p. 53.

30 Cf. *Braumüller, P.* (1999): Versicherungsaufsichtsrecht: internationale Standards, europäische Richtlinien und österreichisches Recht, Springer Verlag, Wien, New York, p. 159.

The protection of the member's interests in the supreme bodies corresponds to the protection of the interests of the insured person, because the insurance is part of the membership. The supreme body of representation of a mutual insurance company is composed of members and their representatives; therefore, it is possible to ensure the interest of the policyholder on a corporate level, i.e. in the annual general meeting. This is the main difference between mutual insurance companies and joint stock companies. The latter differentiates between the interests of the insured person and the shareholder. The shareholder's main goal is to earn a high dividend. In contrast, the policyholder has to argue his/her interests on a contractual level.[31]

Other main principles of mutual insurance companies are, for example, that the articles of association have to contain provisions concerning funding by the members, i.e. internal financing (§ 44 Abs. 1 VAG), and the members' right of sharing the profit (§ 47 Abs. 1 VAG). With regard to the mutuality principle, members have to provide the financial funding for the association due to their membership obligation. Therefore, § 44 Abs. 1 VAG displays the principle of members' financial covering. At the same time, this section prohibits an adjustable contribution procedure when stating that the annually required amount of funding has to be determined in advance[32]. The members' contributions are overhead costs (insurance premium) and therefore dealt with from an insurance contractual point of view. According to § 1 Abs 2 of the insurance contracts law, financial contributions by members of a mutual insurance company are the same as insurance premiums. In reality, mutual insurance companies have to calculate financial contributions beforehand according to their business activities to remain competitive on the market. Before the VAG 1978 became law, adjustable contribution procedures were legal.[33]

After the foundation phase has ended, a mutual insurance company is only capable of creating its own capital from taxable profits. However, Austrian law introduced the possibility to float participation and supplementary capital due to an amendment in 1986.[34]

---

[31] Cf. *Pressl, A.* (1993): Die Einbringung des Geschäftsbetriebes eines Versicherungsvereins auf Gegenseitigkeit in eine Aktiengesellschaft, Unpublished dissertation University Salzburg, p. 30.

[32] The adjustable contribution procedure states that the amount of the annually required financial funding has to be based on the net income of the last financial year. Therefore, the insurance benefits will be distributed among the members retrospectively.

[33] Cf. *Braumüller, P.* (1999): Versicherungsaufsichtsrecht: internationale Standards, europäische Richtlinien und österreichisches Recht, Springer Verlag, Wien, New York, p. 177.

[34] Cf. *Pressl, A.* (1993): Die Einbringung des Geschäftsbetriebes eines Versicherungsvereins auf Gegenseitigkeit in eine Aktiengesellschaft, Unpublished dissertation

Legally, the raised up capital does not belong to the members but to the mutual insurance company as a corporate entity. According to § 40 Abs. 3, the members are not liable towards the association's creditors.[35]

It is possible that the mutual insurance company has a surplus, because the financial contributions of the members are based on the expected amount of damage, similar to joint stock companies. As a result, the insurance principle is given priority over the principle of self-help. Each member has the right of shares. § 47 Abs. 1 VAG states that the management board makes a proposal regarding the distribution of the year's net income, as shown by the financial statements, among the members, and presents it to supervisory board. If the latter agrees, then the proposal and the supervisory board's report of the financial year have to be submitted to the supreme body for the final resolution. This is true unless the net income is allocated to the contingency reserve or to other reserves stipulated in the articles of association, or used for the repayment of the initial fund or the payment of remunerations in accordance with the articles of association, or carried forward to the next financial year. The management board's decision has to be made on the basis of objective reasons and it is neither allowed to favour the distribution of the surpluses among the members over the contingency reserve for reasons of competition nor to build up an unduly contingency reserve to pre-empt the members for having their surpluses' share.[36]

The bylaws define the principles for distributing the net income, but they cannot deprive the members' right of their surpluses' shares or grant them to non-members. The distribution ways include cash payment, the netting with the insurance premium, and the increase of benefits. The bylaws specify in particular whether the net income is also to be distributed to members who withdrew during the financial year.[37]

According to § 47 Abs. 3 VAG, any distribution of the net income has to be excluded in the event that such distribution would result in falling below the last reported level of the Solvency Capital Requirement. Therefore, the Solvency Capital Requirement is given the highest priority compared to all other business aims of mutual insurance companies.[38]

In case of dissolution of the association, the members are entitled to a share of the dissolution capital (§ 58 Abs. 5 VAG). The assets remaining after all debts have been defrayed or secured are to be distributed

University Salzburg, p. 31.

35 Cf. Ibid., S., p. 35.

36 Cf. *Bartl, K.* (2016): §§ 35-67, in: *Korinek, S. / Saria, G. / Saria, S.* (eds.): Versicherungsgesetz VAG, Vienna, p. 26.

37 Cf. Ibid.

38 Cf. Ibid., p. 27.

in accordance with the principles governing distribution of the net income to those persons who were members at the time of the dissolution, unless otherwise specified in the articles of association, in the dissolution's resolution, or in legal rules.[39] The distribution depends on the amount of the insurance premium or the insurance sum. The distribution according to the members is only allowed in exceptional cases, because all contracts of a member have to be considered the surplus capital. The surplus can also be distributed to others than members, for example to charity organizations, when the articles of association state these possibilities.[40]

Persons who were no longer members of the association at the time of the dissolution have no claim to society assets, because the latter belong to the association as a legal entity and not to its members. The reason is that when a member enters a mutual insurance company no capital contribution is made which is related to any kinds of contingencies. Additionally, leaving members do not have a claim to any shares of such society assets which increased during their membership.[41]

The obligation to make supplementary contributions, which mirrors the distribution of surpluses, does not apply to members who withdrew. § 44 Abs. 2 VAG states that the articles of association is allowed to stipulate whether and to what extent members shall be obliged to make supplementary contributions in the event that other funds do not suffice to cover losses. Reductions of insurance benefits instead of or in addition to the obligation to make supplementary contributions are also possible. Supplementary contributions are specific to mutual insurance companies and originate from the membership. In the case of contracts without any kind of membership supplementary contributions are ruled out.[42] According to the law, supplementary contributions are not obligatory to prevent any kind of competitive disadvantages between mutual insurance companies and joint stock companies. De facto it is not used.

The obligation for supplementary contributions has also implications concerning insolvency law. § 315 Abs. 1 VAG states that with regard to the evaluation of a mutual insurance company's excessive indebtedness, supplementary contributions which have been written out and not paid in within six months after becoming due are no longer to be considered assets of the association. However, other written out and paid supplementary contributions are to be considered as assets of the association. As a result, the obligation for supplementary contributions and the reduction of insurance benefits (§ 44 Abs. 2 VAG) may prevent

[39] Cf. Ibid., p. 55.
[40] Cf. Ibid., p. 49.
[41] Cf. Ibid.
[42] Cf. Ibid., p. 20.

insolvency (§ 66 KO) or excessive indebtedness (§ 67 KO) as well as any reasons for the commencement of bankruptcy proceedings. In this particular case, the management board and/or the administrative board and the managing directors or liquidators have no obligation to notify the FMA (§ 309 Abs. 1 VAG), which solely is allowed to file the petition to institute bankruptcy proceedings (§ 309 Abs. 2 VAG).[43]

4.5 Participatory rights

One of the main characteristics of mutual insurance companies is self-administration, performed by its members in the supreme body. Due to the identity of member and insured person, the latter has corporate rights, which is unique compared to other legal insurance forms.

The constitution of mutual insurance companies is modelled on that of joint stock companies, i.e. the legal development of joint stock companies was crucial for the organizational rules of mutual insurance companies. This process was almost completed at the end of the 19th century. According to § 48 Abs. 1, a mutual insurance company must have a management board, a supervisory board and, as its supreme body, a general meeting of members or a council of members. This organization is similar to that of joint stock companies with the exception of the general assembly of the shareholders which is substituted with the general meeting of members or a council of members. The supreme body is only in name the highest body, because neither management board nor supervisory board are subordinated.[44] Both the general assembly of shareholders and the supreme body of mutual insurance companies are limited to decisions regarding the constitutional and economic structure of the company or association. With regard to the latter, this organizational structure should strengthen the rights of the members, in particular in such cases when a council of members will be part of the mutual insurance company structure.[45]

If, according to the articles of association, the supreme body is not a general meeting of members, then, according to § 51 Abs. VAG, the articles of association states how the council of members is build and organized. Therefore, the bylaws determine the rules for the composition of the council of members and the appointment of its representatives and not the law.

---

[43] Cf. *Korinek, S.* (2008): Der österreichische Versicherungsvereine auf Gegenseitigkeit; in: *Bürke, J.* (ed.): Rechtliche Rahmenbedingungen für Versicherungsvereine auf Gegenseitigkeit – Festschrift zum 100 jährigen Bestehen der Stuttgarter Lebensversicherung a.G., Karlsruhe, p. 162.

[44] Cf. *Bartl, K.* (2016): §§ 35-67, in: *Korinek, S. / Saria, G. / Saria, S.* (eds.): Versicherungsgesetz VAG, Vienna, p. 36.

[45] Cf. Ibid., p. 35.

With regard to the historical development and the situation of the regional insurance offices, provinces or provincial bodies are entitled to perform certain functions at existing mutual insurance companies as specified in the articles of association. In such cases, the articles of association may continue to stipulate the performance of functions by those provincial bodies, provided the bodies otherwise necessary for the mutual insurance companies are established (§ 48 Abs. 2 VAG). This includes for example the right to preside over the supervisory board, the appointment of the management board or the position of a particular number of supervisory board's members. These rights were exercised directly by the province government, its member and its head.[46] Practical politics emphasise these rights, while the law only demands that the necessary organizational bodies for mutual insurance companies have to be established.[47] However, it is not possible to be part of the administration of a mutual insurance company without financial support but due to political reasons. *Bartl* ascribes this right of the provincial government to the right of providing the necessary initial funds for establishing mutual insurance companies and states therefore, according to § 41 Abs. 6 VAG, that a new regional social insurance office is a valid option when the initial fund is provided by the regional government.[48]

Nevertheless, the inalienable member's right to be part of the general meeting or the meeting of the members' representatives can only be gained due to a valid insurance contract (§ 51 Abs. 2 VAG). As a result, the articles of association have to state that the withdrawal of the membership results in a withdrawal from the council of members.

According to § 51 Abs. 1 VAG, the members, as a legal entity or natural person (§ 40 VAG), exercise their rights in matters of the association within the supreme body, unless otherwise specified by law. The supreme body can make decisions regarding questions of conduct of business when the management board or the supervisory board (§ 51 Abs. 1 VAG), in cases of businesses with mandatory consent (§ 95 Abs. 5 AktG), demand it. The right to vote are stated in the article of association (§ 122 AktG). According to the law, each member has one vote regardless the number of insurance contracts. However, the articles of association can decide otherwise if it is self-justifying. For example, the bylaws can state that each insurance contract means a vote, or that voting depends on the insurance premium or on the amount assured. If several insured persons share one insurance contract, only one vote is possible.[49]

---

[46] Cf. Ibid., p. 28.

[47] Cf. Ibid.

[48] Cf. Ibid.

[49] Cf. Ibid., p. 36.

Although the concept of a general meeting of members is preferable for mutual insurance companies, the greater the number of members is the more difficult it becomes. Large mutual insurance companies with approximately with one million members have problems for example regarding the invitation and the necessary information of members and would be stretched to their limits. If the supreme body is a general meeting of members the voting right can be exercised by a proxy (§ 51 Abs. 8 VAG and § 113 Abs. 1 AktG), who does not to be a member of the association. The rules regarding a proxy can be modified by the bylaws so far that they cannot contravene, limit or remove them.[50]

According to § 51 Abs. 2, the supreme body can be either a general meeting of members or a council of members, who must be members of the association. Otherwise the task of composition and the appointment of its representatives are left to specification by the articles of association. The number of representatives has to be at least four, because some of the decisions of the supreme body need a three-quarters majority.

Theoretically it is possible that the voting is accomplished by all members (primary election) or by protest or to co-opt someone by the council of members. In a case of a primary election, the representatives are elected by the members, who have both the right to vote or stand for election. Moreover, the articles of association have to include the election procedure, which should comprise an election commission for organizing and conducting the election. Bart states that the form of the primary election is the best option for the participation of the members, the procedure is, however, as complex as a general meeting of members.[51] In cases of mutual insurance companies with a high number of members, this kind of voting is only practical when remaining mute regarding a public nomination is identified as consent. In reality, nominations made by members are usually the exception, which is in particular true for such large mutual insurance companies in which no personal connection among the members exists.

When the voting is done by protest, the council of members is elected by a committee and later a list of the elected people will be presented to the members. The nomination of the elected people is accepted by the members when within a specific deadline not a certain number of members object to it.[52] *Bartl* argues that this kind of election is complex when each member has to be informed or problematic regarding demo-

[50] Cf. Ibid.

[51] Cf. Ibid., p. 37.

[52] Cf. *Braumüller, P.* (1999): Versicherungsaufsichtsrecht: internationale Standards, europäische Richtlinien und österreichisches Recht, Springer Verlag, Wien, New York, p. 171.

cratic and political issues if the information is released via the "Vienna Newspaper" or on the Internet.[53]

In reality, the system of co-option, as the simplest solution, became prevalent and perceived as legitimate[54] even though it offers relatively reduced members' participation. Basically the system of co-option means that when a member resigns or leaves after the end of term, the council of members elects his/her successor. However, the supreme body has to be elected differently at least once. The general problem of this kind of system is that the mutual insurance company becomes a closed community. Only persons who are close to the council stand a chance to be elected to the supervisory and supreme body. It is obvious that this way of replacing members jeopardizes an effective control of the management.[55] *Pachler* criticizes the system of co-option at all due to its undemocratic character.[56] *Reich-Rohrwig* and *Priemayer* state that this kind of system does not represent the insured person democratically or typical for shareholders in the council of members due to its form of election.[57] As a form of compensation, *Korinek* argues that during the process of approving the articles of association, the FMA should pay attention that mutual insurance companies which have the system of co-option offer their members additional rights that give them influence within the association. *Korinek* states that these rights should be considered as compensation for the lost right to elect top bodies. For example, a certain number of members could have the right to present their own list of nominees for the council of members which will be coordinated with the official list and then vote on the nominees or members can make motions to the council of members. With establishing the latter members have no influence on the mutual insurance company's business which is a weakness regarding the organization of the insurance association. Therefore, the election of the members of the council and the preparation of the list of the nominees are essential parts of the articles of association. It is possible that mutual insurance companies with a large number of life insurance or health insurance

---

[53] Cf. *Bartl, K.* (2016): §§ 35-67, in: *Korinek, S. / Saria, G. / Saria, S.* (eds.): Versicherungsgesetz VAG, Vienna, p. 37.

[54] Cf. *Korinek, S.* (2008): Der österreichische Versicherungsvereine auf Gegenseitigkeit; in: *Bürke, J.* (ed.): Rechtliche Rahmenbedingungen für Versicherungsvereine auf Gegenseitigkeit – Festschrift zum 100 jährigen Bestehen der Stuttgarter Lebensversicherung a.G., Karlsruhe, p. 163.

[55] CCf. *Bartl, K.* (2016): §§ 35-67, in: *Korinek, S. / Saria, G. / Saria, S.* (eds.): Versicherungsgesetz VAG, Vienna, p. 37.

[56] Cf. *Pachler, H.* (1995): Die versicherungsrechtliche Bestandsübertragung in Österreich, dissertation University Salzburg, Salzburg,, p. 122.

[57] Cf. *Reich-Rohrwig, J.; Priemayer, B.* (2005): Versicherungsvereine a.G: Umwandlung in Privatstiftung wird möglich, in: ecolex, p. 698.

contracts exclude members with small insurance premiums or short contracts from council of members' election.[58]

Bartl argues that the council of members should not represent the strongest group of members but all of them.[59] § 51 Abs. 2 states that the articles of association of mutual insurance companies must have specific rules for the composition and appointment of the council of members and which also have to allow the possibility of a qualified minority of members to nominate members for election. The supreme body or the election committee give the council of members the nominations and the members of the association or the members' representatives vote on these according to the articles of association.

The mixed system is based on the principle of the primary election, but members who have already left the mutual insurance company are still part of the council of members.[60]

Generally, the following articles of the AktG. are relevant for the supreme body, whereas instead of share-holders the members are the supreme body: § 102 Abs.2 to 6, § 104, § 105, § 106 Z 1 to 4, 7 lit. b. first half-sentence, § 107 Abs. 1, 2 and 4, § 108 Abs. 1 to 3 and 5, § 109 Abs. 1 and 2 first and second sentence, § 116, § 118, § 119 Abs. 1 and 3, § 120, § 121 Abs. 1, § 122 Abs. 1, 3 and 4, § 127 Abs. 1, 3 and 4, § 128 Abs. 1 and 3.

All members of a mutual insurance company have, according to § 55 Abs. 1 VAG and § 100 Abs. 3 AktG., violability regardless if a mutual insurance company consists of a general meeting or a council of members. They have the right to contest a resolution adopted by the supreme body on grounds of breach of law or the articles of association. Such an action can also be on grounds that a member of the supreme body has intentionally attempted through exercising voting rights to gain, for himself or a third party and to the detriment of the association or its members, special advantages not in the interests of the association, where the resolution is suited to this purpose.

---

58 Cf. *Korinek, S.* (2008): Der österreichische Versicherungsvereine auf Gegenseitigkeit; in: *Bürke, J.* (ed.): Rechtliche Rahmenbedingungen für Versicherungsvereine auf Gegenseitigkeit – Festschrift zum 100 jährigen Bestehen der Stuttgarter Lebensversicherung a.G., Karlsruhe, p. 163f.

59 Cf. *Bartl, K.* (2016): §§ 35-67, in: *Korinek, S. / Saria, G. / Saria, S.* (eds.): Versicherungsgesetz VAG, Vienna, p. 37.

60 Cf. *Braumüller, P.* (1999): Versicherungsaufsichtsrecht: internationale Standards, europäische Richtlinien und österreichisches Recht, Springer Verlag, Wien, New York, p. 172.

4.6 Management board

The management board, which is appointed by the supervisory board (§ 75 Abs. 1), has to manage the association on its own responsibility as required for the good of the association, taking into consideration the interests of the members and employees as well as the public interest (§ 49 Abs. 1 VAG). The management board has to consist of at least two persons or two executive directors, who have to pass a test by the FMA to prove their professional qualifications. The FMA has the right to recall the members of the management board, but not to execute it by itself; as a last consequence the FMA can revoke the association's licence.[61] Members of the management board have to manage the business with diligence.

The management board has to respect the restrictions, which the supervisory board or the articles of association have established regarding the power of proxy or which are caused by the resolution of the supreme body.[62]

4.7 Supervisory board

The supervisory board consists of three members unless the bylaws of association intend a greater number of not more than 20 members for the board. A member of the board has to be a person, who is capable of acting, but not necessarily an association's member. The articles of association can require a membership of the supervisory board's member or other qualifications obligatory for the right to vote or to be elected. However, these requirements may not influence the supreme board's right to vote freely. With regard to the professional qualifications, members of the supervisory board have to fulfil the requirements of § 120 Abs. 1 VAG. According to § 90 AktG., members of the supervisory board cannot be members of the management board at the same time.

The supervisory board supervises the management and is allowed to convene the supreme body when required by the good of the association (§ 50 Abs. 4 VAG). The management informs tells the supervision about the business in general and discusses important activities. The supervision board reviews the annual accounts' auditor report regarding the

---

[61] Cf. *Bartl, K.* (2016): §§ 35-67, in: *Korinek, S. / Saria, G. / Saria, S.* (eds.): Versicherungsgesetz VAG, Vienna, p. 30.

[62] Cf. *Braumüller, P.* (1999): Versicherungsaufsichtsrecht: internationale Standards, europäische Richtlinien und österreichisches Recht, Springer Verlag, Wien, New York, p. 169.

annual financial statement. Management issues cannot be assigned to the supervisory board.

The supreme body elects the members of the supervisory board (§ 50 Abs. 1). With regard to the election, the withdrawal, and the commission of supervisory board's members, the incompatibility of a supreme body and supervisory board membership at the same and the obligation for the publication of changes concerning the supervisory board § 86 Abs. 1 to 3, 5 and 6 AktG, § 87 Abs. 1 second sentence, Abs. 2 to 5 and 7 to 10 AktG. and § 89 to § 91 AktG. are to be applied to mutual insurance companies.

4.8 Principle of equal treatment regarding the law of association

The principle of equal treatment as the foundation and demand of the mutuality principle is, apart from the fundamental principles of self-responsibility and self-government, the crucial point which causes a domination of the interests of the policyholders.

According to § 40 Abs. 2 VAG, dues and further contributions of members and services of associations for members have to be equal if they are based on equal terms.[63] Therefore, the output of both partners of an insurance contract is the same when the benefit of the insured person equals the insurance premium, i.e. it is a fair treatment (fairness and equality). Moreover, fairness and equality means that no distinctions between existing insurance portfolio and new business are allowed.[64] The principle of equal treatment derives from the non-discrimination norm for associations and companies and is based on the principle that members form a permanent risk community, in which they are indentured to further contributions and liable for losses, which are caused by one-sided favoritisms of individual members or member groups. In this case only actuarial circumstances have to be considered, which influence the insured risk. Other factors such as the economic situation of a member or the durance of the membership are not relevant for the principle of equal treatment.[65]

---

[63] Cf. *Braumüller, P.* (1999): Versicherungsaufsichtsrecht: internationale Standards, europäische Richtlinien und österreichisches Recht, Springer Verlag, Wien, New York, p. 166.

[64] Cf. *Korinek, S.* (2008): Der österreichische Versicherungsvereine auf Gegenseitigkeit; in: *Bürke, J.* (ed.): Rechtliche Rahmenbedingungen für Versicherungsvereine auf Gegenseitigkeit – Festschrift zum 100 jährigen Bestehen der Stuttgarter Lebensversicherung a.G., Karlsruhe, p. 160.

[65] Cf. *Braumüller, P.* (1999): Versicherungsaufsichtsrecht: internationale Standards, europäische Richtlinien und österreichisches Recht, Springer Verlag, Wien, New York, p. 166.

This principle does not prohibit any kind of differentiation between members, but at the same time it restricts the room for decisions regarding business policy, because it forbids dealing with same facts differently. Therefore, it is not allowed to raise the insurance premium for new insurance contracts in order to compensate losses from the existing insurance portfolio. This is also true when for business expansion's reasons the insurance premium rates of new contracts are lower compared to them of existing.[66]

However, the principle of equal treatment has not the same importance in Austrian law compared to German law, because in the first the legal interpretation is rather broader.[67]

While *Korinek* views § 40 Abs. 2 VAG as an amendment to § 275 VAG which focuses on the principle of correct business activities and as a result expands the principle of equal treatment to the clients of joint stock companies[68], *Braumüller* disagrees, because in his opinion the connection between insurance relationship and membership does not exist.[69]

4.9 Small mutual insurance companies

Small mutual insurance companies are a special form according to Austrian law, which are limited with regard to territory, type of business, and group of persons (§ 68 Abs. 1 VAG), i.e. their scope of activities and their organizational structure is limited. With regard to territory, small mutual insurance companies are limited to the federal province in which the association has its head offices as well as to certain immediately neighboring regions. The FMA limits these to clearly regional or political defined territories of adjacent federal provinces. The FMA decides if a mutual insurance company can be considered as small.[70] Small mutual insurance companies need a licence granted by the FMA.

---

[66] Cf. Ibid.

[67] Cf. *Bartl, K.* (2016): §§ 35-67, in: *Korinek, S. / Saria, G. / Saria, S.* (eds.): Versicherungsgesetz VAG, Vienna, p. 12.

[68] Cf. *Korinek, S.* (2008): Der österreichische Versicherungsvereine auf Gegenseitigkeit; in: *Bürke, J.* (ed.): Rechtliche Rahmenbedingungen für Versicherungsvereine auf Gegenseitigkeit – Festschrift zum 100 jährigen Bestehen der Stuttgarter Lebensversicherung a.G., Karlsruhe, p. 160.

[69] Cf. *Braumüller, P.* (1999): Versicherungsaufsichtsrecht: internationale Standards, europäische Richtlinien und österreichisches Recht, Springer Verlag, Wien, New York, p. 167.

[70] Cf. *Bartl, K.* (2016): §§ 35-67, in: *Korinek, S. / Saria, G. / Saria, S.* (eds.): Versicherungsgesetz VAG, Vienna, p. 8.

Figure 2: Bodies of a mutual insurance company

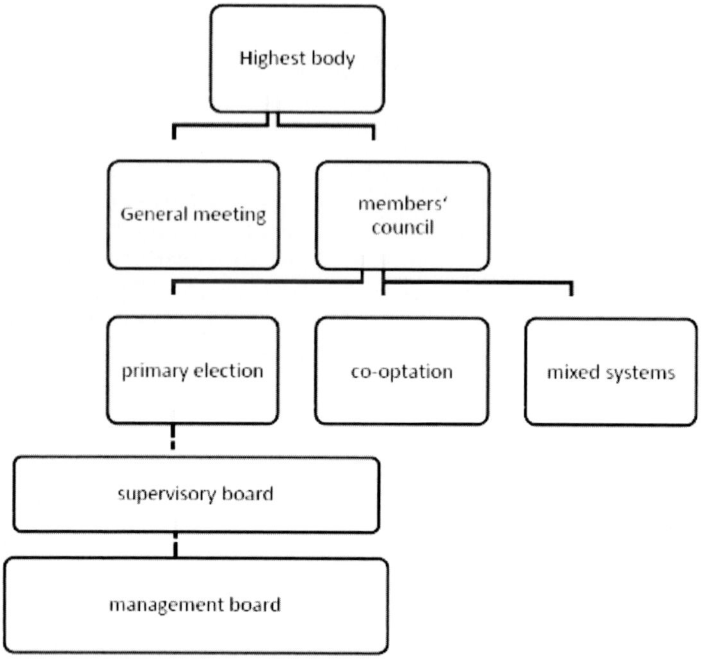

Source: Based on *Farny*, D. (2000): Versicherungsbetriebslehre, 3rd edition, Karlsruhe, p. 194.

All mutual insurance companies are subject to the VAG and therefore controlled and reviewed by the FMA. This is also true for the insurance contract law and other rules regarding insurance activities.

Many small mutual insurance companies have existed for more than 200 years; the oldest can be found in *Kremsmünster* (Upper-Austria). It was established in 1710[71]. Small mutual insurance companies are the oldest form of contract insurance.

The business activities of small mutual insurance companies usually include fire damage and livestock insurance. The restricted type of business activities comprises fire damage, burglary, tap water and livestock insurances.[72] Moreover, small mutual insurance companies are not allowed to comprise more than 20,000 members (§ 68 Abs. 1

[71] Cf. *Ehrenberger, H.* (1889): Zur Statistik der localen Versicherungsvereine gegen Feuerschäden (Bauern-Assecuranzen) in Oesterreich, Statistisches Monatsschrift, Mittheilungen und Miscellen, Wien, p. 149.

[72] Cf. Number 8 and 9 plant A of VAG.

VAG) and restricted to an income of not more than 5 million Euro resulted from insurance premium earnings (including reinsurance) for each year. Small mutual insurance companies may apply for entry in the company register on a voluntary basis (§ 69 Abs. 4 VAG), an option which has not been used yet. As a result, only the FMA has consecutive records about the activities of small mutual insurance companies.

The Austrian lawmaker has adopted the exception clause from the VAG 1978 for the VAG 2016, because the system of Solvency II is not applicable to small mutual insurance companies.[73]

According to § 70 Abs. 1 VAG, the own funds requirements of small insurance undertakings are determined on the basis of the retained earned premiums and the retained total sum insured. The FMA defines by regulation the detailed provisions for determining the own funds requirements, giving consideration to the special circumstances of small mutual insurance companies and in particular to their limited scope of activities. Their own funds consist of the initial fund, provided that it may be used for the coverage of losses, the contingency reserve, the risk reserve, and other reserves (§ 71 Abs. 1 VAG). Restrictions regarding investments are defined by the articles of associations.

Small mutual insurance companies must have a management board and, as its supreme body, a general meeting of members or a council of members. A one-person voluntary management board is sufficient and commonly used and neither the four-eyes-principle nor the prohibition of a full-time employment out of the insurance or bank area is applicable as well as internal control is not necessary. The management must have the necessary professional qualifications and reliability to fulfil their duties. The supreme body appoints the management board and the daily business is usually conducted by the business executive. Small mutual insurance companies with more than 2,000 members must have a supervisory board (§ 75 VAG).

Both small and "large" mutual insurance companies have a supreme body, either in the form of a general meeting of members or a council of members.

Small mutual insurance companies are only allowed to merge by absorption of an association or via the formation of a new association through a merger by consolidation of associations with other small mutual insurance companies. However, small mutual insurance companies can be absorbed by other mutual insurance companies. Apart from § 81 § 60 Abs. 1 and 2 VAG are applicable to small mutual insurance companies, i.e. either via merger by absorption or merger by consolidation.[74]

---

[73] Cf. Ibid., p. 4.

[74] Cf. *Bartl, K.* (2016): §§ 68-81, in: *Korinek, S. / Saria, G. / Saria, S.* (eds.): Versicherungsgesetz VAG, Vienna, p. 44.

In 2017, there were 33 property and 16 cattle insurance mutuals with 45,314 members, who were conceived as small mutual insurance companies. There was also a reinsurance mutual based in Vienna.

Small mutual insurance companies covering property insurance are mostly located in the Eastern part of Austria, while in the west associations with livestock insurance dominate.

The general rules regarding the own funds requirements are not applicable to small insurance undertakings, but their calculation and restrictions concerning investments are stated by the articles of association. The example of the storm damage insurance presents the different kinds of problems of small mutual insurance companies, because the usual requirement of a 10 percent retention maximum for mutual insurance companies by the FMA is not applicable to small associations. The reason is that several small mutual insurance companies may cover the same scope of a storm.

5. Insurance joint stock companies

An insurance joint stock company has its own entity and its legal rules are similar to those of other joint stock companies. However, several rules from the joint stock companies and the companies act are replaced by regulations of the VAG or some regulations of the FMA are added.[75] Shareholders of an insurance joint stock company with a licence for insurance contracts have shares of the capital in form of stocks, but without liability regarding any kinds of financial losses.[76]

5.1 Legal form

Joint stock companies acquire and sell insurances for profit. This differentiates them from mutual insurance companies.[77] The policyholders are connected with the company by contract, but not via a personal bond. The shareholders as a form of "members" carry the risk. On an

[75] Cf. *Farny, D.* (2011): Versicherungsbetriebslehre, 5th edition, VVW, Karlsruhe, p. 173.

[76] Cf. *Braumüller, P.* (1999): Versicherungsaufsichtsrecht: internationale Standards, europäische Richtlinien und österreichisches Recht, Springer Verlag, Wien, New York, p. 157.

[77] Cf. *Großfeld, B.; Merdausl, C. (*1995:) Der Versicherungsverein auf Gegenseitigkeit im System der Unternehmensformen, in: *Peiner, W.* (ed.): Grundlagen des Versicherungsvereins auf Gegenseitigkeit, Köln p. 107ff.

organizational level, the company works independently from the policyholders.[78]

The joint stock company has to calculate the premium in such a way that after all damage is paid a profit remains. This dividend from the deposited capital goes to the shareholders. There is no obligation on the part of the owners of the company to make further contributions.

A joint stock company is bound to the rules established in the company law. § 3 AktG. states that a joint stock company is to be treated as a trading company, even when its business undertaking is not part of commercial trade. Therefore, a joint stock company is always listed in the trade due to its legal form. The scope of the company or the question if it operates commercial trade is not relevant in that respect. Its business undertakings are always considered to be commercial transactions according to Austrian commercial law.[79]

5.2 Executive bodies

A company in the legal form of an insurance stock corporation has the same organizational structure as any other joint stock company: management board, supervisory board, and general meeting. This is also true for their functions. The shareholders' decision-making process takes place in the general meeting, in which the members of the supervisory board are being elected. The management board represents and acts for the joint stock company. Additional boards, such as advisory councils, are not bodies of the joint stock company and have only advisory function.[80]

5.3 Management board (executive body)

The management board manages the joint stock company without supervision and represents the company (§ 70 Abs. 1 AktG.) legally and out-of-court (§ 71 Abs. 1 AktG.) and reports constantly to the supervisory board. The management board makes the annual financial statements and the company report and convoke the general meeting.

---

[78] Cf. *Braumüller, P.* (1999): Versicherungsaufsichtsrecht: internationale Standards, europäische Richtlinien und österreichisches Recht, Springer Verlag, Wien, New York, p. 157f.

[79] Cf. *Pressl, A.* (1993): Die Einbringung des Geschäftsbetriebes eines Versicherungsvereins auf Gegenseitigkeit in eine Aktiengesellschaft, Unpublished dissertation University Salzburg, p. 25f.

[80] Cf. *Farny, D.* (2011): Versicherungsbetriebslehre, 5th edition, VVW, Karlsruhe, , p. 177.

Members of the management board are not allowed to be members of the supervisory board at the same time.[81]

5.4 Supervisory board (monitoring body)

The supervisory board consists of a minimum of three people – the bylaws of association can determine a higher number of people – and is elected by the general meeting for a maximum period of four years. The supervisory board has no management powers, because supervision and management are strictly separated in joint stock companies. However, the supervisory board needs the approval of the management board when the law dictates it. The bylaws of association can also state if an additional approval is necessary. The supervisory board appoints the management board and is entitled to recall it if necessary (delinquency, incompetence). [82]

5.5 General meeting (owners' meeting)

The general meeting functions as the acting sovereign for the insurance stock corporation. The general meeting consists of the shareholders. In general, each share means one vote if the articles of association do not state otherwise, for example the issuance of preference shares, i.e. shares which confirm a higher dividend pay-out in combination with a renouncement of the right to vote in the general meeting. The general meeting has to be convoked annually by the management or supervisory board. The company law grants the non-controlling partners the right to convoke the general meeting in exceptional circumstances. The general meeting decides for example regarding capital change, transformation and dissolution of the joint stock company. In each meeting it is decided about the assessment of the annual accounts and the distribution of profits as well as the approval of the actions of the management and supervisory board. Additionally, the general meeting is entitled to elect the members of the supervisory board. Decisions are made with majority or qualified majority (3/4 majority) if the articles of associations do not state otherwise.[83]

---

[81] Cf. §§ 70 to 85 AktG.

[82] Cf. §§ 86 to 99 AktG.

[83] Cf. §§ 102 to 136.

6. European Company[84]

The legal relationships of the European Company are regulated by the act (EG) 2157/2001 and by the SE-law, BGBl I 2004/67. The European Company is a joint stock company and it differs from an Austrian joint stock company in so far as it permits both the dualistic and the single board system. The latter system does not distinguish between management and supervisory board and allows an administrative board only.[85]

7. Merger

Mutual insurance companies can merge with other mutual insurance companies. A merger offers mutual insurance companies the same possibilities as joint stock companies have due to the AktG. There are no specific textual variations between AktG. and VAG.

According to § 60, associations can merge (consolidate) while avoiding winding-up procedures. The merger can take place:

- through a transfer of the entirety of an association's (transferring association's) assets to another association (transferee association), with the members of the association to be transferred becoming members of the receiving association (merger by absorption); or
- by establishing a new association to which the entirety of the assets of each of the merging associations is transferred, with the members of the merging associations becoming members of the new association (merger by consolidation).

The membership change over by submitting the merger or the new association into the company register. The merger does not offer the right to withdraw from the membership or the right of cancellation.

The merger has to be approved by the FMA and by at least three-quarters of the casted votes of the mutual insurance companies in-

[84] Europäischen Gesellschaft, Societas Europaea – SE.

[85] Cf. *Baran, P.* (2016): Das Österreichische Versicherungsaufsichtsrecht, 3rd edition, Vienna, p. 43f.

volved if the articles of associations do not suggest otherwise.[86] In case of a merger the concept of branch separation is still in effect.

Since 1978 only one merger of mutual insurance companies took place in Austria. In 1991 the „Wiener Verein Lebens- und Bestattungsversicherung a.G., Wien“ and the „Wiener Städtischen Wechselseitigen Versicherungsanstalt“ merged.[87]

7.1 Changes regarding mutual insurance companies

Until 1978 Austrian's VAG was based on the VAG of Germany (1939). It contained no regulations regarding the transformation of mutual insurance companies. § 42 governed the dissolution of mutual insurance companies and § 44 the transfer of a part or the entire insurance portfolio to another insurance company. This regulation was changed by the Austrian VAG (1979).

There are some disadvantages to the legal form of mutual insurance companies. For example the lack of share capital as well as the difficulties regarding the formation of a corporation. This raises the question how a change of the legal forms can be done without any disadvantages regarding civil law or dues. With regard to civil law, this problem is solved when the change of the legal form lead the several existing legal relationships to a universal succession. In this case, the legal successor assumes automatically (*ex lege*) the legal status of the predecessor, including rights and obligations. This occurs with a legal act (*uno actu*) without the necessity of transferring the rights and obligations of each property separately. Before the amendment of 1991, the VAG knew three possibilities to continue the business of a mutual insurance company via a joint stock corporation. These are the transfer of the portfolio, the transformation, and the transfer of assets and liabilities. The latter was not implemented into the VAG 2016 due to the absence of any application in the last 25 years.[88]

It is important to note that all decisions which led to the disappearance of mutual insurance companies or the transfer of their insurance undertakings to joint stock companies were made in agreement with the general meeting without considerable discussion.[89]

---

[86] Cf. *Bartl, K.* (2016): §§ 68-81, in: *Korinek, S. / Saria, G. / Saria, S.* (eds.): Versicherungsgesetz VAG, Vienna, p. 59.

[87] Cf. *Mayer, L.* (2001): Die Demutualisierung von Versicherungsvereinen auf Gegenseitigkeit (VVaG) in Österreich, in: *Geib, G.* (Hrsg.): Rechnungslegung von Versicherungsunternehmen, Düsseldorf, p. 214.

[88] Cf. Ibid. In 1989, the Montanverein used this possibility to transfer its capital to the Montanversicherung AG, which was established by the Montanverein.

[89] f. *Mayer, L.* (2001): Die Demutualisierung von Versicherungsvereinen auf Gegenseitigkeit (VVaG) in Österreich, in: *Geib, G.* (ed.): Rechnungslegung von Versiche-

7.2 Transfer of a mutual insurance company's portfolio

According to § 28 Abs. 1 VAG, an insurance company can transfer with the FMA's approval (§ 29 VAG) all or part of the portfolio of insurance and reinsurance contracts concluded in accordance to this federal act without the policyholders' consent to prevent the enticement of positive risks. In case of an entire portfolio transfer, i.e. of all insurance contracts, the insurance company closes its business and loses its licence. If only a part of the insurance contracts are transferred, i.e. a limited number of contracts defined according to specific features, the insurance company continues to exist reduced by the transferred portfolio.[90]

The transfer of the portfolio of mutual insurance companies is liable to the VAG regulations § 29 to 32. § 59 states additional regulations which are also apply to small mutual insurance companies. According to § 59 Abs. 1, agreements by means of which the insurance portfolio of an association is entirely or partially transferred to another undertaking require the supreme body's consent. In case of a transfer of the entire portfolio a majority of at least three quarters of the votes cast are required. And § 59 Abs. 2 states that the FMA has to supervise the members' interests arising from the membership relationship. This is crucial, because when the insurance contracts are transferred to a joint stock company the membership relationship expires while the members still have the right to a fair compensation. *Jud* excludes the transfer of the portfolio as an option for mutual insurance companies to improve their situation regarding capital and the formation of a corporation.[91]

In the case of a portfolio transfer to another mutual insurance company the memberships are transferred too unless the articles of association state otherwise. The protection of membership interests is crucial in particular regarding the distribution of surpluses.[92]

The principle of branch separation has still to be kept in mind.

In 1983, the "Jupiter Versicherungsverein a.G." transferred their portfolio to the "Volksfürsorge-Jupiter Allgemeine Versicherungs-AG" due to difficulties ensuing from its financial performance. The latter merged with the „Wüstenrot Versicherungs-AG" in 2001. The „Erste

rungsunternehmen, Düsseldorf, p. 203.

90 Cf. *Bartl, K.* (2016): §§ 68-81, in: *Korinek, S./Saria, G./Saria, S.* (eds.): Versicherungsgesetz VAG, Vienna, p. 66.

91 Cf. *Jud, W.* (1992): Die Einbringung des Versicherungsbetriebes eines Versicherungsvereins auf Gegenseitigkeit in eine Versicherungs-Aktiengesellschaft im System der versicherungsaufsichtsrechtlichen Strukturmaßnahmen, in: *Doralt, P./Nowotny, Ch.* (ed.): Kontinuität und Wandel, Wien, p. 206.

92 Cf. *Bartl, K.* (2016): §§ 68-81, in: *Korinek, S./Saria, G./Saria, S.* (eds.): Versicherungsgesetz VAG, Vienna, p. 57.

Wiener Spiegelglas-Versicherungsgesellschaft" transferred its capital to the „NÖ Versicherungs-AG".

7.3 Transformation of a mutual insurance company into a joint stock company

According to § 61 Abs. 1, an association can be transformed into a joint stock company through a resolution by the supreme body. This requires a majority of at least three quarters of the votes cast and the approval of the FMA. This rule does not apply to small mutual insurance companies. The approval can be withheld where the transformation would pose a threat to the members' interests, for example when the share capital participation of the joint stock company or the damages based upon failure to receive such participation are not based on objective aspects or the principle of equal treatment (§ 61 Abs. 4 VAG).

The management board has to inform all members of the mutual insurance company concerned of the intended transformation resolution according to the bylaws of association (Abs. 5 and 6). This has to happen no later than when the supreme body is convened. Every member is entitled to object to the transformation by submitting a registered letter by the end of the third day before the resolution is to be adopted. This means that in this case a member has the right to object to the decision of the council of members. This feature results from the organizational structure of a mutual insurance company: When the supreme body consists of a council of members the objection of the members cannot take place at the supreme body, because not all members have access to it. When the supreme body states the form of a general meeting members' objections are possible but difficult to carry out, in particular if the meeting consists of a large number of members. In practice, such disclosure shall indicate the option of raising an objection and the rights ensuing from such action. However, the decision regarding the transformation is based on the ratio of the votes.[93]

The intention to object to the transformation and the subsequent rights has to be announced. However, the legal consequences of an objection are limited. According to § 61 Abs. 12, any member of the association objecting to the transformation is entitled to hand over their stocks to the company, which sells them at the stock exchange price. If members are not being taken into account when determining the share because of the low par value of their shares or due to the exclusion of members' stockholding as part of the transformation process any objection is ineffectually. Members cannot fight the criteria for redistribution

[93] Cf. Ibid., p. 64.

if they believe they are disadvantaged by them or receive a higher stock exchange price for their stocks.[94]

The registration of a transformation has to be submitted to the company register. It needs a notification of approval by the FMA. With the registration the change of the legal form is completed and the mutual insurance company continues as a joint stock company. The membership rights are terminated.

In this case as well as in case of a transformation of a Ltd into a joint stock company (§ 239 to §253) both transformations are a change of the legal form and not of the legal entity. This means the legal form of an insurance company changes without changing the legal entity. The membership relationship of a mutual insurance company is tied to its legal form and is terminated its change (§ 40 VAG).

Due to the legal form no asset transfer, dissolution or processing as well as tax exemption occur.[95] The essential parts of the company's regulation are the transformation of the membership rights into stocks, the definition of the transformation requirements, and their realization according to the regulations of the company law as well as their legal consequences. The mutual insurance company's members participate in the share capital unless the transformation resolution states otherwise. If this is the case, § 61 Abs. 6 states that members shall receive damages in form of cash settlement, stocks, or involving their insurance benefits. If the members have a share of the capital, which is usual when the legal form changes, than a fair compensation is unproblematic. The compensation exists in the form of sharing. The rights of the former members of the mutual insurance company, who are now share-holders, equal the rights of the membership relationship of mutual insurance companies.

Greater problems arise when the members receive a cash settlement, because in this case the settlement has to be suitable compared to the proprietary claim of the former members. In this case the income value of the mutual insurance company is used. The maximum compensation limit is the equity capital of the mutual insurance company, because the company integrity has to stay stable. The legal position of the members is not very strong regarding the settlement for the loss of their proprietary claims. The FMA has a heavy responsibility taking care of

---

[94] Cf. *Braumüller, P.* (1999): Versicherungsaufsichtsrecht: internationale Standards, europäische Richtlinien und österreichisches Recht, Springer Verlag, Wien, New York, p. 186.

[95] Cf. *Jud, W.* (1992): Die Einbringung des Versicherungsbetriebes eines Versicherungsvereins auf Gegenseitigkeit in eine Versicherungs-Aktiengesellschaft im System der versicherungsaufsichtsrechtlichen Strukturmaßnahmen, in: *Doralt, P. / Nowotny, Ch.* (ed.): Kontinuität und Wandel, Wien, p. 209.

the members' interests due to its previous approval of the transformation (§ 61 Abs. 4).

During the transformation process, a capital inflow from a third party is, apart from members' share capital participation, possible. This is important from an economic point of view, because otherwise the members' cash settlement would endanger the company integrity, i.e. all stocks would become stocks of their own, which contradicts the entity of a joint stock company. The transformation process works only without problems regarding the members' share capital participation when traditional methods are used. According to *Baran*, this was the primary problem for introducing a new method when using a joint stock company to operate a mutual insurance company.[96]

Due to the transformation of a mutual insurance company into a joint stock company the new company obtains legal advantages compared to mutual insurance companies regarding capital market issues, cooperation law issues, and company law issues.

According to § 61 Abs. 5, the share capital, the par value in the case of par value shares, and the number of shares in the case of no-par value shares has to be specified in the resolution authorizing the transformation. The par value of the share capital must not exceed the value of those assets of the association which remain after deduction of debt. The par value of the shares issued on the occasion of the transformation or the amount of the share capital attributable to the individual no-par value share must not exceed EUR 100. It has to reach the stipulated amount stated in § 7 AktG., which is EUR 70,000 at the moment. The transformation of the association concerns solely the membership; the insurance contracts are left untouched.[97]

§ 61 Abs. 6. VAG states that unless the resolution authorizing the transformation states otherwise, the association's members shall participate in the share capital. Unless all members hold an equal share in the share capital, the amount of participation may only be determined in accordance with one or more of the following criteria:

- the amount of the sum insured;
- the amount of the contributions;
- the amount of the life/health insurance provision;
- the principles governing distribution of the net income; or
- the duration of membership.

96 Cf. *Baran, P.* (1992): Die Fortführung des Betriebes von Versicherungsvereinen durch Aktiengesellschaften, in: Versicherungsrundschau, p. 79.

97 Cf. *Bartl, K.* (2016): §§ 68-81, in: *Korinek, S. / Saria, G. / Saria, S.* (eds.): Versicherungsgesetz VAG, Vienna, p. 63.

When changing the structure of a mutual insurance company the future ownership of the stocks is still uncertain. To meet this challenge, considerations regarding the restriction of the transferability of registered stocks (§ 62 AktG.), the changes how the supervisory board is elected (§ 87 AktG.), the right to appoint somebody to the supervisory board (§ 88 AktG.), modification of the voting right (§ 114 AktG.), issuing of preference shares without the right to vote (§§ 115-117 AktG.), and the right of confiscation have to be made.[98]

The transformation is in such cases unproblematic when the members' share in the capital stock raise no problems, which apply to such mutual insurance companies, which are rooted historically in the mutual self-help of companies accomplishing their risks. Here the number of members is manageable; they are willing to continue their commitment in the role of shareholders and if necessary to raise additional capital. The transformation is also unproblematic if a mutual insurance company has started to be active in retail banking but the core of the members stayed strong enough to pay off the rights of the members.[99]

During recent years, the transformation of mutual insurance companies was put into practice several times, e.g. "Versicherungs-Verband für Papier-Industrie a. G.", "Versicherungsverband der Industriellen VVaG", "GLEIMAG" Wechselseitige Haftpflicht- und Sachschaden-Versicherungsanstalt für Gleis- und Magazinanlagen. However, this way to transform a mutual insurance company became less significant due to amendment in 1991 which made it admissible to incorporate an entire mutual insurance company into a joint stock company.

7.4 Incorporation into a joint stock company

The development of the amendment of the VAG in 1991 is interpreted differently by the decision-makers involved. The primary arguments for incorporation and against a transformation that changes the legal form are based on the commentary of the VAG regarding the replacement of the members' rights with shares. At that time when a mutual insurance company transforms into a joint stock company the former members have usually a share of 100 percent of the company, i.e. at that time there are no other shareholders than former members of the mutual insurance company. It is important to note that members receive a share of the capital in exchange for the loss of the cooperative

98 Cf. *Jud, W.* (1992): Die Einbringung des Versicherungsbetriebes eines Versicherungsvereins auf Gegenseitigkeit in eine Versicherungs-Aktiengesellschaft im System der versicherungsaufsichtsrechtlichen Strukturmaßnahmen, in: *Doralt, P. / Nowotny, Ch.* (ed.): Kontinuität und Wandel, Wien, p. 210.

99 Cf. *Baran, P.* (1992): Die Fortführung des Betriebes von Versicherungsvereinen durch Aktiengesellschaften, in: Versicherungsrundschau, p. 80.

rights, which leads to a large number of minor shareholders. The latter are usually indifferent regarding the company or sell their shares.[100]

This behavior leads to such results regarding the shareholders' structure as the legal interpretation displayed. These consequences would be intensified, when the capital is increased to improve the solvability or companies integrate. When such companies are launched at the stock exchange the structure of the company's shareholder will lead automatically to negative actions for the company.

The Austrian lawmakers emphasized these problems insofar that mutual insurance companies which are incorporated into a joint stock company have the legal possibility to be in existence and the stocks are unified. In this way the demands of the large mutual insurance companies to use the advantages of a joint stock company could be followed without dealing with the complicated partnership of members in a joint share company resulting from § 61 (transformation) or § 236 AktG. (merger to a joint stock company). The lawmaker decided for a solution similar to that of banks (§ 8a KWG), which cannot be run as a joint stock company. How strong this solution has influenced that of mutual insurance companies' is obvious due to the used terminology. Instead of the term "Versicherungsbestand" the term "Versicherungsbetrieb" was used in analogy to § 8a KWG to show that such transfers are subject to preferential treatments regarding taxes and rates of the Corporate Restructuring Tax Act.[101]

The transfer included the offer of structural changes such as the merger of several mutual insurance companies into one joint stock company, the division of a mutual insurance company into several joint stock companies or the combination of these two possibilities.

However, from the practical perspective one has to be cautious when considering the effects of the 1991 amendment. *Eckert* refers to the confidential relationship, i.e. risk community, between the insured person and the insurer of mutual insurance companies. This corporate relationship is founded between the member and the institution members, although the opportunity of a member to participate in the supreme body has become rare. Each measure to change the legal form is an undue interference in the intangible fixed assets, because it affects this tangle of relationships.[102]

---

[100] Cf. *Jud, W.* (1992): Die Einbringung des Versicherungsbetriebes eines Versicherungsvereins auf Gegenseitigkeit in eine Versicherungs-Aktiengesellschaft im System der versicherungsaufsichtsrechtlichen Strukturmaßnahmen, in: *Doralt, P. / Nowotny, Ch.* (ed.): Kontinuität und Wandel, Wien, p. 210.

[101] Cf. *Eckert, F.* (1993): Die Einbringung von Versicherungsbetrieben aus Versicherungsvereinen auf Gegenseitigkeit in Versicherungs-Aktiengesellschaften, in: Zeitschrift für Versicherungsrecht, p. 395.

[102] Cf. Ibid., p. 392.

Eckert states that in practice the appearance and the consistent structure of the organs of large mutual insurance companies are more important than the corporate rights and obligations of the members. For example, during the discussion regarding the 1991 amendment, the problematic nature of the possible expiration of contingent rights of members to liquidation proceeds share within the transformation process was not discussed anymore. The question concerning the future development of surplus participation of members in the case of investments was answered satisfactorily by referring to a similar contribution refund for insured persons through joint stock companies. In case of a merger of several mutual insurance companies into one joint stock company the primary concern of the general meeting was if the members should "keep to themselves" or if "the others" will "seize power".[103] It was less important for the members if the insurance activities are managed in the legal form of a mutual insurance company or a joint stock company.

Some objections to the legal form of a joint stock company are based on criticism on the principle of free-market regulation and related to the traditional common good principle of mutual insurance companies. According to this opinion, if a joint stock company has better access to the capital market the management will seize the opportunity to spend the easy obtained money.[104]

Lorenz has already stated in the 1980s that there are no differences between the corporate philosophy of large mutual assertions and joint stock companies.[105] One argues that managers in the insurance industry do the sociopolitical and free-market challenges of the goal justice who are able to justify the company policy's decisions. This means that neither the pursuit of profit is preferred over the principle of mutuality nor competitive disadvantages are condoned. The consequences were that the insurance coverage of the insurer would be undermined and principles such as mutuality or insurance endangered.

The transformation of a mutual insurance company into a joint stock company would not be viewed as a necessity or possibility to rethink on the operational and member levels. This is in particular true when the supreme body of a mutual insurance company keeps its duties while adding that of a joint stock company, i.e. for the duration of being the sole shareholder of the mutual insurance company in the joint stock company while functioning as its own general meeting. A later admittance of third-party shareholders to the joint stock company does not change the general picture. However, a capitalistic joint stock

---

103 Cf. Ibid., p. 393.

104 Ibid.

105 *Lorenz, W.*: Stellungnahme zu der Untersuchung von Dieter Farny, in: ZVersWiss 84, p. 378.

company policy within the narrow limits of the market is possible, in case third-party shareholders pursue different goals compared to the mutual insurance company as existing shareholder and influence the supreme body as well as the supervisory board despite supervision. In case of an amendment regarding mutual insurance companies problems such as the structural disadvantages when own capital has to be raised and the formation of company groups should be addressed. The latter concerns the transfer of several mutual insurance companies into one homogenous joint stock company to raise temporarily the existing synergy potential to fulfil the solvency requirement.[106]

Towards the end of the year 1990, two well-known Austrian mutual insurance companies ("Austria Versicherungsverein auf Gegenseitigkeit" and the "Collegialität Versicherung auf Gegenseitigkeit") turned to a lawyer's office to combine these competitive companies without destroying each other's association structure. At the same time, the existing synergy potential should be raised, advantages of all possible ways to procure capital as established in company law should be taken of, and later inclusions of shares in other group of companies should be allowed.

For this plan it was necessary to develop a legal foundation for the transfer of mutual insurance companies into a joint stock company by maintaining the legal entity of the association through the supervisory authority. Preliminary drafts of the amendment of the VAG were handed over by a lawyer's office to the supervisory authority, several times revised and finally submitted to an examination with shortened datelines.[107] The National Council passed a law (Bundesgesetzblatt No. 411/1991) on August, 2 1991, which offers mutual insurance companies the opportunity to transfer their entire insurance activities to one or several joint stock companies by means of universal legal succession at the end of the financial year as a contribution in kind of book values.[108] § 63 VAG is not applicable to small mutual insurance companies.

In reality, the "Austrian Collegalität" merger initiated the legislation, because the basis model, i.e. several mutual insurance companies transfer into one joint stock company, has not been used so far. In 2005, the two above mentioned associations initiated an additional legislation (change of legal form into a private foundation) and another in 2011 (abolishment of the blocking minority of 26 percent). *Bartl* states

[106] Cf. *Eckert, F.* (1993): Die Einbringung von Versicherungsbetrieben aus Versicherungsvereinen auf Gegenseitigkeit in Versicherungs-Aktiengesellschaften, in: Zeitschrift für Versicherungsrecht, p. 393.

[107] Cf. Ibid.

[108] Cf. *Korinek, S.*: Der österreichische Versicherungsvereine auf Gegenseitigkeit; in: *Bürke, J.* (ed.): Rechtliche Rahmenbedingungen für Versicherungsvereine auf Gegenseitigkeit – Festschrift zum 100 jährigen Bestehen der Stuttgarter Lebensversicherung a.G., Karlsruhe, 2008, p. 169.

critically that the little practical significance of these regulations is in striking disproportion to the legal effort.[109]

With the amendment 1991, mutual insurance companies were able to change legally into a joint stock company (§ 61 VAG). It is now also possible to transfer the assets individually or jointly with other associations into one or more existing or for this purpose established insurance joint stock companies without changing the legal form (§ 63 Abs. 3 VAG). Also other mutual insurance companies can join this transfer in the future. The reason is that a gradual change from a mutual insurance company to a joint stock company has to be feasible. The transfer is only valid when a mutual insurance company joins one or several exciting joint stock companies or for this purpose established joint stock companies as the sole shareholders or joins together with other mutual insurance companies.[110]

The transfer has to take place as a contribution in kind at book values (§ 20 Abs. 1 AktG) as per the end of the financial year (§ 62 Abs. 2, 5 VAG). A revaluation of the assets due to the transfer is not possible, the balance sheet of the transfer has to take over the book values from the mutual insurance company's balance sheet. After the balance sheet of the transfer had been checked and confirmed by the balance sheet auditor it is presented to the company register. The own funds of the mutual insurance company with the exception of additional capital or untaxed reserves are allocated to the share capital or to the tied-up capital reserves of the joint stock company (§ 130 Abs. 2 AktG). This is not applicable to subordinated debts.[111] The entire assets of the mutual insurance company and its rights and obligations belonging to the insurance activities have to be transmitted to the joint stock company. With the transfer of the insurance activities to the joint stock company, all insurance contracts, insurance-specific funds and assets of the own funds requirement follow. All other assets which are not necessary either for the insurance activities or the capital resources of the joint stock company including the liabilities can be withhold by the mutual insurance company. This applies to real estates and corporate holdings of the association that are not part of the guarantee stock, necessary for operating insurance activities or the solvency of the joint stock company. The mutual insurance company is able to cover its tax-deductible outlays by using the taxable income of such retained property regardless of the tax-free dividend yield of their share in the joint stock company.

[109] Cf. *Bartl, K.*: §§ 68-81, in: *Korinek, S. / Saria, G. / Saria, S.* (eds.): Versicherungsgesetz VAG, Wien 2016, p. 89.

[110] Cf. Ibid., p. 68.

[111] Cf. Ibid., p. 71.

The insurance industry intended to keep most of the means with the association so that in case of a future capital increase of the joint stock company the association is able to match it. The FMA, however, regarded the retained capital as a protection of the members' interests, which cannot be taken away by the entry of new shareholders. Today's view regards § 63 Abs. 2 as problematic, because the assets of an insurance association is part of the insurance activities. The assets of the remaining mutual insurance company are comprised basically the shares of the joint stock company to which the insurance activities had been transmitted.[112]

After the transfer the association is limited to asset management, which means, according to the legislature, the management of its own assets. The mutual insurance company cannot be forced to manage the assets of a third party.[113]

The transfer requires the consent of the supreme body and the resolution requires a majority of at least three quarters of the votes cast, which is subject to the company law and if necessary to civil and criminal law. The transfer requires a licence due to the universal legal succession. The FMA can withhold the approval of the transfer as referred to in § 29 VAG when the members' interests as insurant people and arising from the membership relationship are not sufficiently safeguarded (§ 62 Abs. 4 VAG). The regulations made by the lawmaker regarding the change of legal form, in particular the universal legal succession and possibilities to divide the various insurance branches justify overall the detailed control by the FMA.

It is possible that differences occur between the different areas of interest during the distribution of the assets between the mutual insurance company and the joint stock company. Then it is necessary to find a balance of interest between the operational provision for the joint stock company and the safeguard of the assets of the former mutual insurance company. Another disadvantage may develop due to the insufficient safeguarding of the members' interests in the articles of the joint stock company.[114] The supervision of the FMA is limited to such rules and actions which concern the interests of the members arising from the membership relationship.

§ 63 Abs. 2 VAG states that with the transmission of title by means of universal legal succession the licence for contractual insurance activities and the approvals granted for the insurance activities are transmitted too. The membership relationship does not expire, but stays the same. Before the transfer the membership and the insurance are related to the same legal entity. After the transfer the right of the

112 Cf. Ibid., p. 74.
113 Cf. Ibid.
114 Cf. Ibid.

members is only related to the participation in the administration. The membership of a mutual insurance company is established due to the conclusion of new insurance contracts with a joint stock company. In case of the participation of several associations a membership is established for each association. It is not clear why in such cases these associations are not jointed.[115] The membership can be established due to the takeover of the insurance activities of another insurance association or joint stock company, in which the insurance activities of an insurance association are transferred according to § 62. That requires regulations with which part of the premium in each association the member claims the demands concerning the membership, in particular regarding profit participation based on the premium.

The membership relationship is separated from the insurance relationship. However, the membership and insurance relationship have to be connected, although to another legal entity. The insured persons are regarded as members of the mutual insurance company and can have a share of the annual statement, which is now a payment from the insurance joint stock company to the association instead coming from the insurance activities.[116] The principle of non-discrimination (§ 40 Abs. 2 VAG) is not applicable anymore.[117]

The joint stock company can conclude insurance contracts without establishing a membership, provided this is expressly specified in the articles of association (§ 63 Abs. 4VAG). However, this should be the exception and not the norm, because if non-membership contracts were used exclusively associations of shareholders would be extinct. This action would contradict the intention of the amendment to secure such mutual insurance companies. Additionally, the consequences regarding the shareholders' structure of joint stock companies were hardly

[115] Cf. Ibid., p. 77. At first, the membership does not change at the time of transfer. Members of the associations became insured persons of the joint stock company und keep their association's membership. Merely new policyholders of the joint stock company – beyond non-member business – acquire all association's memberships that increase due to the progressive expiration of insurance contracts. Only when all existing insurance contracts are replaced by new, all associations, which participated in the joint stock company due to the previous transfer, have the same members. As a result, these mutual insurance companies can be merged without problems. The structural refinement starts at the operational level and can be repeated smoothly at the level of the owners. Due to historical reasons, it is possible that the mutual insurance companies continue to exist isolated despite the identical structure of the members.

[116] Cf. *Korinek, S.*: Der österreichische Versicherungsvereine auf Gegenseitigkeit; in: *Bürke, J.* (ed.): Rechtliche Rahmenbedingungen für Versicherungsvereine auf Gegenseitigkeit – Festschrift zum 100 jährigen Bestehen der Stuttgarter Lebensversicherung a.G., Karlsruhe, 2008, p. 169.

[117] Cf. Ibid., p. 168.

governable anymore. Therefore, the FMA's approval of insurance joint stock companies' provision of articles which privilege non-membership contracts has to be restrictive.[118]

The members' interests have to be settled uniformly, including the interest of the operational level of joint stock companies: This means that if it is necessary to supply the joint stock company with own funds due to solvency reasons or to extend its business and a third-party shareholder is willing to subscribe for new shares from an joint stock company's capital increase on appropriate issuing conditions such measures are in the members' interests. This is also true if the mutual insurance company is not able to exercise its stock right regarding its share of new stocks which equals its previous share in the capital stock due to the lack of own funds. As a result, the mutual insurance company has to accept a decrease of its participation quota in the joint stock company or even to lose its majority. The minority interest of a mutual insurance company in a joint stock company represents the interests of the members better than to hold on to the majority at the cost of solvency or the growth of the company.[119]

However, it is important to note that the basic problem concerning the members' compensation is simply transferred to the future but not solved.[120] This means that the insurance company is removed from the members. In case of a future capital increase of the joint stock company people who are unrelated to the association are now allowed to purchase shares. The association can also sell directly to them. This supports the investment purpose, i.e. the incorporation of new capital by selling shares to non-association members. The lower limits of voting shares stated in § 63 Abs. 5, § 65 Abs. 1 and § 66 Abs. 3 Z 3 and the closeness to a joint stock company only postpones the transaction. The transfer can only be made with a majority of at least three quarters of the votes cast of the supreme body. This shows the free decision of the mutual insurance company members', but only when the decision was made by a written inquiry of all members. If it was made by a council of members which was elected in the form of co-optation (cf. § 51) then the true purpose was missed. It is still unclear what the consequences for the owners' structure and the capital market will be if the members' rights are replaced by share rights. It seems, by and large, that the lawmaker has created a solution which represents to a large degree the

[118] Cf. *Eckert, F.* (1993): Die Einbringung von Versicherungsbetrieben aus Versicherungsvereinen auf Gegenseitigkeit in Versicherungs-Aktiengesellschaften, in: Zeitschrift für Versicherungsrecht, p. 397.

[119] Cf. Ibid.

[120] Cf. *Bartl, K.* (2016): §§ 68-81, in: *Korinek, S. / Saria, G. / Saria, S.* (eds.): Versicherungsgesetz VAG, Vienna, p. 68.

interests of the insurance companies, although the economic success agrees with the lawmaker.[121]

In case of a transfer, the mutual insurance company is the sole shareholder of the joint stock company. Additional founders are not necessary even only a single mutual insurance company (one-man-foundation) is transferred.[122] It is important to note that the transferring mutual insurance company continues to exist, but from now on its object is limited to asset management (cf. § 63 Abs. 3 VAG). The joint stock company, however, pursues contractual insurance activities. The members of the mutual insurance company continue to be members. Its object is now to manage its share in the insurance joint stock company. Any amendments to the bylaws of association require the approval of the FMA.

The members of the management board still use the four-eyes principle, but adequate knowledge and experience of the insurance business as well as personal responsibility are no longer mandatory requirements for them (cf. § 120 and § 121 VAG). The reason is that their occupation is no longer considered as a full-time occupation such as stated in § 120 Abs. 2 Z 4 VAG. It is taken into account that the object of the association is now limited and, therefore, the members of the management board are not fully occupied anymore. It is no obstacle that they are members of both the management board of the association and of the joint stock company. This is common when a mutual insurance company is the sole shareholder or the majority shareholder in a joint stock company. However, *Bartl* argues that in this case any form of control, especially in the sense of "good governance" is not possible anymore.[123] The appointment of new members of the management and supervisory board has to be announced by the FMA a month in advance.

Baran states that the members' rights are weakened by the transfer but from a constitutional point of view they are not affected substantially. The reason can be found in § 64 Abs. 1 Z 1 VAG which states that the management board of the association has to request additionally a resolution of the supreme body in all matters falling within the scope of responsibility of the annual general meeting of a joint stock company. The members' right to demand information includes matters of the joint stock company related to the subject of the resolution.[124]

[121] Ibid.

[122] Cf. *Jud, W.* (1992): Die Einbringung des Versicherungsbetriebes eines Versicherungsvereins auf Gegenseitigkeit in eine Versicherungs-Aktiengesellschaft im System der versicherungsaufsichtsrechtlichen Strukturmaßnahmen, in: *Doralt, P. / Nowotny, Ch.* (ed.): Kontinuität und Wandel, Wien, p. 210.

[123] Cf. *Bartl, K.* (2016): §§ 68-81, in: *Korinek, S. / Saria, G. / Saria, S.* (eds.): Versicherungsgesetz VAG, Vienna, p. 75.

[124] Cf. *Korinek, S.* (2008): Der österreichische Versicherungsvereine auf Gegenseitigkeit; in: *Bürke, J.* (ed.): Rechtliche Rahmenbedingungen für Versicherungsvereine

This influence of the supreme body regarding the joint stock company pushes to the limits of the company law. In the simplest case, the association is the single shareholder in the operative joint stock company and is represented by the management board. The general meeting of the joint stock company comprises the management board of the association or its proxies, who appoints the supervisory board of the joint stock company and, therefore, influences indirectly the management board. As mentioned above, § 64 VAG states that the management board of the association has to request additionally a resolution of the supreme body in all matters falling within the scope of responsibility of the annual general meeting of a joint stock company. This is plausible, because the object of the association comprises asset management and the protection of the members' rights. The management board is bound by the decisions of the supreme body. The functionality of this kind of influence depends on the extent of information the management board of the association receives and the passing on to the supreme body as well as the timing of the sessions. The supreme body of the association needs a majority in the general meeting of the joint stock company so that the resolution made earlier by the association's supreme body passes. It is important to note that in case the joint stock company has several shareholders than the importance of the supreme body's decision is based on the level of the association's share.[125]

For the purpose of auditing transactions occurring during the joint stock company's establishment or management, the supreme body of the asset management society has the right to appoint auditors with a simple majority of votes (§ 64 Abs. 1 Z 2 VAG). Moreover, it can assert the claims of the joint stock company arising from the management on the members of the management board or the supreme body (§ 64 Abs. 1 Z 3 VAG).

The claim on participation of the net income gained by the insurance activities, turns into a claim on a participation of the dividend income related to the association's share on the joint stock company. Another source of net income is the profit gained by the association's sale of shares. In this case, § 47 is also applicable. The Austrian lawmaker states that the dividend resulted from the association's shareholder position have to be distributed immediately to the members, because a longer-term accumulation of funds is not compatible with this regulation. However, § 47 does not forbid that the association uses the profits to increase the capital of the joint stock company. In the VAG 2016, the lawmaker has not given the FMA any legal possibility to prevent

auf Gegenseitigkeit – Festschrift zum 100 jährigen Bestehen der Stuttgarter Lebensversicherung a.G., Karlsruhe, p. 171.

125 Cf. *Bartl, K.* (2016): §§ 68-81, in: *Korinek, S. / Saria, G. / Saria, S.* (eds.): Versicherungsgesetz VAG, Vienna, p. 80.

such an accumulation of funds, which is common practice. As a result, associations are allowed to accumulate profits and to use them to participate in an increase of capital by the joint stock company in order to prevent a decrease of their interests under the critical limit of 26 percent. Although this approach of companies is understandable, the question arises why members should have any kind of interest in the long-term existence of associations, when they do not receive their annual profits, when the capital would be distributed among the members in case of dissolution.[126]

After the transfer of the insurance undertaking into the joint stock company the latter can support the insured association members by using favorable fees, i.e. to refund premiums in a reasonable way. These expenditures of the joint stock company reduce their taxable income and therefore from a tax platinizing point of view the payments are made from the correct source. This is true as long as the compensations conform to market conditions and all insured people of the joint stock company (including non-members) receive them without any distinctions.

The question how much share insured people, i.e. members, have in the profits of the insurance undertakings, is not easy to answer. In case of life insurances, members of the asset management society and insured people of a joint stock company have the same share in the profit. The profit participation, which results from the terms of the insurance contract, takes place in the joint stock company and not in the asset management society. This is also true for profit participation of health insurances.

In Austria, the refund of the premium to the members of the asset management society is not so important in the case of indemnity/accident insurances due to economic reasons. In the insurance branch, the profits are rather low due to competition. With the approval of the supreme body, the asset management societies use either the entire or a large part of their profit to support the reserve fund and to fulfil the solvency regulations.

The share of the members of the asset management society in the profit of the joint stock company can be found in such insurance branches, which are significant for the joint stock company. However, in asset management societies with shareholder functions the dividends distributed by the insurance joint stock companies are poured into the reserve fund and accumulate for future capital inflow. This action has to be granted by the supreme body. Any other approach would be improper regarding the taxation, because usually the associations make tax-free incomes. Therefore, any kinds of premium refunds to the members would not decrease the taxable income, in contrast to joint

[126] Cf. Ibid., p. 75f.

stock companies. However, it is important to note that the refund of the premium is difficult in such insurance branches where the claim is not based on the insurance contract. This is also true in case many shares of the insurance joint stock company belong to other shareholders.

The lawmaker predetermined that the share of the mutual insurance company in the joint stock company decreases, because its transfer into a joint stock company is commonly used to raise capital. The smaller the association's share the less the possibility of the members to have any kind of influence on the joint stock company. Moreover, the question rises how high the share of the mutual insurance company in the joint stock company has to be that the principle of mutuality still exists to a sufficient extent. Similar legal constructions can be found in the United States at first regarding credit activities and later insurance activities. In the latter, when mutual insurance companies function as holding companies they need a voting share of at least 51 percent.[127] In Austrian law, the limit lies at 26 percent and it states that important changes regarding articles of associations, transfers, merger, and investments need a three-quarters majority. If the asset management society's voting share is below 26 percent due to shares' sale or capital increase of the joint stock company the influence of the association is dwindling and does not justify its right to exist anymore. As a consequence, the association should be dissolved and the members compensated for the loss of the membership.[128]

In case of falling below the limit, the FMA has to be notified immediately (§ 65 Abs. 3 VAG) and has to order the association to restore compliance with statutory provisions within an appropriate period of time. However, in the event of repetition or continuation the FMA has to dissolve the association. If more than one mutual insurance company is transferred to a joint stock company and their total voting share falls under 26 percent, the procedure is the same, as mentioned above. After the dissolution, the supreme body of the association has to resolve a FMA approved winding-up plan for the distribution of the assets between the members. The FMA is allowed to refuse the plan when the members' interests are not protected sufficiently.

According to § 63 Abs. 5 VAG, the association is not to be dissolved when the supreme body resolves within the appropriate period of time given by the FMA to transform the association into a private foundation (§ 66 VAG). In this event, the FMA sets a deadline for the transformation. The asset management society has to be dissolved

[127] Cf. *Mayer, L.* (2001): Die Demutualisierung von Versicherungsvereinen auf Gegenseitigkeit (VVaG) in Österreich, in: *Geib, G.* (Hrsg.): Rechnungslegung von Versicherungsunternehmen, Düsseldorf, p. 219.

[128] Cf. *Bartl, K.* (2016): §§ 68-81, in: *Korinek, S. / Saria, G. / Saria, S.* (eds.): Versicherungsgesetz VAG, Vienna, p. 77.

if the deadline is not met. *Bartl* argues that this is a useful solution, because, according to § 66 Abs. 3, private foundations have no strict voting shares. However, it raises the question if the dissolution would not be the better solution for the members.[129]

Another reason against the dissolution is when members who are insured by a joint stock company receive a compensation in the full amount of their rights pursuant to § 58 Abs. 5 VAG and other participations of at least 26 percent continue to exist (§ 62 VAG). The determination of the total compensation amount requires the approval of the FMA and the members' interests arising from membership have to be sufficiently safeguarded (§ 63 Abs. 6 VAG).

The possibility to transfer a mutual insurance company into a joint stock company has also attracted attention across borders. *Peiner* refers to an "Austrian model" and states that the lawmaker created something new when combing the membership in a mutual asset management society and the characteristic of an insured party by a joint stock company. However, the legal argument should be questioned, because it refers to the intention of changing the corporate culture gradually, i.e. the legal possibility to change from a mutual insurance company to a joint stock company. As a result, the membership rights are replaced by participation rights. This change influences both the structure of the ownership and the capital market in an unpredictable way.[130]

Between 1991 and 1994 the following mutual insurance companies used the possibility to transfer into a joint stock company:

- the "Austria Versicherungsverein aus Gegenseitigkeit" and the „Collegialität Versicherung auf Gegenseitigkeit" transferred into the „Austria-Collegialität Österreichische Versicherungs AG" (1991),
- the "Wiener Städtische Wechselseitige Versicherung" into the "Wiener Städtische Allgemeine Versicherung Aktiengesellschaft" (1992),
- the "Grazer Wechselseitige Versicherung" into the „Grazer Wechselseitige Versicherung AG" (1992),
- the "Merkur Wechselseitige Versicherungsanstalt" into the „Merkur Versicherung AG" (1992) and
- the "Wechselseitige Oberösterreichische Versicherungsanstalt" into the "Oberösterreichische Versicherung AG" (1994).

129 Ibid., p. 78.

130 *Peiner, W.*: Probleme der Konzernbildung bei Versicherungsvereinen auf Gegenseitigkeit, in: *Peiner, W.* (ed.): Grundlagen des Versicherungsvereins auf Gegenseitigkeit, Köln 1995, p. 196.

7.5 Effects of the restructuring

§ 65 VAG applies when a joint stock company is not able to continue the insurance activities of a mutual insurance company, which earlier transferred these activities to the company, due to tasks concerning the holding company. According to § 63 Abs. 4 and 5 VAG, such actions are not possible, because this regulation is based on a participation of the association in the joint stock company. When a holding company is integrated, the association would not be longer part of the company pursuing the insurance activities. As a result, the association has to be dissolved and the assets distributed between the members. To prevent the dissolution, the law permits an indirect participation of the association in the operational joint stock company under certain circumstances.[131]

This regulation was originally created for the reconstruction of the Vienna Insurance Group (VIG) in 2009, i.e. the reason for this legislation, and in the event of the separation of the mutual insurance activities from the operational joint stock company and the foundation of a new joint stock company. *Bartl* states that when this regulation is applied, problems occur due to the use of ambiguous legal terms (especially in Abs. 1 Z 2 lit. c).[132]

7.6 Transformation of legal form into a private foundation

Mutual insurance companies, which transferred their entire insurance activities in one or several joint stock companies (§ 62ff. VAG), have the options to change their legal form into a private foundation (§ 66 VAG). The members of the association become beneficiaries of the private foundation. This regulation was introduced on September 1, 2005 (BGBl. 2500/93) following the example of the act concerning saving banks. According to § 1 Abs. 3 of the saving banks act (BGBl. 1998/184), saving banks are allowed to transfer their banking operations into a joint stock company (Anteilverwaltungssparkassen[133]).

It is argued that the reasons which are in favour for the transformation of Anteilverwaltungssparkassen into private foundations apply to

[131] Cf. *Bartl, K.* (2016): §§ 68-81, in: *Korinek, S. / Saria, G. / Saria, S.* (eds.): Versicherungsgesetz VAG, Vienna, p. 82.

[132] Cf. Ibid.

[133] § 2 Abs. 1 and § 27a Abs. 1 of the saving banks law, the term “take-in saving bank” is defined as a saving bank which transferred its company or sub-banking business into a joint stock company. In common practice both terms “saving banks holding” and “Anteilverwaltungssparkasse” are used.

a large extent to mutual insurance companies, because saving banks associations and mutual insurance companies share several characteristics.[134] For example, both have no owners[135]; however, they do not share the non-profit character. In contrast to the saving banks sector, private foundations, which have been arisen from insurance associations, have no external beneficiaries.[136]

Moreover, it is argued that both the Anteilsverwaltungssparkassen and the asset management societies are unknown internationally, although they have important responsibilities. The introduction of the transformation into a private foundation, a legal form which is accepted nationally and internationally, is the starting point for a modern organizational law following international examples.[137] At the same time, the insurance branch and the saving banks branch are equated.[138]

The legal materials (ErlRV 984 VlgNR 22. GP) sustain the transformation in particular with similarities of insurance associations and saving banks association as well as with positive experiences of saving banks' transformation into private foundations. The latter regulations have been in effect since 1999. The regulations of the saving banks act (§§ 27a ff. SpG.) served as a model for the regulations concerning the transformation of mutual insurance companies and were either adopted directly or partly.

---

[134] Some of the regulations do not apply to the saving banks of societies. Firstly, the society remains, and secondly, the supervision board is appointed by the general meeting of the society. In case of a private foundation, which was established by modifying conversion of a according to § 3 established saving bank, a supervisory board has to be created; the members of the supervisory board are elected, with the exception of the first supervisory board, by the general meeting of the society. (§ 27a/5/3 SpG)

[135] Like saving banks are ownerless legal entities, which belongs to themselves, the assets of the association belongs to the association and not to the members. In contrast, *Hauser* argues that mutuals can have owners, even if there are many and the ownership relation is limited temporally. This means the existence of an insurance relation with that joint stock company in which the insurance portfolio was originally transferred to. (Cf. *Hauser, P.*, Die interne Revision und Whistleblowing, in: Versicherungsgeschichte Österreichs, vol. XI, Ethik-Nachhaltigkeit-Versicherung, Beograd-Wien 2013, p. 397.

[136] Cf. 984 der Beilagen XXII. GP – Regierungsvorlage – Materialien. § 27a Abs. 4 Z 3 states that the declaration of a private foundation has to name one or several beneficiaries, whose only scope of duties are to pursue non-profit, charitable, and clerical causes.

[137] *Bartl* disagrees with this argumentation, because although private foundations are common internationally, they are problematic due the international increasing importance of ownership control. (Cf. *Bartl, K.* (2016): §§ 68-81, in: *Korinek, S. / Saria, G. / Saria, S.* (eds.): Versicherungsgesetz VAG, Vienna, p. 89).

[138] Cf. *Reich-Rohrwig, J.; Priemayer, B. (*2005): Versicherungsvereine a.G: Umwandlung in Privatstiftung wird möglich, in: ecolex p. 695.

A prerequisite for the legal transformation of a mutual insurance company is the transfer of its entire insurance activities or several parts of it into one or several joint stock companies.[139] After the transfer into a joint stock company and the entry in the company register, the former mutual insurance company is allowed to transform into a private foundation.

In case that several associations transfer their insurance activities into the same joint stock company and that both association and private foundation coexist, the shares cannot be added together. The reason is that the prerequisites for these two legal forms differ. In the case of associations an influence on the operative joint stock company is necessary, while in case of private foundations a substantial share in the holding to which the joint stock company belongs is necessary. It seems that the used mixed solution considered the special circumstances of the UNIQA-group, but it does not appear to be very practicable.[140]

§ 66 Abs. 1 states that the transformation is a transformation of the legal form. The Austrian lawmaker states that the association exists as a private foundation with the entry of the transformation in the company register (§ 66 Abs. 7 VAG). This is similar to the right of joint stock companies. If the VAG does not state otherwise, the association is subject to the Private Foundation Act (PSG - Privatstiftungsgesetz).[141] Changing back to a mutual insurance company is prohibited.

The founder of the private foundation is the mutual insurance company, which management board draw up a foundation deed via a notary's office. This foundation deed has to be signed by people who are entitled to act as substitutes. They also need to be sufficient in number. The foundation deed has to include the basic legal requirements which are stated in § 9 PSG. After the change of the legal form and registration into the company register, the private foundation does not have a legal entity which appears as a founder. The reason is that the mutual

---

139 Compare the corresponding regulations of the saving banks act (§ 27a Abs. 1 Sparkassengesetz).

140 Cf. *Bartl, K.* (2016): §§ 68-81, in: *Korinek, S. / Saria, G. / Saria, S.* (eds.): Versicherungsgesetz VAG, Vienna, p. 90.

141 The private foundation is a legal entity that was dedicated an asset by the founder. Its use is allowed for administration and to fulfil a certain purpose stated by the founder. (§ 1/1 PSG). The foundation is based on certain ideas/purposes, which can be realized better, more determined and more lasting by the ownerless assets, connected with the founder's destiny and legal successor (ErlB der RV zum PSG 1132 dB XVIII GP). The idea of a private foundation is that the founder's assets is brought into a foundation to fulfill a certain foundation purpose even after the physical or legal end.

insurance company continue to exist as a private foundation and the private foundation cannot be its own founder.[142]

According to § 1 Abs. 1 PSG, the purpose of the private foundation cannot be decided by the founder. The purpose is to preserve and manage the foundation's funds and to keep the participation in the joint stock company. When the profit reserves, which are necessary for future additional capital funds of the joint stock company, are formed, then the annual net profit has to be distributed to the beneficiaries. A longer-term accumulation is not possible.[143] According to § 66 Abs. 3 Z 2 VAG, the private foundation has to be established for an indefinite period.

§ 66 Abs. 1 states that a resolution by the supreme body of the mutual insurance company is necessary for its transformation into a private foundation. This is also the last action of the supreme body, because it initiates the dissolution of the mutual insurance company and transforms it into a private foundation, which does not have a supreme body. The resolution needs a three-quarters majority of the votes. Within a month before the assembly of the supreme body votes on the transformation, the foundation deed and the closing balance sheet have to be available for the members at the headquarter of the mutual insurance company. All members have to be informed about this action before the documents are available. This has to be done according to the way of publication stated in the bylaws of association. Additionally to the publication in the official gazette of the "Wiener Zeitung", the members of the council have to be informed personally, because all asset management societies have a council of members.[144]

The association as the founder is not allowed to amend the foundation deed, to establish an appendix to the deed, to revoke the private foundation or to exercise other rights to influence legal relationships. Therefore, the former mutual insurance company is unable to react to new developments by changing the foundation deed.[145]

The resolution authorizing the transformation requires the approval of the FMA (§ 66 Abs. 2). The company register can withheld the approval when the foundation deed does not comply with the provisions of the VAG or when the transformation in conjunction with the contents of the foundation deed pose a threat to the interests of the members as future beneficiaries of the private foundation. The lawmaker does not specify the kind of members' restriction, alone the threat to the mem-

---

[142] Cf. *Bartl, K.* (2016): §§ 68-81, in: *Korinek, S. / Saria, G. / Saria, S.* (eds.): Versicherungsgesetz VAG, Vienna, p. 90.

[143] Cf. *Frotz, St.*: Vom Versicherungsverein zur Stiftung, in: RdW2/2006, p. 75.

[144] Cf. *Bartl, K.* (2016): §§ 68-81, in: *Korinek, S. / Saria, G. / Saria, S.* (eds.): Versicherungsgesetz VAG, Vienna, p. 90.

[145] Cf. *Reich-Rohrwig, J.; Priemayer, B.* (2005): Versicherungsvereine a.G: Umwandlung in Privatstiftung wird möglich, in: ecolex, p. 698.

bers' interests is sufficient. It is important to note that the interests of present and future members have to be considered. The association's assets as shown by the closing balance sheet become the assets of the private foundation. The assets are dedicated permanently to the private foundation and have to be maintained. According to §§ 66, the private foundation is neither a charitable nor non-profit organization, therefore, the interests of the beneficiaries consists of the annual profit and that their claim for the private foundation's assets is not reduced in the event of the dissolution. Such events would take place when beneficiaries are not designated to receive shares of the annual profit or when non- beneficiaries receive shares.[146]

As mentioned before, the association's assets as shown by the closing balance sheet are dedicated permanently to the private foundation and have to be maintained (§ 66 Abs. 3 Z 7). Any net income as shown by the financial statements have to be distributed to the beneficiaries unless it is allocated to the profit reserves or other reserves provided for in the foundation deed, or used for remunerations stipulated in the PSG or is carried forward to a new account. However, the same paragraph states that the amounts required maintaining the participation of the private foundation in the joint stock company to which the transformed association transferred its insurance activities may always be allocated to the reserves. This also includes sums in the amount of the participation of the original capital and subordinated liabilities regarding the company. As a result, the beneficiaries can be excluded from receiving their shares of the profits when the profits are needed otherwise.[147]

Within nine months, beginning with the closing balance sheet deadline, the documents for the company register have to be submitted to the company register court which has the jurisdiction for the mutual insurance company. The submission has to be signed by the members of the management board, because the management board of the private foundation starts to exist not before the registration into the company register.[148]

Later changes to the foundation deed have to be decided by the foundation organs according to Abs. 3 Z 5 and need to be granted by the FMA. These later changes also need to protect the interests of the beneficiaries. It is important to note that in this case an integration of the task of the foundation's declaration, the interests of the members, beneficiaries, employees, and the public interest is not planned. According to § 33 PSG, the management board of the private foundation

[146] Cf. *Bartl, K.* (2016): §§ 68-81, in: *Korinek, S. / Saria, G. / Saria, S.* (eds.): Versicherungsgesetz VAG, Vienna, p. 90.

[147] Ibid., p. 95.

[148] Cf. *Frotz, St.*: Vom Versicherungsverein zur Stiftung, in: RdW2/2006, p. 77.

has the right to change the foundation deed when the circumstances have changed, even without the permission of the supervisory board. However, they need the permission of the FMA and the changes have to be made according to the purpose of the foundation. Then the changes have to be submitted to the company register[149]

The private foundation needs to have a management board, a supervisory board and a foundation auditor. The former members of the management board of the asset management society become automatically members of the first foundation management board as well as the members of the supervisory board become members of the first foundation supervisory board (legal transfer).

Other or additional appointments of management board members are made by the supervisory board. The FMA has to be notified about these appointments at least a month before. The foundation deed can state that the supervisory board can recall members from the management board due to important reasons. The management board has to comprise at least two persons and the articles of foundation has to exclude the right to represent, the power of attorney and the authority to act for the entire business activities. After the appointment of the management board the election of the chair and his/her proxy follows. There are no regulation regarding the professional qualifications and personal reliability of the members of the management board. However, the foundation deed has to include such regulations.[150]

The management board of the foundation manages and represents the private foundation and guaranties that the foundation purpose is fulfilled. Additionally, the board manages the bookkeeping and observes the regulations concerning the protection of creditors. The foundation auditor controls the annual statement of accounts, the bookkeeping and the situation report. The management board has a supervisory function regarding the conduct of business and business practices of the private foundation as well as the right to approve legal business with members of the management board.

The insurance foundation has no members' council, because it has no members. The former members are now beneficiaries and excluded from the management of the foundation and the appointment of its bodies. Even when an advisory council as an informal committee or body is introduced, this advisory council cannot has the power of another body, in contrast to the supervision board. To fulfil the foundation purpose, it is stated that additional boards, such as an advisory board or a committee with the right for consultation and hearings, can be established (§ 14 Abs. 2 PSG).

---

[149] Cf. *Bartl, K.* (2016): §§ 68-81, in: *Korinek, S. / Saria, G. / Saria, S.* (eds.): Versicherungsgesetz VAG, Vienna, p. 91.

[150] Cf. Ibid.

The VAG does not state a period of office for the management board members' of the private foundation.[151] In case the foundation deed states no regulation regarding the period of office, the supervisory board decides on it and recalls the members of the management board. The occupation of the members of the management board is not perceived as full-time (cf. § 120 Abs. 2 Z 4 VAG).

Additional or succeeding appointments of members of the supervisory board take place by co-optation (self-completion) - in contrast to a general regulation of the law regarding private foundations, which states that the supervision board, with the exception of the first, is appointed by the court (§ 24/1 PSG). Co-optation needs a majority vote from the remaining supervisory board members. Each intended appointment has to be announced in advance in the official gazette "Amtsblatt zur Wiener Zeitung" and notified to the FMA. The prolongation by itself, which can only be obstructed but not prevented, is not part of the saving banks law. Regulations in case of the co-optation failure are not available. According to § 15 PSG, the supervisory board comprises at least three natural people. Beneficiaries cannot hold the majority in the supervisory board. The foundation deed has to state the period of office and an age limit, because such resolutions are not stated in the act.

The officials of the three level organized insurance society at this time, which is in its structure a joint stock company, are set free from the members' will (without any explanation), and the members become beneficiaries of the foundation, who have according to the founder's idea no right to be consulted regarding the administration of the foundation. The beneficiaries have only a non-binding right of nomination for the members of the supervisory board. The foundation deed has to specify the number of beneficiaries required to support the appointment proposal in order for it to be discussed. The appointment proposal has to be submitted to the management board within three weeks after the announcement. If more than one nomination meets this condition, only the appointment proposal supported by the majority of the beneficiaries must be discussed. However, no regulations exist in case several appointment proposals are supported by the same number of members. The appointment proposal is not binding, but if the supervisory board does not yet include a member nominated by the beneficiaries, a deviation from the appointment proposal requires a majority of two thirds of the remaining supervisory board members. The announcement has to be made in time, i.e. the beneficiaries need sufficient time for the submission of the appointment proposal; in total a period of six weeks are necessary.[152]

---

[151] Cf. Ibid., p. 92.

[152] Cf. Ibid..

The supervisory board has the right to recall a member of the management board before time due to important reasons, but only if the foundation deed states this. Such reasons are a gross dereliction of duty, incompetence of the administration of office, or financial unreliability. According to § 27 Abs. 2 Z 3, reasons for the recall from members are the institution of insolvency proceedings regarding the assets of the management board member, the rejection of such proceeding due to the lack of cost-covering assets or several unsuccessful seizures of the assets.

The conclusion of an insurance contract with the joint stock company to which the transformed association transferred its insurance activities establishes beneficiary status in the private foundation and in the case of the participation of several private foundations a beneficiary status in all those private foundations. The former members of the mutual insurance company become beneficiaries of the private foundation. The joint stock company is allowed, provided that this is expressly specified in the articles of association, to conclude insurance contracts without establishing beneficiary status in the private foundation. This means that the joint stock company's articles of association influence the legal status of beneficiaries of the private foundation. It is sensible to stipulate legally the detailed conditions by contract between the private foundation and the joint stock company. Even without such a contractual arrangement, the joint stock company is to be obliged to disclose to the private foundation the names and addresses of those persons who acquired beneficiary status by concluding an insurance contract. However, for the disclosure a written request of the private foundation is necessary. The joint stock company assumes automatically the agreement of the insurant, because otherwise problems regarding data protection occur. The end of the insurance relationship results in the end of the beneficiary status and in the loss of any kinds of claim on the assets.

In case of the coexistence of several private foundations or associations and private foundations, it is important to note that the regulations concerning the grant of the membership and the status of being a beneficiary are the same.[153]

The main difference between the insurance associations and the private foundation is that the latter requires no substantial influence on the operational joint stock company. According to § 66 Abs. 3 Z 3, it is sufficient that the private foundation invests more than half of its total assets, based on the foundation's most recently audited balance sheet, in companies belonging to the same group as the joint stock company to which the transformed association transferred the insurance activities. This participation shows the closeness to the operational joint

[153] Cf. Ibid., p. 95.

stock company and secures the influence of the private foundation as the most important shareholder of the holding, but is not sufficient to influence the business activities of the operational joint stock company. A similar regulation as § 64 regarding the involvement of the private foundation into the decision making of the operational joint stock company does not exist.[154]

In addition, the companies belonging to the group continue to hold jointly more than 50 percent of the voting shares in the joint stock company to which the transformed association transferred the insurance activities. This majority has to be verified by the statutory auditor when auditing the financial statements. With this action it should be guaranteed that the operational joint stock company is dominated by the holding in which the private foundation has invested. It is not of interest which company of the holding has what share in the joint stock company; it only counts the total of the voting shares of the holding. In the interests of the beneficiaries, the foundation's management board has to ensure ongoing compliance with this provision and in the event of a violation the board has to inform the FMA immediately. However, it is not clear what the remark concerning the "interests of the beneficiaries" means. The only possibility is that it refers to financial matters, i.e. an annual high profit and to keep the right of receiving the assets of the private foundation as beneficiaries, because there is no substantial influence on the operational joint stock company. Therefore, the beneficiaries have no interest, if the shares of the private foundation are assessed in companies of the holding or in other joint stock companies as far as the assessments are secure and profitable. Only the holding has a serious interest in an assessment within the holding.[155]

In the event that the assessment falls below the minimum limit of 50 percent, proceedings according to § 63 Abs. 5 VAG take place, however, without the option of transforming into a private foundation. The provision is re-established when more than 50 percent of the total assets of the private foundation are assessed in the company according to § 195 Abs. 1 Z 3 lit. a VAG.

The provision of Z 3 is fulfilled and the private foundation continues to exist when the share of the transformed association in the joint stock company in which the insurance activities was transferred to is higher than 26 percent of the voting shares. This happens when the private foundation holds more than 26 percent of the voting shares in the joint stock company although less than 50 percent of the assets are assessed in shares of the company.[156]

---

[154] Cf. Ibid., p. 93.

[155] Ibid.

[156] Cf. Ibid.

Only two asset management societies transformed into a private foundation:

- In 2005, the "Austria Versicherungsverein auf Gegenseitigkeit" transformed into the "Austria Versicherungsverein auf Gegenseitigkeit Privatstiftung", which changed in 2013 its name into "UNIQA Versicherungsverein Privatstiftung" due to the change of the name of the "UNIQA Personenversicherung AG" into "UNIQA Österreich Versicherungen AG".
- In 2012, the "Collegialität Versicherung auf Gegenseitigkeit" transformed into "Collegialität Versicherungsverein Privatstiftung".

§ 67 deals with the merger of private foundations, which were established by the transformation of their legal form into a private foundation (§ 66 VAG). It is possible that several private foundations merge. According to § 66 Abs. 5 and 6, this is a merger by absorption.[157] In Austria, this regulation has not been realized yet, because only two private foundations have been established yet in the way mentioned above.

7.7 Assimilation of the legal form[158]

Today, the mutual insurance companies and joint stock companies have been adapted to each other in general and developed to today's existing form of insurance, i.e. they have been assimilated legally and actually. While earlier the legal and actual differences between these two legal forms emphasized the competition about customers, now adaptation tendencies led to an adaptation between companies of different forms: negative side effects and disadvantages were removed and improvements and simplifications via imitation of successful methods were gained; moreover, changed basic conditions demand that members adapt to them.

With regard to the insurance contract, the policyholder recognizes no difference between an insurance association and a joint stock company. The adaptation process, which removed the disadvantages of both legal forms for the policyholder, was a result of the legal forms.[159]

Another element of this assimilation can be found in the Austrian version of the VAG of 1978, of which several drafts were composed in

157 Cf. Ibid., p. 97.

158 Cf. *Nemson, J.* (2014): Geschäftsmodell VVaG: Rahmenbedingungen, Herausforderungen und Chancen. Band 18, Leipziger Schriften zur Versicherungswissenschaft, VVW, Karlsruhe, p. 31ff.

159 Cf. *Pressl, A.* (1993): Die Einbringung des Geschäftsbetriebes eines Versicherungsvereins auf Gegenseitigkeit in eine Aktiengesellschaft, unpublished dissertation University Salzburg, p. 58.

1952 and 1953. A resolution was made after the Austrian Stock Corporation Act in 1965 had been created. The lawmaker did not want to create special regulations before the VAG 1978 would come into effect. After the Austrian Stock Corporation Act had been enacted, the work on an amendment continued.[160]

Besides the specific insurance regulations, the commercial law, labour law, tax law, and labour constitutional right apply equally to the insurance companies. All these basic legal regulations, which are applicable to all legal forms, are the norms and framework for insurance joint stock companies and mutual insurance companies; these provisions have a standardised effect.

Additionally to the legal framework, insurance associations as a group supported the assimilation process of the different legal forms.[161] Since the middle of the 19th century, private insurance companies of both legal forms have worked together. Their work comprised public relations, exchange of ideas, and lobbying. In particular, they worked together on mutual specific insurance issues such as corporate statistics, the development of a specimen for general terms and conditions, or information services.

The customers and their requirements provide the general framework for the work of the insurer. *Farny* sees the conduct of the policyholder as an important element in the assimilation process.[162] Usually the legal form of an insurance company is not well known among the Austrian population. However, it is possible to argue that not the customer's conduct and expectation influence the companies, but the absent or weak boundaries between the different legal forms in the insurance industry lead to an indifferent customer perception.

Additionally, the competition for customers and employees supported the assimilation process of both legal forms. The direct competition between the insurance joint stock companies and the mutual insurance companies triggered serious assimilation effects: it led to the exclusion from the additional payment liability in case of carefully calculated rates by large mutual insurance companies as well as to the adoption of profit-sharing and refunds by insurance joint stock companies. Similar assimilation effects had the competition for staff, in particular in the upper management.

Other reasons for the assimilation of the legal forms were the aim to expand the business area. Fast growing numbers of members, contribu-

---

160 Cf. *Fenyves / Korinek* (1999): Das österreichische Versicherungsaufsichtsrecht im Über-blick, in: ZfV 1999/2, p. 151.

161 On October 4, 1945 the union of the Austrian insurance companies established. It supports its members regarding legal, fiscal, commercial, and international issues.

162 Cf. *Farny, D.* (2011): Versicherungsbetriebslehre, 5th edition, VVW, Karlsruhe, p. 134.

tion capacity and business areas were enabled by the close collaboration between mutual insurance companies and insurance joint stock companies since the 1880s. These elements were also required for high-volume business transactions under a risk point of view. As a result, the newly developed large mutual insurance companies adapted the organization structures and management proceedings of the insurance joint stock companies for their own companies. This action was obvious, because the company structure of insurance joint stock companies have already been proved successful for the insurance business. Additionally, before 1939 no legal regulations regarding the organizational structure of mutual insurance companies existed, although various heterogeneous association structures were used. The reference in the VAG 1978 to the organization of stock companies for large mutual insurance companies mirrored simple the economic reality.

The increased size and the work on a non-regional level of mutual insurance companies led to a weakening of the specific characterizations of their legal form: The VAG from 1939 introduced the co-optation in Austria, because with a growing number of members and business areas the members' participation was only achievable via co-option. This proceeding became widely accepted. As a result, the core elements of mutual insurance company such as the membership rights of policyholders and the annual general meetings fell into oblivion. Therefore, the "law of oligarchy" can be observed. This expression that comes from behavioral science means the development of oligarchic structures within associations.

Another reason for the assimilation of the legal forms is the task to optimize the business. The principle of actuarial practice is the basis of all insurance companies, i.e. operations and production technology are largely unified. Similar business strategies, proceedings and product developments can be identified due to homogenous tasks: mutual insurance companies and joint stock companies seek profits, but with different motives and to a different degree.[163] The restriction when distributing the profits to members in favour of self-financing is reasoned in the assumption that financial covering by large insurance companies has economic advantages (economic growth needs more own capital) and that own capital brings stability.[164] The assimilation is even more obvious regarding the proceedings: *Farny* refers to factual enforcement. He means that proceedings are optimized in the interest of the best profitableness, a development which concerns insurers of

[163] Cf. *Pressl, A.* (1993): Die Einbringung des Geschäftsbetriebes eines Versicherungsvereins auf Gegenseitigkeit in eine Aktiengesellschaft, unpublished dissertation University Salzburg, p. 30ff.

[164] Cf. *Farny, D.* (2011): Versicherungsbetriebslehre, 5th edition, VVW, Karlsruhe, p. 235.

both legal forms.[165] All large insurance companies have programmes to optimize their proceedings and to increase efficiency. Both mutual insurance companies and insurance joint stock companies have similar solutions regarding the design of their product selection: The offer of all insurance branches for diversification reasons and sales policy has led to assimilation. The products of different companies became similar due to similar calculations and with the help of larger and better data regarding damage.[166]

In conclusion, the Austrian insurance industry diverges from the ideal legal form due to many reasons which influence various levels. In particular after the Second World War, the insurer had no reasons to emphasise the differences due to homogenous frameworks in a regulated market. The traditional differences between the legal forms have been levelled due to balance the mutual advantages and disadvantages of the system. This is in particular true regarding the calculations of the rates. Today, no differences between policyholders of large mutual insurance companies and insurance joint stock companies are recognizable anymore.

The results of an analysis regarding the financial efficiency of all mutual insurance companies and hybrid forms and one joint stock company used as benchmark, on the basis of combined ratio in the insurance classes elementary and casualty and of cost ratio in the class of life insurance in the period 1970 to 2014, show no clear differences between these two legal forms regarding an efficient use of premium income. The analysis shows a slightly lower combined ratios and cost ratio regarding mutual insurance companies, because they are not able to raise equity capital on the market, in contrast to joint stock companies, but from retained capital. The joint stock companies that operate in form of a hybrid have similar results as the benchmark company, with the exception of one regional insurance company.

[165] Cf. Ibid., p. 236.

[166] Cf. Ibid.

Bibliography

Baran, P. (2016): Das Österreichische Versicherungsaufsichtsrecht, 3th edition, Vienna

Baran, P. (1992): Die Fortführung des Betriebes von Versicherungsvereinen durch Aktiengesellschaften, in: Versicherungsrundschau

Bartl, K. (2016): §§ 35-67, in: *Korinek, S. / Saria, G. / Saria, S.* (eds.): Versicherungsgesetz VAG, Vienna

Bartl, K. (2016): §§ 68-81, in: *Korinek, S. / Saria, G. / Saria, S.* (eds.): Versicherungsgesetz VAG, Vienna

Braumüller, P. (1999): Versicherungsaufsichtsrecht: internationale Standards, europäische Richtlinien und österreichisches Recht, Vienna, New York

Büchner, F. (1957): Zur Geschichte der Versicherung, in: Versicherungswissenschaftliches Archiv

Eckert, F. (1993): Die Einbringung von Versicherungsbetrieben aus Versicherungsvereinen auf Gegenseitigkeit in Versicherungs-Aktiengesellschaften, in: Zeitschrift für Versicherungsrecht

Ehrenberger, H. (1889): Zur Statistik der localen Versicherungsvereine gegen Feuerschäden (Bauern-Assecuranzen) in Oesterreich, Statistisches Monatsschrift, Mittheilungen und Miscellen, Vienna

Farny, D. (2011): Versicherungsbetriebslehre, 5th edition, VVW, Karlsruhe

Fenyves / Korinek (1999): Das österreichische Versicherungsaufsichtsrecht im Überblick, in: ZfV 1999/2

FMA (ed.): Bericht über die Lage der Versicherungswirtschaft 2015

Frotz, St. (2006): Vom Versicherungsverein zur Stiftung, in: RdW2

Großfeld, B. (1985): Der Versicherungsverein auf Gegenseitigkeit im System der Unternehmensformen, Tübingen

Großfeld, B.; Merdausl, C.: Der Versicherungsverein auf Gegenseitigkeit im System der Unternehmensformen, in: *Peiner, W.* (ed.): Grundlagen des Versicherungsvereins auf Gegenseitigkeit, Köln 1995

Hauser, P. (2013): Die interne Revision und Whistleblowing, in: Versicherungsgeschichte Österreichs, vol. XI, Ethik-Nachhaltigkeit-Versicherung, Beograd-Wien

Jud, W. (1992): Die Einbringung des Versicherungsbetriebes eines Versicherungsvereins auf Gegenseitigkeit in eine Versicherungs-Aktiengesellschaft im System der versicherungsaufsichtsrechtlichen Strukturmaßnahmen, in: *Doralt, P. / Nowotny, Ch.* (eds.): Kontinuität und Wandel, Vienna

Korinek, S. (2008): Der österreichische Versicherungsvereine auf Gegenseitigkeit; in: *Bürke, J.* (ed.): Rechtliche Rahmenbedingungen für Versicherungsvereine auf Gegenseitigkeit – Festschrift zum 100 jährigen Bestehen der Stuttgarter Lebensversicherung a.G., Karlsruhe

Lorenz, W.: Stellungnahme zu der Untersuchung von Dieter Farny, in: ZVersWiss 84

Mayer, L. (2001): Die Demutualisierung von Versicherungsvereinen auf Gegenseitigkeit (VVaG) in Österreich, in: *Geib, G.* (ed.): Rechnungslegung von Versicherungsunternehmen, Düsseldorf

Nemson, J. (2014): Geschäftsmodell VVaG: Rahmenbedingungen, Herausforderungen und Chancen. Band 18, Leipziger Schriften zur Versicherungswissenschaft, VVW, Karlsruhe

Pachler, H. (1995): Die versicherungsrechtliche Bestandsübertragung in Österreich, Dissertation Universität Salzburg, Salzburg

Peiner, W. (1995): Probleme der Konzernbildung bei Versicherungsvereinen auf Gegenseitigkeit, in: *Peiner, W.* (ed.): Grundlagen des Versicherungsvereins auf Gegenseitigkeit, Köln

Pressl, A. (1993): Die Einbringung des Geschäftsbetriebes eines Versicherungsvereins auf Gegenseitigkeit in eine Aktiengesellschaft, unpublished dissertation University Salzburg, Salzburg

Reich-Rohrwig, J.; Priemayer, B. (2005): Versicherungsvereine a.G: Umwandlung in Privatstiftung wird möglich, in: ecolex

The Idea of Solidarity in Mutual Insurance Societies and Cooperatives in the Habsburg Monarchy

Wolfgang Werner[1]

1. Insurances

Cooperative associations are regarded as the origins of today's insurance business.[2] "Among the most beautiful flowers in the field of associations we find without doubt the insurance associations against damage by the elements. Few hours or minutes are often suffice to destroy the results of a life of human labour and to reduce hundreds of family to beggary. Even help by the public authorities is not capable of as being an effective help…Only an association is able to heal those wounds and to rescue of what has fallen prey to the fury of the elements. Where the individual is too weak, united force has to heal."[3]

The idea of insurance is closely connected to the increase of global trade. The first insurance companies were specialised in maritime transport insurances and were established in the 18th century in Trieste[4], which was at that time the main port in the Austrian Empire. The first insurances for the general public offered fire insurances and developed historically from the principle of mutual help in the event of fire. The social union of the manorial system[5], the guilds of craftspeople and merchants in the Middle Ages[6] were organisations covering all areas of life and were obligated to help their members.

---

1 My particular gratitude goes to *Dr. Karl Holubar*, archive of the monastery Klosterneuburg, *Dr. Manfred Haltrich*, library of the monastery Klosterneuburg, *Johann Hanslik* and *Dipl.-Ing. Dr. Gerhard Schreiber* from the Generali historical archive, *Angelika Egger* from the underwriting association "Austria" and *Mag. Dr. Elke Hammer-Luza* from the archive in Styria.

2 Cf. *Dreher Meinrad*, Die Versicherung als Rechtsprodukt (Tübingen 1991) 15.

3 Cf. *Stubenrauch Moriz von*, Statistische Darstellung des Vereinswesens im Kaiserthume Österreich (Wien 1857) 316.

4 Cf. *Rohrbach Wolfgang*, Versicherungsgeschichte Österreichs, Band 1, Von den Anfängen bis zum Börsenkrach des Jahres 1873 (Wien 1988) 160 et seq.

5 Cf. *Bruckmüller Ernst*, Sozialgeschichte Österreichs (Wien, München 1985) 41 et seq.

6 Cf. *Hoke Rudolf*, Österreichische und deutsche Rechtsgeschichte (Wien, Köln, Weimar 1992) 95 et seq.

The manorial system developed from the feudal system of the Early Middle Ages.[7] In the event of fire each villager was bound to help fire-fighting operations and to provide buckets, ladders, and other kinds of equipment.[8] The claimant was allowed to fetch timber from the village's forest and neighbours were obligated to help the rebuilding.[9] The manorial system was, therefore, a kind of insurance contract comprising more than military protection.[10][11] From this support small local finsurance societies developed, which were called peasant insurances (Bauernassekuranzen).[12] The landlords were interested in these local friendly societies, because they protected their tenants.[13] The insurances changed the original customs to contractual regulations, which constitute a legal demand of compensation.[14] This kind of organisations could be found in particular in Upper Austria and Salzburg[15], e.g. in villages such as Kremsmünster and Spital/Pyhrn.[16]

Additionally, the regional law generated regulations. For example, Emperor Maximilian I ordered on May 24, 1518 that people of the Austrian hereditary lands, who were the victims of fire, receive extensions up to three years regarding their dues.[17] However, it is questionable if resolutions of the hereditary lands' conference (Innsbruck) became effective in Lower Austria due to the Emperor's illness and death on January 12, 1519 and the following changes in administration.[18] In the

---

7 Cf. *Henning Friedrich-Wilhelm*, Landwirtschaft und ländliche Gesellschaft in Deutschland, Band 1, 800 bis 1750 (Paderborn 1979) 39.

8 Cf. *Feigl Helmuth*, Die niederösterreichische Grundherrschaft, Forschungen zur Landeskunde von Niederösterreich, XVI. Band (²St. Pölten 1998) 236.

9 Cf. *Buchinger Josef*, Der Bauer in der Kultur- und Wirtschaftsgeschichte Österreichs (Wien 1952) 239.

10 Cf. *Feigl Helmuth*, Grundherrschaft op.cit. 71 et seq.

11 Cf. *Rohrbach Wolfgang*, Von den Anfängen op.cit. 83.

12 Cf. *Buchinger Josef*, Bauer op.cit. 240.

13 Cf. Das Jubelfest der Wechselseitigen Brandschaden-Versicherungs-Anstalt in Graz am 4. Juni 1879 (Graz 1879) 14.

14 Cf. *Göttlicher Erich*, Staat und Versicherungswesen in Österreich, in: *Henn Rudolf/Schwebler Robert* (ed.), Staat, Wirtschaft, Assekuranz und Wissenschaft, Festschrift für Robert Schwebler (Karlsruhe 1986) 188.

15 Cf. *Gluth (Oskar)*, Feuerpolizei, in: *Mischler Ernst/Ulbrich Josef* (ed.), Oesterreichisches Staatswörterbuch, Erster Band (Wien 1895) 466.

16 Cf. *Rohrbach Wolfgang*, Von den Anfängen op.cit. 148 et seq.

17 Cf. Stiftsarchiv Klosterneuburg, Codex provincialis oder Bedenck Buch der Löbl. Herren Ständen des Erzherzogthum Österreich unter der Enns: Erster Band. Anno 1723. Von Litt: A: bis K., Abbrändler.

18 Cf. *Niederstätter Alois*, Das Jahrhundert der Mitte, Österreichische Geschichte 1400-1522 (Wien 1996) 290 et seq. – In the monastery archive of Klosterneuburg a collection of committee documents can be found brought along by provost Georg II Hausmanstetter from Innsbruck (Cf. *Ludwig Vinzenz Oskar*, Propst Georg II. Hausmanstetter. Beiträge zur Kultur- und politischen Geschichte Niederösterreichs im 16. Jahrhundert, in: Jahrbuch des Stiftes Klos-

Austrian lands, the estates of the realm objected to fire insurances, but were advised to regard the benefits for their subjects.

With the increasing development of the absolutism negative developments occurred. For example, landlords did not meet their obligations anymore. *Maria Theresia* enacted regulations which determined the amount of labour obligations and the relationship between landlords and tenants. This relationship was put under supervision.[19] Emperor Joseph II enacted laws which enabled to replace the tenant's labour obligations for the landlord.[20] Major changes of the relationship between tenants and landlords were made by the agrarian reform in 1848,[21] which eliminated all feudal rights and privileges.[22]

1.1 Fire damage

After *Maria Theresia* became Empress in 1740, the discussion about fire insurances started in the Austrian hereditary lands. The introduction of similar organisations which were already in use in England, Prussia, and Saxony failed due to the opposition of the aristocracy. Two arguments were brought up against the introduction of insurances: it was argued that, firstly, the various provinces of the Austrian monarchy had a sufficient number of firefighting plans and, secondly, insurances would lead to abuse, because the owners of indebted or dilapidated buildings would set them on fire to claim illegal compensation.[23]

Baron Astfeld of Widrzy[24] proposed in 1750 the introduction of fire insurance organisations in Austria similar to them initiated by *Fred-*

terneuburg, Band IV. (Wien 1912) 222). The documents are still available in the monastary archive. (Cf. *Holubar Karl* (ed.), Das Augustiner-Chorherrenstift Klosterneuburg, geschichtliche und statistische Daten (^{3}Klosterneuburg 2014) 124).

19 Cf. *Ogris Werner*, Staats- und Rechtsformen, in: *Koschatzky Walter*, Maria Theresia und ihre Zeit (^{2}Salzburg, Wien 1980) 61 et seq.

20 Cf. *Feigl Helmut*, Landwirtschaft und Grundherrschaft. Ihre Entwicklung unter Joseph II., in: Österreichs zur Zeit Kaiser Joseph II., Katalog der niederösterreichischen Landesaustellung 1980 (Wien 1980) 49 et seq.

21 Cf. *Rumpler Helmut*, Eine Chance für Mitteleuropa, Österreichische Geschichte, 1804-1914 (Wien 1997) 347 et seq.

22 Cf. *Bruckmüller Ernst*, Sozialgeschichte op.cit. 362.

23 Cf. *Leimdörfer Max*, Entwicklung und Organisation der Brandschadenversicherung in Österreich 1700-1848 (Wien 1905) 53.

24 *Astfeld Baron of Widrzy* was Professor at the Further Austrian University Freiburg at the age of 20, and then he became diplomat, joined the military in 1730, and became 1731 senior civil servant in Glatz. During the first Silesian War, he was appointed as imperial and royal higher regional commissioner in 1741, and worked as actual imperial and royal highest war and country commissioner during the Seven Years War. In 1760, he became the imperial and royal represent and political head in the county of Glatz and in 1761 the administrator of

eric II of Prussia[25]. His plan was, however, rejected. The court chancellery had sent to this effect documents to all regional offices, but only the offices of Lower Austria and Further Austria responded. In 1763, the Austrian kingdom of Bohemia submitted a proposal based on Prussian documents, but again no result was achieved. The officials of the different territories argued that people who had suffered from fire damage had already received replacements in form of timber etc. and the landlords had granted them tax benefits.[26]

Another initiative was suggested under the reign of Emperor *Francis II*. In 1798, the heads of the regional offices in the Austrian hereditary lands were prompted to submit proposals to establish fire insurance companies. The Galician court chancellery suggested that these companies should be based on voluntariness and mutuality, restricted buildings and administrated by the estates of the realm. This proposal was approved by the Emperor. In October 1802, it was referred again to the resolution of 1798 and to the Galician proposal. In 1811, Salzburg and Upper Austria, at that time part of Bavaria, organised fire insurance companies based on these principals. Tyrol did the same in 1823.[27]

1.1.1 The impulse of the Emperor

For the further development of the insurance business and the establishment of fire insurances the so-called "kaiserliche Entschließung", i.e. the Emperor's resolution, from September 4, 1819 is important. "His majesty fully appreciated the advantages of such institutions for the participants and for the state in general and offered protection and support."[28] The resolution states that insurances should be established and work under the Emperor's protection. It also emphasises the advantages of such companies for the common good. It does not surprise that the idea of insurance is based on the principle of commen good regarding fire damage. At that time almost all buildings were built with timber and had a thatched roof.[29] Moreover, the industry started to

---

the Austrian princedoms Schweidnitz and Jauer. In this capacity, he learned about fire insurances initiated by Friedrich II. – Curriculum vitae: Cf. Leimdörfer Max, Entwicklung op.cit. 36.

25 Cf. *Leimdörfer Max*, Entwicklung op.cit. (36).

26 Cf. *Leimdörfer Max*, Entwicklung op.cit. 44 et seq. – A summary of Maria Theresia's efforts can be found in the following booklet: *Seefeldner Othmar*, Die Frage der Einführung der Feuerversicherung in Österreich zur Zeit der Kaiserin Maria Theresia (Linz o. J.)

27 Cf. *Fachini E(rnst)*, Entstehung, Grundsätze und Entwicklung des Versicherungswesens in Oesterreich-Ungarn (Wien 1888) 62.

28 Cf. Wiener Zeitung (3. November 1819): Amtsblatt (357) Kundmachung

29 Cf. *Eigner Peter / Helige Barbara* (ed.), Österreichische Wirtschafts- und Sozialgeschichte im 19. und 20. Jahrhundert (Wien 1999) 41.

use steam boilers more often which led to an increase of fire hazards.[30] The number of steam boilers used in the Austrian industry increased from 1841 to 1851 from 49 to 2.019.[31] As a result, the industrialisation in the 19th century caused an increased demand of life and non-life insurances.[32]

Around 1800, the idea of insurances was already advanced in Saxony. The Austrian officer, *Major Georg Ritter von Högelmüller*,[33] got to know the Saxon fire insurance model in Dresden and brought this idea back to Austria. From 1803 onwards, he tried to initiate a similar facility but his work was at first in vain.[34]

1.1.2 k.k. privilegierte wechselseitige Brandschaden-Versicherungs-Anstalt

In 1822, *Högelmüller* published a proposal concerning non-profit fire insurances.[35] He argued that fire hazards caused despair and that the wish to put things right was huge. The companies should be mutual insurance societies without pecuniary benefit, in contrast to joint stock companies. Several declarations of approval concerning this idea were already available by the government.[36] He emphasised mutuality due to his extensive experience. Mutual insurance societies could be found in almost all European countries, some governments even commanded

---

30 Cf. *Baumgartner Isabella*, 175 Jahre Grazer Wechselseitige (Graz 2003) 16.

31 Cf. *Chaloupek Günther* et al., Die vorhandene Chance, in: Österreichische Industriegeschichte GmbH (ed.), Österreichische Industriegeschichte 1700 bis 1848 (Wien 2003) 36.

32 Cf. *Zedtwitz Clemens*, Die rechtsgeschichtliche Entwicklung der Versicherung, Diss. Univ. St. Gallen (Zürich 2000) 163.

33 *Georg Ritter von Högelmüller*, * 6. February 1770 in Vienna, +14. April 1826 in Vienna. He was the son of wealthy parents and was educated between 7 and 16 in Strasburg. He joined the military as officer. He participated in all campaigns of the Napoleonic era until 1815, the year in which he became adjutant of the field marshal-lieutenant Count *Radetzky*. After peace had been restored, *Högelmüller* retired due to his injuries. He was convinced of the usefulness of fire insurances and worked for many years for the implementation of this idea. With his power of persuasion and restless eagerness, he was able to interest many people in this topic. Finally, in 1824 the mutual fire insurance society was established. This society was restricted to Lower Austria, but its foundation triggered several other new companies in other crown countries. – Curriculum vitae: Wurzbach Constant von, Biographisches Lexikon des Kaiserthums Oesterreich. Neunter Theil (Wien 1863) 107 et seq.

34 Cf. *Fischer Carl*, Festschrift aus Anlass des Fünfzigjährigen Jubiläums der k. k. priv. wechselseitigen Brandschaden-Versicherungs-Anstalt in Wien (Wien 1875) 4 et seq.

35 Cf. Generali Historisches Archiv, *Hoegelmüller Georg von*, Vorschlag zur Theilnahme an den in Oesterreich unter der Enns, in Oesterreich ob der Enns mit Salzburg, in Böhmen, in Mähren mit Schlesien, in Illyrien und in Steyermark zu errichtenden Brandschaden-Versicherungs-Privat-Anstalten (Wien 1822).

36 Ibid. (IV et seq.).

mandatory membership for their subjects. He had great knowledge about the societies in Saxony and Mecklenburg.[37]

The appendix of *Högelmüller's* proposal listed the proponents of his initiative and included clergy and non-clergy estate owners, agents of agriculture companies, and representatives of the agricultural office in Lower Austria. The mundane estate owners comprised princes, earls, barons, and knights, while the clerical estate owners included the prince-archbishop of Vienna, the archbishop and abbot general of the Mechitaristm order, abbots of monasteries, the Vienna cathedral chapter, and the Theresian Knight-Academy. Among the monasteries Klosterneuburg[38] was also listed, which is the partner of the insurance association to this day.[39] The positive attitude of the clerical circles was confirmed by the court chancellery in 1828, which enacted an appeal for fire insurances concerning public buildings, including churches.[40]

The preliminary general principles[41] of a private fire insurance company under the protection of a sovereign prince[42] are the following:

I. Definition of the company and its size (§ 1-6)
II. Favours and advantages from the sovereign for the members (§ 7-13)
III. Suitable and unsuitable objects for membership (§ 14-16)
IV. The ways and modalities for the admittance, leaving, and re-admission into the company (§ 17-19)
V. About the buildings (§ 20-21)
VI. About the obligation of contributions (§ 22-23)
VII. About the way of collecting the contributions (§ 24)
VIII. About the way of ascertaining fire damage (§ 25-27)
IX. Cases in which the right of compensation becomes effective (§ 28-31)
X. Scale, type, and time of the compensation (§ 32-34)
XI. About the distribution of the contributions (§ 35)
XII. About the administration of the company (society) (§ 36-40)

---

37 Ibid. (2 et seq.).

38 Ibid. (Beylage Lit. B.) 41 et seq.

39 Cf. *Geyer Günter/Backovsky Bernhard*, Ringturmausstellung 2014: 190 Jahre Wiener Städtische Versicherungsverein – 900 Jahre Stift Klosterneuburg, in: Wiener Städtische Wechselseitiger Versicherungsverein (ed.), Arnulf Rainer-Schleier der Agnes (Wien 2014).

40 Cf. *Lehner Ulrich Peter*, Kirche und Versicherung. Zur Geschichte einer fast vergessenen Beziehung, in: An der Schwelle zum 3. Jahrtausend – Retrospektiven und Perspektiven. Versicherungsgeschichte Österreichs, Band VI (Wien 2000) 1197.

41 Cf. Vorläufige allgemeine Grundsätze einer unter landesfürstlichem Schutz zu errichtenden Brandschaden-Versicherungs-Privat-Anstalt, in: Generali Historisches Archiv, Hoegelmüller Georg von, Vorschlag op.cit. 7 et seq.

42 The sovereign was Francis I., Archduke of Austria and Emperor of the Empire Austria.

Högelmüller's association comprises the owners of the buildings (§ 1), who ensure each other to compensate the fire damage of the buildings. In case of a fire, the compensation of the costs was paid in cash after they were ascertained. According to § 3, the company became effective in the particular province after a certain amount of money was registered for the insured buildings. For Lower Austria, the value of the buildings was determined with 30 Million in Convention-Coin. According to § 12, the compensations are paid on the condition that they were used for rebuilding.

Article 22 states the exact requirements for paying contributions. The following example is for the company of Lower Austria which had a foundation capital (value of the insured buildings) of 20 million. The fire damage of one year amounted to 50.000 fl., which was a quarter percent or 15 Kreuzer of 100 fl. of the foundation capital. As a result, the owner had to pay for a house which was registered with 200fl. 30 Kreuzer for insurance, after the contribution quota was emitted. To offer faster help and according to § 32 a reserve fund was created which contribution payments are based on the type of the insured building (§ 33).

Högelmüller sent these preliminary principles for evaluation to experts and a report to the Count of Dietrichstein, the country marshal of Lower Austria.[43][44] The numerous suggestions for improvement were summed up and revised by *Josef Kudler*, professor at the University of Vienna.[45] The new classification of the bylaws was the following:[46]

I. Section: Definition and amount of the company (society) (§ 1-4)
II. Section: Insured objects (§ 5-9)
III. Section: The obligations of the members in general and before the admittance to the society (§ 10-18)

---

[43] *Joseph Karl von Dietrichstein*, *19. October 1763, + 17. September 1825, the last of the Hollenburg'schen line of the Count and prince of Dietrichstein, country marshal of the estates of the country in Lower Austria (1811-1825), and president of Lower Austria (1804-1805). – Curriculum vitae: *Wurzbach* Constant von, Biographisches Lexikon des Kaiserthums Oesterreich. Dritter Theil (Wien 1858) 295 and Wikipedia.

[44] Cf. Generali Historisches Archiv, Umschlag zu: Hoegelmüller Georg von, Vorschlag op.cit..

[45] *Josef Ritter von Kudler*, * 10. Oktober 1786 in Graz, + 6. Februar 1853 in Vienna. Before he received his PhD, he taught statistic and political sciences at the Grazer Lyceum for eleven years. In 1821, he became Professor for political sciences and Austrian political legal issues at the University of Vienna. In 1848, he was elected into the Imperial Council and advocated for basic rights. In 1851, he was raised to the hereditary rank of Knights. He was an acknowledged academic and author. – Curriculum Vitae: *Wurzbach* Constant von, Biographisches Lexikon des Kaiserthums Oesterreich. Dreizehnter Theil (Wien 1865) 298 et seq.

[46] Cf. Landesarchiv Steiermark, K. 31, Nr. 3078, Statuten der k. k. priv. wechselseitige Brandschaden-Versicherungs-Anstalt in Wien (Wien 1824).

IV. Section: Regulations regarding the value of the insured buildings (§ 19-28)
V. Section: The obligation of the society to pay their members compensations (§ 29-37)
VI. Section: Evaluation of fire damage (§ 38-53)
VII. Section: Compensations (§ 54-59)
VIII. Section: Apportionment of fire damage and regulations about the contribution quota (§ 60-67)
IX. Section: The payment of contributions (§ 68-75)
X. Section: Creation and regulations of the surplus funds (§ 76-83)
XI. Section: Conciliation of disputes between the society and its members (§ 84-90)
XII. Section: About leaving the society (§ 91-99)
XIII. Section: Administration of the society (§ 100-118)
XIV. Section: The privileges of society granted by the sovereign (§ 119-123)

The number of sections shows that a lawyer, accomplished in contract law, handled the revision of the bylaws. All sections were revised and supplemented, but without changing the man principles.

According to the bylaws of 1824, the society was created by the owners of the buildings, who mutually compensate each other's fire damage on buildings. The necessary funds come from the members (§ 1). The society is based on voluntary membership (§ 2) and easily combustible buildings e.g. powder mills or smelting works, are excluded from insurance (§ 8). The to-be insured buildings had to be registered with their insurance value at the society (§ 20) and constructional changes as well as their value increase had to be reported (§ 28). Fire damage which was caused by careless behaviour was excluded from compensation (§ 35). The payment of the compensation was due four weeks after the damage evaluation (§ 58).

According to the nature of mutuality, the funds for compensation and administrative costs are raised by the members' contribution. However, the expenditure varies from year to year, therefore, the contributions had to be re-determined each year. In the following year, the expenditure is allocated to all members (§ 62). The society wanted to help fast and efficiently, but the total amount of damage could only be allocated to the members in the next year. Therefore, the creation of a surplus fund was necessary (§ 79). The fund was created by the deposits and subsidy of the members (§ 80) and the surplus funds replaced the reserve fund.

Article § 82 is in particular interesting, because it states that the fund can only be at most one percent of the value of the insured objects. All surpluses above this sum had to be given to the parishes in form

of interest-free loans for buying fire extinguishing equipment, as facilities for members when paying their contributions and for a fast compensation of fire damage.

The collection of the contribution was done in form of an administrative execution, a privilege which regional insurance societies and privileged mutual societies could claim.[47] In § 72 of the bylaws, it is stated that members who did not pay their contributions, were treated in the same way as in the case of land contribution's arrears. This means a warning and later the execution without court order. After three years of non-payment the member will lose the society's membership.

Another new regulation concerned the conciliation of disputes. To avoid legal problems, arbiters should settle the claims of members, but also conciliate between directors and their co-workers (§ 84). Articles 87 and 88 had their own conciliation proceedings.

The approval of the Emperor was officially proclaimed on August 24, 1824. It stated: "Se. k. k. Majestät haben soeben mit landesväterlicher Huld die von allen Einsichtsvollen und Wohlgesinnten sehnlichst gewünschte wechselseitige Brandschaden-Versicherungs-Anstalt allergnädigst zu bestätigen, und dieselbe nicht nur mit ausgezeichneter Begünstigung auszustatten, sondern noch insbesondere die Nied. Oesterr. Landesregierung zu ermächtigen geruht, eine dem Gegenstande entsprechende Aufforderung zur kräftigen Beförderung an die Ortsobrigkeiten zu erlassen."[48] Due to the approval the society became effective on January 1, 1825.[49] 364 prominent people participated in the society's foundation including princes, counts, barons, and industrialists as well as churchly institutions like monasteries and convents.

The early insurance business was patriarchal. It gave the insurer a caring authority. The regulations of the contract were considered by the policyholders similar to governmental regulations and the insurance claim as beneficiation.[50] This is evident in the granted privileges of the draft and bylaws. § 119 states that the society is under the protection of the Emperor and § 121 emphasises the procedure, mentioned in § 72, which excludes a judge in case of an execution.

Soon the society had 31,841 members with 57,956 insured buildings.[51] These numbers show that the urban real estate owners were interested in insurances to the same extent as landlords were.

---

47 Cf. Ibid. (89).

48 Cf. Wiener Zeitung (24. December 1824) 1259: Wien.

49 Cf. *Fischer Carl*, Festschrift op.cit. 11 et seq.

50 Cf. *Ogris Werner*, Zur Entwicklung des Versicherungsrechts und des Versicherungsvertragsrechts in Österreich von der Mitte des 19. Jahrhunderts bis zum Ende der Monarchie, in: Versicherungsgeschichte Österreichs, Band 2, Die Ära des klassischen Versicherungswesens (Wien 1988) 89.

51 Cf. *Buchinger Josef*, Bauer op.cit. 242.

After four years an improved version of the bylaws was published.[52] The changes included putting the term "mutual" into the title and several amendments. Section III got two new articles which concerned members. The new § 15 enabled the admission of people who were not members but beneficiaries and at the same time sustainers of the buildings. The new § 25 clarifies the position of the owner when stating the value of the damage. With these amendments the number of Articles increased from 123 to 125.

This mutual society was the first private insurance company of Austria. It served as model for the Grazer mutual insurance society and for the Brno institution.[53] *Kudler's* contract with the associated companies was not renewed after six years. The Viennese society comprised even before it became effective 30.000 insured people.[54] Today the Viennese society is the "Wiener Städtische Wechselseitige Versicherungsverein",[55] a company and major shareholder of the Vienna Insurance Group.[56]

1.1.3 k.k. priv. innerösterreichische wechselseitige Brandschaden-Versicherungs-Anstalt

The Viennese society became the role model for the 1828 finally established "k.k. priv. innerösterreichische wechselseitige Brandschaden-Versicherungs-Anstalt"[57], today's GRAWE.[58]

The initiator of the insurance was in particular Archduke *Johann of Austria*[59], who, as the founder of the agricultural society, had already

---

[52] Cf. Stiftsarchiv Klosterneuburg, K 793 Nr. 1, Verbesserte Statuten der k. k. priv. wechselseitige Brandschaden-Versicherungs-Anstalt in Wien (Wien 1828).

[53] Cf. 100 Jahre Wechselseitige Brandschaden-Versicherungs-Anstalt (Wien 1924) 7.

[54] Cf. *Eigner Peter / Helige Andrea* (ed.), Österreichische op.cit. 41.

[55] Eine relativ leicht zugängliche Geschichte der Wiener Städtischen bis 1988 enthält: *Lehner Ulrich*, Der Konzern der Wiener Städtischen – Ein Wegbereiter des österreichischen Versicherungswesens, in: Versicherungsgeschichte Österreichs, Band 3, Das Zeitalter des modernen Versicherungswesens (Wien 1988) 1007 et seq.

[56] Cf. Die Entwicklung in Schlagworten im Internetportal Wiener Städtische – Geschichte.

[57] Cf. *Baumgartner Isabella*, 175 Jahre Grazer op.cit. 31.

[58] The historical development of the GRAWE until 2003, in form of a table, can be found in: *Baumgartner Isabella*, 175 Jahre Grazer op.cit. 151 et seq.

[59] *Archduke Johann of Austria*, * 20. January 1782 in Florence, + 10. May 1859 in Graz was a member of the House Habsburg, Austrian field marshal and German realm administrator. In the Dukedom Styria, he was for more than half a century patron and moderniser of industry, agriculture, and railroads as well as culture and education. All his initiatives and measures in Styria were made as a private person and not in his capacity as Archduke. Due to his numerous connections and his power of persuasion and discussion, he was able to implement his innovative ideas. For example, in 1811 he used them for the Joanneum in Graz, the forerunner of the Technical University, the Styrian regional library, 1817 for the Styrian regional archive, and in 1819 for the Styrian agricultural society. In 1822, his uncle Albert of Sachsen-

discussed the idea of fire insurances.[60] The society was also the kick off for insurance foundations. The insurance is based on the mutuality principle, which means that the total amount of money which members have to pay later is determined for a certain period of time.[61] The bylaws[62] differ in various points from the Viennese bylaws, while the outline remained the same. The main concerns were focused on more detailed regulations.

Major changes concerned the following Articles: § 3 defines the geographical area of the Grazer insurance society, § 5 is new and determines when the society comes into effect after the announcement, and § 8 describes § 7 of the Viennese bylaws regarding the parts of buildings. § 12 is new and states that the society has to create membership lists. § 19 is also new and concerns the insurance of public buildings. The Articles § 22 and 23 determine methods of payment upon admission in a more detailed way than § 17 of the Viennese bylaws.

Sections IV (determination of the value of the insured buildings) and V (the obligations of the society to pay members compensation) are more detailed. § 66 is new and determines the execution during the time of compensation payment and damage repair.

Due to the more detailed version of the bylaws the number of Articles increased from 125 to 131. Additionally, the contract between the Viennese and Grazer society can be found in the appendix of the bylaws. The court chancellery approved the contract with a resolution from November 20, 1828. The contract was limited to six years and its most important regulation was the following:

a) Both societies are joined for common compensation of all concerning fire damage and for mutual support via their surplus funds and credit.[63]

This was exactly the point which eliminated a possible renewal of the contract. The reasons were several major fires in Lower Austria, Moravia, and Silesia.[64] The driving force behind this refusal was Archduke

---

Teschen passed away and he inherited 200,000 Gulden. Now he was able to extend his agricultural model property Brandhof near Mariazell and bought in Vordernberg a facility for metallurgy. He was impressed of steam-engines, which he became acquainted with during his visit in England in 1815, and supported vehemently the building of railroads. – Curriculum vitae: *Hamann Brigitte*, Die Habsburger. Ein biographisches Lexikon ([2]Wien 1988) 175 et seq.

[60] Cf. Das Jubelfest der wechselseitigen Brandschaden-Versicherungs-Anstalt in Graz am 4. Juni 1879 (Graz 1879)16

[61] Cf. *Baumgartner Isabella*, 175 Jahre Grazer op.cit. 32.

[62] Cf. Landesarchiv Steiermark, K. 31, Nr. 3122: Statuten der k. k. privilegierten inneröster-reichischen wechselseitigen Brandschaden-Versicherungs-Anstalt (Grätz 1829).

[63] Ibid. (48 f).

[64] Cf. *Fischer Carl*, Festschrift op.cit. 16.

Johann of Austria.[65] Already at the end of May 1826 buildings with a value of 6.046,525 fl. were registered in these three countries.[66] The Grazer society had thirty years after their foundation 69,983 members and 150,414 insured buildings.[67]

Until 1872, the business of the society was based on rate assessment[68], but the bylaws of 1879 introduced the premium system.[69] In 1991, the legal basis changed[70] and the society became a holding company.[71]

1.1.4 Erste österreichische Brandversicherungs-Gesellschaft in Wien

On March 9, 1824 the Viennese joint stock company "Erste österreichische Brandversicherungs-Gesellschaft in Wien" came into effect. The foundation was initiated by a group of wealthy aristocrats and bankers.[72] This company needs to be mentioned, because it competed with mutual insurance societies for a time.

According to the bylaws[73], a fund of two Million Gulden (Convention-coins) was established in form of shares, in which one share had a nominal value of 1000 Gulden (Convention-coins) (1st section § 1). Additionally, a reserve fund for emergency was established by using a part of the dividend of the first five years (1st section § 12). The insurance premium depended on the value of buildings (3rd section § 6).

1.1.5 Mutual insurance society vs. joint stock company

Soon after mutual insurance societies were established fierce competition developed between mutual societies and joint stock companies. The latter accused the societies to lure customers by using low commissions and to demand high additional payments at the end of the year. Thus the members would only recognise afterwards the actual

65 Cf. *Baumgartner Isabella*, 175 Jahre Grazer op.cit. 31.

66 Cf. Ibid. (31).

67 Cf. *Hlubek F(ranz) X(aver)*, Ein treues Bild des Herzogthumes Steiermark als Denkmal dankbarer Erinnerung an Weiland Se. Kaiserlichen Hoheit den durchlauchtigsten Erzherzog Johann (Gratz 1860) 406.

68 Cf. *Baumgartner Isabella*, 175 Jahre Grazer op.cit. 33.

69 Cf. Ibid. (40).

70 Cf. *Zedtwitz Clemens von*, Die rechtsgeschichtliche Entwicklung der Versicherung. Diss. Univ. St. Gallen (Zürich 2000) 172.

71 Cf. *Baumgartner Isabella*, 175 Jahre Grazer op.cit. 106 et seq.

72 Cf. *Rohrbach Wolfgang*, Von den Anfängen op.cit. 225 et seq.

73 Cf. Stiftsarchiv Klosterneuburg, K 793 Nr. 1, Statuten der ersten österreichischen Brandversicherungs-Gesellschaft in Wien vom 18. Oktober 1824, mit Zusätzen vom 1. August 1826.

amount of the premium. On the other hand, mutual societies insinuated that joint stock companies are only interested in shareholders' profits and skimped on compensation.[74] On the occasion of extending the business of the Viennese joint stock company to Hungary in 1829, a press campaign concerning this topic was initiated. In the attachment "Aehrenlese" of the "Pressburger Zeitung" a three-part instalment was published, which emphasised the advantages of mutual insurance societies. These articles were published as an offprint.[75]

The first instalment presented the importance of fire insurances and the advantages of mutuality. It states that sufficient money is always available to cover the insurer's compensation. Although it is possible that in some years the payments are higher compared to the long-term average but in the end they are counterbalanced. Examples from Austria and foreign countries show the advantages of mutual insurances. According to the article, it is a patriotic duty to have such kind of insurance.[76] The second instalment investigated payments and stated that it is wrongfully argued that insured have to wait for 13 to 14 months before receiving payments. This is prevented by the surplus fund. The adversaries of mutual insurances also state that the indecisiveness of the yearly payments lead to uncertainty, which is unfounded. In contrast, insurances based on the premium system have to adapt the premiums to the claims experience, and in general they are more expensive.[77] The third instalment sumed up the advantages once again. How efficient the Viennese mutual insurance society works, is shown that no trials were necessary since it was founded five years ago. And even the country sovereign has insured his lands in Lower Austria.[78]

The problematic relationship between these two legal forms is presented by various advertisements. For example, mutual societies argued that they neither have to pay interests for a large foundation capital nor dividends to shareholders. Every three years a balance will be made and the profits among the members are distributed, according to the bylaws[79], among the members, which decrease their original payments. A joint stock company announced in an advertisement that the company is liable with its own capital and does not demand, in contrast to mutual societies, additional payments.[80]

---

[74] Cf. *Schreiber Gerhard*, Die Interunfall Versicherung und die Riunione Adriatica di Sicurtà in Wien, 1890-2004 (Diss. Univ. Wien 2007) 41.

[75] Cf. Stiftsarchiv Klosterneuburg, K 793 Nr. 1, Drey Briefe eines Ungarn an seinen Freund über die gegenseitige Versicherung gegen Brandschaden.

[76] Cf. Ibid. (3 f).

[77] Cf. Ibid. (5 et seq.).

[78] Cf. Ibid. (10 et seq.).

[79] Cf. § 85 der Statuten op.cit.

[80] Cf. *Graf Baldur*, Werbung damals – Assekuranz-Reklame in Österreich-Ungarn von 1825 bis 1918, in: Versicherungsgeschichte Österreichs, Band 2, (Wien 1988) 209.

Mutual societies had the reputation to offer generous compensations.[81] This was connected with the absence of the necessity to generate a good dividend which is characteristic for joint stock companies.

German experts analysed life insurances and asserted, however, that no essential differences between these two legal forms exist. Additional payments were rather infrequent in mutual societies and the dividends of joint stock companies were around three to four percent.[82]

The principle of mutuality was also established in different industry branches, e.g. the sugar industry, of the Austro-Hungarian Monarchy. In literature, it was argued that mutual associations offered a favourable price, because they only charged the net premiums and a minimal performance surcharge and also offered additionally the possibility of a dividend. On the other hand, joint stock companies work to gain profit.[83]

1.2 Life insurance

On May 27, 1760, the "Witwen- und Waisen-Pensions-Gesellschaft" was established by the PhD collegium of the law faculty. It was not a life insurance company, but a benefit society with the goal to improve the salary of widows of faculty members. Its forerunner was the so-called "Witibkassa", founded by the medical faculty in 1758.[84]

At the beginning of 1821, several experts, under the leadership of Joseph Count of Dietrichstein, submitted the proposal of a general pension fund institution for Austrian subjects to the Emperor. The idea was that the payer of 200 fl. C.M should receive a lifelong pension. The increase of capital should be generated by interests and by the capital of early deceased insured. However, the plan failed, because the Lower Austria's court of appeal decided that it was not able to realise.[85]

On May 21, 1839 the first life insurance company of Austria the "Allgemeine wechselseitige Kapitalien- und Renten-Versicherungs-Anstalt" was established due to the instigation of *Josef Salomon*[86],

81 Cf. *Ogris Werner*, Zur Entwicklung op.cit. 95.

82 Cf. Oesterreichische Revue, Organ für Assecuranz und Volkswirthschaft (17. Mai 1880) 77: Actie oder Gegenseitigkeit.

83 Cf. Österreichische Bürgerkunde. Handbuch der Staats- und Rechtskunde in ihren Beziehungen zum öffentlichen Leben. Zweiter Band (Wien o. J.) 611 et seq.

84 Cf. Die Witwen- und Waisen-Pensions-Gesellschaft des Juridischen Doctoren-Collegiums in Wien. Denkschrift anlässlich ihres hundertfünfzigjährigen Bestandes. 1760-1910 (Wien 1910) 5.

85 Cf. *Thausing Friedrich*, 100 Jahre Sparkassen. Anlässlich des 100jährigen Bestandes der Ersten Österreichischen Sparkasse 1819-1919 (Wien 1919) 59 et seq.

86 *Salomon Johann Michael Joseph*, * 22nd February 1793 in Oberdürrbach/Würzburg, + 2nd July 1856 in Vienna, studied mathematics at the University of Würzburg and worked at the

professor of mathematics, and with the support of the Emperor.[87] The society was a public company, based on mutuality, and open for people of all different social ranks, religions, and nationalities. The provisions could be made for the policyholder as well as for family members etc.[88] The society had six sections:[89]

1. Capital insurance association:

   This section insured capital between 10fl. to 20,000fl and was paid out to a specific person after a particular time-span, when this person was still alive. The amount of the original payment depended on the to-be insured capital, the age of the insured person, and the time-span.

2. Capital insurance association: in the event of death (life insurance society):

   In this section a certain amount of money, based on the earlier paid premium, was paid out in the event of death.

3. Tontine:

   This section obligated itself to pay out an annual pension from a certain point of time onwards. The amount of the deposit depended on age, time of out-payment and the amount of the pension.

4. General retirement pension insurance:

   This section insured pensions for a certain amount of years or lifelong in return of payment.

5. Pension fund institute:

   Out-payment of a pension in return for a one-time payment.

6. Pension fund institute with increasing pensions:

Academic high school in Vienna from 1816 onwards. From 1816 to 1817, he attended the lectures of higher mathematics and physics at the polytechnic institute. In 1821, after teaching at this institute, he was appointed Professor for elementary mathematics and 1838 Professor for higher mathematics at the polytechnic institute. Moreover, he was acclaimed author and teacher. With regard to English and German models, he became interested in life insurances from 1830 onwards and he instigated the foundation of the "Allgemeinen wechselseitige Kapitalien- und Renten-Versicherungs-Anstalt" in Vienna (1839). He was supported by the banks of Rothschild, Sina, Arnstein-Eskeles, Geymüller, and Stametz. In 1848, he became member of the PhD collegium at the University of Vienna and corresponding member of the Academy of Sciences in Vienna. – Curriuculm vitae: Wurzbach Constant von, Biographisches Lexikon des Kaiserthums Oesterreich. Achtundzwanzigster Theil (Wien 1874) 151 et seq.

87 Cf. *Rohrbach Wolfgang*, Versicherungsgeschichte op.cit. 395.

88 Cf. Die allgemeine wechselseitige Capitalien- und Renten-Versicherungsanstalt in Wien (Wien 1857) 3.

89 Cf. Ibid. (3 et seq.).

Bonds can be bought in form of numerous deposits. The amount of the pension depended on the age at entry.
After 1859 the sections were renamed to the following:[90]

I. Insurance for life (endowment insurance or children provision through a certain amount of capital)
II. Insurance in the event of death
III. Life annuity insurance (old age pension)
IV. Insurance of pensions, viability-pension or widow's pension
V. Insurance of educational grant for children
VI. Provision through increasing pensions

The society was regarded as a blessing for the common good, because it insured family members against the unexpected event of death.[91] Life insurance was in particular important for dangerous professions, e.g. miners.[92]

This insurance society was not a company of speculators, but a mutual society[93] based on European models. According to a report, it was one of the best organised institutes of its kind.[94] However, major damage was caused by mismanagement in the administrative sector, which led to supervision by a revision committee[95] and to proposals of revising the bylaws.[96]

In 1866, the society changed its name to "Janus wechselseitige Lebensversicherung-Anstalt"[97], which merged 1923 with "Gemeinde Wien-Städtische Versicherungsanstalt", the formerly "Wechselseitige k.u.k. priv. Brandschadenversicherungsanstalt" (till 1919).[98] From 1924 onwards, the company was called "Wechselseitige Brandschaden und Janus allgemeine Versicherungsanstalt auf Gegenseitigkeit".[99]

90 Cf. Die allgemeine wechselseitige Capitalien op.cit. 4.
91 Cf. *Ebersberg J. S.* (ed.) Der Österreichische Zuschauer. Zeitschrift für Kunst, Wissenschaft und geistiges Leben. Dritter Band (Wien 1840) 1134: Die wechselseitige Capitalien- und Renten-Versicherungsanstalt.
92 Cf. *Urbanski Hans*, 150 Jahre Generali, 100 Jahre Erste Allgemeine (Wien, München, Zürich, New York 1982) 51.
93 Cf. *Springer Johann*, Statistik des österreichischen Kaiserstaates, Band 2 (Wien 1840) 83
94 Cf. *Werdmüller Otto v. Elgg*, Die allgemeine wechselseitige Capitalien- und Renten-Versicherungs-Anstalt. Mängel und Anträge zur beabsichtigten Statutenrevision (Wien 1861) 1.
95 Cf. Ibid. (6 et seq.).
96 Cf. Ibid. (29 et seq.).
97 Cf. *Graf Baldur*, Werbung op.cit. 208.
98 Cf. *Lehner Ulrich Peter*, Konzern op.cit. 1051.
99 Cf. 100 Jahre Wechselseitige Brandschaden-Versicherungs-Anstalt 1824-1924 (Wien 1924) 5.

1.3 Livestock insurance

Livestock insurance was discussed in the German countries since the middle of the 18th century.[100] In 1765, Frederic II of Prussia introduced in the newly-won province Silesia the mandatory mutual livestock insurance. The society was governed by the state and necessary due to instances of occurring cattle-plague, introduced by cattle imports from Austria-Hungary and Russia. In 1842, the insurance was extended so that damage could also be claimed beyond the quarantine period.[101] The insurance was based on mutuality, which means the insured person was also insurer and participated in profit and loss, e.g. like in the 1833 established "Leipziger Verein".[102]

In the Austrian Empire, livestock insurance was introduced in 1845 by two joint stock companies, the "Riunione" and the "Generali".[103]

In the Austrian-Hungarian Monarchy, the interest regarding mutual livestock insurances came from the agricultural district association Weitra and hence from the imperial and royal agricultural association in Vienna.[104] The first foundation was the association Tetschen/Bohemia in 1864.[105] The association "Taurus" was the first mutual livestock society officially registered in Vienna in 1864[106], but was regarded very critically by the imperial and royal agricultural association in Vienna.[107]

According to § 1 of the bylaws, the society is based on limited mutual members' liability (§ 9 conditions of insurance), and has the purpose to compensate the loss of livestock caused by animal disease and other illnesses. The society had the name "Erster allgemeiner wechselseitiger Viehversicherungs-Verein Taurus".[108]

The conditions of insurance state that the insurance premium is changeable due to the principle of mutuality and can be increased or decreased according to the amount of losses. The increase cannot be

100 Cf. *Hülsemann Hermann*, Ueber Vieh-Versicherung (Berlin 1899) 9.

101 Cf. *Brämer Hermann / Brämer Karl*, Das Versicherungswesen (Leipzig 1894) 336.

102 Cf. *Freyenmuth, Johann Conrad, Pöhlmann Robert von*, Statuten der in Leipzig errichteten Viehversicherungs-Anstalt für Deutschland begründet auf Gegenseitigkeit und Oeffentlichkeit (Leipzig 1833) § 1.

103 Cf. *Mayer Gabriele,* Die Einführung der Viehversicherung in Österreich, in: Versicherungsgeschichte Österreichs, Band 2 (Wien 1988) 842 et seq.

104 Cf. Allgemeine Land- und Forstwirthschaftliche Zeitung, XIV. Jahrgang (1864) 259: Programms-Entwurf für die Errichtung einer Viehversicherungs-Anstalt im Bezirke Weitra – available from the Austrian national Library via ANNO (online newspapers).

105 Ibid. (342): Der Viehversicherungs-Verein in Tetschen.

106 Cf. Statuten des Ersten allgemeinen wechselseitigen Viehversicherungs-Vereines „Taurus" (Wien 1864) 16.

107 Cf. Allgemeine op.cit. 1124: Vieh-Versicherungsverein "Taurus".

108 Cf. Statuten op.cit. § 1.

more than four times of the yearly insurance premium as stated in the insurance contract.[109] Insured could be farm animals, e.g. horses, pigs, geese, donkeys, sheep, and cattle, but only within certain age limits.[110]

The society "Taurus" did not exist for long, because the shortage of veterinary surgeons and suitable people restrained the business.[111] Already after a short time, the society had to be liquidated due to lack of capital and misjudgement.[112]

The livestock insurance bank "Apis" was founded in 1865 in Vienna, and several other companies followed in the crown countries.[113] The bank insured livestock at insurer's option against diseases, non-contagious illnesses, or accidents. The premiums for horses ranged between 0.5 and 9 percent of the value insured, depending on keeping and feeding, and for cattle between 0.5 and 5.5 percent.[114] However, "Apis" was also liquidated soon due to the same reasons as Taurus, i.e. lack of capital and misjudgements.[115]

Nevertheless, the livestock insurance was in general a good idea, but, according to experts, did not function properly, because they were carried by agricultural associations.[116]

2. Mutuality and cooperatives

A mutual insurance society is similar to a cooperative regarding its structure, because, according to the mutuality principle, in both institutions members are also policyholders. As members of the society they carry the economic risk, receive a share of the profit, but also have to carry the losses.[117] Both members of a cooperative and a mutual insurance society are fully entitled and receive insurance at net cost price. Moreover, profits are used on behalf of the entire community.[118]

[109] Ibid. (11): Versicherungs-Bedingungen § 9.

[110] Ibid. § 1.

[111] Cf. *Kallbrunner Hermann*, Der Väter Saat. Die österreichische Landwirtschafts-Gesellschaft von 1807 bis 1938 (Wien o. J.) 59.

[112] Cf. Revue op.cit. 25. December 1876 (42): Die Viehversicherung in Oesterreich I.

[113] Cf. *Mayer Gabriele*, Einführung op.cit. 843.

[114] Cf. *Kallbrunner Hermann*, Väter op.cit. 59.

[115] Cf. Revue op.cit. 25. December 1876 (42): Die Viehversicherung in Oesterreich I.

[116] Cf. Ibid. (8. Jänner 1877) 6: Die Viehversicherung in Oesterreich III.

[117] Cf. *Pollak Robert*, Versicherungsaufsicht (Wien 1979) § 42 (33 f).

[118] Cf. *Schwarz Hermann*, 50 Jahre Städtische Versicherung, 1898-1948 (Wien 1948) 69.

Modern cooperatives are a part of today's civil society, i.e. in particular in the German-speaking part are industrial and provident societies according to *Hermann Schulze-Delitzsch*[119] and *Friedrich Wilhelm Raiffeisen.*[120] They developed due to insufficient social circumstances in the middle of the 19th century.[121] They are characterised by the principles of self-help, self-responsibility, and self-administration.[122] In the original form, the cooperative members had a joint guarantee, i.e. the well of one means the well of all and the damage of one is the damage of all.[123] Therefore, the cooperatives are based on the mutuality principle.

Schulze-Delitzsch took the view that associations, this is the name for cooperatives in the middle of the 19th century, are the concerns of the participating people, while governmental help was excluded.[124] The main principle to improve the social circumstances was solidarity "one for all".[125] However, *Schulze-Delitzsch* did not think of insurances, but established the health and funeral expenses fund of Delitzsch (1849).[126] This was the first step towards insurance, because a funeral expenses fund is a special case of life insurance.

Friedrich Wilhelm Raiffeisen also regarded his loan association, which was founded in 1862 in Anhausen,[127] as starting point for future

---

[119] *Schulze-Delitzsch Hermann*, *29. 8. 1808 in Delitzsch, + 29. 4. 1883 in Potsdam, lawyer, judge, and politician. He started his cooperative work by founding a health and funeral expenses fund in Delitzsch in 1849, founded 1850 the first corporative credit associations, 1862 the advocacy of the German industrial and provident societies, and worked full-time for the cooperative system since 1871. He established in 1866 the Prussian cooperative law, which was adopted by the North German Confederation and later from the German Empire. He argued with Raiffeisen regarding different cooperative systems between 1866 and 1879. — Curriculum vitae: www.deutsche-biographie.de.

[120] *Raiffeisen Friedrich Wilhelm*, cooperative founder, and social reformer, * 30. 3. 1818 in Hamm/Sieg, + 11. 3. 1888 in Heddesdorf. At the age of 17, he joined the 7th Prussian artillery brigade. He had to quit the army due to eye problems and worked then in administrative service. In 1845, he became the mayor of the 22 joined parishes of Weyerbusch, 1848 mayor of Flammersfeld, and from 1852 to 1865 mayor of Heddesdorf. After the foundation of several friendly societies, he started to establish his loan societies in Anhausen in 1862. In those societies the principal of charity was replaced with self-help. After he retired in 1865, he became devoted to extend his organisation, to the formation of province associations, to an advocacy, and a central bank. — Curriculum vitae: www.deutsche-biographie.de

[121] Cf. *Faust Helmut*, Geschichte der Genossenschaftsbewegung (3Frankfurt/Main 1977) 33 et seq.

[122] Cf. Ibid. (58 et seq.).

[123] Cf. *Mändle Eduard / Swoboda Walter* (ed.), Genossenschaftslexikon (Wiesbaden 1992) 585.

[124] Cf. *Schulze H(ermann)*, Mittheilungen über gewerbliche- und Arbeiter-Associationen (Leipzig 1850) 3.

[125] Cf. Ibid. (6).

[126] Cf. Ibid. (11 et seq.).

[127] Cf. *Richter Heinrich*, Friedrich Wilhelm Raiffeisen und die Entwicklung seiner Genossenschaftsidee (München 1966) 25.

cooperative foundations.[128] For Raiffeisen the most important duty of a member was joint guarantee.[129] Governmental help was not only possible but even favoured.[130] The goal of loan associations was to improve the moral and financial position of the members,[131] but *Raiffeisen's* wish was to establish a pension and old age insurance.[132] The existing insurances were, according to him, not sufficient for the poor population, which also had hardly knowledge about the effects of such insurances.[133] He recommended his associations to use the 1876 founded "Lebensversicherung- und Ersparnisbank zu Stuttgart". The bank was a mutual society and, therefore, based on the same principles like loan associations.[134] However, he was not able to realise these plans as well as to establish insurance business with the help of provincial banks and the advocacy.[135]

Besides from life insurances, livestock insurances were necessary, because cattle farming was the most important agricultural branch. Therefore, he published in the third edition of his book bylaws for livestock insurance societies.[136] As a result, loan associations and insurances developed as mutual aid organisations.[137]

However the danger was that: "If one piece of cattle falls, the tradesman and insurer comes willingly and offers a substitute. Countless

---

128 Cf. *Raiffeisen F(riedrich) W(ilhelm)*, Die Darlehenskassen-Vereine als Mittel zur Abhilfe der Noth der ländlichen Bevölkerung, sowie auch der städtischen Handwerker und Arbeiter (Neuwied 1866) 16.

129 Cf. Ibid. (23).

130 Cf. *Raiffeisen F(riedrich) W(ilhelm)*, Die Darlehenskassen-Vereine in Verbindung mit Consum-, Verkaufs-, Winzer-, Molkerei-, Viehversicherungs-Gant- ect. Genossenschaften, als Mittel der Abhilfe der Noth der ländlichen Bevölkerung. Praktisch Anleitung zur Gründung und Leitung solcher Genossenschaften. Dritte, vollständig umgearbeitet und bedeutend vermehrte Auflage (Heddesdorf-Neuwied 1881) IV.

131 Cf. *Raiffeisen F(riedrich) W(wilhelm)*, Die Darlehenskassen-Vereine op.cit. 16.

132 Cf. *Raiffeisen F(riedrich) W(wilhelm)*, Die Darlehenskassen-Vereine in Verbindung mit Consum-, Verkaufs-, Gant- etc. -Genossenschaften als Mittel zur Abhilfe der Noth der ländlichen Bevölkerung, sowie auch der städtischen Arbeiter. Zweite, vermehrte und verbesserte Auflage (Neuwied und Leipzig o. J.) 63.

133 Cf. *Raiffeisen F(riedrich) W(ilhelm)*, Denkschrift zur Begründung der Nothwendigkeit der "Deutschen landwirthschaftlichen Generalbank, ein getragene Genossenschaft" in Verbindung mit einem Lebens-, Pensions- und Rentenversicherungs-Institute, sowie zur Begründung der anliegenden Statuten (o. O., o. J.), Teilabdruck in: *Werner Wolfgang*, Raiffeisenbriefe erzählen Genossenschaftsgeschichte (Wien 1988) 132.

134 Cf. *Richter Heinrich*, Friedrich Wilhelm Raiffeisen op.cit. 121 et seq.

135 Cf. *Tomanek Peter*, Versicherung – die unbeachtete Dimension der Raiffeisenidee, in: Versicherungsgeschichte Österreichs, Band 9, Österreich über alles, wann es nur will (Wien 2008) 421.

136 Cf. *Raiffeisen F(riedrich) W(ilhelm)*, Die Darlehenskassen-Vereine op.cit. 291 et seq.

137 Cf. *Wuttig Martin*, Versicherungs- und Genossenschaftswesen als wechselseitige Hilfsorganisationen. Deutsche ländliche Genossenschaftsbücherei Band 5 (Berlin 1914).

examples show that their substitutions of this kind have cost farmers all their belongings".[138] The bylaws state that the people, who signed the contract, form a livestock society which compensates the losses of their livestock based on the mutuality principle. However, it was necessary that the damage was not caused by them.[139]

The connection between agricultural savings and loan associations was recommended by experts, because the maintenance of the working capital is secured by fire and livestock insurances.[140] This was also true for the connection between cooperative savings organisations and life insurances.[141]

3. The statutory framework

At the end of the 18th and during the 19th century, several variations of legal forms for insurance companies were established. Many of them were not able to provide sufficient security for their clients. The three most well-known and economic most important legal forms in the Austrian insurance business are joint stock companies, mutual insurance societies, and public corporations. The last two forms are based on the mutuality principle. The insurance joint stock company is a company with the purpose of selling insurances against premiums on a commercial basis. A peculiarity is, for example, that joint stock companies distribute parts of their profits among the insured of life insurances.[142]

In the 19th century, the Civil Code from 1811, in effect on January 1st, 1812,[143] was the basis for insurances due to the absence of insurance law. An insurance contract arises when someone takes over the damage of someone else (blameless) and promised to compensate the damage against a certain price. The insurer is liable for a coincidental damage and the insured for the promised price.[144]

[138] *Raiffeisen F(riedrich) W(ilhelm)*, Die Darlehenskassen-Vereine op.cit. 284.

[139] Cf. Ibid. (291): Statuten des Viehversicherungs-Vereins, § 1.

[140] Cf. Revue op.cit. 16. April 1877 (62): Das Versicherungswesen als Stütze der landwirthschaftlichen Spar- und Vorschusscassen.

[141] Cf. Ibid. (14. Jänner 1878) 5: Die Verbindung von Credit-Genossenschaften mit der Lebensversicherung.

[142] Cf. *Rohrbach Wolfgang*, Von den Anfängen op.cit. 158 et seq.

[143] Cf. Allgemeines bürgerliches Gesetzbuch für die gesamten Deutschen Erbländer der Oesterreichischen Monarchie, III Theile (Wien 1811).

[144] Gesetzbuch op.cit. Theil II (375) § 1288.

Before the creation of a specific insurance law in 1880, RGBl No. 110, "Regulation of the Home Office, ministry of justice, of trade, and finance" from August 18, 1880, which regulated the licence and the governmental supervision of insurance company, the Associations Act of 1852 was in effect. This law featured for the first time the mandatory permission for insurance companies.[145] The Association Act of 1862 excluded insurances and referred to special regulations.[146] However, a special regulation for insurances came into effect in 1880. The regulation referred to § 1 of the Associations Act's from 1852, RGBl No. 253, and the Commercial law of 1862, RGBl No. 1 ex 1863. The regulation stated that insurances needed governmental supervision and either the legal form of a joint stock company or of a mutual society (paragraph 2).

For mutual insurance societies the paragraphs 2 and 5 were in particular important. § 2 comprises the start of the business and the foundation fund, which is necessary for covering the losses of mutual societies, as well as the common liability of society members. § 4 defines the foundation fund, including the amount of capital.

§ 5 refers to the bylaws of mutual societies and defines the regulations of the bylaws. These have to be the following:

1. About the company and the place of business
2. About the appointment and composition of the management and the forms of legitimation of its members and other bodies of the company
3. About the voting right of members and the kind of its exercise
4. About the form of the mandatory announcement, including to state the names of the public papers in which it had to be published.
5. About the calling of the general meeting on demand of members.

Modernisation forced a new legal framework for insurances and cooperatives. Cooperatives based legally on the Association Act at first.[147] In 1866, *Schulze-Delitzsch* (cf. footnote 119) created the Prussian Cooperative law, which was adopted by the North German Confederation and in 1889[148] by the German Empire.[149]

[145] Cf. RGBl. Nr. 253/1852, Kaiserliches Patent vom 26. November 1852, wirksam für den ganzen Umfang des Reiches, mit Ausnahme der Militärgränze, wodurch neue gesetzliche Bestimmungen über Vereine (Vereinsgesetz) angeordnet werden. §. 2. h.

[146] Cf. RGBl. Nr. 134/1867, Gesetz vom 15. November 1867 über das Vereinsrecht. §. 2.

[147] Cf. *Werner Wolfgang*, Zur Vorgeschichte der österreichischen Raiffeisenbewegung. Forschungen zur Wirtschafts-, Finanz- und Sozialgeschichte, Band 2 (Frankfurt/Main 1993) 39.

[148] Cf. Deutsches Reichsgesetzblatt Band 1889, Nr. 11 (55 et seq.).

[149] Cf. *Honikel Franz*, Genossenschaftsrecht, deutsches, in: *Mädle Eduard* (ed.), Genossenschafts Lexikon (Wiesbaden 1992) 284.

The bylaws must include the regulation, according to § 3 lit 12 of the law, that all cooperatives are liable for obligations of the cooperative and with their entire assets (joint guarantee).[150]

In Austria, the Law about industrial and provident societies, a law which is modelled after the German law, from April 9, 1873 (RGBl No 70) was in effect.[151] The main difference is in § 2 about limited liability. The idea of solidarity can also be found in § 2.

4. Conclusion

The Austrian example shows that mutual insurances and cooperatives are examples of practical self-help, which serve the interests of members.[152] They are private companies and are based on the principles of self-responsibility and self-administration. They are well tested socio-economic support organisations, which were and still are essential for the development of modern economy.

[150] Cf. Bundesgesetzblatt des Norddeutschen Bundes Band 1868, Nr. 24 (415).

[151] Cf. 96 der Beilagen zu den stenographischen Protokollen des Abgeordnetenhauses, VII. Session (1023).

[152] Cf. *Wagner-Braun Margarete*, Das genossenschaftliche Bank- und Versicherungswesen im 19. und zu Beginn des 20. Jahrhunderts – das Beispiel des „Wirtschaftlichen Verbandes“, in: Historischer Verein bayerischer Genossenschaften e. V. München (ed.), Die Anfänge der modernen Genossenschaftsbewegung in Bayern, Österreich und Südtirol, Band 1 (München 1998) 114 et seq.

Bibliography

Archives

Generali Historisches Archiv, Hoegelmüller Georg von, Vorschlag zur Theilnahme an den in Oesterreich unter der Enns, in Oesterreich ob der Enns mit Salzburg, in Böhmen, in Mähren mit Schlesien, in Illyrien und in Steyermark zu errichtenden Brandschaden-Versicherungs-Privat-Anstalten (Wien 1822)

Landesarchiv Steiermark, K. 31, Nr. 3078, Statuten der k. k. priv. wechselseitige Brandschaden-Versicherungs-Anstalt in Wien (Wien 1824)

Landesarchiv Steiermark, K. 31, Nr. 3122: Statuten der k. k. privilegierten innerösterreichischen wechselseitigen Brandschaden-Versicherungs-Anstalt (Grätz 1829)

Stiftsarchiv Klosterneuburg, Codex provincialis oder Bedenck Buch der Löbl. Herren Ständen des Erzherzogthum Österreich unter der Enns: Erster Band. Anno 1723. Von Litt: A: bis K., Abbrändler

Stiftsarchiv Klosterneuburg, K 793 Nr. 1, Drey Briefe eines Ungarn an seinen Freund über die gegenseitige Versicherung gegen Brandschaden

Stiftsarchiv Klosterneuburg, K 793 Nr. 1, Statuten der ersten österreichischen Brandversicherungs-Gesellschaft in Wien vom 18. Oktober 1824, mit Zusätzen vom 1. August 1826

Stiftsarchiv Klosterneuburg, K 793 Nr. 1, Verbesserte Statuten der k. k. priv. wechselseitige Brandschaden-Versicherungs-Anstalt in Wien (Wien 1828)

Laws and supplements

RGBl. Nr. 134/1867, Gesetz vom 15. November 1867 über das Vereinsrecht. §. 2.

RGBl. Nr. 253/1852, Kaiserliches Patent vom 26. November 1852, wirksam für den ganzen Umfang des Reiches, mit Ausnahme der Militärgränze, wodurch neue gesetzliche Bestimmungen über Vereine (Vereinsgesetz) angeordnet werden (§. 2. h)

16396 der Beilagen zu den stenographischen Protokollen des Abgeordnetenhauses, VII. Session

Books and articles

100 Jahre Wechselseitige Brandschaden-Versicherungs-Anstalt 1824 – 1924 (Wien 1924)

Allgemeines bürgerliches Gesetzbuch für die gesamten Deutschen Erbländer der Oesterreichischen Monarchie, III Theile (Wien 1811)

Baumgartner Isabella, 175 Jahre Grazer Wechselseitige (Graz 2003)

Brämer Hermann / Brämer Karl, Das Versicherungswesen (Leipzig 1894)

Bruckmüller Ernst, Sozialgeschichte Österreichs (Wien, München 1985)

Buchinger Josef, Der Bauer in der Kultur- und Wirtschaftsgeschichte Österreichs (Wien 1952)

Chaloupek Günther et al., Die vorhandene Chance, in: Österreichische Industriegeschichte GmbH (Hg.), Österreichische Industriegeschichte 1700 bis 1848 (Wien 2003)

Das Jubelfest der Wechselseitigen Brandschaden-Versicherungs-Anstalt in Graz am 4. Juni 1879 (Graz 1879)

Die allgemeine wechselseitige Capitalien- und Renten-Versicherungsanstalt in Wien (Wien 1857)

Die Witwen- und Waisen-Pensions-Gesellschaft des Juridischen Doctoren-Collegiums in Wien. Denkschrift anlässlich ihres hundertfünfzigjährigen Bestandes. 1760 - 1910 (Wien 1910)

Dreher Meinrad, Die Versicherung als Rechtsprodukt (Tübingen 1991)

Ebersberg J. S. (Hg.) Der Österreichische Zuschauer. Zeitschrift für Kunst, Wissenschaft und geistiges Leben. Dritter Band (Wien 1840) 1134: Die wechselseitige Capitalien- und Renten-Versicherungsanstalt

Eigner Peter / Helige Barbara (Hg.), Österreichische Wirtschafts- und Sozialgeschichte im 19. und 20. Jahrhundert (Wien 1999)

F(riedrich) W(ilhelm), Denkschrift zur Begründung der Nothwendigkeit der „Deutschen landwirthschaftlichen Generalbank, ein getragene Genossenschaft“ in Verbindung mit einem Lebens-, Pensions- und Rentenversicherungs-Institute, sowie zur Begründung der anliegenden Statuten (o. O., o. J.)

Fachini E(rnst), Entstehung, Grundsätze und Entwicklung des Versicherungswesens in Oesterreich-Ungarn (Wien 1888)

Faust Helmut, Geschichte der Genossenschaftsbewegung (^{3}Frankfurt/ Main 1977)

Feigl Helmut, Landwirtschaft und Grundherrschaft. Ihre Entwicklung unter Joseph II., in: Österreichs zur Zeit Kaiser Joseph II., Katalog der niederösterreichischen Landesaustellung 1980 (Wien 1980)

Feigl Helmuth, Die niederösterreichische Grundherrschaft, Forschungen zur Landeskunde von Niederösterreich, XVI. Band (^{2}St. Pölten 1998)

Fischer Carl, Festschrift aus Anlass des Fünfzigjährigen Jubiläums der k. k. priv. wechselseitigen Brandschaden-Versicherungs-Anstalt in Wien (Wien 1875)

Freyenmuth, Johann Conrad, Pöhlmann Robert von, Statuten der in Leipzig errichteten Viehversicherungs-Anstalt für Deutschland begründet auf Gegenseitigkeit und Oeffentlichkeit (Leipzig 1833)

Geyer Günter / Backovsky Bernhard, Ringturmausstellung 2014: 190 Jahre Wiener Städtische Versicherungsverein - 900 Jahre Stift Klosterneuburg, in: Wiener Städtische Wechselseitiger Versicherungsverein (Hg.), Arnulf Rainer - Schleier der Agnes (Wien 2014)

Gluth (Oskar), Feuerpolizei, in: *Mischler Ernst / Ulbrich Josef (Hg.)*, Oesterreichisches Staatswörterbuch, Erster Band (Wien 1895)

Göttlicher Erich, Staat und Versicherungswesen in Österreich, in: *Henn Rudolf / Schwebler Robert (Hg.)*, Staat, Wirtschaft, Assekuranz und Wissenschaft, Festschrift für Robert Schwebler (Karlsruhe 1986)

Graf Baldur, Werbung damals - Assekuranz-Reklame in Österreich-Ungarn von 1825 bis 1918, in: Versicherungsgeschichte Österreichs, Band 2, (Wien 1988)

Hamann Brigitte, Die Habsburger. Ein biographisches Lexikon ([2]Wien 1988)

Henning Friedrich-Wilhelm, Landwirtschaft und ländliche Gesellschaft in Deutschland, Band 1, 800 bis 1750 (Paderborn 1979)

Hlubek F(ranz) X(aver), Ein treues Bild des Herzogthumes Steiermark als Denkmal dankbarer Erinnerung an Weiland Se. Kaiserlichen Hoheit den durchlauchtigsten Erzherzog Johann (Gratz 1860)

Hoke Rudolf, Österreichische und deutsche Rechtsgeschichte (Wien, Köln, Weimar 1992)

Holubar Karl (Hg.), Das Augustiner-Chorherrenstift Klosterneuburg, geschichtliche und statistische Daten ([3]Klosterneuburg 2014)

Honikel Franz, Genossenschaftsrecht, deutsches, in: Mädle Eduard (Hg.), Genossenschafts Lexikon (Wiesbaden 1992)

Hülsemann Hermann, Ueber Vieh-Versicherung (Berlin 1899)

Kallbrunner Hermann, Der Väter Saat. Die österreichische Landwirtschafts-Gesellschaft von 1807 bis 1938 (Wien o. J.)

Lehner Ulrich, Der Konzern der Wiener Städtischen - Ein Wegbereiter des österreichischen Versicherungswesens, in: Versicherungsgeschichte Österreichs, Band 3, Das Zeitalter des modernen Versicherungswesens (Wien 1988)

Lehner Ulrich Peter, Kirche und Versicherung. Zur Geschichte einer fast vergessenen Beziehung, in: An der Schwelle zum 3. Jahrtausend - Retrospektiven und Perspektiven. Versicherungsgeschichte Österreichs, Band VI (Wien 2000)

Leimdörfer Max, Entwicklung und Organisation der Brandschadenversicherung in Österreich 1700 - 1848 (Wien 1905)

Ludwig Vinzenz Oskar, Propst Georg II. Hausmanstetter. Beiträge zur Kultur- und politischen Geschichte Niederösterreichs im 16. Jahrhundert, in: Jahrbuch des Stiftes Klosterneuburg, Band IV. (Wien 1912)

Mändle Eduard / Swoboda Walter (Hg.), Genossenschaftslexikon (Wiesbaden 1992)

Mayer Gabriele, Die Einführung der Viehversicherung in Österreich, in: Versicherungsgeschichte Österreichs, Band 2 (Wien 1988)

Niederstätter Alois, Das Jahrhundert der Mitte, Österreichische Geschichte 1400 - 1522 (Wien 1996)

Ogris Werner, Staats- und Rechtsformen, in: Koschatzky Walter, Maria Theresia und ihre Zeit ([2]Salzburg, Wien 1980)

Ogris Werner, Zur Entwicklung des Versicherungsrechts und des Versicherungsvertragsrechts in Österreich von der Mitte des 19. Jahrhunderts bis zum Ende der Monarchie, in: Versicherungsgeschichte Österreichs, Band 2, Die Ära des klassischen Versicherungswesens (Wien 1988)

Österreichische Bürgerkunde. Handbuch der Staats- und Rechtskunde in ihren Beziehungen zum öffentlichen Leben. Zweiter Band (Wien o. J.)

Pollak Robert, Versicherungsaufsicht (Wien 1979)

Raiffeisen F(riedrich) W(ilhelm), Die Darlehenskassen-Vereine als Mittel zur Abhilfe der Noth der ländlichen Bevölkerung, sowie auch der städtischen Handwerker und Arbeiter (Neuwied 1866)

Raiffeisen F(riedrich) W(ilhelm), Die Darlehenskassen-Vereine in Verbindung mit Consum-, Verkaufs-, Gant- etc. -Genossenschaften als Mittel zur Abhilfe der Noth der ländlichen Bevölkerung, sowie auch der städtischen Arbeiter. Zweite, vermehrte und verbesserte Auflage (Neuwied und Leipzig o. J.)

Raiffeisen F(riedrich) W(ilhelm), Die Darlehenskassen-Vereine in Verbindung mit Consum-, Verkaufs-, Winzer-, Molkerei-, Viehversicherungs-Gant- ect. Genossenschaften, als Mittel der Abhilfe der Noth der ländlichen Bevölkerung. Praktisch Anleitung zur Gründung und Leitung solcher Genossenschaften. Dritte, vollständig umgearbeitet und bedeutend vermehrte Auflage (Heddesdorf-Neuwied 1881)

Richter Heinrich, Friedrich Wilhelm Raiffeisen und die Entwicklung seiner Genossenschaftsidee (München 1966)

Rohrbach Wolfgang, Versicherungsgeschichte Österreichs, Band 1, Von den Anfängen bis zum Börsenkrach des Jahres 1873 (Wien 1988)

Rumpler Helmut, Eine Chance für Mitteleuropa, Österreichische Geschichte, 1804 - 1914 (Wien 1997)

Schreiber Gerhard, Die Interunfall Versicherung und die Riunione Adriatica di Sicurtà in Wien, 1890 - 2004 (Diss. Univ. Wien 2007)

Schulze H(ermann), Mittheilungen über gewerbliche- und Arbeiter-Associationen (Leipzig 1850)

Schwarz Hermann, 50 Jahre Städtische Versicherung, 1898 - 1948 (Wien 1948)

Seefeldner Othmar, Die Frage der Einführung der Feuerversicherung in Österreich zur Zeit der Kaiserin Maria Theresia (Linz o. J.)

Springer Johann, Statistik des österreichischen Kaiserstaates, Band 2 (Wien 1840)

Statuten des Ersten allgemeinen wechselseitigen Viehversicherungs-Vereines "Taurus" (Wien 1864)

Stubenrauch Moriz von, Statistische Darstellung des Vereinswesens im Kaiserthume Österreich (Wien 1857)

Thausing Friedrich, 100 Jahre Sparkassen. Anlässlich des 100jährigen Bestandes der Ersten Österreichischen Sparkasse 1819 - 1919 (Wien 1919)

Tomanek Peter, Versicherung - die unbeachtete Dimension der Raiffeisenidee, in: Versicherungsgeschichte Österreichs, Band 9, Österreich über alles, wann es nur will (Wien 2008)

Urbanski Hans, 150 Jahre Generali, 100 Jahre Erste Allgemeine (Wien, München, Zürich, New York 1982)

Vorläufige allgemeine Grundsätze einer unter landesfürstlichem Schutz zu errichtenden Brandschaden-Versicherungs-Privat-Anstalt, in: Generali Historisches Archiv

Wagner-Braun Margarete, Das genossenschaftliche Bank- und Versicherungswesen im 19. und zu Beginn des 20. Jahrhunderts – das Beispiel des „Wirtschaftlichen Verbandes“, in: Historischer Verein bayerischer Genossenschaften e. V. München (Hg.), Die Anfänge der modernen Genossenschaftsbewegung in Bayern, Österreich und Südtirol, Band 1 (München 1998)

Werdmüller Otto v. Elgg, Die allgemeine wechselseitige Capitalien- und Renten-Versicherungs-Anstalt. Mängel und Anträge zur beabsichtigten Statutenrevision (Wien 1861)

Werner Wolfgang, Raiffeisenbriefe erzählen Genossenschaftsgeschichte (Wien 1988)

Werner Wolfgang, Zur Vorgeschichte der österreichischen Raiffeisenbewegung. Forschungen zur Wirtschafts-, Finanz- und Sozialgeschichte, Band 2 (Frankfurt/Main 1993)

Wurzbach Constant von, Biographisches Lexikon des Kaiserthums Oesterreich. Dritter Theil (Wien 1858)

Wurzbach Constant von, Biographisches Lexikon des Kaiserthums Oesterreich. Neunter Theil (Wien 1863)

Wurzbach Constant von, Biographisches Lexikon des Kaiserthums Oesterreich. Achtundzwanzigster Theil (Wien 1874)

Wuttig Martin, Versicherungs- und Genossenschaftswesen als wechselseitige Hilfsorganisationen. Deutsche ländliche Genossenschaftsbücherei Band 5 (Berlin 1914)

Zedtwitz Clemens, Die rechtsgeschichtliche Entwicklung der Versicherung, Diss. Univ. St. Gallen (Zürich 2000)

Journals and papers

Allgemeine Land- und Forstwirthschaftliche Zeitung, XIV. Jahrgang (1864) 1124: Vieh-Versicherungsverein “Taurus“

Allgemeine Land- und Forstwirthschaftliche Zeitung, XIV. Jahrgang (1864) 259: Programms-Entwurf für die Errichtung einer Viehversicherungs-Anstalt im Bezirke Weitra

Oesterreichische Revue, Organ für Assecuranz und Volkswirthschaft (25. December 1876) 42: Die Viehversicherung in Oesterreich I
Oesterreichische Revue, Organ für Assecuranz und Volkswirthschaft (16. April 1877) 62: Das Versicherungswesen als Stütze der landwirthschaftlichen Spar- und Vorschusscassen
Oesterreichische Revue, Organ für Assecuranz und Volkswirthschaft (14. Jänner 1878) 5: Die Verbindung von Credit-Genossenschaften mit der Lebensversicherung
Oesterreichische Revue, Organ für Assecuranz und Volkswirthschaft (17. Mai 1880) 77: Actie oder Gegenseitigkeit
Wiener Zeitung (24. December 1824) 1259: Wien
Wiener Zeitung (3. November 1819): Amtsblatt (357) Kundmachung

Mutual insurance society in Austria Developments of a principle

Johann Brazda

1. Ancient forerunners

The insurance business in Austria did not develop from one decade to the next so quickly, but it is based on different early forms and it developed in different regions. Although the focus of this paper is Austria, it is important to keep in mind that insurance was and still is both a European invention and cultural concept.

One ancient forerunner for the transport insurance was the maritime loan that was introduced by the Phoenician to the Romans during the 4th century BC and was taken over by the Teutons and England. A maritime loan was carried out the following way: Before the journey, one or several wealthy people gave the captain of a ship a loan, which was paid back, when the ship reached safely, and undamaged its destination. In the event of an accident, the loan was used for the damage.[1] This was the starting point for the development of the marine insurance (the first transport insurance), first in Upper Italy, then in Spain and Portugal, and finally in England. Later this type of insurance was introduced in the Netherlands from which it came to Hamburg and Trieste.

Early forms of supporting associations and death funds can be found in the first centuries AC in all existing Roman provinces. They were called "collegia tenuiorum". These were associations for people of lower social rank (tenuiores), that paid the widows and orphans of members funeral money, and looked after them economically.[2] Later, the structures of these associations were taken over by Christian institutions. According to the concept of caritas: Wealthy people endowed monasteries with assets, the latter organized the care, and help for poor, old, and

---

1 This is the beginning of the professional insurance. (Cf. *Rohrbach, W.* (1988), Versicherungsgeschichte Österreichs, vol. I, Von den Anfängen bis zum Börsenkrach des Jahres 1873, Vienna, p. 161.

2 Cf. *Zedtwitz, von C.* (2000), Die rechtsgeschichtliche Entwicklung der Versicherung, Zurich, p. 41.

Figure 1: Trends of the historical insurance business in Austria

Commercial insurance	Mutual insurance			Landesanstalten (regional insurance institutions)	Public insurance
Initiative by entrepreneurs and capitalists	Mutual benefit societies	Mutual insurance societies	National mutual insurance societies	Initiative by ranks and local authorities	Initiative by the state
Corporate forms	Forms based on *law of association* (1852)			Public contractual insurance (öffentliche Vertragsversicherung)	Forms based on public law
4th century: maritime loans Phoenician → Romans → Teutons → Britons	Early Roman period: *collegia, tennorum* Early Christianity: *caritas* Early and High Middle Ages: *all risk insurance of the landlords* 17th century: *mutual clubs of peasant farmers, brotherhoods, societas*				Insurance for civil servants (1749) Brand-Vergütung-Sicherheits-Gesellschaft (Sozietät) in Austrian Forelands (1764-1805)
Since the 17th century development of the probability theory in England, the Netherlands, and Germany: catalyst for life insurance					
From 1766 respectively 1822 onwards joint stock companies in Trieste National joint stock companies: 1843 respectively 1857 Hungary Galicia (1870) Anker (1858) *life insurance* Companies Act (1874)		From 1824 onwards: *life insurances* From 1862 onwards: *industrial insurance societies*	1st wave of foundations: Galicia (1862) Rumania (1868) Bohemia (1869)	Fire insurers: Salzburg/Upper Austria (1815) Lower Austria (1824) Tyrol (1825) Bohemia (1827) Styria (Grawe) (1829) Moravia (1830)	

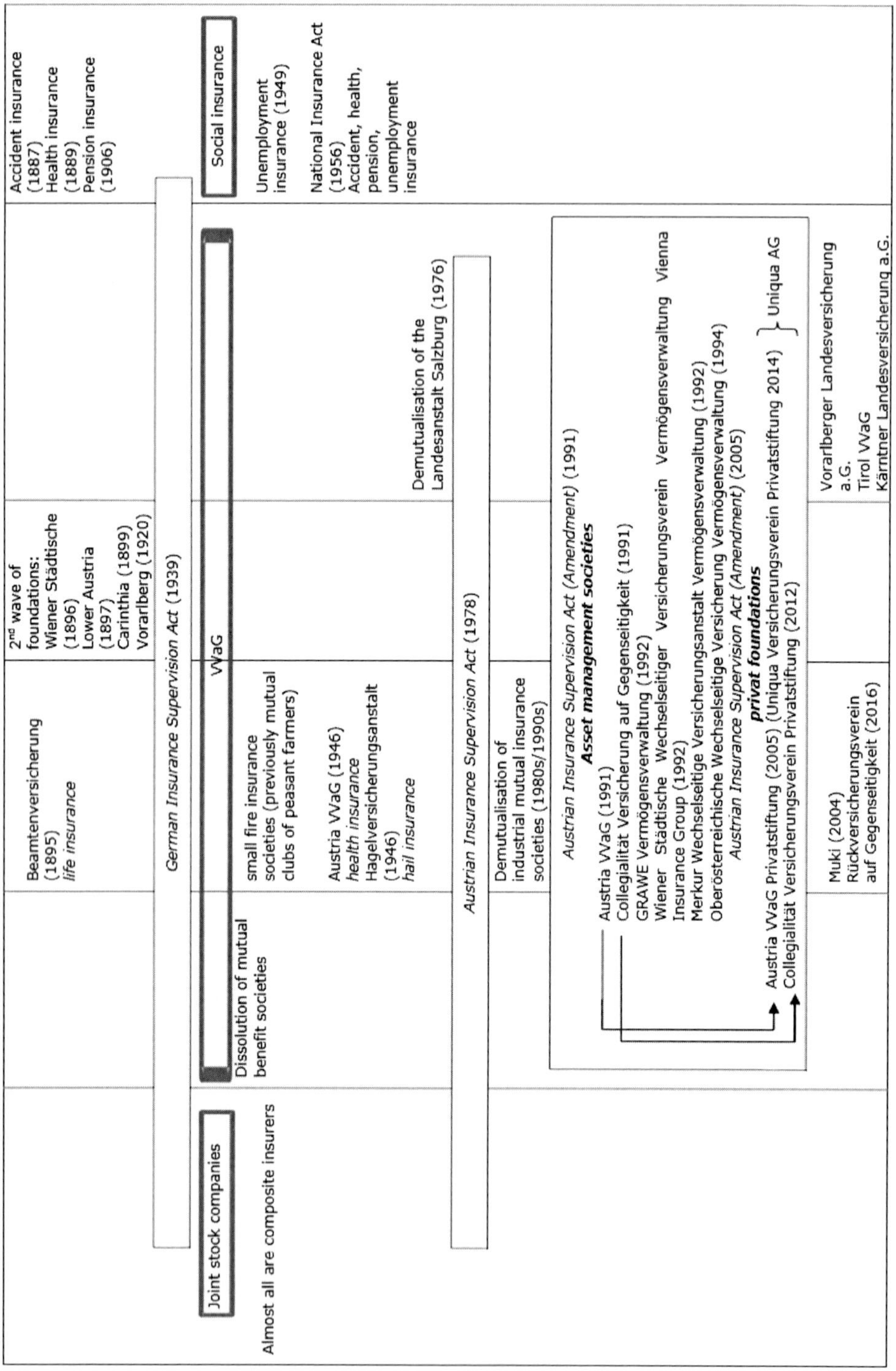
Joint stock companies
Almost all are composite insurers
Social insurance
Accident insurance (1887)
Health insurance (1889)
Pension insurance (1906)
Beamtenversicherung (1895) life insurance
2nd wave of foundations: Wiener Städtische (1896) Lower Austria (1897) Carinthia (1899) Vorarlberg (1920)
German Insurance Supervision Act (1939)
VVaG
Dissolution of mutual benefit societies
small fire insurance societies (previously mutual clubs of peasant farmers)
Austria VVaG (1946) health insurance
Hagelversicherungsanstalt (1946) hail insurance
Unemployment insurance (1949)
National Insurance Act (1956) Accident, health, pension, unemployment insurance
Austrian Insurance Supervision Act (1978)
Demutualisation of the Landesanstalt Salzburg (1976)
Demutualisation of industrial mutual insurance societies (1980s/1990s)
Austrian Insurance Supervision Act (Amendment) (1991)
Asset management societies
Austria VVaG (1991)
Collegialität Versicherung auf Gegenseitigkeit (1991)
GRAWE Vermögensverwaltung (1992)
Wiener Städtische Wechselseitiger Versicherungsverein Vermögensverwaltung Vienna Insurance Group (1992)
Merkur Wechselseitige Versicherungsanstalt Vermögensverwaltung (1992)
Oberösterreichische Wechselseitige Versicherung Vermögensverwaltung (1994)
Austrian Insurance Supervision Act (Amendment) (2005)
privat foundations
Austria VVaG Privatstiftung (2005) (Uniqua Versicherungsverein Privatstiftung 2014)
Collegialität Versicherungsverein Privatstiftung (2012)
Uniqua AG
Muki (2004)
Rückversicherungsverein auf Gegenseitigkeit (2016)
Vorarlberger Landesversicherung a.G.
Tirol VVaG
Kärntner Landesversicherung a.G.

sick people ("Foundations for spiritual welfare"). As a result, hospitals developed, financed by donations of the Christian community. In this way health insurance premiums developed. During the 15th and 16th century, the need for these institutions grew immensely. This action released monasteries from the obligations of a lifelong (care) pension. This was the beginning of life insurance.

2. Peasant insurance unions

During the unsafe times of the Early and High Middle Ages, i.e. from the 8th to 14th century, states in the modern sense did not exist. Many free farmers became dependent on property owners due to the fear of damage by natural forces. The farmers handed over their land to the property owners and received in return the land as fief to work on it. The farmers, however, had to pay contributions. This created a kind of "all-risk-insurance" between the property owner and his subject. This was a lifelong contract. The proprietor had to guarantee the safety of the peasants in exchange for their work and contributions. The so-called feudal system thus included an aspect of immense protection as well as a bond of loyalty. However, during the 15th century, many property owners neglected the protection towards their peasants, due to the development of the monetary and credit system. As a result, the peasants organized their own protection in form of mutual and voluntary support in case of emergencies. In the 17th century, small mutual fire insurance societies ("Bauernassekuranzen") of local farmers developed in the alpine areas. These institutions were used among villagers to help their neighbors with materials, labour, and money to rebuild houses and farm buildings in the aftermath of fires. *Pearson* refers to them as "mutual clubs of peasant farmers"[3]. Originally, this was just a habit but it developed later into a regular form due to contracts. A legal right regulating damages in the event of fire, harvest, and cattle losses as well as war damage. This was an important step forward to the development of insurances. The organization of each association, however, differed very much. In any case, they were mutual aid institu-

[3] Cf. *Pearson, R.* (2015), Organizational forms in insurance: A comparison of the USA and Germany during Industrialization, in: *Pearson, R.* / *Yoneyma, T.* (eds.): Corporate forms and organizational choice in international insurance, Oxford, p. 122.

tions. The first Austrian small fire insurance society was probably the one in Kremsmünster in 1710, belonging to the respective monastery.[4]

3. Private health insurance

Since the 17th century, the towns in Central Europe flourished again. They were the centres of two independent groups of professions, the artisans, active in the production of goods, and the businessmen (traders). Their contributions and their safety were not closely connected any longer with the land property. Therefore, they needed different institutions for security and provisions.

In the realm of material production, the guilds became important. They were based on the so-called brotherhoods (confratemitates) or societies (societates) and were free elected or arbitrary associations based on corporation. They regarded themselves as partly religious and partly mundane associations for mutual support with the aim to secure the individual against injustice and violence. The guilds offered their members services similar to insurances in the event of illness, disability or death as well as against damage by natural forces. The early forms of premiums were regular contributions to the society's cash box (Bruderlade), which was financed in particular by small deductions of the wages. In the field of trade, on the other hand, the Hanseatic League and the trade guilds dominated. Entry fees, regular contributions, and fines financed the trade guilds. They were important in particular for salespersons working in foreign countries. Due to the international connections of the trade guilds, the security of the individual people and the transported goods were guaranteed even in foreign countries. Many trade guilds were so wealthy that they were able to build their own provision houses for ill and poor members.[5]

During the middle Ages, thousands of miners in iron and other metal mines worked in hostile conditions in the less populated regions of the Alps. In these areas, the danger of illness, accidents, and disability was much higher than in other regions. Therefore, religious and charitable brotherhoods, which were mining brotherhoods, developed to insurance-similar miners' guilds. Their main tasks were to provide medical treat-

---

4 Cf. *Gollowitsch, J.* (1950), Die geschichtliche Entwicklung des österreichischen Versicherungswesens bis zur Zulassung ausländischer Gesellschaften, Graz, p. 20.

5 Cf. *Pressl, A.* (1993), Die Einbringung des Geschäftsbetriebes eines Versicherungsvereins auf Gegenseitigkeit in eine Aktiengesellschaft, Salzburg, p. 18.

ments in miners' hospitals, payments similar to health and unemployment does, and provisions for widows and orphans.

4. The development in Austria

In 1773, the Austrian Empress *Maria Theresa* enacted a regulation for miners (Bruderladenverordnung). This was the first step towards a pension fund run by the state. She thus created a sociopolitical regulation that was based on measures developed since the 15th and 16th century.[6]

During the 18th century, many of these early forms of insurances developed into true insurance companies. Already during the 17th century, brotherhoods had contracts with hospitals for the care of their ill members. When it was possible to receive regular contributions from the members and to relinquish the repayment of loans in the event of illness, the services and benefits became closer to a private health insurance. In 1683, the probably oldest insurance association for civil servants in Austria was founded. It was called: "Privatverein der in Wien befindlichen Rechnungs- und Kontrollbeamten zu wohltätigen Zwecken für sich und ihre Familienmitglieder", which was probably an insurance precursor.[7]

The first institution that had health insurance but was still organized in the legal form of a guild was the "Kranken-Hilfs-Confraternität für Handlungs-Commis in Wien", established in 1729 in Vienna. In this case, all members paid the same amount of fees. When they entered the society, the members received a book for paid up fees with the picture of Saint Joseph, the patron saint of the "Confraternität". All paid fees were confirmed monthly in this book and upon showing this book, the member received free medical treatment or care in a hospital connected with the society. During the last quarter of the 18th century, the "Confraternität" had already its own hospital with comfortable bedrooms and a kitchen of its own. In 1798, *J.B. Huber* founded in Graz the "Institut zur Unterstützung armer, kranker, dienstloser,

---

6 Cf. *Rohrbach, W.* (2004), Vorläufer, Wegbereiter und Träger der altösterreichischen „Versicherungsweltmacht", in: Versicherungsgeschichte Österreichs, vol. VII, Teil 1, Die altösterreichischen Regionen Zentral- und (Süd)Osteuropas: Gestern – Heute – Morgen, Vienna, p. 181.

7 Cf. *Megner, K.* (1995), Lebensversicherungen, Vereine und Selbsthilfeprinzip, in: Österreichische Beamtenversicherung (ed.): Vertrauen, Fairness, Solidarität, Verbundenheit, Verantwortung, Sicherheit, Vienna, p. 27.

Alters und Gebrechlichkeiten wegen zum Dienen unfähig gewordener Handlungsdiener" (a society for servants), which was modelled after the "Confraternität" in Vienna. It became later the "Merkur Wechselseitige Krankenversicherungs-Anstalt".

In 1749, *Maria Theresa* introduced social benefits for civil servants (e.g. provisions for illnesses, for old age for the widows and orphans), stated more precisely between 1770 and 1772, and received finally a legal basis by Emperor *Joseph II* on March 24, 1781 (Pensionsnormale). This was valid until the 1850s. At the same time, officers, medical officers, lawyers, and notaries established a private pension system geared towards the upper middle classes and supporting associations for widows and orphans, influenced by the basic care provisions of the state. At the Faculty of Medicine of the University of Vienna, an association, a "Sozietät", developed to provide for widows and orphans of the doctors working there ("Suspendations-Cassa"), which existed until 1959. It was then included into the "Wiener Ärztekammer" (Viennese chamber of medical doctors). In 1760, the "Witwen- und Waisen-Pensionsgesellschaft des juridischen Doktorenkollegium" of the Faculty of Law was founded. In 1774, a manufacturers association, the "Witwen-Pensionsinstitut der bürgerlichen Seifenzeug-, Sammt- und Dünntuchfabrikanten" (soap and cloth-maker) was founded and in 1780 the "Witwen-Sozietät des bürgerlichen Handelsstande in Wien" (civil trade) was established. They provided support for their members and their widows and orphans.[8] Due to a low number of members in these societies and missing actuarial principles, the societies were prone to crises and huge fluctuations regarding their performance in the event of insurance damage. Moreover, the access to these associations was restricted according to religious or professional criteria.

The first Austrian insurance joint stock company in the field of insurance can be found in today's Belgium, which belonged at that time to Austria. Again, Empress *Maria Theresa* recognized the importance of transportation insurance and founded the "Compagnie Royale des assurances"[9] in Antwerp in 1756.[10]

[8] Cf. *Stubenrauch, M.* (1857). Statistische Darstellung des Vereinswesens im Kaiserthume Österreich, Vienna, p. 110ff.

[9] In German sources, the name was "Kaiserlich und Königliche Versicherungsgesellschaft".

[10] Cf. *Rohrbach, W.* (2004), Vorläufer, Wegbereiter und Träger der altösterreichischen „Versicherungsweltmacht", in: Versicherungsgeschichte Österreichs, vol. VII, Teil 1, Die altösterreichischen Regionen Zentral- und (Süd)Osteuropas: Gestern – Heute – Morgen, Vienna, p. 190.

5. Marine companies

The arrival of the steam engine revolutionized manufacturing as well as the tertiary sector notably transporting. The upswing of the manufacturing and trade took place at the same time as the revolution in transport. The development of the steam engine and the transport systems on land and water helped the marine companies in Austria to a first and quick upswing. The marine companies were able to contribute to the upswing. The first foundations of marine companies took place in Trieste, Austria-Hungary's most important Mediterranean port, in the legal form of a joint stock company. Between 1764 and 1803, numerous joint stock companies were established.

Since November 12, 1787, a special regulation existed that formed a basic legal and institutional frame regarding share issues. The first Trieste Company functioned also as a credit bank for local merchants. Since the late 1760s, Trieste's fire and marine companies insured grain and tobacco in transit over land and on river from Hungary to the Adriatic port. Both, the marine insurance and the domestic transport insurance were active on an international level. However, they lost their importance when the Adriatic Sea was blocked by *Napoleon*. With the second attempt after the Congress of Vienna, the insurance industry established itself in Trieste as combined insurers, with branches in all larger trade and industry centres in Middle and South/East Europe. The "Nuova Società d'Assicurazione" was established in 1835 as a pure transport insurance company. The "Riunione Adriatica di Sicurtà" (established in 1838) founded branches at all important moorings of the Danube, i.e. at the 2,500 km long navigable part of the Danube. The "Azienda Assecuratrice" (established in 1822) became the railway insurer of Europe, while the "Assicurazioni Generali" (established in 1831) became the universal insurer for the monarchy from their bases in Trieste and Venice. From its headquarter in Trieste, it soon opened agencies in major cities of the Habsburg Empire, such as Vienna, Prague, and Budapest, as well as in the major French port cities of Marseilles and Bordeaux, shortly followed by Munich, Hamburg, and Königsberg (now Kaliningrad). The second office in Venice, which was responsible for Italian business, expanded its business into the States of the Italian peninsula as far south as Naples and later to Sicily. The "Assicurazioni Generali" and the "Azienda Assecuratrice" expanded their lines of business to life insurances in 1832 respectively 1854. While the "Azienda Assecuratrice" offered tontine business[11], the "Assicurazioni Generali"

[11] This is named after *Lorenzo Tonti* (1630-1695), who connected insurance with gambling to raise revenue for the French royal treasury in 1652. The principle was based on a one-off payment of a specific amount of capital. The circle of members

offered regular life insurances.[12] In Milan, which was part of the Austrian-monarchy at that time, the "Compagnia d'Assicurazione", a fire and life insurance company, was established in 1825.

Additionally, a ship register was introduced in Trieste, modelled after *Edward Lloyd's* register, to supply Austrian merchants and insurers with reliable news about trade and shipping in major ports. It was modelled after *Lloyd's*. This London coffeehouse owner collected since 1686 news about ocean and goods traffic for his customers and printed them since 1692 in his newspaper "Lloyd's News". *Lloyd's* was the first coffeehouse that collected systematically intelligence on shipping movements and political developments affecting trading routes. These features of the early market developments indicate that good information was critical for the success of durable and large-scale marine underwriting. Later this information was formally organized in "Lloyd's List" (1734) and "Lloyd's Register of Shipping" (1760). The "Society of Lloyd's", an official association, was founded in 1771. In 1832/33, the insurance experts in Trieste created the "Lloyd Austriaco" that developed later to the very successful shipping company "Österreichischer Llyod".[13] Trieste's major insurance companies were the driving forces behind the dynamism that helped the Habsburg Empire to develop into an important exporter of insurances until World War I, with activities in all neighboring states.

6. Life Insurance

The insurance of life began in the 14th century in the Mediterranean Area as a by-product of marine insurance when policies on ships and cargoes were extended to cover passengers or slaves on board. Life insurance in the form of wagers on life was in many European countries

was closed, which means the insurance became active when the circle was completed. The rate of interest for the money was fixed and the life annuity was paid to the members with respect to the capital. In the event of death, the pension was allocated to the other members, which means the society became a mutual pension inheritance association. Apart from the provision function, the financial office, which carried out the tontine business, hoped to raise money very quickly. (Cf. *Wortner, M.* (1972), Wandlungen der Lebensversicherung; eine rechtliche und demographische Untersuchung, Linz, p. 112).

[12] Cf. *Gollowitsch, J.* (1950), Die geschichtliche Entwicklung des österreichischen Versicherungswesens bis zur Zulassung ausländischer Gesellschaften, Graz, p. 73.

[13] Cf. *Rohrbach, W.* (1988), Versicherungsgeschichte Österreichs, vol. I, Von den Anfängen bis zum Börsenkrach des Jahres 1873, Vienna; p. 164.

forbidden. The origin of the modern life insurance was in England. Between 1706 and 1721, for instance, sixty mutual life insurance schemes – mostly short-lived – were launched in London. The first foundation was the "Amicable Society for Perpetual Assurance Office" that had simple principles for taken-out insurances and disbursements. The age (12 to 45 years) and the number of the members were restricted and everyone paid the same annual premium. At the end of the year, all deposited premiums were allocated to the heirs of the deceased policyholders in equal shares after cost deduction.[14] In 1762, the "Society of Equitable Assurance on Lives and Survivorships (Equitable Life)" was established in London and worked since 1776 with a statistical mathematical approach. It was an insurance pioneer and the basis for modern life insurance. The way to estimate premiums was new and quite innovative, because the premiums were based on the age and life expectation of the policyholder by using mortality tables. It was possible to relinquish age restrictions of the members and, as a result, a wide range of the population got access to the life insurance system. The focus of the insurance was now the gainful work and saving ability of the policyholder, respective the economic loss due to death, and not any longer life per se.[15] The idea behind this innovation was the conviction that the world could be predicted and computed, which was later on embodied in the principle of rational calculation by *Max Weber*.[16] In sum, English life insurance initially developed on a non-premium non-actuarial basis, with variable or fixed contributions and benefits distributed according to mortality. This system was the basis for all future foundations. The success of the "Equitable Life" encouraged a number of new premium-based life assurance companies to appear. Some were founded as mutuals, but the majority of them were established as joint stock companies.

Until the beginning of the 19th century, no traditional life insurance company existed in Austria with the exceptions of the "Witwen und Waisen-Pensionsinstitut für herrschaftliche Beamte", founded in Vienna in 1787, and the "Wiener allgemeines Witwen- und Waisen-Pensionsinstitut", established in 1823, which can be regarded as insurance precursors. The latter still worked with empirically fixed premium rates, which forced the institution to reduce the pensions by one third in 1833.[17] In 1825, the "Allgemeine Versorgungs-Anstalt für die Unterthanen des österreichischen Kaiserstaates" was established

---

[14] Cf. *Bridgewater, A.* (1995), The Modern Mutual Insurance Company in Britain, in: *Preiner, W.* (ed.) Grundlagen des Versicherungsvereins auf Gegenseitigkeit, Köln/ Göttingen, p. 30.

[15] Cf. Ibid.

[16] Cf. *Weber, M.* (1980), Wirtschaft und Gesellschaft, Tübingen, p. 13.

[17] Cf. *Rohrbach, W.* (1988), Versicherungsgeschichte Österreichs, vol. I, Von den Anfängen bis zum Börsenkrach des Jahres 1873, Vienna, p. 388.

and merged with the "Erste österreichische Spar-Casse". Although its bylaws were based partially on tontines, the terms "policyholder" and "insurer" were already in use. In 1839, the first mutual life insurance company the "Allgemeine wechselseitige Kapitalien- und Renten-Versicherungs-Anstalt" was founded in Vienna, following the English model. From 1865 onwards, the institution was named "Janus, Wechselseitige-Lebensversicherungs-Anstalt". The institution was a non-profit organization, in which its members worked in the administration without payments. It published its statement of accounts to present the public that their savings were earned by reasonable mortality rates and a good use of their assets.[18] The institution used statistics based on registers of death and mortality probability, modelled after the system of the British company "Equitable Life".[19] In 1860, the "Austria, allgemeine wechselseitige Capitalien- und Rentenversicherungs-Gesellschaft" was founded.

The first life assurance joint stock company in Austria was "Der Anker, Gesellschaft für Lebens- und Rentenversicherungen" (1858). The company introduced commission payments, i.e. remunerations for concluding insurance contracts based on the insurance sum or premium in percent.[20] Successors were the "Österreichischer Gresham, Gesellschaft für Lebens- und Renten-Versicherung" 1861 in Vienna and the "Haza" Ungarische Lebensversicherungsbank 1867 in Pesth.

7. Hail insurances

Apart from life insurance companies, some companies started to offer hail insurances. In 1828, the "Mailänder wechselseitiger Versicherungs-Verein gegen Hagelschlag" was established and worked until 1845 outside Italy. Later this business segment was taken over by the joint stock company "Azienda assicuratrice" in Trieste. Since 1839, the "Erste Österreichische (Brand-) Versicherungs-Gesellschaft (AG)" in Vienna insured damage caused by hail. In 1842, the Hungarian mutual "Ungarischer Verein für die Gegenseitige Versicherung von Hagelschäden" was founded while in Klausenburg the "k.k. siebenbürgische wechselseitige Hagel- und Feuerversicherungs-Gesellschaft", which offered hail and later fire insurances, was established (1843/45). In

[18] Cf. Ibid., p. 396.

[19] Cf. Ibid., p. 400.

[20] Cf. *Braun, H.* (1963), Geschichte der Lebensversicherung und der Lebensversicherungstechnik, Berlin, p. 293.

1853 followed the "k.k. privilegierte Hagelversicherungs-Gesellschaft" in Prague.[21]

Hail insurance remained the most problematic segment of the entire insurance industry. In the Austrian-Hungarian monarchy, joint stock companies became in particular important. In 1879, when the liberalism of the belle époque declined, the hail insurance market dominated. While eight joint stock companies insured 86.2 percent of the total insurance sum, only 13.8 percent was by six mutual insurance societies. In 1879, the amount of the business volume of Trieste's company Assicurazioni Generali amounted to almost double of the volume of all six mutuals together. All insurance companies were composite insurers and offered in addition to hail insurance other insurance segments such as life, fire, or transportation insurances, while accident and glass insurances were still not very common. The main concern of all companies, in particular during the two last decades before the turn of the century, was to keep the important fire insurance segment. The latter was so profitable, despite a fierce competition regarding market shares, that large joint stock companies accepted immense deficits in the hail insurance segment by offering insurances with very low premiums. Within a period of 25 years (1877-1901) profits were only achieved 11 times.[22]

8. Fire Insurance

While the growth of different forms of financial protection and the expansion of public and private welfare provisions in early modern Europe can be regarded as a major innovation in the sense of improved levels of security for private property and incomes, actuarial science or underwriting techniques were excluded from this development. From the late 17th century onwards, fire insurance developed via three basic types of organization: public, proprietary, and mutual.

It is important to keep in mind that the catastrophic earthquake of Lisbon in 1755 triggered the development of the insurance industry. It shook the belief in god and in the sense of harmony between heaven and earth. The theologians struggled to explain this devastating intervention of god and the optimism of the philosophers wavered that the

[21] Cf. *Rohrbach, W.* (1988), Versicherungsgeschichte Österreichs, vol. I, Von den Anfängen bis zum Börsenkrach des Jahres 1873, Vienna, p. 268ff.

[22] Cf. *Schneider, B.* (1988), Die Geschichte der Hagelversicherung in Österreich-(Ungarn) von 1880 bis 1938, in: Die Ära des klassischen Versicherungswesens, Versicherungsgeschichte Österreichs, vol. II, Vienna, p. 809.

rational order of things would always lead to a good end. Indeed, the catastrophe served for some people as proof that a caring all-powerful god did not exist. The more than 100,000 victims argued that if god is all-powerful, then he cannot be good or if he is good, then certainly he is not all-powerful. With this earthquake, the European concept of nature began to change. It became now increasingly rare that nature was perceived as the display of a holy plan or as a single, harmonic order. Rather it was more likely regarded as a tragic play of chance. It was then, after Lisbon 1755, that Europe took a decisive step towards managing catastrophes. Shortly afterwards, enlightened leaders and businessmen began to develop techniques to deal with risks including preventative measures such as fire protection and building regulations. In many countries state fire-funds emerged.[23]

In 1666, the Great Fire of London destroyed 13,000 houses and gave rise to the proprietary and the mutual forms of insurances. Since 1591, the residents of Hamburg voluntarily joined into groups to draw up "fire contracts", written agreements between groups of property owners. Members, whose property was destroyed by fire, received compensations from a mutual fund accumulated from post-hoc flat rate calls on members for losses incurred, calls that were not proportional to the sum insured by each of them. In 1676, the difficulty of spreading risk in a confined area led Hamburg's Senate to the action of combing all private agreements in town into one new insurance fund, the "Feuercasse", administered by council officials. There was no compulsion on existing householders to join the fund – full compulsion was first introduced in 1817 – but whoever built, bought, or inherited a house was required to join within six months. This was the world's first public association for the insurance of buildings. The new fund was accumulated from ex ante payments at fixed rates, but if the fund should be insufficient to cover the payments for losses, members were liable for further contributions at rates proportional to the sums they had insured. No actuarial calculations were involved. They mostly charged flat fees for all types of property, which were paid in the same way as taxes, but without any profit considerations. Accumulated funds were used, firstly, to pay for the rebuilding of property destroyed by fire – there was often an obligatory rebuilding clause attached to policies – and, secondly, to supplement other public costs.[24] During the following century, similar public insurance societies, some with compulsory memberships, were formed across northern and central Europe.

The first debate about establishing fire insurances started in Austria in the 1750s under the Empress *Maria Theresa*. However, many

[23] Cf. Ibid., p. 115.

[24] Cf. *Rohrbach, W.* (1988), Versicherungsgeschichte Österreichs, vol. I, Von den Anfängen bis zum Börsenkrach des Jahres 1873, Vienna, p. 197.

court offices were against this idea and resisted, which led to a general standstill. As a result, Austria, compared to other European countries, lost fifty years of practical experience in the insurance business. The discussion was about the introduction of a public insurance system based on mutuality and modelled after the German insurance system. In practice, however, with the exception of the Austrian Forelands (West-Austria, Vorderösterreich)[25], insurance against damage by natural forces was limited to local small mutual fire insurance societies (Bauernassekuranzen). In the Austrian Forelands, a "Brand-Vergütung-Sicherheits-Gesellschaft" (fire reimbursement and security society) was established in 1764 modelled after the fire associations in West Germany. It was dissolved with Austria's loss of the Forelands in 1805 due to the Napoleonic Wars.[26]

The end of the Napoleonic Wars was the starting point for the next phase of the development of the Austrian insurance system in 1814. Bavaria became a kingdom in 1806 and received parts of Austria as a gift due to its fight on *Napoleon Bonaparte's* side during the war. In the main towns of Bavaria, local fire societies and "Feuercassen" existed since the 18th century, while in the newly added parts from Austria small mutual fire insurance societies (Bauernassekuranzen) existed. According to the mercantilism and with the goal to centralise fire societies under governmental influence, King *Max Joseph of Bavaria* established in 1811 a public insurance, the "Königlich-baierische Landes-Brandversicherungsanstalt". It was modelled after the system in Hamburg[27] and based on mutuality and compulsory insurance. Its structural principals functioned as a model for the Austrian insurance companies. The Bavarian institution had public features, i.e. it was welfare-orientated, limited to buildings and regions, the corporation had its own legal entity, its reimbursement was based on an adjustable contribution procedure, compulsory membership, and the bylaws as well as the administration were carried out, independently by the participation and wishes of the members, by the state.[28]

With the reunification of Tyrol in 1814 and the splitting up of *Napoleon's* Empire on the Viennese congress (1814/15), Tyrol, the Innviertel, parts of the Hausruckviertel, and Salzburg returned from Bavaria to Austria, and, as a result, Tyrol was separated from the "Königlich-

[25] The Austrian Forelands is a collective term for the previous estates of the Habsburg's territories west of Tyrol and Bavaria.

[26] Cf. *Leimdörfer, M.* (1905), Entwicklung und Organisation der Brandschadenversicherung in Österreich, Vienna, p. 55ff.

[27] Cf. *Lehner, U.* (1997), Abschied von der Gegenseitigkeit, in: Versicherungsgeschichte Österreichs, vol. V, Assekuranzmosaik des ausgehenden 20 Jahrhunderts, Vienna, p. 1100.

[28] Cf. *Rohrbach, W.* (1988), Versicherungsgeschichte Österreichs, vol. I, Von den Anfängen bis zum Börsenkrach des Jahres 1873, Vienna, p. 197.

baierische Landes-Brandversicherungsanstalt". The good experience with this institution led to the idea to draft bylaws for the foundation of an insurance company, based on the bylaws of the Bavarian company. In 1825, the "Tirolisch-Vorarlberg'sche Feuer-Versicherungs-Anstalt"[29] was established. In Salzburg and parts of Upper Austria, the insurance business was continued based on Bavarian laws and in form of the "Wechselseitige Brand-Assekuranz in Salzburg-Oberösterreich". The district office and the provincial government continued with the company temporarily, a fact, however, that did not change even with the splitting of the insurance company into the "Wechselseitigen Landes-Brandschaden-Versicherungs-Anstalt im Erzherzogtum Österreich ob der Enns"[30] and the "Wechselseitige Landesbrandschaden-Versicherungs-Anstalt für das Herzogtum Salzburg"[31] in 1850.[32]

In addition to the insurance companies in Salzburg/Oberösterreich and Tyrol, *Major Ritter von Högelmüller* initiated a public insurance company, based on his experiences as an officer with fire insurance in Dresden. His plan was to establish a similar model for the entire Austrian monarchy. His first draft of the bylaws propagated a management by the minister of state, compulsory insurance, and the administration by the provincial authorities.[33]

However, in the meantime in Vienna, the resolution of the Emperor from September 4th, 1819 stated that all insurance foundations had to be of a private nature, either in the legal form of mutual societies or joint stock companies, and not public institutions. Only then, the insurance companies were under the protection of the state. This meant that the followers of *Adam Smith*, who wanted to exclude any economic influence by the state, were successful in the Viennese court office.[34] The current foundations, which did not fit into this schema, had to adapt and reacted differently:

- Herzogtum Salzburg (Salzburg/Oberösterreich) kept the temporary solution, i.e. the Bavarian regulations were used.
- In Tyrol, a typical Austrian solution existed. With the resolution from September 5th, 1821, Tyrol obtained new bylaws from the court office that

[29] Today "Tiroler Versicherungs VaG". The Vorarlberger stock was transferred in 1927 to the "VLV Vorarlberger Landes-Versicherung V.a.G".

[30] Today "Oberösterreichische Versicherung AG".

[31] Today part of the "UNIQA Versicherungen AG".

[32] Cf. *Plöchl, G.* (1972), Vereine als öffentliche Unternehmen, Vienna, p. 14.

[33] Cf. *Rohrbach, W.* (1988), Versicherungsgeschichte Österreichs, vol. I, Von den Anfängen bis zum Börsenkrach des Jahres 1873, Vienna, p. 222.

[34] Cf. Ibid., p. 215.

stated that their private company is under the management of the local authorities.[35]

- After considering the pros and cons for a private company, *Högelmüller* opted for a voluntary participation, but with the use of insurance agents such as financial officers and higher public officials (according to the Bavarian principal). He established in quick succession the "k.k. priv. Wechselseitige Brandschaden-Versicherungs-Anstalt"[36] ("Wechselseitige Brandschaden") (1824), the "k.k. priv. Innerösterreichische Wechselseitige Brandschaden-Versicherungs-Anstalt"[37] (1829), the "k.k. priv. Erste böhmische wechselseitige Brand- und Hagelschaden-Versicherungs-Anstalt" (1827), and the "k.k. priv. mährisch-schlesische wechselseitige Versicherungsanstalt" (1830). The economist *Josef von Kudler*, an advocate for the mutuality principle, supported him. *Kudler* propagated an ideal of this principle and took the view that in a mutual insurance society each member should work in an interested and responsible way for establishing preventive measures, such as the foundation of fire departments. To him, the main purpose of this insurance type was the increase of the well-being of all members. Additionally, he expected lower administration costs. However, such ideals were not realistic.[38]

As a result, three different "private" mutual insurance models can be found in Austria, instead of the previously envisaged public insurance system. The three models, which comprised also elements of a joint stock company and the public insurance system, created the type of a provincial institution ("Landesanstalt" or "Anstalt"[39]) of the 1st generation. This type based on the mutuality principle without compulsorily legal membership of the building owners and received advanced payments from the class of gentry to cover damages caused by fire. The money was payed out of the Domistikalfonds.[40]

- The above-mentioned model for "Salzburg" and "Upper Austria" based on Bavarian regulations.
- The model of Tyrol, which is established by the initiative of the Tyrolean gentry, is very similar to a public institution and does not have any partici-

[35] Cf. *Gollowitsch, J.* (1950), Die geschichtliche Entwicklung des österreichischen Versicherungswesens bis zur Zulassung ausländischer Gesellschaften, Graz, p. 44.

[36] "Priv. wechselseitige Brandschaden-Versicherungs-Gesellschaft in österr. u. d. Enns". Merged with "Janus" 1923 and with "Wiener Städtische Wechselseitige allgemeine Versicherungsanstalt auf Gegenseitigkeit" 1938.

[37] Today "Grazer Wechselseitige Versicherung AG".

[38] Cf. *Carinthia* from September 11th, 1824, pp. 151-155.

[39] "Ständische Landes-Assecurranzanstalt" (Cf. *Winckler, J.* (1872), Feuerschäden, Feuerlösch- und Versicherungswesen, in: Mittheilungen aus dem Gebiete der Statistik, Neunzehnter Jahrgang, Heft 3, p. 46.

[40] Cf. Ibid.

pation of its members, with the exception of paragraph 25 of the bylaws. § 25 states that two members have to be appointed for assistance by the public body for the local insurance committee. Local gentry and provincial department work in the administration and organization and receive help and support by the Emperor's command in form of instructions (§ 26 of the bylaws of 1825).[41]

Both insurance systems were under the protection of the state, i.e. their insurance business was regional limited and their administration was done with the help of public officials.

- The *Högelmüller*-model comprised elements from company law (e.g. the appointment of the manager for life) and elements from public institutions (e.g. the participation of public officials regarding administration). The member side was organized by election with postal vote (no general meetings), a list of proposed candidates by the management, and voting rights of the members. The latter's weight in terms of voting rights was determined with the amount of the insured value of the building. Moreover, there was a collective voting right for a whole borough instead of a per-capita voting right in the event the amount of the insured value of the building was too low.[42]

  Even contemporary people regarded the work, management, and administration of these insurance companies as "patriarchal", i.e. a small group leads and the people maintain in their positions permanently due to cooptation (the group appoints its members on their own).[43] Another example for a serious violation of the mutuality principle can be found in the actions of the "k.k. priv. Erste böhmische wechselseitige Brand- und Hagelschaden-Versicherungs-Anstalt". During the crisis of 1867, it became evident that the bylaws of 1827 were still valid and that no general meeting had taken place during the last 11 years.[44]
- Another model, which caused a sensation, was the foundation of the "Wechselseitige Versicherungsgesellschaft in Krakau", the so-called "Floryanka", named after the Saint of the company Saint Florian, in 1860 in Galicia. This region was regarded as the "poor house" of the Habsburg monarchy but also as the testing ground for legal innovations. The com-

---

[41] Cf. Bylaws of the Feuer-Versicherungs-Anstalt für Tirol 1825 in: *Wörz, J. G.* (1835) Gesetze und Verordnungen in Bezug auf die Kultur des Bodens in ihrer Provinz Tirol und Vorarlberg, nach Materien gesammelt, und in diesen chronologisch dargestellt, 2. Theil, Erste Abtheilung, Innsbruck, p. 402ff.

[42] Cf. §§ 104-106 of the bylaws of the "k.k. privilegierten Wechselseitigen Brandschadenversicherungs-Anstalt in Österreich unter der Enns" (1825), and §§ 114-117 of the 1829 established "Wechselseitige Brandschaden-Versicherungsanstalt in Steyermark, Kärnten und Krain" (today's "Grazer Wechselseitige Versicherung AG"); *Ilwof, F.* (1879), Geschichte der wechselseitigen Brandschaden-Versicherungs-Anstalt in Graz von 1829 bis 1879. Graz, p. 36.

[43] Ibid. p. 33.

[44] Cf. *Leimdörfer, M.* (1905), Entwicklung und Organisation der Brandschadenversicherung in Österreich, Vienna, p. 162f.

pany became the role model of a mutual insurance company and the most successful enterprise.[45] It was structured according to a system that was introduced by the German businessman *Ernst-Wilhelm Arnoldi* in 1820 in Gotha, on which the "Gothaer Feuerversicherungs-Bank auf Gegenseitigkeit", today's "Gothaer Versicherungsbank VVaG" is based on. It worked across borders and therefore on international markets with the goal to cover the needs, to make profits, and to achieve growth by securing its business at the same time.[46]

- Additionally, mutual industrial insurance societies existed, such as the "Assecuranzverein von Zuckerfabrikanten in der österr.-ungarischen Monarchie" (sugar manufacturers) in Prague (1861), the mutual "Gegenseitiger Versicherungs-Verein für Montanwerke, Maschinen- und Metallfabriken" (coal and steel industry) (1867), and the "Erste Wiener Spiegelglas-Versicherungsgesellschaft" (glass and plate glass) in Vienna. All had business in the entire monarchy and were characterized by a small number of members and considerable annual reimbursements for their members.[47]

When considering the economic success and failures of the mutual insurance companies during this time, the main problems were – with the exception of the "Wechselseitige Versicherungsgesellschaft in Krakau" – the regional limitation and the adjustable contribution procedure. The latter caused highly fluctuating annual contributions in the event of high financial damage which led, on the one hand, to mass resignations and, on the other hand, to several foundations of small mutual fire insurance societies (Bauernassekuranzen), which were still based on barter, in particular in Upper Austria.[48] Many of the mutual insurance companies were only able to survive due to their connections to the provincial governments. For example, from 1860 until its reorganization in 1872, the "k.k. priv. Innerösterreichische Wechselseitige Brandschaden-Versicherungs-Anstalt" had a phase of financial difficulties and narrowly escaped bankruptcy.[49]

---

45 E.g., the reorganization of the building register, introduction of furniture and hail insurance.

46 The Gothaer Modell distributes the risks, just like joint stock companies, to insurance classes and level of risks and calculates then the premium. The company took advance premiums, dividends were paid, and if necessary additional payments had to be made. (Cf. Excerpt from Grazer Volksblatt from July 17th, 1879, supplement to No. 162, p. 10f.)

47 Cf. *Rohrbach, W.* (1988), Versicherungsgeschichte Österreichs, vol. I, Von den Anfängen bis zum Börsenkrach des Jahres 1873, Vienna, p. 357.

48 Cf. Ibid., p. 150ff.

49 Cf. Grazer Volksblatt from July 17th, 1879, supplement to No. 162.

9. Re-insurance companies

During the first half of the 19th century, insurers in small regions offered co-insurances, i.e. the customer had two or three insurance partners on the insurance contract. Additional regional re-insurance contracts were concluded in the way that the first insurer gave its main risk to one or two other policyholders in form of a re-insurance. For the submitted premium part, the insurer received in the event of damage proportional insurance service.

During the second half of the 19th century, these forms of co- and re-insurances were not sufficient anymore. The business became international and professional and re-insurers became the norm. In the Habsburg monarchy, Hungary was the pioneer in this insurance segment by establishing 1861 the re-insurance company "Pannonia, Ungarische Rückversicherungs-Ges." in Budapest. In 1865 followed, in collaboration with the "Erste Ungarische Allgemeine Assekuranz-Gesellschaft" and the "Pannonia, Ungarische Rückversicherungs-Ges.", the re-insurance company "Rückversicherungs-Gesellschaft Securitas" in Vienna.

10. First reports regarding the insurance sector

10.1 The Journal "Union. Zeitschrift für Versicherungswesen" 1872[50]

In 1872, the journal "Union Zeitschrift für Versicherungswesen" published an article about the situation of insurance companies in Austria with the following content: Until 1858, the Austrian-Hungarian insurance market was dominated by the joint stock companies in Trieste, in particular by four companies ("Azienda Assecuratrice" (1822), "Assicurazioni Generali" (1831), "Riunione Adriatica di Sicurtà" (1838), and "Nuova Società d'Assicurazione" (1835, 1866 liquidated), which were composite insurers (transport-, fire-, life-, and hail insurance) working in the entire monarchy (especially in Hungary, Bohemia, Galicia) as

[50] Cf. Zur Situation, in: Union. Zeitschrift für Versicherungswesen vom 21.1.1872, p. 1.

well as internationally. Their total insurance capital was more than 2.400 Million Gulden. In addition to these four companies the "Erste Österreichische (Brand-)Versicherungs-Gesellschaft (AG)" (1824) existed in Vienna with an insurance capital of 400 Million Gulden, while all mutual fire insurance companies together had only a total of 250 Million Gulden deposit value. Therefore, the distribution of the insurance sum at this time was the following: the four largest insurance companies in Trieste had 78.68 percent, the "Erste Österreichische (Brand-)Versicherungs-Gesellschaft (AG)" 13.14 percent, and the mutual companies 8.18 percent. After 35 years of insurance business, mutuals had only a share of 8.18 percent of the insurance sum compared to 91.82 percent of joint stock companies, which meant mutuals were in need of action. It is important to note that only after the insurance business was taken up and operated by industrial enterprises, it is possible to talk about an actual start of insurance business in Austria.

10.2 Statistics regarding fire damage in 1870[51]

In addition to the number of fire insurances, their spreading, i.e. the actual demand by building owners, are important as well. However, in this period the importance of insurances can only be determined indirectly by looking at the fire damage covered by insurance companies. The reason is that neither the number of insurance policies nor the value of the insured buildings was known. The data, i.e. the fire damage, were provided by the "k.k. statistische Central-Commission" in 1870. The commission was able to record the fire frequency, intensity, and cause of fire on the municipality level.

In 1870, the fire insurance business was characterized by the fact that less than the half of the damaged buildings was already insured. According to the statistic above, the average insurance frequency was only 47.09 percent, which means that from 8,934 buildings damaged by fires only 4,207 were insured. The highest insurance density can be found in Lower Austria with 83.38 percent, followed by Upper Austria (82.47 percent), Bohemia (68.18 percent), Salzburg (62.22 percent), Moravia (61.58 percent), Tyrol/Vorarlberg (60.80 percent), and Silesia (56.84 percent). On the other hand, the lowest insurance density can be found in Dalmatia (0.61 percent), Galicia (19.38 percent), and the Bukovina (11.50 percent). However, it is important to note that from this statistics it is not possible to detect if the insured buildings were sufficient insured or not. The only exception is the area of Bukovina in which the fire insurance was almost exclusively handled by big

[51] Cf. *Winckler, J.* (1872), Feuerschäden, Feuerlösch- und Versicherungswesen, in: Mittheilungen aus dem Gebiete der Statistik, Neunzehnter Jahrgang, Heft 3, p. 64ff.

landowners, who usually insured their assets up to the full amount. In general, it can be noticed that in 1870 the damage for buildings and furnishings were 10,983.811 fl., while the insured damage of buildings was only 3,335.611 fl. respectively 527.235 fl. for furnishings. As a result, it is evident that 47 years after the first insurance wave, the idea of fire insurance had not been successful so far.[52]

Table 1: Comparison of the number of buildings damaged by fire to the number of insured buildings in the Austrian Monarchy in 1870

		Number and percent of the insure buildings which were damaged by fire in percent	
Lower Austria	668	557	83.38
Upper Austria	291	240	82.47
Bohemia	1,848	1,260	68.18
Salzburg	45	28	62.22
Moravia	1,114	686	61.58
Tyrol and Vorarlberg	385	234	60.80
Silesia	190	108	56.84
Styria	383	187	48.83
Coast area	70	32	45.71
Carinthia	409	184	44.98
Carniola	359	147	40.95
Galicia	2,730	529	19.38
Bukovina	113	13	11.50
Dalmatia	329	2	0.61
Total	**8,934**	**4,207**	**47.09**

Source: *Winckler, J.* (1872): Feuerschäden, Feuerlösch- und Versicherungswesen, in: Mittheilungen aus dem Gebiete der Statistik, Neunzehnter Jahrgang, Heft 3, p. 64.

This is also obvious regarding the insurance types and different legal forms. While mutuals offered, in particular, fire, hail, and life insurances, joint stock companies underwrote combined insurances. Additionally, during this time mutuals became more similar to joint stock companies regarding their business operations. For example, in

[52] Cf. Ibid.

1885, according to the annual Assecuranz report, 19 out of 29 mutual societies were pure fire or combined insurers (inclusive fire), 6 were pure life insurers, one was a pure accident insurer and three insured glass or cattle. From 18 joint stock companies, 14 were fire or combined insurers, 3 pure life insurers, and one was an accident insurer.[53]

In the new hail insurance segment, joint stock companies dominated until 1879, although they offered hail insurances always in combination with other insurance types. Apart from the "k.k. priv. Versicherungsgesellschaft Österreichischer Phönix", the "Erste Österreichische (Brand-) Versicherungs-Gesellschaft (AG)", and the large insurance companies in Trieste, three Hungarian companies and the mutual society in Lower Austria offered hail insurances. The "k.k. priv. Innerösterreichische Wechselseitige Brandschaden-Versicherungs-Anstalt" offered this insurance type since 1909, however, it was not profitable until the end of World War I.[54]

10.3 Reports about the emergency sessions of the mutual insurance societies

Since 1865, the deputies of the mutual societies held assemblies ("Wanderversammlungen") with the goal to make general reforms of mutual companies. They criticized that it had become the norm to be insured by a joint stock company and only in few cases by mutual societies. With that trend, the major progresses of the last 42 years in the insurance business were lost for many Austrian mutual insurance societies. One of the main problems was the missing risk classification – this means buildings were not classified regarding their fire risks based on their roof structures, designs, locations, or special purposes. As a result, the adjustable contribution rate was the same amount for buildings with tiled roofs as for a small thatched hut and the payments for low risks buildings were higher than for highly flammable ones. Consequently, this did not lead to an improvement of the existing flammable method of construction. The majority of the policyholders was insured by joint stock companies and not by mutuals, because the former were cheaper and insurance payments were paid much faster. Another problem was that joint stock companies, compared to mutuals, did not need a minimum value to conclude an insurance contract. Moreover, the societies had not developed further or adapted to new challenges since their foundation, in particular regarding their organization. This included the regional limitation that had led to their low prominence.

[53] Cf. Assecuranz-Jahrbuch, Vienna 1887, pp.68-69 (Table A).

[54] Cf. *Baumgartner, I.* (2003), 175 Jahre Grazer Wechselseitige, Festschrift anlässlich des 175-jährigen Jubiläums der Grazer Wechselseitigen Versicherung, Graz, p. 53.

Mutual insurance societies were regarded as mere provincial companies, which was also visible in the company's name.[55]

Although mutual societies survived this challenging period, they only worked on their necessary re-organization in a middle and long-term sense (see Table 2). At the same time, the adaptation of mutuals to joint stock companies became more evident. To emphasize this argument, the next chapter presents the historical events, which underline this hypothesis.

11. The major events for the development of mutuals

Six major events were responsible for the further development of mutuals:

- the stock market crash in 1873,
- consequences of the end of the Austrian-Hungarian monarchy because of World War I
- the first phase of group formations: the example of the "Wiener Städtische Wechselseitige Versicherungsanstalt"
- the bankruptcy of the "Phoenix" life insurance company in 1936
- the effects of the "Anschluss"[56] in 1938
- the development after World War II
- the second phase of group formations: the example of the "Austria Versicherungsverein auf Gegenseitigkeit"

At the same time, three important political events happened in this period:

- the foundation of the "Österreichische Beamtenversicherung",
- the foundations of national insurance companies in various provinces of the monarchy, and
- the debate about nationalisation as well as the introduction of the social security system on the governmental level.

---

[55] Cf. Excerpt from the newspaper "Die Assecuranz" about the travelling assemblies on October 1st, 1865 in Vienna. Auszug aus der Zeitschrift „Die Assecuranz" über die am 1. Oktober 1865 in Wien abgehaltene Wanderversammlung der Wechselseitigen Versicherungs-Gesellschaften und kurzer Bericht über die Beschlüsse und Berathungen der zweiten Versammlung Wechselseitiger Institute in Graz am 26. und 27. Juni 1871. Krakau 1873. p. 10f.

[56] In March 1938, Austria became a part of Hitler's "Third Reich". Whether this happened voluntarily or not is still a matter of discussion. (Some prefer) the term "occupation".

Table 2: Re-organizations of mutual societies

"k.k. priv. Wechselseitige Brandschaden-Versicherungs-Anstalt"[56] („Wechselseitige Brandschaden") (1824)

Year	1824	1828	1860	1870	1890
Adjustable contribution procedure/premium system	adjustable contribution procedure				Premium advance payment
Insurance classes	5 building categories	6 building categories	8 building categories	Estimated by the director	
Management/Administration	Under the protection of the state				
Insurance type	Fire insurance for buildings			Fire insurance for buildings and furnishings	
Court	Valuation by the policyholder				
Territory	Lower Austria	Entire monarchy			

"k.k. priv. mährisch-schlesische wechselseitige Versicherungsanstalt" (1825)

Year	1825	1835	1868	1870
Adjustable contribution procedure/premium system	adjustable contribution procedure			
Insurance classes		11 insurance categories for buildings with 44 subcategories		
Insurance types	Fire insurance for buildings		Fire insurance for buildings and furnishings	Fire insurance for buildings and furnishings

"k.k. priv. Innerösterreichische Wechselseitige Brandschaden-Versicherungs-Anstalt" (1829

Year	1829	1865	1872
Adjustable contribution procedure/premium system	adjustable contribution procedure		premium system
Insurance types	Fire insurance for buildings		
Insurance classes	6 building categories	Revising of the cadastre according to fire risk	Classification premium for the entire insurance area according to the fire risk of villages
Management/Administration	Under the protection of the state		
Courts [57]	Valuation by the policyholder and the agent of the society	Permanent extraordinary committee (administrative board) assembles once a year	
Territories	Styria, Carinthia, and Carniola		

57 "k.k. priv. Wechselseitige Brandschaden-Versicherungs-Anstalt". Merged with "Janus, Wechselseitige-Lebensversicherungs-Anstalt" 1923 and with "Wiener Städtische Wechselseitige Versicherungsanstalt".

"Tirolisch-Vorarlberg'sche Feuer-Versicherungs-Anstalt" (1823)

Year	1823	1864	1874	1891	1905	1918	1920
Adjustable contribution procedure/premium system	adjustable contribution procedure			Calculation based on average of the last 10 years			
Insurance classes		Introduction of 3 building categories	5 building categories	6 building categories			
Insurance type	Fire insurance for buildings						
Management/ Administration	Private insurance society under the protection of the estates of the province	Exact definition of the authority of the federal state parliament and state committee		Cooperation of other departments: tax office and municipal council; insurance agents; municipality;	Municipality is now obligated for collecting the premium (by state law)		
Courts	Administration by civil servants of the province	arbitration panel					
Territory	Regional limited					Separation from South Tyrol	Separation of Tyrol and Vorarlberg

"Wechselseitige Brand-Assekuranz in Salzburg-Oberösterreich" (1816)

Year	1811/1814	1839	1848
Adjustable contribution procedure/premium system	adjustable contribution procedure		
Insurance type	Fire insurance for buildings		
Management/ Administration	Under the protection of the state; management by the federal officials	Supervision by the political authorities	
Courts	Joint work with local authorities; local insurance committees;	Estate committee (functions as administrative authority)s	
Territory	Upper Austria and Salzburg land	Liechtenstein	Separation of Upper Austria and Salzburg

"Wechselseitigen Landes-Brandschaden-Versicherungs-Anstalt im Erzherzogtum Österreich ob der Enns (1850)

Year	1848	1850	1865	1873	1876	1904	1918
Adjustable contribution procedure/premium system		adjustable contribution procedure	Premium advance payment				
Insurance classes				4 building categories			
Insurance type		Fire insurance for buildings	Classification according to fire risk		Fire insurance for buildings and furnishings		
Management/ Administration		The former Bavarian bylaws are no longer in force; the overall management of business by the state board manages; head is the state representative; society under state protection; not compulsory society		Management by the state committee		Damage had to reported to the state committee (direction of the society)	Regional institution; general regulations and terms of insurance policy
Courts		Overall management by the state representative; own agents of the society with cooperation of local authorities;		arbitration panel in the event of disagreements between the society and policyholders		No arbitration panel anymore; experts evaluate damage;	
Territory		Upper Austria and other crown lands	Upper Austria and other crown lands	Only Upper Austria anymore due to bad economic results	also other crown lands		

"Wechselseitige Landesbrandschaden-Versicherungs-Anstalt für das Herzogtum Salzburg" (1848)

Year	1848	1861	1864	1867	1874	1881	1888	1895	1918	1923
adjustable contribution procedure/ premium system	adjustable contribution procedure						Premium system only for furnishings insurance	Premium system for buildings and furnishings		Profit share of the members
Insurance classes	No classification				5 building categories			Decides by the state committee		
Insurance type	Fire insurance for buildings					Fire insurance for buildings and furnishings				
Management/ Administration	administrative district office	Management by Salzburg's state representative and the state committee	Society of building owners; under the protection of the state; managed by the state representative		Separation of the jurisdiction between federal state parliament and state committee			Non-compulsory society under state law	In bylaws legal status not stated; biasness managed by the society's management; constituent assembly has the supervision, administrative, and top management power)	
Courts	arbitration panel in case of disagreements between society and policyholder		State committee manages administration; arbitration panel in case of disagreements; Evaluation of damage by political local authorities	Evaluation of damage by political local authorities				Evaluation of damage by society's agents	arbitration panel; general terms of insurance policy	
Territory	Crown land Salzburg	Crown land Salzburg	Crown land Salzburg							

"Wechselseitige Versicherungsgesellschaft in Krakau" (1860)

Year	1860	1864	1869
Insurance type	Fire insurance for buildings	Hail insurance	Life insurance

11.1 The stock market crash in 1873

During the liberal period (1859-1873), often referred to as "belle époque" (until 1914), it was believed that the market did not need governmental control or severe laws because it would be able to regulate itself. Although the first selling problems of the textile industry became evident in 1872, the government maintained the economic liberal way. Some people even believed in an economic upswing due to the Viennese World Exhibition in 1873.[58] From 1872 to 1874, many banks, insurance companies, and construction companies were founded in a rush by frauds and speculators and without solid capital basis. With the stock market crash on the 9th of May 1873, this economic phase ended abruptly. While in May 1873, 147 banks existed in Austria, by the end of the year the number decreased to 102. With only 53 financial institutions in the years 1878 and 1879 and 18 joint stock companies in Vienna, the low point was reached.[59] While between 1867 and 1873 more than 1,005 licenses for the foundation of joint stock companies were granted, it was only 43 during the next six years.[60] The same development can also be found regarding insurance joint stock companies: only five were founded in 1871, twenty in 1872 but only one in 1873 and in 1874 respectively. Most of these did not survive. In 1874, 18 insurance joint stock companies had to be dissolved and four had to declare bankruptcy.[61] Already in 1873, three mutuals had to be dis-

[58] Cf. *Sandgruber, R.* (1995), Ökonomie und Politik. Österreichische Wirtschaftsgeschichte vom Mittelalter bis zur Gegenwart, Vienna, p. 248.

[59] Cf. *März, E.* (1968), Österreichische Industrie- und Bankpolitik in der Zeit Franz Josephs, Vienna, p. 171ff.

[60] Cf. Die Gründung von Aktiengesellschaften 1867-1882, in: Der österreichische Ökonomist, 1883, p. 14.

[61] Austria: "Atlas" (Rückversicherungsgesellschaft), "Aetna", "Der Bund", "Continental" (Rückversicherungsbank), "Elementar-Versicherungsbank", "Europa", "Österreichische Hagelversicherungsgesellschaft", "Wiener- Hagel- und Rückversicherungs-Gesellschaft", "Allgemeine Hypothekar-Versicherungs-Bank", "Juventus", "Kosmos", "Landwirtschaftliche Rückversicherungs-Bank", "Merkur", "Minerva", "Österreichische Rentenanstalt", "Allgemeine wechselseitige Rückversicherungs-Bank", "Österreichische Rückversicherungs-Gesellschaft", Rückversicherungsgesellschaft "Salus", "Allgemeine Transport-Versicherungs-Gesellschaft", "Union", Rückversicherungsbank "Universelle", "Vindobona", "Wiener Lebensversicherungs-Gesellschaft", "Slovenija", "Galizische Allgemeine Versicherungsbank", "Gesellschaft für Mit- und Rückversicherung", "Allgemeine böhmische Aktiengesellschaft für Elementar- und Lebensversicherungen", "Böhmische wechselseitige Viehversicherungsbank", "Erste böhmische allgemeine Rückversicherungs-Gesellschaft", Erste böhmische Versicherungs-Bank "Moldau", etc.
Hungary: "Centrale", "Haynal", Internationale Lebensversicherungs-Gesellschaft "Karmentö", "Kronos", "Allgemeine Lebens- und Renten-Assekuranz", "Ungari-

solved.[62] Not only the joint stock companies but also mutual insurance societies did not have sufficient financial assets that were necessary for such institutions. The adjustable contribution system was not able to guarantee immediately insurance payments, caused by the lack of statistical data and the existing governmental supervision. As a result, many disappointed policyholders suffered financial losses[63] and one third of the 81 current insurance companies disappeared from the market. These foundations gave the insurance sector a bad name and these "bad sheep" companies damaged their clients by using commissions to play insurers against each other. With the crash in 1873, this phase of alienating insurances ended.

Winckler, too, reported that between 1865 and 1870 110 new fire insurances (including small local fire insurance societies) were established. This increased the competition between companies and led to a cost-ineffective way of doing business.[64]

However, with the stock market crash in 1873, the perception regarding the insurance industry changed drastically towards a pessimistic and distrustful point of view. Both joint stock companies and mutuals lacked the financial background, a fact that shows again the similar way of doing business of both legal forms. Now many people asked for a supervision of the insurance industry and the question of nationalization was raised. However, some people spoke against this trend, for example the newspaper "Neue Freie Presse". Nevertheless, the main idea was that the state should only let continue such companies that could guarantee their policyholders no damage due to their administration and management.[65]

The companies established during the first foundation wave (1822-1850) came out stronger from this crisis. While mutuals continued their adaptation to joint stock companies, at the same time, the insur-

sche wechselseitige Viehversicherungsbank", "Tisza" (the latter was liquidated in 1884) etc.. From the companies founded between 1866 and 1869 the following were also liquidated due tot he financial crisis: the "Ungarische Nationalversicherungs-Gesellschaft", "Erste ungarische Viehversicherungs-Ges.", and the "Victoria", Klausenburg.

62 "Allgemeine wechselseitige Rückversicherungs-Bank", "Union", allgemeine Versicherungs-Bank auf Gegenseitigkeit, "Moldau", wechselseitige Feuer-, Hagel- u. Lebensversicherungs-Bank (auf Gegens.).

63 Cf. Assecuranz-Jahrbuch 1880, Vienna, p. 171.

64 Cf. *Winckler, J.* (1872), Feuerschäden, Feuerlösch- und Versicherungswesen, in: Mittheilungen aus dem Gebiete der Statistik, Neunzehnter Jahrgang, Heft 3, p. 48.

65 Cf. *Egl, H. / Ludwig, B.* (1988), Die Geschichte der Feuerversicherung von 1873 bis 1918, in: Die Ära des klassischen Versicherungswesens, Versicherungsgeschichte Österreichs, vol. II, Vienna, p. 707f.; *Morgenstein, O.* (1937), Von Sonnenfels bis Lueger Beiträge zur Geschichte des österreichischen Versicherungswesens, Vienna, p. 74f.

ance industry established itself and acted as one sector. An example of this can be seen in the since 1880 published annual yearbook, the "Assecuranz-Jahrbuch".

During this period, no regulations for the relationship between insurers and policyholders existed either for joint stock companies or for mutuals. Only in 1917, the first Insurance Contract Act[66] was established. As a result, both legal forms established their own general terms of contracts in form of customary rights, although they would have need permission by the government.[67] Nevertheless, almost identical regulations developed, which were forced on the policyholders.[68]

In conclusion, the crisis year of 1873 was an important watershed for the Austrian economic and social history. The Austrian economic system was now based on economic small-scale thinking resulted from a striving for security that was founded on risk aversion.[69]

The state took the necessary actions and in 1874, a new Companies Act and a year later a new Financial Services Act (1875) came into force, which led in combination with a rigorous state supervision and severe taxation of joint stock companies to a rejection of the former liberal way. Additionally, in 1880 the state introduced the Versicherungsregulativ for insurance companies and improved it in 1896. It included a severe insurance supervision (§ 24) that was able to ban a company from business. From now on, a licence was needed, the products were supervised as well as the insurance regulations, the management, and the business practices including capital investments. With its supervision function, the state decided for unified legal regulations for all insurance companies and, as a result, the trend for the adaptation of mutuals to insurance joint stock companies intensified.

The Versicherungsregulativ 1880 stated unsuitable and unsafe investment forms. The authors of the amended Versicherungsregulativ in 1896 knew that in the life insurance segment assets' shares have to be appropriated for a specific purpose. The knowledge came from the bankruptcy of the 1860 founded insurance company "Austria, allgemeine wechselseitige Capitalien- und Rentenversicherungs-

66 Österr. VVG 1917 vom 23. Dezember 1917 RGBl 501. Without an insurance supervision act the policyholders and insurers were exposed to the insecurity of locally diverse sentences.

67 Cf. *Kraus, H.* (1971), Versicherungsaufsichtsrecht – Eine Studie zum deutschen und zum österreichischen Recht, in: Forschungen aus Staat und Recht, vol. 16, Vienna, p. 14.

68 Cf. *Ogris, W.* (1988), Zur Entwicklung des Versicherungsaufsichtsrechts und des Versicherungsvertragsrechts in Österreich von der Mitte des 19. Jahrhunderts bis zum Ende der Monarchie, in: Die Ära des klassischen Versicherungswesens, Versicherungsgeschichte Österreichs, vol. II, Vienna, p. 118.

69 Cf. *Sandgruber, R.* (1995), Ökonomie und Politik. Österreichische Wirtschaftsgeschichte vom Mittelalter bis zur Gegenwart, Vienna, p. 250.

Gesellschaft".[70] As a result, the guarantee stock regulations were created in several steps (1896/1923/1936). The guarantee stock of an insurance is a special asset, which has to be invested and to be managed separately from other assets. In the life, accident, legal liability, and health insurance segments this share of assets are used for securing the direct claims of the policyholders. Only the lawmaker can decide which assets are used for the guarantee stock. Until 1936, the "Versicherungsregulativ" and later the Insurance Supervision Act regulated which assets could be included into the guarantee stock.

During the course of the 1870s economic liberalism weakened, the liberal phase ended and led to the "Versicherungsregulativ" of 1880 that put insurances under severe governmental supervision. Although from now on, the requirements for insurance companies were stricter, the "Versicherungsregulativ" also required general principles that were useful for the soundness of insurances. During the last two decades of the 19th century, an economic upswing of the overall economy was accompanied by an expansion of the insurance industry. The winners of this development were again the joint stock companies. A ten-year comparison of the business of insurance companies (1878-1887) shows a sevenfold higher premium growth of joint stock companies compared to mutuals. In 1887, insurance joint stock companies had a market share of 77 percent regarding their premium incomes. They insured primarily risks in the industrial field and gained more of a profit from the economic upswing than mutuals that restricted their business to building insurances. The drawback of this development, however, was a fiercer competition among insurance joint stock companies leading to such a drastic decrease of their profit margins (between 1883 and 1887 from 10.8 to 3.00 percent) that even regulating premiums by the state was discussed.[71]

The economic upswing in the life insurance segment was with a share of 1.5 percent of the insured regarding the entire population re-

---

[70] In this case, life insurances have to consider the risk of death regarding the creation of reserves and the process of savings, because different to other insurance sectors the insurance sum will be paid out one day. However, this principle was neglected completely On the one hand, the company used the reserve premiums of the life insurance to cover the costs of the health insurance, and, on the other hand, the company issued too high and too man policy loans. As a result, the premium reserves were too low. (Cf. Assecuranz-Jahrbuch 1897, III. Teil, p. 40ff.). To cover-up the damage to the company's image a new joints stock company was founded with the help of the "Assicurazioni Generali" and the "Riunione Adriatica di Sicurtà". The new "Universale, allgemeine Volksversicherungs-Gesellschaft" took over the liquidation of the "Austria". (Cf. Ibid.).

[71] Cf. *Israel* (1889), Die Feuerversicherungs-Gesellschaften in Oesterreich während der Jahre 1878-87, in: Mittheilungen und Miscellen, Statistische Monatsschrift XV. Jahrgang, p. 275ff.

mained, however, rather small. In particular, the decreasing percentage mortality rate due to better sanitary measures and medical developments were positive for the expansion of life insurances.[72] In combination with the development of the monetary economy, the life insurance segment was a way to satisfy the increasing need of the population for saving their money. Additionally, the competition was less compared to other states, the number of companies lower, and only a few of the foreign 1873 licenced companies were successful despite their aggressive promotional measures. With regard to domestic companies, joint stock companies and mutuals were similar in their numbers. The larger part of the life insurance portfolio belonged to insurance joint stock companies (e.g. in 1892 the two-and-a-half of mutuals[73]), however, the branches of foreign companies got closer with their transactions while mutuals held the last place. The customers of joint stock companies belonged mainly to the upper class while people from lower social ranks with lower insurance sums were insured by mutuals.[74]

At the end of the 19th century, the cooperation between insurance companies improved. For example, in 1878 the "Fachverein der Österreichisch-Ungarischen Assecurateure", a platform for managerial staff of insurance companies, was established. In 1899, the foundation of the "Österreichisch-Ungarischer Verband der Privat-Anstalten", a precursor of today's Insurance Association ("Versicherungsverband Österreich" VVO), followed. The association became the platform for the education and training of insurance companies and mutual societies. Due to the practical cooperation, an association culture developed and, as a result, a common identity.[75] This harmony, however, ended with the dissolution of the monarchy.

11.2 Consequences of the end of the Austrian-Hungarian monarchy because of World War I

The end of World War I signified the complete collapse of the Austrian-Hungarian monarchy. It created a state of six million people with 13.2 percent of the former national territory, 12.6 percent of the population, 34.2 percent of the commercial and industrial production and

[72] Cf. *Roloff, M.* (1988), Die Entwicklung der Lebensversicherung in Österreich zwischen 1873 und 1936, in: Die Ära des klassischen Versicherungswesens, Versicherungsgeschichte Österreich, vol. II, Vienna, p. 321.

[73] Cf. Die österreichischen Assecuranz-Gesellschaften im Jahre 1892, in: Mittheilungen und Miscellen, Statistische Monatsschrift XX. Jahrgang, p. 41.

[74] Cf. Ibid.

[75] Cf. *Roloff, M.* (1988), Die Entwicklung der Lebensversicherung in Österreich zwischen 1873 und 1936, in: Die Ära des klassischen Versicherungswesens, Versicherungsgeschichte Österreichs, vol. II, Vienna, p. 360.

30 percent of the workers employed in industry and trade. A third of the current population lived in Vienna and had to be fed by the rest of the sparsely populated areas. Additionally, a major financial burden, e.g. in form of pensions, resulted from the immigration of civil servants and employees from all parts of the former monarchy as well as the new created succession states in which the head offices of industry and public transport services now existed.

The insurance industry was confronted by the fragmentation of the monarchy[76], in particular because now former domestic insurance companies had their head offices in foreign countries.[77]

Due to the new nationalistic succession states of the monarchy, the insurance industry ended in these regions and concepts of financial, personal, and insurance-specific structures were destroyed. Additionally, many assets of the insurance companies were lost due to the division of the former monarchy into succession states. The consequence was an even tighter cooperation of the remaining insurance companies in Austria. They were now forced to look at their similarities and not at their differences.

At the same time, World War I tore apart many of the international links that had been established over the course of more than a century. The growth of nationalism, the dramatic degree of currency depreciation, and the state intervention following the Great Depression, led even the most outward-looking European insurance markets to narrow their activities. The governments in London and Paris annulled all insurance contracts with policyholders from enemy countries at the outbreak of the war. German and Austrian ship-owners lost their insurance cover on the London market. The same as German industrialists who held policies with English fire insurers.[78]

In addition, cross-border insurance relationships continued to decline in Europe. A wave of chauvinism swept over the continent, global trade collapsed because of new tariff barriers and the impoverishment of wide sections of the population.

The majority of European primary insurers was forced to rein considerably their foreign business after 1918. The Treaties of Versailles

---

76 For example, only one third of the fire insurance business and half of the life insurance business were done within the borders of the new Austrian state, while for example, hail insurance was mainly done in Hungary and therefore its part of the total business was much smaller. (Cf. *Leimdörfer M.* (1919), Versicherungswesen 1914-1918, Separatabdruck aus dem Bericht der niederösterreichischen Handels- und Gewerbekammer, Vienna, p. 16).

77 This was in particular true for the joint stock companies of Trieste, such as the "Assicurazioni Generali" or the "Riunione Adriatica di Sicurtà", which had now their head offices in foreign countries, namely Italy.

78 Cf. *Borscheid, P.* (2012), Europe: Overview, in: *Borscheid, P. / Haueter, N.* (eds.): World Insurance, Oxford, p. 37.

and Saint-Germain led to the confiscation of assets of Austrian insurers in the former crown countries. In addition, companies from the central powers were forbidden to engage in any activities in those countries for several years.

To resolve these problems in Austria, the decree from the 21st of March 1919 stated that all joint stock companies and mutuals that had their head offices in another part of the monarchy then Austria before the 1st of November 1919 were licensed for the insurance business.[79] However, they had to choose a representation and to license their business in Austria within 4 weeks. Mutuals had also to prove that their business in the succession state was based on the mutuality principal. A few days later additional regulations were introduced:

- a temporary committee for the supervision of insurance companies by the state was created,
- the "Versicherungsregulativ" was changed in so far that insurance companies in economic emergency situation had the right to calculate their premium reserves in a for them favorable way, and
- the costs for the state supervision had to be paid by the insurance companies.

In addition to the decrease of production during the last war year, a shortage of raw materials, and insufficient investments in the non-armaments sector, the currency was demonetized during the period of inflation (1919-1922). This resulted, eventually, in the fall of 1921 into a hyperinflation, caused by poor economic circumstances (poor harvests, shortfall in production) and increasing budget deficits[80] that were financed exclusively by banknote production.[81] At this time, this action was considered the sole alternative to avoid anarchy and rebellion and to secure the unstable political and social order.

A firm control of foreign exchange would have alleviated the situation. The government at that time reacted, however, differently and introduced in November 1920 the free foreign exchange trade. This also happened in other European states. As a result, the period of the first globalization – with open foreign exchange and trade – ended in a wave of national isolation. The latter was based on an independent domestic economy with a free private capitalism and less governmental influence. In Austria, after the end of the first Great Coalition between

79 This was established in Art. 272 of the peace treaty of St. German and confirmed by a ten years' time limit.

80 Due to interest and redemption payments for war debts, monetary supporting for the large number of unemployed and to support the prices of goods.

81 Cf. *Sandgruber, R.* (1995), Ökonomie und Politik Österreichische Wirtschaftsgeschichte vom Mittelalter bis zur Gegenwart, Vienna, p. 354.

Social democrats and the Christian social party a hard monetary policy was aimed at. Private property and private economy were, with the exception of few sectors, unregulated and without control. Only during the 1930s, the first signs of governmental interventionism are evident, for example when reorganizing the "Creditanstalt-Bankverein" after its bankruptcy in 1931 or redevelopments regarding the Phoenix scandal in 1936.

Insurance companies became victims of this development. In the fire insurance segment as in the entire non-life sector, the recording of the full value was the main endeavour of the insurers. However, it became clear that this was not possible when looking at the dramatic increase of the prices of insurers from month to month, even per week. This meant that after a quarter of the year an insurance based on a carefully conducted contract became a fatal underinsurance in the event of damage.[82]

After 1918, the low exchange rate of Austrian's currency the Krone promoted in the insurance sector as well as in other fields of the economy the process of foreign control. The Austrian insurance industry was very internationally during peace times and had close connections in particular to the German re-insurance market. German and Italian shareholders had a crucial role in the domestic insurance industry. Since the end of World War I, the foreign influence increased in the Austrian insurance business.[83]

In contrast to the 1870s, less foreign companies were established. It was much easier for a company to establish business on the Austrian market by buying into an existing insurance company. As a result, the infiltration of Austrian companies with foreign capital started. Due to the inflation, shares and property that was originally too expensive became cheap within a few weeks. It was only necessary to restrain stable foreign capital reserves for a time. *Leimdörfer* analyzed the influence of foreign companies on the domestic insurance business as follows:

He states that the requirements of regulating the pre-war debts according to the peace treaty of St. Germain and the need of finding new capital for the organization body, favoured the infiltration of foreign capital. For example, new Italian companies expanded their spheres of interest by including companies such as the "Der Anker, Lebens und Renten-Versicherungs-Gesellschaft" and international re- and co-insurers. German re-insurers were part of the mergers of the "Allianz and the Gisela-Verein" respectively of the "Janus" and the "Erster allgemeiner Beamtenverein der österr.-ungar. Monarchie". The company

[82] Cf. *Reisser, N. / Rohrbach, W.* (1988), Arbeitsverhältnisse und Arbeitssysteme in der Versicherungswirtschaft 1873 bis 1938, in: Versicherungsgeschichte Österreichs, vol. III, Das Zeitalter des modernen Versicherungswesens, p. 180.

[83] Cf. Ibid.

"Universale" came under Rumanian influence, while the "Elementar" and "Lloyd" followed English insurance companies.[84]

The alienation was realized by the increase in share capital and by mergers and new foundations:

- In 1921, two large life insurers the "Allianz, Lebens- und Renten-Versicherungs-Aktiengesellschaft" (1890) and the mutual "Gisela-Verein, Lebens- und Aussteuer-Versicherungsanstalt auf Gegenseitigkeit" (1869/1880) merged to "Allianz und Gisela-Verein, Versicherungs-Aktiengesellschaft".[85].
- The second major merger took place in 1922, when two mutual insurance societies the "Erste allgemeine Beamtenverein der österr.-ungar. Monarchie" (1864) merged with the life insurer "Janus Wechselseitige Lebens-Versicherungs-Anstalt".[86]

Apart from mergers, another strategy of many life insurers was to start non-life insurances or pure insurers expanded their business into

[84] *Leimdörfer, M.* (1921), Das Versicherungswesen während der Jahre 1919 und 1920. Separatabdruck aus dem Bericht der niederösterreichischen Handels- und Gewerbekammer, Vienna, p. 3.

[85] In 1938, it was renamed "Ostmärkische Volksfürsorge Lebensversicherungs-AG der Deutschen Arbeitsfront" and in 1941 it took over the Slovenian portfolio of "Der Anker, Lebens und Renten-Versicherungs-Gesellschaft", was renamed in 1945 in "Österreichische Volksfürsorge", 1968 in "Österreichische Volksfürsorge Lebensversicherungs-AG" and in 1973 in "Österreichische Volksfürsorge Allgemeine Versicherungs-Aktiengesellschaft". In 1983, the company merged with the "Jupiter" and became the joint stock company "Volksfürsorge – Jupiter Allgemeine Versicherungs-AG".

[86] The "Janus Wechselseitige Lebens-Versicherungs-Anstalt" was established in 1839 as the mutual society "Allgemeine Wechselseitige Kapitalien- und Renten-Versicherungs-Anstalt" and renamed into "Janus, Wechselseitige-Lebensversicherungs-Anstalt" in 1866. In 1923, the company merged with *Högelmüller's* "k.k. priv. Wechselseitige Brandschaden-Versicherungs-Anstalt" and was called from now on "Wechselseitige Brandschaden- und Janus, Allgemeine Versicherungs-Anstalt auf Gegenseitigkeit". In 1926, it started a syndicate, based on a reinsurance contract, with the "Anglo-Danubian Lloyd". In 1928, the "Wechselseitige Brandschaden- und Janus, Allgemeine Versicherungs-Anstalt auf Gegenseitigkeit" took over the Austrian non-life insurance portfolio of the "Ungarisch-Französische Versicherungs-AG" and in 1934 "Wechselseitige Brandschaden- und Janus, Allgemeine Versicherungs-Anstalt auf Gegenseitigkeit" transferred the German life insurance portfolio to the "Zukunft, Lebensversicherungs-Bank AG", and the rest of the life insurance portfolio to the "Oevag Österreichische Versicherungs-AG" (ÖVAG). In 1938, the "Wechselseitige Brandschaden- und Janus, Allgemeine Versicherungs-Anstalt auf Gegenseitigkeit" took over the "Domus" and transferred the non-life insurance portfolio to the "Wiener Städtische wechselseitige Versicherungsanstalt" insurance company.

other insurance segments. All these developments led to higher competition that increased the crisis even more.

From 1923 on, a phase of monetary stabilization ended and of revaluation started and the share price increased dramatically, triggered by the undervaluation of joint stock companies. The share index was far under the price level, i.e. the value of companies was much higher as their market value, and therefore dealing with shares was very profitable. Many foundations and mergers resulted from this development, in 1922/1923 265/250 new foundations of joint stock companies and 236/151 capital increases occurred. Most of this capital came from scaled down flight capital and from foreign speculators.[87]

In the insurance industry a foundation wave occurred with the support of foreign capital. The reasons were the inflationary flight of goods and the need to insure these goods.

Most of the new founded insurance companies, both joint stock companies and mutuals, were non-life insurers. Founded were[88]

- the "Anglo Danubian Lloyd, Allgemeine Versicherungs-Aktiengesellschaft" 1918 in Vienna with support of English capital,[89]
- the "Fortuna", Lebens- und Renten-Versicherungs-AG" 1919 in Vienna
- the "Globus, Versicherungs-Aktiengesellschaft" 1920 in Vienna under Italian influence[90],
- the "Vorarlberger Landes-Feuerversicherungs-Anstalt" 1920 in Bregenz,
- the "Heimat, Allgemeine Versicherungs-Aktiengesellschaft" 1921 in Vienna with capital of the "Bodenkreditanstalt", the "Unionbank", the "Leipziger Feuerversicherungsanstalt", the "Assicurazioni Generali", and the "Erste Allgemeinen Assekuranzgesellschaft" in Budapest[91],
- the "Domus, Erste österreichische Hausschaden-Versicherungs-Aktien-Gesellschaft" 1922 with the support of Vienna's property owners,
- with federal law the "Versicherungsanstalt der österreichischen Bundesländer"[92] 1922 in Vienna
- the "Austro Union, Versicherungs-Aktiengesellschaft" 1923 in Vienna with the help of an enterprise from Frankfurt,

[87] Cf. *Jobst, C. / Kernbauer, H.* (2016), Die Bank. Das Geld. Der Staat Nationalbank und Währungspolitik in Österreich 1816-2016, Frankfurt a.M., p. 163.

[88] Cf. *Rohrbach, W.* (2004), "… der Rest ist Österreich!", in: Versicherungsgeschichte Österreichs, vol. VII, Teil 1, Die altösterreichischen Regionen Zentral- und (Süd) Osteuropas: Gestern – Heute – Morgen, Vienna, p. 742.

[89] Under the management of the "London Guarantee and Accident Company Limited", which was merged with the "Phönix" Insurance Company Limited, London.

[90] Majority shareholding of the "La Riassicuratrice" in Milano.

[91] Took over the Austrian customer portfolio of the "Leipziger Feuerversicherung" (1837).

[92] Took over the insurance portfolio of the former "Niederösterreichische Landes-Brandschaden-Versicherungsanstalt".

- the “Erste n.ö. Brandschaden-Versicherungsaktiengesellschaft” 1923 in Vienna,
- the “Europäische Güter- und Reisegepäck-Versicherungs-Aktiengesellschaft” 1923 in Vienna,
- the “Steirer Versicherungs AG” 1923 in Graz, and the
- “Wechselseitige Hypotheken-Versicherungs-Gesellschaft” 1923 in Vienna.

For the insurance industry, the process of evaluation was an advantage, because their obligations towards their policyholders were devaluated faster than their assets. However, the insurance almanac regards this period as a time of the destruction of the insurance business.[93] The process of devaluation could only be stopped by ending the financing the deficit and financing the import surplus by a foreign loan. The solution was the League of Nations’ loan in connection with the Geneva rescue operation in 1922.

The Austrian Chancellor *Ignaz Seipel* was able to connect the League of Nations’ loan – initiated by the Geneva Protocols from the 4th of October 1922 – with the independence of the Austrian republic.[94] Austria received a guaranteed loan of 650 million Gulden, but had in return to mortgage the proceeds of tariffs and the tobacco monopoly. The term of the League of Nations’ loan was 20 years. The announcement of the loan was sufficient to end the inflation and with the introduction of the Schilling as new currency on the 1st of January 1925, the devaluation had officially ended.

Soon after the stabilization of the currency, the economy developed in various ways. On the one hand, the inflation had increased consumption, because nobody wanted to keep devaluated money. Therefore, goods for future uses were bought. Austrian insurers offered contracts with gold and currency clauses (insurance sum in form of gold or stable foreign currency) for higher premiums and secured so their policyholders against losses in value.

With the introduction of the Schilling, the economy was poor due to low production and cutting back of operations caused by the inflation, short-time work, and increasing unemployment. The population had to adjust the consumption to low income and to limit the demand. This situation intensified by shortage of loans and the increasing prices of loans.

On the other hand, a different economic system developed, in which a large quantity of foreign currencies and goods were imported. The capital was not used for production, but at the stock exchange. The profit from major share transactions was transferred into foreign countries

---

93 Cf. Oesterreichischer Versicherungs-Almanach 1929, Vienna, p. V.

94 Cf. *Sandgruber, R.* (1995): Ökonomie und Politik Österreichische Wirtschaftsgeschichte vom Mittelalter bis zur Gegenwart, Vienna, p. 361.

with the help of banks. As a result, the state was deprived of taxes and the domestic economy was confronted with an increasing shortage of money.

The domestic insurers suffered from this development in several ways. The growth of the insurance industry was, with the exception of life insurances, low due to the stabilization policy. Many companies grew slower and as a result, the competition in the insurance industry increased.[95] Fire insurers were affected in particular, because they had despite reinsurances negative damage results. 80 percent of the gross premiums had to be used for reinsurances and paying for damage. For many companies the remaining 20 percent were not sufficient and investment income had to be made.[96]

Some policyholders had to cancel their insurances to have enough money for goods, while others did insurance fraud. Long unemployment and poverty mad many people angry and prone to the misuse of insurers, i.e. fraud became normal.

Similar things happened in the agriculture sector. The years from 1925 to 1933 were terrible for fire insurers, in particular in the alpine areas where agricultural business was not profitable and the number of fires increased. The reason was usually arson. However, not only old and damaged buildings were set on fire, but also new ones. In the beginning, no evidence for arson existed and the owners received money, which was in particular difficult to get during this time. They received the insurance sum and were able to build a new house with low costs and at the same time, workers became employed. For a short time, this insurance fraud was helpful and the swindler believed their actions only affected the rich insurance companies.

From an economic point of view, this situation was a problem. Due to high damage costs of the insurers their capital investments plans were destroyed. The state got less taxes and supporting money was reduced. The high fire insurance damage resulted in a general increase of higher insurance premiums for all policyholders.

With the new currency, the economy was stable, but not healthy. The economy was more prone to the negative effects of the Great Depression in 1929.

Similar the situation of banks after the end of the monarchy was in particular problematic. Banks did not change their policy and instead of a general retreat from the Danube area and reducing their bank machinery with a focus on the Austrian economy, they insisted on their former business area supported by foreign partners and a large part of the domestic industry. Their credo was Austrian knowledge

---

[95] Cf. Oesterreichischer Versicherungs-Almanach 1929, Vienna, p. V.

[96] Cf. Ibid., p. IX.

and Western capital.[97] However, the insufficient growth of production during the 1920s and the world economic crisis led to major losses for Austrian banks, which they were not able to cover. This development led to the bank crisis in 1931, which had to solve by the national bank and a guarantee of the Republic of Austria for the deposits and payment agreements with foreign creditors were made.[98]

A similar development happened in the insurance industry, which also had finical problems and had to be rescued. The insurance almanac reported that the insurance industry was affected by the economic crisis severely in 1930 and had major losses.[99] From 1931 on, the almanac reported about the decrease of premium incomes due to the poor economic circumstances, delayed because a depression effects insurances later.[100]

In particular, life insurances expanded their business after WWI to compensate their losses. The insurance almanac reported for 1929 about a major development in the life insurance sector[101] However, this strategy led to new losses, they were not evident in the public balance sheets. The life insurance "Phönix", a multinational Austrian enterprise that had business in 22 countries collapse after the death of its director *Dr. Wilhelm Berliner* in the spring of 1936. The total loss of the company was 5 percent of the Austrian national income of 1936. The result was a major change in the insurance industry, which effected all insurance companies. Other the bank crisis, the losses of the Phönix had to be covered by the policyholders and the insurance industry. It also damaged the reputation of the state due to connection of the insurance business with the government and the national socialist propaganda used this bankruptcy for anti-Semitic slogans. The view that Vienna was the centre of finance that was able to finance and insure the industry of neighbor states was proofed to be wrong. [102]

---

97 Cf. *Sandgruber, R.* (1995): Ökonomie und Politik Österreichische Wirtschaftsgeschichte vom Mittelalter bis zur Gegenwart, Vienna, p. 367.

98 Cf. Ibid., p. 389.

99 Cf. Oesterreichischer Versicherungs-Almanach 1932, Vienna, p 7.

100 Cf. Oesterreichischer Versicherungs-Almanach 1933, Vienna, p. 9.

101 Cf. Oesterreichischer Versicherungs-Almanach 1931, Vienna, p. 7.

102 Cf. *Sandgruber, R.* (1995), Ökonomie und Politik Österreichische Wirtschaftsgeschichte vom Mittelalter bis zur Gegenwart, Vienna, p. 390.

11.3 The first phase of group formation: the example of the „Wiener Städtische Wechselseitige Versicherungsanstalt“

The “Städtische Kaiser Franz Joseph-Jubiläums-Lebens- und Renten-Versicherungs-Anstalt” was established under the Viennese mayor *Karl Lueger* in 1898 on the 50-year jubilee of the Emperor *Franz Joseph*. At this time, it belonged to the governmental district of Lower Austria. Its rise coincides with the foundation of Vienna as a federal state in 1922. Already, in 1919 the company changed its name to “Gemeinde Wien - Städtische Versicherungsanstalt”. The name change, on the one hand, was meant to signify a new start for the company. On the other hand, the deletion of the characteristic phrase “Lebens- und Rentenversicherungsanstalt” meant that from now on non-life insurances were also offered.[103]

In addition to appointing a director, a new more efficient supervisory board was established. This reorganization included a downsizing of the organizational structure, i.e. the board of management was reduced from 15 to six members and a supervisory board of three members was created. At the same time, the new Versicherungsregulativ (1921) made non-life insurances possible, starting with a contract in 1922 when the “Erste n.ö. Brandschaden-Versicherungsaktiengesellschaft” was established. Already the contract of 1897 contained such as clause. The contract had been agreed on by the “Wiener Magistrat” (city Viennese town administration) and the “Niederösterreichische Landesausschuss” (Lower Austrian federal committee). It stated that the city council of Vienna pays 65 percent of the foundation costs and in return, the future Viennese fire insurance company is going to receive the existing portfolio of the fire insured buildings.[104] With that, it was possible to transfer holdings within the later established group for the first time. Additional non-life insurances such as burglary (1922), accident, third-party insurance, and vehicle insurance (1923) as well as glass insurance (1924) were offered for the first time. In 1925, transport, hail, and cattle insurances followed. At the same time as the expansion of the business, the headquarters in Graz, Linz, Innsbruck, and Salzburg were converted into regional offices and new ones were founded in Carinthia and Lower Austria. To cope with the increasing administrative work caused by the growth, the “Gemeinde Wien - Städtische Versicherungsanstalt” introduced as the first Austrian insurance company a punch card system (including the necessary technology) in 1929. With these innovations

[103] Cf. *Lehner, P.*, Der Konzern der Wiener Städtischen – Ein Wegbereiter des österreichischen Versicherungswesens, in: Versicherungsgeschichte Österreichs, vol. III, Das Zeitalter des modernen Versicherungswesens, Vienna 1988, p. 1051.

[104] Ibid., p. 1052.

the "Gemeinde Wien - Städtische Versicherungsanstalt" rose to the rank of one of Austria's top insurers of the interwar period of the First Republic.[105] Strengthened by the new efficient organizational structure, the "Gemeinde Wien - Städtische Versicherungsanstalt" started to support endangered insurance companies and at the same time to continue the formation of its company as a group:

- In 1929, the company took part in the rescue operation of the "Union Allgemeine Versicherungs-AG", whose owner, the German Frankfurter insurance group[106], was bankrupted.
- In 1934, the "Wiener Wechselseitigen Krankenversicherungsanstalt auf Gegenseitigkeit" became part of the enterprise and got involved into the health insurance business (1956 contract of merger)
- In 1934, the company established the Leichenkostenverein "Vorsorge" (funeral provision society)
- In 1936, the company participated when the "Oevag Österreichische Versicherungs-Aktiengesellschaft" (ÖVAG), the rescue company for the life insurance company "Lebens-Phönix", was established.
- In 1938, the company merged with the mutual life insurance society "Wechselseitigen Brandschaden und Janus" to escape the merger with the German economic group of public insurances and was renamed in "Wiener Städtische und Wechselseitige Janus allgemeine Versicherungs-Anstalt auf Gegenseitigkeit".

Due to this merger, the "Wiener Städtische und Wechselseitige Janus allgemeine Versicherungs-Anstalt auf Gegenseitigkeit" had to be reorganized, on the one hand, to be valid as an acceptable mutual insurance society, and on the other hand, not to lose the traditional connection with the Viennese town administration. The new organization signified also the rising authoritarian principle regarding the structure of companies. To show the mutuality principle publicly a members' council was introduced as the highest body, however, the company tried to avoid laborious elections. Therefore, it was decided that the Viennese mayor could appoint the primary members' council. With that, the authoritarian principle was evident. The members' council appointed the supervisory board, but with the guideline that the members of the board had to come from employees of the Viennese district or town administration. The supervisory board appointed the management board, a body that was introduced by the German insurance supervision act.

105 Ibid., p. 1067f.

106 "Frankfurter Allgemeine Versicherungs- AG" and "Frankfurter Lebensversicherungs-AG".

The Viennese mayor acted as the chairman of the supervision act due to its political position.[107]

With that, it was possible that in addition to the Viennese mayor as chairman of the supervisory board the bylaws stated that

- the Viennese supervision department was responsible for the continuous supervision of the management
- the administration had small influence on the organization of the balance sheet
- the historical connection to Vienna maintained.[108]

This is an instrumentality of the mutuality principle. In 1942, the former name of the company was changed to "Wiener Städtische Wechselseitige Versicherungsanstalt".

The development to a large mutual group can be shown by the following mergers:[109]

- With the "Anglo-Danubian Lloyd Allgemeine Versicherungs-Aktiengesellschaft" (1938) and the
- 1940 take-over of the life insurance portfolio of the "Allgemeine wechselseitige Versicherungsbank Transsylvania"
- "Wiener Verein Lebens- und Bestattungsversicherung auf Gegenseitigkeit" (1956).

The development of the "Wiener Städtische Wechselseitige Versicherungsanstalt" to a group has three steps:

- cross-wide
- cross-divisional
- mergers

[107] Ibid., p. 1064.
[108] Ibid., p. 1065.
[109] Ibid., p. 1066.

11.4 The bankruptcy of the "Phönix" life insurance company in 1936

The Phoenix is a mythical fire bird who is indestructible and able to revive itself out of its ashes.[110] Several Austrian companies used the name to suggest an image of security, constancy, and indestructibility.

The "k.k. priv. Versicherungsgesellschaft "Österreichischer Phönix"" was established in 1860 as a subsidiary of the Dresdner fire insurance company. It started with the life insurance business in 1867. When in 1868 its parent company had financial problems, a committee of Austrian industrialists bought the Phönix. In 1881, the Phönix had financial difficulties caused by the depression after the stock market crash in 1873 and was bought by the "Azienda Assecuratrice", which founded in 1889 two new legally independent joint stock companies, the non-life company "Elementar-Phönix" and the life insurance company "Lebens-Phönix".[111] The latter expanded its business continuously and soon after its foundation, it had business connections across borders and in every important centres, for example in Italy, Alsace-Lorraine, the Orient, and Germany. This fast internationalization was possible due to the take-over of several insurance portfolios of other companies, a strategy that it used during the next decades.[112]

With a market share of almost 67 percent[113], the "Lebens-Phönix" became the largest life insurer in Austria and the third largest in Europe during the inter-war period. Similar to the Creditanstalt's strategy, this was based on a dangerous expansion policy in the succession states of the former monarchy. This was in particular true for the purchase of customer portfolios with high risks. The "Lebens-Phönix" engaged in high-risk speculative transactions without restrain and did not shy away from corruption. Due to a co-optation system the governmental supervision bodies became inactive and so the loss of 250 Million Schilling was concealed.

The main reason for the failure of this strategy was the key person itself: executive director *Wilhelm Berliner*. Originally, he wanted to increase the prosperity of the impoverished Austrian state by establishing an Austrian insurance empire. However, with his huge ambition

---

110 Cf. *Lembke, H.* (2016), Ph2nix, Wiener und Berliner, Wiesbaden, p. 1.

111 Cf. *Rohrbach, W.* (1988), Versicherungsgeschichte Österreichs, vol. I, Von den Anfängen bis zum Börsenkrach des Jahres 1873, Vienna, p. 416.

112 Cf. *Lembke, H.* (2016), Phönix, Wiener und Berliner, Wiesbaden, p. 129.

113 The portion of the "Lebensversicherungs-Gesellschaft Phönix" regarding the total of domestic insurance companies increased from 9.5 percent in 1913 to 67 percent in 1934. (Cf. *Roloff, M.* (1988), Die Entwicklung der Lebensversicherungin Österreich zwischen 1873 und 1936, in: Versicherungsgeschichte Österreichs vol. II, Die Ära des klassischen Versicherungswesen, Vienna, p. 560.)

to transform the "Lebens-Phönix" into the largest insurance company on the continent he used gambling methods and practiced an extreme dumping policy regarding insurance contracts. He offered the policyholders insurance contracts, which were not economic. Additionally, he deceived the customers and the creditors with falsified balance sheets. After *Berliner's* death in February 1936, the house of cards collapsed and the "Lebens-Phönix" went bankrupt.[114]

The government and the insurers agreed that immediate action had to be taken to prevent both panic reactions of the policyholders, in particular pensioners, as well as a complete image loss for life insurances. The result was a solidarity solution, an enormous joint effort to overcome the problems. Thus, another step was taken to treat joint stock companies and mutuals in a parallel way. At the end of April 1936, the "Oevag Österreichische Versicherungs-AG" (ÖVAG) was established as a rescue company by an insurance and bank consortium and without a federal level. The "Oevag Österreichische Versicherungs-AG" (ÖVAG) was supposed to take over the financial commitments of the customers and pensioner in Austria as quickly as possible. The company took over the business without larger losses.[115] Only foreign customers of the "Lebens-Phönix" were not taken care off by Austria.[116] Two banks, the "Creditanstalt" and the "Österreichisches Creditinstitut" as well as two insurance companies, the "Assicurazioni Generali" as a joint stock company and the "Gemeinde Wien - Städtische Versicherungsanstalt" as a mutual society contributed two-third of the share portfolio.[117] However, a solidarity solution means including of all main players on the insurance market. With the "insurance fund act", a solidarity liability of all insurers[118], their employees, and customers, was introduced to secure the insurance service for the next 25 years. A 4 percent surcharge on all premiums of all insurance types as well as a 2 percent discount on damage payments was made. Additionally, the salaries of insurance employees were reduced up to 25 percent. The money receiving from the surcharges and discounts was allocated to the fund from which the insurance services of the "Lebens-Phönix" were paid. The government

[114] Cf. Ibid. The deficit of the Phönix was a twentieth of the annual national product. A third of the insurance policies were affected by this scandal and 1,300 of the employees lost their job. (Cf. *Lembke, H.* (2016), Phönix, Wiener und Berliner, Wiesbaden, p. 134.)

[115] Cf. Ibid., p. 234.

[116] Cf. Ibid., p. 222. A briefly considered foundation of a German-Austrian rescue company, with a large participation of "Münchner Rück", "Allianz" und "Elementar-Phönix" did not take place. (Cf. Ibid.).

[117] Cf. Ibid., p. 134.

[118] On the active side of the ÖVAG assets of 269 Million Schilling existed, from them 250 Million were obligations, which were covered by a permanent share of the costs by all Austrian insurers. (Cf. Ibid.).

strengthened its supervision of the insurance industry by transferring the jurisdiction from the Federal Chancellor's Office to the finance ministry in September 1936.[119] With the "Lebens-Phönix" bankruptcy, the image of insurers became worse and led to more governmental supervision and to a reform of the private insurance system, which eventually led to a stronger supervision of insurance companies.[120]

However, all these stronger supervision measures due to the Phönix scandal came hardly into effect. With the "Anschluss" of Austria by *Hitler* in March 1938, Austrian law was replaced respectively on March 1st with German law, which supervision act was characterized by a much severer and stricter governmental supervision.

11.5 The effects of the "Anschluss" in 1938

With the integration of Austria into the Third Reich, the insurance companies became part of a market, in which they were only a small part of a much larger insurance industry. With that, a process of adjusting was necessary. At the same time, the first phase of an independent Austrian insurance supervision ended.[121] Due to the law "Gesetz über die Wiedervereinigung Österreichs mit dem Deutschen Reich" the German insurance supervision act (Deutsches Versicherungsaufsichtsgesetz VAG 1931) was issued on March 1st, 1939. Austria did not have a supervision law of its own, however, only because of the practice of the supervision authority and several regulations concerning insurance business a supervision law developed.[122] In the German supervision act which was put in effect, the mutual insurance society was defined as a legal form for insurance business (§§ 15 and following paragraphs). Additionally, the members' relationship (§ 20), the principle of equality (§ 21), and the society's bodies (§ 29) were regulated. All other insurance laws, such as the Versicherungsregulativ 1921 were abolished, including the regulations regarding mutual associations (Vereinspatent 1852).[123] The Supervisory Office in Berlin carried out the insurance supervision.

---

119 Cf. Ibid.

120 Cf. *Fenyves, A. / Korinek, S.* (1999), Das österreichische Versicherungsaufsichtsrecht im Überblick, in: Zeitschrift für Verwaltung, 24. Jahrgang 2/99, p. 160f.

121 Cf. *Baran, P.* (2015), Das Österreichische Versicherungsaufsichtsrecht, Vienna, p. 1f.

122 Cf. *Kraus, H.* (1971), Versicherungsaufsichtsrecht – Eine Studie zum deutschen und zum österreichischen Recht, in: Forschungen aus Staat und Recht, vol. 16, Vienna, p. 15.

123 Cf. Ibid.

A practical reorganization of insurance companies in Austria[124] was supposed to happen via dissolutions, mergers, new foundations, by determining the jurisdiction of the bodies, and the regulation of the supervision. This also included the insurance societies based on the Vereinspatent from 1852. Since 1942, it was possible that provincial fire insurance societies (Landes-Brandschadenversicherungsanstalten) with the exception of Styria and Vienna converted into a public insurance company[125], a legal form that was unknown in Austria at this time. The main goal was to bring all Austrian insurance companies into line with the German insurance industry. All foreign connections were ended and to take out insurances in foreign countries was regarded as a crime and punished severely. The main reason for such a forced loyalty was the intention to provide large capital reserves to the insurance companies of the war industry. Most of the Austrian insurance companies were liquidated compulsory and their customer portfolios and capital were transferred to German companies.

Institutions and societies that made an effort to continue the Austrian insurance tradition, for example the "Österreichische Gesellschaft für Versicherungsfachwissen", were closed and their capital was confiscated. Employees who resisted where imprisoned or put into concentration camps.

With regard to this transformation process of the insurance companies, it is important to note that many mutual support societies in Austria based legally on the Vereinsgesetz 1867.[126] However, with the "Gesetz über die Überleitung und Eingliederung von Vereinen, Organisationen und Verbände"[127], these societies were based legally on a new regulation that determined that these organizations had to be orientated according to the NS-politics under the supervision of the Stillhaltekommissär[128]. By 1940, the realization of this law had enormous consequences for 1,400 mutual insurance societies. Approximately 1,000 societies, which had almost a tenth of the Austrian population as members, were dissolved, an act that was considered as a disruption for the political and economic growth of the Ostmark. [129]

---

[124] LGBl. 178/1938.

[125] *Kraus, H.* (1971), Versicherungsaufsichtsrecht – Eine Studie zum deutschen und zum österreichischen Recht, in: Forschungen aus Staat und Recht, vol. 16, Vienna, p. 176.

[126] With the exception of Brandschaden- and Viehversicherungsvereine.

[127] LGBl. 136/1938.

[128] Cf. *Lehner, U.* (1988), Österreichische Versicherungswirtschaft im Deutschen Reich, in: Versicherungsgeschichte Österreichs, vol. III, Das Zeitalter des modernen Versicherungswesens, Vienna, p. 682.

[129] Schlußbericht der Überleitungsstelle für die 67er Vereine mit Versicherungs- oder versicherungsähnlichen Einrichtungen in der Ostmark, Vienna 1940, p. 18. Quoted in *Lehner, U.* (1988), Österreichische Versicherungswirtschaft im Deutschen Reich,

At the same time, a large amount of assets were withdrawn from the societies and transferred to national socialist organizations such as "Reichsbund der deutschen Beamten", the "Deutscher Arbeiterfront", or the "Aufbaufonds Vermögensverwaltungs-Gesellschaft m.b.H." due to political reasons.[130]

The created status quo maintained after 1945, although the law from June 25, 1952 (BGBl 127/1952) regarding the re-establishment of an independent, free, and democratic Austria a re-establishing of this societies would have permitted.[131] With that a long tradition of mutual supporting societies, which can be found in many other countries today, was lost forever.

The large 1852 societies, in combination with small 1852 societies and several 1867 societies were transformed, according to the German insurance supervision law, into mutual insurance societies. For example, the "Österreichische Beamtenversicherung", the "Collegialität Krankenversicherung auf Gegenseitigkeit", the "Jupiter", or the later "Merkur Wechselseitige Krankenversicherungs-Anstalt" were converted.[132]

However, in this period developments in a different direction, i.e. establishing mutuality, can also be found such as the merger of the "Gemeinde Wien - Städtische Versicherungsanstalt", with the "Wechselseitigen Brandschaden und Janus“ which is the best example how it was occasionally possible to cross the plans of the Nazi government. In this case, the starting point was the imminent threat of integrating the "Gemeinde Wien - Städtische Versicherungsanstalt" into the association of public insurances due to its close connection to the Viennese City council. The "Wechselseitige Brandschaden", on the other hand, should have been integrated into the German "Gothaer Lebensversicherungs-Bank a.G." insurance society. However, the "Gemeinde Wien - Städtische Versicherungsanstalt" was able to establish a members' representation in the last minute, which enabled this insurance company to argue against a merger with German public institutions and in favour to existing mutual insurance societies.[133] With that and after a change of the bylaws a jumbo merger of the "Gemeinde Wien - Städtische Versicherungsanstalt" with the "Wechselseitige Brandschaden", and the "Janus" became possible in November 1938. As a result, in conformity with a patriotic system the foundation of an Austrian insurance corporation was possible.[134]

in: Versicherungsgeschichte Österreichs, vol. III, Das Zeitalter des modernen Versicherungswesens, Vienna, p. 689.

[130] Cf. Ibid., p. 690ff.

[131] Cf. Ibid.

[132] Cf. Ibid.

[133] Cf. Ibid.

[134] Cf. Ibid.

11.6 The development after World War II

After 1945, in most of the European states a state-controlled and partly administered economy was imposed. This was a result of the wartime economy and the economy of short supply and a completely different situation compared to the time after 1918. The economy became more centralized and nationalized, in particular in the basic industry built and developed during the period of National Socialism, and in the oil and electricity economy. While the major banks were concerned, insurance companies were excluded from this development, because due to the high losses of assets during the war, no actions seemed to be needed. Moreover, insurers were not the primary goal of the compensation demands of the Allied Forces.

With this type of economic policy, a Golden Age with high growth rates started in Austria that lasted until 1973. The main instruments were

- the Marshall-Plan, European Recovery Program commonly referred to as the ERP that initiated since 1947 financial investments and an increase in productivity,
- a restrictive monetary stability policy (1945-1951),
- a radical wages and price policy,
- the "Social Partnership", i.e. the institutionalized co-operation between the representations of employers and labour in Austria,
- an Austro-Keynesianism with the *Raab-Kamitz*-course.[135]

A crucial element during this period was the further fate of the "German property", i.e. all assets and enterprises at which a third party had a stake of more than 10 percent. In the insurance industry this comprised

- the German property before 1938
- the property of the German Reich created due to transfer of ownerships and new foundations on Austrian soil
- of private assets that became German assets after Austria became part of the Third Reich.

The insurance portfolios and the assets had to be divided. It was only possible to re-convert German property into Austrian assets.[136] Addi-

[135] Cf. *Rathkolb, O.* (2015), Die paradoxe Republik: Österreich 1945 bis 2015, Aktualisierte Neuausgabe, Vienna.

[136] Cf. *Lehner, P.* (1988), Das Versicherungswesen in der Zweiten Republik, in: Versicherungsgeschichte Österreichs, vol. III, Das Zeitalter des modernen Versicherungswesens, Vienna, p. 828ff. The branches of German companies were under pub-

tionally, the insurance industry had become to a high degree creditor of the German Reich due to the compulsory capital investments in war loans.[137]

The consolidation of the Austrian insurance industry after 1945 was characterized by problems in politics and economy such as inflation and unsolved financial circumstances and unclear ownerships. The Austrian insurance industry had to be rebuilt and completely reorganized. The war had caused considerable losses for the individual insurance companies. On the one hand, premiums were not paid and forcibly drawn war bonds and collateral damages (interest bearing houses and flats) had to be compensated. In fact, the insurance industry was bankrupt, that way its reconstruction became a public task. The state received powers of intervention into existing insurance relationships due to an amendment oft the insurance supervision Act in 1949.

While in the property and casualty insurance and health insurance sector, the situation stabilized by the beginning of the 1950s, the life insurance sector had many problems. The latter was characterized by an unclear situation regarding the insurance portfolios from before 1946, the question of the government bonds and their unearned premium reserve as well as the rapid inflation between 1945 and 1952. The currency protection law from 1947 (Währungsschutzgesetz) was a major tool for the survival of insurances.[138] While the premiums of property and casualty and health insurances quadrupled between 1945 and 1955 (1945: 50, 1955: 225) and the payment increased tenfold in real terms (1945: 12, 1955: 125), the results of the life insurance in 1955 in real terms (39) were lower compared to 1945 (44). The life insurance became so an insignificant part of the property and casualty insurance.[139]

lic administration and the companies were only allowed to look after but not to expand their insurance portfolios.

137 Cf. *Rohrbach*, W. (1988), Gesundheitswesen und Privatversicherung in Österreich, in: Versicherungsgeschichte Österreichs, vol. III, Das Zeitalter des modernen Versicherungswesens, Vienna, p. 876.

138 Everyone was allowed to exchange 150 old Schilling into 150 new Austrian Schilling, any additional amount of money was exchange with the ratio 3:1.

139 *Stiefel, D.* (2006), Der Wiederaufbau der österreichischen Versicherungswirtschaft 1945-1955, in: *Stiefel, D.* (ed.), "Unusual Business", Vienna, p. 256.

Table 3: Premiums of the direct domestic business and payments 1945-1955 in million Austrian Schilling

Year	Total premiums	From them		Insurance payment	From them	
		Life	Non-life		Life	Non-life
1945	94	44	50	25	13	12
1946	174	66	108	72	35	37
1947	281	67	214	114	39	74
1948	391	70	320	162	42	120
1949	501	85	416	169	30	139
1950	423	101	322	244	35	210
1951	802	121	681	284	40	245
1952	993	145	848	397	42	355
1953	1.191	174	1.017	515	49	466
1954	1.394	208	1.186	603	43	550
1955	1.645	245	1.400	839	62	777

Table 4: Mio. Schilling real: consumer price index 1945=100

Year	Total premiums	From them		Insurance payment	From them	
		Life	Non-life		Life	Non-life
1955	264	39	225	135	10	125

Source: *Hollmayer, A.* (2000), Makrodaten der Österreichischen Assekuranz 1875-2000, in: Versicherungsgeschichte Österreichs, vol. 6, An der Schwelle zum 3. Jahrtausend – Retrospektiven und Perspektiven, Vienna, p. 1407f.

The main challenge was the legal reconstruction of the Austrian insurance industry. The major part of the active (Reichsanleihen[140]) was devalued, while the obligations continued to exist. Life insurances were concerned mostly from this problem.[141] In this situation, a financial

[140] Almost 70 percent of the in 1944 working insurance companies had government bonds. (Cf. *Mahlberg, B.* (2006), Analyse der Finanzlage österreichischer Versicherungsunternehmenin den Jahren 1944 bis 1955, in: *Stiefel, D.* (ed.), "Unusual Business", p. 295).

[141] For them, the Reich bonds made up 72 percent of the total reserves. (Cf. Ibid.)

statement was not possible and an international regulation was necessary for the definition of the insurance portfolio and the guarantee stock.[142] This was possible when the unclear ownerships and the separation of the insurance assets with the German insurance companies were solved by the international treaty and the law regarding the reconstruction of the insurance industry in 1955 (Versicherungswiederaufbaugesetz)[143]. This law established a unified regulation for the war losses of all insurance companies and enabled them the restoration of their business with the help of public funding. The organization structure of the insurance industry was re-regulated and economic processes were controlled. The insurance companies were now able to do a reconstructing financial statement with profit and loss accounts for the time 1945 to 1954, which was the basis for the first financial statement in Austrian Schilling. With that, the necessary requirements for a fast upswing of the insurance industry were established. If it was not possible to establish a balanced financial statement, then the government had to help with loans and funding. For that, the government made 356 million Schilling available. However, only two domestic companies the "Oevag Österreichische Versicherungs-Aktiengesellschaft" (ÖVAG), and the "Österreichische Volksfürsorge" and a foreign life insurance company needed this kind of help.[144]

After the reconstruction phase was finished, the activities of the insurance industry returned to normal. Now the still existing legal regulations from the period of National Socialism were replaced by Austrian norms: in 1959, the law on insurance contracts was enacted, 1979 the amended insurance supervision act.[145]

11.7 The second phase of group formations: the example of the "Austria Versicherungsverein auf Gegenseitigkeit"

Until World War I, the private health insurers in the monarchy were insignificant due to the introduction of the statuary health insurance

---

[142] Cf. *Stiefel, D.* (2006), Der Wiederaufbau der österreichischen Versicherungswirtschaft 1945-1955, in: *Stiefel, D.* (ed.), "Unusual Business", Vienna, p. 257.

[143] BGBl. Nr. 185/1955. It determined a shortening of the life insurances established before January 1st, 1946 of 60 percent, similar to the procedures of cash and bank account.

[144] Cf. *Stiefel, D.* (2006), Der Wiederaufbau der österreichischen Versicherungswirtschaft 1945-1955, in: *Stiefel, D.* (ed.), "Unusual Business", p. 262.

[145] Cf. *Lehner, P.* (1988), Das Versicherungswesen in der Zweiten Republik, in: Versicherungsgeschichte Österreichs, vol. III, Das Zeitalter des modernen Versicherungswesens, Vienna, p. 847f.

(1884). However, the consequences of the war opened them new business lines due to the poverty of the middle class. Nevertheless, compared to other sectors the private health insurance until 1945 had no economic upswing, therefore, no joint stock company was established. The existing supporting associations, with the exception of middle class societies "Mittelstandskrankenverein vom Gelben Kreuz" (founded in 1919 and converted in "Krankenschutz - Erste Allgemeine Krankenversicherungsanstalt auf Gegenseitigkeit" in 1921) and the "Wiener Wechselseitigen Krankenversicherungsanstalt auf Gegenseitigkeit", which had already cross-country business, had only local significance.[146] Other exceptions were the "Merkur Wechselseitige Krankenversicherungs-Anstalt", which was founded in 1789 to support poor trade employees in Graz and the "Collegialität Krankenversicherung auf Gegenseitigkeit", founded in 1899 by the "Verein österreichischer Handelsangestellter" (Society of Austrian trade employees).[147]

The "Krankenschutz - Erste Allgemeine Krankenversicherungsanstalt auf Gegenseitigkeit" developed continuously to become the largest private insurance company in Austria. In 1937, it had approximately 67,000 members and offices in 6 provinces. After 1938, it was merged with the "Münchener Verein Lebens- und Altersversicherungsanstalt a.G." due to the "Stillhalteabkommen".

After World War II, its re-establishing was not possible and to avoid problems when transferring the portfolios of the "Münchener Verein Lebens- und Altersversicherungsanstalt a.G." to the reactivated insurer – the danger was that the entire portfolio would be confiscated by Allied Forces Troops[148] –, it was decided to establish a new insurance society. To minimize difficulties when transferring the former members of the "Krankenschutz", the legal form of a mutual society was chosen. Therefore, it was possible to argue that the policyholders were as members the legal assets owners.[149] To make it clear that this was an Austrian insurance company for the Austrian population, the firm "Austria Versicherungsverein auf Gegenseitigkeit"[150] was chosen, which already had in 1948 139,000 members and a premium income of 13 million Schilling. This made it the top private health insurer concerning the expansion of the range of services as well as the premium increase. Until 1970, the number of members increased to 428,000 and

---

146 Cf. *Dickinger, G.* (1999), Vom Krankenversicherer zum Gesundheitssicherer, Linz, p. 37.

147 Cf. Ibid.

148 Cf. *Rohrbach*, W. (1988), Gesundheitswesen und Privatversicherung in Österreich, in: Versicherungsgeschichte Österreichs, vol. III, Das Zeitalter des modernen Versicherungswesens, Vienna, p. 879.

149 Cf. Ibid., p. 881.

150 Cf. *Dickinger, G.* (1999), Vom Krankenversicherer zum Gesundheitssicherer, Linz, p. 70.

the premium income increased to 445 million Schilling.[151] This increase was possible in spite of the expansion of the social security. The losses of policyholders with complete insurances could be replaced by supplementary insurances, i.e. with expansion of the welfare state the private health insurance expanded too. The period between 1955 and 1975 was signified by an exorbitant expansion of the private health insurance segment and by a sharp increase of premium incomes. The premium volume increased from 178 million Schilling in 1955 to 1.652 million Schilling in 1970.[152] Between 1965 and 1975 the highest growth of new customers occurred.[153]

During this period of economic boom, the insurance sectors expanded. For example, the "Austria Versicherungsverein auf Gegenseitigkeit" developed very fast to a composite insurer.[154] The development to a composite insurer was possible because in 1959 the company bought 80 percent of the share of the "Oevag Österreichische Versicherungs-Aktiengesellschaft" (ÖVAG) from the Austrian Republic. A connection of both enterprises offered the chance for large future economic success of an Austrian all-round insurer. 1960, the "ÖVAG" was renamed "Austria Österreichische Versicherung AG" after recapitalization. With that, it was possible to expand its business to the non-life and life insurance sector. It was the beginning of the Austria-Versicherungskonzerns.[155] By 1964, the "Austria Versicherungsverein auf Gegenseitigkeit" increased its ÖVAG's parcel of stocks to 95 percent and in 1974, it took over the remaining 5 percent. In 1961, the "Austria Versicherungsverein auf Gegenseitigkeit" took over the branch offices of the former German companies "Leipziger Verein-Barmenia", "Mittelstandshilfe", and the "Münchener Verein" from the Austrian Republic.

Soon the question rose, if the Austrian insurance industry should be contended with staying on a small local market. In the 1960s, the "Austria Versicherungsverein auf Gegenseitigkeit" developed health insurance products, which allowed the company to build up business connections to countries with a larger insurance tradition (Italy, West Germany, and Switzerland). The goal of the "Austria Versicherungsverein auf Gegenseitigkeit" was always to strengthen the own capital above average and to use this capital to expand its market position

---

151 Cf. Ibid., p. 71.

152 Cf. *Rohrbach*, W. (1988), Gesundheitswesen und Privatversicherung in Österreich, in: Versicherungsgeschichte Österreichs, vol. III, Das Zeitalter des modernen Versicherungswesens, Vienna, p. 929.

153 Cf. Ibid., p. 948.

154 Cf. *Dickinger, G.* (1999), Vom Krankenversicherer zum Gesundheitssicherer, Linz, p. 71.

155 Cf. *Rohrbach*, W. (1988), Von der ÖVAG zur Austria-ÖVAG, in: Versicherungsgeschichte Österreichs, vol. III, Das Zeitalter des modernen Versicherungswesens, Vienna, p. 743ff.

internationally by establishing subsidiary companies in foreign countries. In 1966, the company established its first foreign subsidiary, the Austria Assicurazioni S.p.A. with its head office in Milano. By mixing in the line with demand of service and special products in the health insurance segment, the company was able to be successful in Italy, the traditional insurance country, and to gain profits already in 1973.[156] In 1971, another branch as health insurer followed in Switzerland (with an additional insurance for disability and active re-insurance and by establishing the Spanish Austrian subsidiary "Chasyr Salud S. A." in 1985.[157]

Dr. Herbert Schimetschek is one of the prestigious figures of the Austrian financial sector and had formed the history of the insurance business over decades. Alongside of the development of the "Austria Versicherungsverein auf Gegenseitigkeit" his career as the responsible manager is worth looking at more closely. His career path is a mirror of the group foundation from the "Austria Versicherungsverein auf Gegenseitigkeit" to the "UNIQA Versicherungen AG". He regarded the mutuality principle in the insurance industry as a management tool and knew how to use it as an instrument for the creation of an insurance group from the insurance holding construction within asset management (1991) to an insurance holding construction within a private foundation (2005).

During his law studies at the University of Vienna, he started to work at the "Austria Versicherungsverein auf Gegenseitigkeit" in 1957. 1959, the "Austria Versicherungsverein auf Gegenseitigkeit" bought 80 percent of the shares of the "Österreichische Versicherungs-Aktiengesellschaft" (ÖVAG) and changed the name to "Austria Österreichische Versicherung AG".[158] In 1977, *Schimetschek* became in addition to be chairperson in the "Austria Versicherungsverein auf Gegenseitigkeit" also chairperson of the joint stock company. He held this position until 1991, when the operative insurance business of the "Austria Versicherungsverein auf Gegenseitigkeit" and the "COLLEGIALITÄT Versicherungsverein auf Gegenseitigkeit" were transferred into the joint stock company "Austria-COLLEGIALITÄT Versicherungen AG" in which he became director and CEO. In the same year, the two mutual societies moved their assets into asset management societies in which *Schimetschek* became also the director. In 1991, Schimetschek was director of the "Austria Österreichische Versicherung AG" and

[156] Cf. *Rohrbach*, W. (1988), Von der ÖVAG zur Austria-ÖVAG, in: Versicherungsgeschichte Österreichs, vol. III, Das Zeitalter des modernen Versicherungswesens, Vienna, p. 950.

[157] Cf. *Dickinger, G.* (1999), Vom Krankenversicherer zum Gesundheitssicherer, Linz, p. 71.

[158] Cf. Ibid; Versicherungs-Compass 1960.

of the "Austria Versicherungssverein auf Gegenseitigkeit" as well as Generalrat of the "Oesterreichische Nationalbank".[159] Since 1991 he was also Sparkassenrat of the Erste Österreichische Spar-Casse and which established in 1993 a joint stock company ("Ersten Österreichischen Spar-Casse - Bank AG") and an asset management society ("Anteilsverwaltung der Ersten oesterreichischen Spar-Casse"). He was crucial for the conversion of the "Anteilsverwaltung" into the "DIE ERSTE österreichische Spar-Casse Privatstiftung", i.e. "ERSTE Stiftung", in 2003. 1997, the "Austria-COLLEGIALITÄT Versicherungen" and the "Versicherungsanstalt der österreichischen Bundesländer AG" merged to the "Barc Versicherungs-Holding AG", in which *Schimetschek* became director and CEO from 1997 to 1999. In 1997, he held, in addition to other functions, the following positions: CEO of the "Austria-COLLEGIALITÄT Versicherungen", CEO of the "Versicherungsanstalt der österreichischen Bundesländer AG", and chairperson of "BARC Versicherungs-Holding AG".[160] In 1999, the "UNIQA Versicherungen AG" emerged, which was under his management as chief executive director and chairperson until 2001.[161] *Schimetschek* resigned as CEO of the supervisory board of the Erste Bank with August 31, 2003 due to his new position as president of the Oesterreichische Nationalbank.[162] When in 2005, the "AUSTRIA Versicherungsverein Beteiligungs-Verwaltungs GmbH" was established as a 100 percent subsidiary of the "UNIQA Versicherungsverein Privatstiftung", i.e. the former asset management society "Austria Versicherungsverein auf Gegenseitigkeit", *Schimetschek* became chairperson of the GmbH as well as director of the private foundation. He was also chair of the supervisory board of the UNIQA group from 2006 to 2008.[163] In 2011, *Schimetschek* resigned from all his position but stays honorary president of the "UNIQA Versicherungsverein Privatstiftung", although he is now 82 years old.

159 Cf. Personen-Compass 1990/1991; Governors and Presidents of the Osterreichische Nationalbank. Vienna 2015.

160 Cf. Personen-Compass 1997.

161 http://www.uniqagroup.com/gruppe/versicherung/press/press_release/archive/adpa_bilanzpk99_veraenderungen_vorstand.de.html (06.12.2019)

162 https://www.derstandard.at/story/1347167/portraet-herbert-schimetschek-folgt-adolf-wala; https://www.erstegroup.com/content/dam/at/eh/www_erstegroup_com/de/ir/2003/News_de/IR_News_030903de.pdf (06.12.2019)

163 http://www.uniqagroup.com/gruppe/versicherung/press/press_release/archive/adpa_bilanzpk99_veraenderungen_vorstand.de.html (06.12.2019)

11.8 The foundation of the "Österreichische Beamtenversicherung" (Austrian civil servant insurance company)

In the Austro-Hungarian monarchy and in contrast to Germany, civil servants were most important for the development of mutual insurance companies. The group of civil servants were the only part of the population that had since 1848 disadvantages during a time of general economic and social developments.[164] Although a large administrative machinery was needed for enforcing a centralist public administration and while the number of civil servants increased rapidly (mass civil service), their salary maintained on the level of 1848. Due to the inflation caused by the war, the lower civil servants impoverished and were at the mercy of profiteering people. Even the middle civil servant had to live with considerable restrictions and the higher civil servant suffered losses compared to a former good livelihood. In general, civil servants were confronted with a pre-March 1848 era tradition in particular regarding their insufficient employment law, which had numerous different salary levels, as well as with an unquestioning faith in governmental authority. Moreover, the number of private civil servants had increased immensely with the construction of new railways, the foundations of banks, credit institutions, and industrial enterprises, were confronted by a price rise of rents and food. Therefore, the question of improving their circumstances became a crucial question.

Only after the reintroduction of the constitutionalism in 1860, civil servants had the opportunity to improve their situation legally, in particular by founding associations and societies, which helped them to survive economically. In addition to a consumer cooperative (1861) and a thrift and loan association (1862), the "Erster allgemeine Kranken- und Leichenverein für k.k. Beamte in Wien" (1863) and in 1864 the "Verein zur gegenseitigen Kranken- und Lebensversicherung" were established to guarantee sick pay and life insurance as well as to establish a thrift and loan department.[165] In addition, a connection between the principles of mutuality and self-help according to *Schulze-Delitzsch* developed. The main goal was to guarantee economic supporting instruments with reasonable shopping facilities, credit granting and help in the event of illness and death of family members.

At first, most of the civil servants were sceptical regarding the principle of self-help practiced by societies, because they were used to wait for help from above. This hierarchical way of thinking was opposed to

[164] Cf. Gedenkschrift zum fünfzigjährigen Bestände des Ersten allgemeinen Beamten-Vereines der österreichisch-ungarischen Monarchie, Vienna 1915, p. 1.

[165] Cf. *Rohrbach, W.* (1988), Versicherungsgeschichte Österreichs, vol. I, Von den Anfängen bis zum Börsenkrach des Jahres 1873, Vienna, p. 359.

this new type of organizational structures of achieving self-help. This mistrust had two possible effects: firstly, it could prevent the foundations of societies if civil servants with strict beliefs in authority had main decision position, and secondly, potential society members, e.g. lower and middle civil servants, were scared off by their superior's attitude. Therefore, private civil servants working at banks, savings banks, insurance companies, or railway companies established most of the self-help associations. The latter were mostly in private hands and their employees tended more towards to realize new social ideas.

The legal basis of civil servants associations was the Vereinspatent 1852, which gave the state the authority of supervising societies and prohibiting the foundation of such associations that intervene with law making and administration. With the Vereinsgesetz 1867, the foundation of political societies, i.e. political in a very broad sense, became possible. Instead of the previously required and explicit approval, the government had now just the right to prohibit illegal, unlawful or seditious societies or to dissolve such associations. With a strict interpretation of this regulation, joining of civil servants, a right that was regulated in the bylaws would have been a problem. This was solved by emphasizing the non-political idea of self-help. The already established insurance companies were alarmed by this development and opposed to the foundation of the "Erster Allgemeiner Beamtenverein der österr.-ungar. Monarchie". A phenomenon that repeated itself even in later decades.

The Geneva Protocols from 1922, the international treaty between Austria and the victorious powers for maintaining the independence of Austria, caused the dismissal of 80,000 civil servants. This affected the insurance department of the "Erster Allgemeiner Beamtenverein der österr.-ungar. Monarchie" economically and led to the merger with "Janus", and as a result to the precursor of the "Gemeinde Wien - Städtische Versicherungsanstalt".[166]

A second line of development for the foundation of insurances for civil servants was triggered by establishing the "Verein der k.k. Staatsbeamten zur Wahrung der Standesinteressen" (1885) and the "Verein der Staatsbeamten Österreichs in Wien" (1895), a renamed self-help association. The latter was rather sceptical towards the "Erster Allgemeine Beamtenverein der österr.-ungar. Monarchie", which was dominated by higher civil servants.[167] The "Erste Allgemeine Beamtenverein der österr.-ungar. Monarchie" initiated the foundation of a

[166] Cf. *Megner, K.* (1995), Lebensversicherungen, Vereine und Selbsthilfeprinzip, in: Österreichische Beamtenversicherung (ed.): Vertrauen, Fairness, Solidarität, Verbundenheit, Verantwortung, Sicherheit, Vienna, p. 54.

[167] Cf. *Lehner, U.* (1995), Eine beständige Selbsthilfe, in: Österreichische Beamtenversicherung (ed.): Vertrauen, Fairness, Solidarität, Verbundenheit, Verantwortung, Sicherheit, Vienna, p. 108ff.

department concerning the financial support for funeral expenses for the surviving dependents of society's members and based on the legal regulation "Hilfskassengesetz" from 1892[168]. This law enables a new legal possibility for private health insurances and insurance for funeral expenses, but also for invalidity, old age, widows', and orphans' insurances. In this way, the freedom of the Vereingsgesetz 1867 was connected with the requirements of the reliability of insurances, without being subject of the severe regulations of the insurance law.[169] In 1895, the "Unterstützungs-Sozietät der Staatsbeamten Österreichs in Wien" was established and was able to convert into the "Sterbekasse öffentlicher Angestellter Österreichs Versicherungsverein auf Gegenseitigkeit", based on the Vereinspatent 1852.[170] This created the conditions to convert into the "Österreichische (at this time the "Ostmärkische") Beamtenversicherungsanstalt Versicherungsverein auf Gegenseitigkeit" caused by the national socialist measures regarding associations from 1939 and later the opportunity to expand considerably.[171]

11.9 The foundation of national insurance companies in various regions of the monarchy

As has been noted before, nationalism became more important in the insurance industry after 1848. That led to competition mainly based on different nationalities.[172] The four leading insurance companies regarding hail, fire, transport, fire, and life insurances were the Trieste insurance companies "Azienda Assecuratrice", "Assicurazioni Generali", "Riunione Adriatica di Sicurtà" and "Nuova Società d'Assicurazione". They had branches in Hungary, Bohemia, Galicia, and other parts of the monarchy.

Hungary was the first part of the Austrian monarchy with nationalistic tendencies and with its independence movement's peak in 1848/49. The bloody oppression of the revolution in Hungary strengthened the national identity and increased striving for political and economic independence from Vienna. The first national foundation of a Hungarian insurance company was in 1843. It was done with the help of the "Riunione Adriatica di Sicurtà". This company and in particular its general

[168] RGBl. 202/1892.

[169] Cf. *Lehner, U.* (1995), Eine beständige Selbsthilfe, in: Österreichische Beamtenversicherung (ed.): Vertrauen, Fairness, Solidarität, Verbundenheit, Verantwortung, Sicherheit, Vienna, p. 110.

[170] Cf. Ibid., p. 122.

[171] Cf. Ibid., p. 124ff.

[172] Cf. Zur Situation, in: Union. Zeitschrift für Versicherungswesen vom 21.1.1872, p. 1.

agent *B. F. Weisz* had great sympathies for the Hungarian patriotism. *Weisz* became even the first director of the new “Ungarischer Verein für die Gegenseitige Versicherung von Hagelschäden” (Hungarian mutual hail insurance). He was able to establish this society successfully as a competitor to the Trieste insurance companies. In addition to this new form of patriotism, the increasing premium fees of the Trieste companies led to the decision of *Heinrich Levai*, a former employee of the “Riunione Adriatica di Sicurtà”, to establish the first large pure Hungarian joint stock company, the “Erste Ungarische Allgemeine Assekuranz-Gesellschaft”, in 1857. Patriots had already subscribed for shares, provided in this way capital for the new insurance, and were ready to bear the economic risk.[173] As a result, the Trieste companies and the “Erste Österreichische (Brand-)Versicherungs-Gesellschaft (AG)” lost business, while the national company grew stronger. From now on, the Hungarian patriots insured themselves, without considering other insurance companies, at the “Erste Ungarische Allgemeine Assecuranz-Gesellschaft”. They even tolerated financial losses in favour of the domestic insurance company and in defiance of foreign companies.[174] They replaced the political oppression with economic activity[175], which served the national pride within the insurance industry. Due to the economic upswing of the “Erste Ungarische Allgemeine Assekuranz-Gesellschaft”, the “Pannonia Ungarische Rückversicherungs-Ges.” (1861), the first re-insurance company in the Austrian monarchy, and the “Pester Versicherungs-Anstalt” (1864) were established.[176]

At the same time, other national companies were founded in the monarchy. Poland was the first crown country that followed the example. However, their willingness to take risks was lower and, as a result, they established in 1861 a mutual insurance society, the “Wechselseitige Versicherungsgesellschaft in Krakau“, which caused a sensation after it had given up its national character.

In an unsuccessful attempt, the Czech patriots tried to establish the “Böhmische wechselseitige Brandschaden-Versicherungsanstalt” in Prague as a mere Czech company. Therefore, in 1869 they established the mutual insurance bank “Slavia gegenseitige Versicherungsbank in Prag”, which was led by national employees and agents. However, it was also unsuccessful, because other Slavic nations such as Moravia or Slovenia were not interested in this company.

---

173 Cf. *Rohrbach, W.* (1988), Versicherungsgeschichte Österreichs, vol. I, Von den Anfängen bis zum Börsenkrach des Jahres 1873, Vienna, p. 291.

174 Cf. Zur Situation, in: Union. Zeitschrift für Versicherungswesen vom 21.1.1872, p. 1.

175 Cf. *Rohrbach, W.* (1988), Versicherungsgeschichte Österreichs, vol. I, Von den Anfängen bis zum Börsenkrach des Jahres 1873, Vienna, p. 291.

176 Cf. Ibid. p. 292.

Rumania, which followed the Slavic example, established national insurance companies, for example in 1868 the "Allgemeine wechselseitige Versicherungsbank Transsylvania" in Sibiu (Hermannstadt) and the insurance company "Nationale" in Bucharest.

Other national foundations were for example the joint stock company "Galizische Allgemeine Versicherungs-Gesellschaft (AG)" (1870), the mutual society "Dnister, wechselseitige Versicherungsgesellschaft" (1892) in Lemberg, and later, at the turn of the century, the two mutual societies "Gesellschaft zur wechselseitigen Versicherung der Privatbeamten" (1906) and "Wechselseitige Volks-Versicherungs-Gesellschaft" (1909) as well as the "Weichsel Vers. Ges." (1909) and the "Karpathia Vers.-Ges." (1911).[177]

The newspaper "Union" summarized critically that the national mutual insurance companies had made political damage by expanding the problem of nationalism to a wider area while their economic success in particular compared to joint stock companies was minimal. The only exception was the "Erste Ungarische Allgemeine Assecuranz-Gesellschaft", which gave up its nationalistic trend, even after Hungary became independent.[178]

11.10 The debate about nationalisation and the introduction of the social security system on the governmental level

The independence or nationalization of insurance companies was a crucial topic since the 1860s especially after the stock market crash in 1873 and its consequences for the monarchy. Between 1861 and 1880, 48 insurance companies were established, 31 in Austria and 17 in Hungary, but only 11 existed for a longer period (7 in Austria and 4 in Hungary). 20 companies, almost all were joint stock companies, had speculated very badly at the stock exchange or were part of frauds and vanished from the market. This applied to both legal forms, because the adjustable contribution procedure of mutuals did not guarantee the immediate cover in the event of problems. The low point of this development was in 1877 with the end of the liberal period of laissez-faire,

[177] Cf. *Rohrbach, W.* (2004), Vorläufer, Wegbereiter und Träger der altösterreichischen „Versicherungsweltmacht", in: Versicherungsgeschichte Österreichs, vol. VII, Teil 1, Die altösterreichischen Regionen Zentral- und (Süd)Osteuropas: Gestern – Heute – Morgen, Vienna, p. 303.

[178] Cf. Zur Situation, in: Union. Zeitschrift für Versicherungswesen vom 21.1.1872, p. 1.

followed by an interventionist state that started to control process of industrialization by focusing on costs and fiscal policy.

The debate was on several levels and to different times. First, the French social utopist *Louis Blanc* (1811-1882) developed a plan of reform in his book "Organisation du travail" (1839) to reduce the consequences of capitalism. This plan was based on the political supremacy of the working class and included the "Centralisation des Assurances" – a centralisation of the insurance industry. The plan was a logical consequence of *Blanc's* general demands such as establishing national workshops and factories, the management of the production by the state, and the organization of the public transport system for a better and steadier distribution of products. According to *Blanc*, the state should manage all-important economic institutions. More than 40 years later, academics and politicians in the conservative Germany used these revolutionary ideas from France:

Adolf Wagner, professor for national economy, was one of the harshest adversaries of private insurance companies and wanted to convert the most important insurance sectors from private organization forms to public forms. Similar how the financial system, mail, and the telegraph system were nationalistic in a modern state, the insurance industry should also be a public domain due to its economic importance. According to *Wagner*, this was the best way to secure the material welfare of the citizens. Private insurance companies were, however, fuzzy and, therefore, policyholders were not able to understand their rights completely.

According to him, private insurance companies, joint stock companies as well as mutuals, wasted work capacity and capital of an entire national economy due to their disorganised and free competition. Although this principle and the private insurance industry had original effective working capacity and efficiency, it lacked a centralised, economically and unified management. The national economic and social political interest should be used in a public form, i.e. in form of a public insurance industry. *Wagner* wanted to re-establish "Sozietäten".

The German imperial chancellor *Otto von Bismarck* followed *Wagner's* argumentation and held the opinion that no institution should profit from solving the social question. He stated that accidents and mishaps should not be used for achieving high interests and dividends, but the working class should have an affordable insurance, which is in the interest of the workers, the industry, the employers, and the employees. In his opinion, this is only possible by a public insurance system. He argued that some private insurers, e.g. joint stock companies offering fire insurances, had paid out dividends between 38 and 50 percent annually. This, he argued, was amoral.

While in Germany, the law for accident insurances was introduced in July 1884 and the health insurance law in December 1844 and there-

fore a part of the demanded objectives were achieved, the Habsburg monarchy chose a different way.

The debate of nationalization in the monarchy was led by the gentry and academics and not by social revolutionaries. Its aim was to declare fire insurances as a federal matter and to establish them as compulsory insurances. The private insurance industry started to be part of this discussion when a committee, which had to examine the problems and the inadequacies of the existing companies, was introduced. In particular, mutuals under federal supervision reacted harshly, because they felt to be accused of false management. As a reaction, the insurance industry as a whole fought against these accusations. This was another step towards adaptation and unified presentation of joint stock companies and mutuals.

In 1885, *Dr. Karl Lueger* demanded as member of the imperial council the gradual nationalization of the insurance industry. In 1888, the diets of Galicia and Vorarlberg had already accepted the draft law for the nationalization of insurances. They had sent them for the final decision to Vienna. In 1889, Styria followed this example. In 1891, *Kaiser Franz Joseph* declared in his King‘s speech that his government is working on a legal draft regarding the introduction of a compulsory fire insurance concerning property. This idea has based on the wishes of several federal diets and due to important reasons.[179] In 1891, a draft law was presented to the imperial council that outlined the essentials regarding the regulations of fire insurances by the federal law. However, it was problematic to create compulsory insurance companies, because the existing private companies had already acquired certain rights, which could not be taken away so easily. For this, a law of its own would have been necessary. The civil law applies to the existing insurance contracts; therefore, a compulsory federal insurance company that excluded other insurance contracts could only be established if such a law would have already been existed. However, such an enactment did never come about.

Nevertheless, the nationalization in form of federal supervision developed further and a founding wave of second generations of provincial institution (“Landesanstalt” or “Anstalt”) started.

The first was Lower Austria. Since 1876, it was discussed to transform the “Wechselseitige Brandschaden” into a company under federal supervision by Lower Austria. In 1897, it was agreed to establish the “Niederösterreichische Landes-Brandschaden-Versicherungsanstalt”, followed by the “Niederösterreichische Landes-, Lebens- und Renten-

[179] Quoted by *Otruba, G.* (1980), Die Feuerversicherung und die damit befaßten Gesellschaften in Österreich von ihren Anfängen bis zur Gegenwart, in: *Henning, F.* (ed.): Entwicklung und Aufgaben von Versicherungen und Banken in der Industrialisierung, Berlin, p. 111.

versicherungsanstalt" (life and pension insurances) in 1898, and later by hail and cattle insurance companies. The company was designed as a transition form from a private to a public compulsory insurance company with monopoly character, which, however, was never realized.

A similar insurance company under regional supervision was established in Carinthia in 1899, the "Kärntner Landes-Brandschaden-Versicherungs-Anstalt"[180], modelled after the company in Lower Austria. In Carinthia's diet (Landtag) the members discussed the introduction of a monopoly as well as of the company's compulsory nature.

The third foundation was the "Städtische Kaiser Franz-Joseph-Jubiläums-Lebens- und Rentenversicherungsanstalt", the later "Wiener Städtische Wechselseitige Versicherungsanstalt" in Vienna in December 1898. The company was established as a mutual society, because at this time it was legally not possible to establish a public insurance company. In 1900, another insurance company under federal supervision was established in Moravia, while the Bohemian federal committee decided firmly against the foundation of such an "Anstalt" for fire and hail insurances. Others followed in Upper Austria and Tyrol in 1901 in Oberösterreich and Tirol, 1916 in Salzburg, and 1918 in Styria.[181]

At the time of the debate about the nationalization of the insurance industry, a discussion about the so-called social question started to rise in the Austrian monarchy as well as in other European nations. The main point was the consequence of child labour and the serious housing shortage in cities and later the working conditions in factories. Nevertheless, an active social policy by the state cannot be found before the cabinet of *Earl Eduard von Taaffe,* the conservative prime minister in 1897. During his time and with the help of high civil allies in various ministries a statutory accident insurance (1887) and a statutory health insurance (1888) were established. The main point for the new social policy was the interest of the state in itself: With the introduction of the social insurances, the state and its leaders reacted to the endangerment of their power position by the organization of the workforce. The main actors here were the state leaders; therefore, it can be regarded as "social policy from above". With that, the foundation for a social policy focusing on wages was established, i.e. the performance is connected with wages. For the first time, nation-wide laws were passed that applied to all wage depending employees, not only certain groups of professions, in the event of general disability. In contrast, other European countries, i.e. Great Britain, introduced a state welfare system for all citizens to decrease poverty.

---

180 Today "Kärntner Landesversicherung auf Gegenseitigkeit (KLV)".

181 Cf. *Rohrbach, W.* (2004), "… der Rest ist Österreich!", in: Versicherungsgeschichte Österreichs, vol. VII, Teil 1, Die altösterreichischen Regionen Zentral- und (Süd) Osteuropas: Gestern – Heute – Morgen , Vienna, p. 743.

Taaffe's reform plan was based on the ideas of the Christian-conservative social reformer *Karl Freiherr von Vogelsang*, whose publications drew attention to the social problems of an increasing group of workers since 1870. The studies were about the financial situation of workers and collected data regarding the average wages in different professions and areas and the costs of living (food and clothes). The studies showed that very often the income of workers were not sufficient for the daily life due to increasing prices. The reasons could be found in the economic liberal principles of the 1870s. Therefore, the plan based on the principles of social joint ownership and the corporatism of the society. Unions for financial security in the event of illness had a long tradition in the Austrian monarchy. Even before the introduction of the public health insurance, laws for establishing health insurances in certain profession existed: for example, the mining law (1858) obliged mine operators to establish "Bruderladen", while the industrial code (1883/85) introduced provisions in form of "Fabrikskassen" for industrial enterprises and provisions were made by co-operatives for employees of small businesses. Additionally, workers established on their own supporting associations in form of self-help. With the new created health insurance law, the existing health insurance systems were integrated into a public compulsory insurance and were admitted as part of the health insurance system if they fulfilled minimum requirements. As a result, the number of the existing mutual supporting associations decreased.

11.11 Development of legal regulations for mutuals

The first convergence tendencies between mutuals and joint stock companies can be found in the early legal regulations of the monarchy. In the civil law, the lawmaker had only 5 paragraphs to regulate the insurance business (§§ 1288 to 1292) in the Austrian Civil Law Code (Allgemeines Bürgerliches Gesetzbuch, ABGB) of 1812.

The first step towards a company law with the licence or privileges system.[182] The early companies were based on privileges given by the lawmaker. A privilege was a kind of official document, which concerned a certain group of people, which received certain rights. It organized the legal relationships between the state and the beneficiary and between the company and the shareholders, the organization of the bodies and the delimitation of powers as well as the civil law relationships. The focus was hereby to provide the companies with a legal entity. In this way, the state tried to organise and supervise the market, and, at the same time, to motivate the entrepreneurs to be active on certain mar-

[182] Cf. *Kalss, S. / Burger, C. / Eckert, G.* (2003), Die Entwicklung des österreichischen Aktienrechts, Vienna, p. 47ff.

kets, in various lines of business, or regions. Therefore, a continuous state supervision was given priority very early instead of introducing a company law applying to all companies.[183]

From 1821 onwards, the privilege system followed the license system, which was based on a general legal basis that was the foundation for official decisions and a continuous state supervision. A license gives the beneficiary a personal favouring. It is not connected either to the legal form or to the line of business and requires the existence of personal features such as reliability of the people involved, personal suitability, and capital resources.[184] This development opens the way to a general applicable law, the Vereinspatent 1852[185]. In addition to joint stock companies, this law regulated insurance institutes (Versicherungsanstalten) (§ 2 lit. h). Insurance companies were, according to § 4 paragraph 3 subject to a licence, i.e. for their foundation an approval by the Home Office was required and they were under state supervision (§ 22).[186] However, a fixed organization of the body was still missing. The Vereinspatent only regulated that the bylaws of a society had to state:

- the management and executives of the business,
- the laws and duties of the society's members,
- the representation towards a third party, and
- the way how binding decisions of the society are made (§ 9).

The name, number, appointment, and competence of the bodies were left to the autonomous legislation of the societies' bylaws. As a result, this led to great differences between the various insurance institutes.[187]

The Vereinsgesetz 1867, which signifies the transition from the license system to a system based on legal regulations, kept the Vereinspatent 1852 valiant for all insurance companies.[188] With that, the state police regulation of the absolutistic state became the legal basis for the

---

[183] Cf. Ibid.

[184] Cf. Ibid.

[185] RGBl 1852, p. 1109.

[186] Cf. *Kraus, H.* (1971), Versicherungsaufsichtsrecht – Eine Studie zum deutschen und zum österreichischen Recht, in: Forschungen aus Staat und Recht, vol. 16, Vienna, p. 13.

[187] Only the association of shareholders was regulated regarding its internal structure. It was stated that an annual general meeting of shareholders has to take place (§ 12). However, until a legal regulation in the Commercial Code 1862/63 (Gesetz vom 17.12.1862, RGBl. Nr. 1/1863), a tripartite organisation structure in form of general meeting, administrative board, and management developed (Cf. *Kalss, S. / Burger, C. / Eckert, G.*, p. 82.)

[188] § 2 des Gesetzes vom 15. November 1867 über das Vereinsgesetz RGBl 134/1867.

introduction of a modern economic police institution, which developed in other states independently. In Austria, the material state supervision became via contractual insurance a part of the association police.

The first legal rules for regulations for insurance companies were part of the Versicherungsregulativ 1880[189]. The regulation was enacted to secure the fulfilment of the duties of the insurance companies and for the protection of the policyholders' interests.[190] It was also an execution order to the Vereinspatent 1852. The state continued with the license proceedings and the governmental supervision of insurance companies, which were under strict regulations regarding the organization of bodies. This differed from the open organization rules of bodies in the Vereinspatent. Therefore, according to § 5, the mutual insurance society's bylaws have to state:

- the name and headquarter of the society
- the appointment and composition of the management board and the forms to legitimize its members and the rest of the society's body
- the voting rights of members and its way of execution, and
- the calling of the general meeting on the members' demand.

However, the realization of this specific body organization failed in reality, because most of the insurance associations did not integrate these regulations into their bylaws.[191] The reason was a less experienced supervision authority (a department of Home Office) and without sufficient funding. A contemporary criticized that in addition to their missing knowledge of the governmental commissioners the supervisory bodies did not carry out their control obligation and supervision regarding insurance companies.[192] In reality, the unsolved legal nature, i.e. the current mixed system, and the inconsistent legal situation of

[189] "Verordnung des Ministeriums des Innern, der Justiz, des Handels und der Finanzen vom 18. 8. 1880, womit Bestimmungen *für* die Konzessionierung und staatliche Beaufsichtigung von Versicherungsanstalten kundgemacht werden" (RGBl. Nr. 110).

[190] *Herzfeld, E.* (1896), Bemerkungen zum neuen österreichischen Assekuranzregulativ, in: Zeitschrift für die gesamte Versicherungs-Wissenschaft 2, p. 399.

[191] Cf. *Hannak, K.* (1969), Die Rechtsform der Landes-Versicherungsanstalten, in: Die Versicherungs-Rundschau. Heft 2, p. 50.

[192] *Ogris, W.* (1988), Zur Entwicklung des Versicherungsaufsichtsrechts und des Versicherungsvertragsrechts in Österreich von der Mitte des 19. Jahrhunderts bis zum Ende der Monarchie, in: Die Ära des klassischen Versicherungswesens, Versicherungsgeschichte Österreich vol. II, Vienna, p. 64.

insurance associations resulted in problems. In addition, the nature of mutual insurance societies per se was criticized.[193]

In 1896, the next insurance regulation (Regulativ)[194] followed as a mechanism to eliminate irregularities[195] and as a reaction to the public outrage caused by the bankruptcy of the mutual life insurance society "Austria", which resulted in losses of policyholders' claims of up to 40 percent. The regulation stated that the bylaws of mutual insurance societies should contain exact prescriptions regarding the way in which the liability of members could be enforced and how losses could be covered and repaired (§ 2). Additionally, it was new that from now on only joint stock companies or mutual societies were allowed to run an insurance business. However, the decision to exclude all other current forms was met by a lack of understanding of the policyholders.[196] Despite the improvements that were made by the new law, the self-government of mutual insurance societies was not regulated although in practice it was in particular prone to mistakes. The problem of corruption was discussed fiercely due to manipulations during the general meeting, the abuse of voting rights, or the use of front men.[197] However, the new

[193] Ibid., p. 67. Due to luck and the work of the insurance companies, the interests of the policyholders were not violated more often during the last 15 years. „Man kann nur von Glücksagen und es gereicht den in Österreich thätigen Versicherungsgesellschaften zur Ehre, wenn in diesen 15 Jahren nicht häufiger gegen die Interessen der Versicherten gesündigt wurde."; in: *Herzfeld, E.*, (1896), Bemerkungen zum neuen österreichischen Assekuranzregulativ, in: Zeitschrift für die gesamte Versicherungs-Wissenschaft 2, p. 399.

[194] A select committee, was also held comprising civil servants, university professors, members of the Parliament, and people with business experience, but without publishing a report after the event.

[195] This was the first time that the mutuality principle was opposed publicly, because it was regarded as obsolete (Cf. parliamentary debates during this time).

[196] Cf. *Ogris, W.;* Zur Entwicklung des Versicherungsaufsichtsrechts und des Versicherungsvertragsrechts in Österreich von der Mitte des 19. Jahrhunderts bis zum Ende der Monarchie, in: Die Ära des klassischen Versicherungswesens, Versicherungsgeschichte Österreich vol. II, Vienna, 1988, p. 72.

[197] Cf. Ibid., p. 73. The following statement criticizes the way how general meetings were conducted, in particular that the members' lack of understanding was used by others to drive them into decisions which led e.g. to the reduction of insurance sums and the cover of damage and, eventually, effected the economic circumstances of the members in a negative way. "The writer of these paragraphs had the opportunity to observe that the general meetings usually comprise regular people and that the majority of the members have a severe lack of understanding. The writer also observed how easy it is that speculative speakers or the ones with the most powerful voices are able to drive these excitable souls to incomprehensible and absurdest decisions. Moreover, the writer was able to observe how fierce the fight regarding the election of the collector of votes by secret ballots is. It can also be observed how easy a decision that is based on numbers and on incomprehensible

law continued with the existing framework of organizing the bodies as stated in the Regulativ 1880 and, therefore, confirmed the autonomy of the bylaws. At the top of the new department for private insurance an expert from a joint stock company, experienced in all insurance sectors, was appointed.[198]

A debate about the necessary reforms for the insurance institutes, which had become problematic, was conducted not until the end of the World War I. The pressure of the life insurance sector caused by post-war crisis evoked the development of the Versicherungsregulativ 1921.[199] Nevertheless, in § 6 only the formal framework regarding the organization of the bodies, which were stated in the laws of 1880 and 1896, were used word-by-word (§ 7(2) 1-5). An addition could be found in the transitional provision of § 7 paragraph 6 that stated that all mutual insurance societies had to adjust their bylaws after a period of three years. Therefore, the organization of the bodies was not compulsory and the status quo of the insurance companies remained the same as well as the mutual insurance associations were not addressed in terms of special regulations.[200]

The cleavages and the political conflicts of the interwar years prevented any kind of reforms. However, during the dictatorial German regime in Austria, the German Insurance Supervision Act (ISA, VAG) from 1901 was enacted on the 1st of March 1939. This act was based on the law about the "reunification of Austria with Germany" ("Gesetz über die Wiedervereinigung Österreichs mit dem Deutschen Reich") from March 13th, 1938 and the regulation based on this law from the 28th of February 1939. With this act, all other previous laws were re-

---

details which concerns the reduction of the insurance sums and the down scaling of losses is made and that cut deeply into the small economic circumstances of people. The writer also observed the heated meeting of the administrative board starting with insulting utterances and wildest threats and finally that the new administrative board had the order of asserting compensation claims against the former administrative board and of electing a member of the former administrative board who probably had to sue himself. Therefore, every observer will approve that the highly esteemed autonomy of mutual societies should be restricted from the beginning on and that the members do not have a completely arbitrary decision-making power that are beyond their horizon." (*Herzfeld, E.*, (1896), Bemerkungen zum neuen österreichischen Assekuranzregulativ, in: Zeitschrift für die gesamte Versicherungs-Wissenschaft 2, p. 399.)

198 Cf. Ibid.

199 "Verordnung des Bundesministeriums für Inneres und Unterricht im Einvernehmen mit den beteiligten Bundesministerien, betreffend die Neufassung des „Versicherungsregulativs“ (BGBl. 141).

200 Cf. *Ehrenzweig, A.* (1929), Die Rechtsordnung der Vertragssicherung. Vienna. p. 501f.; *Rohrbach, W.*, Versicherungsgeschichte Österreichs, vol. I, Von den Anfängen bis zum Börsenkrach des Jahres 1873, Vienna 1988, p. 86f.

pealed. Mutual insurance societies as private companies replaced now the insurance institutes. Additionally, there was a plan to introduce the legally required bodies, as stated in the ISA, i.e. the management board, supervisory board, and the highest decision-making body, as well as in the Company law regarding mutual insurance societies. A comparison regarding the organization of insurance institutes with the organization regulations for mutual insurance societies shows that the institutes differed considerably from the legal regulations. With regard to the German ISA, a transitional provision for insurance institutes existed at first. It stated that their highest decision-body should decide about new bylaws according to the ISA by the end of 1939 and present them to the supervision authority (Reichsaufsichtsamt) for approval.[201] However, only the institutes of Carinthia[202] and Salzburg changed their bylaws, all other historic developed institutes[203] were able to escape adjustments to mutual insurance societies by arguing that in mutuals with more than one hundred thousand members a working democratic organization would be hard to find. In their opinion, it seemed better that the bodies of the individual regions should represent the interests of the policyholders than the usual bodies of mutuals.[204] These institutes remained legally based on the Vereinspatent 1852.[205]

The institute in Carinthia changed in 1943 its line of business, the formation of the reserve fund and provisions as well as the use of the surpluses, however, not the regulations concerning the organizational structure.[206] The institute in Salzburg converted to a public corporation and to an institution of the Reichsgau self-government, which is connected to the head of the provincial government (later governor "Reichsstatthalter).[207] In 1942, a regulation was enacted that made the

[201] Cf. *Plöchl, G.* (1972), Vereine als öffentliche Unternehmen, Vienna, p. 53ff.; *Hannak, K.* (1969), Die Rechtsform der Landes-Versicherungsanstalten, in: Die Versicherungs-Rundschau. Heft 2, pp. 50; 55f.

[202] The insurance company was modelled after the Lower Austrian company and had an advisory board, a federal committee for complains, regulations regarding asset investment including the possibility to give loans to the dukedom of Carinthia. However, a definition of institute ("Anstalt") is missing. The company is managed by the federal committee and has federal executive bodies. (Cf. *Plöchl, G.* (1972), Vereine als öffentliche Unternehmen, Vienna, p. 35).

[203] "Oberösterreichische Landes-Brandanstalt“, "Tiroler Landes-Brandschaden-Versicherungs-Anstalt“, "Vorarlberger Landes-Feuerversicherungs-Anstalt“.

[204] Cf. *Kraus, H.* (1971), Versicherungsaufsichtsrecht – Eine Studie zum deutschen und zum österreichischen Recht, in: Forschungen aus Staat und Recht, vol. 16, Vienna, p. 177.

[205] Cf. Ibid., p. 178.

[206] Cf. *Plöchl, G.* (1972), Vereine als öffentliche Unternehmen, Vienna, p. 57.

[207] Cf. Ibid., p. 55.

Prussian Sozietätengesetz from 25th of July 1910[208] applicable to public insurance companies. The institute in Salzburg took this opportunity.[209]

After the end of World War II, the German ISA, as amended at the 8th of May 1945, was kept valid in Austria as transitional law.[210] The problem of the insurance institute, however, maintained, in particular regarding the public insurance company in Salzburg. At first, the institute was denoted as an organization of the province Salzburg a solution, which was regarded as incorrect by the Supreme Constitutional Court. The term "public" was still included in the bylaws of 1966, although the character of a public-law corporation was dropped.[211] Until 1967, the bylaws still stated compulsory insurance and the prerogative of the political execution[212], while the bylaws of 1968 still included relics of the official regulations of the Prussian Sozietätengesetz from 1910. In general, it can be stated that even after 1945 the historic developed provincial insurance institutes and mutual insurance societies still created special particularities concerning the bylaws or other topics. For example, some positions in the decision-making bodies of the "Grazer Wechselseitige" insurance company were taken by well-known figures of the public life.[213] In the 1970s, several extensive legal changes were made, e.g. by the institute in Salzburg.

With the introduction of the Austrian Insurance Supervision Act (ISA, VAG) in 1978, the problem of the former provincial insurance institutes was "solved". According to § 43 paragraph 1, the bylaws of a mutual insurance society has to state the required bodies[214]. With regard to the former provincial insurance institutes, § 43 paragraph 3 states that in case provincial organs perform certain functions in existing mutual insurance societies then the bylaws can state that these provincial organs continue their work if the required bodies for mutual

[208] The Prussian Sozietätengesetz from 1910 stated that all public institutes on the national territory were united by this regulation and, as result, confirmed that these institutes were monopoly and compulsory institutes. (Cf. *Homburg, A.* Legitimität des öffentlichen Versicherungswesens in der Bundesrepublik Deutschland. Vienna 2004. p. 88f.).

[209] Cf. *Koch, P.*, Geschichte der Versicherungswirtschaft in Deutschland, Karlsruhe 2012, p. 107.

[210] Rechtsüberleitungsgesetz, StGbl. Nr. 6/1945.

[211] Cf. *Plöchl, G.* (1972), Vereine als öffentliche Unternehmen, Vienna, p. 63.

[212] Ibid., p 195.

[213] *Cf. Kraus, H.* (1971), Versicherungsaufsichtsrecht – Eine Studie zum deutschen und zum österreichischen Recht, in: Forschungen aus Staat und Recht, vol. 16, Vienna, p. 176.

[214] The society has to have a management board, a supervisory board, and a general meeting (members' representative) as the highest decision-making body.

insurance society exist.[215] With that, the legal foundation for provincial insurance institutes in the Austrian legal system was established.

12. Insurance statistics

In 1756, the first modern insurance joint stock company of the Austrian monarchy was established in Antwerp. Until 1859 Trieste was the key area of insurance foundations and consequently of joint stock companies. However, initially stock companies were only founded for a specific duration, similar to marine insurances that were connected with the duration of sea voyages and therefore with the risk undertaking based on. Later businesses were for an unlimited period of time, although portfolio transfers, mergers, or bankruptcies of companies limited their existences. During 1756 and 1918, no mutual society was founded in Trieste.

Between 1890 and 1909, predominantly mutuals were founded in the Austrian-Hungarian monarchy, with Austria as the core area between 1890 and 1899. Foreign branches were established in particular between 1870 and 1889, dominating the foundation waves.

The beginning of statistical reports concerning the insurance business in Austria can be traced back to the 1830s, when the first figures were published in the "Tafeln zur Statistik des Kaisertums Österreich"[216]. In 1845, the King decided that at the end of year all federal offices had to present the Home Office a proof of all licenced associations in tabular form. Since 1853, a commission concerning the business of associations ("Kommission für Vereinsangelegenheiten") collected the data.[217] As a result, *Prof. Moritz von Stubenrauch*, Professor for administrative law at the University of Vienna, was asked by the Home Secretary to create the first statistics about the insurance

[215] VAG vom 30. November 1978; Cf. *Krejci, H. / Weilinger, A.* (ed.) (1988), Österreichisches Versicherungsrecht. Gesetze, Verordnungen und ausgewählte Materialien. Vienna, p. 205.

[216] Tafeln zur Statistik der österreichischen Monarchie, 3. Jg., Vienna 1830-1840; k.k. Direction der administrativen Statistik (ed.): Tafeln zur Statistik der österreichischen Monarchie für das Jahr [Jahr], [Jg.] Jahrgang, Vienna 1841-1848; Direction der administrativen Statistik (ed.): Tafeln zur Statistik der österreichischen Monarchie, Neue Folge [Jg.] Band, [Jahre], k.k. Hof- und Staatsdruckerei, in Commission bei [Commission], Vienna 1849-1859.

[217] Cf. *Randow, v. A.* (1885), Die Statistik des österreichischen Vereinswesens seit dem Jahre 1867, in: Statistische Monatsschrift, Vienna, p. 226.

industry in Austria, which were published in 1857.[218] The first attempt of the Ministry of State (December 13th, 1866) to transfer the statistics concerning associations to the k.k. statistische Central-Commission failed due to the resistance of the insurance companies by referring to the business secret.[219] Finally, after a symposium about the standardization of balance sheets and external accounting, the regulation of the Home Office (Ministeriums des Inneren, der Justiz, des Handels und der Finanzen) from August 18, 1880[220] (Assekurnz-Regulativ from 1880) was successful.

12.1 "Tafeln zur Statistik des Kaisertums Österreich" (Statistics concerning the Austrian Empire)

The statements regarding the beginning of industrialization, its course, and dynamics in Austria differed extremely. On the one end of the scale, the empire was regarded as economical depressed area, while on the other end it was presented as the leader of the industrial revolution. Additionally, the beginning was either regarded as very early or rather late and included the theory of a growth process with a very slow start and setbacks respectively with a jolt.[221] The industrial production in Austria was already successful in 1825/30 and followed the pre-industrial regional distribution of the Austrian manufacturing production. The centres were mainly in the Austrian part of the monarchy. Dominant were the Bohemina-Moravian and the Austrian-Silesian areas with their labour-intensive textile industry, the Vienna Basin (Wiener Becken), the lower and upper Austrian Eisenwurzen as well as East-Styria and parts of Carinthia.[222] At the same time, the insurance industry functioned as a supporter of the industrialization.

After the destabilization of Europe due to the French July-Revolution in 1830, the state authority of the monarchy seemed to be able to deal with all problems at first. The "system Metternich" ruled the political scenery, the police state repressed all political unrests. From an economic point of view, the period was quiet. During this time, the first important attempts for the development of traffic in the entire realm and the beginning of the industrialization of several areas were made.

[218] Cf. *Stubenrauch, v. M.* (1857), Statistische Darstellung des Vereinswesens im Kaiserthume Österreich, Vienna.

[219] Cf. *Süss, R.* (1882), Das österreichische Versicherungs-Geschäft im Jahre 1880, Statistische Monatsschrift, Vienna, p. 202.

[220] RGBl. Nr. 110.

[221] Cf. *Sandgruber, R.* (1995), Ökonomie und Politik. Österreichische Wirtschaftsgeschichte vom Mittelalter bis zur Gegenwart, Vienna, p. 176.

[222] Cf. *Good, D.* (1986), Der wirtschaftliche Aufstieg des Habsburgerreiches, Vienna, p. 61.

At the end of this period, a brief crisis shook the Austrian economy. In Great Britain, economic difficulties arose due to problems with commodity credits between the USA and Great Britain in 1837, problems that were transferred to other European states the following years. They led to drastic decreases in commerce and to an enormous price increase in Austria, followed by bankruptcies of several trading companies in Vienna and in the provinces in 1841, which shook the trusts of the depositors. Additionally, political unrests in 1840/41 occurred, triggered by a conflict in the Middle East, which led to severe tensions between Austria and France.[223]

The new growth-orientated scientific research does not perceive the year 1848 any longer as an economic-historical watershed point in time. The revolution of 1848 was not the trigger of a new society order. However, it helped to remove bonds and to create prerequisite that made a powerful development of the dynamics of the industrial capitalism in the monarchy possible. In this revolution several chains of reasons met: the increasing oppositions of the intellectuals and the trading middle class, the increasing immobilization and paralysis of the political system that was unable to handle the increasing problems. The revolutionary potential of the industrial proletariat multiplied the explosive force of famines, which were from a historical point of view nothing new. All these developments were aspects of the general development towards an industrial capitalism.[224]

The Austrian economy developed despite many negative influences well until 1857, mainly to the work of the great economic politician *Karl Ludwig Freiherr von Bruck*. He contributed to the success of the economic liberalism in Austria, which was, however, much less distinctive than in Germany, France, and Great Britain. Later an international economy crisis followed due to an enormous raw material shortage in the textile industry, the American Civil War, and the wars in 1859 and 1866. As a result, the economy came to a standstill.[225]

During the period of neo-absolutism, a new institutional framework developed in the monarchy that created the preconditions for the development of an economic order for the industrial period. Those were characterized by the removal of feudal values by introducing the absolute discharge (1848), the foundation of a Trade Ministry (1848), establishing chambers of trade and commerce (1850), a standardization of a common market by lifting the taxation system between Austria and Hungary (1851), the removal of the taxation system (1851), and

---

[223] Cf. *Sandgruber, R.* (1995), Ökonomie und Politik. Österreichische Wirtschaftsgeschichte vom Mittelalter bis zur Gegenwart, Vienna, p. 108.

[224] Cf. Ibid., p. 233.

[225] Cf. *Good, D.* (1986), Der wirtschaftliche Aufstieg des Habsburgerreiches, Vienna, p. 208.

the foundation of liberal laws regulating commercial and industrial business (1859). These important institutional reforms improved the rights of the individuals in the economic process.

For the period 1830 to 1859, the "Tafeln zur Statistik des Kaisertums Österreich" provide official data regarding the scale of the insurance business of few insurance companies. The data shows a dominance of the joint stock companies regarding fire insurance premium incomes (76.07 percent), although many foundations of insurance joint stock companies in Trieste were later compared to mutuals.[226] Between 1830 and 1835, mutuals increased their premium market share from 23.93 percent to 34.96 percent, which increased again between 1837 and 1842 from 25.48 percent to 36.75 percent. The risks in the provinces, where mutuals dominated, were much higher than in towns, where joint stock companies dominated.[227] The dominance of the latter increased since 1842 and their market share increased from 63.75 percent in 1842 to 81.05 percent in 1851. As a result, the structural weaknesses of the mutuals became more evident.

When looking at the data of non-life insurances, the dominance of joint stock companies since 1854 is even more obvious. Their market share increased from 92.67 percent to 94.79 percent until 1859.

The fire insurance market was highly concentrated. Both market leaders had always with over 50 percent the largest market shares. Until 1839 the "Azienda Assecuratrice" dominated, then from 1840 to 1844 the "Erste Österreichische (Brand-)Versicherungs-Gesellschaft (AG)", and until 1851 again the "Azienda Assecuratrice". It is interesting that the market entry of the "Riunione Adriatica di Sicurtà" in 1854 and of the "Assicurazioni generali" in 1856/57 were always connected with a leading market position.

Between 1830 and 1859, the mutual market leader was almost continuously the "k.k. priv. Wechselseitige Brandschaden-Versicherungs-Anstalt" in Vienna, followed by the "k.k. priv. Erste böhmische wechselseitige Brand- und Hagelschaden-Versicherungs-Anstalt", and the "k.k. priv. mährisch-schlesische wechselseitige Versicherungsanstalt" (see tables 5 and 6 und figures 2 and 3.

[226] "Assicurazioni generali" (1831), "Nuova Socetà d'Assicurazione" (1835), "Riunione Adriatica di Sicurtà" (1838).

[227] Cf. *Otruba, G.* (1980), Die Feuerversicherung und die damit befaßten Gesellschaften in Österreich von ihren Anfängen bis zur Gegenwart, in: *Henning, F.* (ed.): Entwicklung und Aufgaben von Versicherungen und Banken in der Industrialisierung, Berlin, p. 84.

Table5: Fire insurance societies 1830		
name of society	total premium income in thousand	market share in percent**
Azienda Assecuratrice (Triest)	360.0	42.46
Erste Österreichische (Brand-)Versicherungs-Gesellschaft (AG)	197.0	23.23
* k.k. priv. Wechselseitige Brandschaden-Versicherungs-Anstalt	92.2	10.88
Compagnia d'Assicurazione (Mailand)	88.0	10.38
* k.k. priv. Erste böhmische wechselseitige Brand- und Hagelschaden-Versicherungs-Anstalt	60.2	7.10
* k.k. priv. Innerösterreichische Wechselseitige Brandschaden-Versicherungs-Anstalt	25.4	3.00
* Wechselseitige Brand-Assekuranz in Salzburg-Oberösterreich	18.5	2.18
* k.k. priv. mährisch-schlesische wechselseitige Versicherungsanstalt	4.5	0.50
* Tirolisch-Vorarlberg'sche Feuer-Versicherungs-Anstalt	2.0	0.30

* Landesanstalten
** Conversion from the contribution quote
Source: Tafeln zur Statistik des Kaisertums Österreich.

12.2 *Stubenrauch's* statistics of associations (1857)

At the end of 1856, 1,878 private associations respectively 6,123 (including religious and sociable associations) societies can be found in the monarchy, however the data for the latter is not sufficient for an analysis.[228] The mutual funeral associations (349) and the mutual health benefit societies (359) had the largest portion as well as mutual provision societies (114) in the category charitable and humanity ("Wohltätigkeits- und Humanitätsvereine").

- The function of funeral associations was to secure mutually a decent funeral in a mutual way.
- The health benefit societies were similar to the "sociétés de sécours mutuels" in France or Belgium and offered help and support in the event of illness. They were divided into general benefit societies and societies that were restricted to certain social classes, professions or factory workers. While the first group offered membership to all healthy men and women between 18 and 50 years old, the latter did not. The general benefit societies could mainly be found in large cities, for example, 60 were in Vienna. There were 193 general benefit societies in the Austrian monarchy, while

[228] Cf. *Stubenrauch, v. M.*(1857), Statistische Darstellung des Vereinswesens im Kaiserthume Österreich, Vienna, p. 10.

Table 6: Property and casualty insurance societies 1854		
name of society	total premium income in thousand	market share in percent**
Riunione Adriatica di Sicurtà (Triest)	2150.5	30.11
Assicurazioni generali (Triest)	1705.5	23.88
Azienda Assecuratrice (Triest)	1269.2	17.77
Erste Österreichische (Brand-)Versicherungs-Gesellschaft (AG)	1138.7	15.95
Compagnia d'Assicurazione (Mailand)	354.0	4.96
* k.k. priv. Wechselseitige Brandschaden-Versicherungs-Anstalt	171.1	2.40
* k.k. priv. Erste böhmische wechselseitige Brand- und Hagelschaden-Versicherungs-Anstalt	90.0	1.26
* k.k. priv. Innerösterreichische Wechselseitige Brandschaden-Versicherungs-Anstalt	75.1	1.05
* Wechselseitigen Landes-Brandschaden-Versicherungs-Anstalt im Erzherzogtum Österreich ob der Enns	69.5	0.97
* Tirolisch-Vorarlberg'sche Feuer-Versicherungs-Anstalt	57.0	0.80
* k.k. priv. mährisch-schlesische wechselseitige Versicherungsanstalt	45.2	0.63
* Wechselseitige Landesbrandschaden-Versicherungs-Anstalt für das Herzogtum Salzburg	15.5	0.22
Versicherungsverein gegen Hagelschlag in Pest	-	-
Privat-Assekuranz-Gesellschaft für die Donau- u. Theiss-Schifffahrt in Raab	-	-
Brandschaden-Versicherungsanstalt in Miskolcz	-	-
Feuer- und Hagelschaden-Versicherungsanstalt in Klausenburg	-	-

* Landesanstalten
** Conversion from the contribution quote
Source: Tafeln zur Statistik des Kaisertums Österreich.

from the 166 special ones 36 were for crafts journeymen and domestic servants.[229]

- Mutual provision societies offered their members or their widows and orphans retirement money, and were restricted to a certain social class or profession.[230]

In the category associations for economic promotion, *Stubenrauch* distinguishes between two types of insurance companies: mutuals and joint stock companies. Most of the latter with fix premiums were ma-

[229] Cf. Ibid., p. 102ff.
[230] Cf. Ibid., p. 106ff.

Figure 2: Fire insurance societies 1830-1845

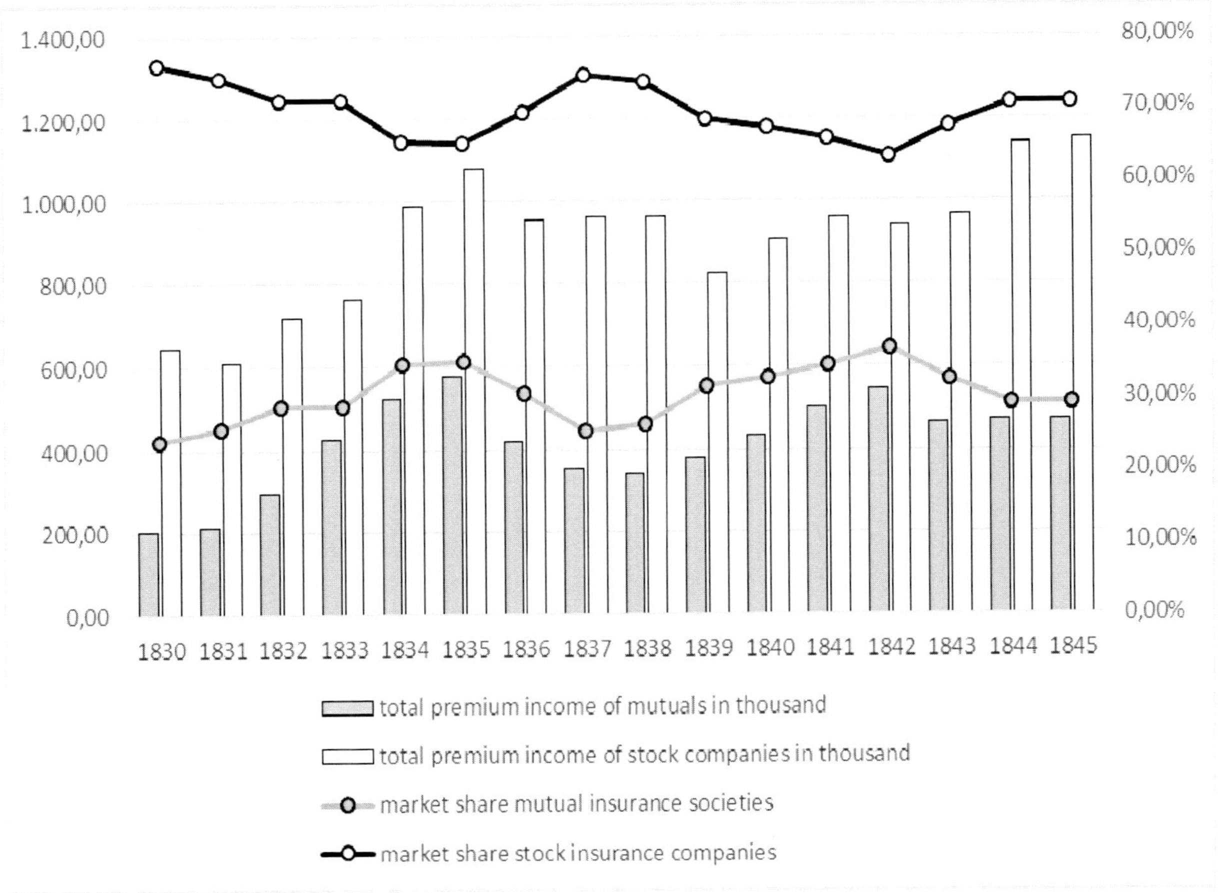

Source: Tafeln zur Statistik des Kaisertums Österreich.

Figure 3: Fire insurance societies (1845-1851) and property and casualty insurers (1854-1859)

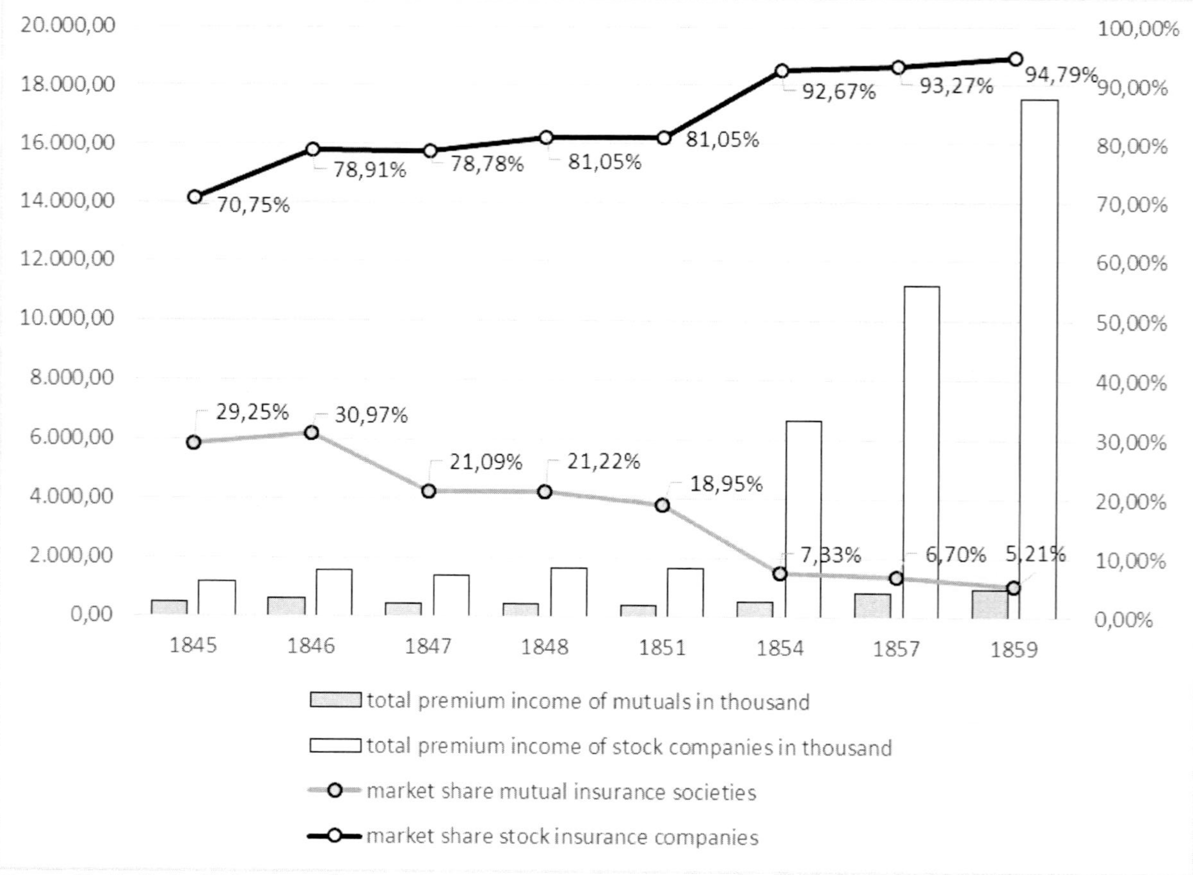

Source: Tafeln zur Statistik des Kaisertums Österreich.

rine insurances in Trieste, while mutual insurances offered fire, water damage, and environmental damage insurances.[231] Mutuals and joint stock companies differed regarding their legal form as following: Joint stock companies offered insurances for fix premiums based on the management's calculation of the value of the insured building (goods) for the insurance duration. The premium is classified into hazard classes from which the insured building (goods) is endangered. Members of mutual insurance societies assure each other the reimbursement of their property's damage. The value of the insured building or parts of it has to be stated by the new member. To provide fast support by paying compensation after the damage happened as quickly as possible, an advance fund is created from which the necessary payments are made of. Later the damage will be split between all members; therefore, the adjustable contribution will be fixed from year to year.[232]

In 1856, 120 non-life insurance companies worked in the Austrian Monarchy, from them 13 were mutual insurance societies and 38 joint stock companies. Most of these 51 insurance companies were pure insurers (39), offering fire, life, hail, or transport insurances, while 12 were composite insurers that combined insurance types such as fire, life, hail, or transport. The oldest and numerous strongest insurance type was fire.

Joint stock companies dominated the market with a share of 85.56 percent regarding premiums, while mutuals had a market share of 14.44 percent (regional insurance institutions held 13.27 percent).

Additionally, 69 small mutual fire insurance societies (Bauernassekuranzen) offered fire, hail, or cattle insurances. Despite monetary compensation, non-cash benefits in form of seeds and building materials were still the prevalent form of mutual compensation forinsurance societies. A members' elected board managed the latter.[233]

Stubenrauch also reports about the first division of the Austrian Lloyds in Trieste (division of the united insurance chamber).[234]

The tables 7 and 8 present the large mutual insurance societies and joint stock companies in 1856 as well as their insurance capital/ deposit value, the premiums/adjustable contribution, and number of members as far as available (see tables 7 and 8).

In the category associations for economic promotion, *Stubenrauch* analyzed also the data regarding provision and pension societies in 1856 (see table 9).

Since 1835, the "Assicurazioni Generali" in Trieste offered life insurances, while the "Azienda-Assicuratrice" and the "Riunione Adriatica di Sicurtà" offered this insurance type since 1851 respectively 1854.

[231] Cf. Ibid., p. 316.
[232] Cf. Ibid.
[233] Cf. Ibid., p. 319.
[234] Cf. Ibid., p. 320.

Table 7: Mutual insurances societies in 1856

Name	foundation year	capital/ deposit value	premiums /adjustable contribution in thousand	market share in percent	number of members
* Tirolisch-Vorarlberg'sche Feuer-Versicherungs-Anstalt	Innsbruck 1825	39,095.730	586.4	3.80%	n.a.
* k.k. priv. Wechselseitige Brandschaden-Versicherungs-Anstalt (Wechselseitige Brandschaden)	Vienna 1824	61,355.825	405.0	2.62%	62,986
* Wechselseitige Landesbrandschaden-Versicherungs-Anstalt für das Herzogtum Salzburg	1815	11,044.462	451.0	2.92%	33,118
* k.k. priv. Innerösterreichische Wechselseitige Brandschaden-Versicherungs-Anstalt	Graz 1829	53,643.125	182.8	1.18%	67,390
* k.k. priv. Erste böhmische wechselseitige Brand- und Hagelschaden-Versicherungs-Anstalt	Prague 1827	34,834.304	156.1	1.01%	39,962
* k.k. priv. mährisch-schlesische wechselseitige Versicherungsanstalt	Brünn 1830	17,904.180	142.3	0.92%	n.a.
* Wechselseitigen Landes-Brandschaden-Versicherungs-Anstalt im Erzherzogtum Österreich ob der Enns	1850	54,107.220	126.3	0.82%	57,300
Compagnia d'Assicurazione	Milan 1825	n.a.	88.0	0.57%	n.a.
Wechselseitige Versicherungs-Verein gegen Hagelschlag zu Pesth	Pesth 1842	1,976.640	40.5	0.26%	1,422
k. k. siebenbürgische wechselseitige Hagel- und Feuerversicherungs-Gesellschaft	Klausenburg 1843	3,006.214	47.9	0.31%	1,605
Eula und Wilsdorfer Feuerverein	1849	2,380.000	4.7	0.03%	3,900
Markersdorfer Feuerverein	1849	1,446.030	1.1		n.a.

* regional insurance institution (Landesanstalt)

Table 8: Joint stock companies in 1856

Nuova Societa d'Assicurazioni	Triest 1835	-	1,539.0	9.10
Azienda assicuratrice	Trieste 1822	741,516.309	1,298.0	8.41
Erste Österreichische (Brand-) Versicherungs-Gesellschaft (AG)	Vienna 1824	354,938.872	1,214.6	7.87
La Fortuna Stabilimento d'Assicurazione	Triest 1854	14,078.389	439.2	2.85
Adriatico Banco di Assicurazioni	Triest 1826	25,484.841	429.7	2.79
Nuovo Stabilimento d'Assicurazione	Triest 1812	11,061.923	391.1	2.53
Stabilimento Commerciale d'Assicurazioni	Triest 1852	4,471.013	174.6	1.13
Socj Assicuratori	Triest 1839	6,833.139	147.2	0.95
Banco Veneto d'Assicurazioni	Triest 1853	630.110	137.0	0.89
Societa assicuratrice	Triest 1845	3,429.567	111.0	0.72
Austria Assicuratrice	Triest 1851	3,808.778	106.5	0.69
Compagnia Nazionale d'Assicurazioni	Triest 1850	2,956.569	78.1	0.51
Nuova Alleanza d'Assicuratori	Triest 1850	2,409.187	74.2	0.48
Nuova Compagnia patriotica d'Assicurazioni	Triest 1852	2,187.587	66.6	0.43
Mediterraneo Banco d'Assicurazioni	Triest 1849	-	64.0	0.41
Greca concordia d'Assicuratori	Triest 1846	2,961.885	64.0	0.41
Feuerversicherungsanstalten an der Theiss zu Miskolecz	1847	3,617.783	62.2	0.40
Banco Orientale d'Assicurazioni	Triest 1845	-	58.5	0.38
Societa Elvetica d'Assicurazioni Marittime	Triest 1829	2,336.210	45.4	0.29
Unione Assicuratrice	Triest 1853	1,672.022	43.6	0.28
Intrepida Compagnia d'Assicurazioni	Triest 1832	-	42.8	0.28
Associazione Assicuratrice	Triest 1832	1,131.420	39.2	0.25
Liburna riunione Assicuratrice in Lussin piccolo	1839	672.000	35.1	0.23
Compagnia Filemporica d'Assicurazione	Triest 1855	170.670	3.8	0.03
Compagnia degli Amici Assicuratori	Triest 1818	50.596	0.1	
Compagnia d'Assicurazione	Milan 1825	n.a.		-
k.k. priv. Hagelversicherungs-Gesellschaft im Königreich Böhmen	Prague 1853	300.000		
Società die Veneti assicuratori	Venice 1852	n.a.		-
Hagelschaden-Versicherungs-Gesellschaft in Cremona	Cremona 1852	n.a.		-

Table 9: provision and pension societies 1856

Name	foundation year	capital	number of members
Wiener allgemeines Witwen- und Waisen-Pensionsinstitut	Vienna 1822	1.239,079	772
Allgemeine Versorgungs-Anstalt für die Unterthanen des österreichischen Kaiserstaates	Vienna 1825	11.422,673	n.a.
Allgemeine wechselseitige Kapitalien- und Renten-Versicherungs-Anstalt (Janus)	Vienna 1839/1855	858,513	104
Pensionsinstitut für schuldlos verunglückte Männer, für Witwen und Waisen in Prag	1804	505,859	1.210
Kronstädter allgemeine Pensions-Versorgungsanstalt	Kronstadt 1844	90,172	36

12.3 Statistics of insurance companies in 1867

According to the newspaper "Die Assecuranz" from November 2nd, 1867[235], 34 insurance companies existed in the Austrian-Hungarian Monarchy at this time. From them 20 were fire insurances (from them 7 also insured hail, transport, and life insurances), 9 were pure life insurers, 2 pure cattle insurers, 1 offered mortgage insurances, and 2 were re-insurance banks. This statistic is based on the directory of all existing insurance companies in the Austrian-Hungarian monarchy in 1867, which was published in *Pappenheims* journal "Österreichisches Handels-Journal". It is interesting that the statistics differ between private mutual insurance societies and mutual insurances under federal/regional administration. This distinction can also be found in the early issues of the "Statistische Monatsschrift" (until 1889), but not later. The "Assecuranz-Jahrbuch", which had been published since 1870, did not make this kind of differentiation. About the reason, why this statistics were published in 1867 and in particular in this form can only be speculated. It is possible that the compromise between Austria and Hungary in 1867 was the trigger to reflect about the state of the insurance industry at this time. It is also possible that the travelling assemblies, which were organized and initiated by the mutual "Wechselseitige Versicherungsgesellschaft in Krakau" since 1865, were the reason for this publication. In these assemblies, the "Krakauer" insurance society offered other mutual insurance societies the opportunity to improve their insurance business by informing them about new business opportunities and developments in the insurance industry. At this time, the "Krakauer" was a very successful company, while many mutual insurance societies had financial difficulties (see table 10).

[235] Cf. Die Assecuranz, November 2, 1867, No. 44.

Table 10: Statistics of insurance companies in 1867

1. Fire, transport, and hail insurances
a) Mutual insurances (under federal/regional administration)

name	foundation year
Based on former Bavarian system	
* Wechselseitigen Landes-Brandschaden-Versicherungs-Anstalt im Erzherzogtum Österreich ob der Enns	1850
* Wechselseitige Landesbrandschaden-Versicherungs-Anstalt für das Herzogtum Salzburg	1815
Under governmental administration	
* Tirolisch-Vorarlberg'sche Feuer-Versicherungs-Anstalt	Innsbruck 1825
Based on *Högelmüller's* model	
* k.k. priv. Wechselseitige Brandschaden-Versicherungs-Anstalt (Wechselseitige Brandschaden)	Vienna 1828
* Innerösterreichische wechselseitige Brandschaden-Versicherungs-Anstalt	Graz 1829
* k.k. priv. Erste böhmische wechselseitige Brand- und Hagelschaden-Versicherungs-Anstalt	Prague 1827
* k.k. priv. wechselseitige Brandschaden-Versicherungsanstalt für Mähren und Schlesien	Brünn 1830
Under governmental administration	
* Wechselseitige Versicherungsgesellschaft in Krakau	Krakau 1860

* regional insurance institution (Landesanstalt)

b) Mutual insurances (private companies)

Name	foundation year
Assecuranzverein von Zuckerfabrikanten in der österr.-ungarischen Monarchie	Prague 1862
Gegenseitiger Versicherungsverein für Montanwerke, Maschinen- und Metallfabriken	Vienna 1866

c) Joint stock companies

name	foundation year	capital
Azienda assicuratrice	Trieste 1822	4.000,000
Erste Österreichische (Brand-) Versicherungs-Gesellschaft (AG) (since October 1st 1867 joint with Donau insurance)	Vienna 1824	3.150,000
Assicurazioni generali	Trieste 1831	4.200,000
Riunione Adriatica di Sicurtà	Trieste 1838	4.000,000
Erste Ungarische allgemeine Assecuranzgesellschaft (*national foundation*)	Pesth 1858	3.150,000
Versicherungsbank Austria	Vienna 1867	2.000,000
k.k priv. Versicherungsgesellschaft Österreichischer Phönix	Vienna 1860	2.000,000
Versicherungs-Bank „Hungaria" (*national foundation*)	Bratislava 1864	3.000,000
Pester Versicherungs-Anstalt (*national foundation*)	Pesth 1865	3.000,000
"Victoria" Versicherungs-Aktiengesellschaft in Klausenburg	Klausenburg 1865	1.000,000

2. Life insurance

a) Mutual insurances

name	foundation year
Allgemeine Versorgungs-Anstalt für die Unterthanen des österreichischen Kaiserstaates	Vienna 1825
Janus Wechselseitige Lenens-Versicherungs-Anstalt	Vienna 1839
Austria, allgemeine wechselseitige Capitalien- und Rentenversicherungs-Gesellschaft	Vienna 1860
Erster allgemeiner Beamten-Verein der österr.-ungar. Monarchie	Vienna 1864
"Patria" Gegenseitige Lebensversicherungs-Bank	Vienna 1866
Kronstädter allgemeine Pensionsanstalt	Kronstadt 1864

b1) Joint stock companies (pure life insurers)

name	foundation year	capital
"Der Anker" Gesellschaft für Lebens- und Rentenversicherungen	Vienna 1858	2.000,000
Österreichischer Gresham,l Gesellschaft für Lebens- u. Renten-Versicherung	Vienna 1861	1.000,000
"Haza" Ungarische Lebensversicherungsbank (*national foundation*)	Pesth 1867	2.000,000

b2) Joint stock companies (with additional fire insurance)

name	foundation year	capital
Erste Österreichische (Brand-) Versicherungs-Gesellschaft (AG)	Vienna 1824	3.150,000
k.k priv. Österr. Versicherungs-Gesellschaft "Donau"	Vienna 1867	2.000,000
k. k. priv. Lebensversicherungs-Gesellschaft österreichischer Phönix in Wien	Vienna 1860	2.000,000
Assicurazioni generali	Trieste 1831	4.200,000
Riunione Adriatica di Sicurtà	Trieste 1838	4.000,000
Azienda assicuratrice	Trieste 1822	4.000,000
Erste Ungarische Allgemeine Assekuranz-Gesellschaft (*national foundation*)	Pesth 1857	3.150,000

3. Cattle insurances

name	foundation year
"Apis" Vieh-Versicherungs-Bank	Vienna 1865
Versicherungsverein der Wiener Milchmeier	Vienna 1867

4. Mortgage insurance

name	foundation year	capital
"Vindobona" Gesellschaft für Hypotheken-Versicherung (in liquidation)	Vienna 1869	10.000,000

5. Re-insurances

name	foundation year	capital
Rückversicherungs-Gesellschaft Securitas	Vienna 1865	2.000,000
Versicherungsverein der Wiener Milchmeier	Vienna 1867	2.000,000

12.4 Statistical report about fire damage, fire fighting, and insurance business in 1870[236]

A special report about fire damage, fire fighting, and insurance business in the journal "Mittheilungen aus dem Gebiete der Statistik" (1872) presents a list of all fire insurance companies in the monarchy.

At the end of 1870, 242 fire insurance companies existed in Austria (see table 11). From them

- 11 were joint stock companies with a share capital of 28.472,900 fl.;
- 16 were mutual insurance societies (8 were regional insurance institution - Landesanstalt) with 672,385 members and insurance assets of 911.050,500 fl., and
- 216 were small local insurance societies with 150,713 members and insurance assets of 154.716,400 fl.

Table 11: Fire insuranc 1870

Joint stock companies

name	foundation year	paid-up capital
Azienda assicuratrice	Trieste 1822	1.200,000
Assicurazioni generali	Trieste 1831	2.260,000
Riunione Adriatica di Sicurtà	Trieste 1838	1.060,000
Erste Ungarische allgemeine Assecuranzgesellschaft (*national foundation*)	Pesth 1858	945,000
k.k. priv. Versicherungsgesellschaft Österreichischer Phönix	Vienna 1860	600,000
Pester Versicherungs-Anstalt (*national foundation*)	Pesth 1865	810,000
"Victoria" Versicherungs-Aktiengesellschaft in Klausenburg	Klausenburg 1865	1.000,000
k.k. priv. Österr. Versicherungs-Gesellschaft "Donau"	Vienna 1867	502.382,553
"Europa" Actien-Gesellschaft für Versicherungen	Vienna 1867	800,000
Galizische Allgemeine Versicherungs-Gesellschaft (AG)	Lemberg 1870	2.000,000

[236] Cf. *Winckler, J.* (1872), Feuerschäden, Feuerlösch- und Versicherungswesen, in: Mittheilungen aus dem Gebiete der Statistik, Neunzehnter Jahrgang, Heft 3, p. 64ff.

Mutual insurances societies

name	foundation year	insurable value	number of members
* Salzburger wechselseitige Landes-Brandschaden-Versicherungsanstalt	Salzburg 1815	18.501,175	32,363
* Oberösterreichische wechselseitige Brandschadenversicherungsanstalt	Linz 1850	61.483,870	51,205
* Feuerversicherungsanstalt für Tirol und Vorarlberg und das Fürstenthum Liechtenstein	Innsbruck 1825	46.704,730	55,496
* k. k. priv. niederösterreichische wechselseitige Brandschaden-Versicherungsanstalt	Vienna 1828	102.743,725	61,318
* Innerösterreichische wechselseitige Brandschaden-Versicherungs-Anstalt	Graz 1828	73.486,125	80,739
* k. k. priv. Erste böhmische wechselseitige Brand- und Hagelschaden-Versicherungs-Anstalt	Prague 1827	91.044,044	77,198
* k.k. priv. wechselseitige Brandschaden-Versicherungsanstalt für Mähren und Schlesien	Brünn 1830	66.170,207	76,914
* Wechselseitige Versicherungsgesellschaft in Krakau	Krakau 1860	258.044,302	68,711
Assekuranzverein von Zuckerfabriken in der österr.-ungarischen Monarchie	Prag 1861	90.504,894	162
Gegenseitiger Versicherungs-Verein für Montanwerke, Maschinen- und Metallfabriken	Vienna 1866	22.115,363	190
"Concordia", Reichenberg-Brünner gegenseitige Versicherungs-Anstalt	Reichenberg 1867	43.672,474	23,875
"Providentia" Gesellschaft für Landwirtschaft und Realitäten-Versicherungen	Vienna 1868	-	-
Wechselseitiger Leinengam-Versicherungs-Verein "Kosmos" - Mährisch-Schönberg	Vienna 1868	-	-
Österreichische Mobiliar-Versicherungs-Bank „Aetna"	Vienna 1869	12.299,210	22,649
"Slavia", gegenseitige Versicherungsbank in Prag	Prag 1869	17.354,904	12,905
Wechselseitiger Versicherungsverein gegen Feuer und Hagelschlag des Prinzen Rohan	Lissa a.d. Elbe 1869	6.925,515	8,677

* regional insurance institution (Landesanstalt)

12.5 Performance review of the Austrian-Hungarian insurance industry from its beginning until 1872

For *Friedrich Fachini,* the owner of the journal "Union" Zeitschrift für Versicherungswesen, the world exhibition in Vienna 1873 was the reason to publish a performance report of the insurance industry. His goal was to present Austria as a modern industrial state. At the same time, *Fachini* wanted to show the importance of Austria's inclusion as a competitor on the world market. However, to compete successfully against other companies on the international market, the existing insurance companies had to reduce their costs. A crucial part of the costs were the insurance premiums that were criticized by the indus-

try as too high. As a result, a market opening for branch offices was demanded.[237] The insurance penetration in the monarchy was in 1875 at 3.4 percent (see table 12).[238]

The performance review of the insurance industry since its beginning shows a dominance of joint stock companies with a premium market share of 86.21 percent and 84 percent regarding compensatory payments, despite the fact that the data of the largest insurance company in Trieste the "Azienda assicuratrice" is missing. Moreover, the market leaders were the two joint stock companies the "Assicurazioni generali" and the "Riunione Adriatica di Sicurtà" with a market share of over 50 percent.

12.6 Reports in the monthly statistical journal (Statistische Monatsschrift)

Since the year 1886 (12th year of publication) the journal ("Statistische Monatsschrift vom k.k. statistischen Central-Kommission in Vienna") published irregularly reports about the insurance industry in the monarchy, at first only about the life insurance segment, since 1889 (15th year of publication) also about the fire insurance segment, and later (1893, 19th year of publication) about the entire insurance industry.

12.6.1 Reports about the life insurance segment[239]

In 1880, 22 domestic life insurance companies (11 joint stock companies and 11 mutuals) existed in the monarchy. Additionally, 13 foreign companies existed. The economic development during the last two de-

[237] Cf. *Rohrbach, W.* (1988), Versicherungsgeschichte Österreichs, vol. I, Von den Anfängen bis zum Börsenkrach des Jahres 1873, Vienna, p. 116.

[238] *Hollmayer, A.* (2000), Makrodaten der Österreichischen Assekuranz 1875-2000, in: Versicherungsgeschichte Österreichs, vol. VI, An der Schwelle zum 3. Jahrtausend – Retrospektiven und Perspektiven, Vienna 2000, p. 1394.

[239] Cf. *Israel, B.* (1886) Die Geschäfts-Resultate der österr.-ungar. und der ausländischen Lebensversicherungs-Gesellschaften in Oesterreich-Ungarn im Jahre 1885, in: Mittheilungen und Miscellen, Statistische Monatsschrift XII., p. 483ff.; *Ehrenberger, H.* (1987), Die Geschäftsresultate der österr.-ungar. Lebensversicherungs-Gesellschaften und der ausländischen Lebens-Versicherungs-Gesellschaften in Oesterreich im Jahre 1886, in: Mittheilungen und Miscellen, Statistische Monatsschrift XIII., p. 469ff.; *Israel, B.* (1888), Die Geschäftsresultate der österr.-ungar. Lebensversicherungs-Gesellschaften und der ausländischen Lebens-Versicherungs-Gesellschaften in Oesterreich im Jahre 1887, in: Mittheilungen und Miscellen, Statistische Monatsschrift XIV., p. 432ff.; *Israel, B.* (1889), Die Geschäftsresultate der österr.-ungar. Lebensversicherungs-Gesellschaften und der ausländischen

Table 12: Performance review of the Austrian-Hungarian insurance industry since its establishing and until 1872

Joint stock companies

Name	foundation year	insurable value since the company's foundation	premiums /income since company's foundation	market share in percent	insurance payments since company's foundation
Azienda assicuratrice	Trieste 1822	-	-		-
Assicurazioni generali	Trieste 1831	17.096.886,113	123.915,879	31.96	86,800.365
Riunione Adriatica di Sicurtà	Trieste 1838	15.008.977,418	80.357,931	20.73	55,812.537
Erste Ungarische Allgemeine Assecuranzgesellschaft	Pesth 1858	7.034.974,210	57.532,191	14.84	35,936.933
k.k. priv. Versicherungsgesellschaft Österreichischer Phönix	Vienna 1860	4.542.868,958	26.424,080	6.82	17,470.934
Pester Versicherungs-Anstalt	Pesth 1865	3.792.928,293	15.598,451	4.02	9,140.152
k. k. priv. Österr. Versicherungs-Gesellschaft „Donau"	Vienna 1867	3.265.153,440	10.913,572	2.82	6,295.780
"Victoria" Versicherungs-Aktiengesellschaft in Klausenburg	Klausenburg 1865	1.220.19,583	7.934,638	2.05	2,814.717
"Europa" Actien-Gesellschaft für Versicherungen	Vienna 1867	887.796,342	5.331,856	1.38	3,267.9 12
Allgemeine Transport-Versicherungs-Gesellschaft	Vienna 1868	1.058.044,855	3.648,927	0.94	2,314.975
Galizische Allgemeine Versicherungs-Gesellschaft (AG)	Lemberg 1870	207.869,080	1.672,818	0.43	871.331
Allgemeine böhmische Actien-Gesellschaft für Elementar- u. Lebens-Versicherungen	Prague 1872	30.494,484	287,263	0.07	10.615
Erste böhmische allgemeine Versicherungs-Bank (AG)	Prague 1873	25.266,962	284,991	0.07	34.380
Erste allgemeine Versicherungsbank "Slovenija" (AG)	Laibach 1872	29.603,681	273,892	0.07	10.000
Versicherungs- u. Hypotheken-Bank "Tisza"	Depreczia 1872	5.395,376	45,469	0.01	3.169
sum				86.21	

Mutual insurances societies

name	year	insurable value since the company's foundation	premiums/ income since the company's foundation	market share in percent	insurance payments since the company's foundation
* k. k. priv. niederösterreichische wechselseitige Brandschaden-Versicherungsanstalt	Vienna 1828	2.810.623,722	16.225,746	4,18	14.318,018
* Oberösterreichische wechselseitige Brandschadenversicherungsanstalt	Linz 1850	2.509.810,145	10.033,402	2,59	8.283,012
* Innerösterreichische wechselseitige Brandschaden-Versicherungs-Anstalt	Graz 1828	1.996.332,311	8.454,118	2,18	7.443,833
* k.k. priv. wechselseitige Brandschaden-Versicherungsanstalt für Mähren und Schlesien	Brünn 1830	965.392,017	7.320,705	1,89	6.040,738
* Feuerversicherungsanstalt für Tirol und Vorarlberg und das Fürstenthum Liechtenstein	Innsbruck 1825	50.490,280	3.106,812	0,80	3.197,977
Assekuranzverein von Zuckerfabriken in der österr.-ungarischen Monarchie	Prague 1861	694.689,142	2.098,206	0,54	947,089
"Slavia", gegenseitige Versicherungsbank in Prag	Prag 1869	125.370,716	1.760,351	0,45	581,532
"Concordia", Reichenberg-Brünner gegenseitige Versicherungs-Anstalt	Reichenberg 1867	278.230,492	1.399,361	0,35	383,472
Gegenseitiger Versicherungs-Verein für Montanwerke, Maschinen- und Metallfabriken	Vienna 1866	102.899,188	841,750	0,21	69,320
Wechselseitiger Versicherungsverein „St. Florian"	Eger 1867	35.000,000	552,539	0,14	381,380
* Salzburger wechselseitige Landes-Brandschaden-Versicherungsanstalt	Salzburg 1815	192.157,234	549,381	0,14	483,990
Österreichische Mobiliar-Versicherungs-Bank „Aetna"	Vienna 1869	44.657,980	385,153	0,09	67,840
Prager städtische Versicherungsanstalt	Prague 1865	307.630,780	257,433	0,07	76,934
Allgemeine wechselseitige Versicherungsbank "Transsylvania"	Hermannstadt 1868	22.929,993	125,777	0,03	41,114
Erste Wiener Spiegelglas-Versicherungsgesellschaft	Vienna 1867	1.992,908	88,366	0,02	20,824
"Moldau", wechselseitige Feuer-, Hagel- u. L[illegible]ensversicherungs-Bank	Prague 1872	3.036,565	65,446	0,02	8,363
* k. k. priv. Erste böhmische wechselseitige Brand- und Hagelschaden-Versicherungs-Anstalt	Prague 1827	-	-		-
* Wechselseitige Versicherungsgesellschaft in Krakau	Krakau 1860	-	-		-
sum				13,79	

* regional insurance institution (Landesanstalt)

Total sum		64.347.722,268	386.954,504		263.353,101

cades of the 19th century, the 1880s introduced a new foundation wave of companies, ensured a fast development of the insurance industry. Between 1880 and 1913, the number of life insurers doubled (from 22 to 45), however, joint stock companies and mutuals balanced out one another regarding their numbers. The number of foreign companies increased until the turn of the century to 24. The phase of growth shows an increased total premium income for the life insurance segment and was over 25 percent in 1887, 33.68 percent in 1900, and increased nearly to 40[240] percent until 1914. With regard to premium income, the life insurance segment became the most important insurance segment in the monarchy. Positive influential factors for the expansion of the life insurance segment were better sanitary measures and medical developments during this period. The competition was lower compared to neighboring countries, the number of companies was moderate, and from the since 1873 licenced foreign companies only a few were able to compete successfully. With the fast expanding business and the increasing competition, the production costs increased, and, therefore, became a measure for the development of the life insurance segment. Theoretically, the premiums should have been increased and the costs reduced. However, the opposite occurred by introducing preferential treatments without compensations. The largest life insurance portfolio held the domestic joint stock companies, while mutuals had the smallest. The medium insurance sum of joint stock companies was at least twice the sum of mutuals. The reasons for the different success was the business politics of mutuals, which needed revision, and that the system of mutuality was successful in Germany.[241] Due to the immense competition pressure, the mutual company "Austria, allgemeine wechselseitige Capitalien- und Rentenversicherungs-Gesellschaft" had financial difficulties during the 1890s. The reason was not fraud but human error and that led to a heavy loss of face for the life insurance segment.

From the 1880s onward, mutuals were able to increase their market share regarding premium income from 7.33 percent (1880) to 30.11 percent (1891), stagnated but later on. Joint stock companies, on the other hand, secured their leading market position with a market share of 70 percent between 1880 and 1896.

In general, the life insurance market was highly concentrated. Only four joint stock companies, the "Assicurazione Generali", the "Erste Ungarische allgemeine Assecuranzgesellschaft", the "Riunione Adriatica di Sicurtà", and the "Der Anker, Lebens und Renten-Versicherungs-

Lebens-Versicherungs-Gesellschaften in Oesterreich im Jahre 1888, in: Mittheilungen und Miscellen, Statistische Monatsschrift XV., p. 468ff.

[240] Cf. *Roloff, M.* (1988), Die Entwicklung der Lebensversicherung in Österreich zwischen 1873 und 1936, in: Die Ära des klassischen Versicherungswesens, Versicherungsgeschichte Österreichs, vol. II, Vienna, p. 317.

[241] Cf. Ibid., p. 320.

Gesellschaft" dominated the market between 1880 and 1896 with a share of more than 50 percent. With 8.44 percent, the mutual company "Erster allgemeiner Beamten-Verein der österr.-ungar. Monarchie" held the fifth rank (see tables 13 and 14 and figure 4).

12.6.2 Report about fire insurances between 1878 and 1887[242]

The 1880s also introduced a foundation wave for the fire insurance segment that was characterized by an intensive competition among the companies with a higher pressure regarding premiums, new business strategies, and progressive insurance conditions. For example, the "Erste Ungarische allgemeine Assecuranzgesellschaft" offered the first insurance year free, an action that became a signal for further premium reductions. Stable competition conditions started when the insurance supervision of the state prohibited the foundation of new insurance companies as well as fraudulent competition methods. The increased offer occurred in a period with a lot of damage. For example, in 1880 and 1881 the fire insurance segment had the worst results since decades. After several bad business years, the companies had to accept the disadvantageous change of risk. As a result, companies had to increase their insurance premiums.[243]

In 1887, 9 joint stock companies, 15 mutuals, and two foreign joint stock companies offered, in addition to 305 local small fire insurance societies, fire insurances in the monarchy. The official statistic data distinguished between mutuals and regional insurance institutions (Landesanstalten). The latter are characterized by the involvement of governmental bodies regarding their business activities, for example concerning advertising and premium collection. Without the help of the state, these companies would have required to act according to the necessities of the market. In practice, however, they concentrated on their business connections with saving banks and local authorities. The two exceptions were the "k.k. priv. niederösterreichische wechselseitige Brandschaden-Versicherungsanstal" and the "k.k. priv. wechselseitige Brandschaden-Versicherungsanstalt für Mähren und Schlesien". The latter was able to increase its annual premiums greatly between 1878 and 1887. In general, during this period the mutuals' premium income and their insurance payments decreased. Another main difference

[242] Cf. *Israel, B.* (1889), Die Feuerversicherungs-Gesellschaften in Oesterreich während der Jahre 1878-87, in: Mittheilungen und Miscellen, Statistische Monatsschrift XV. Jahrgang, p. 275ff.

[243] Cf. *Egl, H. / Ludwig, B.* (1988), Die Geschichte der Feuerversicherung von 1873 bis 1918, in: Die Ära des klassischen Versicherungswesens, Versicherungsgeschichte Österreichs, vol. II, Vienna, p. 719.

Table 13: Life insurance companies 1885		
name of society	total premium income (in Gulden)	market share in percent
Assicurazione Generali	3.598,529	20.97
Erste Ungarische allgemeine Assecuranzgesellschaft (national foundation)	2.131,035	12.42
Riunione Adriatica di Sicurtà	1.595,159	9.29
Der Anker, Lebens und Renten-Versicherungs-Gesellschaft	1.551,094	9.04
Erster allgemeiner Beamten-Verein der österr.-ungar. Monarchie	1.448,430	8.44
Allgemeine wechselseitige Kapitalien- und Renten-Versicherungs-Anstalt (Janus)	1.138,623	6.63
Azienda assicuratrice	983,833	5.73
Magyar Franczia	770,648	4.49
Wechselseitige Versicherungsgesellschaft in Krakau	580,332	3.38
k. k. priv. Versicherungsgesellschaft "Donau"	575,916	3.36
"Austria", allg. wechsels. Capitalien- u. Renten. Versicherungs. Gesellschaft	553,253	3.22
Pester Versicherungs-Anstalt (national foundation)	531,384	3.10
k.k. priv. Versicherungsgesellschaft Österreichischer Phönix	463,536	2.70
Wr. Leb. U. R.-V.-A.	389,864	2.27
"Slavia", gegenseitige Versicherungsbank in Prag	374,425	2.18
"Praha", wechselseitiger Lebens-Versicherungs-Verein	128,920	0.75
Gisela-Verein	109,680	0.64
Allgemeine wechselseitige Versicherungsbank "Transsylvania"	84,322	0.49
Enterprise d. p. f.	84,297	0.49
"Concordia", Reichenberg-Brünner gegenseitige Versicherungs-Anstalt	69,946	0.41

Source: Statistische Monatsschrift.

Table 14: Life insurance industry development 1880-1896 (in Gulden)

year	mutual insurance societies' gross-premium income	mutual insurance societies' market share in percent	stock insurance companies' gross-premium income	domestic stock insurance societies' market share in percent	mutual insurance societies' net-insurance payments	stock insurance companies' net-insurance payments
1880	919,000	7.33	11.622,000	92.67	271,000	2.405,000
1885	4,487,931	26.15	12.675,295	73.85	1.990,765	4.033,828
1886	4,809,035	26.59	13.278,831	73.41	2.120,237	6.970,248
1887	5,228,383	26.53	14.479,402	73.47	2.335,201	7.113,914
1888	5,534,213	24.65	16.915,139	75.35	2.487,861	7.897,937
1891	7,061,630	30.11	16.391,893	69.89	3.440,822	6.509,510
1892	7,695,720	29.93	18.012,911	70.07	4.874,887	6.786,203
1893	8,216,617	29.30	19.830,993	70.70	5.329,160	6.795,003
1894	9,116,249	29.91	21.358,351	70.09	5.834,223	7.163,579
1895	9,609,781	30.10	22.314,973	69.90	5.981,824	7.782,091
1896	10,056,216	30.84	22.547,183	69.16	5.895,933	8.557,909

Source: Statistische Monatsschrift.

Figure 4: Life insurance industry development 1880-1896 (in Gulden)

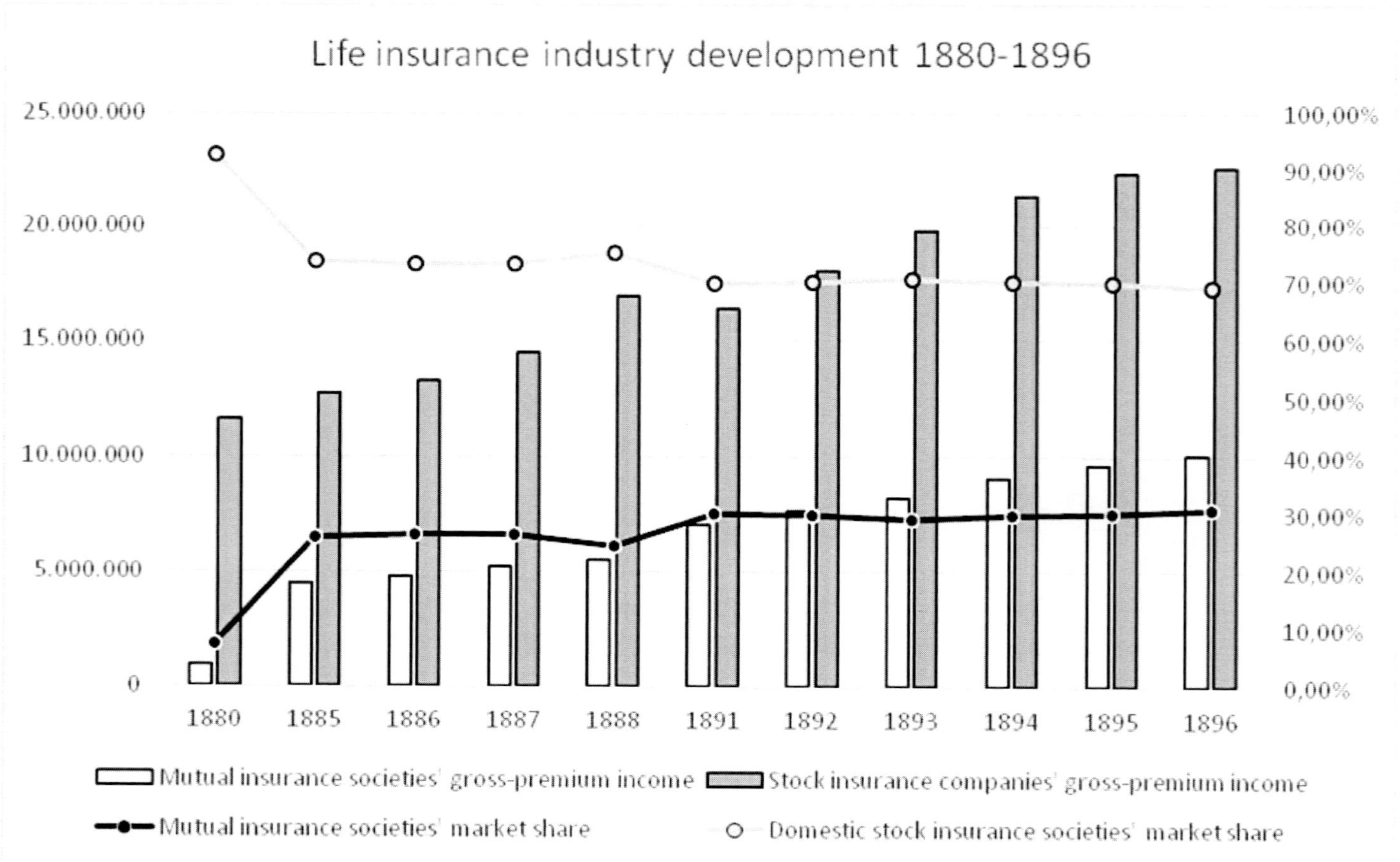

Source: Statistische Monatsschrift.

between joint stock companies and mutuals was that with the exception of the “Wechselseitige Versicherungsgesellschaft in Krakau” all mutuals limited their business to the monarchy, while joint stock companies had also international transactions. The latter participated, for example, via re-insurance contracts in fire insurance transactions in all European states and on the other hand gave foreign companies a large part of their own business (see tables 15 and 16 and figure 5).[244]

In total, the market share of mutuals decreased continuously between 1878 and 1887 from 24.28 percent to 19.75 percent, while the joint stock companies' increased from 71.53 percent to 80.25 percent. Moreover, the premium income of mutuals increased half of those of joint stock companies. During this period, the re-insurers achieved the biggest growth in particular in Hungary, where mutuals caught up strongly. During this period, the insurance sum of mutuals increased over 50 percent. This is an indicator for the strong growth of the insurance business in the monarchy.[245] The fire insurance market was highly concentrated. The five largest companies (exclusive joint stock companies) had a market share of 55.40 percent, including their international business. In 1890, 6.2 percent of the total premiums and 7.1 percent of damage payments belonged to foreign insurance companies.[246]

12.6.3 Reports about the development of the entire insurance industry between 1891-1896[247]

From 1891 onwards, reports and analyses about the entire insurance industry of the monarchy can be found in the journal “Statistische Monatsschrift“.

[244] Cf. *Israel, B.* (1889), Die Feuerversicherungs-Gesellschaften in Oesterreich während der Jahre 1878-87, in: Mittheilungen und Miscellen, Statistische Monatsschrift XV. Jahrgang, p. 276.

[245] Cf. Ibid., p. 281.

[246] Cf. *Otruba, G.* (1980), Die Feuerversicherung und die damit befaßten Gesellschaften in Österreich von ihren Anfängen bis zur Gegenwart, in: *Henning, F.* (ed.): Entwicklung und Aufgaben von Versicherungen und Banken in der Industrialisierung, Berlin, p. 105.

[247] Cf. *Krickl, R.* (1893), Die österreichischen Assecuranz-Gesellschaften im Jahre 1891, in: Mittheilungen und Miscellen Statistische Monatsschrift XIX. Jahrgang, p. 449ff und 527ff.; *Krickl, R.* (1894), Die österreichischen Assecuranz-Gesellschaften im Jahre 1892, in: Mittheilungen und Miscellen, Statistische Monatsschrift XX. Jahrgang, p. 513ff und 575ff.; *Krickl, R.* (1895), Die österreichischen Assecuranz-Gesellschaften im Jahre 1893, in: Mittheilungen und Miscellen, Statistische Monatsschrift XXI. Jahrgang, p. 433ff und 543ff.; *Krickl, R.* (1896), Die österreichischen Assecuranz-Gesellschaften im Jahre 1894, in: Mittheilungen und Miscellen, Statistische Monatsschrift XXII. Jahrgang, p. 620ff und 704ff.; *Krickl, R.* (1897), Die österreichischen Assecuranz-Gesellschaften im Jahre 1895, in: Mittheilungen und Miscellen, Statistische Monatsschrift XXIII. Jahrgang, p. 691ff und

Table 15: Fire insurance societies 1887		
name of society	total premium income	market share in percent
Assicurazione Genrali	6.954,994	15.30
Riunione Adriatica di Sicurtà	5.776,334	12.71
Franco-Hongroise	4.213,657	9.27
k.k priv. Versicherungsgesellschaft Österreichischer Phönix	4.181,625	9.20
Erste Ungarische allgemeine Assecuranzgesellschaft (national foundation)	4.053,236	8.92
Pester Versicherungs-Anstalt (national foundation)	2.888,891	6.35
* Wechselseitige Versicherungsgesellschaft in Krakau	2.724,421	5.99
Azienda assicuratrice	2.610,450	5.74
Wiener V.-G.	2.356,393	5.18
k. k. priv. Österr. Versicherungs-Gesellschaft „Donau"	1.906,566	4.19
+ North British	1.096,919	2.41
"Slavia", gegenseitige Versicherungsbank in Prag	864,234	1.90
* k.k. priv. wechselseitige Brandschaden-Versicherungsanstalt für Mähren und Schlesien	816,596	1.80
* k. k. priv. Erste böhmische wechselseitige Brand- und Hagelschaden-Versicherungs-Anstalt	789,177	1.74
Assekuranzverein von Zuckerfabriken in der österr.-ungarischen Monarchie	771,814	1.70
* k. k. priv. niederösterreichische wechselseitige Brandschaden-Versicherungsanstalt	753,420	1.66
* Innerösterreichische wechselseitige Brandschaden-Versicherungs-Anstalt	626,812	1.38
"Concordia", Reichenberg-Brünner gegenseitige Versicherungs-Anstalt	512,766	1.13
+ Leipziger Feuer-V.-G.	439,000	0.97
* Oberösterreichische wechselseitige Brandschadenversicherungsanstalt	334,332	0.74
* Feuerversicherungsanstalt für Tirol und Vorarlberg und das Fürstenthum Liechtenstein	243,652	0.54
St. Florian	168,017	0.37
Landwirtschaftlich. Prag	141,073	0.31
Transsylvania	88,619	0.19
* Salzburger wechselseitige Landes-Brandschaden-Versicherungsanstalt	82,135	0.18
Prager städt. Vers.-Anstalt	67,711	0.15

* regional insurance institution (Landesanstalt)
\+ foreign joint stock companies
Source: Statistische Monatsschrift.

Table 16: Fire insurance industry development 1878-1887 (in Gulden)

year	mutual insurance societies' gross-premium income	mutual insurance societies' market share in percent	stock insurance companies' gross-premium income	domestic stock insurance societies' market share in percent	foreign stock insurance companies market share in percent	mutual insurance societies' net-insurance payments	stock insurance companies' net-insurance payments
1878	6.942,000	24.28	21.647,000	71.53	4.19		
1879	7.047,000	24.33	21.923,000	71.51	4.17		
1880	7.498,000	23.78	24.035,000	72.32	3.90	14.447,000	49.870,000
1881	7.872,000	22.06	27.811,000	74.45	3.36		
1882	8.190,000	21.60	29.732,000	75.05	3.18		
1883	8.385,000	20.75	32.015,000	75.95	3.04		
1884	8.733,000	20.67	33.518,000	76.22	2.84	12.874,462	53.142,783
1885	8.672,000	20.06	34.552,000	76.78	2.79		
1886	8.732,000	20.19	34.519,000	79.81	2.84		
1887	8.976,000	19.75	36.478,000	80.25	2.64	3.309,538	15.188,217

Source: Statistische Monatsschrift.

Figure 5: Fire insurance industry development 1878-1887 (in Gulden)

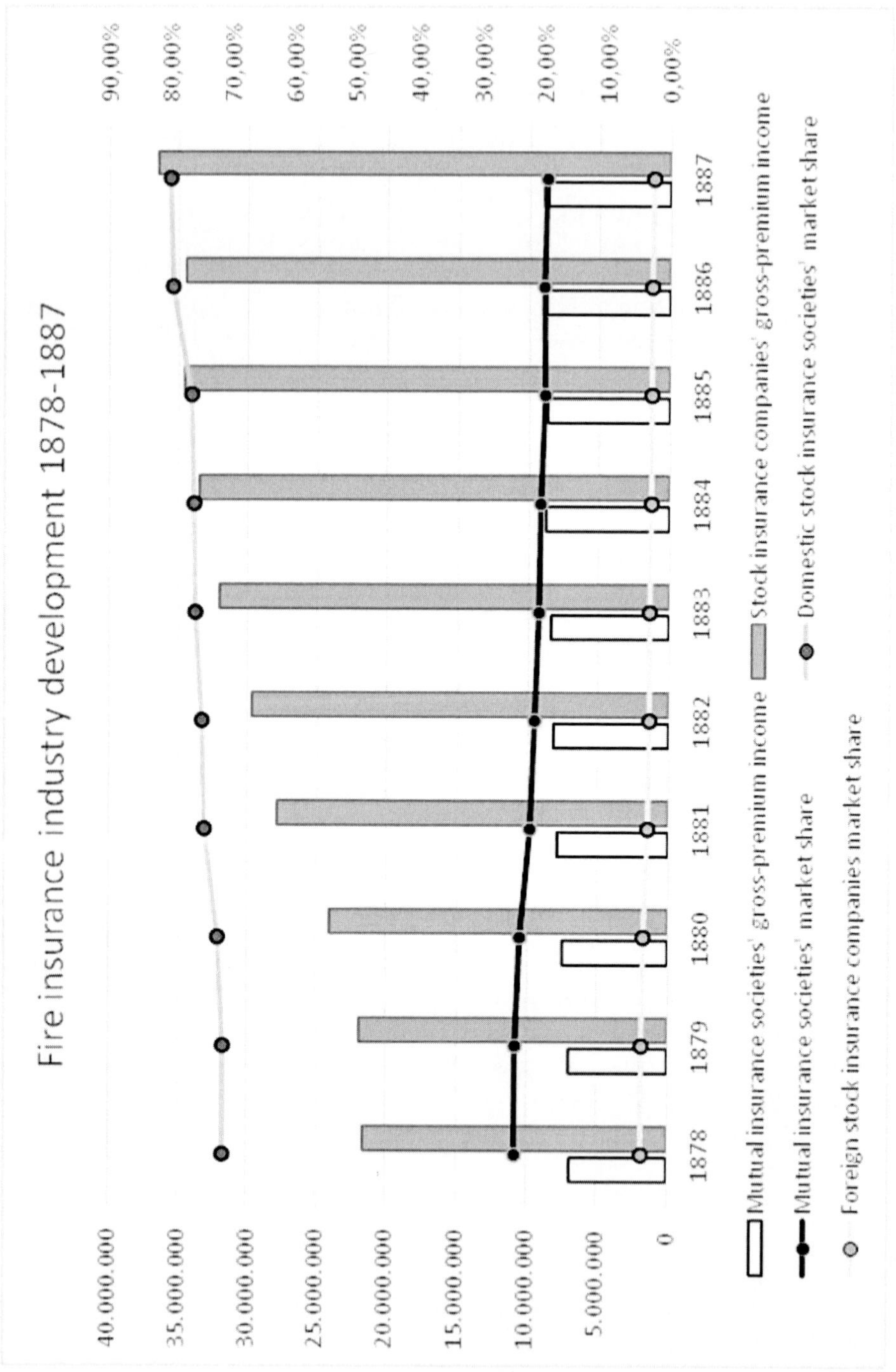

Source: Statistische Monatsschrift.

During this period 1891-1896, the insurance portfolio had only increased from 50 to 52 percent, excluding the local small fire insurance societies that could be found in particular in Lower Austria, Upper Austria, and Bohemia. At the end of 1891, 15 joint stock companies and 35 mutuals existed. From them 19 offered life insurances (from them six were composite insurers) and 31 were non-life insurers (from them six were composite insurers), joint stock companies had business in several insurance segments.[248] The new foundations during this period were the mutual company "Dniester" in Lemberg and the "Universale allgemeine Volksversicherungs-Gesellschaft" in Vienna. The non-life insurance segment had 68.15 percent from the total premium income in 1896. The share decreased to 64.50 percent until 1896. The insurance penetration increased from 4.9 to 5.9 percent during this period (see tables 17 and 18).

The market share of joint stock companies and mutuals in the property and casualty insurance industry, which was hardly cost covering, stayed constant between 1891 and 1896. The re-insurers decreased regarding the market share between 1875 and 1880 but increased fast until 1895 (see tables 19, 20 and 21 and figure 6).

The life insurance segment was 1896 highly concentrated. Joint stock companies had a market share of 69.39 percent, from which the three largest companies, the „Assicurazione Generali", the "Der Anker, Lebens und Renten-Versicherungs-Gesellschaft", and the "Riunione Adriatica di Sicurtà", comprised 53.88 percent. Only in the property and casualty insurance segment a mutual company, the "Wechselseitige Versicherungsgesellschaft in Krakau", could be found among the top five insurers. These five companies had a total market share of 68.97 percent, which indicates a high concentration of the insurance market (see table 22).

Fachini was one of the first who refers in his publications about the insurance industry to the enormous economic importance of the insurance business in the monarchy, which had 49,811 employees in 1888. These people worked under very good working conditions. With England as the starting point, it became common on the continent that insurance officials had a share in the net-profit. Additionally, in Austria several forms of employees' bonus existed. For example, during the 1880s pension and widows funds were established such as

768ff.; *Krickl, R.* (1898), Die österreichischen Assecuranz-Gesellschaften im Jahre 1896, in: Mittheilungen und Miscellen, Statistische Monatsschrift XXIV. Jahrgang, p. 637ff und 711ff.

[248] Cf. *Krickl, R.* (1893), Die österreichischen Assekuranz-Gesellschaften im Jahre 1891, in: Statistische Monatsschrift, Vienna, p. 452.

Table 17: Austrian-Hungarian Monarchy insurance market 1891			
	life insurer	non-life and accident insurer	all sectors
number of companies (composite insurer)	19 (6)	31 (6)	50
premium (in Gulden)	23.453,523	50.183,089	73.636,612
insurance payments (in Gulden)	9.950,332	21.065,318	31.015,650
insurance penetration in percent	1.56 (1890)	3.34 (1890)	4.9 (1890)

Table 18: Austrian-Hungarian Monarchy insurance market 1896			
	life insurer	property and casualty insurer	all sectors
number of companies (composite insurer)	19 (7)	39 (7)	52
premium (in Gulden)	32.638,900	59.276,786	91.915,686
insurance payments (in Gulden)	14.453.842	22.109,040	36.562,882

Source: Statistische Monatsschrift.

the "Unterstützungsverein für Assekuranzangehörige" by *Ritter von Colditz*in 1885.[249]

[249] Cf. *Fachini E.* (1888), Entstehung, Grundsätze und Entwicklung des Versicherungswesens in Österreich-Ungarn, Vienna.

Figure 6: Property and casualty insurance industry 1891-1896

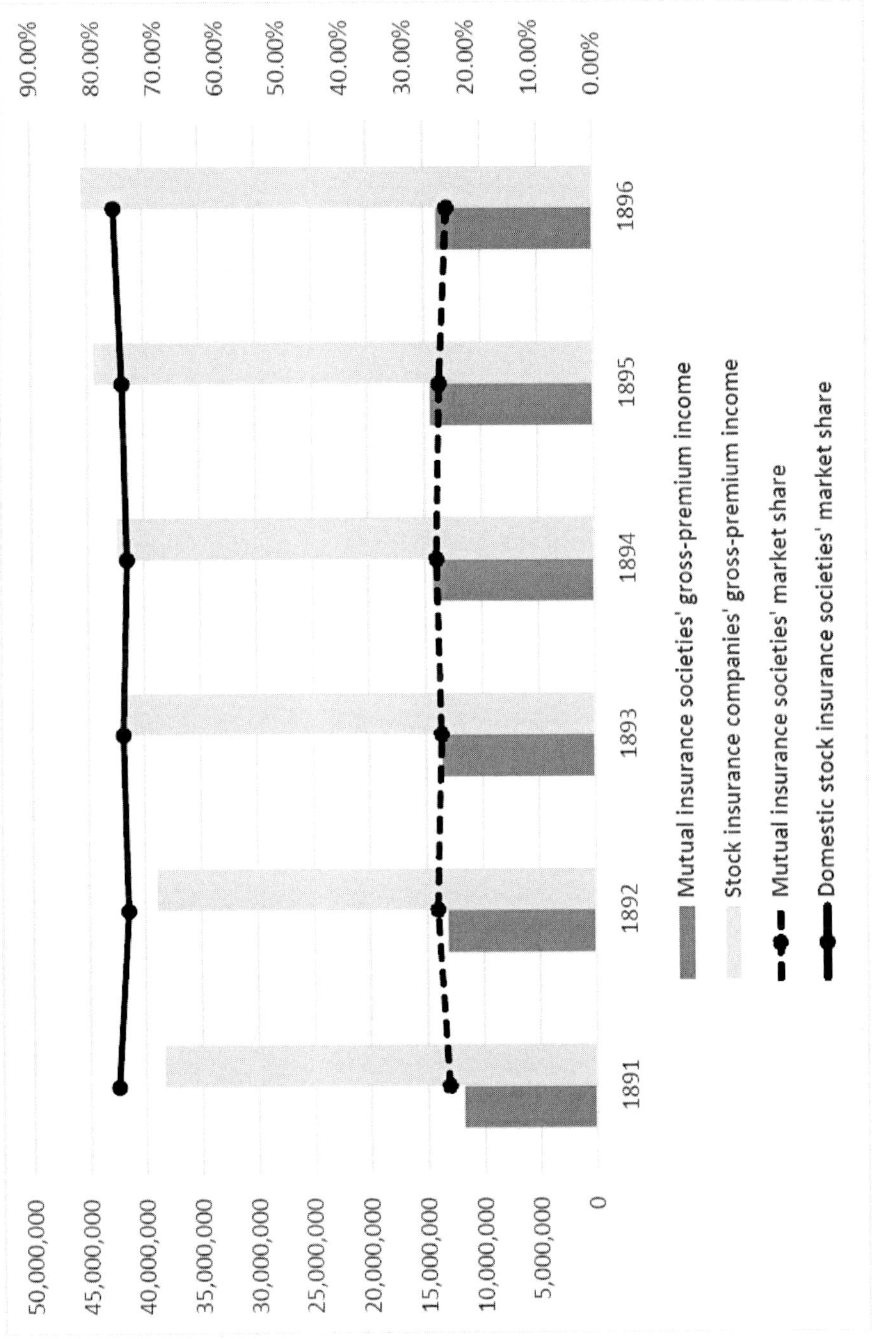

Source: Statistische Monatsschrift.

Table 19: Property and casualty insurance industry 1891-1896 (in Gulden)

year	mutual insurance societies' gross-premium income	mutual insurance societies' market share in percent	stock insurance companies' gross-premium income	domestic stock insurance societies' market share in percent	mutual insurance societies' gross-insurance payments	stock insurance companies' gross-insurance payments
1891	11.837,421	23.59	38.345,668	76.41	4.909,906	16.155,392
1892	13.177,288	25.30	38.913,797	74.70	5.203,394	16.878,574
1893	13,55..099	24.59	41.571,372	75.41	4.802,656	17.389,110
1894	14.328,374	25.26	42.391,142	74.74	5.064,903	18.453,493
1895	14.502,949	24.63	44.379,112	75.37	5.734,020	17.588,932
1896	13.854,589	23.37	45.422,197	76.60	4.589,352	17.519,708

Source: Statistische Monatsschrift

Table 20: Property and casualty insurance 1891		
name of society	total premium income	market share in percent
Assicurazione Genrali	8.937,188	20.73
Riunione Adriatica di Sicurtà	8.119,839	18.83
k.k. priv. Versicherungsgesellschaft Österreichischer Phönix	7.329,831	17.00
Wechselseitige Versicherungsgesellschaft in Krakau	3.824,969	8.87
Wiener Versich.-Ges.	3.632,559	8.42
k.k. priv. Österr. Versicherungs-Gesellschaft „Donau"	2.672,651	6.20
„Slavia", gegenseitige Versicherungsbank in Prag	1.043,729	2.42
Erste öst. Allg. Unfall-Vers.	1.000,236	2.32
Assekuranzverein von Zuckerfabriken in der österr.-ungarischen Monarchie	912,740	2.12
* k.k. priv. Wechselseitige Brandschaden-Versicherungs-Anstalt	871,749	2.02
* k.k. priv. wechselseitige Brandschaden-Versicherungsanstalt für Mähren und Schlesien	707,747	1.64
* Salzburger wechselseitige Landes-Brandschaden-Versicherungsanstalt	621,131	1.44
* k.k. priv. Erste böhmische wechselseitige Brand- und Hagelschaden-Versicherungs-Anstalt	548,627	1.27
„Concordia", Reichenberg-Brünner gegenseitige Versicherungs-Anstalt	526,729	1.22
* Oberösterreichische wechselseitige Brandschadenversicherungsanstalt	323,940	0.75
Intern. Unfall-Vers.-A.G.	315,749	0.73
* Feuerversicherungsanstalt für Tirol und Vorarlberg und das Fürstenthum Liechtenstein	294,273	0.68
Gegenseitiger Versicherungs-Verein für Montanwerke, Maschinen- und Metallfabriken	227,658	0.53
Verein von Indust. Z. Vers. Gegen körperl. Unfälle	211,092	0.49
Landwirtsch. Gegs. Versich.-Anstalt	200,640	0.47
St. Florian	169,377	0.39
Vers. Verb. F. Papier-Industrie	141,782	0.33
Gegens. Brandschaden-Versich.-Verb. Öster. Eisenbahn	92,793	0.22
Erste Wiener Spiegelglas-Versicherungsgesellschaft	92,572	0.21
* Innerösterreichische wechselseitige Brandschaden-Versicherungs-Anstalt	86,953	0.20
Prager städt. Vers.-Anst.	78,780	0.18
* Tirol-Vorarlberg Mobilien Brandvers.-Anst.	58,775	0.14
Unio Catholica	31,049	0.07
Vorarlberger Viehvers.-Ver.	23,690	0.05
Wechsels. Viehvers.-Anst.	11,086	0.03
Deutsch-böhm. Wechselseit. Brandsch.- Versich.- Ver.	8,539	0.02
Dampfkessel-Untersuch. U. Versich.-Gesellschaft	0	0.00

* regional insurance institution (Landesanstalt)
Source: Statistische Monatsschrift.

Table 21: Property and casualty insurance 1896		
name of society	total premium income	market share in percent
Assicurazione Genrali	11.210,333	22.47
k.k. priv. Versicherungsgesellschaft Österreichischer Phönix	8.121,317	16.28
Riunione Adriatica di Sicurtà	7.295,879	14.62
Wechselseitige Versicherungsgesellschaft in Krakau	4.083,121	8.18
Wiener Versich.-Ges.	3.702,386	7.42
k.k. priv. Österr. Versicherungs-Gesellschaft „Donau"	2.856,908	5.73
Hagel- und Rückvers.-Gesellschaft "Meridionale"	1.502,311	3.01
Erste öst. Allg. Unfall-Vers.	1.465,007	2.94
Assekuranzverein von Zuckerfabriken in der österr.-ungarischen Monarchie	1.235,994	2.48
* k.k. priv. Erste böhmische wechselseitige Brand- und Hagelschaden-Versicherungs-Anstalt	1.203,691	2.41
„Slavia", gegenseitige Versicherungsbank in Prag	1.158,458	2.32
Intern. Unfall-Vers.-A.G.	1.048,506	2.10
* Innerösterreichische wechselseitige Brandschaden-Versicherungs-Anstalt	740,256	1.48
* k.k. priv. wechselseitige Brandschaden-Versicherungsanstalt für Mähren und Schlesien	649,746	1.30
* k.k. priv. Wechselseitige Brandschaden-Versicherungs-Anstalt	586,051	1.17
„Concordia", Reichenberg-Brünner gegenseitige Versicherungs-Anstalt	553,586	1.11
* Feuerversicherungsanstalt für Tirol und Vorarlberg und das Fürstenthum Liechtenstein	362,535	0.73
* Oberösterreichische wechselseitige Brandschadenversicherungsanstalt	338,277	0.68
Gegenseitiger Versicherungs-Verein für Montanwerke, Maschinen- und Metallfabriken	277,988	0.56
Verein von Indust. Z. Vers. Gegen körperl. Unfälle	220,812	0.44
Landwirtschaft. Gegs. Versich.-Anstalt	217,879	0.44
St. Florian	186,951	0.37
Wechsels. V.-G. "Dniester"	185,233	0.37
Erste Wiener Spiegelglas-Versicherungsgesellschaft	133,058	0.27
* Salzburger wechselseitige Landes-Brandschaden-Versicherungsanstalt	118,642	0.24
Vers. Verb. F. Papier-Industrie	105,200	0.21
Prager städt. Vers.-Anstalt	101,518	0.20
* Tirol-Vorarlberg Mobilien Brandvers.-Anst.	87,261	0.17
Unio Catholica	54,140	0.11
Gegens. Brandschaden-Versich.-Verb. Öster. Eisenbahn	55,216	0.11
Vorarlberger Viehvers.-Ver.	28.985	0.06
Deutsch-böhm. Wechselseit. Brandsch.- Versich.- Ver.	9,235	0.02
Dampfkessel-Untersuch. U. Versich.-Gesellschaft	0	0.00

* regional insurance institution (Landesanstalt)
Source: Statistische Monatsschrift.

Table 22: Life insurance companies 1896		
name of society	total premium income	market share in percent
Assicurazione Generali	7.887,185	24.19
Der Anker, Lebens und Renten-Versicherungs-Gesellschaft	6.197,856	19.01
Riunione Adriatica di Sicurtà	3.482,368	10.68
Erster allgemeiner Beamten-Verein der ölsterr.-ungar. Monarchie	2.679,734	8.22
Gisela-Verein	2,302,712	7.06
k.k. priv. Lebens-Versicherungs Gesellschaft "Österr. Phönix"	1.849,328	5.67
Allgemeine wechselseitige Capitalien- und Renten-Versicherungs-Anstalt (Janus)	1.409,950	4.32
Wiener Lebens- und Renten-Versicherungs-Gesellschaft	1.296,274	3.98
Wechselseitige Versicherungsgesellschaft in Krakau	1.150,680	3.53
k.k. priv. Versicherungsgesellschaft "Donau"	1.084,972	3.33
„Slavia", gegenseitige Versicherungsbank in Prag	1.011,063	3.10
Allianz, Lebens und Renten Versicherungs Actien Gesellschaft	702,842	2.16
"Praha", wechselseitiger Lebens-Versicherungs-Verein	426,875	1.31
"Austria", allg. wechsels. Capitalien- u. Renten. Versicherungs. Gesellschaft	422,307	1.30
„Concordia", Reichenberg-Brünner gegenseitige Versicherungs-Anstalt	293,039	0.90
Allgemeine Vorsorgungs-Anstalt	189,229	0.58
Lebens-Versich.-Verein v. Eisenb.-Bedienst.	96,536	0,30
"Patria", gegenseitige Lebens-Versicherungs-Bank	74,091	0.23
Garantierte Association	46,358	0.14

Source: Statistische Monatsschrift.

12.6.4 The development during the interwar years

In 1919, as mentioned before, a foundation wave of predominant domestic insurance joint stock companies, which were supported by foreign capital, started. Most of them were composite insurers. A restructuring of the insurance industry occurred due to the foundations of many new successor states after World War I.

While the business of the life insurance segment collapsed, the fire insurance segment was less affected. Many people dissolved or canceled their life insurance policies due to the high inflation, because they could not longer afford the premiums. The 11 life insurance companies working in Vienna (including two mutuals, the "Wiener Städtische Wechselseitige Versicherungsanstalt" and the "Wechselseitige Brandschaden

Table 23: Total premium income and market shares of the 17 largest fire insurance companies in 1923

	premium income (in 1,000 Schilling)	part in percent	market share in percent
Donau Allg. Vers.-AG	10.389,299	47.7	19.1
Allg. Vers.-Gesellschaft Phönix	7.645,423	37.2	14.1
Heimat Allgemein	6.000,660	57.4	11.0
Anglo-Elementar Vers.-A.G.	4.897,458	30.8	9.0
Vers.-Anst. d. österr. Bundesländer	4.772,623	14.5	8.8
Providentia Allg. Versicherungsgesellschaft	3.950,252	34.7	7.3
Wiener Städtische Wechselseitige Versicherungsanstalt	3.588,108	51.9	6.7
Wiener Rückversicherungs-Gesellschaft	3.414,387	34.3	6.3
„Domus", Erste österr. Hausschaden-Versicherungs- A.G.	2.904,681	48.9	5.3
* Wechselseitige Brandschaden und Janus	2.068,077	23.3	3.8
Anglo-Danubian Lloyd Allgemeine Versicherungs-AG	1.510,755	11.6	2.8
Erste Allgemeine Unfall- u. Schadensversicherung	1.005,010	43.5	1.8
Der Anker Allg. Vers.-AG	681,519	28.9	1.3
Internationale Unfall- und Schadensvers.-Gesellschaft	589,555	46.1	1.1
Universale allg. Volksversicherungs-Gesellschaft	483,135	49.4	0.9
Erste österr. Versicherungsgesellschaft gegen Einbruch A.G.	225,494	6.6	0.4
Kosmos Allgemeine Versicherungs-A.G.	213,283	47.7	0.4

* regional insurance institution (Landesanstalt)

Source: *Egl, H.* (1988): Maktstrukturen der österreichischen Versicherungswirtschaft zwischen 1925 und 1938, in: Versicherungsgeschichte Österreichs, vol. III, Das Zeitalter des modernen Versicherungswesens, p. 570.

Janus") lost almost 200,000 insurance contracts in 1923.[250] In 1924, the life insurance business improved.

The 17 largest fire insurance companies (including the above-mentioned mutuals with a market share of 10.5 percent) show a noticeable increase: During the first years after the war, the turnovers of non-life insurers decreased due to a heavy underinsurance of the insured

[250] Cf. *Egl, H.* (1988), Maktstrukturen der österreichischen Versicherungswirtschaft zwischen 1925 und 1938, in: Versicherungsgeschichte Österreichs, vol. III, Das Zeitalter des modernen Versicherungswesens, p. 569.

buildings/goods. The year 1922 was a turning point, in which many people became policyholders. According to the publication "Assecuranz-Compass" from 1925, another increase occurred in 1924, in particular in the former crown lands, which were now foreign countries. In these states, the insurance companies wanted to restore the expired insurance contracts as well as the policyholders were willing to pay higher premiums (see table 23).

From 1925 onwards, the risk in the fire insurance segment shifted to the insurance companies when owners set their highly insured property on fire for the insurance money to cover their debts. Unfortunately, the "Abbrennen" (arson) was often well conducted and the companies were not able to proof the arson[251], which happened more often by mutual policyholders. *Otruba* reports a significant growth of the original rather low market share of mutuals since 1925.[252]

At the end of 1925, Austria had 53 domestic insurance companies and 43 subsidiaries of foreign companies: 2 British, 24 German, 2 Italian, 6 Swiss, 3 Czech, and 6 Hungarian. From the 53 domestic companies, 29 were joint stock companies with a market share of 92.32 percent, and 24 mutuals with 7.68 percent (from them 6 were regional insurance institutions with a market share of 3.89 percent) (see table 24).

The Great Depression influenced in Austria in particular the export-orientated sectors and the industry concerning investment goods. As a result, the volume of the foreign trade was halved and a dramatic intensification of the job market occurred.[253] The insurance industry was not excluded from this crisis. The "Assekuranz-Jahrbuch" stated in 1930 that the Austrian insurance industry was one of the few economic branches that were able to maintain its stability and developments despite the economic crisis.

In 1928 the share of the life insurance segment was rather low (36.92 percent), increased stronger than the non-life insurance segment until 1930 (42.72 percent), but decreased continuously during the Great Depression. In 1933, the premium income in the life insurance segment was as high as in the non-life segment (49.47 percent), but decreased dramatically until 1936 (29.5 percent). With regard to insurance payments, the life insurance segment was still a better business

[251] Cf. Ibid., p. 570.

[252] Cf. *Otruba, G.* (1980), Die Feuerversicherung und die damit befaßten Gesellschaften in Österreich von ihren Anfängen bis zur Gegenwart, in: *Henning, F.* (ed.): Entwicklung und Aufgaben von Versicherungen und Banken in der Industrialisierung, Berlin, p. 123.

[253] Cf. *Sandgruber, R.* (1995), Ökonomie und Politik Österreichische Wirtschaftsgeschichte vom Mittelalter bis zur Gegenwart, Vienna, p. 383.

Table 24: Premium income and market share on the insurance market 1925

	premium income (in 1,000 Schilling)	market share in percent
Allg. Vers.-Gesellschaft Phönix	28,516	12.37
Lebensversicherungs-Gesellschaft Phönix	23,230	10.08
Providentia Allg. Versicherungsgesellschaft	22,972	9.97
Donau Allg. Vers.-AG	22,177	9.62
Anglo-Elementar Vers.-A.G.	16,969	7.36
Erste Allgemeine Unfall- u. Schadensversicherung	12,859	5.58
Vers.-Anst. d. österr. Bundesländer	12,830	5.57
Internationale Unfall- und Schadensvers.-Gesellschaft	11,407	4.95
Der Anker Allg. Vers.-AG	10,527	4.57
Riunione Adriatica di Sicurta, Direktion für Österreich	7,116	3.09
Intern. Rück-u. Mitversicherungs A.G.	8,389	3.64
Assicurazioni Generali, Direktion für Österreich	5,523	2.40
Erste österr. Versicherungsgesellschaft gegen Einbruch A.G.	4,804	2.08
Wiener Städtische Wechselseitige Versicherungsanstalt	4,273	1.85
Wiener Rückversicherungs-Gesellschaft	3,330	1.44
* Wechselseitige Brandschaden und Janus	3,170	1.38
Anglo-Danubian Lloyd Allgemeine Versicherungs-AG	2,848	1.24
* OÖ Landes-Brandschaden-Versicherungsanstalt	2,539	1.10
Erste n.ö. Brandschaden-Versicherungs-A.G.	2,497	1.08
Heimat Allgemein	2,229	0.97
Universale allg. Volksversicherungs-Gesellschaft	1,429	0.62
* Tiroler Landes-Brandschanden-Versicherungs-Anstalt	1,350	0.59
Allianz und Gisela-Verein Versicherungs-A.G.	1,312	0.57
„Securitas"	1,277	0.55
Victoria Feuer-Versicherungs-A.G.	1,142	0.50

Gegenseitiger Versicherungsverein für Montanwerke, Maschinen- und Metallfabriken	1,077	0.47
Steirer-Versicherungs-A.G.	1,023	0.44
Kosmos Allgemeine Versicherungs-A.G.	1,004	0.44
Mannheimer Vers.-Gesellschaft	910	0.39
Rück-Vers.-Ver. f. Elementar-Vers.	878	0.38
* Kärntnerische Landes-Versicherungs-Anstalt	861	0.37
Ung.-Französ. Versicherungs-A.G.	708	0.31
Erste Ungarische. Allg. Assekuranz Gesellschaft	677	0.29
Wechsels. Brand, Graz	653	0.28
Versicherungsverband der Industriellen VVaG	629	0.27
* Salzburger Landes-Brandschaden-Versicherungs-Anstalt	601	0.26
Globus Versicherungs-A.G.	496	0.22
Europäische Güter u. Reisegepäck-Versicherungs AG	473	0.21
„Zürich" Versicherungs-Gesellschaft, Direktion für Österreich	473	0.21
Fortuna, Lebens- u. Rückversicherungs-A.G.	471	0.20
Erste Wiener Spiegelglas-Versicherungsgesellschaft	455	0.20
* Vorarlberger Landes-Feuerversicherungs-Anstalt	442	0.19
Assek.-Ver. d. Zuck. Ind., Prag	416	0.18
Frankfurter Allg. Versicherungs- A.G.	411	0.18
Basler Versicherungs-Gesellschaft gegen Feuerschaden, Direktion für Österreich	390	0.17
Versicherungs-Verband für Papier-Industrie a.G.	364	0.16
Eidgenössische Versicherungs-AG, Zweigniederlassung für Österreich	303	0.13
Allg. Versicherungs Gesellschaft „Helvetia"	265	0.11
„Concordia" Allgemeine Versicherungs-A.G.	199	0.09
„Domus", Erste österr. Hausschaden-Versicherungs- A.G.	188	0.08
Vaterländische Allg. Versicherungs- A.G.	178	0.08
„Hammonia", Glas Versicherungs-A.-G.	163	0.07
„Agrippina" Allg. Verswicherungs A.G.	116	0.05
„Albingia" Versicherungs- A.G.	114	0.05

„Hungaria", Allg. Assekuranz A.G.	110	0.05
Gegens. Steir. Ind.-Vers.-Ver.	104	0.05
Slavische Versicherungs A.G.	88	0.04
Assekuranz Union v. 1865	86	0.04
Württembergische Transport Versicherungsgesellschaft	85	0.04
Badische Assekuranz Gesellschaft	82	0.04
Norddeutsche Versicherungs Gessellschaft	81	0.04
„Allianz" Versicherungs A.G.	55	0.02
Vaterländische u. „Rhenania"	48	0.02
„GLEIMAG" Wechselseitige Haftpflicht- und Sachschadenversicherungsanstalt für Glas- und Magazinanlagen	24	0.01
Versicherungs Gesellschaft „Thuringia"	22	0.01
„Deutscher Lloyd" Transportversicherungs- A.G.	21	0.01
Transatlantische Güter-Versicherungsgesellschaft	21	0.01
„Schweiz", Allg. Versicherungs- A.G.	12	0.01
Minerva, Allg. Versicherungs- A.G.	3	0.00
Dampfkesseluntersuchungs u. Versicherungsgesellschaft	1	0.00
Versicherungs A.G. früher Pensionsverein für Handel. Industrie und Gewerbe	1	0.00

* regional insurance institution (Landesanstalt)
Source: *Egl, H.* (1988): Maktstrukturen der österreichischen Versicherungswirtschaft zwischen 1925 und 1938, in: Versicherungsgeschichte Österreichs, vol. III, Das Zeitalter des modernen Versicherungswesens, p. 567ff.

for the companies than other segments, although its premiums' share maintained the same as before the war.[254]

During the interwar years, the insurance segments accident, car (obligatory since 1930), and the third-party insurance developed. Smaller segments such as water pipe and hail insurance did also well.

[254] Cf. *Otruba, G.* (1980), Die Feuerversicherung und die damit befaßten Gesellschaften in Österreich von ihren Anfängen bis zur Gegenwart, in: *Henning, F.* (ed.): Entwicklung und Aufgaben von Versicherungen und Banken in der Industrialisierung, Berlin, p. 123.

During this period, a new segment, the health insurance, was established.[255] In 1930, the insurance penetration was 1.5 percent.[256]

Foreign insurance companies were of great importance during the First Republic, their market shares increased significantly between 1925 and 1933, but these companies ceased to exist under the National-socialism regime. On the other hand, the market share of re-insurance companies decreased enormously at first, but increased during the National socialism. After the bad experience with the joint stock company "Phönix" in 1936, a new trend towards more security in the insurance business developed, which supported the regional insurance institutions and the mutual fire insurance companies as well as the rise of the insurance company "Versicherungsanstalt der österreichischen Bundesländer".[257]

The "Insurance Almanac" presents from volume 1 (1929) to volume 8 (1937) data that can be used to calculate the premium income and the market shares of the insurance companies.

The market was dominated by joint stock companies, which were founded during the foundation wave with the support of foreign capital. Their market share in the life insurance segment was around 93 percent and between 84 and 89 percent in the non-life segment (see figures 7 and 8).

During the interwar years, the market share of mutuals increased continuously compared to earlier times. Their premium share increased from 7.68 percent in 1925 to 15.92 percent (1933), and to 26.2 percent during the war (1942/44) due to the structural improvements that started since the 1870s and led to an adjustment to the structures of joint stock companies (see tables 25 and 26).

The level of concentration in the property and casualty insurance segment was very high in 1928. The top five companies (all joint stock companies) had a market share of 52.66 percent that increased until 1932 to 60.47 percent. The largest non-life insurance company was the "Allgemeine Versicherungsgesellschaft Phönix" with a market share of 22.28 percent in 1932. Even before the Phönix scandal, among joint stock companies a certain concentration process developed. This process was further promoted by the Nazi regime due to companies' merg-

[255] Cf. *Egl, H.* (1988), Maktstrukturen der österreichischen Versicherungswirtschaft zwischen 1925 und 1938, in: Versicherungsgeschichte Österreichs, vol. III, Das Zeitalter des modernen Versicherungswesens, p. 632.

[256] *Hollmayer, A.* (2000), Makrodaten der Österreichischen Assekuranz 1875-2000, in: Versicherungsgeschichte Österreichs, vol. VI, An der Schwelle zum 3. Jahrtausend – Retrospektiven und Perspektiven, Vienna 2000, p. 1394.

[257] Cf. *Otruba, G.* (1980), Die Feuerversicherung und die damit befaßten Gesellschaften in Österreich von ihren Anfängen bis zur Gegenwart, in: *Henning, F.* (ed.): Entwicklung und Aufgaben von Versicherungen und Banken in der Industrialisierung, Berlin, p. 123.

Figure 7: Insurance force and market share of mutual and stock life insurance companies on the Austrian insurance market 1927-1932

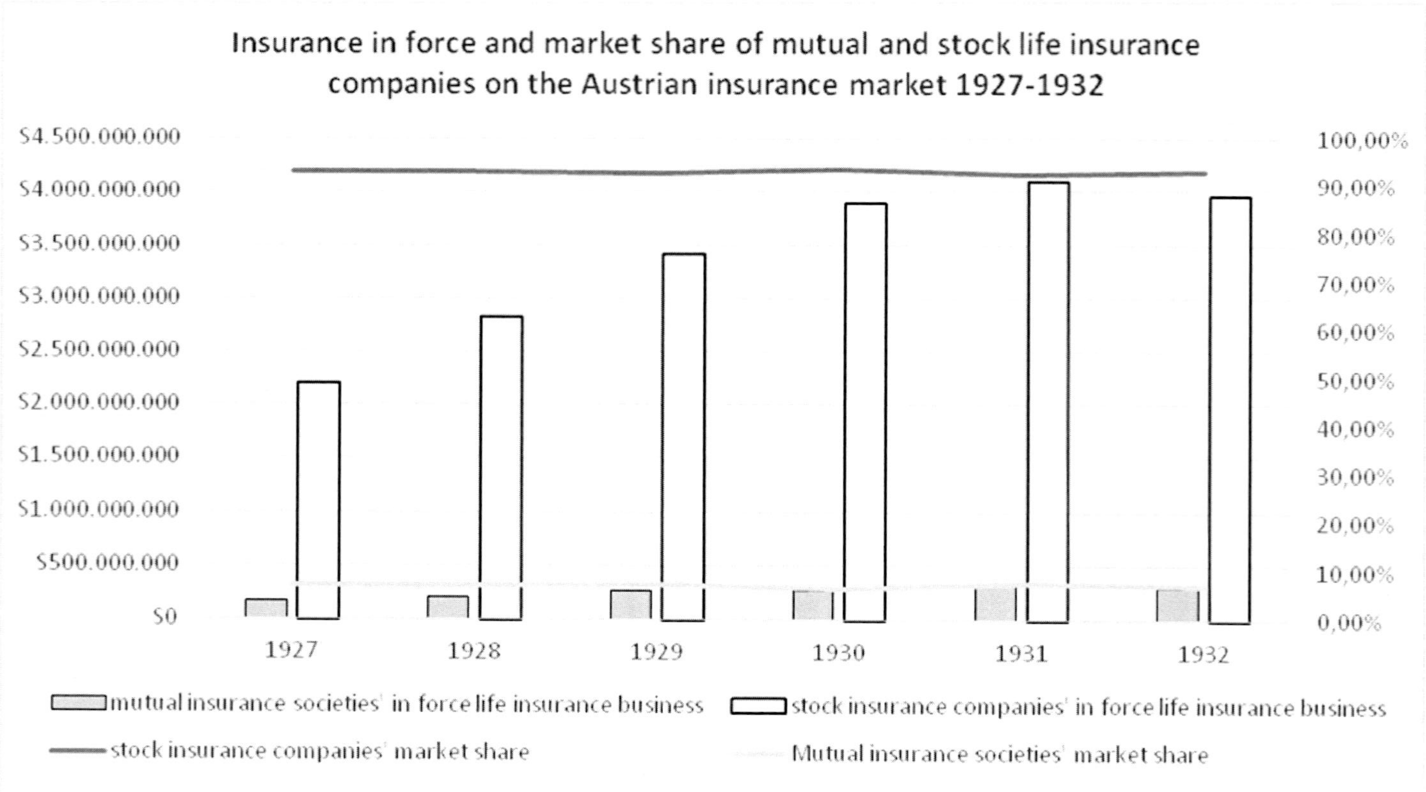

Source: Versicherungs-Almanach

Figure 8: Gross premium and market share of mutual and stock property and casualty insurance companies on the Austrian insurance market 1928-1932

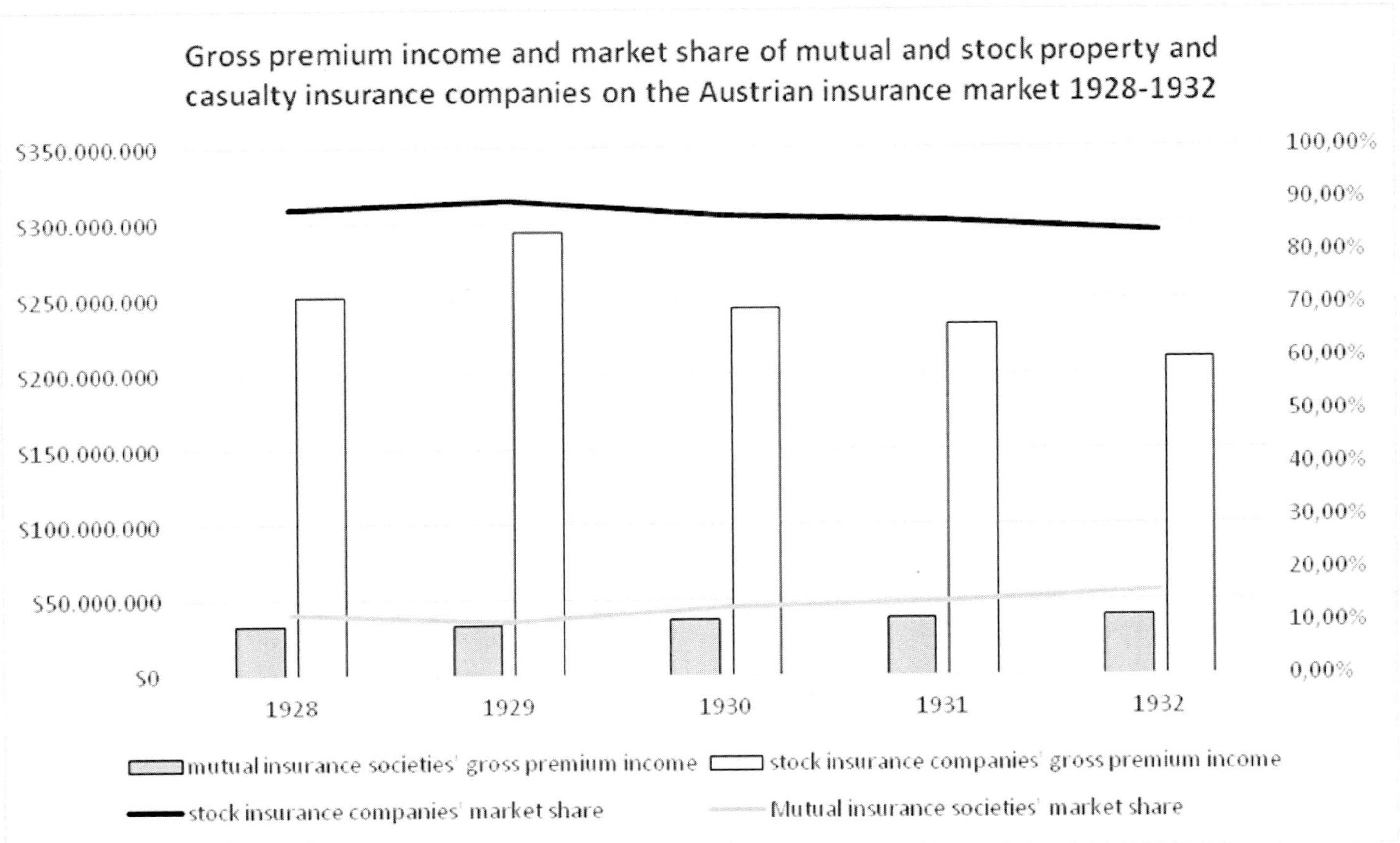

Source: Versicherungs-Almanach

Table 25: Top 5 property and casualty insurers on the Austrian insurance market 1928		
name	premium income (in Schilling)	market share in percent
Allg. Vers.-Gesellschaft Phönix	59.228,519	20.86
Anglo-Elementar Vers.-A.G.	25.313,198	8.91
Donau Allg. Vers.-AG	24.505,342	8.63
Erste Allgemeine Unfall- u. Schadensversicherung	21.715,178	7.65
Internationale Unfall- und Schadensvers.-Gesellschaft	18.761,541	6.61

Source: Versicherungs-Almanach.

Table 26: Top 5 property and casualty insurers on the Austrian insurance market 1932			
name	premium income (in Schilling)	market share in percent	insurance payments
Allg. Vers.-Gesellschaft Phönix	55.559,691	22.28	31.282,337
Internationale Unfall- und Schadensvers.-Gesellschaft	27.328,232	10.96	13.547,341
Donau Allg. Vers.-AG	23.771,752	9.53	13.373,689
Erste Allgemeine Unfall- u. Schadensversicherung	22.927,477	9.20	10.489,079
Vers.-Anst. d. österr. Bundesländer	21.183,933	8.50	14.775,473

Source: Versicherungs-Almanach.

ers. As a result, the joint stock companies' market share decreased from 88.41 percent in 1928 to 84.04 percent in 1932.

In the life insurance segment, which was extremely concentrated, mutuals were able to increase their market share slightly from 6.87 percent in 1927 to 7.01 in 1932. In 1927, the market share of the top five insurers (all joint stock companies) was 88.58 percent with the "Lebensversicherungs-Gesellschaft Phönix" on the first rank with 59.27 percent. The share of life insurers increased until 1932 to 88.64 percent and that of the "Lebensversicherungs-Gesellschaft Phönix" to 62.34 percent. This shows again the ambitious business transactions of the "Phoenix" director *Berliner* (see tables 27 and 28).

The last Austrian insurance statistics of the interwar period can be found in the "Assekuranz-Jahrbuch" 1938 and comprises the statistical

Table 27: Top 5 Life Insurers on the Austrian insurance market in 1927		
name	business in force (in thousand Schilling)	market share in percent
Lebensversicherungs-Gesellschaft Phönix	1.398,460	59.27
Der Anker Allg. Vers.-AG	322,878	13.68
Donau Allg. Vers.-AG	180,785	7.66
* Wechselseitige Brandschaden und Janus	104,002	4.41
Vers.-Anst. d. österr. Bundesländer	84,090	3.56

* regional insurance institution (Landesanstalt)
Source: Versicherungs-Almanach

Table 28: Top 5 Life Insurers on the Austrian insurance market in 1932		
name	business in force (in thousand Schilling)	market share in percent
Lebensversicherungs-Gesellschaft Phönix	2.694,065	62.34
Der Anker Allg. Vers.-AG	450,117	10.41
Donau Allg. Vers.-AG	344,137	7.96
Vers.-Anst. d. österr. Bundesländer	210,763	4.88
* Wechselseitige Brandschaden und Janus	174,853	4.05

* regional insurance institution (Landesanstalt)
Source: Versicherungs-Almanach.

data including the 31st of December 1936. Later no statistics of that kind were published. This can be explained by the dictatorial regime in Austria until 1945. With the reconstruction of the private Austrian insurance industry by legislative acts such as the Insurance Transaction Act and the Insurance Restitution Law, the insurance industry became reinstated and created so the necessary preconditions for a new insurance statistics.[258]

The following section covering the period 1945 to 1955 is based on the data from *Dieter Stiefel's* publication from 2006.[259] For the

[258] Cf. Veröffentlichungen des Bundesministeriums für Finanzen, betreffend die Vertragsversicherung, 1963, No. 1, p. 1.

[259] Cf. *Stiefel, D.* (ed.) (2006), "Unusual Business", Vienna.

time 1959 to 1969, the data is drawn from the official publication "Veröffentlichungen des Bundesministeriums für Finanzen, betreffend die Vertragsversicherung".[260]

12.6.5 The development of the insurance industry in Austria between 1945 and 1955

The relationship between joint stock companies and mutuals[261] in terms of premium income in 1945 was 75 percent to 25 percent (see table 29).

By the end of 1955, 35 domestic and 16 branches of foreign insurance companies existed. From the 35 domestic companies 16 were joint stock companies, 14 mutual insurance societies, and five insurance companies were "Landesanstalten". Three companies, two mutuals ("Austria Versicherungsverein auf Gegenseitigkeit" (1946)[262], "Österreichische Hagelversicherungsanstalt auf Gegenseitigkeit" (1946) and one joint stock company ("Österreichische Kreditversicherungs-AG") were new on the market. (cf. Table 30).[263]

[260] Cf. Veröffentlichungen des Bundesministeriums für Finanzen, betreffend die Vertragsversicherung, 1963, No. 1, Versicherungsstatistik für die Jahre 1959, 1960 und 1961; Veröffentlichungen des Bundesministeriums für Finanzen, betreffend die Vertragsversicherung, 1967, No. 1, Versicherungsstatistik für die Jahre 1962, 1963, 1964 und 1965; Veröffentlichungen des Bundesministeriums für Finanzen, betreffend die Vertragsversicherung, 1972, No. 1, Versicherungsstatistik für die Jahre 1966, 1967, 1968 und 1969.

[261] Data only for mutual societies with head office in Vienna.

[262] The "Österreichische Hagelversicherungsanstalt auf Gegenseitigkeit" was founded by 18 Austrian insurance companies, which until then were operating hail insurance as a side business. Doing so, respective companies agreed to suspend their license to operate hail insurance for the duration of the existence of the "Österreichische Hagelversicherungsanstalt". In 1961 the hail insurance support legislation, under which the Austrian state as well as the country's federal states obligated themselves in equal shares to partially refinance farmers that signed up for hail insurance for premium rates paid.

[263] Cf. *Mahlberg, B.* (2006), Analyse der Finanzlage österreichischer Versicherungsunternehmenin den Jahren 1944 bis 1955, in: *Stiefel, D.* (ed.), "Unusual Business", Vienna, p. 309.

Table 29: Premium income of Austrian insurance companies in 1,000 Austrian Schilling in 1945

Austrian joint stock companies

	premium income in 1000 Schilling	Market share in percent
Oevag Österreichische Versicherungs-Aktiiengesellschaft (ÖVAG)	7,349	14.54
Donau-Concordia	6,679	13.22
Versicherungsanstalt der österreichischen Bundesländer Versicherungs-AG	12,195	24.13
Wiener Allianz Versicherungs-AG	5,911	11.70
Österreichische Volksfürsorge Lebensversicherungs-AG	4,267	8.44
Erste Allgemeine Unfall- und Schadens-Versicherungs-Gesellschaft	3,845	7.60
Erste n.ö. Brandschadenversicherungsaktiengesellschaft	2,800	5.54
Anglo-Elementar Versicherungs-AG	2,715	5.37
Der Anker Allgemeine Versicherungs-AG	2,334	4.62
Internationale Unfall- und Schadensversicherungsanstalt (Interunfall)	1,507	2.30

Mutual societies with head office in Vienna[264]

	premium income in 1000 Schilling	market share in percent
Wiener Städtische Wechselseitige Versicherungsanstalt	10,794	63.77
Wiener Verein Lebens- und Bestattungsversicherung a.G.	1,525	9.00
Jupiter Versicherungsverein a. G.	1,337	7.90
Wiener Wechselseitigen Krankenversicherung	1,322	7.82
Collegialität Kankenversicherung a. G.	986	5.83
Österreichische Beamtenversicherung	363	2.14
Versicherungsverband der Industriellen VvaG	250	1.48
Versicherungsverband für Papierindustrie (a. G.)	177	1.05
Gegenseitiger Versicherungsverein für Montanwerke, Maschinen- und Metallfabriken	104	0.61
Erste Wiener Spiegelglas-Versicherungsgesellschaft	68	0.40
	16,926	25

Source: *Stiefel, D.*, Der Wiederaufbau der österreichischen Versicherungswirtschaft 1945-1955, in: *Stiefel, D.* (ed.), "Unusual Business", p. 171.

264 The companies "Union Allgemeine Versicherungs-Aktiengesellschaft" and "Anglo-Danubian Lloyd Allgemeine Versicherungs-Aktiengesellschaft" are included in the results of the "Wiener Städtische Wechselseitige Versicherungsanstalt“ since May 1945.

Table 30: Insurance companies 1955

Austrian joint stock companies
Anglo-Danubian Lloyd Allgemeine Versicherungs-AG
Anglo-Elementar Versicherungs-AG
Der Anker Allgemeine Versicherungs-AG
Donau Allgemeine Versicherungs-AG
Erste Allgemeine Unfall- und Schadens-Versicherungs-Gesellschaft
Erste n. ö. Brandschadenversicherungs-AG
Europäische Güter u. Reisegepäck-Versicherungs AG
Heimat Allgemeine Versicherungs-Aktiengesellschaft
Internationale Unfall- und Schadensversicherungs-AG (Interunfall)
Kosmos Allgemeine Versicherungs-AG
Oevag Österreichische Versicherungs-Aktiiengesellschaft (ÖVAG)
Österreichische Kreditversicherungs-AG
Österreichische Volksfürsorge Lebensversicherungs-AG
Union Versicherungs-AG
Versicherungsanstalt der österreichischen Bundesländer AG
Wiener Allianz Versicherungs-AG

Mutual societies
Austria Versicherungsverein auf Gegenseitigkeit
Collegialität Krankenversicherung a.G.
Erste Wiener Spiegelglas-Versicherunggesellschaft
Gegenseitiger Versicherungsverein für Montanwerke, Maschinen- und Metallfabriken
„GLEIMAG" Wechselseitige Haftpflicht- und Sachschaden-Versicherungsanstalt für Glas- und Magazinanlagen
Jupiter Versicherungsverein a.G.
* Kärntnerische Landes-Versicherungs-Anstalt
Merkur Wechselseitige Krankenversicherungs-Anstalt
* OÖ Landes-Brandschaden-Versicherungsanstalt
Österreichische Beamtenversicherung VVaG
Österreichische Hagelversicherungsanstalt a.G.
* Salzburger Landes-Brandschaden-Versicherungs-Anstalt
* Tiroler Landes-Brandschanden-Versicherungs-Anstalt
Versicherungsverband der Industriellen VVaG
Versicherungs-Verband für Papier-Industrie a.G.
* Vorarlberger Landes-Feuerversicherungs-Anstalt
* Wechselseitige Versicherungsanstalt in Graz
Wiener Städtische Wechselseitige Versicherungsanstalt
Wiener Verein Lebens- und Bestattungsversicherung a.G.
Wiener Wechselseitige Krankenversicherung

* regional insurance institution (Landesanstalt)

Branch offices of foreign insurance companies
Assicurazioni Generali, Direktion für Österreich
Basler Versicherungs-Gesellschaft gegen Feuerschaden, Direktion für Österreich
Basler Transport-Versicherungs-Gesellschaft, Zweigniederlassung Wien
Österreichische Verwaltung der Deutschen Sachversicherung AG
Eidgenössische Versicherungs-AG, Zweigniederlassung für Österreich
Helvetia Allgemeine Versicherungs-Gesellschaft, Filialdirektion Wien
Mannheimer Versicherungsgesellschaft, Direktion für Österreich
„National" Allgemeine Versicherungs-AG, Direktion für Österreich
Nordstern Allgemeine Versicherungs-AG, Direktion für Österreich
Nordstern Lebenversicherungs-AG, Zweigniederlassung für Österreich
Riunione Adriatica di Sicurta, Direktion für Österreich
"Schweiz" Allgemeine Versicherungs-AG, Zweigniederlassung für Wien
Victoria zu Berlin, Allgemeine Versicherungs-AG, Dire,tion für Österreich
Victoria Feuer-Versicherungs-AG, Direktion für Österreich
Winterthur Versicherungs AG, Direktion für Österreich
„Zürich" Versicherungs-Gesellschaft, Direktion für Österreich

Source: *Mahlberg, B.* (2006): Analyse der Finanzlage österreichischer Versicherungsunternehmenin den Jahren 1944 bis 1955, in: *Stiefel, D.* (ed.), "Unusual Business", p. 346ff.

Their line of business included health, life and property and casualty insurance companies. In 1955, five were health insurers (from them four were mutuals with a market share of 89.02 percent), 11 life insurers (from them three were mutuals with a market share of 34.04 percent), 43 property and casualty insurers (from them 12 were mutuals with a market share of 23.95 percent) and one was a pure re-insurer. Six companies offered insurance services from at least two departments, while the "Versicherungsanstalt der Österreichischen Bundesländer AG" and the "Wiener Städtische wechselseitige Versicherungsanstalt" were active in three departments (cf. table 31).[265]

[265] Cf. Ibid. p. 310.

Table 31: Structure of the insurance market in 1955[266]

	health insurer	life insurer	property and casualty insurer	all sectors
number of companies	5	11	42	51
premium (in Schilling)	227.489.917,32 15.47	205.562.804,09 13.98	1.037.021.950,73 70.55	1.470.074.672,14
insurance payments (in Schilling)	160.054.882,52 20.30	66.123.624,13 8.39	562.080.447,36 71.31	788.258.954,01
capital investment (in Schilling)	138.075.018,32	823.113.234,15	1.717.570.575,87	2.678.758.828,34
Iisurance volume (in Schilling)	32.75	29.59	149.28	211.61
insurance penetration in percent	0.21	0.19	0.97	1.37

Source: *Mahlberg, B.*: Analyse der Finanzlage österreichischer Versicherungsunternehmenin den Jahren 1944 bis 1955, in: *Stiefel, D.* (ed.), “Unusual Business”, p. 310.

266 The data regarding premiums, services, capital investments, insurance volume, and insurance penetration refer exclusively to the companies from the data record that comprises 5 health insurers, 11 life insurer, and 31 property and casualty insurers.

In reference to the data of *Mahlberg's* study it can be seen that in 1955 the property and casualty insurance business was the largest out of the three different existing insurance segments, in which the highest premium incomes (70.55 percent) and insurance payments (71.31 percent) can be found. These insurers also had the highest capital investments. Furthermore, the segment also recorded the highest number of actively operating insurance companies (42).

The second largest insurance segment in 1955 measured in terms of total premium income collected (15.47 percent) and total insurance payments performed (20.30 percent) was the health insurance segment. The market share of health insurance within the insurance industry rose steadily after World War II. This was certainly an advantage because it made it possible that all insurance benefits could be paid without limitations – based on the Insurance Transfer Act (Versicherungsüberleitungsgesetz). The limitation of sickness benefits, which has been in force since 1942, was cancelled, that way the benefits for the insured were increased. The existing premium reserves were actively paid to the insured. This was the beginning of a lasting growth for health insurance, though the number of compulsorily insured expanded significantly. This meant that private health insurances had a smaller share of the insurance market. This development was more than compensated through the considerable growth of the supplementary insurance business and related improvements in performance (for example, the introduction of group tariffs). You could even speak of a period of boom in the private health insurance, which lasted until mid of the 70s. During this time, the number of insured and the premium income rose steadily. The rising standard of living also had a positive impact on health insurers.

Recording the lowest amount of insurance premium payments collected (13.98 percent) and insurance benefits performed (8.39 percent) was the life insurance segment. After 1945, the life insurance transactions were regulated due to the precarious conditions: rights to benefits were restricted or taken over by the state. The premium incomes were very low but increased due to state measures very fast. Until 1955, a continuously improvement of the premium-benefit proportion in the life insurance segment can be observed. Nevertheless, due to a usually longer duration of contracts, the total amount of capital held by Austrian insurers stemming from life insurance was higher than the amount of capital originating from the segment of health insurance.[267]

The insurance density *(premium income pro resident)* was 211.61 Schilling in 1955 and thus was higher in comparison to the year 1937,

[267] Cf. *Mahlberg, B.* (2006), Analyse der Finanzlage österreichischer Versicherungsunternehmenin den Jahren 1944 bis 1955, in: *Stiefel, D.* (ed.), "Unusual Business", p. 309.

the last year before the "Anschluss" of Austria by the German Reich, as well as higher in comparison to the immediate post war era in 1946. On the other hand, the insurance penetration measured for the same year (premium income compared to the economic output) was significantly lower in comparison to the late pre-war era, only accumulating to 1.37 percent in 1946 in comparison to 1.88 percent in 1937. Considering this situation, it can be argued that even ten years after the end of World War II the Austrian insurance industry had not reached its prior state of development during the late 1930s.[268]

The health insurance market was highly concentrated, i.e. the first three companies, all mutuals, had a market share of 80.9 percent. The largest company was the "Austria Versicherungsverein auf Gegenseitigkeit" with a market share of 35.06 percent (see table 32). This company originated 1946 from the Austrian branch of the "Münchner Versicherungsverein a.G." Second was the "Wiener Städtische Wechselseitige Versicherungsanstalt", and the third was the "Merkur Wechselseitige Krankenversicherungs-Anstalt". With the exception of one company, the "Versicherungsanstalt der österreichischen Bundesländer AG", the health insurance companies were mutuals.[269] From these health insurers the "Austria Versicherungsverein auf Gegenseitigkeit" expanded the most.

Table 32: Premium income and market share of health insurers in 1955

	premium income in Schilling	market share in percent
Austria Versicherungsverein auf Gegenseitigkeit	79.767.770,50	35.06
Wiener Städtische Wechselseitige Versicherungsanstalt	60.231.733,34	26.48
Merkur Wechselseitige Krankenversicherungs-Anstalt	43.950.320,20	19.32
Versicherungsanstalt der österreichischen Bundesländer AG	24.983.248,47	10.98
Collegialität Krankenversicherung a.G.	18.556,844.81	8.16
Total	227.489.917,32	100.00

Source: *Mahlberg, B* (2006).: Analyse der Finanzlage österreichischer Versicherungsunternehmenin den Jahren 1944 bis 1955, in: *Stiefel, D.* (ed.), "Unusual Business", p. 312.

[268] Cf. Ibid., p. 311.
[269] Cf. Ibid., p. 312.

Table 33: Premium income and market share of life insurers in 1955

	premium income in Schilling	market share
Versicherungsanstalt der österreichischen Bundesländer AG	50.795.403,26	24.71
Wiener Städtische Wechselseitige Versicherungsanstalt	33.570.614,75	16.33
Assicurazioni Generali, Direktion für Osterreich	28.584,259.31	13.91
Wiener Verein Lebens- und Bestattungsversicherung a. G.	27.152.386,00	13.21
Osterreichische Volksfürsorge Lebensversicherungs-AG	20.764.292,26	10.10
Oevag Osterreichische Versicherungs-Aktiiengesellschaft (OVAG)	18.135.068,35	8.82
Osterreichische Beamtenversicherung VVaG	9.255.058,85	4.50
Der Anker Allgemeine Versicherungs-AG	9.198.680,01	4.47
Riunione Adriatica di Sicurta, Direktion für Osterreich	5.070.258,44	2.47
Donau Allgemeine Versicherungs-AG	2.989.406,35	1.45
Nordstern Lebensversicherungs-AG, Zweigniederlassung für Osterreich	47.376,51	0.02
Total	205.562.804,09	100.00

Source: *Mahlberg, B.*: Analyse der Finanzlage österreichischer Versicherungsunternehmenin den Jahren 1944 bis 1955, in: *Stiefel, D.* (ed.), "Unusual Business", p. 313.

The life insurance market was not so highly concentrated. The three largest companies had together a market share of 55 percent. The largest company was the "Versicherungsanstalt der österreichischen Bundesländer AG"[270] with a market share of 24.7 percent. The „Wiener Städtische Wechselseitige Versicherungsanstalt" and the "Assicurazioni Generali" were the second respectively third largest life insurers (cf. table 33).[271]

The property and casualty market had the lowest market concentration. The three largest companies had a total market share of 46.95 percent. The largest company was the "Erste Allgemeine Unfall- und Schadens-Versicherung-Gesellschaft" with a market share of 21.02 percent, followed by the "Wiener Städtische Wechselseitige Versicherungsanstalt" and the "Versicherungsanstalt der österreichischen Bundesländer AG" at the second respectively third place (cf. Table 34).

---

[270] The "Versicherungsanstalt der österreichischen Bundesländer AG" was able to gain the administration of the Austrian customers' portfolio, although it had not undertaken the statutory required health insurace segement before 1938.

[271] Cf. Ibid.

Table 34 Premium income and market share of property and casualty insurers in 1955

	premium income in Schilling	market share in percent
Erste Allgemeine Unfall- und Schadens-Versicherungs-Gesellschaft	217.938.090,92	21.02
Wiener Städtische Wechselseitige Versicherungsanstalt	140.879.724,58	13.59
Versicherungsanstalt der österreichischen Bundesländer AG	128.018.914,63	12.34
Internationale Unfall- u. Schadenversicherungs-AG (Interunfall)	126.630.961,98	12.21
Wiener Allianz Versicherungs-AG	76.618.996,60	7.39
Anglo-Elementar Versicherungs-AG	55.629.924,71	5.36
* Wechselseitige Versicherungsanstalt in Graz	35.040.689,93	3.38
Riunlone Adriatica di Sicurta, Direktion für Österreich	24.822.451,15	2.39
Kosmos Allgemeine Versicherungs-AG	22.143.439,76	2.14
Erste n. ö. Brandschadenversicherungs-AG	21.983.705,53	2.12
* Tiroler Landes-Brandschaden-Versicherungsanstalt	19.268.495,03	1.86
Anglo-Danubian Lloyd Allgemeine Versicherungs-AG	18.377.936,96	1.77
„Zürich" Versicherungs-Gesellschaft, Direktion für Österreich	15.577.110,57	1.50
Der Anker Allgemeine Versicherungs-AG	12.393.094,86	1.20
* Salzburger Landes-Brandschaden-Versicherungsanstalt	11.602.899,94	1.12
Nordstern Allgemeine Versicherung-AG, Direktion für Österreich	8.610.317,38	0.83
* Kärntnerische Landes-Versicherungs-Anstalt	6.862.132,75	0.66
Heimat Allgemeine Versicherungs- Aktiengesellschaft	6.545.993,09	0.63
Winterthur Versicherung AG, Direktion für Österreich	6.545.993,09	0.63
Österreichische Hagelversicherungsanstalt a. G.	4.960.649,10	0.48
Gegenseitiger Versicherungsverein für Montanwerke, Maschinen- und Metallfabriken	3.976.108,39	0.38
Assicurazioni Generali, Direktion für Österreich	2.937.020,50	0.28
Union Versicherungs-AG	2.299.064,34	0.22
Erste Wiener Spiegelglas-'Versicherungsgesellschaft	1.599.623,59	0.15
Versicherungsverband der Industriellen VVaG	1.564.983,69	0.15

Eidgenössische Versicherungs-AG, Zweigniederlassung für Österreich	1.468.076,05	0.14
Europäische Guter- u. Reisegepäck-Versicherungs AG	1.086.411,91	0.10
„GLEIMAG" Wechselseitige Haftpflicht- und Sachschaden-Versicherungsanstalt für Gleis- und Magazinanlagen	357.727,37	0.03
Versicherungs-Verband für Papier-Industrie a.G	264.347,23	0.03
Österreichische Kreditversicherungs-AG	120.183,28	0.01
Total	**1.037.021.950,73**	**100.00**

Source: *Mahlberg, B.* (2006): Analyse der Finanzlage österreichischer Versicherungsunternehmenin den Jahren 1944 bis 1955, in: *Stiefel, D.* (ed.), "Unusual Business", p. 346ff.

12.6.6 The development of the insurance industry in Austria between 1959-1969

In the period 1964 to 1970, insurance companies belonged to the most rapidly expanding sectors of the Austrian economy. The nominal value of insurance companies increased each year by an average of 6 percent. In the service sector, only the monetary and credit system had a higher real growth. The relative contribution for the real gross domestic product increased from 0.9 percent in 1964 to 1.2 percent in 1970 (see table 38).[272]

This growth was due to several different factors. While the demand for life and health insurances depended on the individual gross income, the demand for non-life insurances was connected with investments, consumption, and the demand for motorized vehicles, i.e. overall economic demand factors. The property and casualty insurer had the highest part in the gross premiums between 1959 and 1969 (1959: 72.4 percent; 1969: 68.3 percent) (see table 39).

The development of the different insurance branches can be shown in connection with global economic development. Therefore, the elasticity of the premium income will be calculated in connection with the gross domestic product for three periods, which are distinguished regarding economic points of view. The premiums grew slower, at the same rate, or faster compared to the gross domestic product and over a specific time span. The calculated "premium elasticities" sank never below one, i.e. the gross premiums from the domestic direct business grew faster in all three insurance sectors than the gross national product. Moreover, it is evident that the premium incomes in the various sectors varied over a long and short duration of time (see table 40).

[272] Cf. *Szopo, P.* (1980), Die Entwicklung der österreichischen Privatversicherungswirtschaft seit 1959, in: Wifo-Monatsbericht 7, p. 356.

Table 35: Premium income and market share of property and casualty insurance in 1959		
	premium income	market share in percent
Erste Allgemeine Unfall- und Schadens-Versicherungs-Gesellschaft	452,714	20.58
Versicherungsanstalt der österreichischen Bundesländer AG	286,605	13.03
Wiener Städtische Wechselseitige Versicherungsanstalt	284,950	12.95
Internationale Unfall- und Schadensversicherungs-AG (Interunfall)	210,235	9.56
Anglo-Elementar Versicherungs-AG	165,953	7.54
Wiener Allianz Versicherungs-AG	154,195	7.01
Donau Allgemeine Versicherungs-AG	109,238	4.97
*Wechselseitige Versicherungsanstalt in Graz	66,264	3.01
Kosmos Allgemeine Versicherungs-AG	50,403	2.29
Anglo-Danubian Lloyd Allgemeine Versicherungs-AG	45,361	2.06
Wiener Rückversicherungs-Gesellschaft	38,924	1.77
* OÖ Landes-Brandschaden-Versicherungsanstalt	38,765	1.76
Erste n. ö. Brandschadenversicherungs-AG	34,720	1.58
„Zürich" Versicherungs-Gesellschaft, Direktion für Österreich	31,042	1.41
Nordstern Allgemeine Versicherungs-AG, Direktion für Österreich	30,968	1.41
Der Anker Allgemeine Versicherungs-AG	30,921	1.41
Riunione Adriatica di Sicurta, Direktion für Österreich	30,405	1.38
Österreichische Hagelversicherungsanstalt a. G	14,370	0.65
„National" Allgemeine Versicherungs-AG, Direktion für Österreich	13,821	0.63
*Tiroler Landes-Brandschanden-Versicherungs-Anstalt	12,900	0.59
Heimat Allgemeine Versicherungs-Aktiengesellschaft	9,748	0.44
* Salzburger Landes-Brandschaden-Versicherungs-Anstalt	9,623	0.44
* Kärntnerische Landes-Versicherungs-Anstalt	9,233	0.42
Gegenseitiger Versicherungsverein für Montanwerke, Maschinen- und Metallfabriken	7,992	0.36
* Vorarlberger Landes-Feuerversicherungs-Anstalt	7,515	0.34

Oevag Österreichische Versicherungs-Aktiengesellschaft (ÖVAG)	6,899	0.31
Mannheimer Versicherungsgesellschaft, Direktion für Österreich	6,404	0.29
Assicurazioni Generali, Direktion für Österreich	4,510	0.20
Victoria Feuer-Versicherungs-AG, Direktion für Österreich	4,203	0.19
DAS Der Automobil Schutz Österreichische Allgemeine Rechtsschutz-Versichgerungs-Aktiengesellschaft	4,018	0.18
Basler Versicherungs-Gesellschaft gegen Feuerschaden, Direktion für Österreich	3,777	0.17
Garant Versicherungs-Aktiengesellschaft	3,645	0.17
Union Versicherungs-AG	3,381	0.15
Allg. Vers.-Gcs. Helvetia	3,011	0.14
Erste Wiener Spiegelglas-Versicherungsgesellschaft	2,355	0.11
Basler Transport-Versicherungs-Gesellschaft, Zweigniederlassung Wien	2,290	0.10
Europäische Güter u. Reisegepäck-Versicherungs AG	2,136	0.10
Versicherungs-Verband der Industriellen VVag	1,890	0.09
Eidgenössische Versicherungs-AG, Zweigniederlassung für Österreich	1,882	0.09
Versicherungs-Verband für Papier-Industrie a. G.	1,058	0.05
Österreichische Kreditversicherungs-AG	964	0.04
Schweiz" Allgemeine Versicherungs-AG, Zweigniederlassung für Wien	419	0.02
„GLEIMAG" Wechselseitige Haftpflicht- und Sachschadenversicherungsanstalt für Glas- und Magazinanlagen	366	0.02

Source: Veröffentlichungen des Bundesministeriums für Finanzen.

With regard to the annual premium income from the direct domestic business, the life insurance sector was the most expanding insurance branch during the period under review as well as in all sub-periods. From 1959 to 1969, the life insurance's proportion of the premium income increased from 14.05 percent to 17.30 percent from the total insurance sector. The premium income of life insurances is based almost exclusively on the domestic direct business. From that originated an average of 96 percent of the gross premiums during the period under review.

The private health insurers business is focused almost exclusively on the domestic direct business. Their proportion of the total premium

Table 36: Premium income and market share of life insurers in 1959		
	premium income	market share in percent
Versicherungsanstalt der österreichischen Bundesländer AG	93,757	20.97
Wiener Städtische Wechselseitige Versicherungsanstalt	82,797	18.51
Assicurazioni Generali, Direktion für Österreich	76,130	17.02
Wiener Verein Lebens- und Bestattungsversicherung a.G	47,743	10.68
Oevag Österreichische Versicherungs-Aktiiengesellschaft (ÖVAG)	37,864	8.47
Österreichische Volksfürsorge Lebensversicherungs-AG	30,300	6.78
Jupiter Versicherungsverein a.G.	23,528	5.26
Österreichische Beamtenversicherung VVaG	15,386	3.44
Riunione Adriatica di Sicurta, Direktion für Österreich	13,253	2.96
Der Anker Allgemeine Versicherungs-AG	11,105	2.48
Victoria zu Berlin, Allgemeine Versicherungs-AG, Direction für Österreich	8,524	1.91
Donau Allgemeine Versicherungs-AG	6,548	1.46
Nordstern Lebenversicherungs-AG, Zweigniederlassung für Österreich	255	0.06
Wiener Rückversicherungs-Ges.	—	—
Internationale Unfall- und Schadensversicherungs-AG (Interunfall)	—	—

Source: Veröffentlichungen des Bundesministeriums für Finanzen

income of the insurance industry increased during the period under review only slightly. In 1969, the health insurance premiums were with 1.5 billion only 14.40 percent of the gross premiums of all insurance sectors.

The proportion of property and casualty insurance companies regarding the income of the gross premiums from the domestic direct business decreased from 72.40 percent to 68.30 percent between 1959 and 1969. The premiums of property and casualty insurance companies increased below average during the period under review as well as in all other sub-periods. However, property and casualty insurance companies formed a very heterogeneous unit. The policyholders were, with different emphasis, business enterprises as well as individual households. Additionally, the various property and casualty branches were connected differently with the development of specific economic

Lehner, U. (1988), Der Konzern der Wiener Städtischen – Ein Wegbereiter des österreichischen Versicherungswesens, in: Versicherungsgeschichte Österreichs, vol. III, Das Zeitalter des modernen Versicherungswesens, Vienna

Lehner, U. (1988), Österreichische Versicherungswirtschaft im Deutschen Reich, in: Versicherungsgeschichte Österreichs, vol. III, Das Zeitalter des modernen Versicherungswesens, Vienna

Lehner, U. (1988), Staat und Versicherung in Österreich, in: Versicherungsgeschichte Österreichs, vol. III, Das Zeitalter des modernen Versicherungswesens, Vienna

Lehner, U. (1995), Eine beständige Selbsthilfe, in: Österreichische Beamtenversicherung (ed.): Vertrauen, Fairness, Solidarität, Verbundenheit, Verantwortung, Sicherheit, Vienna

Lehner, U. (1997), Abschied von der Gegenseitigkeit, in: Versicherungsgeschichte Österreichs, vol. V, Assekuranzmosaik des ausgehenden 20 Jahrhunderts, Vienna

Leimdörfer, M. (1905), Entwicklung und Organisation der Brandschadenversicherung in Österreich, Vienna

Leimdörfer, M. (1919), Versicherungswesen 1914-1918, Separatabdruck aus dem Bericht der niederösterreichischen Handels- und Gewerbekammer, Vienna

Leimdörfer, M. (1921), Das Versicherungswesen während der Jahre 1919 und 1920. Separatabdruck aus dem Bericht der niederösterreichischen Handels- und Gewerbekammer, Vienna

Lembke, H. (2016), Phönix, Wiener und Berliner, Wiesbaden

Mahlberg, B. (2006), Analyse der Finanzlage österreichischer Versicherungsunternehmenin den Jahren 1944 bis 1955, in: *Stiefel, D.* (ed.), "Unusual Business", Vienna

März, E. (1968), Österreichische Industrie- und Bankpolitik in der Zeit Franz Josephs, Vienna

Megner, K. (1995), Lebensversicherungen, Vereine und Selbsthilfeprinzip, in: Österreichische Beamtenversicherung (ed.): Vertrauen, Fairness, Solidarität, Verbundenheit, Verantwortung, Sicherheit, Vienna

Morgenstein, O. (1937), Von Sonnenfels bis Lueger Beiträge zur Geschichte des österreichischen Versicherungswesens, Vienna

Ogris, W. (1988), Zur Entwicklung des Versicherungsaufsichtsrechts und des Versicherungsvertragsrechts in Österreich von der Mitte des 19. Jahrhunderts bis zum Ende der Monarchie, in: Die Ära des klassischen Versicherungswesens, Versicherungsgeschichte Österreichs, vol. II, Vienna

Otruba, G. (1980), Die Feuerversicherung und die damit befaßten Gesellschaften in Österreich von ihren Anfängen bis zur Gegenwart, in: *Henning, F.* (ed.): Entwicklung und Aufgaben von Versicherungen und Banken in der Industrialisierung, Berlin

Pearson, R. (2015), Organizational forms in insurance: A comparison of the USA and Germany during Industrialization, in: *Pearson, R. / Yoneyma, T.* (eds.): Corporate forms and organizational choice in international insurance, Oxford

Plöchl, G. (1972), Vereine als öffentliche Unternehmen, Vienna

Pressl, A. (1993), Die Einbringung des Geschäftsbetriebes eines Versicherungsvereins auf Gegenseitigkeit in eine Aktiengesellschaft, Salzburg

Randow, v. A. (1885), Die Statistik des österreichischen Vereinswesens seit dem Jahre 1867, in: Statistische Monatsschrift, Vienna

Rathkolb, O. (2015), Die paradoxe Republik: Österreich 1945 bis 2015, Aktualisierte Neuausgabe, Vienna

Reisser, N. / Rohrbach, W. (1988), Arbeitsverhältnisse und Arbeitssysteme in der Versicherungswirtschaft 1873 bis 1938, in: Versicherungsgeschichte Österreichs, vol. III, Das Zeitalter des modernen Versicherungswesens, Vienna

Rohrbach, W. (1988), Gesundheitswesen und Privatversicherung in Österreich, in: Versicherungsgeschichte Österreichs, vol. III, Das Zeitalter des modernen Versicherungswesens, Vienna

Rohrbach, W. (1988), Versicherungsgeschichte Österreichs, vol. I, Von den Anfängen bis zum Börsenkrach des Jahres 1873, Vienna

Rohrbach, W. (1988), Von der ÖVAG zur Austria-ÖVAG, in: Versicherungsgeschichte Österreichs, vol. III, Das Zeitalter des modernen Versicherungswesens, Vienna

Rohrbach, W. (2004), "... der Rest ist Österreich!", in: Versicherungsgeschichte Österreichs, vol. VII, Teil 1, Die altösterreichischen Regionen Zentral- und (Süd)Osteuropas: Gestern – Heute – Morgen , Vienna

Rohrbach, W. (2004), Vorläufer, Wegbereiter und Träger der altösterreichischen „Versicherungsweltmacht", in: Versicherungsgeschichte Österreichs, vol. VII, Teil 1, Die altösterreichischen Regionen Zentral- und (Süd)Osteuropas: Gestern – Heute – Morgen, Vienna

Roloff, M. (1988), Die Entwicklung der Lebensversicherung in Österreich zwischen 1873 und 1936, in: Die Ära des klassischen Versicherungswesens, Versicherungsgeschichte Österreich, vol. II, Vienna

Sandgruber, R. (1995), Ökonomie und Politik. Österreichische Wirtschaftsgeschichte vom Mittelalter bis zur Gegenwart, Vienna

Schneider, B. (1988), Die Geschichte der Hagelversicherung in Österreich-(Ungarn) von 1880 bis 1938, in: Die Ära des klassischen Versicherungswesens, Versicherungsgeschichte Österreichs, vol. II, Vienna

Stiefel, D. (2006), Der Wiederaufbau der österreichischen Versicherungswirtschaft 1945-1955, in: *Stiefel, D.* (ed.), "Unusual Business", Vienna

Stiefel, D. (ed.) (2006), "Unusual Business", Vienna

Stubenrauch, M. (1857). Statistische Darstellung des Vereinswesens im Kaiserthume Österreich, Vienna

Süss, R. (1882), Das österreichische Versicherungs-Geschäft im Jahre 1880, Statistische Monatsschrift, Vienna

Szopo, P. (1980), Die Entwicklung der österreichischen Privatversicherungswirtschaft seit 1959, in: Wifo-Monatsbericht 7

Weber, M. (1980), Wirtschaft und Gesellschaft, Tübingen

Winckler, J. (1872), Feuerschäden, Feuerlösch- und Versicherungswesen, in: Mittheilungen aus dem Gebiete der Statistik, Neunzehnter Jahrgang, Heft 3

Wortner, M. (1972), Wandlungen der Lebensversicherung; eine rechtliche und demographische Untersuchung, Linz

Wörz, J. G. (1835) Gesetze und Verordnungen in Bezug auf die Kultur des Bodens in ihrer Provinz Tirol und Vorarlberg, nach Materien gesammelt, und in diesen chronologisch dargestellt, 2. Theil, Erste Abtheilung, Innsbruck